The Top 40 Honest-to-Goodness Unsolicited Quotes about the Previous Edition of *Macworld Photoshop Bible*

(And it wasn't nearly as good as *this* edition!)

"This book saved my job!"
    — David James, Lake Forest, California

"I teach Photoshop classes at the University of Oregon, and have been looking for quite a while for a good Photoshop reference/recipe book. Until about a month ago, I was very disappointed in the stuff available on the market (sad, brooding music). But then I saw (happy music here) Deke's *Photoshop 2.5 Bible*, and I gotta tell you, it's truly excellent. As a reference, it has an enormous amount of information (well indexed, too). As a recipe book, it has many cool effects that I hadn't run across before (well explained, too). Perhaps more importantly, Deke is an excellent writer with a great sense of humor. Two thumbs up. Check it out."
    — Matt Triplett, Portland Oregon

"Yesterday, I purchased what might be the greatest product since Double-Stuffed Oreos, the *Macworld Photoshop 2.5 Bible*. This is no ordinary Deke McClelland book. Sure, *Drawing on the Macintosh* and *Mastering Adobe Illustrator* were great books, but this is your masterpiece. I will constantly keep this book with my Mac for reference at all times. Thank you for writing the first comprehensive tome on Adobe Photoshop."
    — Steven Rubel, Bronx, New York

"At almost 700 pages in length, this encyclopedic effort ought to help both new and experienced users unleash the power of this multidimensional program. Nearly every feature is explored in detail — in McClelland's conversational style. . . .The book provides a truly comprehensive look at Photoshop's first cross-platform version. . . . One imaging topic of importance among Photoshop disciples — Unsharp Masking — gets no less than seven pages in the *Bible*. It's as clear an explanation of USM as has ever been published, backed up with examples showing the effects achieved by varying the Amount, Radius, and Threshold settings. . . . In fact, if you're looking for only one comprehensive Photoshop book, this may be the one."
    — Kurt Foss, *Photo District News*, March 1994

"Just picked up your book today and haven't been able to stop reading it. A veritable gold mine of useful information that will stay right next to my mouse. Just wanted to thank you for writing it."
    — Dan Casselberry, Elizabeth, New Jersey

"I've been enjoying your *Photoshop Bible*. It is definitely the best Photoshop book out there."
    — Kevin Garrett, Woodland Hills, California

"No doubt the *Photoshop 2.5 Bible* is the best. (You should see all the Post-its I've got marking 'favorite' passages — I might as well highlight the whole book!)"
    — Susan Klefstad, Monticello, Illinois

"Hello! I just wanted to say THANK YOU THANK YOU THANK YOU for your *Photoshop 2.5 Bible*. I am an artist who has used Photoshop for the past three years and love it to death. Your book was insightful, had lots of new tricks for me, and was just plain FUNNY. I spent the weekend reading it cover to cover, and couldn't have asked for anything more fun (except for perhaps a trip to Disneyland)."
— Jennifer Melnick, Minneapolis, Minnesota

"Just wanted to take a moment to compliment you on your new Photoshop book. Tremendous effort. . . . This is what should ship with the product as documentation."
— Steve Pollock, Sysop, CompuServe Digital Imaging Forum

"I'm 15 years old and I go to Lowell High School. I'm an editor on the staff of our very fine paper. . . . I decided to make the paper more visual, so I had our teacher buy Photoshop, and now I am learning Photoshop by reading your book. . . . It is very informative, thorough, but most of all, it reads easily. I like it a lot."
— Stephen Dodson, San Francisco, California

"Great book! I highly recommend it to my students. I was fascinated by your treatment on the custom filter."
— Andrew Chan, Singapore

"I bought your *Photoshop 2.5 Bible* and I think it is great! . . . The text is up to your usual excellent standards, and on that strength alone it is a great book. . . . As I continue to get into your book I like it even more; the chapter on 'Selections and Masks' has taken me to another level of skill. That chapter alone is worth the price of the book."
— Dr. Henry F. Domke, Jefferson City, Missouri

"The *Macworld Photoshop 2.5 Bible* is a giant of a book. IDG Books classifies this one as being aimed at intermediate users, but there's plenty of introductory material included. . . . This is author Deke McClelland's 30th book, and he has it down to a science. This one has nearly 700 pages, covering every imaginable aspect of Photoshop's operation."
— Jim Alley, Newsletter of the Savannah Macintosh Users Group

"I can only describe this book as TERRIFIC, since it's turned out to be everything the title would suggest plus a whole lot more; at one and the same time eminently readable, entertaining, and exceptionally enlightening. This book deserves the title *Macintosh Bible*, though it's too late for that, in the sense that Deke goes far beyond Photoshop with his detailed descriptions of file formats and structures and the impact of the various aspects of Photoshop's functionality on them. I've learned more about the inner workings of image files already — and I've only scratched the surface — than in the last five years of self-inflicted Mac addiction."
— Dr. Philip H. H. Nelson, Kent, United Kingdom

"It was fun to read and work with. I laughed out loud! More! More! More!"
— Karyn Kaplan, San Marcos, Texas

"You write with great brevity, clarity, and humor. I'm looking forward to exploring digital imaging with the unexpected bonus of a delightful read. Thanks."
— Teresa Curtin, New York, New York

"The enthusiasm of the author keeps me interested. I've learned more reading this book than going through the instructions and having coworkers help me in the past six months."
— Raymond Chow, Gaithersburg, Maryland

"Let me start off by thanking you profusely for writing the *Photoshop Bible* tome. I truly do not know how I could have slogged this far into the program without it. I don't think I ever get through a Photoshop session without referring to it at least once. (And it has a real index, too!) Huzza, huzza. For better or worse, I am only able to casually sling the digital lingo in the manner exhibited in this letter because of you. Thank you."
— Sharon Morris, Somerville, Massachusetts

"I am on page 15 of your *superb* book on Photoshop 2.5 and laughing my way through learning what is a requisite in my profession (that is, typography). Your chatty, conversational style is so entertaining, I'm beginning to think that restricting myself to reading only five pages a day is a mistake. . . . Bravo! Keep up the good work!"
— Ross L. Pruden, Paris, France

"I thought that I would write to you about your wonderful book, *Photoshop 2.5 Bible*. It is great! I just got my little Mac LC III a couple of months ago before getting Photoshop LE. Although your book concentrates on the full version, I was able to make allowances in the book and get to understand a lot more about the program. I especially like the detail you went to in the first few chapters — about memory allocation, how graphics work, etc. . . . The way you wrote it made it all make sense."
— Warren Sang, Hawkes Bay, New Zealand

"I've been reading your excellent book, the *Macworld Photoshop 2.5 Bible*. I love it. I particularly like the humor you inject into your writing. Life is tough. Keeping up with changing technologies is tough. A touch of humor rewards the reader for plodding through what would otherwise be a heavy read."
— Martin Coles, Montreal, Quebec

"McClelland offers tons of tips, tricks, and procedures. There are more insights than any one person will likely be able to digest, but even a few will prove invaluable for getting more out of the program. . . . One advantage to such a large book is that complicated subjects can be dealt with at length. McClelland takes full advantage of this in the special-effects section, detailing how the different filters work, what the effects of the filters are, and how users can better control the results. . . . *Macworld Photoshop 2.5 Bible* succeeds as a valuable tome for users of all levels. It will be helpful for beginners and relevant to advanced users."
— Richard Koman, *Communication Arts*, May/June 1994

"Deke guides you through some of the most complex functions. He chats, jokes, and draws good analogies to clarify. It's like having a master behind your shoulder. He's informational *and* conversational. . . . Thanks for the *Bible*! I'd be lost without it!"
— Erik Olsen, Ann Arbor, Michigan

"Thank you for the *Photoshop 2.5 Bible*. I teach Photoshop here in New York and I'll definitely be recommending it to my students."
— Ellie Dickson, New York, New York

"Your Photoshop book is a welcome and unique break from the usual 'how to' dreck on the market. I laughed, I cried, and I'm not even done yet! I've even found some stuff I didn't know. Thanks!"
— Paul Sherman, Derry, New Hampshire

"What I really like about the book is that Deke McClelland starts at the basics and takes you step by step as if you knew nothing about scanning or images. He takes nothing for granted, explaining in the introduction such fundamentals as when to use Photoshop and when to use a drawing programme. . . . So what does Photoshop do and how does this book help you in doing it? Mr. McClelland will answer both questions and every other question you can think of within the confines of the Macintosh and Photoshop."
— Sean Gilligan, *Work Place*, University College Dublin, Ireland

"It's the first Photoshop book that actually shows some things that I didn't already know!"
— Alan Boucek, New York, New York

"I work in a service bureau and I must have recommended your *Bible* to every client with whom I've discussed Photoshop. Keep up the solid work."
— Alan Ruthazer, Fair Lawn, New Jersey

"I made the mistake of lending the *Photoshop Bible* to a friend/client and I don't think he's come up for air in a week."
— David Wasson, Saint Paul, Minnesota

"Just a quick note to say 'thank you.' . . . This is the first time I have found ANY book with info on custom filters. Thanks again for presenting the info in the form that I can understand (non-techno-garb). . . . From what I see, it will be one of the best purchases I made since buying Photoshop."
— Ron Dabbs, Clearwater, Florida

"I taught a class for the user group on Photoshop plug-ins three weeks ago. It would have been VERY hard without your book. I finished reading it some weeks before and I must say it really is a very good job. . . . I recommended the book to the class (and whoever asks), and the user group book people will be stocking it for the group. Keep em' coming!!"
— John Ryan, Norwalk, Connecticut

"Coming from the world of natural media, Photoshop hasn't been the easiest thing in the world for me to get ahold of. So, when folks like you are putting down pavement, folks like me have an easier road to follow, and I appreciate it. You have a really fine book."
— Bruce Swan, Albany, Georgia

"I'm a student at the Brooks Institute of Photography in Santa Barbara, California. I'm also a Teaching Assistant in the Brooks Computer Lab. I just want to let you know that your book, the *Macworld Photoshop 2.5 Bible*, is VERY popular in our Digital Imaging classes here at Brooks. . . . It's answered lots of my questions and problems, as well helped our students with their assignments and with their understanding of Photoshop."
— Dan Moran, Brooks Institute, Santa Barbara, California

"Hey, I just have to tell you that your book is fantastic. You are a natural writer and your logic in how you approach things is perfect. . . . I'm going to push this book at every seminar and class I give. I'm putting it on my 'must read' list."
    — Maya McDonald, Minneapolis, Minnesota

"Your book is EXCELLENT — well written, funny, and useful. I couldn't have asked for more (except for another couple hundred pages of good stuff)!"
    — Matthew Frederick, Phoenix, Arizona

"I just wanted to say thanks for one of the most enjoyable books I've read. The combination of technical info plus bizarro humor is way cool, dude. Actually I don't usually speak like that but I thought it might sound hep. Thanks a lot, from a novice Photoshopper."
    — Rick Handville, Granby, Connecticut

"I bought your book (as so many forum-ees recommended), and read it cover to cover (no small task). One week later, the book has doubled my comprehension of how the tools are used, as well as my creativity in manipulating images. And in the time since I bought the book and started lugging it to and from work, three of my coworkers have also bought it. (Can we talk about sharing the royalties?) Thanks for a comprehensive job."
    — Robin E. Johnston, Chicago, Illinois

"I have been telling everyone about your book! No joke. I have learned more from the first 160 pages than from anywhere else. Thank you!! And to everyone that I hear say, 'It's so expensive, I think I'll wait,' I say 'Buy it. You won't be disappointed. And you'll be a much cooler person after reading just the first chapter.' Once again, nice work."
    — Kevin White, Kalamazoo, Michigan

"The *Photoshop 2.5 Bible* is a very rare find in the world of instructional books. While providing the absolute beginner with the information needed to get started using Photoshop, Deke McClelland makes it easy for the intermediate and advanced users to skip the introductory material and get right to the more advanced information. This book is useful for anyone from complete neophytes to those with years of experience using Photoshop.

"Given the technical nature of the topic and the depth of the coverage, you might expect the writing to be rather dry — somewhat less than inspiring. Fortunately, Deke McClelland is as accomplished a writer as he is a Photoshop guru. He has managed to keep a potentially heavy topic from becoming too great a burden on the reader, while maintaining a strong flow of information. His wit and style show through repeatedly in every chapter. I strongly recommend this book to anyone who uses Adobe Photoshop on the Mac or PC."
    — John Jeffries, *Flash*, February 1994

"Will you be writing another *Photoshop Bible?* . . . I hope that your answer is "yes," because your books are straightforward, entertaining, and friendly. . . . I do truly respect and value all you have done to further the knowledge and abilities of us mere mortals."
    — Ren Petrauskas, Chicago, IL

Macworld
Photoshop 3 Bible, 2nd Edition

MACWORLD

MW

AUTHORIZED
EDITION

TM

Macworld
Photoshop 3 Bible,
2nd Edition

by Deke McClelland

Foreword
by John Kunze

IDG
BOOKS

IDG Books Worldwide, Inc.
An International Data Group Company

Foster City, CA ✦ Chicago, IL ✦ Indianapolis, IN ✦ Braintree, MA ✦ Dallas, TX

Macworld Photoshop 3 Bible, 2nd Edition

Published by
IDG Books Worldwide, Inc.
An International Data Group Company
919 E. Hillsdale Blvd., Suite 400
Foster City, CA 94404

Library of Congress Catalog Card No.: 94-7905

ISBN: 1-56884-158-2

Printed in the United States of America

10 9 8 7 6 5 4 3 2

2B/QT/QS/ZV

Distributed in the United States by IDG Books Worldwide, Inc.

Distributed by Macmillan Canada for Canada; by Computer and Technical Books for the Caribbean Basin; by Contemporanea de Ediciones for Venezuela; by Distribuidora Cuspide for Argentina; by CITEC for Brazil; by Ediciones ZETA S.C.R. Ltda. for Peru; by Editorial Limusa SA for Mexico; by Transworld Publishers Limited in the United Kingdom and Europe; by Al-Maiman Publishers & Distributors for Saudi Arabia; by Simron Pty. Ltd. for South Africa; by IDG Communications (HK) Ltd. for Hong Kong; by Toppan Company Ltd. for Japan; by Addison Wesley Publishing Company for Korea; by Longman Singapore Publishers Ltd. for Singapore, Malaysia, Thailand and Indonesia; by Unalis Corporation for Taiwan; by WS Computer Publishing Company, Inc. for the Philippines; by WoodsLane Pty. Ltd. for Australia; by WoodsLane Enterprises Ltd. for New Zealand.

For general information on IDG Books in the U.S., including information on discounts and premiums, contact IDG Books at 800-434-3422 or 415-655-3000.

For information on where to purchase IDG Books outside the U.S., contact IDG Books International at 415-655-3021 or fax 415-655-3295.

For information on translations, contact Marc Jeffrey Mikulich, Director, Foreign & Subsidiary Rights, at IDG Books Worldwide, 415-655-3018 or fax 415-655-3295.

For sales inquiries and special prices for bulk quantities, write to the address above or call IDG Books Worldwide at 415-655-3000.

For information on using IDG Books in the classroom, or ordering examination copies, contact Jim Kelly at 800-434-2086.

 is a registered trademark of International Data Group

About the Author

Deke McClelland

A contributing editor to *Macworld* magazine, Deke McClelland also writes for *PC World* and *Publish*. He has authored more than 30 books on desktop publishing and the Macintosh computer. He started his career as artistic director at the first service bureau in the U.S.

McClelland received the Ben Franklin Award for the Best Computer Book in 1989 and won the prestigious Computer Press Award in 1990 and again in 1992. He is the author of *CorelDRAW! 5 For Dummies, Macworld FreeHand 4 Bible,* and *Pagemaker 5 For Windows For Dummies.*

Welcome to the world of IDG Books Worldwide.

IDG Books Worldwide, Inc. is a subsidiary of International Data Group, the world's largest publisher of computer-related information and the leading global provider of information services on information technology. IDG was founded more than 25 years ago and now employs more than 7,000 people worldwide. IDG publishes more than 220 computer publications in 65 countries (see listing below). More than fifty million people read one or more IDG publications each month.

Launched in 1990, IDG Books Worldwide is today the #1 publisher of best-selling computer books in the United States. We are proud to have received 3 awards from the Computer Press Association in recognition of editorial excellence, and our best-selling *...For Dummies™* series has more than 12 million copies in print with translations in 25 languages. IDG Books, through a recent joint venture with IDG's Hi-Tech Beijing, became the first U.S. publisher to publish a computer book in the People's Republic of China. In record time, IDG Books has become the first choice for millions of readers around the world who want to learn how to better manage their businesses.

Our mission is simple: Every IDG book is designed to bring extra value and skill-building instructions to the reader. Our books are written by experts who understand and care about our readers. The knowledge base of our editorial staff comes from years of experience in publishing, education, and journalism — experience which we use to produce books for the '90s. In short, we care about books, so we attract the best people. We devote special attention to details such as audience, interior design, use of icons, and illustrations. And because we use an efficient process of authoring, editing, and desktop publishing our books electronically, we can spend more time ensuring superior content and spend less time on the technicalities of making books.

You can count on our commitment to deliver high-quality books at competitive prices on topics consumers want to read about. At IDG, we value quality, and we have been delivering quality for more than 25 years. You'll find no better book on a subject than an IDG book.

John J. Kilcullen

John Kilcullen
President and CEO
IDG Books Worldwide, Inc.

Acknowledgments

Thank you to the following people and companies for their aid in providing me with the information and product loans I needed to complete this book.

John Leddy, Matt Brown, Rita Amladi, Scot Reid, Patricia Pane, LaVon Peck, and Russell Preston Brown at Adobe Systems

Bruce Berkoff and Andrew Eisner at Radius/SuperMac

Burton Holmes at Burton Holmes Associates

D.J. Anderson and Tom Mitchell at A&R Partners

Jeff Butterworth and Alien Skin Software

Lisa Wood and Lee Cannon at PictureWorks

Don Kent at PressLink

Tom Hughes at PhotoDisc

Michael Zak at ColorBytes

David and Ria Skernick of Photo 24

Nathan Benn and David Evans, Picture Network International

Bill Davis and David Stone, Planet Art

Charles Smith, Digital Stock

Ann Burgrass, CMCD

Steve Abramson at Trumatch

Rick Barron at Affinity

Thérèse Bruno at Xaos Tools

Frank Colin at Equilibrium

Andrei Herasimchuk and Kelly Ryer at Specular International

Harry Magnan, Kai Krause, and John Wilczak at HSC Software

Tony Graham at Allsport

Robert Stark at Reuter

Peter Rohowsky at Bettmann

Warren Vollmar at 3M

Andrei Lloyd at The Stock Market

A special thank you to John Palmer and Lenny Mizusaka of Palmer Photographic; Mike Mihalik of LaCie Limited; and Traci Hayes of Maples and Associates. Their generous help during the production of this book's CD-ROM prevented at least one nervous breakdown.

Extra special thanks to Julie King, Jim Martin, Beth Jenkins, Ben Barbante, Diane Steele, Mark Collen, Denise McClelland, Russell McDougal, Anne Hines, Diane Fenster, Jim Heid, Jeff Sacilotto, John Kilcullen, the gang at Waterside, and everyone else who was instrumental in creating and producing this book.

(The publisher would like to give special thanks to Patrick J. McGovern, without whom this book would not have been possible.)

Dedication

To Elizabeth, the best companion on this and many other planets.

Credits

Publisher
Karen A. Bluestein

Acquisitions Editor
Gregory Croy

Brand Manager
Melisa M. Duffy

Editorial Director
Mary Bednarek

Editorial Managers
Mary C. Corder
Andy Cummings

Editorial Executive Assistant
Jodi Lynn Semling-Thorn

Editorial Assistant
Nate Holdread

Production Director
Beth Jenkins

Project Coordinator
Cindy L. Phipps

Pre-Press Coordinators
Tony Augsburger
Steve Peake

Project Editor
Julie King

Copy Editor
April S. Holmes

Technical Reviewer
Ben Barbante

Production Staff
Paul Belcastro
J. Tyler Connor
Maridee Ennis
Kim Fry
Drew R. Moore
Carla Radzikinas
Dwight Ramsey
Patricia R. Reynolds
Gina Scott

Proofreader
Michelle Worthington

Indexer
Sharon Hilgenberg

Book Design
Beth Jenkins

Cover Design
Kavish + Kavish

Cover Illustration
Diane Fenster

CD-ROM Compilation
Jim Martin

Contents at a Glance

Table of Contents

Foreword

In the tradition of Adobe Photoshop, *Macworld Photoshop 3 Bible,* 2nd Edition "raises the bar" in providing you with the tools you need to do your work. This book explores the new features and traditional functions of Adobe Photoshop with a uniquely engaging focus on you and your information needs — whether you are the expert, intermediate, or new user.

Deke makes great use of the visual world of graphics, icons, and illustrations, which he has gleaned from his own talents and his rich network of graphics resources, to create the blend of text and art that best presents the world of Adobe Photoshop to any user.

If you are new to Adobe Photoshop, you'll begin to feel comfortable with the program only several pages into the book. If you have been productive with Photoshop for a while but need to learn Version 3.0, you'll find easy access to the program's new features in Deke's practical presentation. If you are looking for a definitive primary reference for Adobe Photoshop, you can rely on *Macworld Photoshop 3 Bible* for its excellent depth and breadth of coverage.

Adobe has been an industry leader in moving beyond the world as it was before computer graphics, and Adobe Photoshop Version 3.0 is on the leading edge of the new graphics universe. You will be well served in your Photoshop adventures if you take along the gospel according to Deke McClelland, the *Macworld Photoshop 3 Bible.*

John Kunze
Director of Product Marketing
Adobe Systems Incorporated
September 1994

Introduction

When I wrote the first edition of this book more than a year ago, I was concerned that I had bitten off more than I could chew. So much had already been written about Photoshop that I honestly wondered if I could add anything to the subject. When I called vendors for support and told them the name of the book, they'd generally say something to the effect of, "You're trying to write a *Bible* on Photoshop?" Then, with muffled laughter and a bit too much sympathy, they'd add, "That's an awfully big topic." In other words, "Little man, you ain't got a chance."

But despite my anxieties, I dug in my heels and ingested and purged as much information as I could possibly locate. What I discovered, much to my amazement and undeniable pleasure, was that although coverage of Photoshop techniques abounded, in-depth analysis of the inner workings of the program were almost nonexistent. Furthermore, many of the techniques described elsewhere were inefficient, based on a limited understanding of Photoshop's higher functions. I was determined to fill in the holes and make this book the foremost tool for mastering this vast program.

It seems to have worked. When the book debuted at the Macworld exposition in Boston in August 1993, a single bookseller, Quantum Books, sold more than 500 copies in three days — a show record that still stands. The book immediately became the best-selling book on any graphics application, both here and abroad. I was so happy, I found myself humming the theme song to "The Jeffersons" all week.

But as much as the success of the first edition might warm my cockles (actually, I only told you that story so that you'd quit browsing through the book and buy the darned thing), act two is every bit as difficult as act one. Every publisher short of Harlequin is coming out with at least one Photoshop book this year. So I figure that the only defense is an all-out Battle of the Bookseller offense. To wit, this edition of the book is bigger and better than ever, including not only completely revised text — you'd expect that from any update — but also more than 200 pages of brand new material and more than 600MB of Macintosh- and Windows-compatible images and software on the CD. (Isn't competition great? For you, I mean. For me, it's kind of a nuisance.)

But before I brag some more about the book, there's always the chance that you're not even sure what Photoshop is, much less why you'd need a book on the subject. Just so that we're all clear, let's take a little peek behind curtain number one.

What is Photoshop?

Photoshop is software for Macintosh and Windows-based computers that enables you to edit photos and artwork scanned to disk and print out your results. Here's an example: Your job is to take a picture of Mr. High-and-Mighty CEO, touch up his crow's feet, and publish his smiling face on the cover of the annual report. No problem. Just shoot the photo, have it digitized to a Photo CD or some other high-tech gizmo, open Mr. H & M inside Photoshop, dab on the digital wrinkle cream, fix his toupee (and for heaven's sake, do *something* about those jowls), and there you go. The man looks presentable no matter how badly the company is doing.

Photoshop, then, is about changing reality. And it goes beyond just reducing the distance between two Giza pyramids on the cover of *National Geographic* or plopping a leaning Tom Cruise, photographed in Hawaii, onto the supportive shoulder of Dustin Hoffman, photographed in New York, for a *Newsweek* spread (both duller-than-fiction applications of photo-editing software). Photoshop brings you full-tilt creativity. Picture a diver leaping from the summit of Mount Everest, or a bright violet zebra galloping toward a hazel-green sunset, or an architectural rendering with wallpaper that looks exactly like the surface of the moon. Photoshop lets you paint snapshots from your dreams. The sky's the limit.

About This Book

If you're familiar with the previous edition of this book, you'll find quite a few differences in this edition. First of all, three introductory chapters have been jettisoned to the CD. This setup freed up 100 pages for a discussion of more advanced information revolving around masking, color correcting, compositing, and a whole bunch of other topics that needed flushing out. Two of the chapters moved to the CD are specially written for Macintosh users who are either new to the computer or thinking of upgrading their machinery, and the third is about scanning and acquiring images. If you're a new user and you need access to these chapters — or if you just want to check them out to make sure that you already know everything — the chapters are provided in the Adobe Acrobat format, which allows you to read chapters on-screen. Another advantage is that these chapters are in color. We don't have any printing constraints on the CD, so color doesn't cost a penny more. Most figures appear in 256 colors so that they'll display properly on any monitor; only Chapter C, the image acquisition chapter, contains a few 16-million-color images.

Speaking of color . . .

The color insert in this book has been bumped up from 16 pages to 32 pages. I also got rid of the stock photos — they're now on the CD — thereby freeing up even more space for images that show off real techniques. Each color plate is numbered according to the chapter that discusses the image; in this way, the color plates serve as a sort of visual index to topics covered in the book.

If you're wondering why the book isn't printed in full color throughout, the answer's simple: It just wouldn't be economically feasible. A full-color book of this size would cost nearly $150. With volume discounts, we could probably pull it off at something in the $85 to $90 range. But even so, that's a little steep for a book that's going to sit on your desk and get coffee stains and pen marks all over it, don't you think? We did, too, and so we opted to forego full color throughout the book and concentrate on giving you what you really need: Tons of useful information at an affordable price.

That silver Frisbee in the back of the book

In the back of this book, you'll find a CD-ROM containing hundreds of pieces of original artwork and stock photography, most in full color. Nearly all the photographs are high-resolution images that you can use and abuse as you see fit. (You won't get that out of a picture book!) The CD holds 650MB of data — and we took full advantage of it.

Jim Martin, formerly chief graphics editor at *Macworld* and one-time executive editor at *Publish*, spent nearly as much time compiling the CD as I spent writing the book. Rather than limiting himself to the same old plug-ins that you find in every book with a disk, Jim knocked himself out to make sure that this CD was valuable in and of itself. In addition to software from Adobe, Aldus, Specular International, HSC Software, Affinity Microsystems, DayStar Digital, Radius, Equilibrium, Light Source, PressLink, Wacom, and others, you'll find digital articles of direct interest to Photoshop users from *Macworld* magazine; stunning digital artwork from some of the best around, including Diane Fenster, Mark Collen, Greg Vander Houwen, John Lund, Bart Nagel, and Glenn Mitsui; royalty-free stock photos from PhotoDisc, ColorBytes, Digital Stock, Letraset, Clement Mok Design, Photo 24, Planet Art, and FotoSets. There's even a Pro Photo CD image from photographer Anne Hines that allows you to experiment with this format without shelling out $20 a shot to produce your own.

Needless to say, if you don't already own a CD-ROM player, you'll want to go out and get one. Or just find a friend whose system is equipped with a CD-ROM player and copy all this stuff onto an enormous hard drive, 15 SyQuests, or 450 floppy disks. (Actually, I rounded down on the floppies. Better bring 500 just in case.)

The CD-ROM is compatible with both Macintosh and Windows machines. Mac and Windows users get different software, but you'll all see the same articles, artwork, and images.

The Guts of the Book

Insofar as the actual pages in this massive tome are concerned, well, there are lots of them. But keep in mind that I don't cover every command or option available in Photoshop. That is the job of the Photoshop manual. My job is to explain the features that really count and explore capabilities that you won't easily glean on your own. I also look at Photoshop's place in the larger electronic design scheme and examine how to best approach Photoshop in ways that will yield the most efficient and accurate results.

This is a big, fat book, so exercise caution. Those of you who like to read in-flight, remember to stow the book under the seat in front of you after you board the plane. It'll just go and damage lesser luggage if you try to stick it in the overhead compartment. If you plan on using the book for self-defense, be sure to spar with a partner armed with a volume of equal size. And please, take out the CD before using the book to prop up a youngster at the dinner table. That way, you can use the CD as a coaster in case of spills.

The images inside the book

Before I proceed so much as one step farther, I should take a moment to credit the folks who contributed the photos that appear throughout this book. For the most part, the artistic embellishments are my own, but the original images derive from a variety of sources, including PhotoDisc, ColorBytes, Reuters, and the Bettmann Archive, as well as independents Russell McDougal, Mark Collen, and Denise McClelland. (In case you're wondering whether there's some kind of nepotism going on here, the answer is bingo. Denise is my sister.) Every one of these folks generously provided me with images for the first edition, so they all have a special place in my heart (even my sister). But rather than clutter every single figure with credits and copyright statements, I provide this information in Appendix B near the end of the book.

How this book is organized

To enhance your enjoyment of Photoshop's mouth-watering capabilities, I sliced the task into five tasty parts and then diced those parts into a total of 18 digestible chapters. Bon appetite.

Part I: Photoshop Fundamentals

Here's all the basic stuff you need to know about Photoshop. I explain the new Photoshop 3.0 interface, show how to edit colors, explain how channels work, and describe how to print full-color artwork. Whether you're new to Photoshop or an old hand, you'll find a lot you didn't know in these first six chapters.

 If you're experienced with Photoshop and you're familiar with the previous edition of this book, read the last section of Chapter 1, all of Chapter 2, and, if you're foggy on the subject of channels, Chapter 5. Then skip to Chapter 7 and keep reading. Nearly every chapter in Parts II, III, IV, and V has been dramatically revised or altogether rewritten.

Chapter 1, Getting to Know Photoshop, explains how Photoshop fits into the larger experience of using the Mac to produce printed pages and on-screen presentations. I also list all the new features in Photoshop 3.0 in case you're trying to decide whether or not to upgrade.

Chapter 2, Inside Photoshop, introduces you to Version 3.0's revamped working environment and examines Photoshop's generous supply of tools, cursors, multi-paneled palettes, and preference settings. The comprehensive shortcuts table will keep you apprised of time-saving techniques and make you more productive.

Chapter 3, Image Fundamentals, describes what it means to be a digitized image and how file formats such as TIFF and JPEG affect the content of an image and its size on disk. You also learn how to resample and crop images within Photoshop.

Chapter 4, Defining Colors, covers the fundamentals of editing colors on a computer screen. I explain how you can manipulate common color models to display predictable results. I also examine the differences and similarities between the commercial printing standards Pantone and Trumatch.

Chapter 5, Navigating Channels, looks at color channels, which are the building blocks of color images, and examines how they work. In a nutshell, channels are so important that even beginning Photoshop users should become comfortable with editing them.

Chapter 6, Printing Images, starts off with a glossary of printing terms that will help you better communicate with the folks at your service bureau or commercial print house. Following that, I explain how to print grayscale and color composites, four-color separations, and duotones, tritones, or quadtones.

Part II: Retouching with a Purpose

Every month or so, some fraudulent photo sparks a new flame of public scorn and scrutiny. Now it's your chance to give people something to talk about. These chapters show you how to exchange fact with a modicum of fantasy.

Chapter 7, Painting and Editing, shows you how to use Photoshop's brush tools to enhance and augment photographic images. It also explores ways to paint images from scratch using pressure-sensitive tablets. The chapter ends with an in-depth analysis of brush modes and how they add to everyday living.

Chapter 8, Drawing Selection Outlines, covers absolutely everything you ever wanted to know about the magic wand and the path tools, antialiasing and feathering, expanding, and growing. I also show you how to send a floating selection to its own independent layer and why layers may be the greatest thing to happen to Photoshop.

Chapter 9, Creating Masks, documents the inherent advantages of masks over the rest of the selection tools. I explain how to paint inside selection masks, how to work in the quick mask mode, how to generate selections automatically using the Color Range command, and how to save masks to a separate channel. You'll also learn how to exploit the three specialized masking options available to independent layers.

Chapter 10, Filling and Stroking, shows how to paint the interiors and outlines of images with solid colors and gradations. It also steps you through the processes of creating drop shadows, halos, and translucent, gradient arrows (of all things). There's a lot more to Photoshop's straightforward fill and stroke functions than meets the eye.

Chapter 11, Duplicating and Reverting, details the operation of the rubber stamp tool, the most versatile and possibly the most frequently overlooked editing tool available to Photoshop users. In addition, you learn how to create seamlessly repeating patterns and textures in Photoshop for use with the rubber stamp and other tools. And finally, you learn how to revert images to their original appearance using the newly improved eraser tool.

Part III: Special Effects

Making manual artistic enhancements is all very well and good, but it's easier to let your computer do the work. These chapters show ways to produce highly entertaining and effective results using fully automated operations.

Chapter 12, Text Effects, tells you how to create word art, including gradient text, characters with tiger stripes, raised letters, custom logos, and a whole mess of other effects guaranteed to make jaws drop and eyes boggle.

Chapter 13, Corrective Filtering, covers how to get the most out of Photoshop's most commonly used filters, including Unsharp Mask, Gaussian Blur, Add Noise, and High Pass. I'll also explain how to clean up a scanned halftone from a magazine and the myriad benefits of floating before you filter.

Chapter 14, Full-Court Filtering, describes every one of the new special effects filters available in Photoshop 3.0. I also document a series of specific applications for these and other of Photoshop's abundant supply of plug-in filters.

Chapter 15, Constructing Homemade Effects, investigates the exact workings of the Custom and Displace filters, which multiply and shift pixels to create user-definable effects. If you're really feeling brave, you can program your own effects using Adobe's new Filter Factory.

Part IV: Corrections and Composites

Here's where you learn what you can do with Photoshop's most powerful color correction commands, how to composite images using overlay modes and channel operations, and what role layers play in all this.

Chapter 16, Mapping and Adjusting Colors, explores ways to change the color balance in scanned photographs to more accurately represent real life — or more radically depart from it. You learn how to make use of Photoshop's straightforward Variations options, how to modify specific colors with Hue/Saturation and other commands, and how to adjust brightness values using Levels and Curves.

Chapter 17, The Fundamentals of Compositing, describes everything you need to know about mixing images from different layers or even different windows. I answer such burning questions as how overlay modes work, where the Composite Controls dialog box went, and what you do when channel operations fail to provide sufficient control.

Chapter 18, Compositing on the March, goes beyond how compositing works and shows you specific ways to mix images in step-by-step form. Fans of channel operations may be amazed to learn how much easier it is to composite images using floating selections.

Part V: Appendixes

Three appendixes follow Chapter 18. The first explains how to install Photoshop onto your hard drive and offers some advice on which files you'll need to get the most out of this book. The second provides complete information on the photographers, image collections, and news services that contributed images to this book. And the third contains a list of vendors whose products I covered in the book, complete with addresses, phone numbers, and retail prices.

Last but not least is an astonishingly comprehensive index. It'll knock your socks off, should you happen to be wearing any.

On-disk chapters

As I mentioned earlier, three chapters have been moved out of the book and onto the CD. These chapters are stored in the Acrobat portable document format (PDF). Just double-click on any one of them to open it and view it on-screen. IDG production manager Beth Jenkins has taken special pains to make these pages visible and legible on 13-inch monitors. All figures are in color. You can even print the chapters, if paper is your idea of a cheap commodity, or open them in your own copy of Illustrator 5.5, if you've a hankering to edit them.

Chapter A, Welcome to Macintosh, explores a range of topics that are fundamental to using a Macintosh computer. Get ready to familiarize yourself with CPUs, system software, random-access memory, fonts, QuickTime, and a whole bunch of other mystifying topics.

Chapter B, Preparing the Soil, explains how to prepare your computer to sustain and nurture Photoshop. RAM, virtual memory, and video display are all covered in this chapter. It also includes an amazing computer-rating chart that includes every new brand of Mac, including the super-fast Power Macs.

Chapter C, Acquiring the Raw Materials, examines the many sources for digitized images, including scanners, video capture boards, on-line photographic libraries, and Kodak's Photo CD technology. Unlike the previous sections, this chapter is required reading not only for novices, but for experienced image editors as well.

Conventions

Every computer book seems to conform to a logic all its own, and this one's no exception. Although I try to avoid pig latin — ellway, orfay hetay ostmay artpay — I do subscribe to a handful of conventions that you may not immediately recognize.

Vocabulary

Call it computerese, call it technobabble, call it the synthetic jargon of propeller heads. The fact is, I can't explain the Mac or Photoshop in graphic and gruesome detail without reverting to the specialized language of the trade. However, to help you keep up, I can and have italicized vocabulary words (as in *random-access memory*) with which you may not be familiar or which I use in an unusual context. An italicized term is followed by a definition.

If you come across a strange word that is *not* italicized (that bit of italics was for emphasis), look it up in the index to find the first reference to the word in the book.

Commands and options

To distinguish the literal names of commands, dialog boxes, buttons, and so on, I capitalize the first letter in each word (for example, *click on the Cancel button*). The only exceptions are option names, which can be six or seven words long and filled with prepositions like *to* and *of.* Traditionally, prepositions and articles (*a, an, the*) don't appear in initial caps, and this book follows that time-honored rule, too.

When discussing menus and commands, I use an arrow symbol to indicate hierarchy. For example, *Choose File⇨Open* means to choose the Open command from the File menu. If you have to display a submenu to reach a command, I list the command used to display the submenu between the menu name and the final command. *Choose Image⇨Map⇨Invert* means to choose the Map command from the Image menu and then choose the Invert command from the Map submenu. (If this doesn't quite make sense to you now, don't worry. Future chapters will make it abundantly clear.)

 For an introduction to menu commands and the like, check out the "Reviewing System Software Elements" section in Chapter A on the CD. For an introduction to Photoshop's tools, see "The Photoshop desktop" section in Chapter 2.

Version numbers

A new piece of software comes out every 15 minutes. That's not a real statistic, mind you, but I bet I'm not far off. As I write this, Photoshop has advanced to Version 3.0. But by the time you read this, the version number may be seven hundredths of a percentage point higher. So know that when I write *Photoshop 3.0*, I mean any version of Photoshop short of 4.0 (if that ever occurs).

Similarly, when I write *Photoshop 2.5*, I mean both Version 2.5 and the more recent 2.5.1. *Photoshop 2.0* means 2.0 and 2.01. *Photoshop 1.0* means anything up to Version 1.0.7.

The term *System 7* includes Versions 7.0, 7.01, 7.1, 7.5, and any other version that begins with a 7. I make a distinction between Illustrator 5.0 and the updated 5.5, but when I write *Illustrator 5.5*, I mean anything short of 6.0. *Illustrator 4.0* indicates the Windows edition and likewise incorporates future updates.

Icons

Like just about every computer book currently available on your green grocer's shelves, this one includes alluring icons that focus your eyeballs smack dab on important information. The icons make it easy for folks who just like to skim books to figure out what the heck's going on. Icons serve as little insurance policies against short attention spans. On the whole, the icons are self-explanatory, but I'll explain them anyway.

The Caution icon warns you that a step you're about to take may produce disastrous results. Well, perhaps "disastrous" is an exaggeration. Inconvenient, then. Uncomfortable. For heaven's sake, use caution.

The Note icon highlights some little tidbit of information I've decided to share with you that seemed at the time to be remotely related to the topic at hand. Then again, even if it's not remotely related, it's still good info.

The Background icon is like the Note icon, except that it includes a modicum of history. I tell you how an option came into existence, why a feature is implemented the way it is, or how things used to be better back in the old days. It's a perfect opportunity to either explain or gripe.

The Photoshop 3.0 icon explains an option, command, or other feature that is brand spanking new to this latest revision. If you're already familiar with previous versions of Photoshop, you might just want to plow through the book looking for Photoshop 3.0 icons and see what new stuff is out there.

Photoshop 3.0 is available on both the Macintosh and Windows platforms. The Windows icon highlights Photoshop features that work differently under Windows. There aren't very many of them, and you could probably figure them out without my help. I'm just trying to justify my job, don't you know.

This book is bursting with tips and techniques. If I were to highlight every one of them, whole pages would be gray with triangles popping out all over the place. The Tip icon calls attention to shortcuts that are specifically applicable to the Photoshop application. For the bigger, more useful power tips, I'm afraid you'll have to actually read the text.

In the previous version of this book, I had a System 7 icon. In another book, I had a Power PC icon. I'm tired of changing this icon all the time, so I decided to come up with one blanket New Technology icon that highlights every one of those weird pieces of software and hardware that you may not have yet, or if you do, that changes everything.

The Cross-Reference icon tells you where to go for information related to the current topic. I included one a few pages back and you probably read it without thinking twice. That means you're either sharp as a tack or an experienced computer-book user. Either way, you won't have any trouble with this icon.

If I'm talking about something that is backed up by something on the CD, I'll try to let you know with this catchy little See CD icon.

I thought of including one more icon that alerted you to every new bit of information — whether Photoshop 3.0-dependent or not — that's included in this book. But I found myself using it every other paragraph. Besides, that would have robbed you of the fun of discovering the new stuff.

How to Bug Me

Even though this book is in its second edition and has been scanned by thousands of readers' eyes and scanned about 60 times by the eyes of my editor, I'll bet that someone, somewhere will still manage to locate errors and oversights. If you notice those kinds of things and you have a few spare moments, please let me know what you think. I always appreciate readers' comments.

If you want to share your insights, comments, or corrections, please contact me on America Online at DekeMc. You can also reach me via CompuServe at 70640,670. Don't fret if you don't hear from me for a few days, or months, or ever. I read every letter and try to implement nearly every idea anyone bothers to send me.

Now, without further ado, I urge you to turn the page and advance forward into the great untamed frontier of image editing. But remember, this book can be a dangerous tool if wielded unwisely. Don't set it on any creaky card tables or let your children play with it without the assistance of a stalwart adult, preferably an All-Star Wrestler or that guy who played the Incredible Hulk on TV. And no flower pressing. The little suckers would be pummeled to dust by this monstrously powerful colossus of a book.

Photoshop Fundamentals

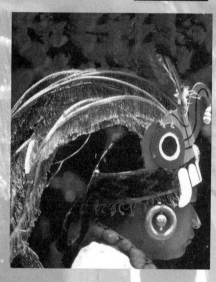

Chapters 1 through 6 are among the most important chapters in this book for developing a thorough understanding of Photoshop and the image-editing environment. By the time you finish reading these six chapters, you'll be prepared not only to begin using Photoshop in earnest, but also to engage in witty repartee with friends, neighbors, and business associates who claim to know everything about the product.

In addition to exploring Photoshop itself, this part of the book examines the core image-editing process, taking you from composition and construction to color theory and output. You learn how to change the size and resolution of an image, how to define colors and navigate among color channels, and how to print images. I also discuss more than 20 file formats that permit you to compress images on disk, trade images with other pieces of software, and export images for use on other computer platforms, such as DOS-based PCs, Microsoft Windows, or high-end imaging systems.

If you're reading this book for the first time, I strongly urge you to read these chapters carefully, because nearly all the discussions are geared toward both beginning and expert users. On the other hand, if you practically memorized the last edition of this book at least read the last section of Chapter 1 to find out which features are new to Photoshop 3.0. Then read all of Chapter 2 to acquaint yourself with the revised interface, the new palette organization, and the slew of additional keyboard shortcuts. Also, if channels have long left you mystified, read through the revised Chapter 5 to gain a clear understanding of how they work. In other words, whoever you are, you'll be sorry if you skip these chapters.

Getting to
Know Photoshop

In This Chapter

- ⚬➤ An introduction to Photoshop
- ⚬➤ The difference between painting and drawing programs
- ⚬➤ How Photoshop fits into the bigger Macintosh design scheme
- ⚬➤ The many uses for Photoshop
- ⚬➤ The new features in Photoshop 3.0

What Is Photoshop? _____

Adobe Photoshop is the most popular image-editing application available for use on Macintosh and Windows-based computers. Despite hefty competition from programs such as Fractal Design's Painter, Aldus PhotoStyler, HSC Software's Live Picture, and Fauve's xRes, industry analysts report that Adobe sells upwards of four times as many copies of Photoshop as any competing image editor. Some estimates say that Photoshop sales exceed those of all its competitors combined.

If you're already familiar with Photoshop and you just want to scope out its new capabilities, skip to "The Fast Track to Version 3.0."

The term *application* — as in *image-editing application* — is just another word for *computer program*. Photoshop satisfies a specific purpose, so programmers abuse the language by calling it an application. I also use the word in the conventional sense throughout the book, as in *Photoshop has many applications*. Hopefully, you won't become hopelessly confused.

The result of Photoshop's amazingly lopsided sales advantage is that Adobe has the capital to reinvest in Photoshop and regularly enhance its capabilities. Meanwhile, other vendors spin their wheels or let their products die on the vine. (Nearly all the programs compared to Photoshop in the last edition of this book, for example, are for all practical purposes dead and gone.) Therefore, the legacy of this program reads like a self-perpetuating fantasy. Photoshop hasn't always been the best image editor, but it's long been perceived as such. So now — thanks to substantial capital injections and highly creative programming on the part of Adobe's staff and Photoshop originators Thomas and John Knoll — it has evolved into the most popular program of its kind.

Image-editing software for the Mac went through its infancy in the late 1980s. The first image editor for the Mac was ImageStudio, a grayscale program from Fractal Design, creators of ColorStudio and Painter. The first Macintosh image editor to feature color was an Avalon Development Group entry called PhotoMac, which is now all but forgotten. But rumor had it that the *best* photo editor during this time was Lumena from Time Arts, a DOS-based program that ran on IBM PCs and compatibles. Meanwhile, Photoshop was a custom program used within the hallowed walls of George Lucas's Industrial Light and Magic that converted file formats and combined images from different sources. We were almost into a new decade before Adobe purchased the product and set it on its current path.

Image-Editing Theory _____

Having used mirrors, dry ice, and some rather titillating industry analysis to convince you of Photoshop's prowess, I now should answer that burning question: What the heck does Photoshop *do*?

Like any *image editor*, Photoshop enables you to alter photographs and other scanned artwork. You can retouch an image, apply special effects, swap details between photos, introduce text and logos, adjust color balance, and even add color to a grayscale scan. Photoshop also provides the tools you need to create images from scratch. These tools are fully compatible with pressure-sensitive tablets, so you can create naturalistic images that look for all the world like watercolors and oils.

Bitmaps versus objects

Image editors fall into the larger software category of *painting programs.* In a painting program, you draw a line, and the application converts it to tiny square dots called *pixels.* The painting itself is called a *bitmapped image,* but *bitmap* and *image* are equally acceptable terms. Every program I've discussed so far is a painting program. Other examples include PixelPaint, Color It, PC Paintbrush, and CorelPhoto-Paint.

 Photoshop uses the term *bitmap* exclusively to mean a black-and-white image, the logic being that each pixel conforms to one *bit* of data, 0 or 1 (off or on). In order to avoid ad hoc syllabic mergers like *pix-map* — and because forcing a distinction between a painting with exactly two colors and one with anywhere from four to 16 million colors is entirely arbitrary — I use the term bitmap more broadly to mean any image composed of a fixed number of pixels, regardless of the number of colors involved.

What about other graphics applications, such as Adobe Illustrator and Aldus FreeHand? Illustrator, FreeHand, Canvas, and others fall into a different category of software called *drawing programs.* Drawings comprise *objects,* which are independent, mathematically-defined lines and shapes. For this reason, drawing programs are sometimes said to be *object-oriented.* Some folks prefer the term *vector-based,* but I really hate that one because *vector* implies the physical components direction and magnitude, which generally are associated with straight lines. Besides, my preference suggests an air of romance, as in, "Honey, I'm bound now for the Object Orient."

 Illustrator and FreeHand are sometimes called *illustration programs,* though this is more a marketing gimmick — you know, like Father's Day — than a legitimate software category. The idea is that Illustrator and FreeHand provide a unique variety of features unto themselves. In reality, their uniqueness extends little beyond more reliable printing capabilities and higher prices.

The ups and downs of painting

Painting programs and drawing programs each have their strengths and weaknesses. The strength of a painting program is that it offers an extremely straightforward approach to creating images. For example, although many of Photoshop's features are complex — *exceedingly* complex on occasion — its core painting tools are as easy to use as a pencil. You alternately draw and erase until you reach a desired effect, just as you've been doing since grade school. (Of course, for all I know, you've been using computers since grade school. If you're pushing 20, you probably managed to log in many happy hours on paint programs in your formative years. Then again, if you're under 20, you're still in your formative years. Shucks, we're *all* in our formative years. Wrinkles, expanding tummies, receding hairlines . . . if that's not a new form, I don't know what is.)

In addition to being simple to use, each of Photoshop's core painting tools is fully customizable. It's as if you have access to an infinite variety of crayons, colored pencils, pastels, airbrushes, watercolors, and so on, all of which are entirely erasable. Doodling on the phone book was never so much fun.

The downside of a painting program is that it limits your *resolution* options. Because bitmaps contain a fixed number of pixels, the resolution of an image — the number of pixels per inch — is dependent upon the size at which the image is printed, as demonstrated in Figure 1-1. Print the image small, and the pixels become tiny, which increases resolution; print the image large, and the pixels grow, which decreases resolution. An image that fills up a standard 13-inch screen (640 × 480 pixels) prints with smooth color transitions when reduced to, say, half the size of a postcard. But if you print that same image without reducing it, you may be able to distinguish individual pixels, which means that you can see jagged edges and blocky transitions. The only way to remedy this problem is to increase the number of pixels in the image, which dramatically increases the size of the file on disk.

Figure 1-1:
When printed small, a painting appears smooth (left). But when printed large, it appears jagged (right).

 Bear in mind that this is a very simplified explanation of how images work. For a more complete description that includes techniques for maximizing image performance, refer to the "How Images Work" section of Chapter 3.

The downs and ups of drawing

Painting programs provide tools reminiscent of traditional art tools. A drawing program, on the other hand, features tools that have no real-world counterparts. The process of drawing might more aptly be termed *constructing,* because you actually build lines and shapes point by point and stack them on top of each other to create a finished image. Each object is independently editable — one of the few structural advantages of an object-oriented approach — but you're still faced with the task of building your artwork one chunk and a time.

Nevertheless, because a drawing program defines lines, shapes, and text as mathematical equations, these objects automatically conform to the full resolution of the *output device,* whether it's a laser printer, imagesetter, or film recorder. The drawing program sends the math to the printer and the printer *renders* the math to paper or film. In other words, the printer converts the drawing program's equations to printer pixels. Your printer offers far more pixels than your screen — a 300 dots-per-inch (dpi) laser printer, for example, offers 300 pixels per inch (dots equal pixels) whereas most screens offer 72 pixels per inch. So the printed drawing appears smooth and sharply focused regardless of the size at which you print it, as shown in Figure 1-2.

Figure 1-2:
Small or large, a drawing prints smooth, but it's a pain to create. This one took more than an hour out of my day, and I didn't even bother with all the letters found in the version created in a painting program, shown in Figure 1-1.

Another advantage of drawings is that they take up relatively little room on disk. The file size of a drawing depends on the quantity and complexity of the objects the drawing contains. Thus, the file size has almost nothing to do with the size of the printed image, which is just the opposite of the way bitmapped images work. A thumbnail drawing of a garden that contains hundreds of leaves and petals consumes several times more disk space than a poster-sized drawing that contains three rectangles.

When to use Photoshop

Thanks to their specialized methods, painting programs and drawing programs fulfill distinct and divergent purposes. Photoshop and other painting programs are best suited to creating and editing the following kinds of artwork:

- Scanned photos, including photographic collages and embellishments that originate from scans

- Realistic artwork that relies on the play between naturalistic highlights, midranges, and shadows

- Impressionistic-type artwork and other images created for purely personal or aesthetic purposes

- Logos and other display type featuring soft edges, reflections, or tapering shadows

- Special effects that require the use of filters and color enhancements you simply can't achieve in a drawing program

When to use a drawing program

You're probably better off using Illustrator, Canvas, FreeHand, or some other drawing program if you're interested in creating more stylized artwork, such as the following:

- Poster art and other high-contrast graphics that heighten the appearance of reality

- Architectural plans, product designs, or other precise line drawings

- Business graphics, such as charts and other "infographics" that reflect data or show how things work

- Traditional logos and text effects that require crisp, ultrasmooth edges. (Drawing programs are unique in that they enable you to edit character outlines to create custom letters and symbols.)

⮕ Brochures, flyers, and other single-page documents that mingle artwork, logos, and standard-sized text (such as the text you're reading now)

If you're serious about computer graphics, you should own at least one painting program and one drawing program. If I had to rely exclusively on two graphics applications, I would probably choose Photoshop and Illustrator. Both are Adobe products, and the two function together almost without a hitch. Much to its credit, however, FreeHand also works remarkably well in combination with Photoshop.

The Computer Design Scheme _____

If your aspirations go beyond image editing into the larger world of computer-assisted design, you'll soon learn that Photoshop is just one cog in a mighty wheel of programs used to create artwork, printed documents, and presentations. Dedicated scanning software such as Light Source's Ofoto can match colors in a photograph to their closest on-screen equivalents and remove moiré patterns that occur when scanning published photos. EFI's Cachet provides color-correction and printing capabilities that exceed those of Photoshop and dramatically improve your ability to match colors between original and printed photographs without losing any image data. These two products go a long way toward turning Photoshop into a professional-quality image production studio.

The natural-media paint program Fractal Design Painter emulates real-world tools such as charcoal, chalk, felt-tip markers, calligraphic pen nibs, and camel-hair brushes as deftly as a synthesizer mimics a thunderstorm. Three-dimensional drawing applications such as Infini-D, Alias Sketch, and Ray Dream Designer enable you to create hyper-realistic objects with depth, lighting, shadows, surface textures, reflections, refractions — you name it. If you're rich as Midas, the $7,000 ElectricImage goes one step further and throws animation into the equation. All these applications can import images created in Photoshop as well as export images you can then enhance and adjust with Photoshop.

Page-layout programs such as Aldus PageMaker and QuarkXPress let you integrate images into newsletters, reports, books (such as this one), and just about any other kind of document you can imagine. If you prefer to transfer your message to slides, you can use Microsoft PowerPoint or Aldus Persuasion to add impact to your images through the use of charts and diagrams. With Adobe Premier, you can merge images with video sequences recorded in the QuickTime format. You even can edit individual frames in Premier movies with Photoshop. MacroMind Director, Passport Producer, and others make it possible to combine images with animation, QuickTime movies, and sound to create multimedia presentations you can show on a screen or record on videotape.

Photoshop Scenarios

All the programs just described run on the Macintosh computer — and many, including Painter, PageMaker, QuarkXPress, PowerPoint, Persuasion, and Premiere, also run on Windows. But the number of programs you decide to purchase and how you use them is up to you. The following list outlines a few specific ways to use Photoshop alone and in tandem with other products:

- ◌ Scan a photograph into Ofoto or another scanning utility or directly into Photoshop. Retouch and adjust the image as desired and then print the final image as a black-and-white composite (like the images in this book) or as color separations using Photoshop or Cachet.

- ◌ After scanning and adjusting an image inside Photoshop, use PageMaker or QuarkXPress to place the image into your monthly newsletter and then print the document from the page-layout program.

- ◌ After putting the finishing touches on a lovely tropical vista inside Photoshop, import the image for use as an eye-catching background inside PowerPoint or Persuasion. Then save the document as a self-running screen presentation or print it to overhead transparencies or slides from the presentation program.

- ◌ Capture an on-screen image (by pressing Command-Shift-3 on the Mac or the Print Screen key in Windows). Then open the screen shot and edit it in Photoshop. Place the corrected image into Illustrator or FreeHand, annotate the screen shot using arrows and labels, and print it from the drawing program.

- ◌ Paint an original image inside Photoshop using a Wacom pressure-sensitive tablet. Use the image as artwork in a document created in a page-layout program or print it directly from Photoshop.

- ◌ Scan a surface texture such as wood or marble into Photoshop and edit it to create a fluid repeating pattern (as explained in Chapter 11). Import the image for use as a texture map in a three-dimensional drawing program. Render the 3-D graphic to an image file, open the image inside Photoshop, and retouch as needed.

- ◌ Create a repeating pattern, convert it to the system software's built-in 256-color palette inside Photoshop, and apply it as a desktop pattern at Finder level, using a utility such as ResEdit or Wallpaper. (Sorry, for the moment, you can only do this on the Mac.)

- Take a problematic Illustrator EPS file that keeps generating errors when you try to print it, open it inside Photoshop, and render it as a high-resolution bitmap. Then place the image in a document created in a page-layout program or print it directly from Photoshop. Many top drawing programs, including FreeHand and CorelDraw, support the Illustrator format.

- Start an illustration in a drawing program and save it as an Illustrator EPS file. Open the file in Photoshop and use the program's unique tools to add textures and tones that are difficult or impossible to create in a vector-based drawing program.

- Record a QuickTime movie in Premier and export it to the FilmStrip format. Open the file inside Photoshop and edit it one frame at a time by drawing on the frame or applying filters. Finally, open the altered FilmStrip file in Premier and convert it back to the QuickTime format.

Obviously, few folks have the money to buy all these products and even fewer have the energy or inclination to implement every one of these ideas. But quite honestly, these are just a handful of projects I can list off the top of my head. There must be hundreds of uses for Photoshop that involve no outside applications whatsoever. In fact, so far as I've been able to figure, there's no end to the number of design jobs you can handle in whole or in part using Photoshop.

Simply put, this is a versatile and essential product for any designer or artist who currently uses or plans to purchase a Macintosh or Windows-based computer. I, for one, wouldn't remove Photoshop from my hard drive for a thousand bucks. (Of course, that's not to say I'm not willing to consider higher offers. For $1,500, I'd gladly swap it to an optical disk.)

The Fast Track to Version 3.0 _____

 If you're already an old hand at Photoshop 2.5 and you're champing at the bit to get on that new version and ride, the following list explains a few of the most prominent features that are new to Photoshop 3.0 and points you to the chapter in which you can pick up the trail:

- **The new palettes:** Photoshop now offers five floating palettes, many of which contain multiple panels. See Chapter 2 to find out how to switch panels and even move them from one palette to another — heck, you can move the Brushes panel to the Info palette if you're so inclined (although why you'd want to do so is beyond me).

↝ **Image annotation:** Choose File⇨File Info to attach a caption, copyright statement, credits, keywords, categories, and a whole lot more textual information to a file. If you work for a stock agency or otherwise distribute images for public consumption, you're going to love this feature. See Chapter 2 for the lowdown.

↝ **Brush size cursor:** Photoshop can now show the actual size of your cursor when you use a brush up to 300 pixels in diameter. Chapter 2 has a bit more to add on this subject.

↝ **Drag and drop:** Want to take a selection from Image A and put it in Image B? Without using the Clipboard or some arcane channel operation? No sweat. Just drag the selection from Image A and drop it into Image B, as explained in Chapter 8.

↝ **Layers:** The newest rage in image editing is layering. As do Painter X2, Specular Collage, Live Picture, and others, Photoshop 3.0 now lets you assign images to separate layers, each of which you can edit independently. When you view a single layer by itself (via the Layers palette), a checkerboard pattern indicates areas that are transparent or translucent. Perhaps Version 3.0's most significant enhancement, layers figure considerably into Chapters 8, 9, and 17. (Hey, it's a big topic.)

↝ **The move tool:** When you first see this tool (just below the lasso in the toolbox), you might wonder why Adobe added it to the program. After all, you can already move selections with the selection tools themselves. The move tool, however, lets you move selections by dragging outside them. You can also move entire layers. For complete information, read Chapter 8.

↝ **New tool modifiers:** No more double-clicking tools to change them; you can access all modifiers inside the Brushes/Options palette. Among the new options at your disposal are a shape-changing eraser (discussed in Chapter 11), the new sponge tool (Chapter 7), and a combined rectangular and elliptical marquee tool (Chapter 8).

↝ **Toolbox shortcuts:** You can now access all tools and controls in the toolbox by pressing keys. For example, press M to select the marquee tool, press L to select the lasso. It's so convenient, you'll swear that you died and went to heaven. You can even get to the quick mask mode by pressing Q. Chapter 2 tells all.

↝ **Automated masking:** Choose Select⇨Color Range to create a mask based on a sample color lifted with the eyedropper. The interface may be a little daunting at first, but with a little practice you'll find it much more useful than the magic wand (to which it bears a strong functional resemblance). For the big picture, see Chapter 9.

- **Out-of-gamut corrections:** Mode⇨Gamut Warning allows you to identify regions of color in an RGB image that have no CMYK equivalents and will therefore print inaccurately. In the past, most folks simply converted their work to CMYK and let Photoshop resolve the color conflicts. But now you can do it yourself using techniques covered in Chapter 16.

- **Filter previews:** That's right, no more guessing what the Unsharp Mask filter will do; now you can preview the filter before you apply it. Photoshop 3.0 provides a small preview inside most dialog boxes and offers the option of previewing the effect in the full image window. Lucky Chapter 13 tells it all.

- **The Filter Factory:** If you get a thrill out of designing your own effects using the Custom filter or displacement maps, you'll absolutely love the new Filter Factory, explained in the last portion of Chapter 15. Even if you can't stand math, you can try out some of the predefined filters on the CD included with this book. And keep an eye out for on-line offerings from fellow artists who manage to make the most out of this powerful new tool.

- **More convenient channel operations:** Gone is the old Image⇨Calculate submenu. It's replaced by a series of commands — Duplicate, Apply Image, and Calculations — that integrate several new options and a fair amount of additional functionality. For the comprehensive analysis, check out Chapter 17.

Version 3.0 also offers new filters (covered in Chapter 14), new color correction options (Chapter 16), new overlay options (Chapter 17), new selection outline modifiers (Chapter 8), and all the other stuff you'd expect to find in your typical better-than-ever upgrade.

■ ■

Summary

- ⇥ Image editors such as Photoshop are painting programs that are designed specifically to facilitate the editing of photographs and artwork scanned to disk.

- ⇥ To fully understand Photoshop, you need to understand how bitmapped images differ from other kinds of computer graphics.

- ⇥ Use a drawing program such as Illustrator or FreeHand to create high-contrast or stylized graphics; use Photoshop to edit scanned images or to paint free-form artwork that features transitional colors.

- ⇥ The new Photoshop is a dramatic upgrade with independent layers, new palette construction and tool modifiers, a powerful filter programming environment, and a whole lot more. It's a gas.

■ ■

Inside Photoshop

A First Look at Photoshop

Photoshop is like a chocolate candy with a rock core. It's soft and sweet on the outside and hard as nails on the inside. It doesn't take long to get up and running with the program — most folks even have a certain amount of fun experimenting with its straightforward image-editing tools — but it takes lots of experience and careful examination to make the program sing.

This chapter deals with the soft candy outside; future chapters look at the rock. Why bother with the candy? Certainly, if you're familiar with other Macintosh or Windows applications, you'll have little problem adapting your skills and knowledge to Photoshop. But a few items just a tad off the beaten path bear mentioning. If you're a new user, I recommend that you read this chapter from start to finish so that you don't inadvertently leave any part of the candy unchewed. Photoshop offers gobs of fundamental capabilities; you don't want to end up discovering some of them a year from now and lamenting how much time they might have saved you. To this end, I've tried to cover the basic functions that you're most likely to miss or that will prove the most valuable. If you're an experienced Photoshop pro, skim through the chapter with an eye peeled for the Photoshop 3.0 icon, which calls out new capabilities and subtle interface changes.

As my old pappy used to say, "A program that's worth learning is worth learning right." Well, actually, my pappy didn't say anything much like that, and I can't honestly say I ever heard anyone call him "pappy," but you get my drift. Read this chapter and you won't be sorry. Or words to that effect.

The Photoshop desktop

Shortly after you launch Photoshop, the Photoshop *splash screen* appears. Shown at the top of Figure 2-1, the splash screen explains the launching process by telling you which plug-in modules are loading. Any time while running Photoshop, you can re-access the splash screen by choosing the About Photoshop command from the Apple menu.

If you're not sure how to launch Photoshop, read the "Starting an Application" section in Chapter A on the CD. If you need help installing the program, read Appendix A, "How to Install Photoshop."

I know no one cares about the splash screen. In fact, the only reason I even mention it is because Photoshop 3.0 conceals two additional splash screens, also shown in Figure 2-1. If you press the Option key while choosing Apple⇨About Photoshop, you get the old Knoll Software screen that has been with Photoshop since Version 1.0. If you press Command and choose Apple⇨About Photoshop, you display the Double-Secret About Box. It's like the toy surprise in a box of Cracker Jacks, only not so sticky. Purposeless but amusing secret features such as these are called *Easter eggs*.

A general note for Windows users: Because this book is a little biased toward the larger audience of Photoshop users on the Mac, I express shortcuts and other keyboard techniques in Macintosh terms — that is, Option-key this, Command-key that. You may even see a Control key reference every once in a while. When you see *Option*, substitute *Alt*; when you see *Command*, substitute *Ctrl*. When you see a Control key reference, there most likely is no Windows equivalent.

Figure 2-1:
The Photoshop 3.0 splash screen and its two hidden companions.

If you choose the About Photoshop command and wait a moment, the list of programmers and copyright statement at the bottom of the splash screen begins to scroll. Press the Option Key to make the list scroll more quickly. The final line of the scrolling message thanks *you*, of all people, for being "one of our favorite customers." Just the thing for the megalomaniac who doesn't get out enough. (Hey, *I* fell for it.)

 Want another Easter egg? After the "favorite customer" message disappears and the names start to recycle, click on the Adobe logo in the upper left corner. A series of entertaining quotes appears, including some from such relatively obscure sources as *This is Spinal Tap* and "Lost in Space." The quotes go on for a while, but definitely hang in there for the Top 10 list that appears.

After the launch process is complete, the Photoshop desktop consumes the foreground. Figure 2-2 shows the Photoshop 3.0 desktop as it appears when an image is open and all palettes are visible.

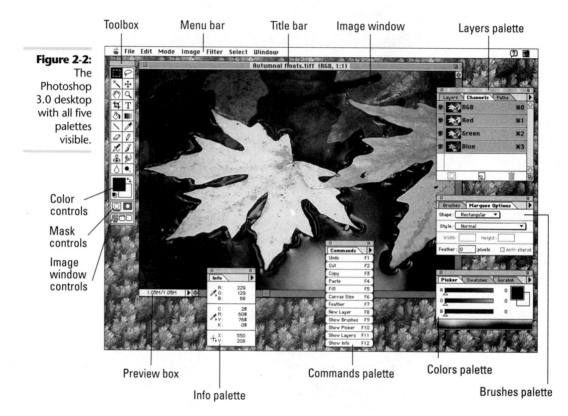

Figure 2-2:
The Photoshop 3.0 desktop with all five palettes visible.

Toolbox   Menu bar   Title bar   Image window   Layers palette

Color controls

Mask controls

Image window controls

Preview box   Info palette   Commands palette   Colors palette   Brushes palette

Many of the elements that make up the Photoshop desktop are well known to folks familiar with the Macintosh computer. They work just like the elements of the Finder desktop and the standard application window. For example, the menu bar provides access to menus and commands, the title bar enables you to move the window around, and the scroll bars let you view the hidden portions of the image inside the window. Other elements of the Photoshop desktop work as follows:

    ⌛ **Image window:** You can open as many images in Photoshop as RAM and virtual memory allow. Each open image resides inside its own window. The lower left corner of the window features the *preview box,* which tells the size of the foreground image on disk.

- **Toolbox:** The toolbox offers 20 *tool icons,* each of which represents a selection, navigation, painting, or editing *tool.* To select a tool, click on its icon. Then use the tool by clicking or dragging with it inside the image window. The lower third of the toolbox features three sets of controls. The *color controls* let you change the colors with which you paint; the *mask controls* let you enter and exit the quick mask mode; and the *image window controls* enable you to change the state of the foreground window on the desktop.

- **Floating palettes:** Photoshop 3.0 offers five *floating palettes:* Layers, Brushes, Colors, Info, and Commands. The term *floating* refers to the fact that each palette is independent of the image window and of other palettes. Three palettes contain multiple *panels,* which offer related but independent options. For example, the Layers palette contains the Layers, Channels, and Paths panels. "The floating palettes" section, later in this chapter, provides a brief explanation of each of these palettes.

The preview box

The preview box in the lower left corner of the image window was expanded in Version 3.0. It now contains two numbers divided by a slash. The first number is the size of the base image in memory. Photoshop calculates this value by multiplying the height and width of the image (both in pixels) by the *bit depth* of the image, expressed in bytes. A 24-bit RGB image takes up 3 bytes per pixel; an 8-bit grayscale image takes up 1 byte; a 1-bit black-and-white image consumes $1/8$ bit. So a 640×480-pixel RGB image takes up $640 \times 480 \times 3 = 921,600$ bytes, which is exactly 900K. (There are 1,024 bytes in one kilobyte.)

The number after the slash takes into account any additional layers in your image. Photoshop only measures the visible portion of each layer, which can take up considerably less space than the base layer. If you transfer a 160×320-pixel selection of an RGB image to a new layer, for example, that layer consumes only $160 \times 320 \times 3 = 153,600$ bytes = 150K, even if the base image is much larger. If the image contains one layer only, the numbers before and after the slash are the same.

Press and hold on the preview box to display a pop-up window that shows the placement of the image on the printed page. The preview even shows the approximate placement of crop marks, captions, and other elements requested in the Page Setup dialog box (File➪Page Setup). Press Option and mouse down on the preview box to view the size and resolution of the image.

The right-pointing arrowhead next to the preview box offers access to a pop-up menu that contains two options, Document Sizes and Scratch Sizes. The first of the two is selected by default and displays the image size values described a moment ago. If you select Scratch Sizes, however, Photoshop changes the values in the preview box to represent memory consumption and availability. The first value is the amount of room required to hold all open images in RAM. This value is generally equal to about 3 $1/2$ times the sum total of all images, including layers. However, the value constantly updates depending on the operations that you perform, growing as large as five times the image size when floating images and complex operations are involved.

The second value indicates the amount of RAM space available to images after the Photoshop application is loaded. This value does not change unless you quit Photoshop and change the amount of RAM dedicated to the application in the Info dialog box (as explained in the "Using the Get Info command" section of Chapter A on the CD). If the value before the slash in the preview box is larger than the value after the slash, Photoshop has to take advantage of virtual memory in order to display the open images. Virtual memory makes Photoshop run more slowly because the program has to frequently load portions of the image off disk. To speed up the application, close one or more images until the first value is smaller than the second value. (If doing so isn't possible, don't sweat it. Virtual memory is an occasional fact of life when using Photoshop.)

Tools

The Photoshop 3.0 toolbox, shown in Figure 2-3, looks a lot like the toolbox from Version 2.5. In fact, there are only superficial differences — the removal of the elliptical marquee tool and the addition of the move tool (which looks like a bunch of arrows pointed in different directions). The other new tool, the sponge tool, is an optional tool available from the toning tool slot (lower right tool icon). Also, Photoshop now calls the dodge, burn, and sponge tools *toning tools,* and the blur and sharpen tools are called *focus tools.*

The following paragraphs explain how to use each tool inside the image window. For example, if an item says *drag,* you click on the tool's icon to select the tool and then drag in the image window, not on the tool icon itself. Keep in mind that these are merely the briefest of all possible introductions to Photoshop's tools. Future chapters reveal the details in their nitty-grittiest form.

Rectangular marquee: Drag with this tool to enclose a portion of the image in a rectangular *marquee,* which is a pattern of moving dash marks that indicates the boundary of a selection. The dash marks are sometimes fondly called *marching ants* (hoorah, hoorah).

Elliptical marquee: Option-click on the marquee tool to change from the rectangular marquee to the elliptical marquee. Then drag with the elliptical marquee tool to enclose a portion of the window in an oval marquee.

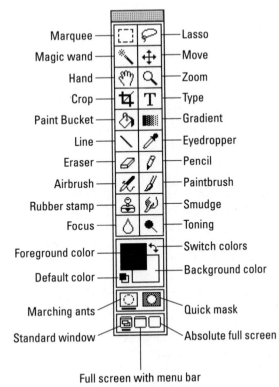

Marquee — Lasso
Magic wand — Move
Hand — Zoom
Crop — Type
Paint Bucket — Gradient
Line — Eyedropper
Eraser — Pencil
Airbrush — Paintbrush
Rubber stamp — Smudge
Focus — Toning
Foreground color — Switch colors
Default color — Background color
Marching ants — Quick mask
Standard window — Absolute full screen

Full screen with menu bar

Lasso: Drag with the lasso tool to select a free-form portion of the image.

Magic wand: Click with this tool to select a contiguous area of similarly colored pixels. To select discontiguous areas, click in one area and then Shift-click in another.

Move: Drag with this new tool to move the selected area of the image, whether you're dragging inside the selection or not. If no portion of the image is selected, dragging with the move tool moves the entire layer.

Hand: Drag an image with the hand tool to scroll the window so that you can see a different portion of the image. The hand tool differs from the move tool in that it doesn't actually move pixels or in any way alter the image; it simply shifts the on-screen view to another part of the image. Double-click on the hand tool icon to magnify or reduce the image so that it fits on-screen in its entirety (as when you first open the image).

Zoom: Click with the zoom tool to magnify the image so that you can see individual pixels more clearly. Option-click to step back from the image and take in a broader view. Drag to enclose the specific portion of the image that you want to magnify. And finally, double-click on the zoom tool icon to restore the image to 100 percent view size.

Crop: Drag with the crop tool to enclose within a rectangular marquee the portion of the image you want to retain. The crop marquee offers *corner handles* so that you can resize the marquee after you create it. Click inside the marquee to crop away the portions of the image that lie outside it.

Type: Click with the type tool to display the Type Tool dialog box, in which you can enter and format text. Note that you cannot use the type tool to edit existing text as you can in page-layout and drawing programs. (Like any other image, bitmapped type is just a bunch of colored dots. If you misspell a word, you must erase it and try again.)

Paint bucket: Click with the paint bucket tool to fill a contiguous area of similarly colored pixels with the foreground color or a predefined pattern.

Gradient: Drag with this tool to fill a selection with a gradual transition of colors (called a *gradient* or *gradation*) that begins with the foreground color and ends with the background color. In Photoshop 3.0, a gradation can also fade from the foreground color to transparent.

Line: Drag with the line tool to create a straight line. Click on the Start or End option in the Line Tool Options panel of the Brushes palette to add arrowheads.

Eyedropper: Click with the eyedropper tool on a color in the image window to make that color the foreground color. Option-click on a color in the image to make that color the background color.

Eraser: Drag with the eraser tool to paint in the background color, which in effect erases portions of the image. Option-drag to access the *magic eraser,* which changes portions of the image back to the way they appeared when last saved. Photoshop 3.0 offers four kinds of erasers, which paint like the paintbrush, airbrush, pencil, and old eraser (now called the *block eraser),* respectively. You can cycle through these erasers by Option-clicking on the eraser tool icon in the toolbox.

Pencil: Drag with the pencil tool to paint hard-edged lines.

Airbrush: Drag with the airbrush tool to paint feathered lines that blend into the image — ideal for creating shadows and highlights.

Paintbrush: Drag with the paintbrush tool to paint soft lines that are not as hard-edged as those created with the pencil but not as soft as those created with the airbrush.

Rubber stamp: Option-click with this tool on an element of your image and then drag to create a clone of that element in another portion of the image. Then drag to *clone* that area to another portion of the image. This method enables you to hide defects in one portion of an image by duplicating another portion. You also can use the rubber stamp tool to paint with a pattern or to change portions of an image to the way they looked when last saved (as you can using the magic eraser) or when last shot using Edit⇨Take Snapshot.

Smudge: Drag with this tool to smear colors inside the image.

Blur: Drag with the blur tool to decrease the contrast between neighboring pixels, which blurs the focus of the image.

Sharpen: Option-click on the blur tool icon in the toolbox to access the sharpen tool. Then drag to increase the contrast between pixels, which sharpens the focus.

Dodge: Drag with the dodge tool to lighten pixels in the image.

Burn: Option-click on the dodge tool icon in the toolbox to access the burn tool, which darkens pixels.

Sponge: Option-click on the dodge tool icon again to get the new sponge tool. Drag with this tool to decrease the amount of saturation in an image, which eventually removes the color from the image and leaves only grayscale values. You can also increase saturation by changing the setting in the Toning Tool Options palette.

You should know something else about tools in Version 3.0: You no longer adjust the performance via a specialized dialog box. You'll now find these same options (and a few more) in the Options panel of the Brushes palette. (To display this panel, choose Window⇨Palettes⇨Show Options and then select the desired tool. Or just double-click on the tool icon like you used to do in the old days.) Only the move tool and type tool lack palette options.

Cursors

Photoshop 3.0 uses more than 50 cursors. Most cursors correspond to the tool you're using, but a few have nothing to do with the tool. Nonetheless, all cursors have unique meanings.

 You may think that learning the meaning of each and every one of these cursors is a big waste of time, and certainly my descriptions don't qualify as a literary treat. But as with the rest of the information in this chapter, taking the time to become familiar with the various cursors leads to a greater understanding of the program. At least, that's the idea. Tell you what, read the following descriptions if you want to; skip them if you don't. You won't find a better deal than that.

Arrow: The left-pointing arrow appears any time the cursor is outside of the image window. You can select a tool, set palette options, or choose a command when this cursor is visible.

Marquee: The cross appears when the rectangular or elliptical marquee tool is selected and the cursor is outside of a selected area. You can access the marquee cursor inside a selected area if you press the Shift or Command key. (Shift adds to the selection; Command subtracts.)

Lasso: The lasso cursor works the same way as the marquee cursor, except that it indicates that the lasso tool is selected.

Wand: Again, this cursor works the same as the lasso and marquee cursors, but it appears when you select the magic wand tool.

Right arrow: The right-pointing arrow appears when the cursor is inside a selected area and the rectangular marquee, elliptical marquee, lasso, magic wand, or type tool is selected. Drag the selected area to move it; Option-drag to clone it.

Move: The omnidirection move icon appears any time the new move tool is selected. Drag to move a selection. If nothing is selected, drag to move the entire image or layer.

Gavel: After you select an area and rotate it, stretch it, or apply some other transformation, you can accept the effect by clicking inside the selection with the gavel cursor. Until you click inside the selection, Photoshop remains in transformation mode, thus allowing you to test out multiple rotation angles, stretching percentages, and so on without diminishing the integrity of the selected image.

Cancel: You can click outside a selection during a rotation or a stretch to cancel the transformation and return the selection to its original size and orientation. The cancel cursor warns you that if you click now, you lose your changes.

Crop: This cursor appears when the crop tool is selected and remains on-screen until you marquee the portion of the image that you want to retain.

Scissors: Click with the scissors cursor inside the crop marquee to cut away the portions of the image that lie outside the marquee. (If you move outside the marquee, the cancel cursor appears.)

Type: The common I-beam cursor indicates that the type tool is selected and ready to use. Click with this cursor to display the Type Tool dialog box. As I mentioned before, you can't use the type tool to edit text.

Pen: This cursor appears when the pen tool is selected from the Paths panel in the Layers palette, enabling you to add points to the path at hand.

Insert point: When a small plus sign accompanies the pen cursor, you can insert points into the current path.

Remove point: When this cursor is active, you can delete points from a path. A new segment joins the remaining points to prevent the path from breaking.

Close path: When you position your cursor over the first point in an open path — that is, a path that has a break in it — this symbol appears. Click with the cursor to close the path.

Convert point: Use this cursor to convert a corner to an arc or an arc to a corner. Just click on a point to change it to a corner; drag from a point to change it to an arc.

Edit path: Press the Command key when using the path tool to access the edit path cursor, which lets you move a point or adjust a control handle.

Drag path: When you're dragging a point, control handle, or whole path, this cursor replaces the edit path cursor.

Clone path: This cursor appears when you Command-Option-drag on a point or whole path. This technique enables you to make a duplicate of the path and store it separately or with the original path.

Hand: The hand cursor appears when you select the hand tool or when you press the spacebar with some other tool selected.

Zoom in: This cursor appears when you select the zoom tool or press Command-spacebar when some other tool is selected. Click or drag to magnify the image on-screen.

Zoom out: The zoom out cursor appears when you press Option with the zoom tool selected or press Option-spacebar with some other tool selected. Click to reduce your view of the image.

Zoom limit: This cursor appears when you're at the end of your zoom rope. You can't zoom in beyond 1,600 percent or out beyond 6 percent ($^1/_{16}$).

Paint bucket: This cursor appears when the paint bucket tool is selected.

Line/gradient: This cursor appears when you select either the line or gradient tool. Drag with the cursor to determine the angle and length of a prospective straight line or gradient fill.

Eyedropper: This cursor appears when you select the eyedropper tool or when you press Option while using the type tool, paint bucket tool, gradient tool, or any painting tool other than the eraser. Click to lift a color from the image window.

Crosshair pickup: If the eyedropper cursor gets in the way, preventing you from seeing what you're doing, press the Caps Lock key to display a crosshair cursor, which zeroes in on an exact pixel. This specific crosshair appears when you use the eyedropper tool or press the Option key with the rubber stamp tool while Caps Lock is down.

Eraser: This cursor appears when you select the eraser tool and the old-style Block option is selected in the Eraser Options panel.

Magic eraser: The magic eraser cursor appears when you press the Option key while using the eraser tool set to the Block mode. You then drag to change portions of the image back to the way they looked when last saved to disk.

Soft eraser: If you select some option other than Block — such as Paintbrush, Airbrush, or Pencil — in the Eraser Options panel, this cursor appears.

Soft magic eraser: When you Option-drag with the soft eraser cursor, Photoshop displays this cursor to show you that any dragging will change the image back to the way it looked when last saved.

Pencil: This cursor appears when you select the pencil tool.

Crosshair: You see this cursor when you press the Caps Lock key while using any painting or editing tool. I find it a particular blessing when I'm using the rubber stamp, smudge, and other editing tools that can sometimes prevent you from seeing what you're doing.

Brush size: This cursor varies in size to show you the exact diameter of the brush that you're using when dragging with the soft eraser, pencil, airbrush, or paintbrush. You can request this special cursor by choosing File⇨ Preferences⇨General and selecting the Brush Size radio button.

Airbrush: You see this cursor by default when you paint with the airbrush.

Paintbrush: When you select the paintbrush, this cursor appears (again, by default).

Stamp: This cursor denotes the selection of the rubber stamp tool.

Stamp pickup: When you press the Option key while using the rubber stamp tool — and the Caps Lock key is up — you see this cursor. You then can specify which portion of an image you want to clone.

Smudge: This cursor appears when the smudge tool is selected.

Blur: When you use the blur tool, you see this cursor.

Sharpen: This cursor appears when you press the Option key in combination with the blur tool or when you switch to the sharpen tool by Option-clicking on the blur tool icon.

Dodge: This cursor appears when you select the dodge tool in order to lighten an image.

Burn: If you prefer to darken portions of an image, press the Option key while using the dodge tool or Option-click on the dodge tool icon to switch to the burn tool. Either way, you get this cursor.

Sponge: Option-click on the burn tool icon in the toolbox to get the sponge tool cursor, which lets you decrease or increase the saturation of colors in an image.

Black eyedropper: This cursor and the two that follow are available only when you work in the Levels and Curves dialog boxes. Click with the black eyedropper to select the color in an image that will change to black.

Gray eyedropper: Click with this cursor to select the color that will change to medium gray (called the *gamma value*).

White eyedropper: Use this cursor to specify the color that will change to white.

Eyedropper plus: New to Version 3.0, this cursor and the next one are available only via the Color Range and Replace Color dialog boxes. Click with this cursor to add colors to the temporary mask generated by these dialog boxes. For complete information on these commands, read Chapters 9 and 16.

Eyedropper minus: Click with this cursor to remove colors from the temporary mask.

Palette hand: This cursor displays inside all panels of the Layers palette. Drag with the cursor to move a layer, channel, or path above or below other layers, channels, or paths listed in the palette.

Move palette item: When you drag a layer, channel, or path, the palette hand changes to the move palette item cursor.

Group layer: Press the Option key and position the cursor over the horizontal line between two layers in the Layers panel to get this cursor. Option-click on the line to group the layers divided by that line.

Ungroup layer: When two layers are grouped, the horizontal line between them becomes dotted. Option-click on the dotted line to ungroup the two layers.

Watch: The watch cursor is the universal Macintosh symbol for hurry up and wait. When you see the cursor inside Photoshop 3.0, you can either sit on your idle hands, waiting for the devil to start playing with them, or you can be industrious, switch to another application, and try to get some work done.

Toolbox controls

You have to love lists. They're fun to write and they're a joy to read. All right, so I'm lying. Making your way through lists of information is a monstrous chore, whether you're on the giving or receiving end. But these particular lists happen to contain essential reference information. So on we go with our newest and most astonishing list yet: the one that explains (gasp) the controls at the bottom of the toolbox. (By the way, in that last sentence, you're not supposed to read "gasp," you're supposed to actually gasp. Try again and see if it works better for you the second time.)

■ **Foreground color:** Click on the foreground color icon to bring up the Color Picker dialog box. Select a color from Photoshop's immense palette and press Return to change the foreground color, which is used by all painting tools except the eraser. (I'm not sure why, but many users make the mistake of double-clicking on the foreground or background color icons when they first start using Photoshop. A single click is all that's needed.)

□ **Background color:** Click on the background color icon to display the Color Picker and change the background color, which is used by the eraser and gradient tools. Photoshop also uses the background color to fill a selected area when you press the Delete key.

↰ **Switch colors:** Click on the switch colors icon to exchange the foreground and background colors. If you want a quick way to make the foreground color white, click on the default colors icon and then click on the switch colors icon.

◼ **Default colors:** Click on this icon to automatically change the foreground color to black and the background color to white.

▣ **Marching ants:** Click on this icon to exit the quick mask mode, which enables you to edit selection boundaries using painting tools. In the marching ants mode, Photoshop represents selection outlines as animated dotted lines that look like marching ants, hence the name. (Adobe calls this mode the *standard mode,* but I think *marching ants mode* better describes the function.)

◉ **Quick mask:** Click here to enter the quick mask mode. The marching ants vanish and the image appears half covered by a translucent layer of red, like a rubylith in traditional paste-up. The rubylith covers the deselected — or masked — portions of the image. Paint with black to extend the areas covered by the rubylith, thereby subtracting from the selection. Paint with white to subtract from the rubylith, thereby adding to the selection.

 The quick mask mode is too complex a topic to sum up in a few sentences. If you can't wait to find out what it's all about, check out Chapter 9, "Creating Masks."

You can change the color and translucency of the rubylith by double-clicking on the marching ants or quick mask icon. You also can change which portion of the image is covered by the color — that is, you can cover the selected area or the masked area.

Standard window: Click on this icon to display the foreground image in a standard window, as shown earlier, in Figure 2-2. By default, every image opens in the *standard window mode*.

Full screen with menu bar: If you can't see enough of your image inside a standard window, click on this icon. The title bar and scroll bars disappear, as do all background windows, but you still can access the menu bar. A black-and-white dotted background fills any empty area around the image. Figure 2-4 shows this option applied to the image from Figure 2-2.

Absolute full screen: Aesthetically speaking, the black-and-white dotted background that accompanies the full-screen with menu bar mode looks awful behind *any* image. I don't know why Adobe didn't just make the background solid gray, or better yet, paisley. But enough griping. To see your image set against a neutral black background — a thoroughly preferable alternative — click on the rightmost of the image window icons. The menu bar disappears, limiting your access to commands (you still can access commands via keyboard equivalents), but you can see as much of your image as can physically fit on-screen. Only the toolbox and palettes remain visible, as shown in Figure 2-5. Adobe calls this mode *Full screen without menu bar;* I call it the *absolute full screen mode,* which seems a bit more descriptive and less cumbersome.

 If the toolbox gets in your way when you're viewing an image in full screen mode, you can hide it and all other open palettes by pressing the Tab key. To bring the toolbox back into view, press Tab again.

The floating palettes

Although palettes have been revised fairly dramatically in Photoshop 3.0, they still share many of the same elements they did in Photoshop 2.5. All palettes, for example, offer most of the standard elements labeled in Figure 2-6. (Some panels lack scroll bars and size boxes.) Many of these elements are shrunken versions of the ones that accompany any window. For example, the close box and title bar work identically to their image-window counterparts. The title bar lacks a title, but you can still drag it to move the palette to another location on-screen. Shift-drag the title bar to align the dragged palette with other palettes or with the edge of the screen.

Figure 2-4:
Click on the full screen with menu bar icon to hide the title bar, scroll bars, and preview box.

Figure 2-5:
Click on the absolute full screen icon to hide everything but the toolbox, floating palettes, and image.

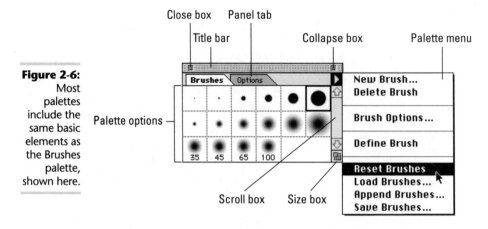

Figure 2-6:
Most palettes include the same basic elements as the Brushes palette, shown here.

Four elements are unique to floating palettes:

- **Palette options:** Each floating palette offers its own collection of options. These options may include tools, icons, pop-up menus, slider bars, you name it.

- **Palette menu:** Drag from the right-pointing arrowhead icon to display a menu of commands specific to the palette. These commands enable you to manipulate the palette options and adjust preference settings.

- **Collapse box:** Click on the collapse box to decrease the on-screen space consumed by the palette. If you previously enlarged the palette by dragging the size box, your first click reduces the palette back to its default size. After that, clicking on the collapse box hides all but the most essential palette options.

 In most cases, collapsing a palette hides all options and leaves only the panel tabs visible. But in the case of the Options, Layers, Paths, and Picker panels, clicking on the collapse box leaves a sliver of palette options intact. To eliminate all options for these panels, Option-click on the collapse box or double-click on one of the panel tabs. Either technique works even if you enlarged the palette by dragging the size box. Figure 2-7 shows how the different palettes appear when partially and fully collapsed.

- **Panel tabs:** Click on a *panel tab* to switch from one panel to another inside a palette. (You can also switch panels by selecting commands from the Window⇨Palettes submenu, but it's more convenient to click.)

Figure 2-7:
The ten palette
panels when
partially collapsed
(left) and fully
collapsed (right).

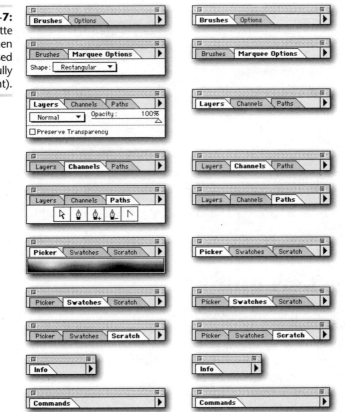

 Photoshop 3.0 allows you to separate and group panels in palettes as you see fit. To separate a panel into its own palette, just drag the panel tab away from the palette, as demonstrated in Figure 2-8. To combine a panel with a different palette, drag the panel tab onto the palette so that the palette becomes highlighted, and then release. The middle and right examples in the figure show off this technique.

The text in this book always assumes the default setup, which may or may not match your configuration. For example, though I may say *check out the Channels panel in the Layers palette*, your Channels panel may be separated into its own palette, or combined with the Info palette. I guess what I'm saying is that you shouldn't take me too seriously.

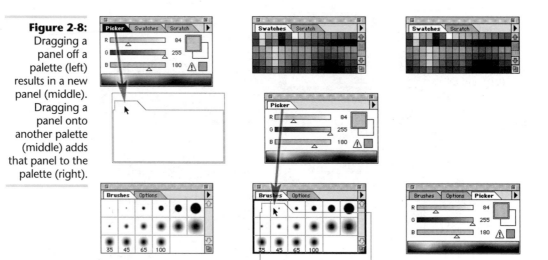

Figure 2-8: Dragging a panel off a palette (left) results in a new panel (middle). Dragging a panel onto another palette (middle) adds that panel to the palette (right).

How to get around

All graphics and desktop publishing programs provide a variety of navigational tools and functions that enable you to scoot around the screen, visit the heartlands and nether regions, examine the fine details, and take in the big picture. Photoshop is no exception. In fact, it provides more navigational tricks per square pixel than just about any other graphics program.

The zoom ratio

In Photoshop, you can change the *view size* — the size at which an image appears on-screen — so that you can either see more of an image or concentrate on individual pixels. Each change in view size is expressed as a *zoom ratio,* which is the ratio between screen pixels and image pixels. A 1:1 zoom ratio means one screen pixel per each image pixel and is therefore equivalent to a 100 percent view size. A 1:2 zoom ratio equates to a 50 percent view size, as shown in Figure 2-9. A 2:1 zoom ratio is equivalent to a 200 percent view size, as shown in Figure 2-10. All told, Photoshop 3.0 provides 31 zoom ratios, ranging from 1:16 to 16:1 in single-digit increments (1:15, 1:14, 1:13, and so on).

When you first open an image, Photoshop displays it at the largest zoom ratio (up to and including 1:1) that permits the entire image to fit on-screen in the standard window mode. Assuming that you don't change the size of the image, you can return to this view size — sometimes called the *fit-in-window view* — at any time during the editing cycle by double-clicking on the hand tool icon in the toolbox.

Figure 2-9:
When viewing an image at the 1:2 zoom ratio, you see only a quarter of the total pixels in the image (half of the pixels vertically and half horizontally).

Figure 2-10:
At the 2:1 zoom ratio, each pixel in the image measures 2 screen pixels tall and 2 screen pixels wide.

The zoom tool

The zoom tool enables you to change view sizes as follows:

↪ Click in the image window with the zoom tool to magnify the image to twice the previous zoom ratio.

↪ Option-click with the zoom tool to reduce the image to half its previous zoom ratio.

↪ Drag with the zoom tool to draw a rectangular marquee around the portion of the image you want to magnify. Photoshop magnifies the image so that the marqueed area fits just inside the image window. If the horizontal and vertical proportions of the marquee do not match those of the image window — for example, if you draw a tall, thin marquee or a short, wide one — Photoshop favors the smaller of the two possible zoom ratios to avoid hiding any detail inside the marquee.

↪ Double-click on the zoom tool icon in the toolbox to restore the foreground image to a 1:1 zoom ratio.

 To temporarily access the zoom tool when some other tool is selected, press and hold the Command and spacebar keys. Release both keys to return control of the cursor to the selected tool. To access the zoom out cursor, press both Option and the spacebar. These keyboard equivalents work from inside many dialog boxes, most notably those that provide preview options (such as the Hue/Saturation, Levels, and Curves dialog boxes discussed in Chapter 16).

When you use the zoom tool, you magnify and reduce the image within the confines of a static image window. To change the dimensions of the window to fit those of the image, click on the zoom box in the upper right corner of the title bar.

 To automatically resize the window along with the image, use the Zoom In (Command-plus) and Zoom Out (Command-minus) commands under the Window menu. Frequently, it's more convenient to use these commands than the zoom tool. And if that's not enough, you can zoom in to the highest level of magnification, 16:1, by pressing Command-Option-plus. Command-Option-minus zooms out to the smallest view size, 1:16.

 Photoshop 3.0 offers one additional zooming command under the Window menu. Called Zoom Factor, it enables you to set the exact zoom ratio numerically. Choose Window⇨Zoom Factor, select the Magnification or Reduction radio button, enter the desired zoom value (from 1 to 16) in the Factor option

box, and press Return. For example, if you select Magnification and enter 3, Photoshop magnifies to a 3:1 zoom ratio. Selecting Reduction with the same Factor value results in a 1:3 zoom ratio.

Creating a reference window

In the old days, paint programs used to provide a cropped view of your image at the 1:1 zoom ratio to serve as a reference when you worked in a magnified view size. Because it's so doggone modern, Photoshop does not, but you can easily create a second view of your image by choosing Window⇨New Window. Use the new window to maintain a 100 percent view of your image while you zoom and edit inside the original window. Both windows track the changes to the image, as shown in Figure 2-11. The paintbrush strokes applied to the leaves appear in both windows.

Figure 2-11:
You can create multiple windows to track the changes made to a single image by choosing the New Window command from the Window menu.

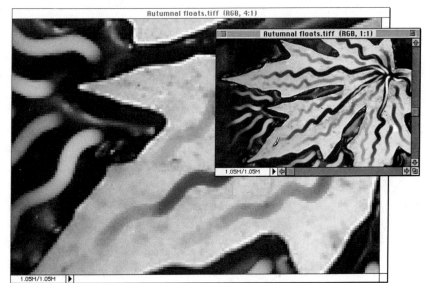

Scrolling inside the window

In the standard window mode, you have access to scroll bars, just as you do in the vast majority of Macintosh and Windows applications. But as you become more proficient with Photoshop, you'll use the scroll bars less and less. One way to bypass the scroll bars is to use the keyboard equivalents listed in Table 2-1. Mac folks who don't own extended keyboards can use the Control key equivalents in the third column.

Table 2-1	Scrolling from the Keyboard	
Scrolling Action	*Extended Keyboard*	*Smaller Mac Keyboard*
Up one screen	Page Up	Control-K
Up slightly	Shift-Page Up	Control-Shift-K
Down one screen	Page Down	Control-L
Down slightly	Shift-Page Down	Control-Shift-L
To upper left corner	Home	Control-A
To lower right corner	End	Control-D

Unfortunately, you can't scroll exclusively left or right from the keyboard. But who cares? You won't be scrolling from the keyboard that often anyway. Most of the time, you'll use the hand tool.

To temporarily access the hand tool when some other tool is selected, press and hold the spacebar. Releasing the spacebar returns the cursor to its original appearance. This keyboard equivalent even works from inside many dialog boxes.

Shortcuts

Shortcuts enable you to access commands and other functions without resorting to the laborious task of choosing commands from menus or clicking on some fool icon until your arm falls off. Many shortcuts are fairly obvious. For example, Photoshop lists keyboard equivalents for its commands next to the command in the menu. You can choose File⇨New by pressing Command-N, choose Edit⇨Undo by pressing Command-Z, choose Select⇨All by pressing Command-A, and so on. But a few of Photoshop's shortcuts are either hidden or can be overlooked easily.

Table 2-2 lists my favorite Photoshop shortcuts. I've already mentioned some of these, but they bear repeating. Italicized table entries indicate shortcuts that are new or revised in Version 3.0.

Be sure to substitute Alt for Option and Ctrl for Command if you're using Photoshop for Windows. The Return key on the Mac is the same as the standard Enter key on a PC keyboard. The Mac's Enter key corresponds to the Enter key on the PC keypad. Macintosh Control-key shortcuts are not available in Windows.

Table 2-2	The Best Photoshop Shortcuts You'll Ever Learn
Operation	*Shortcut*
Navigation tricks	
Scroll image with hand tool	Press the spacebar and drag with any selected tool
Zoom in without changing window size	Command-spacebar-click
Magnify to custom zoom ratio	Command-spacebar-drag
Zoom in and change window size to fit	Command-plus
Zoom out without changing window size	Option-spacebar-click
Zoom out and change window size to fit	Command-minus
Zoom to 100%	Double-click on the zoom tool icon
Fit image in window	Double-click on the hand tool icon
Paint and edit tool tricks	
Display crosshair cursor	Caps Lock
Lift foreground color with eyedropper (when any paint tool is selected)	Option-click
Lift background color	Option-click with the eyedropper tool
Revert image with magic eraser	Option-drag with the eraser tool
Select different kind of eraser	*Option-click on eraser tool icon in toolbox*
Specify an area to clone	Option-click with the rubber stamp tool
Dip into the foreground color when smearing	Option-drag with the smudge tool
Change sharpen tool to blur tool or blur tool to sharpen tool	Option-click on focus tool icon in toolbox
Sharpen with the blur tool or blur with the sharpen tool	Option-drag
Change dodge tool to burn tool, burn tool to sponge tool, or sponge tool to dodge tool	*Option-click on toning tool icon in toolbox*
Darken with the dodge tool or lighten with the burn tool	Option-drag
Paint or edit in a straight line	Click and then Shift-click with the painting or editing tool
Change opacity, pressure, or exposure of paint tools in 10% increments	Press 0 through 9 (1 is 10%, 9 is 90%, 0 is 100%)
Cycle through brush shapes	*Left or right bracket*
Switch to first or last shape in Brushes palette	*Shift-left bracket or Shift-right bracket*

(continued)

Table 2-2 *(continued)*

Operation	Shortcut
Selection and layering tricks	
Select area of contiguous color	*Control-click when marquee or lasso tool is selected*
Add to a selection	Shift-drag with selection tool (Shift-click with magic wand)
Subtract from a selection or delete part of a floating selection	Command-drag with selection tool (Command-click with magic wand)
Drop part of a floating selection	Command-drag with type tool
Subtract all but intersected portion of a selection	Command-Shift-drag with selection tool (Command-Shift-click with magic wand)
Move selection	*Drag inside selection with selection tool or drag anywhere with move tool*
Constrain movement vertically or horizontally	Shift after you begin to drag inside selection with selection tool
Move selection in 1-pixel increments	Any arrow key
Move selection in 10-pixel increments	Shift-any arrow key
Clone selection	Option-drag inside selection with selection tool
Clone selection in 1-pixel increments	Option-any arrow key
Clone selection in 10-pixel increments	Shift-Option-any arrow key
Clone a selection to a different window	*Drag the selection from one window and drop it into another*
Move selection boundary independently of contents	Command-Option-drag inside selection with selection tool
Move selection boundary independently in 1-pixel increments	Command-Option-any arrow key
Move selection boundary independently in 10-pixel increments	Command-Shift-Option-any arrow key
Fill selection with background color	Delete or Clear (or Control-H) when no path is selected
Fill selection with foreground color	Option-Delete (or Control-Option-H)
Display Fill dialog box	*Shift-Delete (or Control-Shift-H)*
Float selection (separate it from the rest of the image)	Command-J
Change opacity of floating selection in 10% increments	Press 0 through 9 when a selection tool is active (1 is 10%, 9 is 90%, 0 is 100%)

Operation	Shortcut
Send a floating selection to a new layer	*Double-click on the Floating Selection layer name in the Layers panel*
Change overlay options for layer	*Double-click on layer name in Layers panel*
Convert mask channel to selection outline	*Option-click on mask channel name in Channels palette or Command-Option-0 through Command-Option-9*
Select contents of active layer	*Command-Option-T*
Toggle quick mask color over masked or selected area	*Option-click on quick mask icon in toolbox*
Hide/show marching ants	Command-H
Deselect everything	Command-D
Pen tool and path tricks (when any tool but a selection tool is active, unless otherwise noted)	
Move selected points	Command-drag on point
Select multiple points in path	Command-Shift-click on point
Select entire path	Command-Option-click on point or segment
Convert corner to arc	Command-Control-drag on point *(no Windows equivalent)*
Convert arc to corner	Command-Control-click on point *(no Windows equivalent)*
Convert arc to cusp	Command-Control-drag the control handle *(no Windows equivalent)*
Insert point in path	Command-Option-click on segment when arrow tool in Paths panel is selected
Remove point from path	Command-Option-click on point when arrow tool is selected
Convert path to selection outline	*Press Enter when selection tool is active*
Add path to current selection	*Shift-Enter when selection tool is active*
Subtract path from current selection or delete path from floating selection	*Command-Enter when selection tool is active*
Subtract all of current selection that isn't intersected by path	*Command-Shift-Enter when selection tool is active*
Apply brushstroke, eraser, rubber stamp, or edit around perimeter of path	*Enter when appropriate tool is active*
Save the current path for future use	*Double-click on the Work Path name in the Paths panel*

(continued)

Table 2-2 *(continued)*

Operation	*Shortcut*
Image and color adjustments	
Resize cropping boundary	Drag corner handle
Rotate cropping boundary	Option-drag corner handle
Move cropping boundary	Command-drag corner handle
Reapply last filter used	Command-F
Display dialog box for last filter used	Command-Option-F
Replace color in Swatches panel of Picker palette with foreground color	Shift-click on color swatch
Delete color from Swatches panel	Command-click on color swatch
Compare unaltered image from inside color correction dialog box	Mouse down on dialog box title bar when Preview check box is not selected
Reset options inside any color correction dialog box	Option-click on Cancel button
General	
Switch between channels	Command-0 through Command-9 (0 is composite of color channels)
Switch to next layer down	*Command-left bracket*
Switch to next layer up	*Command-right bracket*
Switch to layer that contains image	*Command-click on image with move tool*
Move a panel out of a palette	*Drag the panel tab*
Display Options panel of Brushes palette	Double-click on tool icon in toolbox
Fully collapse palette	*Option-click on collapse box or double-click on panel tab*
Preview how image will sit on printed page	Mouse down on preview box
View size and resolution of image	Option-mouse down on preview box
Hide or show toolbox and other floating palettes	Tab
Change a command in the Commands palette	*Shift-click on command name*
Delete a command from the Commands palette	*Command-click on command name*
Change the preference settings	Command-K
Activate Don't Save button	Command-D
Cancel the current operation	Command-period

Toolbox shortcuts

All right, if this next bit of information doesn't make you squeal with delight, nothing will. With Photoshop 3.0, you now can select tools and activate controls from the keyboard. Is that the greatest thing since sliced bread or what? The moment I stumbled on it — I can't find it in the documentation, but then I'm using a beta version of the software — I had to get up and do a little dance around my office. (Isn't it nice to know I still take pleasure in life's little rewards?)

In any case, Figure 2-12 tells the whole, wonderful story. Just press the appropriate key, as shown in the figure — no Command, Option, or other modifiers required. Many of the shortcuts make sense. *M* selects the marquee tool, *L* is for lasso tool. But then there are the weird ones, like *Y* for tYpe, *K* for paint bucKet, *U* for smUdge, *O* for dOdge, and my favorite, *I* for I-dropper. As far as I can tell, the only alphabetical key that doesn't do anything is *J*.

Figure 2-12:
Press these keys to select tools and toggle controls in Photoshop 3.0.

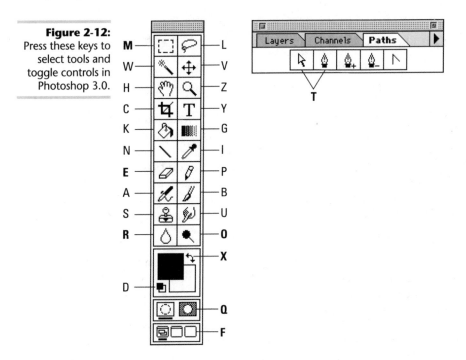

The keys that appear in bold type in Figure 2-12 act as toggles. For example, if you press M once, you get the last marquee tool used (rectangular by default). Press M again to select the other marquee tool. Other toggles work as follows:

- **E** takes you from one kind of eraser to the next. (The only way to monitor which eraser is active is to display the Eraser Options panel.)

- **R** switches between the blur and sharpen tools.

- **O** toggles between the dodge, burn, and sponge tools.

- **X** swaps the foreground and background colors and then swaps them back again.

- **Q** enters the quick mask mode and then exits it.

- **F** takes you from one window mode to another.

- **T** switches between the pen tool and the arrow tool in the Paths panel. It even displays the palette if the palette is hidden.

Establishing function key shortcuts

Though pretty extensive, Table 2-2 doesn't include *every* shortcut, just the best ones. (I left out most of the keyboard equivalents you can see in the menus.)

If you own an extended keyboard, you can specify additional keyboard equivalents by choosing Window⇨Palettes⇨Show Commands. Shown in Figure 2-13, the Commands palette enables you to assign any command to a function key or Shift-function key combination. You can even assign colors to the commands to logically group them, as shown in the second example in the figure. And if you prefer clicking on-screen to pressing function keys, you can simply click on the command name in the palette to initiate the corresponding command.

Using the Commands palette is a little more involved than the old Function Key Preferences dialog box. The best way to assign function-key equivalents en masse is to select the Edit Commands option from the Commands palette pop-up menu, which displays the first dialog box shown in Figure 2-14. From here, you can either edit or delete the commands that have already been assigned or add new commands. To add a command, click on the New button, which displays the second dialog box in the figure. Then choose the desired command from the menu bar along the top of the screen or from any available palette menu. The chosen command appears in the Name option box. Alternatively, you can enter the first few letters of a command name and click on the Find button. When Photoshop finds a match, it automatically displays it in the Name option box.

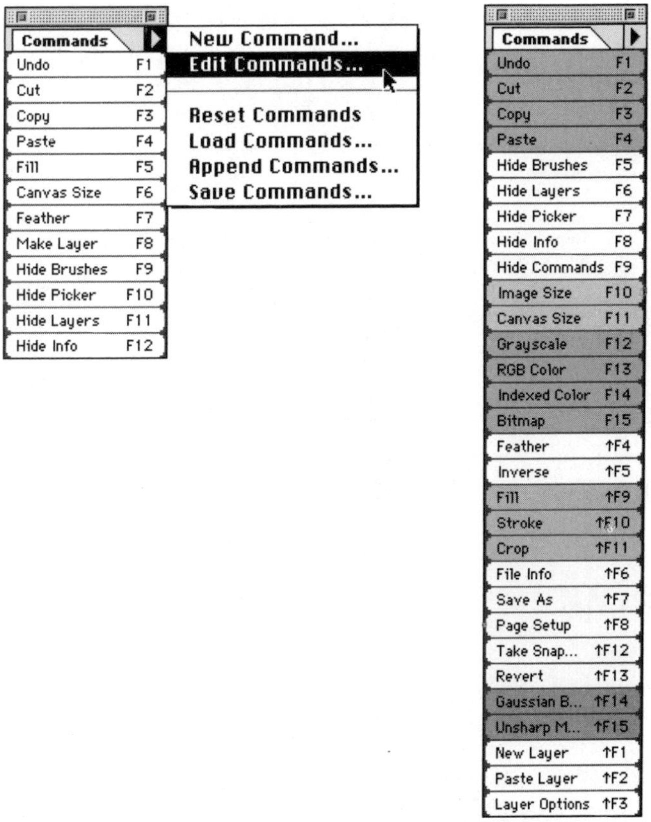

Figure 2-13:
The Commands
palette as it
appears by default
(left) and after I
assigned a
command to every
function key
combination
(right).

Commands	▶
Undo	F1
Cut	F2
Copy	F3
Paste	F4
Fill	F5
Canvas Size	F6
Feather	F7
Make Layer	F8
Hide Brushes	F9
Hide Picker	F10
Hide Layers	F11
Hide Info	F12

New Command...
Edit Commands...

Reset Commands
Load Commands...
Append Commands...
Save Commands...

Commands	▶
Undo	F1
Cut	F2
Copy	F3
Paste	F4
Hide Brushes	F5
Hide Layers	F6
Hide Picker	F7
Hide Info	F8
Hide Commands	F9
Image Size	F10
Canvas Size	F11
Grayscale	F12
RGB Color	F13
Indexed Color	F14
Bitmap	F15
Feather	⇧F4
Inverse	⇧F5
Fill	⇧F9
Stroke	⇧F10
Crop	⇧F11
File Info	⇧F6
Save As	⇧F7
Page Setup	⇧F8
Take Snap...	⇧F12
Revert	⇧F13
Gaussian B...	⇧F14
Unsharp M...	⇧F15
New Layer	⇧F1
Paste Layer	⇧F2
Layer Options	⇧F3

To assign a key equivalent, select an option from the Function Key pop-up menu.
Dimmed options indicate keys that have already been assigned. Select the Shift check
box if you want to press Shift with the function key to access the command. Select an
option from the Color pop-up menu if you want to assign a color to the button in the
Commands palette.

You don't have to assign any key to a command. If you just want to create a
button for the command without any means to access it from the keyboard,
leave the Function Key option set to None. This way, you can access the
command by clicking on its name in the Commands palette, even in the absolute full screen mode when the menu bar is hidden.

To edit a command in the Edit Commands dialog box, double-click on the command
name in the scrolling list. To delete a command, select it and click on the Delete button.

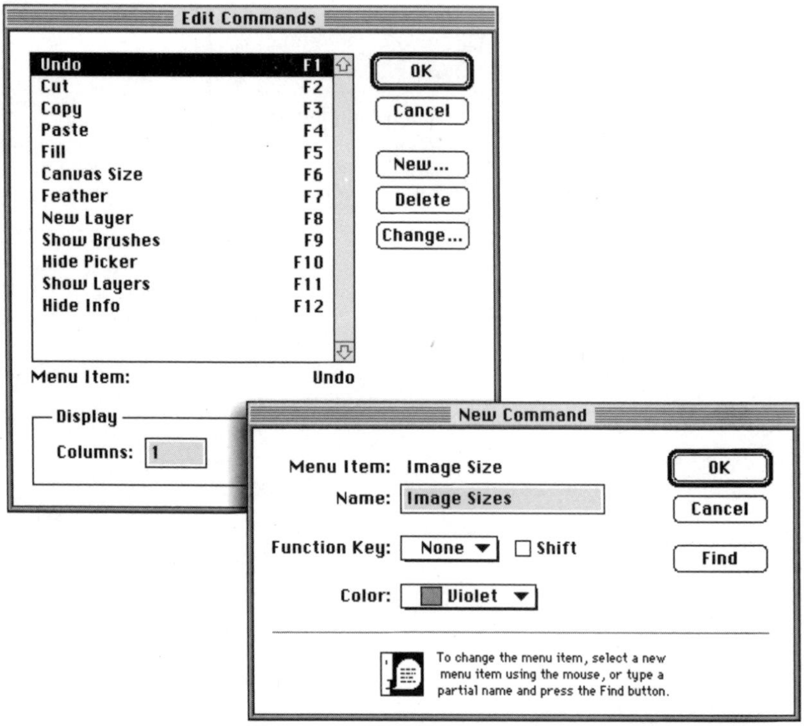

Figure 2-14:
Click on the New button in the Edit Commands dialog box (top) to display the New Command dialog box (bottom).

Edit Commands

Undo	F1
Cut	F2
Copy	F3
Paste	F4
Fill	F5
Canvas Size	F6
Feather	F7
New Layer	F8
Show Brushes	F9
Hide Picker	F10
Show Layers	F11
Hide Info	F12

OK
Cancel
New...
Delete
Change...

Menu Item: Undo

Display
Columns: 1

New Command

Menu Item: Image Size
Name: Image Sizes
Function Key: None ▼   ☐ Shift
Color: ▓ Violet ▼

OK
Cancel
Find

To change the menu item, select a new menu item using the mouse, or type a partial name and press the Find button.

You can also delete a command from the scrolling list by Command-clicking on it. When you press the Command key, the scissors cursor appears to show you that your next click will clip away a command. In addition, you can edit and delete commands from outside the Edit Commands dialog box. Command-click on a button in the Commands palette to delete it; Shift-click (or Control-click) to edit the command.

The Columns option box at the bottom of the Edit Commands dialog box controls the number of columns in the Commands palette. Like colors, columns are simply an organizational issue. If you want a long list of commands going down the side of your monitor, leave the option set to one column. If you prefer a shorter and wider Commands palette, go with two or three columns. You can specify as many as nine columns.

When you're finished adding commands and function-key equivalents, be sure to save your settings to disk by selecting the Save Commands option from the palette pop-up menu. If your preferences file ever becomes corrupted or if someone goes and throws it away, you can retrieve the function keys using the Load Commands option in the pop-up menu.

Using a macro utility

To expand your range of shortcut options beyond a handful of function-key combinations, you need to go outside of Photoshop and take advantage of a separate utility. Generally speaking, you have two software options. You can use Apple's ResEdit, which lets you assign keyboard equivalents that you save inside the Photoshop application, or you can choose one of two macro utility programs, CE Software's QuicKeys or Affinity Microsystems' Tempo, which require that you store keyboard equivalents in a separate file. The advantages and disadvantages of each are as follows:

- ☞ **ResEdit advantages:** Because ResEdit makes keyboard equivalents part of the Photoshop application code, you can access commands when the menu bar is unavailable, as it is when you view an image in the absolute full screen mode. Also, ResEdit shortcuts appear in the menu, just like Photoshop's default shortcuts. You can even change the default shortcuts if you don't like them.

- ☞ **ResEdit disadvantages:** ResEdit enables you to assign Command-key equivalents only, and Photoshop already uses Command plus every key on the keyboard. That means that you must resort to special Option and Shift-Option symbols, which won't necessarily display correctly in the Photoshop menu. Also, with ResEdit, you are actually editing the Photoshop application code, and you can mess it up royally if you're not careful. Make sure to make a backup copy of Photoshop before you even *think* about using ResEdit.

- ☞ **QuicKeys/Tempo advantages:** The first advantage of a macro utility program is safety. Because you store the keyboard equivalents in a separate file, you can't harm the Photoshop application no matter how many mistakes you make. Second, it's easy to use. You can get up and running with QuicKeys, for example, in a matter of minutes. By contrast, ResEdit is one of those programs that takes years to grasp fully — and Apple distributes it without any documentation. (This is because ResEdit is designed with programmers, not end users, in mind.) Third, a macro utility provides access to any keystroke you care to press. Fourth, you can create shortcuts not only for commands but also for options, tools, control icons, and so on. And fifth, you can record *sequences,* which are shortcuts that perform many operations in response to a single keystroke.

- ☞ **QuicKeys/Tempo disadvantages:** Although macro utilities are inexpensive compared to other varieties of software, they do cost money — about $100 through mail-order vendors. ResEdit is distributed free of charge over electronic bulletin boards and the like. Another drawback is that you cannot choose a command unless the menu bar is available, which presents a potential problem when you work in the absolute full screen mode. Luckily, there is a way around this, as explained in the upcoming section "Shortcuts in the absolute full screen mode."

Of the two macro utilities, QuicKeys is the more popular and the easiest to use. But QuicKeys also is limited in its ability to perform conditional operations — "Do X if Y is true." Tempo is more difficult to use but is much more flexible. If you want to do more than launch programs and assign shortcuts to commands, Tempo is the better choice.

You'll find a run-time version of Tempo on the CD, along with some predefined macros that run complicated channel operations. It will give you a taste of what this fine utility is capable of doing.

Shortcut suggestions

In the final analysis, a macro utility wins out over ResEdit. Whether you ultimately select QuicKeys or Tempo, you can increase your speed and efficiency by creating shortcuts of your own. I don't have space in this book to document how to use a macro utility, but I can recommend keyboard equivalents you may want to explore. Table 2-3 contains a list of suggested shortcuts for commands and control icons. Keep in mind that these represent only those commands I consider to be the most useful; I ignore all sorts of filters that are handy but on a less frequent basis.

All keystrokes employ the first letter of the function name when possible. When that keystroke is already taken, an alternate letter is selected. You may occasionally disagree with my reasoning, in which case I encourage you to experiment on your own and come up with shortcuts that work best for you.

As you can see in Table 2-3, I associate certain modifier keys with certain tasks, which helps me remember the shortcuts I've already assigned and their purposes. For example, I use Command-Control combinations exclusively to launch programs. Command-Control-A launches Adobe Photoshop. (Actually, right now I'm using Command-Control-3 for Photoshop 3.0 because Version 2.5 is still on my hard drive. But once I dump the old version, I'll switch over to Command-Control-A again. I knew you'd want to hear that story.) Similarly, I use Command-Shift combinations to edit selections and Command-Option combinations to edit an entire image.

Table 2-3	Potential Photoshop Shortcuts
Operation	**Shortcut**
Displaying palettes	
Window⇨Palettes⇨Show Brushes	Command-Shift-1 (keypad)
Window⇨Palettes⇨Show Layers	Command-Shift-2 (keypad)
Window⇨Palettes⇨Show Picker	Command-Shift-3 (keypad)
Window⇨Palettes⇨Show Info	Command-Shift-4 (keypad)
Window⇨Palettes⇨Show Commands	Command-Shift-5 (keypad)
Editing selections	
Edit⇨Stroke	Command-Shift-S
Edit⇨Define Pattern	Command-Shift-P
Edit⇨Paste Into	Command-Shift-V
Image⇨Flip⇨Horizontal	Command-Shift-H
Image⇨Flip⇨Vertical	Command-Shift-Y
Image⇨Rotate⇨90° CW	Command-Shift-right arrow
Image⇨Rotate⇨90° CCW	Command-Shift-left arrow
Image⇨Rotate⇨Free	Command-Shift-R
Image⇨Effects⇨Scale	Command-Shift-Z
Filter⇨Blur⇨Gaussian Blur	Command-Shift-G
Filter⇨Noise⇨Add Noise	Command-Shift-N
Filter⇨Sharpen⇨Unsharp Mask	Command-Shift-U
Select⇨Inverse	Command-Shift-I
Select⇨Color Range	Command-Shift-O
Select⇨Feather	Command-Shift-T
Select⇨Modify⇨Expand	Command-Shift-plus
Select⇨Modify⇨Contract	Command-Shift-minus
Select⇨Similar	Command-Shift-M

(continued)

Table 2-3 *(continued)*	
Operation	***Shortcut***
Changing the image	
File⇨Revert	Command-Option-V
Mode⇨Bitmap	Command-Option-B
Mode⇨Grayscale	Command-Option-G
Mode⇨Indexed Color	Command-Option-X
Mode⇨RGB Color	Command-Option-R
Mode⇨CMYK Color	Command-Option-K
Mode⇨Lab Color	Command-Option-L
Image⇨Duplicate	Command-Option-D
Image⇨Canvas Size	Command-Option-C
Image⇨Image Size	Command-Option-I
Window⇨Zoom Factor	Command-Option-Z

Shortcuts in the absolute full screen mode

You learned earlier that the menu bar disappears when you work in the absolute full screen mode. That means that you can't access commands via the menu bar. The only way to choose commands is by using preset keyboard equivalents or custom shortcuts that you assign to function keys. So what are you to do if you want to create custom shortcuts for Photoshop commands that will work even in the absolute full screen mode, but you already assigned away all or most of your function keys using a macro program? The answer is to use *keystroke aliases*.

First, you assign commands to function keys inside Photoshop. Then, inside the macro utility, you assign keystrokes to those Photoshop function keys. When you press the keystroke aliases, the macro sends the function key combination to Photoshop 3.0.

Here's an example. Suppose you assigned the F5 key to open the Scrapbook. You've used this keyboard equivalent for years and you would sooner be tarred and feathered than change it just for the sake of Photoshop. By default, however, Photoshop 3.0 assigns F5 to open the Brushes palette. In absolute full screen mode, F5 provides the only access to the palette, because menu commands are unavailable. You want to continue using F5 to open the Scrapbook, but at the same time, you don't want to lose the ability to show and hide the Brushes palette in the absolute full screen mode. So what do you do? Create a keyboard alias for F5.

As illustrated in Figure 2-15, a macro utility intercepts all keystrokes before they go to the foreground application. If the utility doesn't recognize the keystrokes, it lets the keystroke pass. If the keystroke corresponds to one of its macros, it passes the macro on to the foreground application.

When you press F5, the macro utility intercepts the keystroke and converts it into the *Open Scrapbook* operation. F5 goes in, but F5 does not come out. You therefore can instruct the macro utility to convert a different keystroke to F5. In Table 2-3, I suggested assigning Command-Shift-1 to the Windows⇨Show Brushes command. If you also establish Command-Shift-1 as a keystroke alias for F5, the macro not only fulfills the same purpose, it also works inside the absolute full screen mode.

The conclusion, therefore, is to use the Commands palette to assign function and Shift-function keystrokes to your favorite 30 commands that don't already have preset keyboard equivalents. Then create keystroke aliases for the function keys using QuicKeys or Tempo. All 30 aliases will work in the absolute full screen mode.

Figure 2-15:
A macro utility can convert the F5 keystroke into an operation and convert another keystroke into F5.

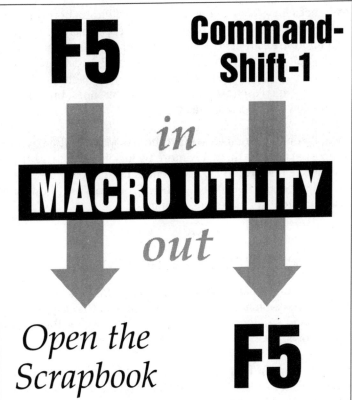

Customizing the Interface

In addition to adding your own keyboard equivalents, you can customize the Photoshop interface by changing the *preference settings.* Photoshop ships with certain preference settings already in force (these are called *factory default settings*), but you can change the settings to reflect your personal preferences.

You can change preference settings in two ways. You can make environmental adjustments using commands from the File⇨Preferences submenu, or you can change the operation of specific tools by adjusting settings in the Options panel of the Brushes palette. Photoshop 3.0 remembers environmental preferences, tool settings, and even the file format under which you saved the last image by saving this information to a file called *Adobe Photoshop 3.0 Prefs* in the Preferences folder inside the System Folder.

 To restore Photoshop's factory default settings, delete the Adobe Photoshop 3.0 Prefs file when the application is *not* running. The next time you launch Photoshop, it creates a new preferences file automatically.

Deleting the preferences file is also a great thing to do if Photoshop starts acting funny. Photoshop's preference file has always been highly susceptible to corruption, possibly because the application writes to it so often. Whatever the reason, if Photoshop starts behaving erratically, quit the program, delete the Adobe Photoshop 3.0 Prefs file, and relaunch Photoshop. You'll have to reload your function key settings — see, aren't you glad you saved them? — and reset other important preferences, but a smooth-running program is worth the few minutes of extra effort.

 After you get your preferences set just the way you like them, you can prevent Photoshop from altering them any more by locking the file. At the Finder level, select the Adobe Photoshop 3.0 Preferences file, choose File⇨Get Info (Command-I), and select the Locked check box. From now on, Photoshop will start up with a consistent set of default settings.

The File⇨Preferences commands

The File⇨Preferences submenu in Photoshop 3.0 differs from its counterpart in Version 2.5 in the addition of two commands — Gamut Warning and Transparency — and the deletion of one command — Function Keys. Whether old or new, the commands in this submenu work as follows:

- ⇨ **General (Command-K):** This command provides access to the preference settings you'll need to adjust most often. The next section of this chapter examines the General Preferences dialog box.

- **Gamut Warning:** This command controls the color that Photoshop uses to highlight screen colors that will not print correctly. You request this feature by choosing Mode⇨Gamut Warning.

- **Plug-ins:** Offered only by Photoshop 3.0, this command lets you change the folder in which Photoshop searches for the plug-in modules it loads during the launch cycle. This setting doesn't take effect until you relaunch the program.

- **Scratch Disks:** Discussed in Chapter B on the CD, this command lets you specify the hard drive or removable media device on which Photoshop stores its temporary virtual memory files. Again, this setting doesn't take effect until you relaunch the program.

- **Transparency:** You may have noticed that Photoshop 3.0 momentarily displays a checkerboard pattern after you open an image or switch application. This checkerboard represents *transparency,* which is the utter absence of data. As explained in Chapter 8, transparency is required to mix one layer with the layer in back of it. You can change the checkerboard pattern by using File⇨Preferences⇨Transparency. The command has no effect on the way transparency or layers work. It's purely a visual thing, as is so often the case with preferences.

- **Units:** This command enables you to change the units of measure that appear in the Info palette, as well as in every dialog box in which you can specify the size of something. If you prefer picas to inches, for example, choose this command.

The lower portion of the File⇨Preferences submenu enables you to adjust the way colors appear on-screen (*monitor calibration*) and when printed (*color separation*). These options are explained in greater depth in Chapter 6, "Printing Images," but here's a quick rundown:

- **Monitor Setup:** This command enables you to change the way Photoshop displays colors on your monitor. You can specify the brand of monitor you use and the lighting conditions of the room in which you work. You also can adjust the *gamma,* which affects the brightness of the medium-range colors (or *midtones*) displayed on your monitor.

- **Printing Inks Setup:** Use this command to control the output of color proofs and CMYK (cyan, magenta, yellow, and black) separations for four-color offset reproduction. Together with the preceding command, Printing Inks Setup determines the way Photoshop converts colors between the RGB and CMYK modes.

- **Separation Setup:** This command lets you control the generation of four-color separations. You can adjust the black separation both independently and in tandem with the cyan, magenta, and yellow separations.

⌘ **Separation Tables:** This command enables you to save the settings you selected in the Printing Inks Setup and Separation Setup dialog box to a special file for later use. Even though both of those dialog boxes provide save options of their own, only the Separation Tables dialog box lets you save both together.

General environmental preferences

Of all the Preferences commands, the General command is the most important. I touch on the other valuable commands throughout the remainder of this book, but the General command deserves your immediate attention because it affects the widest range of Photoshop functions. Why else do you think they call it *General* (as opposed to *Corporal* or *Potato Peeler, 3rd Class*)? Figure 2-16 shows the General Preferences dialog box in all its splendor.

In brief, the options inside this dialog box work as follows:

⌘ **Color Picker:** When you click on the foreground or background color control icon in the toolbox, Photoshop displays one of two *color pickers,* its own or the one provided by the Apple system software. If you are familiar with other Macintosh graphics programs but new to Photoshop, the system software's Color Picker dialog box may be more familiar to you. However, Photoshop's color picker is more versatile.

⌘ **Interpolation:** When you resample an image using Image⇨Image Size or transform it using one of the commands in the Image⇨Rotation or Image⇨Effects submenu, Photoshop has to make up — or *interpolate* — pixels to fill in the gaps. You can change how Photoshop calculates the interpolation by choosing one of the three options demonstrated in Figure 2-17.

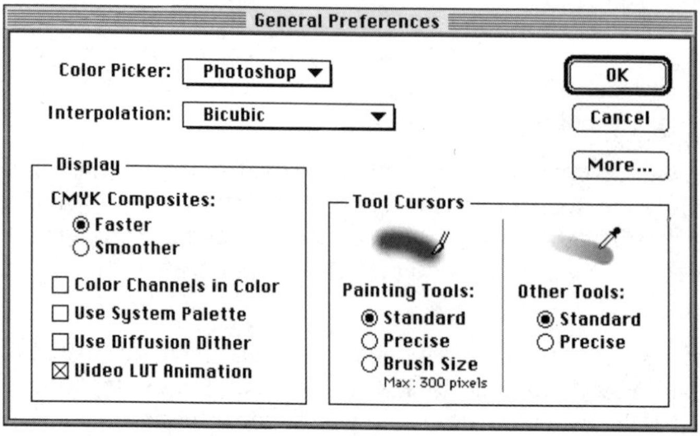

Figure 2-16: The General Preferences dialog box contains the options for the most important environmental settings.

Figure 2-17:
The
Photoshop
application
icon and a
simple box
pattern
shown as
they appear
when
enlarged to
400 percent
and subjected
to the three
different
types of
interpolation.

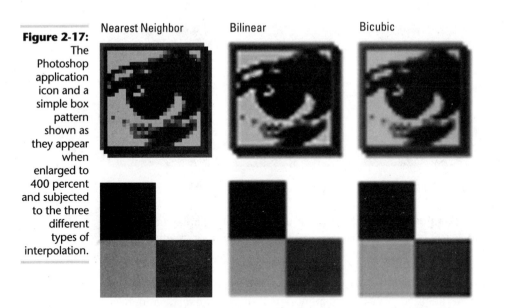

If you choose Nearest Neighbor, Photoshop simply copies the next-door pixel when creating a new one. This is the fastest but least helpful setting. The Bilinear option smoothes the transitions between pixels by creating intermediary shades. It takes more time, but typically, the softened effect is worth it. Still more time-intensive is the default setting, Bicubic, which boosts the amount of contrast between pixels in order to offset the blurring effect that generally accompanies interpolation.

Figure 2-18 shows how the Bicubic setting adds special dips and peaks in color transitions that the Bilinear setting leaves out. (The names *bilinear* and *bicubic* refer to the complexity of the polynomial used to calculate the interpolations. Better names might be *softened* and *softened with enhanced contrast*.) Figure 2-18 shows the gray boxes from the previous figure mapped onto bar graphs. Taller vertical graph lines indicate darker values. You can see that whereas bilinear interpolation simply rounds off the transition between neighboring colors, bicubic interpolation creates dips and peaks in color transitions that accentuate contrast and prevent overblurring.

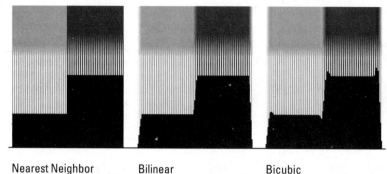

Nearest Neighbor   Bilinear   Bicubic

- **CMYK Composites:** RGB is the color mode used to display images on a monitor; CMYK is the color mode used to print colors on paper. In effect, when you edit a CMYK image, you're trying to display images on-screen in the wrong color mode. Photoshop 3.0 provides two solutions: If you select the Smoother option, Photoshop preserves the actual CMYK color values in an image and converts them on the fly to your RGB display — a precise but excruciatingly slow process. If you specify the Faster option, Photoshop cheats by converting the colors in an image to their nearest RGB equivalents according to a *color lookup table* (CLUT), which speeds up the screen display dramatically but sacrifices image quality. When using CMYK acceleration hardware, such as SuperMac's Thunder II GX•1360 board, select the more accurate Smoother option. Otherwise, you may as well enjoy the speed improvement offered by Faster.

- **Color Channels in Color:** Individual color channels contain only 8 bits of information per pixel, which means that they display grayscale images. Photoshop provides you with the option of colorizing the channel according to the primary color it represents. For example, when this option is turned on, the red color channel looks like a grayscale image viewed through red acetate. However, most experts agree that the effect isn't very helpful and does more to obscure your image than make it easier for you to see what's going on.

- **Using System Palette:** This option applies to using Photoshop on an 8-bit monitor. As discussed in Chapter B on the CD, it's best to use 16-bit video or better, but in case you don't, Photoshop lets you specify how you want it to dither colors on-screen. By default, Photoshop selects the 256 colors that are most suited to your image. In doing so, however, it must switch color palettes every time you bring a new document to the foreground. If you want all open documents to conform to the same color palette — the one built into the Macintosh system software — select this option.

- **Use Diffusion Dither:** 32-bit QuickDraw, built into System 7 and included as a system extension with System 6, automatically dithers colors using a gridlike dot pattern. Photoshop offers a more naturalistic *diffusion dither* that imitates colors slightly more accurately. But because the diffusion dither follows no specific pattern, you sometimes see distinct edges between selected and deselected portions of your image after applying a filter or some other effect.

 To eliminate any visual disharmony that may occur when using the Use Diffusion Dither option, you can force Photoshop to redraw the entire image by double-clicking on the zoom tool icon or performing some other zoom function.

- **Video LUT Animation:** To speed display on 24-bit monitors, Photoshop uses a color lookup table (old *CLUT* again, or in Photoshop lingo, *LUT*). If you've ever worked inside one of Photoshop's color correction dialog boxes — such as Levels or Curves — with the Preview option turned off, you've seen *LUT animation* in progress. Photoshop changes the LUT on the fly according to your specifications and, in doing so, more or less previews the color change over the entire image. It's not a real preview, but it's the next best thing. If LUT animation causes a problem with your video board, you can turn it off using this option. Otherwise, leave it on.

- **Painting Tools:** When you use paint or edit tools in an image, Photoshop can display one of three cursors. The default Standard cursor looks like a paintbrush, airbrush, finger, or whatever. These cursors are great if you have problems keeping track of what tool you selected, but otherwise they border on childishly simplistic. The Precise and Brush Size options are more functional. Precise displays crosshairs, the same ones that appear when you press the Caps Lock key. Brush Size shows the actual size of the brush up to 300 screen pixels in diameter. This means that if the zoom ratio is 1:2 and the brush size is 500 pixels wide, the brush only looks 250 pixels wide on-screen and displays fine. But if you zoom in to actual size, the brush size is too large to display, and the standard cursor appears instead. In the final analysis, the Brush Size option is so great that nine out of ten doctors recommend it.

 When Standard or Brush Size is selected, pressing the Caps Lock key displays the precise crosshair cursors. But when Precise is selected, pressing Caps Lock displays the actual brush size.

- **Other tools:** Again, you can select Standard to get the regular cursors or Precise to get crosshairs. I prefer to leave this option set to Standard, because you can easily access the crosshairs by pressing Caps Lock. The Precise option locks you into crosshairs whether you like it or not.

The number of General Preference options has grown so much that a second dialog box has been created to accommodate them. Click on the More button to display this overflow dialog box, shown in Figure 2-19. The options work as follows:

- **Image Previews:** In Photoshop 3.0, you can select as many as three kinds of image previews. The Icon option creates a tiny preview icon that you can view from the Finder in System 7. In my opinion, this option is hardly worth the extra disk space; lots of custom icons can even cause problems with your system software. The more useful Thumbnail option creates a larger preview that displays inside the Open dialog box when you select a file. The third and newest option, Full Size, creates a 72 dpi preview that can be used for placement inside a page-layout program.

    If you want to decide which previews to assign when saving a file, select the Ask When Saving radio button. All three Image Preview options then appear at the bottom of the Save dialog box.

- **Anti-alias PostScript:** Photoshop can swap graphics with Adobe Illustrator 5.0 and 5.5 and Adobe Dimensions 1.0 and 2.0 via the Clipboard. The Anti-alias PostScript option smoothes out the edges of PostScript paths pasted into Photoshop from the Clipboard. If you don't want antialiased (softened) edges, turn this option off.

- **Export Clipboard:** When selected, this option ensures that Photoshop transfers a copied image from its internal Clipboard to the system's Clipboard when you switch applications. This enables you to paste the image into another running program (as discussed in the "Application Clipboards" section of Chapter A on the CD). Turn this option off if you plan to use copied images only within Photoshop and you want to reduce the lag time that occurs when you switch from Photoshop to another program. Even with this option off, you can paste images copied from other programs into Photoshop.

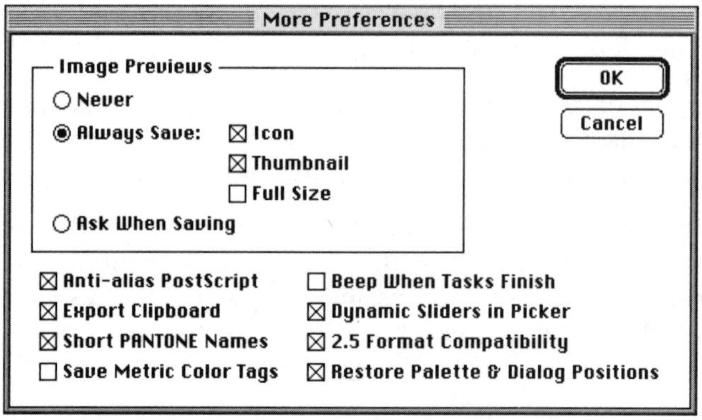

Figure 2-19:
The More Preferences dialog box contains a bunch of ragtag options that no longer fit in the General Preferences dialog box.

- ↝ **Short Pantone Names:** Photoshop uses updated Pantone naming conventions. If you plan to import a Photoshop image that contains Pantone colors into an aging desktop publishing or drawing package, you may need to select this option to ensure that the receiving application recognizes the color names. More recent upgrades, such as QuarkXPress 3.3 and PageMaker 5.0, support the updated names and thus do not require you to select this option. (Incidentally, you only have to worry about this option if you're creating duotones.)

- ↝ **Save Metric Color Tags:** If you use EFI's EfiColor for Photoshop to help with screen and printer calibration, and you import and print most of your images inside QuarkXPress, turn this option on. Photoshop then references the active EfiColor separation table when saving an image in the TIFF or EPS file format, making the table available to XPress and thus maintaining consistent color between the two applications. If you don't use EfiColor, leave the option off.

- ↝ **Beep When Tasks Finish:** You can instruct Photoshop to beep at you whenever it finishes an operation that displays a Progress window. This option may be useful if you find yourself dozing off during particularly time-consuming operations. But I'm a firm believer that computers should be seen and not heard.

- ↝ **Dynamic Sliders in Picker:** When selected, this option instructs Photoshop to preview color effects within the slider bars of the Picker palette. When the option is turned off, the slider bars show the same colors regardless of your changes. Unless you're working on a souped-up SE/30 or some other old-model machine, leaves this option on. It takes a fraction of a second longer to calculate, but it's worth it.

- ↝ **2.5 Format Compatibility:** This option allows Photoshop 2.5 to open files saved in the Photoshop 3.0 format. But this backwards compatibility comes at a price. It works like this: The only file format that retains layers is the Photoshop 3.0 format. Even though Photoshop 2.5 does not support layers, it can open a flattened version of the image in which all the layers are fused together, as long as the 2.5 Format Compatibility option is selected. "So," you say, "I should leave this option on." Ah, not so fast. When the option is on, Photoshop has to insert an additional flattened version of the image into the file, which takes up a huge amount of disk space. You reduce the file size by as much as 50 percent by deselecting 2.5 Format Compatibility. Photoshop 2.5 won't be able to open it — nor will other programs that support the 2.5 format — but unless you're working with folks that are behind the times, who cares?

- ↝ **Restore Palette & Dialog Box Positions:** When this option is selected, Photoshop remembers the location of the toolbox and floating palettes from one session to the next. If you deselect this checkbox, Photoshop displays the toolbox in the upper left corner of the screen and the Brushes, Layers, and Picker palettes in formation at the bottom of the screen each time you run the program.

Out of context like this, Photoshop's preference settings can be a bit confusing. In future chapters, I'll try to shed some additional light on the settings you're likely to find most useful.

Annotating an Image

 If you work for a stock agency or you distribute your work by some other means, you'll definitely be interested in Photoshop 3.0's new image-annotation feature. You can now attach captions, credits, bylines, photo location and date, and other information, as prescribed by the IPTC (International Press Telecommunications Council). We're talking official worldwide guidelines here. Who'd have thought Photoshop would ever become so mainstream?

Choose File⇨File Info to display the five-paneled File Info dialog box. You switch from one panel to another by pressing Command with a number key (1, 2, 3, 4, or 5). All five panels appear in Figure 2-20.

Though sprawling with options, this dialog box is pretty straightforward. For example, if you want to create a caption, enter it into the Caption option box, which can hold up to 2,000 characters. The Keywords panel allows you to enter a list of descriptive words that will help folks find the image if it's added to a large electronic library. Just enter the desired word and press Return (or click on the Add button) to add it to the list. Alternatively, you can replace a word in the list by selecting it and pressing Return (or clicking on Replace). Browser utilities such as Aldus Fetch or Kudo Image Browser let you search images by keyword, as do some dedicated image servers.

The Categories panel may seem foreign to anyone who hasn't worked with a news service. Many large news services use a system of three-character categories to file and organize stories and photographs. If you're familiar with this system, you can enter the three-character code into the Category option box and even throw in a few supplemental categories up to 32 characters long. Finally, use the Urgency pop-up menu to specify the editorial timeliness of the photo. The High option tells editors around the world to hold the presses and holler for their copy boys. Low is for celebrity mug shots that can be tossed in the morgue to be hauled out only if the subject of the photograph decides to do something diverting like lead police on a nail-biting tour of the Los Angeles freeway system, not that anyone would be so passé as to repeat that old saw. (Dang, and I promised myself that I would refrain from Keanu Reeves jokes.)

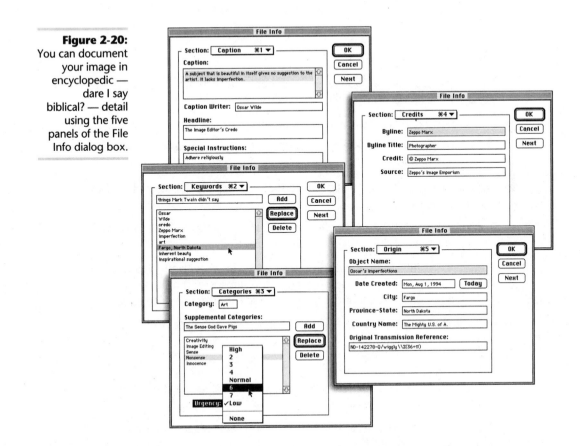

Figure 2-20:
You can document your image in encyclopedic — dare I say biblical? — detail using the five panels of the File Info dialog box.

Although these options are obviously geared toward news photographers, any Joe off the street can take advantage of them. For example, my intrepid sidekick James A. Martin documented a couple of pieces of artwork on the CD, including one from Greg Vander Houwen and one from John Lund, using the File Info command. You can view the captions on-screen by choosing File⇨File Info or you can print them with the image by choosing File⇨Page Setup and selecting the Caption checkbox.

File information is saved with an image regardless of the format you use. Photoshop merely tacks the text on to the image as a resource. Because you cannot format the text in the File Info dialog box, it consumes very little space on disk — one byte per character — which means that all the text in Figure 2-20 doesn't even take up 1K.

Summary

- In many cases, you can access options that let you change the way a tool works by double-clicking on the tool's icon in the toolbox.

- Photoshop's cursors show you what actions you can perform.

- The absolute full screen mode enables you to view as much of an image as will fit on-screen, minus title bar, menu bar, and scroll bars.

- To hide the toolbox and all floating palettes, press the Tab key. Press Tab again to bring them back.

- Click on the collapse box in a floating palette's title bar to hide most of its options so that it takes up less space on-screen.

- You can magnify an image at one of 31 zoom ratios without affecting the resolution or size of the image (much in the same way that looking at an amoeba under a microscope doesn't change the size of the little critter).

- Photoshop lets you initiate many commands and other operations by pressing keystroke combinations.

- You can use QuicKeys or Tempo to automate additional Photoshop functions.

- Photoshop saves your preference settings to disk. You can delete this file to reinstate the factory default settings.

- You can assign captions, append credits, and otherwise annotate an image by choosing File Info and filling in the option boxes.

Image
Fundamentals

How Images Work

Think of a bitmapped image as a mosaic made out of square tiles of various colors. When you view the mosaic up close, it looks like something you might use to decorate your bathroom. You see the individual tiles, not the image itself. But if you back a few feet away from the mosaic, the tiles lose their definition and merge together to create a recognizable work of art, presumably Medusa getting her head whacked off or some equally appetizing thematic classic.

Similarly, images are colored pixels pretending to be artwork. If you enlarge the pixels, they look like an unrelated collection of colored squares. Reduce the size of the pixels, and they blend together to form an image that looks for all the world like a standard photograph. Photoshop deceives the eye by borrowing from an artistic technique older than Mycenae or Pompeii.

Of course, there are differences between pixels and ancient mosaic tiles. Pixels come in 16 million distinct colors. Mosaic tiles of antiquity came in your basic granite and sandstone varieties, with an occasional chunk of lapis lazuli thrown in for good measure. Also, you can resample, color separate, and crop electronic images. We know from the time-worn scribblings of Dionysius of Halicarnassus that these processes were beyond the means of classical artisans.

But I'm getting ahead of myself. I won't be discussing resampling, cropping, or Halicarnassus for several pages. In the meantime, I'll address the inverse relationship between image size and resolution.

Size and resolution

If you haven't already guessed, the term *image size* describes the physical dimensions of an image. *Resolution* is the number of pixels per linear inch. I say *linear* because you measure pixels in a straight line. If the resolution of an image is 72 *ppi* — that is, *pixels per inch* — you get 5,184 pixels per square inch (72 pixels wide × 72 pixels tall = 5,184).

Assuming that the number of pixels in an image is fixed, increasing the size of an image decreases its resolution and vice versa. Therefore, an image that looks good when printed on a postage stamp probably will look jagged when printed as an 11 × 17-inch poster.

Figure 3-1 shows a single image printed at three different sizes and resolutions. The smallest image is printed at twice the resolution of the medium-sized image, and the medium-sized image is printed at twice the resolution of the largest image. One inch in the smallest image includes twice as many pixels vertically and twice as many pixels horizontally as an inch in the medium-sized image, for a total of four times as many pixels per square inch. The result is an image that covers one-fourth of the area of the medium-sized image.

The same relationships exist between the medium-sized image and the largest image. An inch in the medium-sized image comprises four times as many pixels as an inch in the largest image. Consequently, the medium-sized image consumes one-fourth of the area of the largest image.

 The number of pixels in an image doesn't grow or shrink automatically when you save the image or print it, but you can add or subtract pixels using one of the techniques discussed in the "Resampling and Cropping Methods" section later in this chapter. However, doing so may lead to a short-term sacrifice in the appearance of the image.

Figure 3-1:
These three images contain the same number of pixels but are printed at different resolutions. Doubling the resolution of an image reduces it to 25 percent of its original size.

Printing versus screen display

You should select the resolution for an image based on what you want to do with the image. When printing an image, a higher resolution translates to a sharper image with greater clarity. If you plan to use the image in an on-screen presentation, the resolution of the image should correspond to the resolution of your monitor.

Printed resolution

When figuring the resolution of a printed image, Photoshop considers two factors:

- ✪ You can specify the working resolution of an image by choosing Image⇨Image Size and entering a value into the Resolution option box, either in pixels per inch or pixels per centimeter. The default resolution for a Macintosh screen image is 72 ppi. To avoid changing the number of pixels in the image, be sure that the File Size check box is selected.

- ✪ You can instruct Photoshop to scale an image during the print cycle by choosing File⇨Page Setup and entering a percentage value into the Reduce or Enlarge option box.

To determine the printed resolution, Photoshop divides the Resolution value by the Reduce or Enlarge percentage. For example, if the image resolution is set to 72 ppi and you reduce the image during the print cycle to 48 percent, the printed image has a resolution of 150 ppi (72 divided by .48).

At the risk of boring some folks, I'll briefly remind the math haters in the audience that whenever you use a percentage in an equation, you first convert it to a decimal. For example, 100 percent is 1.0, 64 percent is .64, 5 percent is .05, and so on.

Both the Resolution and Reduce or Enlarge values are saved with an image. The Resolution setting determines the size and resolution at which an image imports into object-oriented applications, most notably desktop publishing programs such as PageMaker and QuarkXPress.

Moiré patterns

For best results, the resolution of the image should jibe with the resolution of your printer, which is measured in *dots per inch* (*dpi*). For example, suppose that you are printing a 72 ppi image to a 300 dpi laser printer. Assuming that the Reduce or Enlarge option is set to 100 percent, each image pixel wants to take up $4\,^1/_6$ printer dots (300 ÷ 72 = $4^1/_6$). By definition, a printer dot can't be divvied up into pieces, so there is no such thing as a $^1/_6$ printer dot. Each image pixel must be represented by a whole number of printer dots. But your laser printer can't simply round down every pixel in the image to four printer dots, or it would shrink the image. To maintain the size of the image, the printer assigns four dots to each of the first five pixels and five dots to the sixth. These occasionally larger pixels result in a throbbing appearance, called a *moiré pattern*. (In case you're wondering where this weird term came from, *moiré* — pronounced *moray* — is a French technique for pressing wavy patterns into fabric.)

To eliminate moiré patterns, set the resolution of the image so that it divides evenly into the printer resolution. To avoid moiré patterns in the preceding example, you could set the Resolution value to 100 ppi, which divides evenly into 300 dpi (300 ÷ 100 = 3). Alternatively, you could set the Reduce or Enlarge value to 72 percent, which would effectively change the resolution of the printed image to 100 ppi (72 ÷ .72 = 100).

 Use the Resolution option to account for the final output device resolution; use the Reduce or Enlarge option to account for the proof printer resolution. For example, suppose that you want to print your final image to a 2,540 dpi Linotronic 330 imagesetter and proof it to a 300 dpi LaserWriter. You can account for the imagesetter by setting the Resolution option to 127 ppi. However, although 127 divides evenly into 2,540 dpi, it doesn't divide evenly into 300 dpi. To fudge the difference, set the Reduce or Enlarge option to 127 percent, which changes the image resolution to 100 ppi (127 ÷ 1.27 = 100).

If you use this technique, be sure to change the Reduce or Enlarge option back to 100 percent before printing the final image to the imagesetter.

Screen resolution

Regardless of the Resolution and Reduce or Enlarge values, Photoshop displays each pixel on-screen according to the zoom ratio. (The zoom ratio, displayed in the title bar, is discussed in Chapter 2.) If the zoom ratio is 1:1, for example, each image pixel takes up a single screen pixel. Zoom ratio and printer output are unrelated.

When creating an image for a screen presentation or display, you want the image size to fill every inch of the prospective monitor at a 1:1 zoom ratio. I say *prospective* monitor because although you may use a 16-inch monitor when you create the image, you may want to display the final image on a 13-inch monitor. In that case, you would set the image size to 640 × 480 pixels (the standard resolution of a 13-inch monitor), with no concern for resolution on your 16-inch monitor.

For your information, Table 3-1 lists common Macintosh and DOS-based PC screen sizes. Unless indicated otherwise, the monitors can handle color. On the Mac side, System 7 or System 6 equipped with the 32-bit QuickDraw extension automatically dithers 24-bit images to conform with an 8-bit display, so you don't necessarily need to worry about the number of colors in an image. Most PC systems don't provide access to more than 256 colors, and the system software provides no automatic dithering option.

Table 3-1	Macintosh and PC Monitor Standards	
Monitor	**Pixels wide**	**Pixels tall**
Macintosh		
Most pre-1994 PowerBooks	640	400
9" (monochrome Plus, SE, Classic)	512	342
10" (Color Classic)	512	384
12"	512	384
1994 PowerBooks (and 180c)	640	480
13" or 14"	640	480
15" (portrait)	640	870
16" or 17"	832	624
19" or 20"	1,024	768
21" (two-page)	1,152	870

(continued)

Monitor	Pixels wide	Pixels tall
Table 3-1 (continued)		
IBM compatibles		
Hercules (monochrome)	720	348
EGA (16 colors)	640	350
MCGA (4 colors)	640	480
VGA or XGA	640	480
Video7 VGA	720	512
SuperVGA	800	600
8514/a or TIGA	1,024	768

 Monitors aren't quite as straightforward as Table 3-1 might suggest. On the Mac side, many 16-inch and larger monitors can handle resolutions from 640×480 pixels on up. The professional-level SuperMac Thunder II GX•1360 video board provides resolutions as high as $1,360 \times 1,024$ pixels to 19-inch monitors and up. The Thunder II GX•1600 delivers $1,600 \times 1,200$ pixels, which is more than enough to hold the contents of six 13-inch screens. On the PC, Video7 VGA can accommodate 640×480 pixels, 720×512 pixels, or 800×600 pixels, depending on VRAM. In addition to 640×480 pixels, the XGA adapter can go as high as $1,024 \times 768$ pixels.

How to Open, Duplicate, and Save Images

Before you can work on an image in Photoshop — whether you're creating a brand new document or opening an image from disk — you must first load the image into an image window. Here are the four basic ways to create an image window:

- **File⇨New:** Create a new window by choosing File⇨New (Command-N). After you fill out the desired size and resolution specifications in the New dialog box, Photoshop confronts you with a stark, white, empty canvas. You then face the ultimate test of your artistic capabilities — painting from scratch. Feel free to go nuts and cut off your ear.

- **File⇨Open:** Open an image saved to disk or CD-ROM by choosing File⇨Open (Command-O). Of the four ways to create an image window, you most likely will use this method most frequently. You can open images scanned in other applications, images purchased from stock photo agencies, slides and transparencies digitized to a Kodak Photo CD, or an image you previously edited in Photoshop.

- **Edit⇨Paste:** Photoshop automatically adapts a new image window to the contents of the Clipboard (provided those contents are bitmapped). So if you copy an image inside a different application or in Photoshop and then choose File⇨New, Photoshop enters the dimensions and resolution of the image into the New dialog box. All you have to do is accept the settings and choose Edit⇨Paste (Command-V) to introduce the image into a new window. This technique is useful for editing screen shots captured to the Clipboard and for testing out filtering effects on a sample of an image without harming the original.

- **File⇨Acquire⇨Scan:** If you own a scanner, it probably has a plug-in module that lets you scan directly into Photoshop. Just copy the module into Photoshop's Plug-ins folder and then run or relaunch the Photoshop application. To initiate a scan, choose the scanner driver from the File⇨Acquire submenu. For example, to scan from my Agfa Arcus scanner (alas, it's not really mine, it's just on loan), I choose File⇨Acquire⇨Agfa PhotoScan. A dialog box appears that enables me to scan the photograph or artwork under the scanner lid. When the scan is complete, the image appears in a new image window.

 Scanning is by far the most complex method of loading an image into Photoshop. For a detailed discussion of the scanning process, read the "Scanning" section in Chapter C on the CD.

Creating a new image

Whether you are creating an image from scratch or transferring the contents of the Clipboard to a new image window, choose File⇨New or press Command-N to bring up the New dialog box shown in Figure 3-2. If the Clipboard contains an image, the Width, Height, and Resolution option boxes show the size and resolution of that image. Otherwise, you can enter your own values in one of five units of measurement: pixels, inches, centimeters, picas, or points. (A pica, incidentally, is equal to roughly $1/6$ inch, and a *point* is $1/12$ pica, or roughly $1/72$ inch.) If you're not sure exactly what size image you want to create, enter a rough approximation. You can always change your settings later.

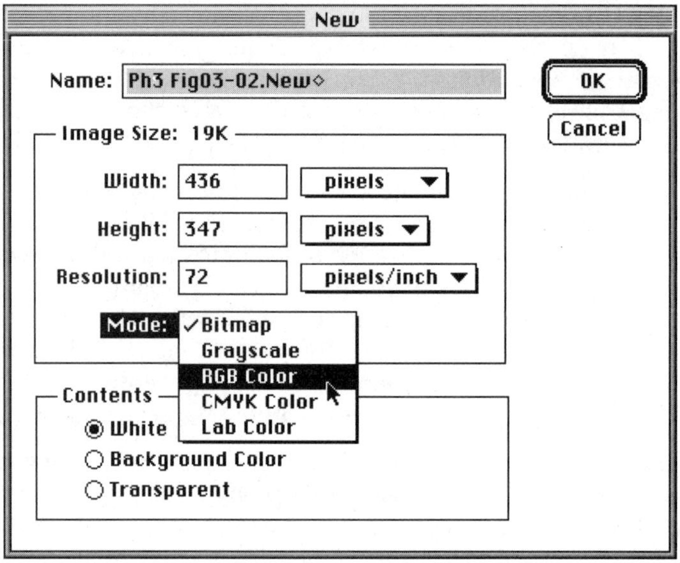

Figure 3-2:
Use the New dialog box to specify the size, resolution, and color mode of your new image.

```
┌─────────────────────── New ───────────────────────┐
│                                                     │
│   Name: │Ph3 Fig03-02.New◇         │     ┌──OK──┐   │
│                                           └───────┘  │
│   ┌─ Image Size: 19K ─────────────┐   ┌─Cancel─┐   │
│   │                                │                │
│   │   Width: │436│   │ pixels ▼│   │                │
│   │                                │                │
│   │  Height: │347│   │ pixels ▼│   │                │
│   │                                │                │
│   │ Resolution: │72│ │pixels/inch ▼│                │
│   │                                │                │
│   │   Mode:│✓Bitmap        │       │                │
│   │         │ Grayscale    │       │                │
│   │         ├─RGB Color────┤       │                │
│   │  ┌─Contents  CMYK Color  ▶     │                │
│   │         │ Lab Color    │       │                │
│   │    ● White                     │                │
│   │    ○ Background Color           │                │
│   │    ○ Transparent                │                │
│   └────────────────────────────────┘                │
└─────────────────────────────────────────────────────┘
```

By default, Photoshop assigns *exactly* 72 points per inch and 6 picas per inch (which works out to be one point per screen pixel). Before the advent of computers, however, picas and points represented their own distinct measurement system. Although there are exactly 12 points in a pica, one inch really equals about 72.27 points, or 6.02 picas. If you prefer to use the traditional system — as when pasting up a page with an X-Acto knife and hot wax — choose File⇨Preferences⇨Units and select the Traditional (72.27 points/inch) radio button.

You can change the default unit of measure that appears in the Width and Height pop-up menus by choosing File⇨Preferences⇨Units and selecting a different option from the Ruler Units pop-up menu. You can also change the unit of measure by selecting Palette Options from the Info palette pop-up menu.

Column width

A sixth unit of measure, Column, is available from the Width pop-up menu. If you want to create an image that fits exactly within a certain number of columns when it's imported into a desktop publishing program, select the Column option. You can specify the width of a column and the gutter between columns by choosing File⇨Preferences⇨Units and entering values into the Column Size option boxes.

The Gutter value affects multiple-column images. Suppose that you accept the default setting of a 15-pica column width and a 1-pica gutter. If you specify a one-column image in the New dialog box, Photoshop makes it 15 picas wide. If you ask for a two-column image, Photoshop adds the width of the gutter to the width of the two columns and creates an image 31 picas wide.

The Height pop-up menu in the New dialog box lacks a Column option because vertical columns have nothing to do with an image's height.

On-screen image size

In most cases, the on-screen dimensions of an image depend on your entries in the Width, Height, and Resolution option boxes. If you set both the Width and Height values to 10 inches and the Resolution to 72 ppi, the new image will measure 720×720 pixels. The exception occurs if you choose pixels as your unit of measurement, as in Figure 3-2. In that case, the on-screen dimensions depend solely on the Width and Height options, and the Resolution value determines the size at which the image prints.

Color mode and background

Use the Mode pop-up menu to specify the number of colors that can appear in your image. Choose Bitmap to create a black-and-white image and choose Grayscale to access only gray values. RGB Color, CMYK Color, and Lab Color all provide access to the full range of 16 million colors, although their methods of doing so differ.

RGB stands for *red-green-blue; CMYK* for *cyan-magenta-yellow-black;* and *Lab* for *luminosity* and two abstract color variables, *a* and *b*. To learn how each of these color modes works, read the "Working in Different Color Modes" section of Chapter 4.

In Photoshop 3.0, the New dialog box provides three Contents radio buttons that allow you to change the color of the background for the new image. You can fill the new image with white, with the current background color (assuming, of course, that the background color is something other than white), or with no color at all. This last setting, Transparent, results in a floating layer with no background image whatsoever, which can be useful when editing one layer independently of the rest of an image, or when preparing a layer to be composited with an image. (For an in depth examination of the more nitty-gritty aspects of layering, see Chapter 17.) White is the default setting.

If you do select a transparent background, you won't be able to save the image in any format other than Photoshop 3.0, because only the Photoshop 3.0 format is capable of saving layers. If you want to save the image in some other format, you'll have to make the image opaque by choosing the Flatten Image option from the Layers palette pop-up menu. (To display the Layers palette, choose Window⇨Palettes⇨Show Layers.) Or choose File⇨Save a Copy to save a flattened copy of the image to disk.

Now, just in case you're thinking, "Cool, Photoshop supports transparent backgrounds. Now I can import images into QuarkXPress and be able to see through the image to text and other page elements behind it," the answer is, *eeeh*, as in, "Ooh, I *am* sorry, Contestant Number Four, but that conclusion is totally false." You can only make a color transparent if the image is black and white — or, more correctly, black and transparent — and you save the image in the EPS format (as I'll discuss in the section "Saving an EPS document" later in this chapter). Otherwise, you have to create a stencil for the image using Photoshop's clipping path function, as explained in the "Retaining transparent areas in an image" section of Chapter 8.

Naming the new image

 The New dialog box now provides a Name option. If you know what you want to call your new image, enter the name now. Or don't. It doesn't matter. Either way, when you choose File⇨Save, Photoshop asks you to specify the location of the file and confirm the file's name, just as in previous versions. So don't feel compelled to name your image anything. The only real reason for this option is to help you keep your images organized on-screen. Lots of folks create temporary images that they never save; Photoshop now offers a way to assign temporary images more meaningful names than *Untitled-4, Untitled-5, Untitled-6*, and so on.

Opening an existing image

If you want to open an image stored on disk, choose File⇨Open or press Command-O to display the Open dialog box (introduced in the "How to navigate dialog boxes" section of Chapter A on the CD.) The scrolling list contains the names of documents Photoshop recognizes that it can open. If you cannot find a desired document, it may be because Photoshop does not recognize the document's four-character *type code*. The type code for a document created or last edited on a Macintosh computer corresponds to the file format under which the image was saved (as explained in the upcoming "Image File Formats" section).

For example, TIFF is the type code for a TIFF image, PICT is the type code for a PICT image, and so on. However, if you transferred a document from another platform, such as the IBM PC or Commodore Amiga, it probably lacks a type code. In the absence of a type code, the Macintosh system software assigns a PC document the default type code TEXT, which indicates a text-only document. Photoshop does not recognize the TEXT code, so it does not list the corresponding document in the Open dialog box.

To see *all* documents regardless of type code, select the Show All Files check box inside the Open dialog box. When you click on a document in the scrolling list, Photoshop displays the format that it thinks the file is saved in — if it has any thoughts to offer — in the Format option. If you disagree, select a different format file from the pop-up menu, as demonstrated in Figure 3-3. If the desired document conforms to the selected format option, Photoshop opens the image after you click on the Open button or press Return. If Photoshop displays an error message instead, you need to either select a different format option or try to open the document in a different application.

Incidentally, you can view and alter the type code for a document using CE Software's DiskTop or Apple's ResEdit, both of which are distributed separately.

Figure 3-3:
Select the
Show All
Files option
to access
any
document
regardless
of its four-
character
type code.

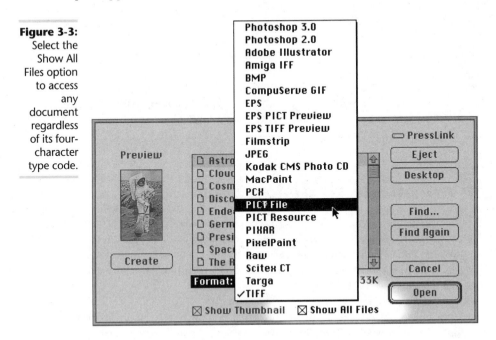

Duplicating an image

Have you ever wanted to try out an effect without permanently damaging an image? Certainly, you can undo the last action performed in Photoshop (by choosing Edit⇨Undo), but what if the technique involves multiple steps? And what if you want to apply two or more effects to an image independently and compare them side by side? And later maybe even merge them? This is a job for image duplication.

Lots of new users think that Window⇨New Window will satisfy this need. But as I discussed in Chapter 2, the New Window command simply creates another view of the same image. It's great for monitoring an effect in two different zoom ratios or two different color modes or whatever, but the two images you see on-screen are not independent.

To create a new window with an independent version of the foreground image, choose Image⇨Duplicate. A dialog box appears requesting a name for the new image. Just like the Name option in the New dialog box, the option is purely an organizational tool that you can use or ignore. If your image contains multiple layers, Photoshop will by default retain all layers in the duplicate document. Alternatively, you can merge all visible layers into a single layer by selecting the Merged Layers Only check box. (Hidden layers remain independent.) Press Return to create your new, independent image. (This image is unsaved; you need to choose File⇨Save to save any changes to disk.)

If you're happy to let Photoshop automatically name your image and you don't care what it does with the layers, press the Option key while choosing Image⇨Duplicate to bypass the Duplicate Image dialog box and immediately create a new window.

Saving an image to disk

The first rule of storing an image on disk is to save it frequently. If the foreground image is untitled, as it is when you work on a new image, choosing File⇨Save displays the Save dialog box, enabling you to name the image, specify its location on disk, and select a file format. After you save the image once, choosing the Save command updates the file on disk without bringing up the Save dialog box.

Choose File⇨Save As to change the name, location, or format of the image stored on disk. By the way, if your only reason for choosing the Save As command is to change the file format, it's perfectly acceptable to overwrite (save over) the original document, assuming that you no longer need that copy of the image. Granted, your computer could crash during the save-as operation, in which case you would lose both the new document and the original. But crashing during the save-as operation is extremely unlikely and no more likely than crashing during any other save operation.

 To speed up the save process, I usually save an image in Photoshop's native format until I'm finished working on it. Before I close the image, I choose File⇨Save As and save the image in the compressed TIFF or JPEG format. By using this method, I only compress each image once during a session. (This is an especially useful technique on 680X0 Macs and Windows machines. On the Power Mac, saving in the TIFF and JPEG formats has been accelerated so successfully that it's almost as fast as saving in the Photoshop format.)

Image File Formats

As you can see back in Figure 3-3, Photoshop 3.0 supports a total of 22 file formats from inside its Open and Save dialog boxes. It can support even more through the addition of plug-in modules, which attach commands to the File⇨Acquire and File⇨Export submenus.

File formats represent different ways to save a file to disk. Some formats provide unique image *compression schemes,* which save an image in a manner that consumes less space on disk. Other formats enable Photoshop to trade images with different applications on the Mac and on different platforms.

The native formats

 Photoshop 3.0 supports two *native formats* (that is, formats that are optimized for Photoshop's particular capabilities and functions), one for Version 2.0 and one for Version 3.0. Photoshop 2.0 and 2.01 support the Photoshop 2.0 format only. But what about Photoshop 2.5? Well, it turns out that the Photoshop 3.0 format is compatible with Photoshop 2.5 *if* the 2.5 Format Compatibility check box is selected inside the More Preferences dialog box (which you reach by pressing Command-K and then clicking on the More button). If this check box is turned off, Photoshop 2.5 will *not* be able to open an image saved in the 3.0 format.

After that explanation, it may come as surprise when I tell you that I leave the 2.5 Format Compatibility check box turned off. If you've made the permanent plunge into Photoshop 3.0 — as I have — and you don't have any friends or neighbors who want to open your images in antiquated versions of Photoshop, you'll actually save disk space by turning the 2.5 Format Compatibility option off, particularly if your image involves layers.

Adobe has specifically optimized both the 2.0 and 3.0 formats to retain every smidgen of data, including additional masking channels and a few other elements that may be lost when saving to other formats. It's also worth noting that Photoshop can open and save in its native format more quickly than in any other format. The Photoshop 3.0 format offers a compression option missing from the earlier format. The compression does *not* result in any loss of data.

Cross-platform formats

Photoshop 3.0 provides seven formats for saving an image you want to transfer to a different computer. If your clients or coworkers use computers other than Macs, you'll find these formats essential.

Amiga's IFF and HAM

Popular among video enthusiasts, the now discontinued Commodore Amiga is a variety of personal computer that offers an operating system similar to the Mac's. I owned the first-model Amiga 1000, a machine that Commodore almost immediately abandoned. You'd think I would have learned my lesson after having previously owned a Commodore Plus/4, possibly the worst computer ever made.

Nowadays, the only reason to use an Amiga — particularly since the company recently bit the dust — is because it supports NewTek's much-celebrated Video Toaster. If you know someone who uses an Amiga, maybe you can talk the poor soul into hawking it at a yard sale and using the money to make a down payment on a Mac. Until then, you can trade images using the IFF (*Interchange File Format*) format, which is the Amiga's all-around graphics format and serves much the same function as PICT on the Mac.

Photoshop includes a plug-in module that lets you export an image to a compressed variation of IFF called HAM (*Hold and Modify*) by choosing File⇨Export⇨Amiga HAM. Unfortunately, HAM is generally useless for images that don't conform to one of two standard image sizes — 320×200 pixels or 320×400 pixels. Most Amiga applications treat nonstandard images as having rectangular as opposed to square pixels, thus stretching the image out of proportion.

Photoshop can open HAM images with up to 256 colors and IFF images with up to 16 million colors.

Windows Paint's BMP

BMP (*Windows Bitmap*) is the native format for Microsoft Paint (included with Microsoft Windows) and is supported by a variety of Windows and OS/2 applications. Photoshop supports BMP images with up to 16 million colors. You also can use RLE (*Run-Length Encoding*), a lossless compression scheme specifically applicable to the BMP format.

 The term *lossless* refers to compression schemes such as BMP's RLE and TIFF's LZW (*Lempel-Ziv-Welch*) that enable you to save space on disk without sacrificing any data in the image. The only reasons *not* to use lossless compression are that it slows down the open and save operations and it may prevent less-sophisticated applications from opening an image. *Lossy* compression routines, such as JPEG, sacrifice a user-defined amount of data to conserve even more disk space.

CompuServe's GIF

CompuServe designed GIF (*Graphics Interchange Format*) as a means of compressing 8-bit images so that users can transfer photographs via their modems to and from the company's commercial bulletin board service more quickly. Like most on-line imagery, the lion's share of the world's GIF images are pornographic. (In fact, I often wonder how many folks never venture beyond using Photoshop and other image editors to view naked women.) Still, many folks do use GIF for purposes their mothers would approve. Like TIFF, GIF uses LZW compression, but unlike TIFF, GIF can't handle more than 256 colors.

PC Paintbrush's PCX

PCX doesn't stand for anything. Rather, it's the extension that PC Paintbrush assigns to images saved in its native file format. By all accounts, PCX is one of the most popular image file formats in use today, largely due to the fact that PC Paintbrush is the oldest painting program for DOS. Photoshop supports PCX images with up to 16 million colors.

PIXAR workstations

PIXAR has created some of the most memorable computer-animated shorts and commercials in recent memory. (That "recent memory" bit is just a saying, of course. *All* computer animation has occurred in recent memory.) Examples include the desk lamps playing with a beach ball from *Luxo, Jr.;* the run-amok toddler from the Oscar-winning *Tin Toy;* and the commercial adventures of a Listerine bottle that boxes Gingivitis one day and swings Tarzan-like through a spearmint forest the next. These folks are *the* reason I entered computer graphics. They're so awesome. Wow weezers.

PIXAR develops a few 3-D graphics applications for the Mac, including MacRenderMan, ShowPlace, and Typestry. But the company works its 3-D magic using mondo-expensive PIXAR workstations. Photoshop enables you to open a still image created on a PIXAR machine or save an image to the PIXAR format so you can integrate it into a 3-D rendering. The PIXAR format supports grayscale and RGB images.

Scitex image-processors

High-end commercial printers use Scitex computers to generate color separations of images and other documents. Photoshop can open images digitized with Scitex scanners and save the edited images to the *Scitex CT* (*Continuous Tone*) format. Because you need special hardware to transfer images from the Mac to a Scitex drive, you'll probably want to consult with your local Scitex service bureau technician before saving to the CT format. It's very possible that the technician will prefer that you submit images in the native Photoshop, TIFF, or JPEG format. The Scitex CT format supports grayscale and CMYK images.

TrueVision's TGA

TrueVision's Targa and NuVista video boards let you overlay Macintosh graphics and animation onto live video. The effect is called *chroma keying* because typically, a key color is set aside to let the live video show through. TrueVision designed the TGA (*Targa*) format to support 32-bit images that include 8-bit *alpha channels* capable of displaying the live video. Though support for TGA is scarce among Macintosh applications, it is widely implemented among professional-level color and video applications on the PC.

Interapplication formats

In the name of interapplication harmony, Photoshop supports a few software-specific formats that enable you to trade files with programs that run on the Mac, including such popular drawing programs as Adobe Illustrator. Photoshop can also trade images directly with two painting pioneers, MacPaint and PixelPaint. And finally, you can use Photoshop to edit frames from a QuickTime movie created with Adobe Premier.

Rendering an Illustrator file

Photoshop supports Adobe Illustrator files saved in the EPS format. EPS (Encapsulated PostScript) is specifically designed for saving object-oriented graphics that you intend to print to a PostScript output device. Every drawing program and most page-layout programs enable you to save EPS documents. However, many versions of EPS exist, and Photoshop supports Illustrator's version only. To make life a little more straightforward, Illustrator uses a small subset of PostScript commands in its EPS files. This way, Illustrator and Photoshop can swap files back and forth with relative ease; if Photoshop tried to support the full gamut of EPS, the size of each program would easily double.

 You may have noticed that the pop-up menu in Figure 3-3 shows several EPS options, including separate EPS and Adobe Illustrator options. This may have led you to believe that Photoshop 3.0 now at least makes an attempt to open a vanilla EPS illustration exported from FreeHand, Canvas, or CorelDraw. *Eeeh.* "Ouch, I'm afraid this is not your day, Contestant Number Four. And you did so well in the rehearsals." The fact is, the EPS format refers to EPS *images* — not objects — such as those created in Photoshop itself. So if you create a drawing in FreeHand, Canvas, or CorelDraw, you still need to export it to the Illustrator format (with the .AI extension if you work on Windows) before opening it in Photoshop.

When you open an Illustrator EPS graphic, Photoshop *renders* (or *rasterizes*) the artwork — that is, it converts it from a collection of objects to a bitmapped image. During the open operation, Photoshop presents the EPS Rasterizer dialog box (see Figure 3-4), which enables you to specify the size and resolution of the image, just as you do in the New dialog box. Because the graphic is object-oriented, you can render it as large or as small as you want without any loss of image quality.

You should always select the Anti-aliased check box unless you're rendering a very large image — say, 300 ppi or higher. *Antialiasing* blurs pixels to soften the edges of the objects so that they don't appear jagged. When you're rendering a very large image, the difference between image and printer resolution is less noticeable, so antialiasing is unwarranted.

 Photoshop 3.0 renders illustrations against a transparent background. Before you can save the rasterized image to a format other than Photoshop 3.0, you have to eliminate the transparency by choosing Flatten Image from the Layers palette pop-up menu. Or save a flattened version of the image to a separate file by choosing File⇨Save a Copy.

Figure 3-4:
You can specify the
size and resolution at
which Photoshop
renders an EPS
illustration.

```
░░░░░░░░░░░░░ EPS Rasterizer ░░░░░░░░░░░░░

┌─ Image Size: 1.13M ──────────────┐     ┌────────────┐
│                                  │     │     OK     │
│     Width:  [437  ]  [ pixels ▼] │     └────────────┘
│                                  │     ┌────────────┐
│    Height:  [675  ]  [ pixels ▼] │     │   Cancel   │
│                                  │     └────────────┘
│ Resolution: [72   ]  [ pixels/inch ▼] │
│                                  │
│      Mode:  [ CMYK Color ▼]      │
│                                  │
└──────────────────────────────────┘

       □ Anti-aliased   ⊠ Constrain Proportions
```

If you want to introduce an EPS graphic into the foreground image rather than render-ing it into a new image window of its own, choose File⇨Place. Unlike other File menu commands, Place supports only the Illustrator variety of the EPS format. After you import the EPS graphic, it appears selected with a great X across it, allowing you to move it into position. (You have to drag it; you can't use the arrow keys.) When the graphic is properly situated, click with the gavel cursor to render the illustration against the bitmapped background. In this way, Photoshop 3.0 lets you combine illustrations that have transparent backgrounds with existing images. (To keep the imported graphic independent from the rest of the image, send the graphic to a separate layer *after* clicking with the gavel cursor. Chapter 8 explains how.)

Rendering an EPS illustration is an extremely useful technique for resolving printing problems. If you work in Illustrator often, you no doubt have encoun-tered *limitcheck errors,* which occur when an illustration is too complex for an imagesetter or other high-end output device to print. If you're frustrated with the printer and you're tired of wasting your evening trying to figure out what's wrong (sound familiar?), use Photoshop to render the illustration at 300 ppi and print it. Nine out of ten times, this technique works flawlessly.

If Photoshop can't *parse* the EPS file — which is a techy way of saying that Photoshop can't break down the individual objects (or that Photoshop doesn't know this EPS file from Shinola) — it attempts to open the PICT (Mac) or TIFF (Windows) preview. Most of the time, this exercise is totally useless, but you may occasionally want to take a quick look at an illustration in order to, say, match the placement of elements in an image to those in the drawing.

(If you select an EPS file in the Open dialog box when the Show All Files check box is selected, the Format pop-up menu displays one of three options: Adobe Illustrator, EPS PICT Preview, or EPS TIFF Preview. If either of the last two appears, you can bet that Photoshop won't be able to parse the file.)

Saving an EPS document

To use a Photoshop image inside Illustrator, you must save it in the EPS format. In my opinion, this is Illustrator's most prominent drawback. Photoshop can open 19 formats, acquire several more, and swap Sanskrit parchments among Buddhist monks. Meanwhile, Illustrator only supports EPS, which wouldn't be so bad if EPS weren't such a remarkably inefficient format for saving images. An EPS image may be three to four times larger than the same image saved to the TIFF format with LZW compression. Granted, EPS is more reliable for PostScript printing, but that's an internal translation issue that Illustrator should be able to handle, as do FreeHand, PageMaker, QuarkXPress, and many other programs.

Griping aside, here's how the process works. When you save an image in the EPS format, Photoshop 3.0 displays the dialog box shown in Figure 3-5. The options in this dialog box are:

✆ **Preview:** Technically, an EPS document comprises two parts: a pure PostScript-language description of the graphic for the printer; and a bitmapped preview that enables you to see the graphic on-screen. If you want to use the image in Illustrator 5.5 on the Mac, select the Macintosh (8 Bits/Pixel) option from the Preview pop-up menu. If you want to import the image into Illustrator 4.0 or some other Windows application, select TIFF (8 Bits/Pixel). The 1-bit options provide black-and-white previews only, which are useful if you want to save a little room on disk. Select the None option to include no preview and save even more disk space. The new option is Macintosh (JPEG), which builds JPEG compression into the EPS image. This saves a lot of room on disk, but it also sacrifices data, as described in the upcoming "JPEG" section.

Only select the Macintosh (JPEG) option if you'll be printing your final artwork from Illustrator, QuarkXPress, or some other program to a PostScript Level 2 printer. Earlier PostScript devices do not support EPS artwork with JPEG compression.

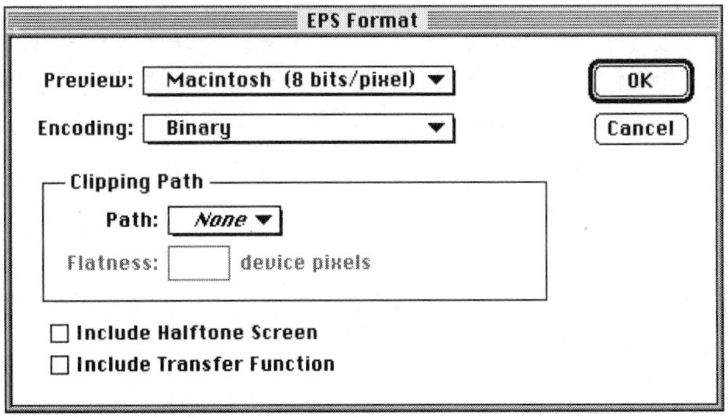

Figure 3-5:
When saving an image in the EPS format, you can specify the type of preview and tack on some printing attributes.

EPS Format
Preview: Macintosh (8 bits/pixel) ▼   [OK]
Encoding: Binary ▼   [Cancel]
┌ Clipping Path ─
Path: None ▼
Flatness: ____ device pixels
☐ Include Halftone Screen
☐ Include Transfer Function

∿ **Encoding:** If you're exporting an image for use with Illustrator, select the Binary encoding option (also known as *Huffman encoding*), which compresses an EPS document by substituting shorter codes for frequently used characters. The letter *a,* for example, receives the 3-bit code *010* rather than its standard 8-bit ASCII code, *01100001* (the binary equivalent of what we humans call *97*). Some programs — namely FreeHand and PageMaker — don't recognize Huffman encoding, in which case you must select the ASCII option. (*ASCII* stands for *American Standard Code for Information Interchange,* which is fancy jargon for *text-only.* In other words, you can open and edit an ASCII EPS document in a word processor, provided you know how to read and write PostScript.)

If you selected the Macintosh (JPEG) option from the Preview pop-up menu, select the quality of the compression that you want to apply. Generally, you'll want to select JPEG (Maximum Quality). For more information, read the "JPEG" section.

∿ **Clipping Path:** These options allow you to select a path that you created using the path tool and saved in the Paths panel of the Layers palette. You can then use that path to mask the contents of the EPS image. For complete information about clipping paths, see the "Retaining transparent areas in an image" section of Chapter 8.

∿ **Include Halftone Screen:** I've been badmouthing EPS pretty steadily, but it does have one advantage over other image formats: It can retain printing attributes. If you specified a custom halftone screen using the Screen button inside the Page Setup dialog box, you can save this setting with the EPS document by selecting the Include Halftone Screen check box.

∿ **Include Transfer Function:** As described in Chapter 6, "Printing Images," you can change the brightness and contrast of a printed image using the Transfer button inside the Page Setup dialog box. To save these settings with the EPS document, select the Include Transfer Function check box.

∿ **Transparent Whites:** When saving black-and-white EPS images in Photoshop, select this option to make all white pixels in the image transparent. (The option doesn't appear in Figure 3-5 because the image being saved is in color.) Incidentally, the EPS format is the only format that offers this option. So if you want to create transparent images, black-and-white and EPS are the ways to go.

QuarkXPress DCS

Quark developed a variation on the EPS format called *DCS* (*Desktop Color Separation*). When you work in QuarkXPress, this format enables you to print color separations of imported artwork. If you save a CMYK image in the EPS format, Photoshop displays the additional Desktop Color Separation options shown in Figure 3-6. When you save to the DCS format, Photoshop creates five files on disk: one master document plus one file each for the cyan, magenta, yellow, and black color channels. Select Off (Single File) to save the image as a single standard EPS document. Select one of the three On options to save the separations as five independent DCS files.

Figure 3-6:
Photoshop
offers four
DCS options
when you
save a CMYK
image in the
EPS format.

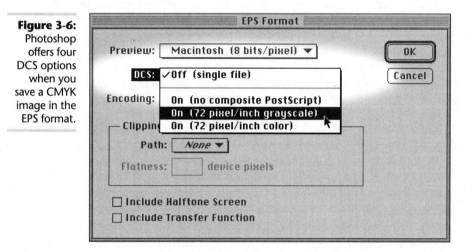

Photoshop also gives you the option of saving a 72 ppi PostScript-language version of the image inside the DCS master document. Independent from the bitmapped preview — which you specify as usual by selecting a Preview option — the 72 ppi *composite* image enables you to print a low-resolution version of a DCS image imported into QuarkXPress to a consumer-quality printer such as a LaserWriter. If you're using a black-and-white printer, select the 72 Pixel/Inch Grayscale option; if you're using a color printer, select the final option. Note that the composite image significantly increases the size of the master document on disk.

You convert an image to the CMYK mode by choosing Mode⇨CMYK Color. Do not choose this command casually. Converting back and forth between RGB and CMYK results in a loss of color information. Only use the CMYK Color command if you want to convert an image to CMYK color for good. For more information, read Chapter 4, "Defining Colors."

Premier Filmstrip

Adobe Premier is the foremost QuickTime movie-editing application for the Mac. The program is a wonder when it comes to fades, frame merges, and special effects, but it offers no frame-by-frame editing capabilities. For example, you can't draw a mustache on a person in the movie, nor can you make brightly colored brush strokes swirl about in the background — at least, not inside Premier.

However, you can export the movie to the Filmstrip format, which is a file-swapping option exclusive to Photoshop and Premier. A Filmstrip document organizes frames in a long vertical strip, as shown on the left side of Figure 3-7. The right side of the figure shows the movie after each individual frame was edited in ways not permitted by Premier. (I believe it's in the Constitution somewhere that a brother has the right to edit his sister's face in bizarre and unusual ways.)

A gray bar separates each frame. The number of each frame appears on the right; the *SMPTE* (*Society of Motion Picture and Television Engineers*) time code appears on the left. The structure of the three-number time code is *minutes:seconds:frames,* with 30 frames per second.

If you change the size of a Filmstrip document inside Photoshop in any way, you cannot save the image back to the Filmstrip format. Feel free to paint and apply effects, but stay the heck away from the Image Size and Canvas Size commands.

I don't really delve into the Filmstrip format anywhere else in this book, so I want to pass along a couple of quick Filmstrip tips right here and now. First, you can scroll up and down exactly one frame at a time by pressing Shift-Page Up or Shift-Page Down, respectively. Second, you can move a selection exactly

Figure 3-7:
Five frames from a
QuickTime movie as
they appear in the
Filmstrip format
before (left) and
after (right) editing
the frames in
Photoshop.

one frame up or down by pressing Shift-up arrow or Shift-down arrow. If you want to clone the selection as you move it, press Shift-Option-up arrow or Shift-Option-down arrow. And finally — here's the great one — you can select several sequential frames and edit them all at once by following these steps:

STEPS: Selecting Sequential Frames in a Movie

Step 1.   Select the rectangular marquee tool by pressing the M key. Then drag with the tool to select the first frame that you want to edit in the movie. (This is the only step that takes any degree of care or coordination whatsoever.)

Step 2.   Switch to the quick mask mode by pressing the Q key. The areas around the selected frame are overlaid with pink.

Step 3.   Double-click on the magic wand tool icon in the toolbox to display the Magic Wand Options panel in the Brushes palette. Enter 0 for the Tolerance value and deselect the Anti-aliased check box.

Step 4.   Click inside the selected frame (the one that's not pink) with the magic wand tool. This selects the unmasked area inside the frame.

Step 5.   Press Shift-Option-down arrow to clone the unmasked area to the next frame in the movie. When you exit the quick mask mode, both this frame and the one above it will be selected.

Step 6.   Keep Shift-Option-down arrowing until you've gotten rid of the pink stuff on all the frames that you want to select.

Step 7.   Exit the quick mask mode by pressing the Q key again. All frames appear selected.

Step 8.   Edit the frames to your heart's content.

If you're new to Photoshop, half of those steps, if not all of them, probably went sailing over your head like so many extraterrestrial spaceships. If you want to learn more about selections and cloning, read Chapter 8. In Chapter 9, I explore the quick mask mode and other masking techniques in depth. After you finish reading those chapters, come back to this section and see if it doesn't make a little more sense.

The process of editing individual frames as just described is sometimes called *rotoscoping,* named after the traditional technique of combining live-action film with animated sequences. You also can try out some *scratch-and-doodle* techniques, which is where an artist scratches and draws directly on frames of film. As if that's not enough, you can emulate *xerography,* in which an animator makes Xerox copies of photographs, enhances the copies using markers or whatever else is convenient, and shoots the finished artwork, frame by frame, on film. In a nutshell, Photoshop extends Premier's functionality by adding animation to its standard supply of video-editing capabilities.

You can save an image in the Filmstrip format only if you opened the image as a Filmstrip document and did not change the size of the image. To do so, just press Command-S.

MacPaint

Now in the hands of Claris, Apple's lethargic software subsidiary, MacPaint was the first painting program for the Mac. In fact, MacPaint and MacWrite preceded all other Macintosh applications and shipped with the first 128K Mac. Last updated in 1987, MacPaint 2.0 is severely lacking by today's standards.

The MacPaint format accommodates 1-bit (black-and-white) images on vertically-oriented, $7 \frac{1}{2} \times 10 \frac{1}{2}$-inch pages. End of story. It's no wonder that Photoshop can open MacPaint images but can't save to the MacPaint format. What would be the point? If you dig, you can find truckloads of old clip art in the MacPaint format, which is the only reason Photoshop bothers to support it at all.

PixelPaint

PixelPaint from Pixel Resources was the first color painting application for the Mac. In its day, it was a show-stopper, easily as remarkable as Photoshop is now. In fact, PixelPaint's demise started about the same time that Photoshop arrived on the scene. Some coincidence, huh?

Photoshop supports the old 8-bit PixelPaint format, the native format for the standard PixelPaint 1.0 and 2.0. PixelPaint Professional offers a 24-bit format that Photoshop does not support. I guess Adobe figures that most of its users gave up on PixelPaint when Photoshop became available. However, the newest upgrade, PixelPaint Professional 3.0, provides a number of capabilities that Photoshop still lacks, including a scripting option for recording operations and more flexible channel operations. To trade an image with PixelPaint Professional 3.0, save it in the TIFF or PICT format.

The mainstream formats

The formats discussed so far are mighty interesting, and they all fulfill their own niche purposes. But the following formats — JPEG, PICT, and TIFF — are the all-stars of Macintosh imagery. You'll use these formats the most because of their outstanding compression capabilities and almost universal support among Macintosh graphics applications.

JPEG

Photoshop supports the JPEG format, named after the folks who designed it, the Joint Photographic Experts Group. JPEG is the most efficient and essential compression format currently available and is likely to be the compression standard for years to come. It is a "lossy" compression scheme, which means that it sacrifices image quality to conserve space on disk. However, you can control how much data is lost during the save operation.

When you save an image in the JPEG format, Photoshop displays the dialog box in Figure 3-8, which offers a scant four compression settings. (That's five fewer than Photoshop 2.5 offered.) Just select a radio button to specify the quality setting. The Low option takes up the least space on disk but distorts the image rather severely; Maximum retains the highest amount of image quality but consumes more disk space.

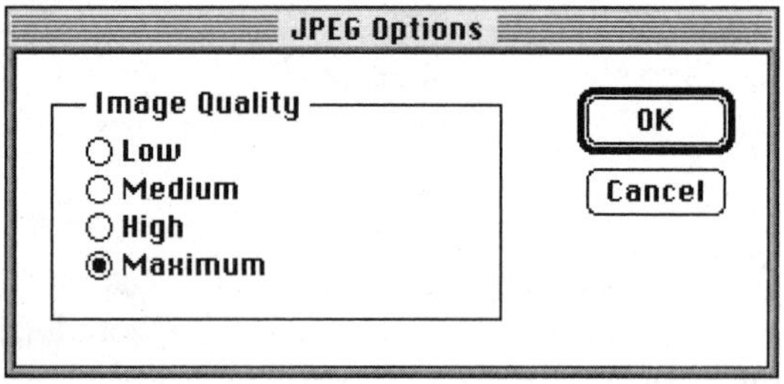

Figure 3-8:
The new JPEG Options dialog box provides four compression settings, ranging from Low image quality (excellent compression) to Maximum image quality (fair compression).

> **JPEG Options**
>
> Image Quality
> ○ Low
> ○ Medium
> ○ High
> ● Maximum
>
> [OK]
> [Cancel]

JPEG evaluates an image in 8×8-pixel blocks, using a technique called *Adaptive Discrete Cosine Transform* (or ADCT, as in *Yes, I'm an acronym ADCT*). It averages the 24-bit value of every pixel in the block (or 8-bit value of every pixel in the case of a grayscale image). It then stores the average color in the upper left pixel in the block and assigns the remaining 63 pixels smaller values relative to the average.

Next, JPEG divides the block by an 8×8 block of its own called the *quantization matrix,* which homogenizes the pixels' values by changing as many as possible to zero. It's this process that saves the majority of disk space and loses data.

When Photoshop opens a JPEG image, it can't recover the original distinction between the zero pixels, so the pixels become the same or similar colors. Finally, JPEG applies lossless Huffman encoding to translate repeating values to a single symbol.

In most instances, I recommend that you use JPEG only at the Maximum quality setting, at least until you gain some experience with it. The smallest amount of JPEG compression saves more space on disk than any non-JPEG compression format and still retains nearly every bit of detail from the original image. Figure 3-9 shows a grayscale image saved at each of the four compression settings.

Figure 3-9:
The four JPEG settings from the preceding figure applied to a single image, with the highest image quality setting illustrated at the upper left and the lowest at bottom right.

Maximum   66K

Medium   33K

High   50K

Low   28K

The samples are arranged in rows from highest image quality (upper left) to lowest quality (lower right). Below each sample is the size of the compressed document on disk. Saved in the only moderately compressed Photoshop 3.0 format, the image consumes 116K on disk. From 116K to 28K — the result of the lowest-quality JPEG setting — is a remarkable savings, but it comes at a price.

I've taken the liberty of sharpening the focus of strips in each image so that you can see more easily how JPEG averages neighboring pixels to achieve smaller file sizes. The first strip in each image appears in normal focus, the second strip is sharpened once by choosing Filter⇨Sharpen⇨Sharpen More, and the third strip is sharpened twice. I've also adjusted the gray levels to make the differences even more pronounced. You can see that although the lower image quality setting leads to a dramatic saving in file size, it also gums up the image excessively. The effect, incidentally, is more obvious on-screen. And believe me, after you familiarize yourself with JPEG compression, you'll be able to spot other people's overly compressed JPEG images a mile away. It's not something that you want to exaggerate in your images.

 To see the impact of JPEG compression on a full-color image, check out Color Plate 3-1. The original image consumes 693K in the Photoshop 3.0 format, but 116K when compressed at the JPEG module's Maximum setting. To better demonstrate the differences between different settings, I enlarged one portion of the image and oversharpened another.

JPEG is a *cumulative compression scheme,* meaning that Photoshop recompresses an image every time you save it in the JPEG format. There's no disadvantage to repeatedly saving an image to disk during a single session, because JPEG always works from the on-screen version. But if you close an image, reopen it, and save it in the JPEG format, you inflict a small amount of damage. Therefore, use JPEG sparingly. In the best of all possible worlds, you should only save to the JPEG format after you finish *all* work on an image. Even in a pinch, you should apply all filtering effects before saving to JPEG, because these have a habit of exacerbating imperfections in image quality.

JPEG is best used when compressing *continuous-tone* images (images in which the distinction between immediately neighboring pixels is slight). Any image that includes gradual color transitions, as in a photograph, qualifies for JPEG compression. JPEG is not the best choice for saving screen shots, line drawings (especially those converted from Illustrator EPS graphics), and other high-contrast images. These are better served by a lossless compression scheme such as TIFF with LZW. The JPEG format is available when you are saving grayscale, RGB, and CMYK images.

Photoshop's built-in JPEG format is not the only way to access JPEG compression. You can also compress PICT images using QuickTime JPEG, as described in the following section.

PICT

PICT (*Macintosh Picture*) is the Macintosh system software's native graphics format. Based on the QuickDraw display language that the system software uses to convey images on-screen, PICT is one of the few file formats that handles object-oriented artwork and bitmapped images with equal aplomb. It supports images in any bit depth, size, or resolution. It even supports 32-bit images, so you can save a fourth masking channel when working in the RGB mode.

If you have installed QuickTime, you can subject PICT images to JPEG compression. When you save an image in the PICT format, Photoshop offers several compression options in the dialog box shown in Figure 3-10. Although this dialog box appears to provide the same compression settings as the one shown in Figure 3-8, it represents the more viable solution because more Macintosh applications recognize QuickTime JPEG than Photoshop's built-in JPEG format. Heck, you can even open JPEG PICT files inside a word processor, including everything from TeachText to Microsoft Word.

Figure 3-10:
If QuickTime is installed, Photoshop provides JPEG compression options when you save an image in the PICT format.

PICT File Options

Resolution
- ○ 16 bits/pixel
- ◉ 32 bits/pixel

OK
Cancel

Compression
- ○ None
- ○ JPEG – low quality
- ○ JPEG – medium quality
- ○ JPEG – high quality
- ◉ JPEG – maximum quality

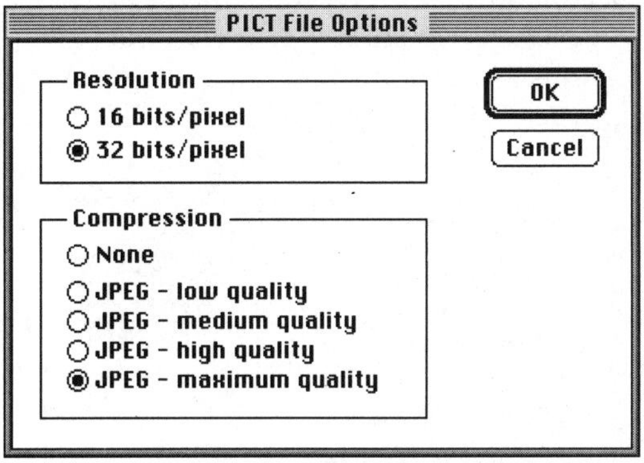

The JPEG format is better than the PICT format when you want to transfer the image to the Windows platform. More Windows applications recognize JPEG than PICT, and it's extremely difficult to find a Windows program that can handle PICT files with QuickTime JPEG compression (particularly because about three Windows machines in the western hemisphere are equipped with QuickTime).

TIFF

Developed by Aldus back in the early days of the Mac to standardize an ever-growing population of scanned images, TIFF (*Tag Image File Format*) is the most widely supported bitmapped format across both the Macintosh and PC platforms. Unlike PICT, it can't handle object-oriented artwork and doesn't support JPEG compression, but it is otherwise unrestricted. In fact, TIFF offers a few tricks of its own that are worth mentioning. When you save an image in the TIFF format, Photoshop displays the TIFF Options dialog box (see Figure 3-11), which offers these options:

- ∞ **Byte Order:** Leave it to Photoshop to name a straightforward option in the most confusing way possible. Byte Order? No, this option doesn't have anything to do with how you eat your food. Rather, because Macintosh TIFF and PC TIFF are two slightly different formats, this option permits you to specify whether you want to use the image on the Mac or on an IBM PC-compatible machine. I'm sure it has something to do with the arrangement of 8-bit chunks of data, but who cares? You want Mac or you want PC? It's that simple.

- ∞ **LZW Compression:** Like Huffman encoding (described earlier in the "Saving an EPS document" section), the LZW (Lempel-Ziv-Welch) compression scheme digs into the computer code that describes an image and substitutes frequently used codes with shorter equivalents. But instead of substituting characters, as Huffman does, LZW substitutes strings of data. Because LZW doesn't so much as touch a pixel in your image, it's entirely lossless. Most image editors and desktop publishing applications — including FreeHand, PageMaker, and QuarkXPress — import LZW-compressed TIFF images, but a few still have yet to catch on.

Figure 3-11:
Photoshop lets you save TIFF files in either the Mac or PC format and compress the image using LZW.

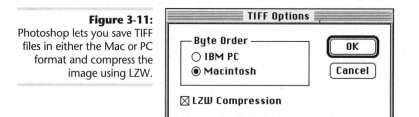

If names like Huffman and LZW ring a faint bell, it may be because these are the same compression schemes used by Aladdin's StuffIt, Salient's AutoDoubler, Bill Goodman's Compact Pro, and other compression utilities. For that reason, there's no sense in using an additional utility to compress a TIFF image that was already compressed using LZW. Neither do you want to compress a JPEG image, because JPEG takes advantage of Huffman encoding. You may shave off a couple of K, but it's not enough space to make it worth your time and effort.

Long-time Photoshop users may have noticed the disappearance of an option, Save Alpha Channels. In Photoshop 3.0, the TIFF format now supports up to 24 channels, which is the maximum number permitted in a document. In fact, TIFF is the only format other than raw and the native Photoshop format that can save more than four channels. To save a TIFF file without extra mask channels, choose File⇨Save a Copy and select the Don't Include Alpha Channels check box. For complete information on channels, read Chapter 5.

The oddball formats

Can you believe it? Sixteen formats down and I still haven't covered them all. The last three are the odd men out. Few programs other than Photoshop support these formats, so you won't be using them to swap files with other applications. Also, these formats don't let you compress images, so you can't use them to conserve disk space. What can you do with these formats? Read the following sections and find out.

Photo CD YCC images

Photoshop can open Eastman Kodak's Photo CD and Pro Photo CD formats directly. This is not an essential capability because a Photo CD contains compressed PICT versions of every image in each of the five scan sizes provided on Photo CDs — from 128×192 pixels (72K) to $2,048 \times 3,072$ pixels (18MB). However, these PICT files are RGB images. The Photo CD format uses the *YCC color model,* a variation on the CIE (Commission Internationale de l'Eclairage) color space discussed in the next chapter. YCC provides a broader range of color — theoretically, every color your eye can see.

The Pro Photo CD format can accommodate each of the five sizes included in the regular Photo CD format, plus one additional size — $4,096 \times 6,144$ pixels (72MB) — that's four times as large as the largest image on a regular Photo CD. As a result, Pro Photo CDs hold only 25 scans; standard Photo CDs hold 100. Like their standard Photo CD counterparts, Pro Photo CD scanners can accommodate 35mm film and slides. But they can also handle 70mm film and 4×5-inch negatives and transparencies. The cost might knock you out, though. While scanning an image to a standard Photo CD costs about $1, scanning it to a Pro Photo CD costs about $9. It just goes to show you; once you gravitate beyond consumerland, everybody expects you to start coughing up the big bucks.

By opening Photo CD files directly, you can translate the YCC images directly to Photoshop's Lab color mode, another variation on CIE color space that ensures no color loss. The Photo CD files are found inside the IMAGES folder in the PHOTO_CD folder, as shown in Figure 3-12. The PICT images are located inside the Photos folder.

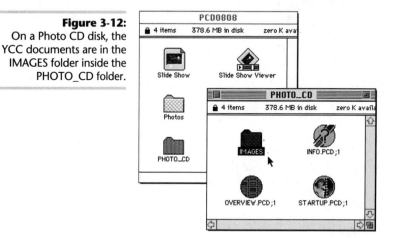

Figure 3-12: On a Photo CD disk, the YCC documents are in the IMAGES folder inside the PHOTO_CD folder.

Photoshop 3.0 includes the new Kodak Color Management Software (CMS), which tweaks colors in Photo CD images based on the kind of film from which they were scanned. When you open a Photo CD image, Photoshop displays the dialog box shown in Figure 3-13. Here you can specify the image size you want to open by selecting an option from the Resolution pop-up menu. The dialog box even shows you a preview of the image. But the options that make a difference are the Source and Destination buttons:

- **Source:** Click on this button to specify the kind of film from which the original photographs were scanned. You can select from two specific Kodak brands — Ektachrome and Kodachrome — or settle for the generic Color Negative Film option. Your selection determines the method by which Photoshop transforms the colors in the image.

- **Destination:** After clicking on this button, select an option from the Device pop-up menu to specify the color model you want to use. Select Adobe Photoshop RGB to open the image in the RGB mode; select Adobe Photoshop CIELAB to open the image in the Lab mode. (A CMYK profile can be purchased separately from Kodak.)

Figure 3-13:
Use these options
to select a
resolution and
calibrate the colors
in the Photo CD
image.

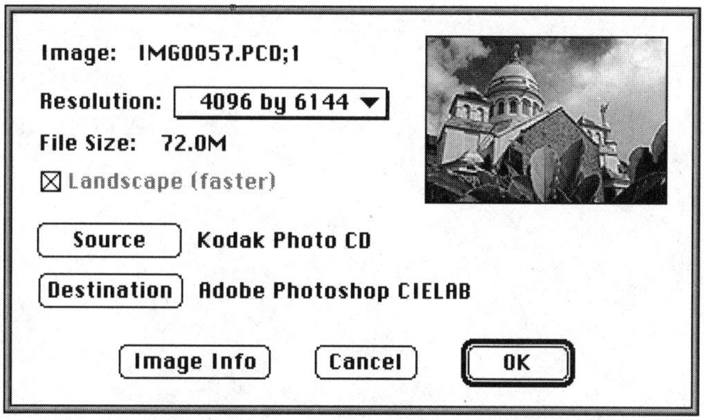

> Image: IMG0057.PCD;1
>
> **Resolution:** [4096 by 6144 ▼]
>
> File Size: 72.0M
>
> ☒ Landscape (faster)
>
> [Source] Kodak Photo CD
>
> [Destination] Adobe Photoshop CIELAB
>
> [Image Info] [Cancel] [OK]

To access Photo CD images, you need a single-session or multi-session CD-ROM device. For more information on Kodak's Photo CD, read the "Using Images on CD-ROM" section of Chapter C on the CD included with this book. For more information on the relationship between YCC, Lab, RGB, and every other color mode you ever thought you might want to learn about, read Chapter 4, "Defining Colors."

Photoshop cannot save to the Photo CD format. So far, Kodak hasn't licensed other vendors to write images using its proprietary code.

PICT resource (startup screen)

If you really want to open a *PICT resource,* such as the splash screen included with Photoshop or the contents of the Scrapbook, choose File⇨Acquire⇨PICT Resource, as described in the upcoming "Lifting PICT resources" section. The PICT Resource option provided by the Open and Save dialog boxes is useful only for opening, editing, and saving *startup screens.*

What is a startup screen? Well, when you boot your computer, a message appears welcoming you to the great big wonderful Macintosh experience. This is the default startup screen included with the system software. However, you can change the startup screen by creating an image and saving it in the PICT Resource file format under the name *StartupScreen* in the root directory of your System Folder. When I recently changed over to a Power Mac 7100, I decided that the old startup screen must die and a new startup screen must dawn. Hence, Figure 3-14. I'm so proud of the darn thing — it shows off a host of third-party filters, many of which are included for your perusal on the CD — that I decided to include a color version of it in the center portion of the book. To wit, check out Color Plate 3-2.

Figure 3-14:
An example of
a custom
startup screen.

To save an image as a startup screen, choose File⇨Save, select the PICT Resource option from the Format pop-up menu, name the image *StartupScreen*, and save it in your System Folder. The PICT Resources Options dialog box appears, asking you to enter a four-character Name code. The secret code is *SCRN*.

If you're saving a 24-bit startup screen, the PICT Resources Options dialog box offers a bunch of QuickTime compression options. *Don't select any of them!* Because QuickTime isn't built into the ROM of your computer, it won't be available when the startup screen appears, and therefore a weird-looking, stretched error message will appear on-screen instead. To avoid this, select None from the Compression options.

For best results, create a startup screen that conforms to the exact dimensions of your screen. If you're unsure what those dimensions are, consult Table 3-1 near the beginning of this chapter.

Opening a raw document

A *raw document* is a plain binary file stripped of all extraneous information. It contains no compression scheme, it specifies no bit depth or image size, and it offers no color mode. Each byte of data indicates a brightness value on a single color channel, and that's it. Photoshop offers this function specifically so that you can open images created in undocumented formats, such as those created on mainframe computers.

To open an image of unknown origin, choose File⇨Open As and select Raw from the File Format pop-up menu. Then select the desired image and click on the Open button or press Return. The dialog box shown in Figure 3-15 appears and features these options:

- ✐ **Width, Height:** If you know the dimensions of the image in pixels, enter the values in these option boxes.

- ✐ **Swap:** Click on this button to swap the Width value with the Height value.

- ✐ **Channels:** Enter the number of color channels in this option box. If the document is an RGB image, enter 3; if it is a CMYK image, enter 4.

- ✐ **Header:** This value tells Photoshop how many bytes of data at the beginning of the file comprise header information that it can ignore.

- ✐ **Retain Header When Saving:** If the Header value is greater than zero, you can instruct Photoshop to retain this data when you save the image in a different format.

- ✐ **Guess:** If you know the Width and Height values but you don't know the number of bytes in the header — or vice versa — you can ask Photoshop for help. Fill in either the size or header information and then click on the Guess button to ask Photoshop to take a stab at the unknown value. Photoshop estimates all this information when the Raw Options dialog box first appears. Generally speaking, if it doesn't estimate correctly the first time around, you're on your own. But hey, the Guess button is worth a shot.

 If a raw document is a CMYK image, it opens as an RGB image with an extra masking channel. To correctly display the image, choose Mode⇨Multichannel to free the four channels from their incorrect relationship. Then recombine them by choosing Mode⇨CMYK Color.

Figure 3-15:
Photoshop requires
you to specify the size
of an image and the
number of color
channels when you
open an image that
does not conform to a
standardized file
format.

```
┌──────────────── Raw Options ────────────────┐
│                                              │
│  Specify parameters of "IMG0007.PCD;1":   ┌────────┐
│  (4466688 bytes)                          │   OK   │
│                                           └────────┘
│                                           ┌────────┐
│     Width:  [2181  ]  pixels              │ Cancel │
│                                           └────────┘
│     Height: [2048  ]  pixels              ┌────────┐
│                                           │  Swap  │
│     Channels: [1    ]                     └────────┘
│                                           ┌────────┐
│     Header: [0      ]        bytes        │  Guess │
│                                           └────────┘
│     ☐ Retain Header When Saving              │
└──────────────────────────────────────────────┘
```

Saving a raw document

Photoshop also allows you to save to the raw document format. This capability is useful when you create files that you want to transfer to mainframe systems or output to devices that don't support other formats, such as the Kodak XL7700 or Hewlett PaintWriter XL.

Do not save 256-color indexed images to the raw format, or you will lose the color lookup table and therefore lose all color information. Be sure to first convert such images to RGB or one of the other full-color modes before saving.

When you save an image in the raw document format, Photoshop presents the dialog box shown in Figure 3-16. The dialog box options work as follows:

- **File Type:** Enter the four-character file type code (TIFF, PICT, and so on) in this option box. (You may want to check the documentation for the application you plan to use to open the raw document.) If you plan to use this file on a computer other than a Mac, you can enter any four characters you like; only Macs use this code.

- **File Creator:** Enter the four-character *creator code,* which tells the system software which application created the file. By default, the creator code is 8BIM, Photoshop's code. Ignore this option unless you have a specific reason for changing it — for example, to open the image in a particular Macintosh application. (You won't hurt anything by changing the code, but you will prevent Photoshop from opening the image when you double-click on the document icon at the Finder desktop.)

- **Header:** Enter the size of the header in bytes. If you enter any value but zero, you must fill in the header using a data editor such as Norton Disk Editor or Central Point Software's MacTools.

↝ **Save Image In:** Select the Interleaved Order option to arrange data in the file sequentially by pixels. In an RGB image, the first byte represents the red value for the first pixel, the second byte represents the green value for that pixel, the third the blue value, and so on. To group data by color channel, select Non-interleaved Order. When you select this option, the first byte represents the red value for the first pixel, the second value represents the red value for the second pixel, and so on. When Photoshop finishes describing the red channel, it describes the green channel and then the blue channel.

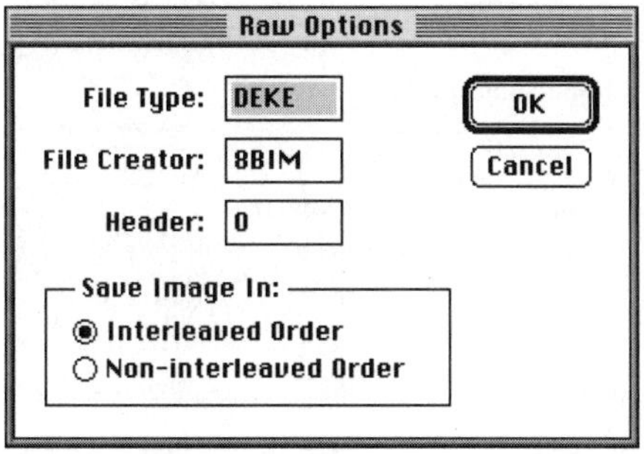

Figure 3-16:
When saving a raw document, enter file type and creator codes and specify the order of data in the file.

How to import PICT elements

I don't think that I ever want to see another format again — I thought my brain was going to dissolve during that last section. Talk about your raw topics! Well, I certainly hope I conveyed my enthusiasm to you. Really, it's the least I could do. (Yawn.)

Anyway, on to bigger and better things, including — do you believe it — more formats! But these last few formats are more interesting. Honest.

The first topic of discussion is importing PICT images into Photoshop via the File⇨Acquire submenu. You can do this using two different methods. These functions enable you to open Canvas and MacDraw Pro documents and extract PICT images from places where you never expected to find them.

Rendering a PICT drawing

As I mentioned back in "The mainstream formats" section, Apple designed the PICT format to handle both images and object-oriented drawings. In fact, if you use Canvas, ClarisDraw, or some other QuickDraw drawing program, you probably save a fair amount of your images to the PICT format. Photoshop provides a plug-in module that lets you render an object-oriented PICT file and convert it to an antialiased image, just as you can render an EPS graphic.

Choose File⇨Acquire⇨Anti-aliased PICT, select the desired drawing, and click on the Open button or press Return. Photoshop displays the Anti-aliased PICT dialog box, shown in Figure 3-17, which allows you to specify the size of the image. The drawing is object-oriented, so you can render it as large or as small as you want without any loss of image quality. Select the Constrain Proportions check box to preserve the width-to-height ratio of the drawing. You also can change the colors in the drawing to gray values or open the drawing as an RGB image. Photoshop automatically antialiases objects to give them soft edges.

Figure 3-17:
You can specify the size and colors of a PICT drawing rendered inside Photoshop.

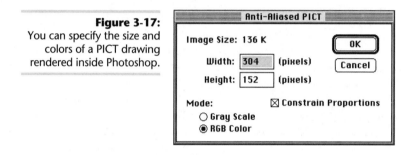

Photoshop renders PICT drawings remarkably well, especially compared to other applications that import PICT — mostly notably PageMaker and QuarkXPress, both of which do a pretty lousy job. However, Photoshop does not support bitmapped patterns in a PICT drawing. Any patterns render to solid color.

Lifting PICT resources

When you choose File⇨Acquire⇨PICT Resource, Photoshop lets you open an application or other resource file on disk and browse through any PICT images it may contain. Figure 3-18 shows the dialog box that appears after you select a file to open. You use the double arrow symbols to advance from one PICT image to the next. Click on the Preview button to display the image in the preview box.

The manual shows how you can use this command to open the Photoshop application, which contains a number of PICT images, including those from the various splash screens shown back in Figure 2-1 in Chapter 2. In fact, many applications include PICT images in their *resource forks,* a special section of code available to some files, usually applications. Most of these images are screen controls and other items you'll probably never want to access.

Figure 3-18:
Choose File⇨Acquire⇨PICT
Resource to browse through
the PICT images inside an
application or other file that
contains a resource fork,
such as the Scrapbook.

 A better use for the File⇨Acquire⇨PICT Resource command is to open images directly from the Scrapbook. In fact, this function becomes phenomenally practical if you use a commercial or shareware screen-capture utility (such as Mainstay's Capture) that can store screens in the Scrapbook, as demonstrated in Figure 3-19. You can process your screen shots *en masse* at your leisure. In fact, this is how I created every screen shot in this book.

Figure 3-19:
Use a commercial or shareware
screen capture utility to save your
screen shots to the Scrapbook and
then use Photoshop to process
them in a single sitting.

If you have problems opening or saving any of the formats listed in this chapter — particularly the PC-type formats, such as BMP, GIF, PCX, and others — you may want to try out DeBabelizer from Equilibrium. Absolutely the best format converter bar none, DeBabelizer handles every format Photoshop handles, as well as Dr. Halo's CUT, Fractal Design Painter's RIFF, the animation formats PICS, FLI, and ANM, as well as UNIX workstation formats for Silicon Graphics, Sun Microsystems, and others. For a preview of this incredible utility, check out the limited edition on the CD. It actually offers a few working formats that you may find useful.

Resampling and Cropping Methods

After you bring up an image — whether you created it from scratch or opened an existing image stored in one of the five billion formats discussed in the preceding pages — its size and resolution are established. However, neither size nor resolution is set in stone. Photoshop provides two methods for changing the number of pixels in an image: resampling and cropping.

Resizing versus resampling

Typically, when folks talk about *resizing* an image (as they're so prone to do these days), they mean enlarging or reducing it without changing the number of pixels in the image, as demonstrated back in Figure 3-1. By contrast, to *resample* an image is to scale it so that it contains a larger or smaller number of pixels. With resizing, there is an inverse relationship between size and resolution — size goes up when resolution goes down, and vice versa — while resampling affects either size or resolution alone. Figure 3-20 shows an image resized and resampled to 50 percent of its original dimensions. The resampled and original images have identical resolutions, but the resized image has twice the resolution of its companions.

Resizing an image

To resize an image, use one of the techniques discussed in the "Printed resolution" section near the beginning of this chapter. To briefly recap, you can either choose File⇨Page Setup and enter a percentage value into the Reduce or Enlarge option box, or you can choose Image⇨Image Size and enter a value into the Resolution option box (assuming that the File Size check box is selected). Neither technique affects the on-screen appearance of the image, only the way it prints.

Resampling an image

You also use Image⇨Image Size to resample an image. The difference is that you turn off the File Size check box, as shown in Figure 3-21. In fact, the File Size option is the key to this dialog box.

Figure 3-20:
An image (top) resized
(bottom left) and
resampled (bottom
right) down to 50
percent.

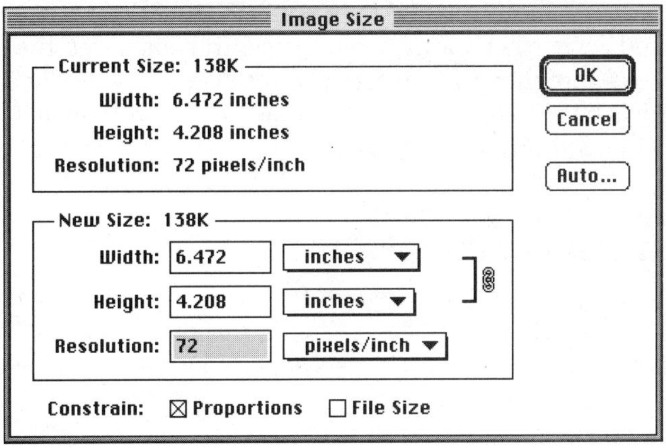

Figure 3-21:
The setting of the
File Size option
determines
whether you resize
or resample an
image.

When selected, File Size ensures that the number of pixels in the image remains fixed. Any change to the Resolution inversely affects the Width and Height values if they are set to any measurement unit but pixels (see the following note).

When File Size is deselected, the Resolution value is independent of the Width and Height values. You then can increase the number of pixels in an image by increasing any of the three values or decrease the number of pixels by decreasing the values. Photoshop stretches or shrinks the image according to the new size specifications. To do so, it must interpolate the pixels in the image, as explained in the "General environmental preferences" section of Chapter 2 (see Figure 2-17).

 If the unit of measurement is pixels, the Resolution option does not affect the Width or Height values regardless of whether File Size is on or off. In fact, the rules change completely. To resize an image, you change the Resolution value. To resample an image, you change the Width and Height values.

Cropping

You also can change the number of pixels in an image by *cropping* it, which means to clip away pixels around the edges of an image without changing the color of any remaining pixel. (The one exception occurs when you rotate a cropped image, in which case pixels in the image change color because Photoshop has to interpolate pixels to account for the rotation.)

Cropping enables you to focus in on an element in your image. For example, Figure 3-22 shows an image my sister photographed for me. It has good color balance, but the image is crooked and we're too far away from the central character, the apprehensive lion. (At least he looks apprehensive. I worry about the guy.) No problem. All I do is crop around the lion's head to delete all the extraneous image elements and focus right in on Mr. Scaredy Cat, as shown in Figure 3-23.

Changing the canvas size

One way to crop an image is to choose Image⇨Canvas Size, which displays the Canvas Size dialog box shown in Figure 3-24. The options in this dialog box enable you to scale the imaginary *canvas* on which the image rests separately from the image itself.

Figure 3-22:
This image
has too much
extraneous
information
in it.

Figure 3-23:
Cropping allows you to focus
in on the essential image
elements.

If you enlarge the canvas, Photoshop surrounds the image with a white background (assuming that the background color is white). If you reduce the canvas, you crop the image. Click inside the Placement grid to specify the image placement on the new canvas. For example, if you want to add space to the bottom of an image, enlarge the canvas size and then click inside the upper middle square. If you want to crop away the upper left corner of an image, create a smaller canvas size and then click on the lower right square.

Figure 3-24:
Choose Image⇨Canvas Size to crop an image or add empty space around the perimeter of an image.

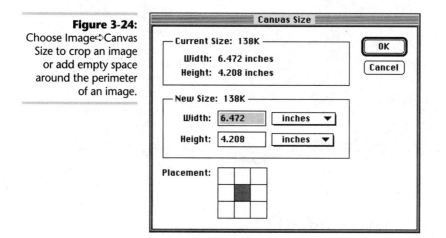

Using the crop tool

Generally speaking, the Canvas Size command is most useful for enlarging the canvas or shaving a few pixels off the edge of an image. If you want to crop away a large portion of an image, using the crop tool is a better choice.

To crop the image, drag with the crop tool to create a rectangular marquee that surrounds the portion of the image you want to retain. If you don't get it right the first time, you can change the horizontal and vertical dimensions of the marquee by dragging any one of the four *corner handles,* as shown in Figure 3-25. When the marquee surrounds the exact portion of the image you want to keep, click inside it with the scissors cursor. This action clips away all pixels except those that lie inside and along the border of the crop marquee.

Figure 3-25:
Drag a corner handle to
resize the crop marquee.

Crop marquee   Crop handle

Rotating and moving a crop marquee

Photoshop enables you to rotate a crop marquee by Option-dragging a corner handle
prior to clicking inside the marquee with the scissors cursor. Straightening out an image
by Option-dragging the corner handle of a crop marquee can be a little tricky, however.
I wish I had a certified check for every time I thought that I had the marquee rotated
properly, only to find that the image was still crooked after I clicked inside it with the
scissors cursor. If that happens to you, choose Edit⇨Undo and try again. Do *not* try
using the crop tool a second time to rotate the already rotated image. If you do,
Photoshop sets about interpolating between already interpolated pixels, resulting in
more lost data. Every rotation gets farther away from the original image.

A better solution is to do it right the first time. Locate a line in your image that
should be straight up and down. Option-drag the crop marquee so that it aligns
exactly with that line, as shown in Figure 3-26. Don't worry that this isn't how
you want to crop the image — you're just using the line as a reference. After
you arrive at the correct angle for the marquee, release the Option key and drag
the handles normally to specify the crop boundary. The angle of the marquee
remains fixed throughout.

Figure 3-26:
Option-drag
exactly over a
long line in
your image to
determine the
proper angle
of rotation.

 You can also move the entire crop marquee by Command-dragging on any one of the handles. This is a great way to reposition a cropping boundary without having to fiddle around with moving each handle separately. I somehow missed this technique in the last edition of the book. Thanks to ace Photoshop artist Greg Vander Houwen for setting me straight.

Cropping a selection

Another way to crop an image is to drag with the rectangular marquee tool around the portion of the image you want to keep and then choose Edit⇨Crop. One of the advantages of this technique is that it lets you crop the canvas to the boundaries of an image pasted from the Clipboard (or dragged and dropped from another image). As long as the boundaries of the pasted image are rectangular, as in the case of an image copied from a different application, you can choose Edit⇨Paste followed by Edit⇨Crop to both replace the former image and to crop the window to fit the new image.

Another reason I like this technique is the speed. I'm becoming increasingly frustrated with how slow the cropping marquee updates when I draw or edit it (and this is on a Power Mac, gang). Though you can't resize a selection marquee so conveniently, it sure as heck responds more quickly.

Summary

- The resolution of an image is measured in pixels per inch; the resolution of a printer is measured in dots per inch.

- You can control the resolution at which an image prints by changing the Resolution value in the Image Size dialog box and/or the Reduce or Enlarge value in the Page Setup dialog box.

- The New dialog box automatically scales a prospective image window to the size of the image in the Clipboard (if any).

- You can now make the background of a new image transparent, which is perfect for temporarily holding an image that you later want to composite with a different background.

- If you can't get a PICT or EPS drawing to print or you simply want to be able to edit a drawing as a bitmapped image, you can render it at any size or resolution inside Photoshop.

- To import an image into Adobe Illustrator, you must save it in the EPS format.

- JPEG is a lossy image compression format, meaning that it sacrifices a minimal amount of data to conserve space on disk.

- With QuickTime installed, you can apply JPEG compression to a PICT image.

- The TIFF format is the most popular image format in use across both the Mac and PC platforms.

- Photoshop enables you to open images directly while inside the Scrapbook by using File⇨Acquire⇨PICT Resource.

- You can crop an image by choosing Image⇨Canvas Size or by using the crop tool.

- Option-drag a corner handle to rotate a crop marquee.

- The time-worn scribblings of Dionysius of Halicarnassus contain no information about Photoshop, except to say that the PICT format was very popular among the plebeians. I think there's something to that.

Defining Colors

░░░

In This Chapter

➼ How to use the color controls in the toolbox

➼ How to select and define colors in the Color Picker dialog box

➼ In-depth examinations of the RGB, HSB, CMYK, and Lab color models

➼ How and why to reduce a full-color image to 256 colors

➼ How to create grayscale and black-and-white images

➼ Introductions to the Trumatch and Pantone color standards

➼ How to use the Picker palette and eyedropper tool

░░░

Selecting and Editing Colors

Every once in a while, the state of Macintosh graphics technology reminds me of television in the early 1950s. Only the upper echelon of Photoshop artists can afford to work exclusively in the wonderful world of color. The rest of us print most of our images in black and white.

Regardless of who you are, however, color is a prime concern. Even gray values, after all, are colors. Many folks have problems accepting this premise — guess we're all so used to separating the worlds of grays and other colors in our minds that never the twain shall meet. But the fact is, gray values are just variations on what Noah Webster used to call "The sensation resulting from stimulation of the retina of the eye by light waves of certain lengths." (Give the guy a few drinks and he'd spout off 19 more definitions, not including the meanings of the transitive verb.) Just as black and white represent a subset of gray, gray is a subset of color. In fact, you'll find that using Photoshop involves an awful lot of navigating through these and other colorful subsets.

Specifying colors

First off, Photoshop provides four color controls in the toolbox, as shown in Figure 4-1. These icons work as follows:

- ✑ **Foreground color:** The foreground color icon indicates the color you apply when you use the type, paint bucket, line, pencil, airbrush, or paintbrush tool or if you Option-drag with the smudge tool. The foreground color also begins any gradation created with the gradient tool. You can apply the foreground color to a selection by choosing Edit⇨Fill or Edit⇨Stroke or by pressing Option-Delete. To change the foreground color, click on the foreground color icon to display the Color Picker dialog box or click in an open image window with the eyedropper tool.

- ✑ **Background color:** The active background color indicates the color you apply with the eraser tool. The background color also ends any gradation created with the gradient tool. You can apply the background color to a selection by pressing the Delete key. To change the background color, click on the background color icon to display the Color Picker dialog box or Option-click in any open image window with the eyedropper tool.

- ✑ **Switch colors:** Click on this icon (or press the X key) to exchange the foreground and background colors.

- ✑ **Default colors:** Click on this icon (or press the D key) to make the foreground color black and the background color white, according to their factory default settings.

Figure 4-1:
The color controls provided with Photoshop 3.0 (along with keyboard shortcuts in parentheses, where applicable).

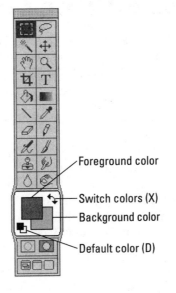

Foreground color

Switch colors (X)

Background color

Default color (D)

Using the Color Picker

When you click on the foreground or background color icon, Photoshop displays the Color Picker dialog box. (This assumes that Photoshop is the active option in the Color Picker pop-up menu in the General Preferences dialog box. If you select the Apple option, the generic Apple Color Picker appears, as described in the "HSB" section later in this chapter.) Figure 4-2 labels the wealth of elements and options in the Color Picker dialog box, which work as follows:

↦ **Color slider:** Use the color slider to home in on the color you want to select. Drag up or down on either of the *slider triangles* to select a color from a particular 8-bit range. The colors represented inside the slider correspond to the selected radio button. For example, if you select the H (Hue) radio button, which is the default setting, the slider colors represent the full 8-bit range of hues. If you select S (Saturation), the slider shows the current hue at full saturation at the top of the slider, down to no saturation — or gray — at the bottom of the slider. If you select B (Brightness), the slider shows the 8-bit range of brightness values, from solid color at the top of the slider to absolute black at the bottom. You also can select R (Red), G (Green) or B (Blue), in which case the top of the slider shows you what the current color looks like when subjected to full-intensity red, green, or blue (respectively), and the bottom of the slider shows every bit of red, green, or blue subtracted.

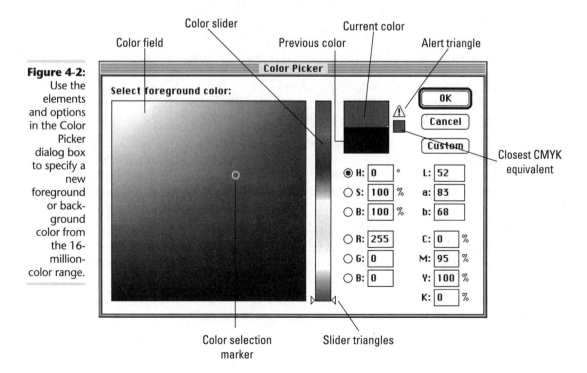

Figure 4-2:
Use the elements and options in the Color Picker dialog box to specify a new foreground or back-ground color from the 16-million-color range.

For a proper introduction to the HSB and RGB color models, including definitions of specific terms such as hue, saturation, and brightness, read the "Working in Different Color Modes" section later in this chapter.

- **Color field:** The color field shows a 16-bit range of variations on the current slider color. Click inside it to move the *color selection marker* and thereby select a new color. The field graphs colors against the two remaining attributes *not* represented by the color slider. For example, if you select the H (Hue) radio button, the field graphs colors according to brightness vertically and saturation horizontally, as demonstrated in the first example of Figure 4-3. The other examples show what happens to the color field when you select the S (Saturation) and B (Brightness) radio buttons.

  Likewise, Figure 4-4 shows how the field graphs colors when you select the R (Red), G (Green), and B (Blue) radio buttons. Obviously, it would help a lot to see these images in color, but you probably wouldn't have been able to afford this big, fat book if we had printed it in full color. Therefore, I recommend that you experiment with the Color Picker inside your version of Photoshop or refer to Color Plate 4-1 to see how the dialog box looks when the H (Hue), S (Saturation), and B (Brightness) options are selected.

Slider and field always work together to represent the entire 16-million-color range. The slider displays 256 colors, and the field displays 65,000 variations on the slider color; 256 times 65,000 is 16 million. Therefore, no matter which radio button you select, you have access to the same colors. It's just that your means of accessing them changes.

- **Current color:** The color currently selected from the color field appears in the top rectangle immediately to the right of the color slider. Click on the OK button or press Return to make this the current foreground or background color (depending on which color control icon in the toolbox you clicked to display the Color Picker dialog box in the first place).

- **Previous color:** The bottom rectangle just to the right of the color slider shows how the foreground or background color — whichever one you are in the process of editing — looked before you displayed the Color Picker dialog box. Click on the Cancel button or press Command-period to leave this color intact.

- **Alert triangle:** The alert triangle appears when you select a bright color that Photoshop can't print using standard process colors. The box below the triangle shows the closest CMYK equivalent, which is invariably a duller version of the color. Click either on the triangle or box to bring the color into the printable range.

Figure 4-3:
The color field graphs colors against the two attributes that are not represented in the slider. Here you can see how color is laid out when you select (top to bottom) the H (Hue), S (Saturation), and B (Brightness) radio buttons.

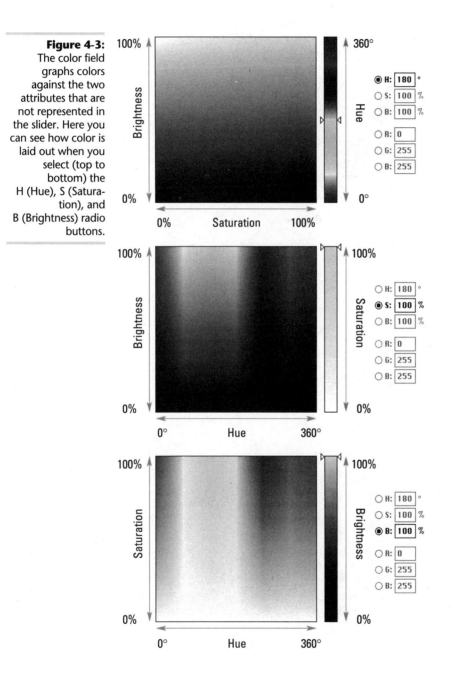

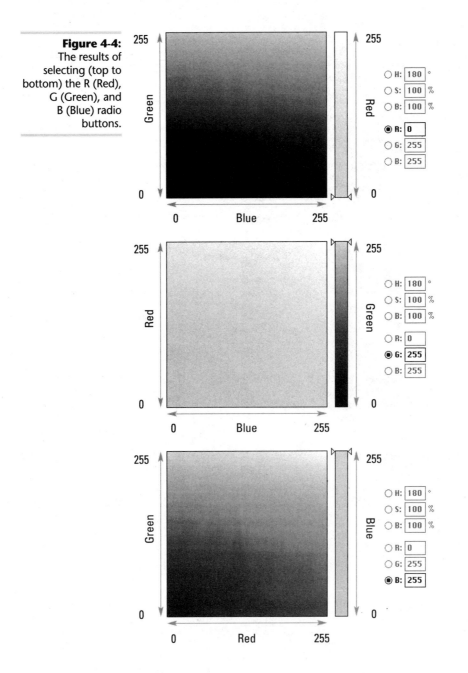

Figure 4-4:
The results of selecting (top to bottom) the R (Red), G (Green), and B (Blue) radio buttons.

Entering numeric color values

In addition to selecting colors using the slider and color field, you can enter specific color values in the option boxes in the lower right region of the Color Picker dialog box. Novices and intermediates may find these options less satisfying to use than the slider and field. However, the options enable artists and print professionals to specify exact color values, whether to make controlled adjustments to a color already in use or to match a color used in another document. These options fall into one of four camps:

- **HSB:** These options stand for hue, saturation, and brightness. Hue is measured on a 360-degree circle. Saturation and brightness are measured from 0 to 100 percent. These options permit access to more than 3 million color variations.

- **RGB:** You can change the amount of the primary colors red, green, and blue by specifying the brightness value of each color from 0 to 255. These options permit access to more than 16 million color variations.

- **Lab:** This acronym stands for *luminosity,* measured from 0 to 100 percent, and two arbitrary color axes, *a* and *b,* whose brightness values range from –128 to 127. These options permit access to more than 6 million color variations.

- **CMYK:** These options display the amount of cyan, magenta, yellow, and black ink required to print the current color. In fact, when you click on the alert triangle, these are the only values that don't change, because these are the values that make up the closest CMYK equivalent.

In my opinion, the numerical range of these options is extremely bewildering. For example, numerically speaking, the CMYK options enable you to create 100 million unique colors, whereas the RGB options permit the standard 16 million variations, and the Lab options permits a scant 6 million. Yet in point of fact, Lab is the largest color space, theoretically encompassing all colors from both CMYK and RGB. The printing standard CMYK provides by far the fewest colors, just the opposite of what you might expect. What gives? Misleading numerical ranges. How do these weird color models work? Keep reading and you'll find out.

Working in Different Color Modes

The four sets of option boxes inside the Color Picker dialog box represent *color models* — or, if you prefer, *color modes* (one less letter, no less meaning, perfect for you folks who are trying to cut down in life). Color models are different ways to define colors both on-screen and on the printed page.

Outside the Color Picker dialog box, you can work inside any one of these color models by choosing a command from the Modes menu. In doing so, you generally change the colors in your image by dumping a few hundred or even thousand colors that have no equivalents in the new color model. The only exception is Lab, which in theory encompasses every unique color your eyes can detect.

 Rather than discuss the color models in the order in which they occur in the Modes menu, I cover them in logical order, starting with the most common and widely accepted color model, RGB. Also note that I don't discuss the duotone or multichannel modes at this time. Mode⇨Duotone represents an alternative method for printing grayscale images, and is therefore discussed in Chapter 6, "Printing Images." The multichannel mode, meanwhile, is not even a color model. Rather, Mode⇨Multichannel enables you to separate an image into entirely independent channels which you then can swap around and splice back together to create special effects. For more information, see the "Using multichannel techniques" section of Chapter 5.

RGB

RGB is the color model of light. It comprises three *primary colors* — red, green, and blue — each of which can vary between 256 levels of intensity (called *brightness values,* as discussed in previous chapters). The RGB model is also called the *additive primary model,* because a color becomes lighter as you add higher levels of red, green, and blue light. All monitors, projection devices, and other items that transmit or filter light, including televisions, movie projectors, colored stage lights, and even stained glass, rely on the additive primary model.

Red, green, and blue light mix as follows:

- **Red and green:** Full-intensity red and green mix to form yellow. Subtract some red to make chartreuse; subtract some green to make orange. All these colors assume a complete lack of blue.

- **Green and blue:** Full-intensity green and blue with no red mix to form cyan. If you try hard enough, you can come up with 65,000 colors in the turquoise/jade/ sky blue/sea green range.

- **Blue and red:** Full-intensity blue and red mix to form magenta. Subtract some blue to make rose; subtract some red to make purple. All these colors assume a complete lack of green.

- ✏ **Red, green, and blue:** Full-intensity red, green, and blue mix to form white, the absolute brightest color in the visible spectrum.

- ✏ **No light:** Low intensities of red, green, and blue plunge a color into blackness.

Insofar as image editing is concerned, the RGB color model is ideal for editing images on-screen because it provides access to the entire range of 24-bit screen colors. Further-more, you can save an RGB image in any file format supported by Photoshop. As shown in Table 4-1, the only other color mode that is compatible with such a wide range of file formats is grayscale. (I should note, however, that GIF is an 8-bit format. So if you save an RGB image in GIF, the image will be reduced to 256 colors.)

Table 4-1	File-Format Support for Photoshop 3.0's Color Models						
	Bitmap	**Grayscale**	**Duotone**	**Indexed**	**RGB**	**Lab**	**CMYK**
EPS	yes	yes	yes	yes	yes	yes	yes
GIF	yes	yes	no	yes	yes	no	no
JPEG	no	yes	no	no	yes	no	yes
PCX	yes	yes	no	yes	yes	no	no
PICT	yes	yes	no	yes	yes	no	no
Scitex	no	yes	no	no	yes	no	yes
TIFF	yes	yes	no	yes	yes	yes	yes

Table 4-1 lists color models in the order they appear in the Modes menu. Again, I left out the multichannel mode because it is not a color model. (Also, the multichannel mode can only be saved in the Photoshop and raw formats.) The native Photoshop format, not listed in the table, supports all color models.

On the negative side, the RGB color model provides access to a wider range of colors than you can print. Therefore, if you are designing an image for full-color printing, you can expect to lose many of the brightest and most vivid colors in your image. The only way to entirely avoid such color loss is to scan your image and edit it in the CMYK mode, which can be an exceptionally slow proposition. The better solution is to scan your images to Photo CDs and edit them in the Lab mode, as explained in the upcoming "CIE's Lab" section.

HSB

Back in Photoshop 2.0, the Modes menu provided access to the HSB — hue, saturation, brightness — color model, now relegated to the Color Picker dialog box and the Picker palette (discussed later in this chapter). *Hue* is pure color, the stuff rainbows are made of, measured on a 360-degree circle. Red is located at 0 degrees, yellow at 60 degrees, green at 120 degrees, cyan at 180 degrees (midway around the circle), blue at 240 degrees, and magenta at 300 degrees. It's basically a pie-shaped version of the RGB model at full-intensity.

To see what the HSB color model looks like, choose Preference⊃General (Command-K), select Apple from the Color Picker pop-up menu, and press Return. Then click on the foreground or background color icon in the toolbox to display the Apple Color Picker window shown in Figure 4-5. The perimeter of the color wheel shows each and every hue at full saturation. The center of the wheel represents lowest saturation. Use the scroll bar to change the brightness.

Saturation represents the purity of the color. A zero saturation value equals gray. White, black, and any other colors you can express in a grayscale image have no saturation. Full saturation produces the purest version of a hue.

Brightness is the lightness or darkness of a color. A zero brightness value equals black. Full brightness combined with full saturation results in the most vivid version of any hue.

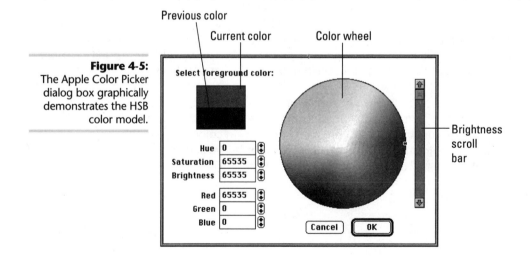

Figure 4-5:
The Apple Color Picker dialog box graphically demonstrates the HSB color model.

If you miss being able to edit images in the HSB mode, the brothers Knoll distribute a complimentary HSL&HSB plug-in via on-line services. Unfortunately, it isn't particularly useful. You can edit an image according to hue, saturation, and brightness, but you can't accurately view the results of your changes until you return to the RGB mode.

(Incidentally, the HSL part of the HSL&HSB plug-in represents another mode abandoned after Photoshop 2.0. Only slightly different than HSB, HSL offers *luminosity* — also called *lightness* — in place of brightness. No luminosity still equals black, but full luminosity turns any hue or saturation value to white. Therefore, medium luminosity is required to produce the most vivid version of any hue.

CMYK

In nature, our eyes perceive pigments according to the *subtractive color model.* Sunlight contains every visible color found on earth. When sunlight is projected on an object, the object absorbs (subtracts) some of the light and reflects the rest. The reflected light is the color that you see. For example, a fire engine is bright red because it absorbs all non-red — meaning all blue and green — from the white-light spectrum.

Pigments on a sheet of paper work the same way. You can even mix pigments to create other colors. Suppose you paint a red brush stroke, which absorbs green and blue light, over a blue brush stroke, which absorbs green and red light. You get a blackish mess that has only a modicum of blue and red light left, along with a smidgen of green because the colors weren't absolutely pure.

But wait — every child knows that red and blue mix to form purple. So what gives? What gives is that what you learned in elementary school is only a rude approximation of the truth. Did you ever try mixing a vivid red with a canary yellow only to produce an ugly orange-brown gloop? The reason you didn't achieve the bright orange you wanted is obvious if you stop and think about it. The fact that red starts out darker than bright orange means that you have to add a great deal of yellow before you arrive at orange. And even then, it had better be an incredibly bright lemon yellow, not some deep canary yellow that already has a lot of red in it.

Commercial subtractive primaries

The subtractive primary colors used by commercial printers — cyan, magenta, and yellow — are for the most part very light. Cyan absorbs only red light, magenta absorbs only green light, and yellow absorbs only blue light. Unfortunately, on their own, these colors don't do a very good job of producing dark colors. In fact, at full intensities, cyan, magenta, and yellow all mixed together don't get much beyond a muddy brown. That's where black comes in. Black helps to accentuate shadows, deepen dark colors, and, of course, print real blacks.

In case you're wondering how colors mix in the CMYK model, it's basically the opposite of the RGB model. However, because pigments are not as pure as primary colors in the additive model, there are some differences:

- **Cyan and magenta:** Full-intensity cyan and magenta mix to form a deep blue with a little violet in it. Subtract some cyan to make purple; subtract some magenta to make a dull medium blue. All these colors assume a complete lack of yellow.

- **Magenta and yellow:** Full-intensity magenta and yellow mix to form a brilliant red. Subtract some magenta to make vivid orange; subtract some yellow to make rose. All these colors assume a complete lack of cyan.

- **Yellow and cyan:** Full-intensity yellow and cyan mix to form a bright green with a hint of blue in it. Subtract some yellow to make a deep teal; subtract some cyan to make chartreuse. All these colors assume a complete lack of magenta.

- **Cyan, magenta, and yellow:** Full-intensity cyan, magenta, and yellow mix to form a muddy brown.

- **Black:** Black pigmentation added to any other pigment darkens the color.

- **No pigment:** No pigmentation results in white (assuming that white is the color of the paper).

Editing in CMYK

If you're used to editing RGB images, editing in the CMYK mode can require some new approaches, especially when editing individual color channels. When you view a single color channel in the RGB mode (as discussed in the following chapter), white indicates high-intensity color, and black indicates low-intensity color. It's just the opposite in CMYK. When you view an individual color channel, black means high-intensity color, and white means low-intensity color.

This doesn't mean that RGB and CMYK color channels look like inverted versions of each other. In fact, because the color theory is inverted, they look pretty much the same. But if you're trying to achieve the full-intensity colors mentioned in the preceding section, you should apply black to the individual color channels, not white as you would in the RGB mode.

Should I edit in CMYK?

Boy, this is a thorny issue, but I'm going to attack it anyway. Here's the deal: RGB doesn't accurately represent the colors you get when you print an image, because RGB allows you to represent many colors — particularly very bright colors — that CMYK can't touch. That's why when you switch from RGB to CMYK, the colors appear duller. (If you're familiar with painting, RGB is like oils and CMYK is like acrylics. The latter lacks the depth of color provided by the former.)

For this reason, lots of folks advocate working in the CMYK mode. I, however, do not. While working in CMYK eliminates color disappointments, it is also much slower because Photoshop has to convert CMYK values to your RGB screen on the fly. (One way to accelerate the CMYK mode is to purchase a Thunder II GX•1360 or GX•1600 from SuperMac. Both make editing in the CMYK mode as fast as editing in the RGB mode. Currently, the GX•1360 will set you back $2,500; the GX•1600 costs more than $3,000. The two boards differ only in resolution.)

Furthermore, your scanner and monitor are RGB devices. No matter how you work, a translation from RGB to CMYK color space must occur at some point in time. If you pay the extra bucks to purchase a Scitex CMYK scan, for example, you simply make the translation at the beginning of the process — Scitex has no option but to use RGB sensors internally — rather than at the end. In fact, every color device on earth is RGB *except* the printer.

Ergo — it makes me sound like a really smart guy in a lab coat if I say "ergo" — you should wait to convert to the CMYK mode until right before you print. After your artwork is finalized, choose Mode⇨CMYK and make whatever edits you deem necessary. For example, you might want to introduce a few color corrections, apply some sharpening, and even retouch a few details by hand. Photoshop applies your changes more slowly in the CMYK mode, but at least you're only slowed down at the end of the job, not throughout the entire process.

This is not to say that you can't edit in the RGB mode and still get a picture of what the image will look like in CMYK. If you choose Mode⇨CMYK Preview, Photoshop displays colors in the CMYK color space on-screen while allowing you to continue to work in the larger world of RGB. This is one of Photoshop 3.0's best new features.

Colors that occur in the RGB color space but are missing from CMYK are said to be "out of gamut." Chapter 16 explains how to use Photoshop 3.0's new capabilities to correct out-of-gamut colors before you switch to the CMYK mode. If you switch modes without first addressing these out-of-gamut colors, Photoshop adjusts the colors automatically. This may result in flat areas in your image because several out-of-gamut colors may automatically gravitate toward a single CMYK value. If you can spare the time, I strongly advise you to check out Chapter 16 before choosing Mode⇨CMYK.

RGB isn't the only mode that responds quickly and provides a bountiful range of colors. Photoshop's Lab color space comprises all the colors from RGB and CMYK and is every bit as fast as RGB. Many high-end users prefer to work in this mode, and I certainly advocate it if you're brave enough to take it on. Read the next section for the full story.

CIE's Lab

Whereas the RGB mode is the color model of your luminescent computer screen and the CMYK mode is the color model of the reflective page, Lab is independent of light or pigment. Perhaps you've already heard the bit about how in 1931, an international color organization called the *Commission Internationale d'Eclairage* (CIE) developed a color model that in theory contains every single color the human eye can see. (Gnats, iguanas, fruit bats, go find your own color models; humans, you have CIE. Mutants and aliens — maybe CIE, maybe not, too early to tell.) Then, in 1976, the significant birthday of our nation, the CIE celebrated by coming up with two additional color systems. One of those systems was Lab, and the other was shrouded in secrecy. Well, at least *I* don't know what the other one was. Probably something that measures how it is that the entire visible spectrum of color can bounce off your retina when using flash photography and come out looking the exact shade of red one normally associates with lab (not Lab) rabbits. But that's just a guess.

The beauty of the Lab color model is that it fills in gaps in both the RGB and CMYK models. RGB, for example, provides an overabundance of colors in the blue-to-green range, but is stingy on yellows, oranges, and other colors in the green-to-red range. Meanwhile, the colors missing from CMYK are enough to fill the holes in Albert Hall. Lab gets everything just right.

Understanding Lab anatomy

The Lab mode features three color channels, one for luminosity and two others for color ranges known simply by the initials *a* and *b*. (The Greeks would have called them alpha and beta, if that's any help.) Upon hearing *luminosity,* you might think, "Ah, just like HSL." Well, just to make things confusing, Lab's luminosity is just like HSB's brightness. White indicates full-intensity color.

Meanwhile, the *a* channel contains colors ranging from deep green (low brightness values) to gray (medium brightness values) to vivid pink (high brightness values). The *b* channel ranges from bright blue (low brightness values) to gray to burnt yellow (high brightness values). As in the RGB model, these colors mix together to produce lighter colors. Only the brightness values in the luminosity channel darken the colors. Therefore, you can think of Lab as a two-channel RGB with brightness thrown on top.

To get a glimpse of how it works, try the following simple experiment.

STEPS: Testing Out the Lab Mode

Step 1. Create a new image in the Lab mode — say, 300×300 pixels.

Step 2. Press the D key to return the default colors — black and white — to the toolbox. Then press Command-2 to go to the *a* channel.

Step 3. Double-click on the gradient tool in the toolbox. Make sure that you see the words *Normal, Foreground to Background,* and *Linear* in the Gradient Tool Options panel of the Brushes palette. If these words aren't visible, select them from the first, second, and third pop-up menus, respectively.

Step 4. Shift-drag with the gradient tool from the top to the bottom of the window.

Step 5. Press Command-3 to go to the *b* channel. Shift-drag from left to right with the gradient tool to create a horizontal gradation.

Step 6. Press Command-0 to return to the composite display, which lets you view all channels at once. If you're using a 24-bit monitor, you should be looking at a window filled with an incredible array of super bright colors. In theory, these are the brightest shades of all the colors you can see. In practice, however, the colors are limited by the display capabilities of your RGB monitor.

Step 7. Just for laughs, compare this color circle to the one included in the Apple Color Picker dialog box. Press Command-K to bring up the General Preferences dialog box. Select Apple from the Color Picker pop-up menu (where's Peter Piper when you need him?) and press Return. Then click on the foreground color icon in the tool box. Drag the scroll box in the brightness scroll bar all the way up and check out the difference. You can see that although it appears slightly rotated, the Lab color space contains the same basic colors as in the hue/saturation circle, but far more of them. Or, at least, far more colors than are discernible to your eye, and that's what ultimately counts.

Step 8.   If you really want a sobering sight, choose ModeÍCMYK and watch those bright colors disappear. Aagh, isn't it pitiful? Luckily, CMYK is capable of doing a slightly better job than this. Choose ImageÍAdjustÍLevels (or press Command-L). Then click on the Auto button and press Return. That's better — much better, in fact — but it's still very much muted compared with its Lab counterpart.

Using Lab

Because it's device independent, you can use the Lab mode to edit any image. Editing in the Lab mode is as fast as editing in the RGB mode and several times faster than editing in the CMYK mode. If you plan on printing your image to color separations, you may want to experiment with using the Lab mode instead of RGB, because Lab ensures that no colors are altered when you convert the image to CMYK, except to change colors that fall outside the CMYK range. In fact, any time you convert an image from RGB to CMYK, Photoshop automatically converts the image to the Lab mode as an intermediate step.

   If you work with Photo CDs often, open the scans directly from the Photo CD format (as opposed to the PICT format) as Lab images. Kodak's proprietary YCC color model is nearly identical to Lab, so you can expect an absolute minimum of data loss; some people claim there is no loss whatsoever.

Indexed colors

In Chapter B on the CD, I mentioned that Photoshop automatically dithers your images to the bit depth of your monitor. Therefore, you can create 24-bit images regardless of the screen you use. However, if you specifically want to create an 8-bit or less-colorful image, you can choose Mode⇨Indexed Color to round off all the colors to a finite palette, known as a *color lookup table (CLUT)*.

Using the Indexed Color command

To index the colors in an image, choose Mode⇨Indexed Color. (It's called *indexing*, incidentally, because you're reining in colors that used to roam free about the spectrum into a rigid, inflexible, maniacally oppressive CLUT. Will you ever be able to look another color in the face?) Photoshop displays the Indexed Color dialog box shown in Figure 4-6, which offers these tempting options:

- ☞ **Resolution:** Select one of these radio buttons to specify the number of colors you want to retain in your image. If the image already contains fewer than 256 colors, Photoshop computes this number and automatically enters it into the Other option box. If the Other option box is empty, you probably will want to select the 8 Bits/Pixel option. This is the default setting.

- ☞ **Palette:** These options determine how Photoshop computes the colors in the CLUT. If the image already contains fewer than 256 colors, select Exact to transfer every color found in the image to the CLUT. The next option is labeled *System* if the 8 Bits/Pixel option is selected; otherwise, it is labeled *Uniform*. Either way, Photoshop computes a CLUT based on a uniform sampling of colors from the RGB spectrum. (I discuss this option in more detail later in this chapter.) The Adaptive option selects the most frequently used colors in the image, which typically delivers the best possible result. Finally, you can select Custom to load a CLUT palette from disk or Previous to use the last CLUT created by the Indexed Color command. This last option is dimmed unless you have previously employed the command during the current session.

You can influence the performance of the Adaptive option by selecting an area of your image before choosing Mode⇨Index. Photoshop will then favor the selected area when creating the palette. For example, when indexing an image of a person wearing a brightly colored costume, you may want to make sure that the flesh colors are not underrepresented in the new palette. To do this, you would select a portion of exposed skin and then choose the Index command.

- ☞ **Dither:** Use the Dither options to specify how Photoshop distributes CLUT colors throughout the indexed image. If you select None, Photoshop maps each color in the image to its closest equivalent in the CLUT, pixel for pixel. This option is useful only if you selected Exact from the Palette options or if you want to perform further editing on an image that requires uninterrupted expanses of color. The Pattern option is available only if you selected System from the Palette options — but even then, avoid it like the plague, because it dithers colors in a geometric pattern, as shown in the lower right example of both Figure 4-7 and Color Plate 4-2. The final option, Diffusion, dithers colors randomly to create a naturalistic effect, as shown in the lower left example of Figure 4-7 and Color Plate 4-2. Nine out of ten times, Diffusion is the option you'll want to use.

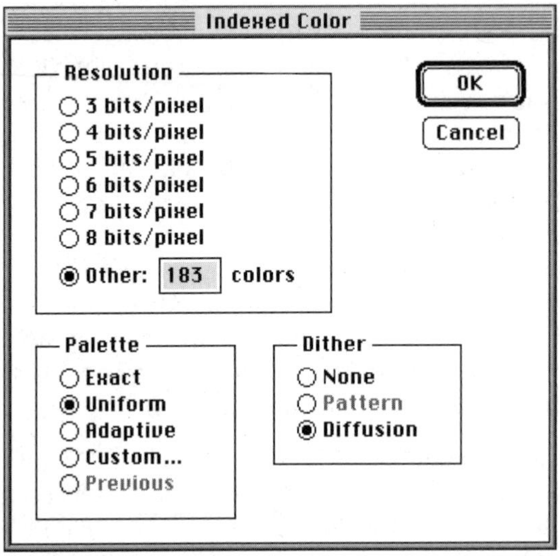

Figure 4-6:
The Indexed Color options let you specify how many colors you want to retain in your image, how Photoshop computes the color lookup table, and the way in which colors are distributed throughout the image.

Indexed Color

Resolution
- ○ 3 bits/pixel
- ○ 4 bits/pixel
- ○ 5 bits/pixel
- ○ 6 bits/pixel
- ○ 7 bits/pixel
- ○ 8 bits/pixel
- ● Other: `183` colors

OK

Cancel

Palette
- ○ Exact
- ● Uniform
- ○ Adaptive
- ○ Custom...
- ○ Previous

Dither
- ○ None
- ○ Pattern
- ● Diffusion

 For some reason, Photoshop doesn't let you index Lab or CMYK images. If the Indexed Color command is dimmed, choose Mode⇨RGB to convert the image to the RGB mode and then choose Mode⇨Indexed Color.

 Some of Photoshop's functions, including the gradient tool, all the edit tools, and the commands under the Filter menu, refuse to work in the indexed color mode. Others, like feathering and the paintbrush and airbrush tools, don't work like they ought to. If you plan on editing an 8-bit image much in Photoshop, convert it to the RGB mode, edit it as desired, and then switch back to the indexed color mode when you're finished.

Creating images for the screen

Many people make the mistake of using the Indexed Color command to make an image smaller on disk. Certainly, an 8-bit indexed image is smaller than its 24-bit counterpart in RAM. However, this savings doesn't necessarily translate to disk. For example, the JPEG format almost always compresses a 24-bit image to a smaller size on disk than the same image indexed to 8-bit and saved in some other format. (As shown back in Table 4-1, JPEG doesn't support indexed images.) Furthermore, JPEG sacrifices considerably less information than does the Indexed Color command.

Therefore, the only reason to index an image is to prepare it for display on an 8-bit monitor. Suppose that you created a repeating pattern that you want to apply to the Finder desktop using a utility such as Thought I Could's Wallpaper. You figure that you may want to show off by distributing it to other users over a bulletin board, so the pattern should be 8-bit compatible. This means that you need to adhere to the Macintosh system software's 8-bit CLUT palette. You can simply copy the pattern from Photoshop and paste it into Wallpaper, but if you do, the system software automatically dithers the image using the hideous Pattern motif. To prevent this from happening, choose the Indexed Color command, select 8 Bits/Pixel from the Resolution options, and select System from the Palette options to use the system software's CLUT palette. Finally, select Diffusion from the Dither options to achieve the most satisfying effect. After indexing the image, you can copy it and paste it into Wallpaper with no dire effects.

Figure 4-7:
The results of converting an image (upper left) to the System CLUT palette subject to each of the three Dither options: (clockwise from upper right) None, Pattern, and Diffusion.

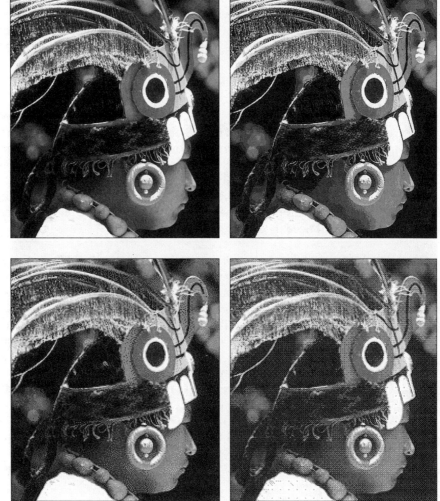

Mind you, Wallpaper represents just one of many ways to customize your system using images from Photoshop. You also can use Photoshop to create custom icons, replace the image in the Puzzle desk accessory, and even edit cursors, dialog boxes, splash screens, and a whole mess of other on-screen items using a customization utility such as ResEdit. In all cases, you should first index the image to the system's CLUT palette in Photoshop.

 Want another example of images prepared specially for the screen? Check out Chapters A, B, and C on the CD. All three chapters contain color figures. But because many readers may only have 8-bit monitors, I indexed most of the figures using the Diffusion option. In those few cases where I included 24-bit figures — all in Chapter C — viewers with 8-bit monitors will see the images automatically dithered as if subjected to the Pattern option. (For the benefit of those viewers, I've also included 8-bit versions of the figures dithered with Diffusion.)

Editing indexed colors

If you're creating images to be displayed in an 8-bit application other than the Finder, such as a presentation program like Microsoft PowerPoint or Aldus Persuasion, you're better off selecting Adaptive from the Palette radio buttons in the Indexed Color dialog box. This setup permits Photoshop to pick the most popular colors from the 24-bit version of the image instead of constraining it to the system palette. But even the Adaptive option doesn't get things 100 percent right. On occasion, Photoshop selects some colors that look noticeably off base.

To replace all occurrences of one color in an indexed image with a different color, choose Mode⇨Color Table. The ensuing Color Table dialog box, shown in Figure 4-8, enables you to selectively edit the contents of the CLUT. To edit any color, click on it to display the Color Picker dialog box, select a different color, and click on the OK button to return to the Color Table dialog box. Then click on the OK button to close the Color Table dialog box and change every pixel colored in the old color to the new color.

The Color Table dialog box also enables you to open and save CLUTs and select predefined CLUTs from the Table pop-up menu. What the Color Table dialog box doesn't let you do is identify a color from the image. For example, if you're trying to fix a color in your image, you can't display the Color Table dialog box, click on the color in the image, and have the dialog box show you the corresponding color in the CLUT. The only way to be sure you're editing the correct color — and be forewarned, this is a royal pain in the behind — is to slog through the following steps, which begin before you choose Mode⇨Color Table.

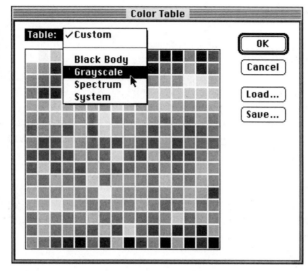

Figure 4-8:
Use the Color Table
command to edit
colors in the color
lookup table.

STEPS: **Editing a Specific CLUT Color**

Step 1. Use the eyedropper tool to click on the offending color in the image, making it the foreground color.

Step 2. Click on the foreground color icon to display the specs for the color in the Color Picker dialog box. Write down the RGB values on a handy piece of paper, the palm of your hand, a bald friend's scalp, or whatever. (Don't edit the color inside the Color Picker dialog box at this time. If you do, you just change the color without changing any pixel in the image associated with that color.) Press Command-period to escape the dialog box.

Step 3. Choose Mode⇨Color Table. Now here's the fun part: Click on a color that looks like it might be the right one. After the Color Picker appears, compare the color's RGB numbers to those you wrote down. If they match, boy, did you ever luck out. Go ahead and edit the color as desired. If the RGB values don't match, press Command-period to return to the Color Table dialog box and try again. And again. And again.

To create a *color ramp* — that is, a gradual color progression — in the CLUT, drag rather than click on the colors in the palette to select multiple colors at a time. Photoshop then displays the Color Picker dialog box, enabling you to edit the first color in the ramp. After you select the desired color and press Return, the Color Picker reappears, this time asking you to edit the last color in the ramp. After you specify this color, Photoshop automatically creates the colors between the first and last colors in the ramp in even RGB increments.

Grayscale

Grayscale is possibly my favorite color mode. It frees you from all the hassles and expense of working with color and provides access to every bit of Photoshop's power and functionality. Anyone who says you can't do just as much with grayscale as you can with color missed out on *Citizen Kane, L'Aventura, To Kill a Mockingbird,* and *Raging Bull.* You can print grayscale images to any laser printer, reproduce them in any publication, and edit them on nearly any machine. Besides, they look great, they remind you of old movies, and they make a hefty book like this one affordable. What could be better?

Other than extolling its virtues, however, there isn't a whole lot to say about grayscale. You can convert an image to the grayscale mode regardless of its current mode, and you can convert from grayscale to any other mode just as easily. In fact, choosing Mode⇨Grayscale is a necessary step in converting a color image to a duotone or black-and-white bitmap.

Search your channels before converting

When you convert an image from one of the color modes to the grayscale mode, Photoshop normally weights the values of each color channel in a way that retains the apparent brightness of the overall image. For example, when you convert an image from RGB, Photoshop weights red more heavily than blue when computing dark values because red is a darker-looking color than blue (much as that might seem contrary to popular belief).

 However, if you choose Mode⇨Grayscale while viewing a single color channel, Photoshop retains all brightness values in that channel only and abandons the data in the other channels. This can be an especially useful technique for rescuing a grayscale image from a bad RGB scan.

Therefore, before switching to the grayscale mode, be sure to take a look at the individual color channels — particularly the red and green channels (the blue channel frequently contains substandard detail) — to see how each channel might look on its own. To browse the channels, press Command-1 for red, Command-2 for green, and Command-3 for blue. Or Command-1 for cyan, Command-2 for magenta, Command-3 for yellow, and Command-4 for black. Or even Command-1 for luminosity, Command-2 for *a*, and Command-3 for *b*. The next chapter describes color channels in more detail.

Dot gain interference

You should be aware of a little item that might throw off your gray value calculations. If the Use Dot Gain for Grayscale Images check box in the Printer Inks Setup dialog box (File⇨Preferences⇨Printer Inks Setup) is selected, Photoshop figures in *dot gain* when calculating the lightness and darkness of grayscale images.

 Dot gain is more thoroughly discussed in the "Printer calibration" section of Chapter 6, but the basic concept is this: Printed images are made up of tiny dots of ink called *halftone cells.* During the printing process, the halftone cells expand — it's sort of like what happens to drops of water plopped onto a paper towel. The Use Dot Gain for Grayscale Images feature lightens the gray values in an image, which reduces the size of the halftone cells, thereby giving the dots some room to bleed.

Suppose that you click on the foreground color icon and change the B (Brightness) value in the Color Picker dialog box to 50 percent. Later, after applying the 50 percent gray to the current image, you move your cursor over some of the medium gray pixels while the Info palette is displayed. You notice that the Info palette interprets the pixels to be 56 percent gray, 6 percentage points darker than the color you specified. This happens because Photoshop automatically darkens the colors in your image to reflect how they will print subject to the dot gain specified in the Printing Inks setup dialog box.

 At this point, I need to insert two bits of information to avoid (or perhaps enhance) confusion. First, as long as the S (Saturation) value is 0, the B (Brightness) value is the only Color Picker option you need to worry about when editing grayscale images. Second, although the B (Brightness) value measures luminosity, ranging from 0 percent for black to 100 percent for white, the K value in the Info dialog box measures ink coverage, thus reversing the figures to 100 percent for black and 0 percent for white. Ignoring dot gain for a moment, this means that a 50 percent brightness translates to 50 percent ink coverage, a 40 percent brightness translates to 60 percent ink coverage, a 30 percent brightness translates to 70 percent ink coverage, and so on.

In theory, automatic dot gain compensation is a good idea, but in practice, it frequently gets in the way. For example, in creating the displacement map gradations in the last chapter, I had a heck of a time trying to achieve a medium gray that didn't slightly move pixels in the affected image. The culprit was dot gain. Luckily, the Use Dot Gain for Grayscale Images check box is no longer selected by default in Version 3.0, but it's still something to keep an eye on.

Black and white (bitmap)

Choose Mode⇨Bitmap to convert a grayscale image to exclusively black and white pixels. This may sound like a pretty boring option, but it can prove useful for gaining complete control over the printing of grayscale images. After all, output devices such as laser printers and imagesetters render grayscale images as series of tiny dots. Using the Bitmap command, you can specify the size, shape, and angle of those dots.

When you choose Mode⇨Bitmap, Photoshop displays the Bitmap dialog box, shown in Figure 4-9. Here you specify the resolution of the black-and-white image and select a conversion process. The options work as follows:

✎ **Output:** Specify the resolution of the black-and-white file. If you want control over every single pixel available to your printer, raise this value to match your printer's resolution. As a rule of thumb, try setting the Output value somewhere between 200 to 250 percent of the Input value.

✎ **50% Threshold:** Select this option to make every pixel that is darker than 50 percent gray black and every pixel that is 50 percent gray or lighter white. Unless you are working toward some special effect — for example, overlaying a black-and-white version of an image over the original grayscale image — this option most likely isn't for you. (And if you're working toward a special effect, Image⇨Map⇨Threshold is the better alternative.)

✎ **Pattern Dither:** This option dithers an image using that worthless geometric pattern I discussed in the "Indexed colors" section. Not only are the images produced by this option ugly, as demonstrated in the left example in Figure 4-10, but the space between dots has a tendency to fill in, especially when you output to a laser printer.

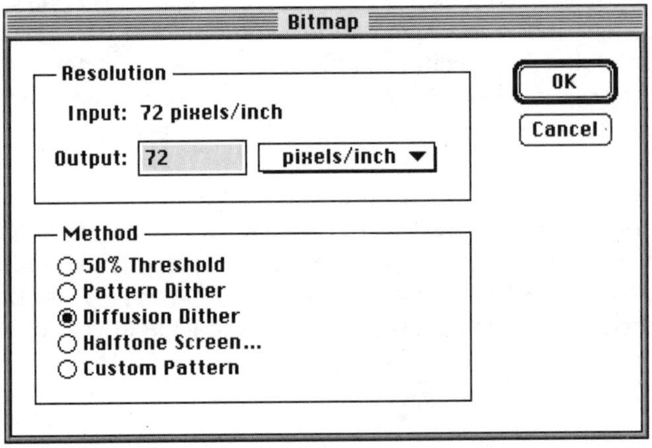

Figure 4-9:
The Bitmap dialog box converts images from grayscale to black and white.

☞ **Diffusion Dither:** Select this option to create a mezzotint-like effect, as demonstrated in the second example in Figure 4-10. Again, because this option converts an image into thousands of stray pixels, you can expect your image to darken dramatically when output to a low-resolution laser printer and when reproduced. Be sure to lighten the image with something like the Levels command, as described in the "Making Custom Brightness Adjustments" section of Chapter 16, before selecting this option.

☞ **Halftone Screen:** When you select this option and press Return, Photoshop displays the Halftone Screen dialog box shown in Figure 4-11, which is nearly an exact duplicate of the one you access by clicking on the Screen button in the Page Setup dialog box. Enter the number of halftone cells per inch in the Frequency option box and the angle of the cells in the Angle option box. Then select a cell shape from the Shape pop-up menu. Figure 4-12 shows examples of four cell shapes, each with a frequency of 20 lpi (lines per inch). (The image appears reduced in the figure; therefore, the halftone frequency appears higher.)

Figure 4-10:
The results of selecting the Pattern Dither option (left) and the Diffusion Dither option (right).

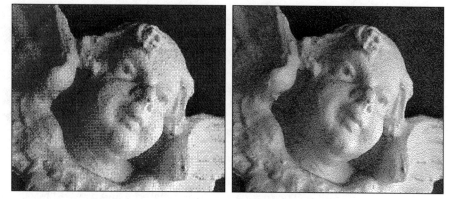

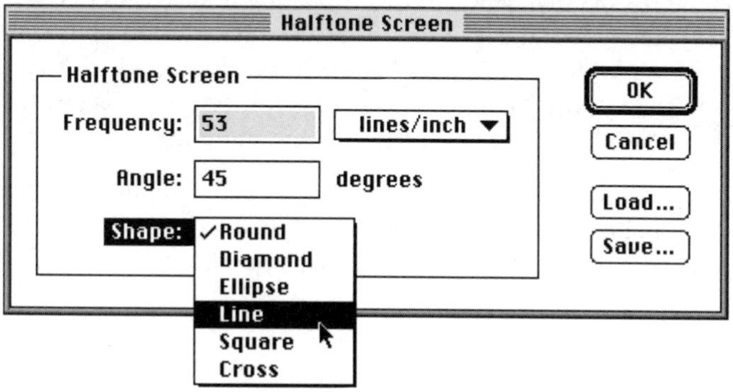

Figure 4-11:
This dialog box appears when you select the Halftone Screen option in the Bitmap dialog box.

Figure 4-12: Four examples of halftone cell shapes, including (clockwise from upper left) Round, Diamond, Line, and Cross.

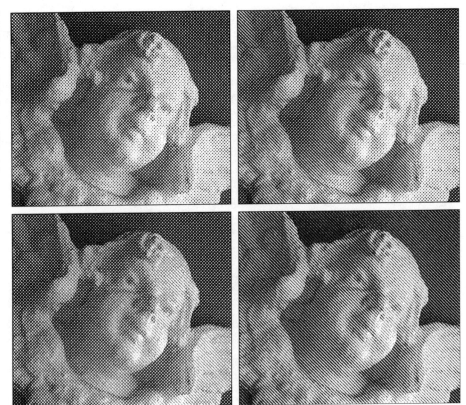

⊶ **Custom Pattern:** If you specified a repeating pattern by choosing Edit⇨Define Pattern, you can use it as a custom halftoning pattern. Figure 4-13 shows two custom examples. The first pattern was created using the Add Noise, Emboss, and Ripple filters (as discussed in the "Creating texture effects" section of (Chapter 15). The second is the Twirl Pattern file, which you'll find in the Displacement Maps folder inside the Plug-Ins folder included with your Photoshop application. (In fact, the Displacement Maps folder contains several images you can use as custom halftoning patterns. Check them out.)

The wackiest image appears in Figure 4-14. It might be hard to tell what's going on this example because it combines an image inside an image. But if you look closely, you can see a bunch of tiny Lenins. You know, the bygone Soviet leader.

I describe how to create this seamless repeating pattern in an exercise in the "How to create patterns" section of Chapter 11. Granted, the Lenin pattern competes with the original image to the extent that you can barely distinguish any of the cherub's features. But what the hey, it's worth a chuckle or two.

Figure 4-13:
Two examples of employing repeating patterns as custom halftoning patterns. The patterns include the Ripple filter texture from the previous chapter (top) and the Twirl pattern image in the Displacement Maps folder (below).

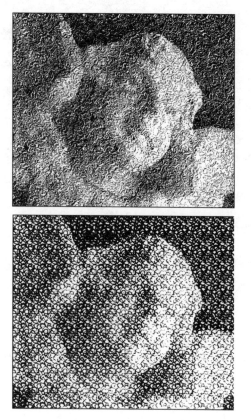

Photoshop lets you edit individual pixels in the so-called bitmap mode, but that's about the extent of it. After you go to black-and-white, you can't perform any serious editing and, worse, you can't expect to return to the grayscale mode. So be sure to finish your image editing before choosing Mode➪Bitmap. More importantly, be sure to save your image before converting it to black-and-white. Frankly, saving is a good idea when performing any color conversion.

Figure 4-14:
A black-and-white cherub composed entirely of itsy-bitsy Lenin faces. Ten years ago, I could have flown to Russia and been deported for this.

Using Photoshop's Other Color Selection Methods

In addition to the Color Picker dialog box, Photoshop provides a handful of additional techniques for selecting colors. The sections that finish out this chapter explain how to use the Custom Colors dialog box, the Colors palette, and the eyedropper tool. None of this information is terribly exciting, but it will enable you to work more efficiently and more conveniently.

Predefined colors

If you click on the Custom button inside the Color Picker dialog box, Photoshop displays the Custom Colors dialog box shown in Figure 4-15. In this dialog box, you can select from a variety of predefined colors by choosing the color family from the Book pop-up menu, moving the slider triangles up and down the color slider to specify a general range of colors, and ultimately selecting a color from the color list on the left. If you own the swatchbook for a color family, you can locate a specific color by entering its number on the keyboard.

The color families represented in the Book pop-up menu fall into seven brands: ANPA (now NAA), DIC, Focoltone, Pantone, Toyo, and Trumatch, all of which get a big kick out of capitalizing their names in dialog boxes. I honestly think that one of these companies would stand out better if its name *weren't* capitalized. Anyway, at the risk of offending a few of these companies, you're likely to find certain brands more useful than others. The following sections briefly introduce the brands in order of their impact on the American market — forgive me for being ethnocentric in this regard — from smallest impact to greatest.

Figure 4-15:
The Custom Colors dialog box enables you to select predefined colors from brand-name libraries.

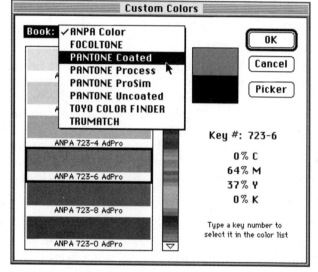

The number-one use for predefined colors in Photoshop is in the creation of duotones, tritones, and quadtones (described in Chapter 6.) You can also use predefined colors to match the colors in a logo or some other important element in an image to a commercial standard.

Focoltone, DIC, and Toyo

Focoltone, Dianippon Ink and Chemical (DIC), and Toyo fall into the negligible impact category. All are foreign color standards with followings abroad. Focoltone is an English company; not English speaking — although they probably do — but English living, as in commuting-to-France-through-the-Chunnel England. DIC and Toyo are popular in the Japanese market, but have next to no subscribers outside Japan.

Newspaper Association of America

ANPA — *American Newspaper Publishers Association* — recently changed its name to NAA, which stands for *Newspaper Association of America,* and updated its color catalog. NAA provides a small sampling of 33 *process colors* (mixes of cyan, magenta, yellow, and black ink) plus 5 *spot colors* (colors produced by printing a single ink). The idea behind the NAA colors is to isolate the color combinations that reproduce most successfully on inexpensive newsprint and to provide advertisers with a solid range of colors from which to choose without allowing the color choices to get out of hand. You can purchase a Pocket Tint Chart from NAA for $175. Members pay only $100.

Trumatch

Trumatch remains my personal favorite process-color standard. Designed entirely using a desktop system and created especially with desktop publishers in mind, the Trumatch Colorfinder swatchbook features more than 2,000 process colors, organized according to hue, saturation, and brightness. Each hue is broken down into 40 tints and shades. Tints are created by reducing the saturation in 15 percent increments; shades are created by adding black ink in 6 percent increments. The result is a guide that shows you exactly which colors you can attain using a desktop system. If you're wondering what a CMYK blend will look like when printed, you need look no farther than the Trumatch Colorfinder.

As if the Colorfinder weren't enough, Trumatch provides the ColorPrinter Software utility, which automatically prints the entire 2,000-color library to any PostScript-compatible output device. The utility integrates EfiColor and PostScript Level 2, thereby enabling design firms and commercial printers to test out the entire range of capabilities available to their hardware. Companies can provide select clients with swatches of colors created on their own printers, guaranteeing that what you see is darn well what you'll get.

The Colorfinder swatchbook retails for $85; the ColorPrinter Software costs $98. Together, swatchbook and utility sell for $133. Support for Trumatch is built into Illustrator, FreeHand, PageMaker, QuarkXPress, Cachet, as well as Corel Draw and Micrografx Designer in the Windows environment.

Pantone

I've been hard on Pantone over the years, and for good reason. Prior to Trumatch, Pantone had a virtual monopoly on the desktop market, and the company acted like it. It was unresponsive to criticism, condescending to service bureaus and desktop designers alike, and slow to improve its product. Since Trumatch came along, however, Pantone has acted like a different company. In fact, I am beginning to warm up to it.

On the heels of Trumatch, Pantone released a 3,006-color Process Color System Guide (labeled *Pantone Process* in the Book pop-up menu) priced at $75, $10 less than the Trumatch Colorfinder. Pantone also produces the foremost spot color swatchbook, the Color Formula Guide 1000, and the Process Color Imaging Guide, which enables you to quickly figure out whether you can closely match a Pantone spot color using a process-color blend or whether you ought to just give it up and stick with the spot color. Pantone spot colors are ideal for creating duotones, discussed in Chapter 6, "Printing Images." Furthermore, Pantone is supported by every computer application that aspires to the color prepress market. As long as the company retains the old competitive spirit, you can most likely expect Pantone to remain the primary color printing standard for years to come.

The Colors palette

Another means of selecting colors in Photoshop is to use the Picker palette, shown in Figure 4-16. If you're willing to sacrifice on-screen real estate for the convenience of being able to define colors on the spot, without having to call up the Color Picker dialog box, the Picker palette is a useful tool indeed.

To display the palette, choose Window⇨Palettes⇨Show Picker. You then can use the elements and options inside the palette as follows:

- **Foreground color/background color:** Click on the foreground or background color icon in the Picker palette to specify the color that you want to edit. If you click on the foreground or background color icon when it's already highlighted — as indicated by a double-line frame — Photoshop displays the Color Picker dialog box.

- **Slider bars:** Drag the triangles in the slider controls to edit the highlighted color. By default, the sliders represent the red, green, and blue primary colors. You can change the slider bars by choosing a different color model from the palette menu.

- **Alert triangle:** Photoshop displays the alert triangle when a color falls outside the CMYK color gamut. The color swatch to the right of the triangle shows the closest CMYK equivalent. Click on the triangle or the color swatch to replace the current color with the CMYK equivalent.

- **Color bar:** The bar along the bottom of the Picker palette displays all colors contained in the CMYK spectrum. Click or drag inside the color bar to lift a color and make it the current foreground or background color (depending on whether the foreground or background icon is selected above). The sliders update as you drag. Option-click or drag to lift the background color if the foreground icon is selected or the foreground color if the background color is selected.

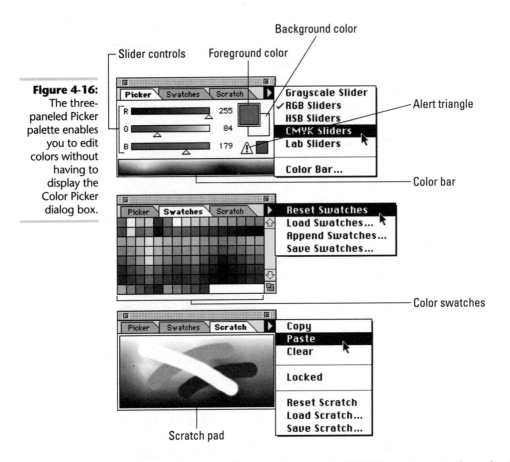

Figure 4-16:
The three-paneled Picker palette enables you to edit colors without having to display the Color Picker dialog box.

Background color

Slider controls   Foreground color

Grayscale Slider
✓ RGB Sliders
HSB Sliders
CMYK Sliders
Lab Sliders

Color Bar...

Alert triangle

Color bar

Picker   Swatches   Scratch

R   255
G   84
B   179

Reset Swatches
Load Swatches...
Append Swatches...
Save Swatches...

Picker   Swatches   Scratch

Color swatches

Copy
Paste
Clear

Locked

Reset Scratch
Load Scratch...
Save Scratch...

Picker   Swatches   Scratch

Scratch pad

↪ **Color Bar option:** You don't have to accept the CMYK spectrum in the color bar. To change to a different spectrum, select the Color Bar command from the palette pop-up menu (or Command-click on the color bar itself). The resulting dialog box lets you change to the RGB spectrum or select a black-to-white gradation (Grayscale Ramp). If you select Foreground to Background, the color bar is filled with a gradation from the current foreground color to the current background color. Unless you select the Lock to Current Colors check box, the color bar continuously updates to represent the newest foreground and background colors.

The Swatches panel

As shown in Figure 4-16, the Picker palette offers two additional panels, Swatches and Scratch. The Swatches panel lets you collect colors for future use, sort of like a favorite color reservoir. To select a color from the reservoir, click on it. To add the current foreground color to the reservoir, Option-click on an existing color swatch to replace the old color or click in an empty swatch to append the new color. In either case, your cursor temporarily changes to a paint bucket. To delete a color from the panel, Command-click on a color swatch. Your cursor changes to a pair of scissors.

You can also save and load color palettes on disk using options in the pop-up menu. The Load Swatches option replaces the colors in the panel with the colors in the file; the Append Swatches option tacks the colors on to the end of the palette. The Color Palettes folder, located inside the same folder that contains the Photoshop application, contains palettes for the major color libraries from Pantone, Trumatch, and others. When one of these palettes is loaded, positioning your cursor over a color swatch makes the name of that color appear in place of the word *Swatches* in the panel tab.

The Scratch panel

The Scratch panel enables you to mix colors outside of the image window. You can paint and edit inside the scratch pad using any of the tools in the toolbox, just as you paint and edit inside the image window. To sample a color from the mix, click on it with the eyedropper tool. To erase the scratch pad, drag inside it with the eraser tool or select the Clear option from the palette pop-up menu.

You can also copy and paste the contents of the scratch pad as well. Just select the portion of the scratch pad you want to copy and select the Copy option in the pop-up menu. Or select the Paste option to paste the contents of the Clipboard into the pad. The pasted image always appears in the scratch pad at actual size. You have the option of moving it around right after you select Paste. To deselect the image, click in the scratch pad with a selection tool.

 You can't access the Copy and Paste options from the keyboard, but that's okay because there's an easier way to transfer images back and forth between image window and scratch pad. Just drag and drop. Select an area inside the image window, drag it over the scratch pad, and drop it in place. You can likewise drag a selection from the scratch pad into the image window. In both cases, Photoshop clones the selection rather than moving it. (For more information about selecting, cloning, and dragging and dropping, see Chapter 8.)

If you only want to lift colors from the scratch pad and not accidentally paint on it, select the Locked option. As long as this option is checked, your cursor will always change to an eyedropper inside the Scratch panel. You will not be allowed to erase the contents of the scratch pad or paste an image inside it.

The eyedropper tool

The eyedropper tool — which you can now select by pressing the I key — provides the most convenient and most straightforward means of selecting colors in Photoshop. It's so straightforward, in fact, that it's hardly worth explaining. But very quickly, here's how it works:

- **Selecting a foreground color:** To select a new foreground color, click on the desired color inside any open image window with the eyedropper tool. (This assumes that the foreground icon in the Picker palette is selected. If the background icon is selected, Option-click with the eyedropper tool to lift the foreground color.) You can even click inside a background window to lift a color without bringing that window to the foreground.

- **Selecting a background color:** To select a new background color, Option-click on the desired color with the eyedropper tool. (Again, this assumes that the foreground icon is selected in the Picker palette. If the background icon is selected, click with the eyedropper to lift the background color.)

- **Skating over the color spectrum:** You can animate the foreground color control box by dragging with the eyedropper tool in the image window. As soon as you achieve the desired color, release your mouse button. To animate the background color icon, Option-drag with the eyedropper tool. The icon color changes as you move the eyedropper tool.

- **Sampling multiple pixels:** Normally, the eyedropper tool selects the color from the single pixel on which you click. However, if you prefer to average the colors of several neighboring pixels, double-click on the eyedropper icon in the toolbox and select a different option from the Sample Size pop-up menu in the Eyedropper Option panel of the Brushes palette.

To temporarily access the eyedropper tool when using the type, paint bucket, gradient, line, pencil, airbrush, or paintbrush tool, press the Option key. The eyedropper cursor remains in force for as long as the Option key is down. You can select only a foreground color while Option-clicking with any of these tools, even if the background color icon is selected in the Picker palette. To select a background color, you must select the eyedropper tool by pressing the I key and then Option-click (or click) in an image window.

Summary

•❖ The color slider and color field change to reflect the selected radio button in the Color Picker dialog box.

•❖ You can save RGB and grayscale images in any file format supported by Photoshop. However, you can save Lab images only in the native, EPS, and TIFF formats. You can save CMYK images in those formats and the JPEG and Scitex CT formats.

•❖ The Lab color model encompasses all colors found in the RGB and CMYK models.

•❖ Use the Indexed Color command to prepare images for display at the Finder desktop or on less capable computer systems. The command reduces the bit depth of the image to 8-bit or less.

•❖ When editing colors in the grayscale mode, set the S (Saturation) option in the Color Picker dialog box to 0 and rely exclusively on the B (Brightness) option.

•❖ To accurately view gray values in the grayscale mode, choose File⇨Preferences⇨Printing Inks Setup and make sure that the Use Dot Gain for Grayscale Images check box is deselected.

•❖ You can use a repeating pattern as a custom halftoning pattern when you convert a grayscale image to a black-and-white painting by choosing Mode⇨Bitmap.

•❖ Trumatch and Pantone are the foremost means for defining custom colors in desktop publishing.

•❖ The Picker palette and its three panels allow you to edit and assemble colors without having to constantly display and close the Color Picker dialog box.

•❖ Use the eyedropper tool to select colors from any open image window.

Navigating Channels

■ ■

In This Chapter

➟ Putting channels in perspective and understanding how they work

➟ Viewing the contents of independent color channels within a full-color image

➟ Using channel editing commands in the Channels palette menu

➟ Improving the appearance of poorly scanned images

➟ Editing channels to achieve special effects

■ ■

Introducing Color Channels _____

Have you ever seen a set of separated CMYK transparencies? Certainly print professionals see these things all the time, but even if you're an absolute beginner, you may have
come in contact with them — perhaps on that grade school field trip to the print shop.
Some nebulous adult — life was a stream of nebulous adults back then — held up four
sheets of acetate. One sheet showed a cyan picture, another showed the same picture
in magenta, a third showed it in yellow, and the last depicted the scene in a rather
washed-out black. By themselves, the pictures appeared exceedingly light and rather
sparse in the detail department. But when they were put together — one layered in
front of another — you saw a full-color picture. Whoa. Neato. Cool.

Sound familiar? Whether it does or not — hey, I can't spend all day conjuring up these
little slices of nostalgia — those sheets of acetate have a functional equivalent inside
Photoshop: *channels*. In a CMYK image, for example, there is one cyan channel, one
magenta channel, one yellow channel, and one black channel. They mix on-screen to

form a full-color image. The RGB mode features a red channel, a green channel, and a blue channel. Because RGB is the color model of light, the three images mix together like three differently colored slides in different projectors aimed at the same screen. In other words, regardless of color mode, channels are distinct planes of primary color.

 Channels frequently correspond to the structure of an input or output device. Each channel in a CMYK image, for example, corresponds to a different printer's plate when the document goes to press. The cyan plate is inked with cyan, the magenta plate is inked with magenta, and so on. Each channel in an RGB image corresponds to a pass of the red, green, or blue scanner sensor over the original photograph or artwork. Only the Lab mode is device independent, so its channels don't correspond to any piece of hardware.

Why you should care

But so what, right? Who cares how many planes of color an image comprises? You want to edit the photograph, not dissect it. "Dammit, Jim, I'm an artist, not a doctor!" Well, even if you don't like to rebuild car engines or poke preserved frog entrails with sharp knives, you'll get a charge out of editing channels. The fact is, channels provide you with yet another degree of selective control over an image.

Consider this example: Your client scanned an image that he wants you to integrate into some goofy ad campaign for his car dealership. Unfortunately, the scan is downright rotten. Maybe it looked good on his computer, but on your screen it looks like dried . . . well, perhaps I shouldn't get too graphic here. Still, you don't want to offend the guy. The image is a picture of his favorite daughter, after all (come on, I'm making this up as I go along), so you praise him on his fine scan and say something to the effect of, "No problem, boss." But after you take it back to your office and load it into Photoshop, you break out in a cold sweat. You try swabbing at it with the edit tools, applying a few filters, and even attempting some scary-looking color correction commands, but the image continues to look like the inside of a garbage disposal. (Not that I've ever seen the inside of a garbage disposal, but it can't be attractive.)

Suddenly, it occurs to you to look at the channels. What the heck, it can't hurt. With very little effort, you discover that the red and green channels look okay, but the blue channel looks like it's melting. Big gobs of gooey detail slide off the kid's face like some kind of mobile acne. Her mouth is sort of mixed in with her teeth, her eyes look like an experiment in expressionism, and her hair has taken on a slightly geometric appearance. (If you think that this is a big exaggeration, take a look at a few blue channels from low-end scanners. They're frequently ripe with tattered edges, random blocks of color, stray pixels, and other so-called *digital artifacts*.)

The point is, you've located the cancer, Doctor. You don't have to waste your time trying to perform surgery on the entire image; in fact, doing so may very well harm the channels that are in good shape. You merely have to fix this one channel. A wave of the Gaussian Blur filter here, an application of the Levels command there, and some selective rebuilding of missing detail borrowed from the other channels — all of which I'll get to in future sections or chapters — result in an image that resembles a living, breathing human being. It may not be absolute perfection, but it's solid enough to pass muster.

How channels work

Photoshop devotes 8 bits of data to each pixel in each channel, thus permitting 256 brightness values, from 0 (black) to 255 (white). Therefore, each channel is actually an independent grayscale image. At first, you may be thrown off by this. If an RGB image is made up of red, green, and blue channels, why do all the channels look gray? Photoshop provides an option in the General Preferences dialog box (Command-K) called Color Channels in Color that, when selected, displays each channel in its corresponding primary color. But although this feature can be reassuring — particularly to novices — it's equally counterproductive. When you view an 8-bit image composed exclusively of shades of red, for example, it's easy to miss subtle variations in detail that may appear obvious when you print the image. You may have problems accurately gauging the impact of filters and tonal adjustments. I mean, face it, red isn't a friendly shade to stare at for a half hour of intense editing. So leave the Color Channels in Color option off and temporarily suspend your biological urge for on-screen color. With a little experience, you'll be able to better monitor your adjustments and predict the outcome of your edits in plain old grayscale.

 Just because you're editing a single channel doesn't mean that you have to work with blinders on. At any time, you can see how your changes affect the full-color image. Simply create a new view of your image by choosing Window⇨New Window. Leave this window set to the standard composite view (presumably RGB, but it could be CMYK, Lab, or any other color mode) and edit away on the individual channel in the first image. (Don't worry, I explain how to switch channels in the very next section.)

Images that include 256 colors or fewer can be expressed in a single channel and therefore do not include multiple channels that you can edit independently. A grayscale image, for example, includes a single channel. A black-and-white image permits only one bit of data per pixel, so a single channel is more than enough to express it. Indexed images represent the only case where a single channel can express different hues, because each of the 256 colors is customized according to a CLUT (as described in the previous chapter). Duotones are the really weird ones. Though they may contain two, three, or four plates of color, Photoshop treats them as a single channel of 8-bit color. I explain duotones in detail in Chapter 6, "Printing Images."

 You can add channels above and beyond those required to represent a color or grayscale image for the purpose of storing masks, as described in the "Creating and Independent Mask Channel" section of Chapter 9. But even then, each channel is limited to 8 bits of data per pixel — meaning that it's just another grayscale image. Mask channels do not affect the appearance of the image on-screen or when it is printed. They rather serve to save selection outlines, as Chapter 9 explains.

How to switch and view channels

 To access channels in Photoshop 3.0, display the Channels panel of the Layers palette by choosing Window⇨Palettes⇨Show Channels. Every channel in the image will appear — including any mask channels — as shown in Figure 5-1. Photoshop 3.0 even shows little thumbnail views of each channel so that you can see what it looks like.

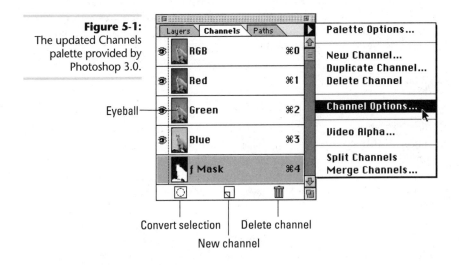

Figure 5-1:
The updated Channels palette provided by Photoshop 3.0.

Eyeball

Convert selection

New channel

Delete channel

To switch to a different channel, click on a channel name in the Channels palette. The channel name becomes gray — like the Mask channel in Figure 5-1 — showing that you can now edit it independently of other channels in the image.

 To edit more than one channel at a time, click on one channel name and then Shift-click on another. You can also Shift-click on an active channel to deactivate it independently of any others.

When you select a channel, Photoshop normally displays the channel that you want to edit on-screen. However, you can view additional channels beyond those that you want to edit. To specify which channels appear on-screen, click in the far left column of the Channels palette. Click on an eyeball icon to make it disappear and hence hide that channel. Click where there is no eyeball to create one and thus display the channel.

When only one channel is visible, that channel appears gray or in color, depending on the setting of the Color Channels in Color check box in the General Preferences dialog box. However, when more than one channel is visible, you always see color. If both the blue and green channels are visible, for example, the image appears blue-green. If the red and green channels are visible, the image has a yellow cast, and so on. If a mask channel and some other channel are visible, the mask appears by default as a pink overlay. (The color of the mask can be changed.) For more information on viewing two or more individual channels simultaneously — and why in the world you'd want to do so — read the "Viewing mask and image" section of Chapter 9.

In addition to the individual channels, Photoshop provides access to a *composite view* that displays all colors in an RGB, CMYK, or Lab image at once. (The composite view does not show mask channels; you have to specify their display separately.) The composite view is listed first in the Channel palette and is displayed by default. Notice that when you select the composite view, all the names of the individual color channels in the Channels palette turn gray along with the composite channel. This shows that all the channels are active. The composite view is the one in which you will perform the majority of your image editing.

 Press Command plus a number key to switch between color channels. Command-1 always takes you to the red (RGB), cyan (CMYK), or luminosity (Lab) channel; Command-2 takes you to the green, magenta, or *a* channel; and Command-3 takes you to the blue, yellow, or *b* channel. In the CMYK mode, Command-4 displays the black channel. Other Command-key equivalents — up to Command-9 — take you to mask channels. Command-0 takes you to the composite view.

The shortcuts are slightly different when you're working on a grayscale image. You access the image itself by pressing Command-1. Command-2 and higher take you to the mask channels.

 Don't freak or in any way feel inadequate if your images don't contain mask channels. As I mentioned earlier, we won't be talking about masks until Chapter 9. In the meantime, I'm just trying to make sure that I don't leave any stone unturned as I explain the many nuances of this many-splendored topic.

Trying Channels on for Size _____

Feeling a little mystified? Need some examples? Fair enough. Color Plate 5-1 shows the yellow-orange dome of the United States Capitol building set against a deep blue evening sky. These colors — yellow-orange and deep blue — are very nearly opposites. Therefore, you can expect to see a lot of variation between the images in the independent color channels.

RGB channels

Suppose that the capitol is an RGB image. Figure 5-2 compares a grayscale composite of this same image (created by choosing Mode⇨Grayscale) with the contents of the red, green, and blue color channels from the original color image. The green channel is more or less in keeping with the grayscale composite because it is the neutral channel in this image (that is, no element in Color Plate 5-1 is predominantly green). But the red and blue channels differ significantly. The pixels in the red channel are lightest on the Capitol dome because the dome contains a high concentration of red. The pixels in the blue channel are lightest in the sky because — you guessed it — the sky is blue.

Notice how the channels in Figure 5-2 make interesting grayscale images in and of themselves? The blue channel, for example, looks like a photo of the Capitol on a cloudy day, when the picture actually was shot at night.

I mentioned this as a tip in the previous chapter, but it bears a bit of casual drumming into the old noggin. When converting a color image to grayscale, you have the option of calculating a grayscale composite or simply retaining the image exactly as it appears in one of the channels. To create a grayscale composite, choose Mode⇨Grayscale when viewing all colors in the image in the composite view, as usual. To retain a single channel only, switch to that channel and then choose Mode⇨Grayscale. Instead of the usual *Discard color information?* message, Photoshop displays the message *Discard other channels?* If you click on the OK button, Photoshop chucks the other channels into the electronic abyss.

Figure 5-2:
A grayscale composite of the image from Color Plate 5-1 followed by the contents of the red, green, and blue color channels.

Grayscale composite

Red

Green

Blue

CMYK channels

In the name of fair and unbiased coverage, Figures 5-3 and 5-4 show the channels from the image after it was converted to other color modes. In Figure 5-3, I converted the image to the CMYK mode and examined its channels. Here, the predominant colors are cyan (the sky) and yellow (the dome). Because this color mode relies on pigments rather than light, as explained in the "CMYK" section of Chapter 4, dark areas in the channels represent high color intensity. For that reason, the sky in the cyan channel is dark, whereas it is light in the blue channel shown in Figure 5-2.

Figure 5-3:
The contents of the cyan, magenta, yellow, and black channels from the image shown in Color Plate 5-1.

Cyan

Magenta

Yellow

Black

Lab channels

To create Figure 5-4, I converted the image in Color Plate 5-1 to the Lab mode. The image in the luminosity channel looks a lot like the grayscale composite because it contains the lightness and darkness values for the image. Because the *b* channel maps the yellows and blues in the image, it contains the highest degree of contrast. Meanwhile, the *a* channel, which maps colors from green to magenta, is almost uniformly gray. The only remarkable greens occur in the statue at the top of the dome and in the bright area inside the rotunda.

You can achieve some entertaining effects by applying commands from the Image⇨Map and Image⇨Adjust submenus to the *a* and *b* color channels. For example, if I reverse the brightness values in the *b* channel in Figure 5-4 by choosing Image⇨Map⇨Invert (Command-I), the building turns bright blue, and the sky changes to a moody orange-brown. If I apply Image⇨Map⇨Equalize to the *a* channel, the sky lights up with brilliant blue and purple sparks, and the Capitol becomes deep emerald.

Grayscale composite   Luminosity

a (black is green, white is magenta)   b (black is blue, white is yellow)

Other Channel Functions

In addition to viewing and editing channels using any of the techniques discussed in future chapters of this book, you can choose commands from the pop-up menu in the Channels palette and select icons along the bottom of the palette (both shown back in Figure 5-1). A few of the commands and all the icons are new to Version 3.0. These commands and icons work as follows:

- **Palette Options:** Here's an exciting one. When you choose this command, Photoshop displays four Thumbnail Size radio buttons, enabling you to change the size of the thumbnail previews that appear along the left side of the Channels palette. Figure 5-5 shows the four thumbnail settings — nonexistent, small, medium, and large.

- **New Channel:** Choose this command to add a mask channel to the current image. The Channel Options dialog box appears, enabling you to name the channel. You also can specify the color and translucency that Photoshop applies to the channel when you view it with other channels. I explain how these options work in the "Changing the red coating" section of Chapter 9. An image can contain no more than 24 total channels, regardless of color mode.

Figure 5-5:
The Channels Palette
Options dialog box
lets you select
between four
thumbnail preview
options.

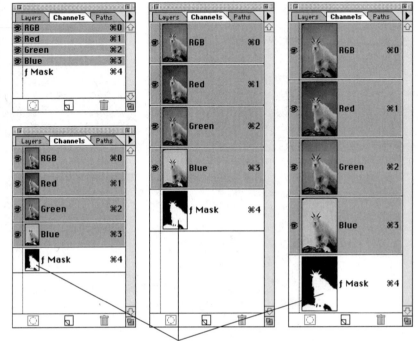

Thumbnail previews

You can also create a new channel by clicking on the new channel icon at the bottom of the Channels palette. (It's the one that looks like a blank page, labeled in Figure 5-1.)

⌖ **Duplicate Channel:** Choose this command to create a duplicate of the selected channel, either inside the same document or as part of a new document. (If the composite view is active, the Duplicate Channel command is dimmed, because you can only duplicate one channel at a time.) The most common reason to use this command is to convert a channel into a mask. Again, you can find real-life applications in Chapter 9.

You can also duplicate a channel by dragging the channel name onto the new channel icon. No dialog box appears; Photoshop merely names the channel automatically. To copy a channel to a different document, drag the channel name and drop it into an open image window. Photoshop automatically creates a new channel for the duplicate.

⌖ **Delete Channel:** To delete a channel from an image, click on the channel name in the palette and choose this command. You can delete only one channel at a time. The Delete Channel command is dimmed when the composite view or any single essential color channel is active or when more than one channel is selected.

If choosing a command is too much effort, just drag the channel onto the delete channel icon (which is the little trash icon in the lower right corner of the Channels palette).

⊷ **Channel Options:** Choose this command or double-click on the channel name in the palette's scrolling list to change the name, color, and translucency settings of a mask channel, as described in the "Viewing mask and image" section of Chapter 9. The Channel Options command is dimmed when the composite view or any of the color channels is active. It is applicable to mask channels only.

⊷ **Video Alpha:** If you own a bona fide 32-bit video board such as TrueVision's NuVista+ or RasterOps' ProVideo32, you can copy a mask channel to the board's built-in 8-bit alpha channel (introduced in the "Video card technology" section of Chapter B on the CD). This *video mask* determines the translucency of the Photoshop image when you lay the image over live video. Black areas in the mask result in opaque image pixels; gray areas result in translucent pixels over video; and white areas result in unobscured video. After you specify the mask channel you want to copy to the board's alpha channel, Photoshop displays a small TV icon in front of the channel name, as shown in Figure 5-6.

Figure 5-6:
A TV icon appears in front of a channel copied to a 32-bit video board's alpha channel.

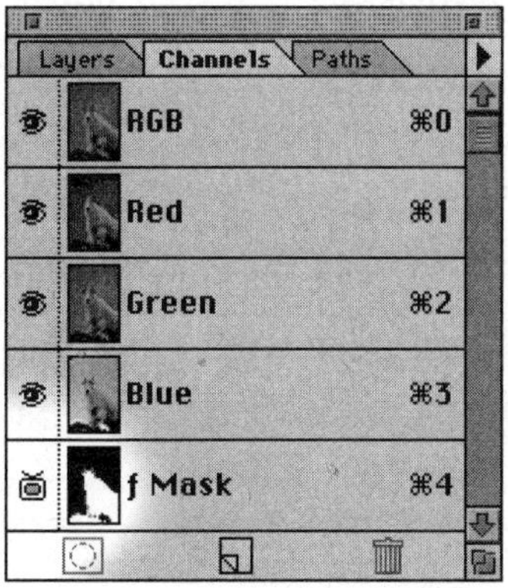

Layers	Channels	Paths	▶
👁	RGB	⌘0
👁	Red	⌘1
👁	Green	⌘2
👁	Blue	⌘3
📺	f Mask	⌘4

⊷ **Split Channels:** When you choose this command, Photoshop splits off each channel in an image to its own independent grayscale image window. As demonstrated in Figure 5-7, Photoshop automatically appends the channel color to the end of the window name. The Split Channels command is useful as a first step in redistributing channels in an image prior to choosing Merge Channels (as demonstrated later in this chapter).

Capitol Dome.Red (1:1)

Figure 5-7:
When you choose the Split
Channels command,
Photoshop relocates each
channel to an independent
image window.

Capitol Dome.Red (1:1)

Capitol Dome.Green (1:1)

Capitol Dome.Blue (1:1)

82K

∽ **Merge Channels:** Choose this command to merge several images into a single
multichannel image. The images you want to merge must be open, they must be
grayscale, and they must be of absolutely equal size — the same number of
pixels horizontally and vertically. When you choose Merge Channels, Photoshop
displays the Merge Channels dialog box, shown in Figure 5-8. It then assigns a
color mode for the new image based on the number of open grayscale images
that contain the same number of pixels as the foreground image.

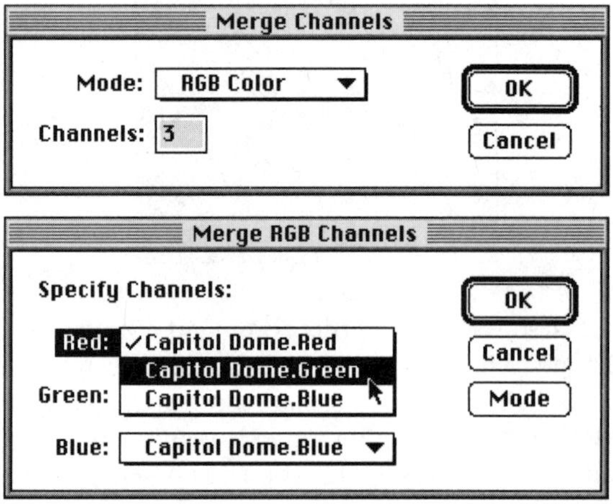

Figure 5-8:
The two dialog boxes
that appear after you
choose Merge Channels
enable you to select a
color mode for the
merged image (top)
and to associate images
with color channels
(bottom).

Merge Channels

Mode: **RGB Color** ▼

Channels: 3

OK

Cancel

Merge RGB Channels

Specify Channels:

Red: ✓Capitol Dome.Red
Capitol Dome.Green
Green: Capitol Dome.Blue

Blue: **Capitol Dome.Blue** ▼

OK

Cancel

Mode

You can override Photoshop's choice by selecting a different option from the Mode pop-up menu. (Generally, you won't want to change the value in the Channels option box because doing so causes Photoshop to automatically select Multichannel from the Mode pop-up menu. I explain multichannel images in the upcoming "Using multichannel techniques" section.) After you press Return or click on the OK button, Photoshop displays a second dialog box. In this dialog box, you can specify which grayscale image goes with which channel by choosing options from pop-up menus, as demonstrated in the second example in Figure 5-8. When working from an image split with the Split Channels command, Photoshop automatically organizes each window into a pop-up menu according to the color appended to the window's name. For example, Photoshop associates the window *Capitol Dome.Red* with the Red pop-up menu.

☞ **Convert selection:** Click on the convert selection outline icon — the one in the bottom left corner of the Channels palette — to convert a selection outline to a new mask channel. Drag a channel name onto the convert selection icon to convert the mask into a selection outline. You can also convert a mask to a selection by Option-clicking on the mask channel name.

Color Channel Effects _____

Now that you know how to navigate among channels and apply commands, allow me to suggest a few reasons for doing so. The most pragmatic applications for channel effects involve the restoration of bad color scans. If you use a color scanner, know someone who uses a color scanner, or just have a bunch of color scans lying around, you can be sure that some of them look like dog meat. (Nothing against dog meat, mind you. I'm sure that Purina has some very lovely dog meat scans in their advertising archives.) With Photoshop's help, you can turn those scans into filet mignon — or at the very least, into an acceptable Sunday roast.

Improving the appearance of color scans

The following are a few channel editing techniques you can use to improve the appearance of poorly scanned full-color images. Keep in mind that these techniques don't work miracles, but they can retrieve an image from the brink of absolute ugliness into the realm of tolerability.

(Don't forget that it's a good idea to first choose Window⇨New Window to maintain a composite view. Be sure to drag the composite view off to an empty portion of your screen so that you can see how applying a change to a single channel affects the full-color image.)

- **Aligning channels:** Sometimes, a scan still looks out of focus even after you use Photoshop's sharpening commands to try to correct the problem, as discussed in Chapter 13. If, on closer inspection, you can see slight shadows or halos around colored areas, one of the color channels probably is out of alignment. To remedy the problem, switch to the color channel that corresponds to the color of the halos. Then choose Select⇨All (Command-A) and use the arrow keys to nudge the contents of the channel into alignment. Use the separate composite view (created by choosing Window⇨New Window) to monitor your changes.

- **Channel focusing:** If all channels seem to be in alignment (or, at least, as aligned as they're going to get), one of your channels may be poorly focused. Use the Command-key equivalents to search for the responsible channel. When and if you find it, use the Unsharp Mask filter to sharpen it as desired. You may also find it helpful to blur a channel, as when trying to eliminate moiré patterns in a scanned halftone. (For a specific application of these techniques, see the "Cleaning up Scanned Halftones" section in Chapter 13.)

- **Bad channels:** In your color channel tour, if you discover that a channel is not so much poorly focused as simply rotten to the core — complete with harsh transitions, jagged edges, and random brightness variations — you may be able to improve the appearance of the channel by overlaying the other channels on top of it. Suppose that the blue channel is awful, but the red and green channels are in fairly decent shape. First, save your image to disk in case this technique does more to harm the image than help it. Then switch to the red channel (Command-1), select the entire image (Command-A), and copy it (Command-C). Switch back to the blue channel (Command-3), paste the contents of the Clipboard (Command-V), and change the opacity of the pasted red channel to somewhere in the neighborhood of 30 to 50 percent. Next, switch to the green channel (Command-2) and repeat the process. The colors in the composite view will change slightly or dramatically depending on the range of colors in your image. But if you can live with the color changes, the appearance of the image will improve dramatically.

 As discussed in Chapter 17, the Calculations command from the Image menu serves as an alternate method for blending one channel with another. At first glance, the dialog box might appear sufficiently complicated to make you feel a mild twinge of panic. But if you give it a chance, you'll find that it works faster than transferring images via the Clipboard, particularly when editing very large images.

When you choose Image⇨Calculations, a dialog box asks you to select two source channels, a method for blending them, and a destination channel. For example, to mix the red and blue channels in a 30 percent/70 percent blend, you would select the red channel as Source 1 and the blue channel as Source 2. Then you'd enter 30 into the Opacity option box, select the same document name from the Result pop-up menu, and choose Blue from the final Channel pop-up menu. If you don't quite understand what the heck I'm talking about, look to Chapter 17 for a full explanation.

Using multichannel techniques

The one channel function I have so far ignored is Mode⇨Multichannel. When you choose this command, Photoshop changes your image so that channels no longer have a specific relationship to one another. They don't mix to create a full-color image; instead, they exist independently within the confines of a single image. The multichannel mode is generally a intermediary step for converting between different color modes without recalculating the contents of the channels.

For example, normally when you convert between the RGB and CMYK modes, Photoshop maps RGB colors to the CMYK color model, changing the contents of each channel as demonstrated back in Figures 5-2 and 5-3. But suppose, just as an experiment, that you want to bypass the color mapping and instead transfer the exact contents of the red channel to the cyan channel, the contents of the green channel to the magenta channel, and so on. You convert from RGB to the multichannel mode and then from multichannel to CMYK as described in the following steps.

STEPS:	Using the Multichannel Mode as an Intermediary Step

Step 1. Open an RGB image. If the image is already open, make sure that it is saved to disk.

Step 2. Choose Mode⇨Multichannel to eliminate any relationship between the formerly red, green, and blue color channels.

Step 3. Choose the New Channel command from the Channels palette pop-up menu to add a mask channel to the image. When the Channel Options dialog box appears, press Return to accept the default settings. This empty channel will serve as the black channel in the CMYK image. (Photoshop won't let you convert from the multichannel mode to CMYK with less than four channels.)

Step 4.   Unfortunately, the new channel comes up black, which would make the entire image black. So make the channel white by choosing Select⇨All (or Command-A) and pressing the Delete key. (This assumes that the background color is white. If it isn't, press the D key.)

Step 5.   Choose Mode⇨CMYK. The image looks washed out and a tad bit dark compared to its original RGB counterpart, but the overall color scheme of the image remains more or less intact. This is because the red, green, and blue color channels each have a respective opposite in the cyan, magenta, and yellow channels.

Step 6.   The one problem with the image is that it lacks any information in the black channel. So although it may look okay on-screen, it will lose much of its definition when printed. To fill in the black channel, convert the image to the RGB mode and then convert it back to the CMYK mode. Photoshop automatically adds an image to the black channel in keeping with your specifications in the Separation Setup dialog box (as described in the "How to prepare CMYK conversions" section of Chapter 6.)

Keep in mind that these steps are by no means a recommended procedure for converting an RGB image to a CMYK image. Rather, they are merely intended to suggest one way to experiment with channel conversions to create a halfway decent image. You can likewise experiment with converting between the Lab, multichannel, and RGB modes, or Lab, multichannel, and CMYK.

Replacing and swapping color channels

If you truly want to abuse the colors in an RGB or CMYK image, there's nothing like replacing one color channel with another to produce spectacular effects. Color Plate 5-2 shows a few examples applied to an RGB image. In the upper left example, I copied the image in the blue channel (Command-3, Command-A, Command-C) and pasted it into the red channel (Command-1, Command-V). The result was a green Capitol against a purple sky. To achieve the upper right example (starting again from the original RGB image), I copied the green channel and pasted it into the blue channel. The result this time was a pink building against a deep jade sky. To create a lemon yellow Capitol against a backdrop of bright blue, shown in the lower left corner of Color Plate 5-2, I copied the red channel and pasted it into the green channel.

Again, instead of copying and pasting, you can transfer images between channels without upsetting the contents of the Clipboard by choosing Image⇨ Calculations. I discuss this and other applications for this command in Chapter 17.

You can create equally amusing effects by swapping the contents of color channels. For example, in the lower right example of Color Plate 5-2, I swapped the contents of the red and blue channels to create a blue Capitol against an orange-brown sky (very similar to the effect of inverting the *b* channel in the Lab mode, as I suggested in the "Lab channels" section of this chapter). To accomplish this, I chose the Split Channels command from the Channels palette menu. I then chose the Merge Channels command and accepted the default settings in the Merge Channels dialog box. When the Merge RGB Channels dialog box appeared, I selected the blue channel from the Red pop-up menu and the red channel from the Blue pop-up menu.

 When experimenting, it's a good idea to keep the original contents of each color channel close at hand just in case you don't like the results. I recommend using the Duplicate Channel command to save each color channel in the image to a separate mask channel. For example, when editing an RGB image, create three duplicates, one each for duplicates of the red, green, and blue channels, for a total of six channels in the image. You then can replace channels with impunity, knowing that you have backups if you need them.

Summary

•◆ Channels fall into three camps: planes of color in a full-color image; mask channels for editing selection outlines; and video alpha channels for masking an image overlaid onto live video.

•◆ The composite view in a RGB, CMYK, or Lab image shows all colors in an image simultaneously.

•◆ Grayscale images, duotones, black-and-white bitmaps, and images with indexed color contain only one color channel apiece.

•◆ You can edit a channel independently by pressing Command plus a number key. Command-1 takes you to the first channel, Command-2 takes you to the second, and so on. Press Command-0 to return to the composite view when working in the RGB, CMYK, or Lab mode.

•◆ To hide or view a channel, click in the far left column of the Channels palette. Click on an eyeball icon to hide both it and the corresponding channel; click in front of a channel name without an icon to make the eyeball reappear and view the channel.

•◆ When editing a single channel, create a new window for the image using Window⇨New Window so that you can monitor your changes in the composite view.

•◆ Use the Split Channels and Merge Channels commands to rearrange color channels in an image to produce special effects.

•◆ Sometimes, a poor full-color scan is the fault of a single color channel. You can remedy the appearance of a channel by nudging it with the arrow keys, applying the Unsharp Mask filter, or blending the two remaining color channels.

Printing Images

CHAPTER 6

In This Chapter

- ➥ A glossary of terms you need to know in order to communicate with a commercial printer
- ➥ How to print grayscale and color composites
- ➥ A complete guide to the Page Setup dialog box
- ➥ The theory behind halftone screens
- ➥ How to assign transfer functions to distribute brightness values
- ➥ A discussion of the color-separation process
- ➥ How to apply color trapping
- ➥ How to convert a grayscale image into a duotone, tritone, or quadtone
- ➥ Some advice on adding spot-color highlights to a CMYK image

Welcome to Printing

On one hand, printing can be a very straightforward topic. You choose the Print command, press the Return key, wait for something to come out of your printer, and admire yet another piece of forestry that you've gone and destroyed. On the other hand, printing can be a ridiculously complicated subject, involving dot gain compensation, hardware calibration, under color removal, toxic processor chemicals, separation table generation, and so many infinitesimal color parameters that you're liable to spend half your life trying to figure out what's going on.

This chapter is about finding a middle ground. Although it is in no way intended to cover every possible facet of printing digitized images, it walks you through the process of preparing and printing the three major categories of output: composites, color separations, and duotones. By the end of the chapter, you'll be familiar with all of Photoshop's printing options. You'll also be prepared to communicate with professionals at your service bureau or commercial printer, if need be, and to learn from their input and expertise.

Understanding Printing Terminology

I'm not a big believer in glossaries. Generally, they contain glib, jargony, out-of-context definitions that are about as helpful in gaining understanding of a concept as a seminar in which all the presenters speak in pig latin. But before I delve into the inner recesses of printing, I thought I should introduce, in a semilogical, sort of random order, a smattering of the printing terms you'll encounter. Ood-gay uck-lay:

➥ **Service bureau:** A service bureau is a shop filled with earnest young graphic artists (at least they were young and earnest when *I* worked there), printer operators, and about a billion dollars worth of hardware. A small service bureau is usually outfitted with a few laser printers, photocopiers, and self-service computers. Big service bureaus offer scanners, imagesetters, film recorders, and other varieties of professional-quality input and output equipment.

➥ **Commercial printer:** Generally speaking, a commercial printer takes up where the service bureau leaves off. Commercial printers reproduce black-and-white and color pages using offset presses, web presses, and a whole bunch of other age-old technology that I don't cover in this mini glossary (or anywhere else in this book, for that matter). Suffice it to say, the process is less expensive than photocopying when you're dealing with large quantities — say, more than 100 copies — and it delivers professional-quality reproductions.

➥ **Output device:** This is just another way to say *printer.* Rather than writing *Print your image from the printer,* which sounds repetitive and a trifle obvious, I write *Print your image from the output device.* Output devices also include laser printers, imagesetters, film recorders, and a whole bunch of other machines.

➥ **Laser printer:** A laser printer works much like a photocopier. First, it applies an electric charge to a cylinder, called a *drum,* inside the printer. The charged areas, which correspond to the black portions of the image being printed, attract fine, petroleum-based dust particles called *toner.* The drum transfers the toner to the page, and a heating mechanism fixes the toner in place. Most laser printers have resolutions of 300 dots (or *printer pixels*) per inch. A few offer higher resolutions, such as 600 and 1,200 dots per inch (*dpi*).

☞ **Color printers:** Color printers fall into three categories: *ink-jet* and *thermal-wax* printers at the low end and *dye-sublimation* printers at the high end. Ink-jet printers deliver colored dots out of disposable ink cartridges. Thermal-wax printers apply wax-based pigments to a page in multiple passes. Both kinds of printers mix cyan, magenta, yellow, and, depending on the specific printer, black dots to produce full-color output. Generally speaking, these printers produce mediocre detail and acceptable, though not necessarily accurate, color. If you want photographic quality prints — the kind you'd be proud to hang on your wall — you must migrate up the price ladder to dye-sublimation printers. Dye-sub inks permeate the surface of the paper, literally dying it different colors. Furthermore, the cyan, magenta, yellow, and black pigments mix in varying opacities from one dot to the next, resulting in a continuous-tone image that appears nearly as smooth on the page as it does on-screen.

☞ **Imagesetter:** A typesetter that is equipped with a graphics page-description language such as PostScript is called an *imagesetter*. Unlike a laser printer, an imagesetter prints photosensitive paper or film by exposing the portions of the paper or film that correspond to the black areas of the image. The process is a lot like exposing film with a camera, but an imagesetter only knows two colors, black and white. The exposed paper or film collects in a light-proof canister. In a separate step, the printer operator develops the film in a *processor* that contains two chemical baths — developer and fixer — a water bath to wash away the chemicals, and a heat dryer to dry off the water. Developed paper looks like a typical glossy black-and-white page. Developed film is black where the image is white and transparent where the image is black. Imagesetters typically offer resolutions between 1,200 and 2,600 dpi. But the real beauty of imageset pages is that blacks are absolutely black (or transparent), as opposed to the deep, sometimes irregular gray you get with laser-printed pages.

☞ **Film recorder:** This device transfers images to full-color 35mm slides that are perfect for professional presentations. Slides also can be useful as a means for providing images to publications and commercial printers. Many publications can scan from slides, and commercial printers can use slides to create color separations. So if you're nervous that a color separation printed from Photoshop won't turn out well, ask your service bureau to output the image to a 35mm slide. Then have your commercial printer reproduce the image from the slide.

☞ **PostScript:** The PostScript page-description language was the first project developed by Adobe, the same folks who sell Photoshop, and is now a staple of hundreds brands of laser printers, imagesetters, and film recorders. A *page-description language* is a programming language for defining text and graphics on a page. PostScript specifies the locations of points, draws line segments between them, and fills in areas with solid blacks or *halftone cells* (dot patterns that simulate grays). PostScript Level 2, an updated version of the original PostScript, speeds up output time and provides improved halftoning options, better color separations, automated antialiasing of jagged images, and direct support for Lab images (discussed in the "CIE's Lab" section of Chapter 4).

- **QuickDraw:** QuickDraw is a competing page-description language developed by Apple. It is the language that displays images on any Macintosh screen. It is also built into a few laser printers, including the LaserWriter SC. QuickDraw GX, a new version that may be available by the time you read this, will automate kerning and other typographic functions, provide better printer spooling, offer new graphics capabilities previously exclusive to PostScript, and integrate Apple's ColorSync color-matching technology to ensure smooth transitions from scanner to screen to printer.

- **Spooling:** Printer *spooling* allows you work on an image while another image prints. Rather than communicating directly with the output device, Photoshop describes the image to the system software. Under System 7, this function is performed by a program called *PrintMonitor.* In Windows, the Print Manager handles the task. When Photoshop finishes describing the image — a relatively quick process — you are free to resume working while the system software prints the image in the background.

- **Calibration:** Traditionally, *calibrating* a system means to synchronize the machinery. However, in the context of Photoshop, it means to adjust or compensate for the color displays of the scanner, monitor, and printer so that what you scan is what you see on-screen, which in turn is what you get from the printer. Colors match from one device to the next. Empirically speaking, this is impossible; a yellow image in a photograph won't look exactly like the on-screen yellow or the yellow printed from a set of color separations. But calibrating is designed to make them look as much alike as possible, taking into account the fundamental differences in hardware technology. Expensive hardware calibration solutions seek to change the configuration of scanner, monitor, and printer. Less expensive software solutions, including those provided by Photoshop, manipulate the image to account for the differences between devices.

- **Brightness values/shades:** As described at length in Chapter 4, there is a fundamental difference between the way your screen and printer create gray values and colors. Your monitor shows colors by lightening up an otherwise black screen; the printed page shows colors by darkening an otherwise white piece of paper. Therefore, on-screen colors are measured in terms of *brightness values.* High values equate to light colors; low values equate to dark colors. On the printed page, colors are measured in percentage values called *shades,* or if you prefer, *tints.* High percentage values result in dark colors, and low percentage values result in light colors.

- **Composite:** A *composite* is a page that shows an image in its entirety. A black-and-white composite printed from a standard laser printer or imagesetter translates all colors in an image to gray values. A color composite printed from a color printer or film recorder shows the colors as they actually appear. Composites are useful any time you want to proof an image or print a final grayscale image from an imagesetter, an overhead projection from a color printer, or a full-color image from a film recorder.

- **Proofing:** To *proof* an image is to see how it looks on paper in advance of the final printing. In professional circles, laser printers are considered proofing devices because they lack sufficient quality or resolution to output final images. Color printers are necessarily proofing devices because commercial printers can't reproduce from any color composite output except slides. (Well, they *can* reproduce from other kinds of color composites, but you don't get the same quality results.)

- **Bleeds:** Simply put, a *bleed* is an area outside the perimeter of a page that can be printed. You use a bleed to reproduce an image all the way to the edge of a page, as in a slick magazine ad. By way of example, this book includes bleeds. Most of the pages — like the page you're reading — are encircled by a uniform two-pica margin of white space. This margin keeps the text and figures from spilling off into oblivion. However, a few pages — including the parts pages and the color plates in the middle of the book — print all the way to the edges. In fact, the original artwork goes two picas beyond the edges of the paper. This ensures that if the paper shifts when printing — as it invariably does — you don't see any thin white edges around the artwork. This two picas of extra artwork is the bleed. In Photoshop, you create a bleed by clicking on the Bleed button in the Page Setup dialog box.

- **Color separations:** To output color reproductions, commercial printers require color separations (or slides, which they can convert to color separations for a fee). A color-separated image comprises four printouts, one each for the cyan, magenta, yellow, and black primary printing colors. The commercial printer transfers each printout to a *plate* that is used in the actual reproduction process.

- **Duotone:** A grayscale image in Photoshop can contain as many as 256 brightness values, from white on up to black. A printer can convey significantly fewer shades. A typical laser printer, for example, provides 26 shades at most. An imagesetter typically provides from 150 to 200 shades, depending on resolution and screen frequency. And that's assuming perfect printing conditions. You can count on at least 30 percent of those shades getting lost in the reproduction process. A *duotone* helps to retain the depth and clarity of detail in a grayscale image by printing with two inks. Suddenly, the number of shades available to you jumps from 150 to 22,000 (150^2). Photoshop also permits you to create *tritones* (three inks) and *quadtones* (four inks). Note, however, that using more inks translates to higher printing costs. Color Plate 6-1 shows a quadtone.

Printing Composites

Now that you've picked up a bit of printer's jargon, you're ready to learn how to put it all together. This section explores the labyrinth of options available for printing composite images. Later in this chapter, I cover color separations and duotones.

Like any Macintosh application, Photoshop can print composite images to just about any output device you hook up to your Mac. Assuming that your printer is turned on, properly attached, and in working order, printing a composite image from Photoshop is a five-step process, as outlined below.

STEPS: Printing a Composite Image

Step 1.   Use the Chooser desk accessory to select the output device to which you want to print. Unless your computer is part of a network that includes multiple printers, you probably rely on a single output device, in which case you can skip this step.

Step 2.   Choose File⇨Page Setup to specify the page size and the size and orientation of the image on the page. (You can also use Image⇨Image Size to control the size of the image by changing its resolution, as explained in the "Printed resolution" section of Chapter 3.)

Step 3.   Click on the Screens button to change the size, angle, and shape of the halftone screen dots. This step is purely optional, useful mostly for creating special effects.

Step 4.   Click on the Transfer button to map brightness values in an image to different shades when printed. This step is also optional, though frequently very useful.

Step 5.   Choose File⇨Print (Command-P) to print the image according to your specifications.

The following sections describe each of these steps in detail.

 When you print from a Windows machine, Step 1 works slightly differently. Rather than having to bother with a separate Chooser program, you can select a printer directly from inside the Page Setup dialog box. You can either accept the default printer or select the Specific Printer radio button and choose a different printer from the accompanying pop-up menu.

If you have QuickDraw GX running with System 7.5, you can also access printers directly from the Page Setup or Print dialog box — at least in theory. In practice, each program has to build in support for this new function. Guess which program doesn't support it? That's right. Photoshop 3.0 is among a throng of programs from Adobe, Aldus, Quark, and other vendors that still require you to mess around with the Chooser, GX or no GX.

Choosing a printer

To select a printer, choose the Chooser desk accessory from the list of desk accessories under the Apple menu. The Chooser dialog box appears, as shown in Figure 6-1. The dialog box is split in two, with the left half devoted to a scrolling list of printer driver icons and network zones, and the right half to specific printer options.

Figure 6-1:
Use the Chooser desk accessory to select the desired output device.

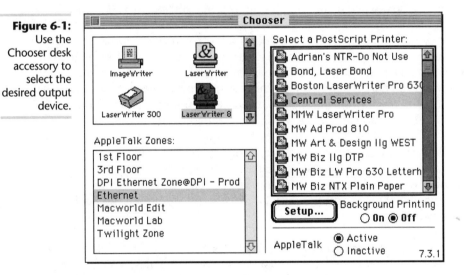

Select the printer driver icon that matches your model of printer. *Printer drivers* help the Macintosh hardware, system software, and Photoshop translate the contents of an image to the printer hardware and the page-description language it uses. If you intend to use a PostScript-compatible printer, you'll generally want to select the LaserWriter driver (although some PostScript printers include drivers of their own). You even can prepare an image for output to a PostScript printer when no such printer is currently hooked up to your computer. For example, you can use this technique prior to submitting a document to be output on an imagesetter at a service bureau.

If the network at your office (or, heaven forbid, at your home) is divided up into multiple zones, you'll see two scrolling lists on the left side of the Chooser dialog box, as in Figure 6-1. Select the zone that contains the desired printer from the lower list. The figure shows how zones are laid out in the vast network at the *Macworld* magazine complex. I gained access remotely — just as might be an option at your workplace — using Apple Remote Access. Once connected, my Chooser can access printers thousands of miles away from my office. (I'm in Boulder, Colorado; *Macworld* is in San Francisco.) Of course, this slows the printing down a bit, and I have to hop aboard a plane to go fetch the page, but it's great for sending a message to some staff member. For example, if I wanted to say hello to *Macworld* editor-in-chief Adrian Mello, I'd select the printer *Adrian's NTR-Do Not Use.* In fact, I plan on printing my electronic book version of *Alice in Wonderland* for him this very afternoon. He'll get a kick out of it.

After you select the required printer driver and, if necessary, gain access to the proper zone, you can select the name of your printer from the scrolling list on the right side of the Chooser dialog box. When using a PostScript printer, you see two sets of radio buttons, Background Printing and AppleTalk. The latter refers to the kind of cabling required to hook up PostScript printers. If you turn it off, you won't be able to access your printer anymore, so by all means leave it turned on. Background Printing, on the other hand, is not so cut and dried. When on, this option lets you print an image in the background while you continue to work in Photoshop or some other application (just as described back in the "Printing in the background" section in Chapter A on the CD). This enables you to take advantage of *spooling*, as defined earlier in this chapter.

Spooling can interrupt foreground tasks and increase the likelihood of printing errors. Photoshop images are particularly prone to spooling problems. For example, a half inch across the middle of the image may print out of alignment with the rest of the image. For perfect image printing, turn off the Background Printing option.

The most recent version of the LaserWriter printer driver — Version 8.1.1 — includes support for *PostScript printer description (PPD)* files. A single driver can't account for the myriad differences between different models of PostScript printers, so each PPD serves as a little guidance file, customizing the driver to accommodate a specific printer model. After selecting a printer from the right-hand scrolling list, you can access the proper PPD by clicking on the Setup button. (Or just double-click on the printer name in the list.) The dialog box shown in Figure 6-2 appears. It contains several buttons — you can display all the ones shown in Figure 6-2 by clicking on the More Choices button — but the most important one is Auto Setup. Click on this button to instruct the system software to automatically select the correct PPD for your printer. If the system fails or if it selects the Generic option, click on the Select PPD button and try to locate the proper PPD files inside the Printer Descriptions folder in the Extensions folder in your System Folder.

Figure 6-2:
Use this dialog box to select the proper PPD file for your specific brand of PostScript printer.

If your printer does not require AppleTalk cabling, as is generally the case with ImageWriters, StyleWriters, and other low-end devices, the right-hand scrolling list contains two icons: one for the printer port, and the second for the modem port. Select the icon that corresponds to the serial port in the back of your Mac that connects to your printer.

When you finish selecting options in the Chooser dialog box, click on the close box in the upper left corner of the title bar to return to the Photoshop desktop.

Setting up the page

The next step is to define the relationship between the current image and the page on which it prints. Assuming that you're using a PostScript output device, choosing File⇨Page Setup displays the LaserWriter Page Setup dialog box shown in Figure 6-3.

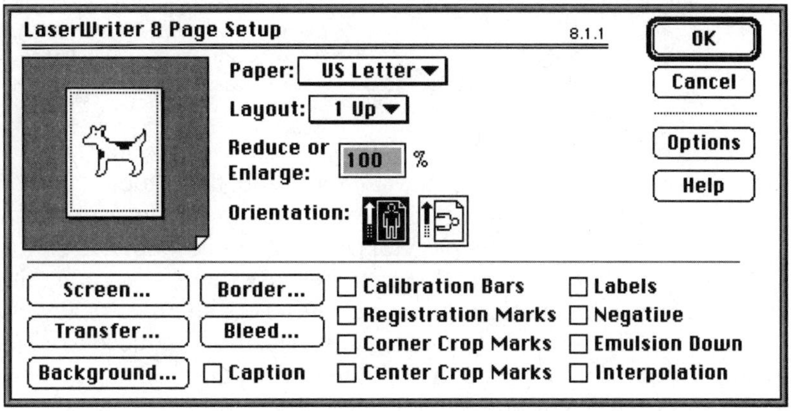

Figure 6-3:
Use this dialog box to specify the relationship between the printed image and the page on which it appears.

Assuming that you're using LaserWriter driver 8 or later, this dialog box provides the following options:

- **Paper:** Select the option from the Paper pop-up menu that corresponds to the size of the paper loaded into your printer's paper tray. The paper size you select determines the *imageable area* of a page — that is, the amount of the page that Photoshop can use to print the current image. For example, the US Letter option calls for a page that measures 8.5×11 inches, but only 7.7×10.2 inches is imageable.

To slightly enlarge the imageable area of a page without changing paper sizes, click on the Options button to display the LaserWriter Options dialog box and select the Larger Print Area check box, as shown in Figure 6-4. For example, when you print to a letter-sized page, this option increases the size of the imageable area from 7.7×10.2 inches to 8.0×10.8 inches. The dotted line in the page preview on the left side of the dialog box enlarges slightly to demonstrate the option's effect.

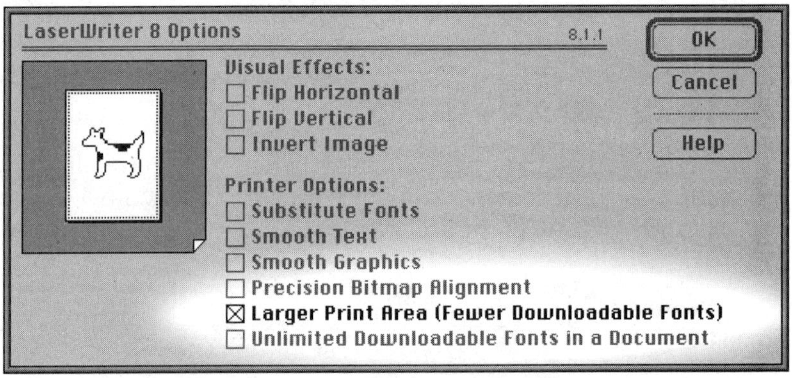

Figure 6-4:
Select the Larger
Print Area check box
to enlarge the size of
the imageable area of
a page printed from
a laser printer.

LaserWriter 8 Options	8.1.1

Visual Effects:
- ☐ Flip Horizontal
- ☐ Flip Vertical
- ☐ Invert Image

Printer Options:
- ☐ Substitute Fonts
- ☐ Smooth Text
- ☐ Smooth Graphics
- ☐ Precision Bitmap Alignment
- ☒ Larger Print Area (Fewer Downloadable Fonts)
- ☐ Unlimited Downloadable Fonts in a Document

[OK] [Cancel] [Help]

- **Layout:** This option allows you to print more than one page per each sheet of paper. For example, if you wanted to proof the layout of a 16-page QuarkXPress document, you could select the 4 Up option to print four quarter-sized versions of each page per each piece of paper. You save paper, kill fewer trees, and even waste a little less time. However, because there is no such thing as a multipage document in Photoshop, this option serves no purpose. If you select the 4 Up option, for example, you simply get one image reduced to 25 percent its normal size in the upper left corner of the printed page. So always leave this option set to 1 Up when printing from Photoshop.

- **Reduce or Enlarge:** Enter a percentage value into this option box to enlarge or reduce the size of the image when printed. For more information on this option, read the "Printing versus screen display" section of Chapter 3.

☞ **Orientation:** You can specify whether an image prints upright on a page (called the *portrait setting*) or on its side (called the *landscape setting*) by selecting the corresponding Orientation icon. The landscape setting is useful when an image is wider than it is tall. (In the Photoshop manual, Adobe recommends that you rotate the image 90 degrees by choosing Image⇨Rotate⇨90° CCW and print it at the portrait setting in order to save on printing time. I personally don't subscribe to this technique because rotating the image takes time and you have to re-rotate it if you want to edit it again. But I suppose that it's an option.)

After specifying the Reduce or Enlarge percentage and Orientation icon, you can check to see how the image fits on the page. To do so, press Return to exit the LaserWriter Page Setup dialog box and click and hold on the preview box in the lower left corner of the image window. The rectangle with the inset X that appears inside the pop-up window represents the image on the page. If the rectangle extends outside the page, you need to further reduce the image or change the page orientation.

If you're using LaserWriter driver 7.1.2 or earlier — as listed in the upper right corner of the LaserWriter Page Setup dialog box — you'll notice a few minor differences. First, the Paper options are presented as radio buttons, not listed in a pop-up menu. Second, there is no Layout option. And third, you get a handful of Printer Effects check boxes that have since been moved to the LaserWriter Options dialog box (see the Visual Effects check boxes in Figure 6-4). These check boxes have no effect, so feel free to ignore them. Heck, go ahead and ridicule their impudence if you're feeling particularly cruel.

Nearly every Macintosh application offers the options described so far because they're a function of the Macintosh system software. However, it's a different story when you descend below the dotted line to the options at the bottom of the LaserWriter Page Setup dialog box. These options are specific to Photoshop. First I'll describe how to use the buttons on the left and then I'll explain the check boxes on the right.

☞ **Screen:** Click on this button to enter a dialog box that allows you to change the size, angle, and shape of the printed halftone cells, as described in the upcoming "Changing the halftone screen" section.

☞ **Transfer:** The dialog box that appears when you click on this button allows you to redistribute shades in the printed image, as explained in the upcoming "Specifying a transfer function" section.

☞ **Background:** To assign a color to the area around the printed image, click on this button and select a color from the Color Picker dialog box, which is described in the "Using the Color Picker" section of Chapter 4. This button and the one that follows (Border) are designed specifically for use when printing slides from a film recorder.

- **Border:** To print a border around the current image, click on this button and enter the thickness of the border into the Width option box. The border automatically appears in black.

- **Bleed:** New to Photoshop 3.0, this button allows you to print outside the imageable area of the page when outputting to an imagesetter. (Imagesetters print to huge rolls of paper or film, so you can print far outside the confines of standard page size. Most other printers use regular old sheets of paper; any bleed — were the printer to even acknowledge it — would print off the edge of the page.) Click on the Bleed button and enter the thickness of the bleed into the Width option box. Two picas (24 points) is generally a good bet. (Bleeds are defined in the "Understanding Printing Terminology" glossary at the beginning of this chapter.)

Now for the check boxes in the lower middle and right-hand sections of the dialog box. Most of these options — all except Negative, Emulsion Down, and Interpolation — append special labels and printer marks to the printed version of the image. These labels and marks are demonstrated in Figure 6-5.

By the way, Figure 6-5 shows the actual labels and marks exactly as they print. This may not sound like much, but in the past, such printer's marks have been very difficult to capture because there was no way to save them in a reliable file format. A book writer like me either had the option of printing the file to disk as an EPS file — which might or might not print accurately when placed into a page-layout program — or simply printing the page independently and manually pasting it up into the book. But thanks to the fact that Illustrator 5.5 opens Adobe Acrobat PDF (*portable document format*) files, I was able to create an editable version of the printed image.

In the name of full disclosure — my job is to pass along information, not store up trade secrets — here's how I accomplished this smallish feat: I first printed the Photoshop image to disk as an EPS file (as described in the "Printing pages" section later in this chapter) — labels, printer's marks, and all. I then converted the EPS file to the PDF format using Acrobat Distiller (included with Illustrator 5.5). Finally, I used Illustrator to convert the PDF file to the more reliable Illustrator EPS format and to assign the callouts — which are those little labels like "Calibration bars" and "Modern youngster."

Here's how the check box options work:

- **Caption:** To print a caption beneath the image, select this option. Then press the Return key to exit this dialog box, choose File⇨File Info, and enter a caption into the File Info dialog box. The caption prints in 9-point Helvetica. It's strictly an image-annotation feature, something to help you 17 years down the road, when your brain starts to deteriorate and you can't remember why you printed the darn thing. (You might also use the caption to keep images straight in a busy

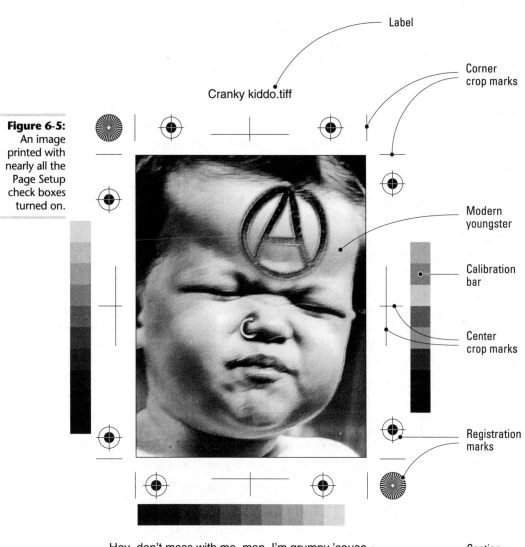

Label

Cranky kiddo.tiff

Corner
crop marks

Figure 6-5:
An image
printed with
nearly all the
Page Setup
check boxes
turned on.

Modern
youngster

Calibration
bar

Center
crop marks

Registration
marks

Hey, don't mess with me, man. I'm grumpy 'cause •————— Caption
I can't change the font for this caption. Aargh!

office where hundreds of folks have access to the same images, but I don't like
this alternative as much because I can't make fun of it.)

❧ **Calibration Bars:** A calibration bar is a 10-step grayscale gradation that starts at
10 percent black and ends at 100 percent black. The function of the calibration
bar is to ensure that all shades are distinct and on target. If not, the output
device isn't properly calibrated, which is a fancy way of saying that the printer's
colors are out of whack and need realignment by a trained professional armed
with a hammer and hacksaw. When you print color separations, the Calibration
Bars check box instructs Photoshop to print a gradient tint bar and progressive
color bar, also useful to printing professionals.

- **Registration Marks:** Select this option to print eight crosshairs and two star targets near the four corners of the image. Registration marks are absolutely imperative when you print color separations because they provide the only reliable means for ensuring exact registration of the cyan, magenta, yellow, and black printing plates. When printing a composite image, however, you can ignore this option.

- **Corner Crop Marks:** Select this option to print eight hairline *crop marks* — two in each of the image's four corners — which indicate how to trim the image in case you anticipate engaging in a little traditional paste-up work.

- **Center Crop Marks:** Select this option to print four pairs of hairlines that mark the center of the image. Each pair forms a cross. Two pairs are located on the sides of the image, one is above the image, and the fourth is below.

- **Labels:** When you select this check box, Photoshop prints the name of the image and the name of the printed color channel in 9-point Helvetica. If you process lots of images, you'll find this option extremely useful for associating printouts with documents on disk.

- **Negative:** When you select this option, Photoshop prints all blacks as white and all whites as black. In-between colors switch accordingly. For example, 20 percent black becomes 80 percent black. Imagesetter operators use this option to print composites and color separations to film negative.

- **Emulsion Down:** The *emulsion* is the side of a piece of film on which an image is printed. When the Emulsion Down check box is turned off, film prints from an imagesetter emulsion side up; when the check box is turned on, Photoshop flips the image so that the emulsion side is down. Like the Negative option, this option is useful only when you print film from an imagesetter and should be set in accordance with the preferences of your commercial printer.

- **Interpolation:** If you own an output device equipped with PostScript Level 2, you can instruct Photoshop to antialias the printed appearance of a low-resolution image by selecting this option. The output device resamples the image up to 200 percent and then reduces it to its original size using bicubic interpolation (as described in the "General environmental preferences" section of Chapter 2), thereby creating a less jagged image. This option has no effect on older-model PostScript devices.

Changing the halftone screen

Before I go any farther, let me explain a bit more about how printing works. To keep costs down, commercial printers use as few inks as possible to create the appearance of a wide variety of colors. Suppose that you want to print an image of a pink flamingo wearing a red bow tie. Your commercial printer could print the flamingos in one pass using pink ink, let that color dry, and then load the red ink and print all the bow ties. But why go to all that trouble? After all, pink is just a lighter shade of red. Why not imitate the pink by lightening the red ink?

Well, unfortunately, with the exception of dye-sublimation printers, output devices can't print lighter shades of colors. They recognize only solid ink and the absence of ink. So how do you print the lighter shade of red necessary to represent pink?

The answer is *halftoning.* The output device organizes printer pixels into spots called *halftone cells.* Because the cells are so small, your eyes cannot quite focus on them. Instead, the cells appear to blend with the white background of the page to create a lighter shade of an ink. Figure 6-6 shows a detail of an image enlarged to display the individual halftone cells.

Figure 6-6:
A detail from an image (left) enlarged so that you can see the individual halftone cells (right).

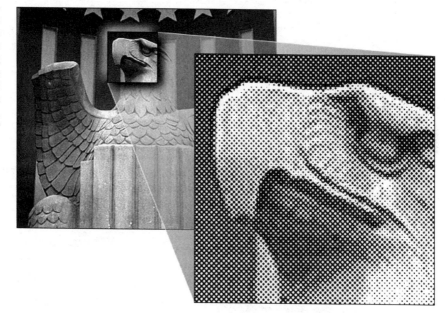

The cells grow and shrink to emulate different shades of color. Large cells result in dark shades; small cells result in light shades. Cell size is measured in printer pixels. The maximum size of any cell is a function of the number of cells in an inch, called the *screen frequency.*

For example, the default frequency of the Apple LaserWriter is 60 halftone cells per linear inch. Because the resolution of the LaserWriter is 300 printer pixels per linear inch, each halftone cell must measure 5 pixels wide by 5 pixels tall ($300 \div 60 = 5$), for a total of 25 pixels per cell (5^2). When all pixels in a cell are turned off, the cell appears white; when all pixels are turned on, you get solid ink. By turning on different numbers of pixels — from 0 up to 25 — the printer can create a total of 26 shades, as demonstrated in Figure 6-7.

Figure 6-7:
5 × 5-pixel halftone
cells with different
numbers of pixels
activated, ranging from
25 (top left) to 0
(bottom right). Each cell
represents a unique
shade from 100 to 0
percent black.

Photoshop lets you change the size, angle, and shape of the individual *halftone cells* used to represent an image on the printed page. To do so, click on the Screens button in the LaserWriter Page Setup dialog box. The Halftone Screens dialog box shown in Figure 6-8 appears.

Figure 6-8:
Use the
Halftone
Screens dialog
box to edit the
size, angle, and
shape of the
halftone cells
for any one ink.

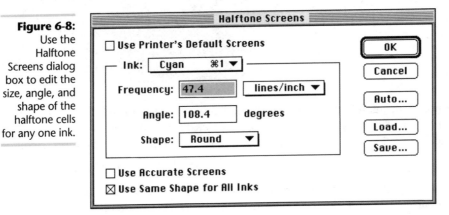

In the dialog box, you can manipulate the following options:

- **Use Printer's Default Screens:** Select this check box to accept the default size, angle, and shape settings built into your printer's ROM. All other options in the Halftone Screens dialog box automatically become dimmed to show they are no longer in force.

- **Ink:** If the current image is in color, you can select the specific ink that you want to adjust from the Ink pop-up menu. When you work with a grayscale image, no pop-up menu is available.

- **Frequency:** Enter a new value into this option box to change the number of halftone cells that print per linear inch. A higher value translates to a larger quantity of smaller cells; a smaller value creates fewer, larger cells. Frequency is traditionally measured in *lines per inch,* or *lpi* (as in lines of halftone cells), but you can change the measurement to lines per centimeter by selecting Lines/cm from the pop-up menu to the right of the option box.

 Higher screen frequencies result in smoother-looking printouts. However, raising the Frequency value also decreases the number of shades an output device can print because it decreases the size of each halftone cell and likewise decreases the number of printer pixels per cell. Fewer printer pixels means fewer shades. You can calculate the precise number of printable shades using the following formula:

$$Number\ of\ shades = (printer\ resolution \div frequency)^2 + 1$$

- **Angle:** To change the orientation of the lines of halftone cells, enter a new value into the Angle option box. In the name of accuracy, Photoshop accepts any value between negative and positive 180.0000 degrees.

 When printing color composites to ink-jet and thermal-wax printers and when printing color separations, Photoshop calculates the optimum Frequency and Angle values required to print seamless colors. In such a case, you should change these values only if you know *exactly* what you're doing. Otherwise, your printout may exhibit moiré patterns, as defined in the "Moiré patterns" section of Chapter 3. When printing grayscale images, however, you can edit these values to your heart's content.

- **Shape:** By default, most PostScript printers rely on roundish halftone cells. You can change the appearance of all cells for an ink by selecting one of six alternate shapes from the Shape pop-up menu. (For a demonstration of four of these shapes, see Figure 4-12 in the "Black and white (bitmap)" section of Chapter 4.) If you know how to write PostScript code, you can select the Custom option to display a text-entry dialog box and code away.

- **Use Accurate Screens:** If your output device is equipped with PostScript Level 2, select this option to subscribe to the updated screen angles for full-color output. Otherwise, don't worry about this option.

- **Use Same Shape for All Inks:** Select this option if you want to apply a single set of size, angle, and shape options to the halftone cells for all inks used to represent the current image. Unless you want to create some sort of special effect, leave this check box deselected. The option is not available when you are printing a grayscale image.

- **Auto:** Click on this button to display the Auto Screens dialog box shown in Figure 6-9, which automates the halftone editing process. Enter the resolution of your output device in the Printer option box. Then enter the screen frequency you would like to use in the Screen option box. After you press the Return key to confirm your change, Photoshop automatically calculates the optimum screen frequencies for all inks. This technique is especially useful when you print full-color images; because Photoshop does the work for you, you can't make a mess of things.

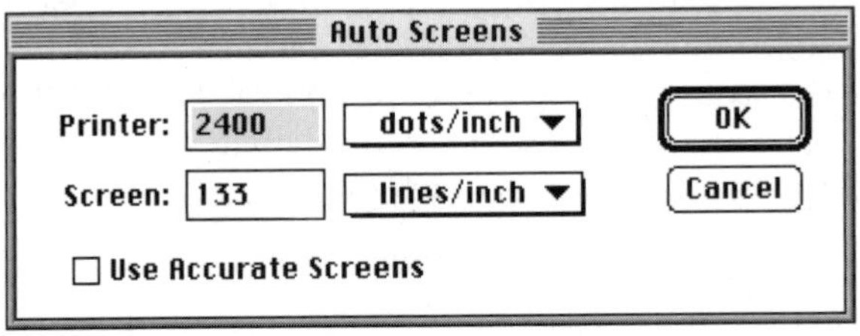

Figure 6-9:
To automate the halftone editing process, enter the resolution of the output device and the screen frequency you want to use into the Auto Screens dialog box.

> **Auto Screens**
>
> Printer: `2400` dots/inch ▼   OK
>
> Screen: `133` lines/inch ▼   Cancel
>
> ☐ Use Accurate Screens

- **Load/Save:** You can load and save settings to disk in case you want to reapply the options to other images. These buttons are especially useful if you find a magic combination of halftone settings that results in a really spectacular printout.

You can change the default size, angle, and shape settings that Photoshop applies to all future images by Option-clicking on the Save button. When you press Option, the Save button changes to read →*Default.* To restore the default screen settings at any time, Option-click on the Load button (← *Default*).

Specifying a transfer function

A *transfer function* enables you to change the way on-screen brightness values translate — or *map* — to printed shades. By default, brightness values print to their nearest shade percentages. A 30 percent gray on-screen pixel (which equates to a brightness value of roughly 180) prints as a 30 percent gray value.

Problems arise, however, when your output device prints lighter or darker than it should. For example, in the course of using my LaserWriter NTX over the last three years or so, I've discovered that all gray values print overly dark. Dark values fill in and become black; light values appear a dismal gray, muddying up any highlights. The problem increases if I try to reproduce the image on a photocopier.

To compensate for this over-darkening effect, I click on the Transfer button in the LaserWriter Page Setup dialog box and enter the values shown in Figure 6-10. Notice that I lighten 30 percent on-screen grays to 10 percent printer grays. I also lighten 90 percent screen grays to 80 percent printer grays. The result is a smooth, continuous curve that maps each gray value in an image to a lighter value on paper.

Figure 6-10:
The transfer function curve lets you map on-screen brightness values to specific shades on paper.

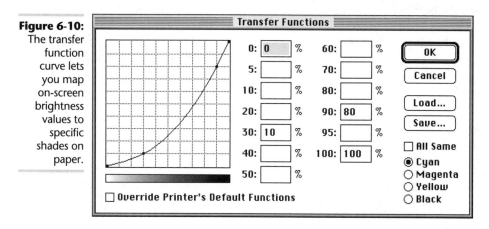

The options in the Transfer Functions dialog box work as follows:

- **Transfer graph:** The *transfer graph* is where you map on-screen brightness values to their printed equivalents. The horizontal axis of the graph represents on-screen brightness values; the vertical axis represents printed shades. The *transfer curve* charts the relationship between on-screen and printed colors. The lower left corner is the origin of the graph — the point at which both on-screen brightness value and printed shade are white. Move to the right in the graph for darker on-screen values; move up for darker printed shades. Click in the graph to add points to the line. Drag up on a point to darken the output; drag down to lighten the output.

 For a more comprehensive explanation of how to graph colors on a curve, read about the incredibly powerful Curves command, covered in Chapter 16.

- **Percentage option boxes:** The option boxes are labeled according to the on-screen brightness values. To lighten or darken the printed brightness values, enter higher or lower percentage values in the option boxes. Note that there is a direct correlation between changes made to the transfer graph and the option boxes. For example, if you enter a value in the 50 percent option box, a new point appears along the middle line of the graph.

⇨ **Override Printer's Default Functions:** As an effect of printer calibration, some printers have custom transfer functions built into their ROM. If you have problems making your settings take effect, select this check box to instruct Photoshop to apply the transfer function you specify regardless of the output device's built-in transfer function.

⇨ **Load/Save:** Use these buttons to load and save settings to disk. Option-click on the buttons to retrieve and save default settings.

⇨ **Ink controls:** When you print a full-color image, five options appear in the lower right corner of the Transfer Functions dialog box. These options enable you to apply different transfer functions to different inks. Select the All Same check box to apply a single transfer function to all inks. To apply a different function to each ink, select one of the radio buttons and edit the points in the transfer graph as desired.

Printing pages

When you finish slogging your way through the mind-numbingly extensive Page Setup options, you can initiate the printing process by choosing File⇨Print (Command-P). The Printer dialog box or its equivalent appears, as shown in Figure 6-11.

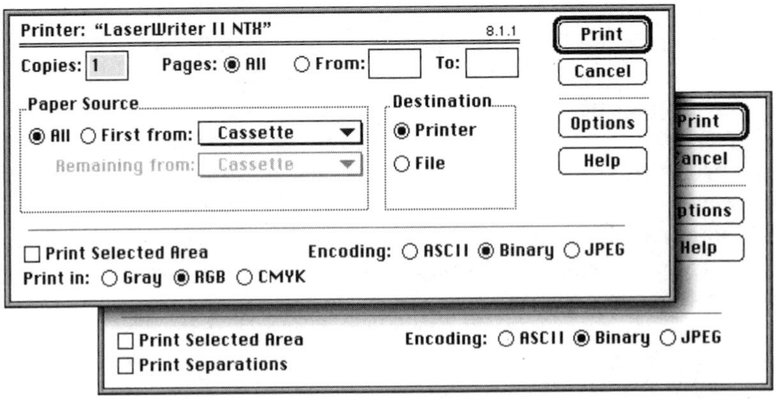

Figure 6-11:
The Print dialog box as it appears when printing an RGB (top) and CMYK (bottom) image.

Most of the options of this dialog box are a function of the Macintosh system software, but a few at the bottom of the dialog box are exclusive to Photoshop. The options work as follows:

⇨ **Copies:** Enter the number of copies you want to print in this option box. You can print up to 999 copies of a single image, although why you would want to do so is beyond me.

☞ **Pages:** There is no such thing as a multipage document in Photoshop, so you can ignore the All, From, and To options.

☞ **Paper Source:** If you want to print your illustration on a letterhead or other special piece of paper, select the Manual Feed radio button. If you're using the LaserWriter driver 8 or later, select the First From radio button and then select Manual Feed from the accompanying pop-up menu. LaserWriter 8 lets you print the first page to different paper than other pages in the document. However, because Photoshop images are never more than one page long, you can pretty well ignore this option.

☞ **Destination:** This option allows you to generate a PostScript-language definition of the file on disk rather than printing it directly to your printer. Select the Printer option to print the image to an output device as usual. Select File (or PostScript File under LaserWriter driver 7.1.2 and earlier) to write a PostScript-language version of the image to disk. Because Photoshop offers its own EPS option via the Save dialog box, you'll probably want to ignore this option. In fact, the only reason to select File is to capture printer's marks, as I did back in Figure 6-5. If you select File, a second dialog box appears, asking you where you want to save the EPS file. You can navigate just as in the Open and Save dialog boxes. For the best results, select the Binary radio button.

☞ **Print Selected Area:** Select this option to print the portion of an image that is selected with the rectangular marquee tool. You can use this option to divide an image into pieces when it's too large to fit on a single page.

☞ **Print In:** Select one of these radio buttons to specify the type of composite image Photoshop prints. Select the first radio button to print the image as a grayscale composite. Select the second radio button to let the printer translate the colors from the current color mode to CMYK. Select the third radio button to instruct Photoshop to convert the image to CMYK colors during the print process. These options are not available when you print a grayscale image. (When printing a CMYK image, the Print In options change to a single Print Separations check box, which is described in the next section.)

 Relying on the output device to translate colors can result in printing errors, thanks to the low memory capabilities of most printers. If an image refuses to print, try selecting either the Gray or CMYK radio button. Use the first option when you print to black-and-white devices such as laser printers and imagesetters; use the last option when printing to color printers and film recorders.

☞ **Encoding:** If your network doesn't support binary encoding, select the ASCII option to transfer data in the text-only format. The printing process takes much longer to complete, but at least it's possible.

The Options button is another little item you can ignore. It brings up a dialog box with three options. The first lets you print a cover page, which is a ridiculous waste of paper in the context of Photoshop. The second option, Print, lets you convert color images to grayscale. Photoshop is not only capable of printing both grayscale and color composites without the assistance of the system software, it actually accomplishes the task more quickly and more expertly than the system. Leave this option set to Black & White unless you want the system's assistance. The final option is the only one that's remotely useful, allowing you to display PostScript printing errors on-screen. My advice is to set this option to Summarize On Screen. Then close the dialog box and never return to it.

Press Return inside the Printer dialog box to start the printing process on its merry way. To cancel a print in progress, click on the Cancel button or press Command-period. If Photoshop ignores you, keep pressing away on those keys. I never have figured out if it does any good, but at least you feel like you're doing everything you can.

Creating Color Separations _____

If printing a composite image is moderately complicated, printing color separations is a terrific pain in the behind. Printer manufacturers and software developers are working to simplify this process, but for the present, Photoshop requires you to stagger through a maze of variables and obtuse options. I wish that I could offer some conciliatory advice like "Hang in there and you'll make it," but every day that I work with Photoshop's color separation capabilities adds to my conviction that this is an unnecessarily complicated process, designed by people who are nearly as confused as we are.

On that cheery note, the upcoming steps explain how to muddle your way through the color-separation process. You'll recognize many of the steps from the process described for printing a grayscale or color composite.

 If you're a prepress professional or computer artist looking for a means to enhance the printing process, you owe it to yourself to check out two substantial products, EFI's Cachet and Light Source's Ofoto. Cachet is capable of adjusting the colors in an image in keeping with a proven reference image that you know prints with superb color definition. Ofoto provides automatic calibration capabilities that match scanner, monitor, and printer at any stage in the image-editing process. Both programs simplify the color-separation process and offer a wealth of capabilities thus far missing from Photoshop.

STEPS: Printing CMYK Color Separations

Step 1. If your computer is part of a network that includes many printers, use the Chooser desk accessory to select the printer to which you want to print, as described previously in the "Choosing a printer" section.

Step 2. Calibrate your system to the specific requirements of your monitor and the selected printer using File⇨Preferences⇨Monitor Setup and File⇨Preferences⇨Printing Inks Setup. You only need to complete this step once for each time you switch hardware. If you always use the same monitor and printer combination, you need to repeat this step very rarely, say once every six months, to account for screen and printer degradation.

Step 3. Use File⇨Preferences⇨Separation Setup to control how Photoshop converts RGB and Lab colors to CMYK color space. Again, you need to perform this step only when you want to compensate for a difference in the output device or if you simply want to fine-tune Photoshop to create better separations.

Step 4. Choose Mode⇨CMYK Color to convert the image from its present color mode to CMYK. The CMYK mode is explained in the "CMYK" section of Chapter 4.

Step 5. Switching color modes can dramatically affect the colors in an image. To compensate for color and focus loss, you can edit the individual color channels as described in the "Color Channel Effects" section of Chapter 5.

Step 6. If your image features many high-contrast elements and you're concerned that your printer might not do the best job of registering the cyan, magenta, yellow, and black color plates, you can apply Image⇨Trap to prevent your final printout from looking like the color funnies.

Step 7. Choose File⇨Page Setup to specify the size of the pages and the size and orientation of the image on the pages, as described earlier in this chapter. Also be sure to select — at the very least — the Calibration Bars, Registration Marks, and Labels check boxes.

Step 8. Click on the Screens button to change the size, angle, and shape of the halftone screen dots for the individual color plates, as described earlier in the "Changing the halftone screen" section. This step and Step 9 are optional.

Step 9. Click on the Transfer button to map brightness values in each of the CMYK color channels to different shades on the printed plates, as described in the "Specifying a transfer function" section earlier in this chapter.

Step 10. Choose File⇨Print (Command-P) and select the Print Separations check box in the lower left corner of the dialog box (see Figure 6-11). Photoshop then prints the color separations according to your specifications.

Steps 1 and 7 through 10 are repeats of concepts explained in earlier sections of this chapter. To fully understand Steps 4 and 5, read the larger color theory discussions contained in Chapter 4. That leaves Steps 2, 3, and 6, which I describe in detail in the following sections.

You also can create color separations by importing an image into a desktop publishing program like QuarkXPress. To do so, export the image in the DCS format, as described in the "QuarkXPress DCS" section of Chapter 3. Then print the separations directly from the desktop publishing program. Because DCS is a subset of the EPS format, it enables you to save halftone screen and transfer function settings. XPress doesn't require that you export the image in the CMYK mode, but I recommend it because it gives you greater control over the separation process.

Monitor calibration

Choose File⇨Preferences⇨Monitor to display the Monitor Setup dialog box shown in Figure 6-12. Along with the Gamma control panel, which offers the added capability of adjusting specific red, green, and blue color intensities, this dialog box represents the extent of Photoshop's monitor-calibration capabilities. However, unlike Gamma, the Monitor Setup dialog box provides options that directly affect the conversion of scanned colors to their CMYK equivalents. These options advise Photoshop that certain on-screen color distortions are in effect and instruct the program to make accommodations when converting between the RGB and CMYK color modes.

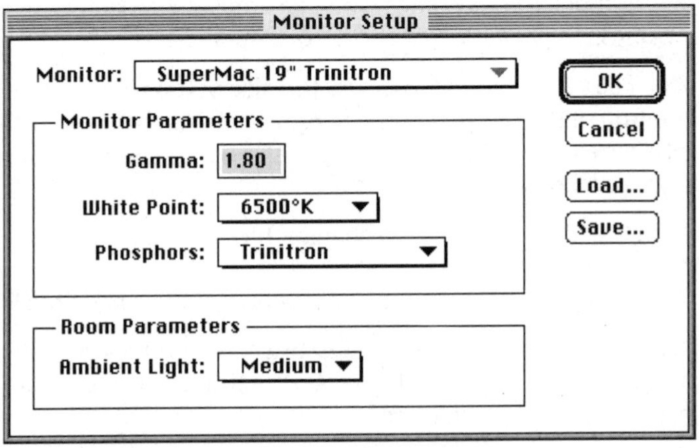

Figure 6-12:
The options in the Monitor Setup dialog box tell Photoshop how to compensate for on-screen colors when preparing color separations.

Monitor Setup

Monitor: SuperMac 19" Trinitron

Monitor Parameters

Gamma: 1.80

White Point: 6500°K

Phosphors: Trinitron

Room Parameters

Ambient Light: Medium

OK

Cancel

Load...

Save...

The options in the Monitor Setup dialog box work as follows:

⌖ **Monitor:** In the best of all possible worlds, you can select your exact model of monitor from this pop-up menu. Photoshop automatically changes the settings in the Monitor Parameters box — Gamma, White Point, and Phosphors — in accordance with the recommendations of the monitor's manufacturer. If you can't find your exact model, look for a model that is made by the same manufacturer and whose *only* difference from your model is screen size. If you can't find a suitable model, select the Other option.

Do *not* assume that all monitors from the same vendor are basically alike. Most vendors sell screens manufactured by different companies. For example, the SuperMac 19-inch Trinitron is manufactured by Sony, while the SuperMac 19-inch Color may come from Hitachi or Ikegami. More importantly, the two screens use different technology (Trinitron versus shadow-masked tridot). Do not select a monitor other than the one you use unless the only difference in the name is screen size.

⌖ **Gamma:** This value represents the brightness of medium colors on-screen. Low values down to 0.75 darken the image to compensate for an overly light screen; high values up to 3.00 lighten the image to compensate for an overly dark screen. Generally speaking, 1.8 is the ideal value for Macintosh RGB screens. When you use an NTSC television monitor — as when editing video images using TrueVision's NuVista+ or RasterOps' ProVideo32 — set Gamma to 2.2.

⌖ **White Point:** This value represents the temperature of the lightest color your screen can produce. Measured on the Kelvin temperature scale, it refers to the heat at which a so-called "black body" would turn to white. So theoretically, if you took the Maltese Falcon and heated it to 6,500 degrees Kelvin, it would turn white (if it didn't catch on fire first). The only way to achieve the correct value for this option is to consult the technical support department for your make of monitor or use a hardware testing device such as Minolta's $10,000 Minolta CRT Color Analyzer CA-100.

⌖ **Phosphors:** This pop-up menu lets you select the kind of screen used in your monitor. About half the monitors used with Macintosh computers — including all monitors sold by Apple — use Trinitron screens. (You can recognize Trinitron screens by the fact that they bow slightly outward horizontally but are flat vertically.) Select the NTSC option if you are using a television monitor. Otherwise, consult your vendor's technical support department.

⌖ **Ambient Light:** Select the amount of light in your office or studio from this pop-up menu. In a dark room, Photoshop slightly darkens the image. In a light room, Photoshop lightens it so that you can see it clearly despite the ambient light.

When you finish setting the options, press Return to close the dialog box. Photoshop takes a few moments to adjust the display of the on-screen image.

Printer calibration

To prepare an image that is to be reproduced on a commercial offset or web press, choose File⇨Preferences⇨Printing Inks Setup to display the Printing Inks Setup dialog box shown in Figure 6-13.

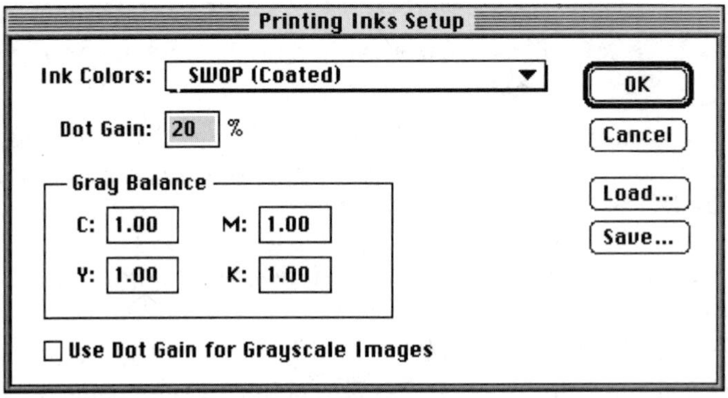

Figure 6-13:
Use the options in the Printing Inks Setup dialog box to prepare an image for printing on a commercial offset or web press.

```
┌─────────────────────── Printing Inks Setup ───────────────────────┐
│                                                                    │
│   Ink Colors:  │ SWOP (Coated)              ▼ │    ┌─ OK ─┐        │
│                                                                    │
│   Dot Gain: │ 20 │ %                             ┌ Cancel ┐        │
│                                                                    │
│   ┌─ Gray Balance ──────────────────────┐        ┌ Load... ┐       │
│   │   C: │ 1.00 │     M: │ 1.00 │        │                         │
│   │                                      │        ┌ Save... ┐       │
│   │   Y: │ 1.00 │     K: │ 1.00 │        │                         │
│   └──────────────────────────────────────┘                        │
│                                                                    │
│   ☐ Use Dot Gain for Grayscale Images                              │
│                                                                    │
└────────────────────────────────────────────────────────────────────┘
```

Like the Monitor Setup options, these settings are very technical and can be properly set only with the assistance of your commercial printer. But just so you have an inkling about inks, here's how the options work:

- **Ink Colors:** Select the specific variety of inks and paper stock that will be used to reproduce the current image. (Consult your commercial printer for this information.) Photoshop automatically changes the settings of the Dot Gain and Gray Balance options to the most suitable values.

- **Dot Gain:** Enter any value from –10 to 40 percent to specify the amount by which you can expect halftone cells to shrink or expand during the printing process, a variable known as *dot gain.* When printing to newsprint, for example, you can expect halftone cells to bleed into the page and expand by about 30 percent. When you convert to the CMYK color mode, Photoshop automatically adjusts the brightness of colors to compensate for the dot gain.

- **Gray Balance:** Assuming that the inks are up to snuff, equal amounts of cyan, magenta, yellow, and black ink should produce gray. But inks can fade and become impure over time. To compensate for this, you can vary the amount of ink that mixes to produce medium gray by entering values from 0.50 to 2.00 in the Gray Balance option boxes. Think of it as a recipe — 0.75 parts cyan mixed with 1.50 parts magenta and so on. Again, consult with your commercial printer before changing these values.

↬ **Use Dot Gain for Grayscale Images:** When this option is turned off, the Dot Gain value only affects the creation and editing of CMYK images. If you select this check box, however, you also can apply the value to grayscale images. Then, any time you select a gray value, Photoshop automatically treats it as if it were lighter or darker depending on whether the Dot Gain value is negative or positive, respectively.

Rather than getting 50 percent gray when you select 50 percent gray, for example, you might get 58 percent gray. This can cause problems when you want to create displacement maps, create precise gradations, or simply achieve exact brightness values. I strongly recommend that you turn this check box off unless you have some specific reason for turning it on, like you've suddenly taken leave of your senses.

How to prepare CMYK conversions

Now that you've told Photoshop how to compensate for the foibles of your screen and commercial printer, you need to explain what kind of separation process you intend to use. To do this, choose File⇨Preferences⇨Separation Setup to display the Separation Setup dialog box, shown in Figure 6-14. Unlike the options in the Printing Inks Setup dialog box, which describe the specific press belonging to your commercial printer, these options describe a general printing process. Even so, you'll probably find it helpful to consult with your commercial printer before changing the settings.

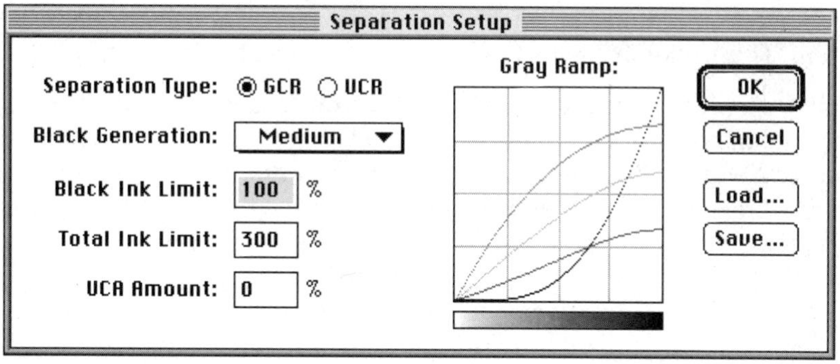

Figure 6-14: Describe the printing process using the options inside the Separation Setup dialog box.

	Separation Setup
Separation Type: ⦿ GCR ◯ UCR	Gray Ramp:
Black Generation: Medium ▼	
Black Ink Limit: 100 %	
Total Ink Limit: 300 %	
UCA Amount: 0 %	

OK · Cancel · Load... · Save...

The options in the Separation Setup dialog box work as follows:

↬ **Separation Type:** When the densities of cyan, magenta, and yellow inks reach a certain level, they mix to form a muddy brown. The GCR (*gray component replacement*) option avoids this unpleasant effect by overprinting these colors with black to the extent specified with the Black Generation option. If you select the UCR (*under color removal*) option, Photoshop removes cyan, magenta, and yellow inks where they overlap black ink. Generally speaking, GCR is the setting of choice except when you're printing on newsprint.

≈ **Black Generation:** Available only when the GCR option is active, the Black Generation pop-up menu lets you specify how dark the cyan, magenta, and yellow concentrations have to be before Photoshop adds black ink. Select Light to use black ink sparingly and Heavy to apply it liberally. The None option prints no black ink whatsoever, while the Maximum option prints black ink over everything. You may want to use the UCA Amount option to restore cyan, magenta, and yellow ink if you select the Heavy or Maximum option.

≈ **Black Ink Limit:** Enter the maximum amount of black ink that can be applied to the page. By default, this value is 100 percent, which is solid ink coverage. If you raise the UCA Amount value, you'll probably want to lower this value by a similar percentage to prevent the image from over-darkening.

≈ **Total Ink Limit:** This value represents the maximum amount of all four inks permitted on the page. For example, assuming that you use the default Black Ink Limit and Total Ink Limit values shown in Figure 6-14, the darkest printable color contains 100 percent black ink. Therefore, the sum total of cyan, magenta, and yellow inks is 200 percent. (You subtract the Black Ink Limit value from the Total Ink Limit value to get the sum total of the three other inks.)

≈ **UCA Amount:** The opposite of UCR, UCA stands for *under color addition,* which lets you add cyan, magenta, and yellow inks to areas where the concentration of black ink is highest. For example, a value of 20 percent raises the amount of cyan, magenta, and yellow inks applied with black concentrations between 80 and 100 percent. This option is dimmed when the UCR radio button is active.

The Gray Ramp graph demonstrates the effects of your changes to any option in the Separation Setup dialog box. Four lines, one in each color, represent the four inks. Though you can't edit the lines in this graph by clicking and dragging on them, as you can in the Transfer Functions dialog box, you can observe the lines to gauge the results of your settings.

Color trapping

If color separations misalign slightly during the reproduction process (a problem called *misregistration*), the final image can exhibit slight gaps between colors. Suppose that an image features a 100 percent cyan chicken against a 100 percent magenta background. (Pretty attractive image idea, huh? Go ahead, you can use it if you like.) If the cyan and magenta plates don't line up exactly, you're left with a chicken with a white halo around it. Yuck.

A *trap* is a little extra bit of color that fills in the gap. For example, if you choose Image⇨Trap and enter 4 into the Width option box, Photoshop outlines the chicken with an extra 4 pixels of cyan and the background with an extra 4 pixels of magenta. Now the registration can be off a full 8 pixels without any halo occurring.

 Continuous-tone images, such as photographs and natural-media painting, don't need trapping because there are no harsh color transitions. In fact, trapping will actually harm such images by thickening up the borders and edges, smudging detail, and generally dulling the focus.

Therefore, the only reason to use the Trap command is to trap rasterized Illustrator drawings. Some state-of-the-art prepress systems trap documents by first rasterizing them to pixels and then modifying the pixels. Together, Photoshop and Illustrator constitute a more rudimentary but nonetheless functional trapping system. When you open an Illustrator document in Photoshop, the latter converts the illustration into an image according to your size and resolution specifications, as described in the "Rendering an Illustrator file" section of Chapter 3. Once the illustration is rasterized, you can apply Image⇨Trap to the image as a whole. Despite the command's simplicity, it handles nearly all trapping scenarios, even going so far as to incrementally reduce the width of the trap as the colors of neighboring areas grow more similar.

Printing Duotones

It's been a few pages since the "Printing terminology" section, so here's a quick recap: A *duotone* is a grayscale image printed with two inks. This technique expands the depth of the image by allowing additional shades for highlights, shadows, and midtones. If you've seen one of those glossy Calvin Klein magazine ads, you've seen a duotone. Words like *rich, luxurious,* and *palpable* come to mind.

Photoshop also allows you to add a third ink to create a *tritone* and a fourth ink to create a *quadtone*. Color Plate 6-1 shows an example of an image printed as a quadtone. Figure 6-15 shows a detail from the image printed in its original grayscale form. See the difference?

Figure 6-15:
This salute to all-around athlete Jim Thorpe by artist Mark Collen looks pretty good, but if you want to see great, check out the quadtone in Color Plate 6-1.

Creating a duotone

To convert a grayscale image to a duotone, tritone, or quadtone, choose Mode⇨Duotone. Photoshop displays the Duotone Options dialog box shown in Figure 6-16. By default, Duotone is the active Type option, and the Ink 3 and Ink 4 options are dimmed. To access the Ink 3 option, select Tritone from the Type pop-up menu; to access both Ink 3 and Ink 4, select Quadtone from the pop-up menu.

You specify the color of each ink you want to use by clicking on the color box associated with the desired ink option. Select a color from the Custom Colors dialog box as described in the "Predefined colors" section of Chapter 4. (In some cases, Photoshop displays the Color Picker dialog box, described in the "Using the Color Picker" section of that same chapter.)

 When creating duotones, tritones, and quadtones, prioritize your inks in order from darkest at the top to lightest at the bottom when you specify them in the Duotone Options dialog box. Because Photoshop prints inks in the order that they appear in the dialog box, the inks will print from darkest to lightest. This ensures rich highlights and shadows and a uniform color range.

After selecting a color, you can use either of two methods to specify how the differently colored inks blend. The first and more dependable way is to click on the transfer function box associated with the desired ink option. Photoshop then displays the

Transfer Functions dialog box, described back in the "Specifying a transfer function" section of this chapter. This enables you to emphasize specific inks in different portions of the image according to brightness values.

Figure 6-16:
The Duotone Options dialog box enables you to apply multiple inks to a grayscale image.

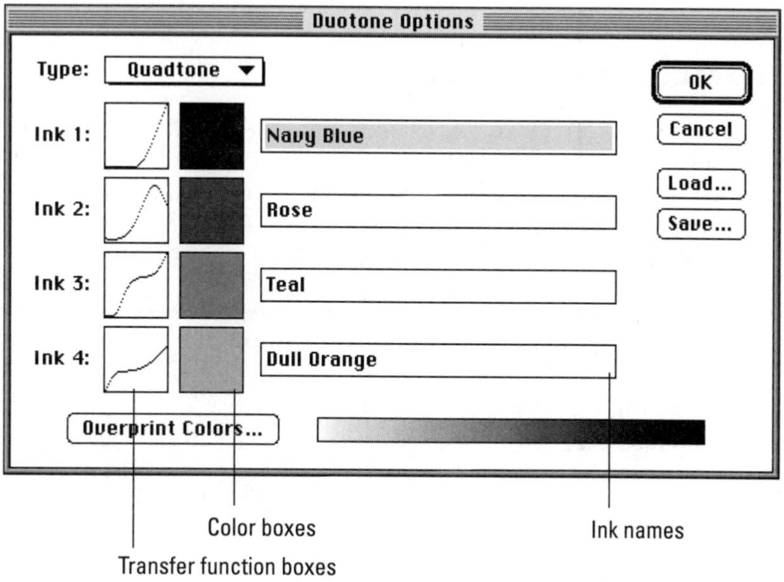

Color boxes

Ink names

Transfer function boxes

For example, Figure 6-16 shows the inks and transfer functions assigned to the quadtone in Color Plate 6-1. The Navy Blue color is associated only with the darkest brightness values in the image; Rose peaks at about 80 percent gray and then descends; Teal covers the midtones in the image; and Dull Orange is strongest in the light values. The four colors mix to form an image whose brightness values progress from light orange to olive green to brick red to black.

The second method for controlling the blending of colors is to click on the Overprint Colors button. An Overprint Colors dialog box appears, showing how each pair of colors will mix when printed. Other color swatches show how three and four colors mix, if applicable. To change the color swatch, click on it to display the Color Picker dialog box.

The problem with this second method is that it complicates the editing process. Photoshop doesn't actually change the ink colors or transfer functions in keeping with your new specifications; it just applies the new overprint colors without any logical basis. Secondly, you lose all changes made with the Overprint Colors dialog box when you adjust any of the ink colors or any of the transfer functions.

To go back and change the colors or transfer functions, choose Mode⇨Duotone again. Instead of reconverting the image, the command now enables you to edit the existing duotone, tritone, or quadtone.

Reproducing a duotone

If you want a commercial printer to reproduce a duotone, tritone, or quadtone, you must print the image to color separations, just like a CMYK image. However, because you already specified which inks to use and how much of each ink to apply, you don't have to mess around with all those commands in the File⇨Preferences submenu. Just take the following familiar steps:

STEPS: Printing a Duotone, Tritone, or Quadtone

Step 1.   Select a printer with the Chooser desk accessory, as described previously in the "Choosing a printer" section.

Step 2.   Choose File⇨Page Setup to specify the size of the pages and the size and orientation of the image on the pages, as described earlier in this chapter, in the "Setting up the page" section. Be sure to select the Registration Marks option.

Step 3.   If you're feeling inventive, click on the Screens button to change the size, angle, and shape of the halftone screen dots for the individual color plates, as described previously in the "Changing the halftone screen" section.

Step 4.   Choose File⇨Print (Command-P). Select the Print Separations check box in the lower left corner of the dialog box to print each ink to a separate sheet of paper or film.

To prepare a duotone to be imported into QuarkXPress, Illustrator, or some other application, save the image in the EPS or DCS format, as described in the "Saving an EPS document" section of Chapter 3. As listed back in Table 4-1 of Chapter 4, EPS (and its DCS variation) is the only file format other than the native Photoshop format that supports duotones, tritones, and quadtones.

If you'll be printing your duotone using CMYK colors, and you can't quite get the effect you want inside the Duotone Options dialog box, you can convert the duotone to the CMYK mode (by choosing Mode⇨CMYK). Not only will all the duotone shades remain intact, but you'll have the added advantage of being able to tweak colors and even add color using Photoshop's standard color correction commands and editing tools. You can even edit invidual color channels, as described in the previous chapter.

Spot-Color Separations

Photoshop 3.0 offers no new capability that accommodates spot-color printing. Photoshop is, after all, designed for creating and editing continuous-tone images; and although spot colors work well for printing duotones, they more often lend themselves to high-contrast artwork created in drawing and page-layout programs.

But what if you want to add a spot-color highlight to an image? For example, suppose that you have a full-color image of a jet ski. The logo along the side of the boat is fully visible, just as the client wants it to be, but the color is off. Normally, the logo appears in Pantone 265 purple. But the CMYK equivalent for this color looks about three shades darker, four shades redder, and several times muddier. The only solution is to assign the proper spot color — Pantone 265 — to the logo. But how do you do it? Here are your options:

ᗮ Paint over the logo in the actual image. Then import the image into Illustrator or FreeHand and recreate the logo as object-oriented text. Then assign the text Pantone 265 and export the document in the EPS format or print it directly from the drawing program. The logo will appear on its own separation.

ᗮ Select the logo using the magic wand tool (or some more exacting method, as described in Chapters 8 and 9) and remove it using Edit⇨Cut (Command-X). Then create a new channel by choosing the New Channel command from the Channels palette pop-up menu. After the Channel Options dialog box appears, click on the Color swatch and change it to a color that matches Pantone 265 as closely as possible. Press Return twice to create the new channel and then press Command-I to invert the channel and make it white. Paste in the logo art (Edit⇨Paste or Command-V). As long as your selection outline is still intact, the logo is pasted in the exact same position as in the original image. To see logo and image together, click on the eyeball icon in front of the CMYK composite view to show all channels at once. The logo will automatically appear in the purple color that you selected in the Channel Options dialog box. Edit the CMYK image and logo as desired.

If you opt for the second option, you can print the image directly from Photoshop in two passes. First, you switch to the CMYK composite view (Command-0) and print the traditional four-color separation. Then you switch to the logo channel (Command-5) and print this channel independently.

However, you cannot import the image into QuarkXPress or some other publishing program. Photoshop doesn't offer any file formats that support more than four color channels, except the native Photoshop format (which most other programs don't support and certainly not for the purpose of printing quality separations). If you were to save the image to the EPS or DCS format, for example, Photoshop would simply jettison the logo channel.

That's where In Software's PlateMaker comes in. This $300 plug-in allows you to export CMYK images with up to 16 additional spot-color channels to the DCS format. When you choose File⇨Export⇨PlateMaker, the plug-in treats each mask channel as a separate plate of spot color. The product supports clipping paths (defined in Chapter 8) and allows you to assign custom halftone screens. The manual even contains instructions for editing the plug-in inside ResEdit to assign different default settings. Certainly, $300 is a lot to spend on what is essentially no more than an export module, and the DCS file doesn't display the spot color correctly inside XPress or any other program, but if you're a print professional, this may be your only solution.

 At least one other spot-color plug-in, called PhotoSpot (from Second Glance) is available for Photoshop. This program, however, works very differently from PlateMaker. Frankly, although PhotoSpot is more automated, it produces far less useful results. It works by boiling down an entire image exclusively into spot colors. You can use a second utility, PaintThinner, to customize which spot colors are used. PhotoSpot is smart enough to name the colors — it sees a light blue and names it Light Blue (technology on the march!) — but it isn't particularly smart about the way it separates them. First of all, it creates color transitions between neighboring areas of spot color by dithering. In other words, though Photoshop provides 256 gray values per channel, PhotoSpot only takes advantage of two of them, black and white. The upshot of this solution is some uniformly ugly results. Second, rather than supporting the standard DCS format, PhotoSpot saves each separation to an independent TIFF file. To print the image from XPress, you have to import each TIFF file separately, stack them on top of each other, color them manually with the desired spot colors, and hope for the best. All this eliminates any real prepress potential for PhotoSpot.

Summary

- The Chooser desk accessory enables you to select a printer connected directly to your Mac or shared over a network.

- Use the Page Setup command to specify the size of the page and the orientation and size of the image on the page.

- Drag on the preview box in the lower left corner of the image window to preview how the image fits on the page before printing it.

- Output devices represent shades of color by printing thousands of tiny color spots called *halftone cells*.

- The number of distinct shades a printer can produce is dependent on the screen frequency. Higher frequencies result in smaller halftone cells and therefore fewer shades.

- A transfer function allows you to compensate for overly dark or overly light printouts by mapping brightness values in an image to lighter or darker printed shades.

- In order to properly calibrate your monitor, consult the technical support department for your make of monitor.

- Consult with your commercial printer before changing the settings in the Printing Inks Setup dialog box.

- Before printing color separations, you must convert an image to the CMYK mode by choosing Mode⇨CMYK.

- Be sure to turn on the Registration Marks check box in the LaserWriter Page Setup dialog box when printing color separations and duotones.

- Color trapping is a get-by solution that helps to eliminate gaps between colors by swelling up shades of ink, with emphasis on dark values.

- Duotones, tritones, and quadtones expand the number of shades available to a grayscale image. You also can add a modicum of color to otherwise drab grayscale images.

- You can add channels to an image to accommodate spot colors. Then print the separations directly from Photoshop or use In Software's PlateMaker to save the spot-color separations in the DCS format.

Retouching with a Purpose

Retouching is perhaps the most controversial of image-editing functions, because an adept artist can dramatically alter the contents of a photo without the viewer being the least bit aware. The idea is particularly worrisome to news and action photographers, because any alteration to such a photo represents a departure from reality. After all, what's the point of risking personal injury to shoot a photo of an underwater shark encounter if some fool in the graphics department is going to enhance the photo by adding a few Great Whites?

In the following chapters, I explain how to edit photos as realistically as possible. However, I recommend that you temper the application of your skills with a smidgen of responsibility. Some retouching is perfectly acceptable. A photographer friend of mine, for example, runs an image-editing service on the side so that he can edit his own photos according to a client's needs. Seems okay. Certainly, retouching is so rampant and blatant in advertising that most consumers have grown savvy enough not to mistake advertising for reality. Not ideal, but again, okay. Where the merit of retouching is most tenuous is in the depiction of real events. In this case, it's not enough to edit the photo with the approval of the photographer; you also need to bring the edit to the attention of the viewer. There has been talk of adopting a symbol to indicate manipulated news photos, such as an *M* in a circle. Even better is an addition to the credit line: *Photo by X. Photo manipulation by Y.*

Ultimately, the whens and whys of image editing are up to you. My job, as I see it, is to show you how to retouch images without lecturing to you any more than I already have. So without further ado, the following chapters show you how to edit an image so that its own mother wouldn't recognize it.

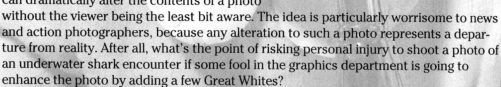

Painting and Editing

- -

In This Chapter

➡ Explanations of Photoshop's paint and edit tools

➡ How to use the Shift key to create straight and perpendicular lines

➡ How to use and customize the smudge tool

➡ Everything you want to know about the new sponge tool

➡ A thorough explanation of the Brushes palette

➡ How to create round and elliptical brush shapes and save any selection as a custom brush

➡ How to paint lines that gradually fade away or taper to a point

➡ An introduction to pressure-sensitive drawing tablets

➡ Thorough examination of the brush modes, including the five new modes introduced in Photoshop 3.0

- -

Paint and Edit Tool Basics _____

In the previous edition of this book, this chapter began with a humorous little anecdote about how late in the game you and I were finally getting around to sinking our teeth into this mighty program. Mind you, most folks who communicated with me seemed to appreciate the introductory stuff and realize that it would prepare them for a better understanding of Photoshop's inner workings, but a few strident eggs let me know that they were much too experienced for anything short of continual, hard-core, image-editing madness. "First 200 pages are largely off the subject. How to use a menu — c'mon!" was one reader's brusque commentary.

To mollify these squeaky wheels — I think we're talking maximum of four or five guys, but my, how they squeaked — I jettisoned three introductory chapters to the CD. And yet here I am discussing the very same topic only one chapter and 20 pages earlier. What is my problem? Can't I get to the point any quicker than this?

No. And you know why? Because the introductory material is *very* important. From this point on, I want you and I to have a common verbal and theoretical vocabulary. I need to be able to communicate with you plainly and effectively. I want you to understand not only how to perform a certain task, but also why I'm approaching the task in the way I am. If I just sit here and fire off a bunch of techniques, you'll probably be able to repeat those techniques with relatively little effort. But if I take the time to explain the larger issues of how image editing works and how Photoshop's specific capabilities relate to the real world, you'll be better prepared to branch out beyond the specific techniques I show you and develop your own. This is when a real mastery of Photoshop begins.

Painting primer

This chapter, in case you're still curious, is about painting and editing images using a bunch of tools in Photoshop's toolbox. Now, you may be thinking that these tools require you to possess a modicum of artistic talent. But in truth, each tool provides options for just about any level of proficiency or experience. Photoshop offers get-by measures for novices who just want to make a quick edit and put the tool down before they make a mess of things. If you have a few hours of experience with other painting programs, such as SuperPaint or PC Paintbrush, you'll find that Photoshop's tools provide at least as much functionality and, in many cases, more. And if you're a professional artist, you'll have no problem learning how to make Photoshop sing. Suffice it to say that no matter who you are, you'll find electronic painting and editing tools to be more flexible, less messy, and more forgiving than their traditional counterparts.

 If you screw something up in the course of painting your image, stop and choose Edit⇨Undo. If that doesn't work, try one of the reversion techniques described in the "Selectively Undoing Changes" section of Chapter 11. As long as a previous version of the image is saved on disk, you have a way out.

Meet your tools

Photoshop provides three paint tools: the pencil, paintbrush, and airbrush. You also get six edit tools: smudge, blur, sharpen, burn, dodge, and sponge. Figure 7-1 shows all these tools. The keyboard equivalent for each tool appears in parentheses.

Chapter 7: Painting and Editing 217

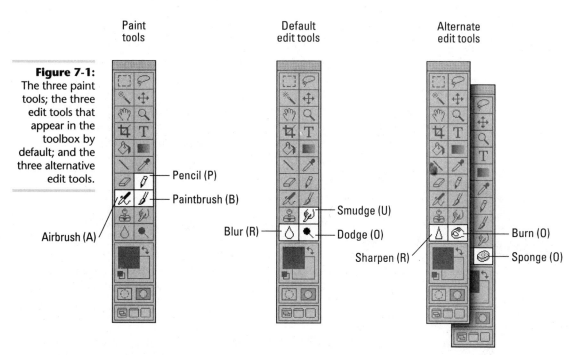

Paint tools | Default edit tools | Alternate edit tools

Figure 7-1: The three paint tools; the three edit tools that appear in the toolbox by default; and the three alternative edit tools.

Pencil (P)
Paintbrush (B)
Airbrush (A)
Smudge (U)
Blur (R)
Dodge (O)
Sharpen (R)
Burn (O)
Sponge (O)

In case you're wondering about all the other tools, Figure 7-2 segregates tools by category and lists the chapter in which you can find more information.

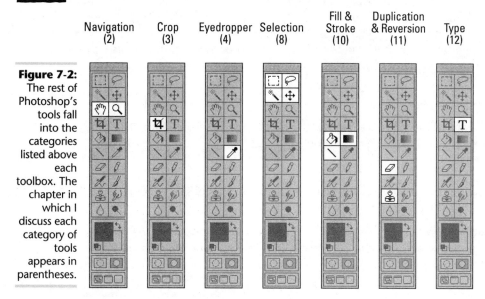

Navigation (2) | Crop (3) | Eyedropper (4) | Selection (8) | Fill & Stroke (10) | Duplication & Reversion (11) | Type (12)

Figure 7-2: The rest of Photoshop's tools fall into the categories listed above each toolbox. The chapter in which I discuss each category of tools appears in parentheses.

The paint tools

The paint tools apply paint in the foreground color. In this and other respects, they work like their counterparts in other painting programs, but there are a few exceptions:

- **Pencil:** The pencil has been a Macintosh standard since the first version of MacPaint. Unlike pencil tools found in most other painting programs — which paint lines one pixel thick — Photoshop's pencil paints a hard-edged line of any thickness. Figure 7-3 compares the default single-pixel pencil line with a fatter pencil line, a paintbrush line, and an airbrush line.

- **Paintbrush:** The paintbrush works just like the pencil tool, except that it paints an antialiased line that blends in with its background.

   In Photoshop 3.0, the paintbrush offers a Wet Edges option. (Double-click on the paintbrush tool icon in the toolbox and you'll see the Wet Edges check box in the bottom left corner of the Paintbrush Options panel of the Brushes palette.) When this option is turned on, the paintbrush creates a translucent line with darkened edges, much as if you were painting with watercolors. Soft brush shapes produce more naturalistic effects. An example of this effect is shown in Figure 7-3.

- **Airbrush:** It's tempting to describe Photoshop's airbrush tool as a softer version of the paintbrush, because it uses a softer brush shape by default. Photoshop's default settings also call for a lighter pressure, so the airbrush paints a semitranslucent line. But if you set the airbrush to the same brush shape and pressure as the paintbrush, you will notice only one distinction. The paintbrush stops applying paint when you stop dragging, but the airbrush continues to apply paint as long as you press the mouse button or stylus. Figure 7-3 shows the dark glob of paint that results from pressing the mouse button while holding the mouse motionless at the end of the drag.

The edit tools

The edit tools don't apply color; rather, they influence existing colors in an image. Figure 7-4 shows each of the five edit tools applied to a randomized background. The tools work as follows:

- **Smudge:** The smudge tool smears colors in an image. The effect is much like dragging your finger across wet paint.

- **Blur:** The first of the two focus tools — as they are now known in Photoshop 3.0 — the blur tool blurs an image by lessening the amount of color contrast between neighboring pixels.

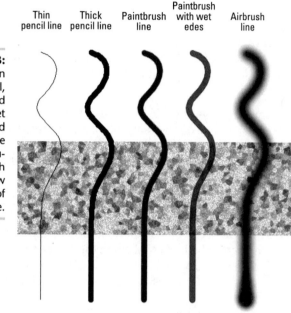

Thin pencil line Thick pencil line Paintbrush line Paintbrush with wet edes Airbrush line

Figure 7-3:
Five lines painted in black with the pencil, paintbrush, and airbrush tools. The Wet Edges option (2nd from right) causes the line to appear translucent. I held the airbrush tool in place for a few moments at the end of the rightmost line.

✑ **Sharpen:** The second focus tool selectively sharpens by increasing the contrast between neighboring pixels. Generally speaking, I find both the blur and sharpen tools to be less useful than their command counterparts in the Filters menu. They provide less control and usually require scrubbing at an image. Maybe I've been using a computer too long, but my wrist starts to ache when I use these tools. If, unlike me, you like the basic principle behind the tools but you want to avoid Carpel Tunnel Syndrome, you can achieve consistent, predictable results without scrubbing by using the tools in combination with the Shift key, as described in the next section.

✑ **Dodge:** The first of three toning tools, the dodge tool lets you lighten a portion of an image by dragging across it. Named after a traditional film exposure technique, the dodge tool is supposed to look like a little paddle thingie — you know, like one of those spoons you put over your eye at the optometrist's — that you wave over an image to diffuse the amount of light that gets to the film and therefore lighten the print. Thank golly we no longer have to wave little paddle thingies in our modern age.

➺ **Burn:** The second toning tool, the burn tool, enables you to darken a portion of an image by dragging over it. The effect is similar to burning a film negative, which you apparently do by holding your hand in a kind of O shape in an effort to focus the light, kind of like frying a worker ant using a magnifying glass (except not quite so smelly). At least, that's what they tell me. Sadly, I've never had the pleasure of trying it out.

➺ **Sponge:** The last toning tool — and one of only two tools added to Photoshop 3.0 — the sponge tool robs an image of both saturation and contrast. Alternately, you can set the tool so that it boosts saturation and adds contrast. For information about the newest of Photoshop's editing tools, stay tuned for the upcoming section "Mopping up with the sponge tool."

To temporarily access the sharpen tool when the blur tool is selected, press and hold the Option key while using the tool. The sharpen tool remains available only as long as you press the Option key. You also can press Option to access the blur tool when the sharpen tool is selected; to access the burn tool when the dodge tool is selected; and to access the dodge tool when the burn tool is selected. (If the sponge tool is active, pressing the Option key has no effect, except maybe to give your finger a cramp.)

Smudge   Blur   Sharpen   Dodge   Burn   Sponge

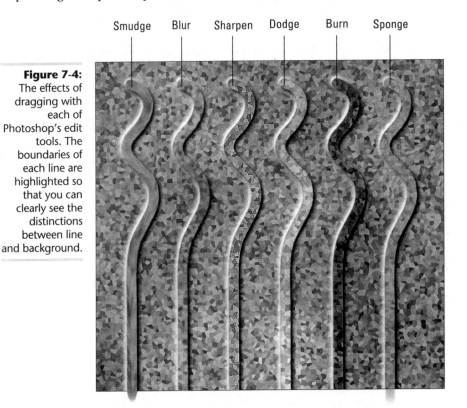

Figure 7-4: The effects of dragging with each of Photoshop's edit tools. The boundaries of each line are highlighted so that you can clearly see the distinctions between line and background.

In Photoshop, you can replace the blur tool with the sharpen tool in the toolbox by Option-clicking on the tool's icon. To *toggle* (switch) back to the blur tool, Option-click on the sharpen icon. Likewise, you can Option-click on the dodge tool icon to toggle between the dodge, burn, and sponge tools.

As explained in Chapter 2, the keyboard equivalents also toggle between the tools. When the blur tool is selected, press R to toggle to the sharpen tool. Another tap of the R key takes you back to blur. When the dodge tool is selected, press O to toggle to the burn tool, then press O again to get the sponge. Press O one more time to take the trail herd back to dodge. (What dodge tool discussion would be complete without at least one "Gunsmoke" joke?)

 To modify the performance of a tool, double-click on its icon in the toolbox to display the customized Options panel in the Brushes palette. Alternatively, you can simply press the Return key while the tool is selected. All the options inside the various Options panels are discussed throughout the remainder of this chapter.

Basic techniques

I know several people who claim that they can't paint, and yet they create beautiful work in Photoshop. Even though they don't have sufficient hand-eye coordination to write their names on-screen, they have unique and powerful artistic sensibilities and they know lots of tricks that enable them to make judicious use of the paint and edit tools. I can't help you in the sensibilities department, but I can show you a few tricks that will boost your ability and inclination to use the paint and edit tools.

Drawing a straight line

You're probably already aware that you can draw a straight line with the line tool. If not, try it out. The line tool is that diagonal line on the left side of the toolbox. After selecting the tool, drag with it inside the image window to create a line. Pretty hot stuff, huh? Well, no, it's actually pretty dull. (Attention, dull guy — check it out.) In fact, the only reason I ever use this tool is to draw arrows like those shown in the upcoming Figure 7-6. If you don't want to draw an arrow, you're better off using Photoshop's other means for drawing straight lines: the Shift key.

 To access options that enable you to add an arrowhead to a line drawn with the line tool, double-click on the line tool icon in the toolbox to display the Line Tool Options panel in the Brushes palette. These options are explained in the "Applying Strokes and Arrowheads" section of Chapter 10.

To draw a straight line with any of the paint or edit tools, click on one point in the image and then press Shift and click on another point. Using the current tool, Photoshop draws a straight line between the two points.

To create free-form polygons, continue to Shift-click with the tool. I drew the left image in Figure 7-5 by Shift-clicking with the airbrush tool. Just to firm things up a bit, I applied the Unsharp Mark filter with a Radius of 8 pixels (as described in great detail in the "Using the Unsharp Mask Filter" section of Chapter 13). The result is shown in the right example. I think it's supposed to be a cross between George Washington and Popeye. But it's hard to say; I only drew the thing.

Figure 7-5:
I traced this image over a lightened scan of Mount Rushmore by clicking and Shift-clicking with the airbrush tool (left). I then sharpened the image using Filter➪ Sharpen➪ Unsharp Mask.

The Shift key makes the blur and sharpen tools halfway useful. Suppose that you want to edit the perimeter of the car shown in Figure 7-6. The arrows in the figure illustrate the path your Shift-clicks should follow. Figure 7-7 shows the effect of Shift-clicking with the blur tool; Figure 7-8 demonstrates the effect of Shift-clicking with the sharpen tool.

Figure 7-6:
It takes one click and 24 Shift-clicks to soften or accentuate the edges around this car using the blur or sharpen tool.

Figure 7-7:
The results of blurring the car's perimeter with the pressure set to 50 percent (top) and 100 percent (bottom). You set the pressure using the slider bar in the Focus Tools Options panel of the Brushes palette.

Figure 7-8:
The results of sharpening the car with the pressure set to 50 percent (top) and 100 percent (bottom).

Drawing a perpendicular line

To draw a perpendicular line — that is, one that is either vertical or horizontal — with any of the paint or edit tools, press and hold the mouse button, press the Shift key, and begin dragging in a vertical or horizontal direction. Don't release the Shift key until you finish dragging or until you want to change the direction of the line, as demonstrated in Figure 7-9. Notice that pressing the Shift key in mid-drag snaps the line back into perpendicular alignment.

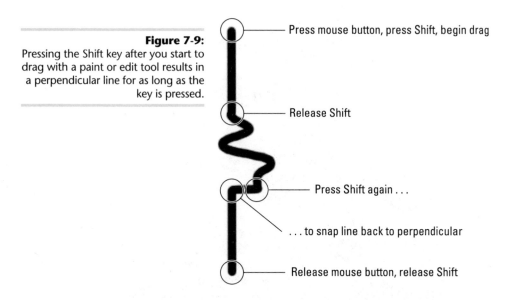

Figure 7-9:
Pressing the Shift key after you start to drag with a paint or edit tool results in a perpendicular line for as long as the key is pressed.

Press mouse button, press Shift, begin drag

Release Shift

Press Shift again . . .

. . . to snap line back to perpendicular

Release mouse button, release Shift

One way to exploit the Shift key's penchant to snap to the perpendicular is to draw "ribbed" structures. Being left-handed, I dragged from right to left with the paintbrush to create both of the central outlines around the skeleton that appears at the top of Figure 7-10. I painted each rib by pressing and releasing the Shift key as I dragged with the paintbrush tool. Pressing Shift snapped the line to the horizontal axis, whose location was established by the beginning of the drag.

In the figure, I represented the axis for each line in gray. After establishing the basic skeletal form, I added some free-form details with the paintbrush and pencil tools, as shown in the middle image in Figure 7-10. I then applied the Emboss filter to create the finished fossil image. Nobody's going to confuse my painting with a bona fide fossil — "Hey Marge, look what I done tripped over in the back forty!" — but it's not half bad for a cartoon.

 It's no accident that Figure 7-10 features a swordfish instead of your everyday round-nosed carp. In order to snap to the horizontal axis, I had to establish the direction of my drag as being more horizontal than vertical. If I had instead dragged in a fish-faced convex arc, Photoshop would have interpreted my drag as vertical and snapped to the vertical axis.

Figure 7-10:
To create the basic structure for our bony pal, I periodically pressed and released the Shift key while dragging with the paintbrush tool (top). Then I embellished the fish using the paintbrush and pencil tools (middle). Finally, I selected a general area around the image and chose Filter⇨Stylize⇨ Emboss to transform fish into fossil (bottom).

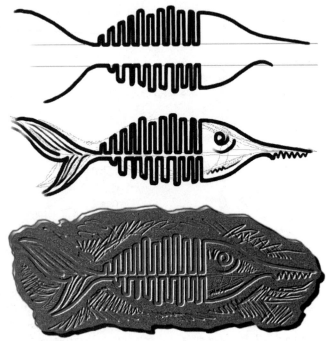

Painting with the smudge tool

Lots of first-time Photoshop artists misuse the smudge tool to soften color transitions. In fact, softening is the purpose of the blur tool. The smudge tool *smears* colors by shoving them into each other. The process bears more resemblance to the finger painting you did in grade school than to any traditional photographic editing technique.

In Photoshop, the performance of the smudge tool depends in part on the settings of the Pressure and Finger Painting options. Both reside in the Smudge Tool Options of the Brushes palette (see Figure 7-11), which you access by double-clicking on the smudge tool icon in the toolbox. These two options work as follows:

- **Pressure:** Measured as a percentage of the brush shape, this option determines the distance that the smudge tool drags a color. Higher percentages and larger brush shapes drag colors farthest. A Pressure setting of 100 percent equates to infinity, meaning that the smudge tool drags a color from the beginning of your drag until the end of your drag, regardless of how far you drag. Cosmic, Daddy-O.

Figure 7-11:
Combined with brush shape, the Pressure and Finger Painting options are the most important considerations when using the smudge tool.

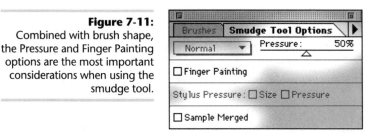

⤳ **Finger Painting:** The folks at Adobe used to call this effect *dipping,* which I think more accurately expressed how the effect works. When you select this option, the smudge tool begins by applying a smidgen of foreground color, which it eventually blends in with the colors in the image. It's as if you dipped your finger in a color and then dragged it through an oil painting. Use the Pressure setting to specify the amount of foreground color applied. If you turn on Finger Painting and set the Pressure to 100 percent, the smudge tool behaves exactly like the paintbrush tool.

For some examples of the smudge tool in action, take a look at Figure 7-12. The figure shows the effects of using the smudge tool set to four different Pressure percentages and with the Finger Painting option both off and on. In each instance, the brush shape is 13 pixels in diameter and the foreground color is set to black.

Figure 7-12:
Eight drags with the smudge tool subject to different Pressure and Finger Painting settings.

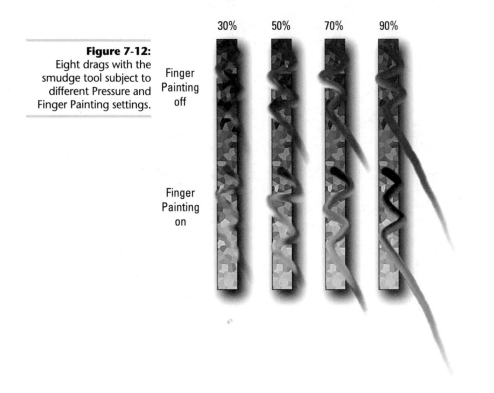

In Version 2.5, you reverse the Finger Painting setting by Option-dragging. If the option is off, Option-dragging dips the tool into the foreground color. If Finger Painting is turned on, Option-dragging smudges normally.

The third option highlighted in Figure 7-11 — Sample Merged — is new to Photoshop 3.0. (You'll also find this option inside the Focus Tools Options panel, which controls the operation of the blur and sharpen tools.) This option allows the smudge tool to grab colors from the background layers and smudge them into the current layer. Whether the option is on or off, only the current layer is affected; the background layers remain intact. For example, suppose that the inverted eyes of the woman at the top of Figure 7-13 are on a different layer than the rest of the face. If I use the smudge tools on the eyes layer with Sample Merged turned off, Photoshop ignores the face layer when smudging the eyes. As a result, details like the nose and teeth remain unsmudged, as you can see in the lower left example. If I turn Sample Merged on, Photoshop lifts colors from the face layer and mixes them in with the eyes layer, as shown in the lower right example.

Figure 7-13:
The original image (top) features inverted eyes on a layer above the rest of the face. I first smudged the eyes with Sample Merged turned off (lower left) and then with the option turned on (lower right).

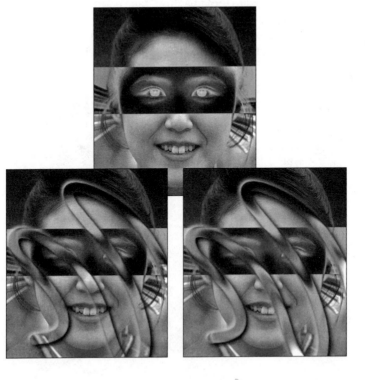

Note that all of this activity occurs exclusively on the eyes layer. Just to give you a better look, the two lower examples on the eyes layer are shown independently of those on the face layer in Figure 7-14. You can now clearly see the proliferation of face details mixed into the eyes in the right example. Meanwhile, the face layer remains absolutely unaffected.

Figure 7-14:
The eyes layer from the previous figure shown by itself.

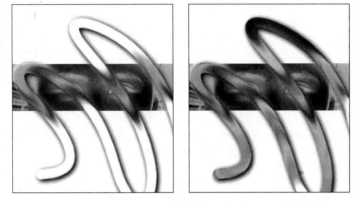

Incidentally, in case you're wondering where the heck the option name *Sample Merged* comes from, Photoshop is saying that it will *sample* — that is, lift colors — as if all layers are merged into one. For more information about setting up and merging layers, read Chapter 17.

Mopping up with the sponge tool

The sponge tool is actually a pretty darn straightforward tool, hardly worth expending valuable space in a book as tiny as this one. In fact, if it wasn't so brand spankin' new, I'd probably breeze right past it. But here's the deal: Double-click on the sponge tool icon in the toolbox to gain access to the Toning Tool Options panel. In the upper left corner of the panel is a pop-up menu that offers two options, Desaturate and Saturate. When set to the former, as by default, the tool reduces the saturation of the colors over which you drag. When editing a grayscale image, the tool reduces the contrast. If you select the Saturate option, the sponge tool increases the saturation of the colors over which you drag or increases contrast in a grayscale image. Higher Pressure settings produce more dramatic results.

Consider Color Plate 7-1. The upper left example shows the original PhotoDisc image. The upper right example shows the result of applying the sponge tool set to Desaturate. I dragged with the tool inside the pepper and around in the corner area. The Pressure was set to 100 percent. Notice that the affected colors are on the wane, sliding toward gray. In the lower right example, the effect is even more pronounced. Here I applied the sponge tools with great vim and vigor two additional times. There's hardly any hint of color left in these areas now.

To create the lower left example in Color Plate 7-1, I applied the sponge tool set to Saturate. This is where things get a little tricky. If you boost saturation levels with the sponge tool in the RGB or Lab color modes, you can achieve colors of absolutely neon intensity. However, these high-saturation colors don't stand a snowball's chance in a microwave of printing in CMYK. Therefore, I recommend that you choose Mode⇨CMYK Preview before boosting saturation levels with the sponge tool. This way, you can accurately view the results of your edits. After you're finished, choose Mode⇨CMYK Preview to turn off the CMYK preview and return to the RGB view.

Figure 7-15 shows the yellow channel from Color Plate 7-1. Because yellow is the most prevalent primary color in the image, it is the most sensitive to saturation adjustments. When I boosted the saturation in the lower left example, the yellow brightness values deepened, adding yellow ink to the CMYK image. When I lessened the saturation in the two right-hand examples, the amount of ink diminished.

Figure 7-15:
The yellow channel from Color Plate 7-1 shows the greatest amount of variation when the saturation is reduced or boosted with the sponge tool.

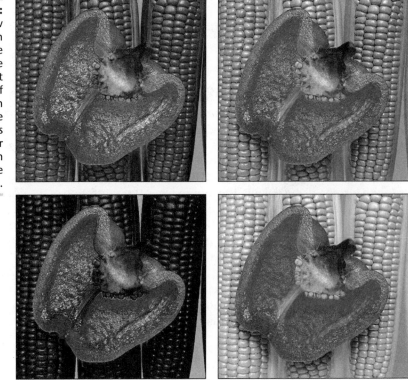

One of Adobe's recommended purposes of the sponge tool is to reduce the saturation levels of out-of-gamut RGB colors before converting an image to the CMYK mode. I'm not too crazy about this use of the tool for the simple reason that it requires a lot of scrubbing. It's generally easier to select the out-of-gamut area and reduce the colors using more automated controls (as discussed in Chapter 16). Instead, you might prefer to use the sponge tool when a more selective, personal touch is required, as when curbing a distracting color that seems to be leaping a little too vigorously off the screen or boosting the saturation of a detail in the CMYK mode.

Brush Shape and Opacity

So far, I mentioned the words *brush shape* seven times and I have yet to explain what the Sam Hill I'm talking about. Luckily, it's very simple. The *brush shape* is the size and shape of the tip of your cursor when you use a paint or edit tool. A big, round brush shape paints or edits in broad strokes. A small, elliptical brush shape is useful for performing hairline adjustments.

 In Photoshop 3.0, brush size is finally treated with the respect it deserves. You now have the option of displaying a cursor whose outline reflects the selected brush shape. To access this incredibly useful cursor, press Command-K to bring up the General Preferences dialog box and then select Brush Size from the Tool Cursors radio buttons. Photoshop then displays the actual size of the brush you're using, up to 300 pixels in diameter. If the brush is bigger — no doubt there's someone out there with some reason for wielding a gigantic 600-pixel brush, though I can't imagine what that reason might be — the standard tool cursor appears instead.

When using very small brushes, as when using the single-pixel pencil to do very precise retouching, the cursor includes four dots around its perimeter, making the cursor easier to locate. If you need a little more help, press the Caps Lock key to access the more obvious crosshair cursor.

The Brushes palette

You access brush shapes by choosing Window⇨Palettes⇨Show Brushes to display the Brushes palette. (Alternatively, you can double-click on one of the painting or editing tools to display the Options panel of the Brushes palette and then click on the Brushes tab to display the brush shapes themselves. I know this doesn't sound any easier, but I hate negotiating submenus.) Figure 7-16 shows the Brushes palette with pop-up menu wide open for your viewing pleasure.

Figure 7-16:
Photoshop 3.0's Brushes
palette is much like the
Brushes palette of its
predecessor.

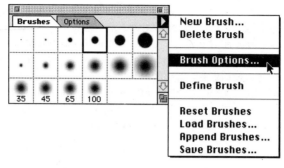

Figure 7-16:
Photoshop 3.0's Brushes
palette is much like the
Brushes palette of its
predecessor.

 You can switch brush shapes from the keyboard without displaying the
brushes palette. Press the left-bracket key to select the previous brush shape in
the palette; press the right-bracket key to select the next brush shape. You can
also press shift-left bracket to select the first brush shape in the palette and
shift-right bracket to select the last shape.

Editing a brush shape

To edit a brush shape in the Brushes palette, select the brush you want to change and
choose Brush Options from the palette menu (as in Figure 7-16). To create a new brush
shape, choose New Brush. Either way, the dialog box shown in Figure 7-17 appears. (If
you choose the New Brush command, the title bar is different but the options are the
same.)

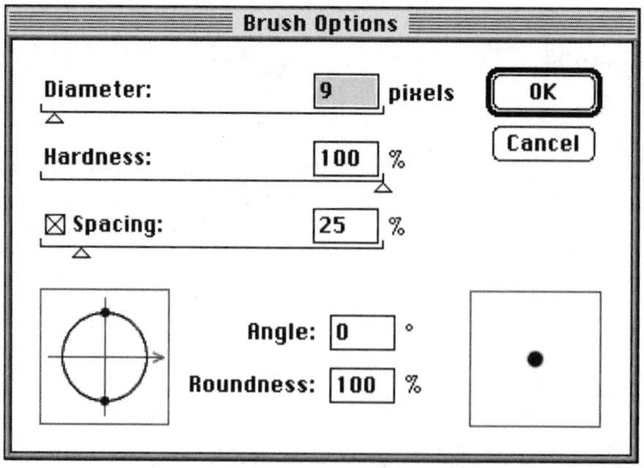

Figure 7-17:
The Brush Options
dialog box lets you
change the size,
shape, and hardness of
the brush shape.

If you hate menus — and who doesn't? — you can more conveniently edit a brush shape by simply double-clicking on it. To create a new brush shape, click once on an empty brush slot, as shown in the first example in Figure 7-18. (Incidentally, you can also delete a brush from the palette. To do so, press the Command key to display the scissors cursor — as in the second example in Figure 7-18 — then click. It's a great little housekeeping tip.)

Figure 7-18:
Clicking on an empty brush slot (left) brings up the New Brush dialog box so that you can create a new brush shape. Command-clicking on a brush shape (right) deletes it from the palette.

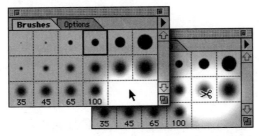

Whether you're editing an existing brush or creating a new one, you have the following options at your disposal:

- **Diameter:** This option determines the width of the brush shape. If the brush shape is elliptical instead of circular, the Diameter value determines the longest dimension. You can enter any value from 1 to 999 pixels. Brush shapes with diameters of 30 pixels or higher are too large to display accurately in the Brushes palette and instead appear as circles with inset Diameter values.

- **Hardness:** Except when you use the pencil tool, brush shapes are always antialiased. However, you can further soften the edges of a brush by dragging the Hardness slider bar away from 100 percent. The softest setting, 0 percent, gradually tapers the brush from a single solid color pixel at its center to a ring of transparent pixels around the brush's perimeter. Figure 7-19 demonstrates how low Hardness percentages expand the size of a 100-pixel brush beyond the Diameter value (as demonstrated by the examples set against black). Even a 100 percent hard brush shape expands slightly because it is antialiased. The Hardness setting is ignored when you use the pencil tool.

Figure 7-19:
A 100-pixel diameter brush shown as it appears when set to a variety of Hardness percentages. Below, I changed the background pixels from white to black so that you can see the actual diameter of each brush shape. The tick marks indicate 10-pixel increments.

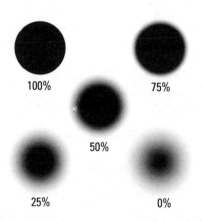

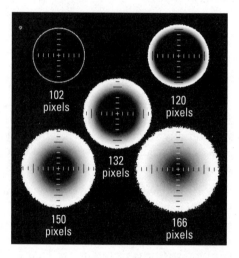

⤿ **Spacing:** The Spacing option controls how frequently a tool affects an image as you drag, measured as a percentage of the brush shape. Suppose that the Diameter of a brush shape is 12 pixels and the Spacing is set to 25 percent (the setting for all default brush shapes). For every 3 pixels (25 percent of 12 pixels) you drag with the paintbrush tool, Photoshop lays down a 12-pixel wide spot of color. A Spacing of 1 percent provides the most coverage, but may also slow down the performance of the tool. If you deselect the Spacing check box, the effect of the tool is wholly dependent on the speed at which you drag, which can be useful for creating nonuniform or splotchy lines. Figure 7-20 shows examples.

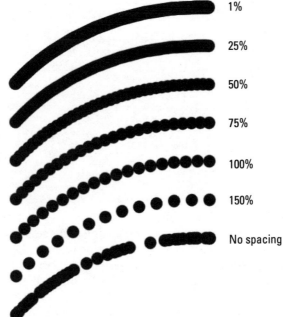

Figure 7-20:
Examples of lines drawn with different Spacing values in the Brush Options dialog box. Gaps or ridges generally begin to appear when the Spacing value exceeds 30 percent. The final line was created by turning off the Spacing option.

1%

25%

50%

75%

100%

150%

No spacing

- **Angle:** This option enables you to pivot a brush shape on its axes. However, it won't make a difference in the appearance of the brush shape unless the brush is elliptical.

- **Roundness:** Enter a value of less than 100 percent into the Roundness option to create an elliptical brush shape. The value measures the width of the brush as a percentage of its height, so a Roundness value of 5 percent results in a long, skinny brush shape.

 You can adjust the angle of the brush dynamically by dragging the gray arrow inside the box to the left of the Angle and Roundness options. Drag the handles on either side of the black circle to make the brush shape elliptical, as demonstrated in Figure 7-21.

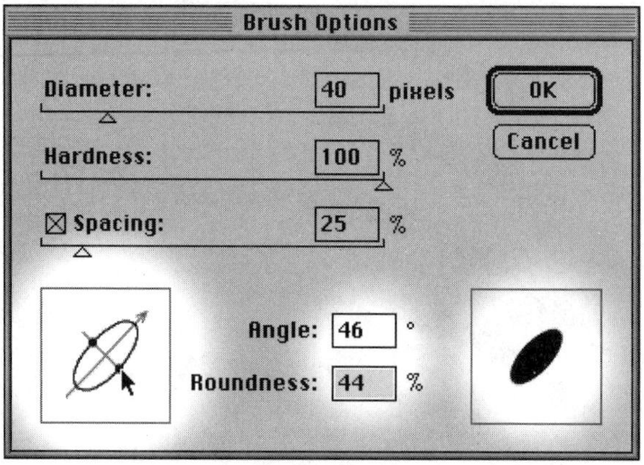

Figure 7-21:
Drag the gray arrow or the black handles to change the angle or roundness of a brush, respectively. The Angle and Roundness values update automatically, as does the preview of the brush in the lower right corner of the dialog box.

I heartily recommend that you take a few moments one of these days to experiment at length with the Brush Options dialog box. By combining paint and edit tools with one or more specialized brush shapes, you can achieve artistic effects unlike anything permitted via traditional techniques. Starting with a PhotoDisc image lightened and filtered to serve as a template, I painted Figure 7-22 using the flat, 45-pixel brush shape shown in the dialog box. (For a color version of the effect, take a look at Color Plate 7-2.) No other brush shape or special effect was applied. Think of what you can accomplish if you don't limit yourself as ridiculously as I did.

Creating and using custom brushes

You can define a custom brush shape by selecting a portion of your image that you want to change to a brush and choosing the Define Brush command from the Brushes palette pop-up menu. You can even draw your brush in the Scratch panel of the Picker palette, select the brush, and choose Define Brush to capture it.

In addition to giving you the flexibility to create a brush out of some element in your image, Photoshop ships with a file called Assorted Brushes that contains all kinds of little symbols and doodads you can assign as custom brush shapes. You can load the contents of the Assorted Brushes file into the Brushes palette by choosing the Load Brushes command from the palette menu (or Append Brushes if you don't want to lose the brush shapes that currently occupy the palette). You'll find Assorted Brushes inside the Brushes and Patterns folder, which resides in the same folder as the Photoshop application. Figure 7-23 shows an inspirational image I created using Photoshop's predefined custom brushes.

Figure 7-22:
Just to show off, I painted over a scanned image with the paintbrush tool, using the brush shape shown in the dialog box at top.

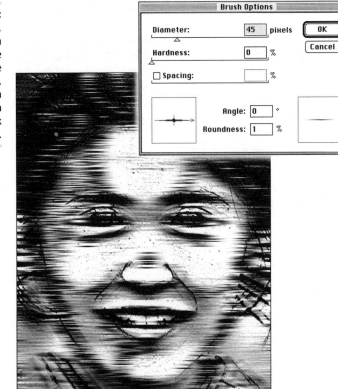

Figure 7-23:
Yes, it's Boris, the sleeping custom-brush guy. If you suspect that this image is meant to suggest that custom brushes are more amusing than utilitarian, you're right. The brushes from the Assorted Brushes file appear on the right.

In Photoshop, you can adjust the performance of a custom brush in the following ways:

☞ **Brush options:** Choose the Brush Options command from the palette menu or double-click on the custom brush in the Brushes palette to bring up the dialog box shown in Figure 7-24. Here you can adjust the spacing of the brush shape and specify whether Photoshop antialiases (softens) the edges or leaves them as is. If the brush is sufficiently large, the Anti-aliased check box appears dimmed. All custom brushes are hard-edged when you use the pencil tool.

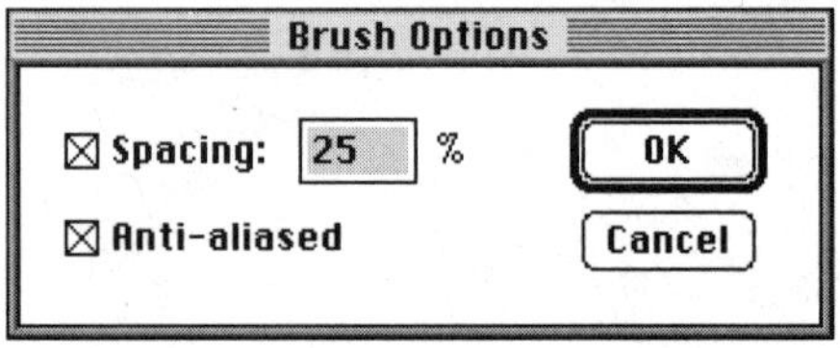

Figure 7-24:
The dialog box that appears when you double-click on a custom brush.

Brush Options

☒ Spacing: [25] %   [OK]

☒ Anti-aliased   [Cancel]

☞ **Brush color:** The foreground color affects a custom brush just as it does a standard brush shape. To erase with the brush, select white as the foreground color. To paint in color, select a color.

☞ **Opacity and brush modes:** The setting of the Opacity slider bar and the brush modes pop-up menu also affect the application of custom brushes. For more information on these options, keep reading this chapter.

You can achieve some unusual and sometimes interesting effects by activating the smudge tool's Finger Painting option and painting in the image window with a custom brush. At high Pressure settings, say 80 to 90 percent, the effect is rather like applying oil paint with a hairy paintbrush, as illustrated in Figure 7-25.

Figure 7-25:
I created this organic, expressive image by combining the smudge tool's dipping capability with four custom brushes. I don't know what those finger-like growths are, but they'd probably feel right at home in an aquarium.

To restore the factory-default brush shapes, choose Reset Brushes from the Brushes palette menu. It's a lot easier than searching around for the Default Brushes file as you had to do in the old days.

Opacity, pressure, and exposure

The brush shapes in the Brushes palette affect two tools other than the paint and edit tools, these being the eraser and the rubber stamp, both discussed in Chapter 11, "Duplicating and Reverting." But the slider bar in the upper right corner of the Options panel of the Brushes palette additionally affects the paint bucket, gradient, and line tools. Photoshop assigns one of three labels to this slider bar, illustrated in Figure 7-26.

⊸ **Opacity:** The Opacity slider bar determines the translucency of colors applied with the paint bucket, gradient, line, pencil, paintbrush, eraser, or rubber stamp tool. At 100 percent, the applied colors appear opaque, completely covering the image behind them. (The one exception is the paintbrush with Wet Edges active, which is always translucent.) At lower settings, the applied colors mix with the existing colors in the image.

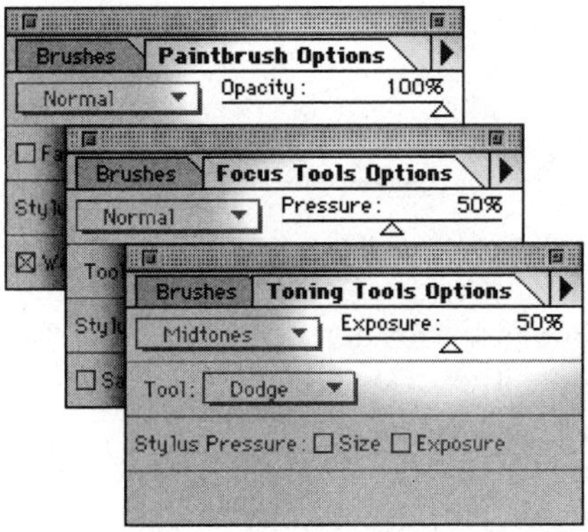

Figure 7-26:
The slider bar in the upper right corner of the Brushes palette assumes one of these functions, depending on the selected tool. The slider disappears altogether when you select one of the navigation tools, one of the selection tools, the crop tool, or the eyedropper.

⊸ **Pressure:** The Pressure slider bar affects different tools in different ways. When you use the airbrush tool, the slider bar controls the opacity of each spot of color the tool delivers. (In this case, the slider bar really ought to be labeled *Opacity*, because your settings produce the same results as the Opacity settings for the pencil or paintbrush tools. The effect appears unique because the airbrush spews out more color than the pencil or paintbrush. I guess the folks at Adobe don't agree with me, however, because they've left the option labeled *Pressure* in Version 3.0.)

When you use the smudge tool, the slider bar controls the distance that the tool drags colors in the image. And in the case of the blur, sharpen, or sponge tool, the slider bar determines the degree to which the tool changes the focus or saturation of the image, 1 percent being the minimum and 100 percent being the maximum.

⌐ **Exposure:** If you select the dodge or burn tool, the slider bar title changes to *Exposure.* A setting of 100 percent applies the maximum amount of lightening or darkening to an image, which is still far short of either absolute white or black.

The factory default setting for all Exposure and Pressure slider bars is 50 percent; the default setting for all Opacity sliders is 100 percent.

 As long as one of the tools listed in this section is selected, you can change the Opacity, Pressure, or Exposure setting in 10 percent increments by pressing a number key on the keyboard or keypad. Press 1 to change the setting to 10 percent, press 2 for 20 percent, and so on, all the way up to 0 for 100 percent. This tip works whether or not the Options panel of the Brushes palette is visible. Believe me, this is one of the best and most easily overlooked Photoshop tips ever. Get in the habit of using the number keys and you'll thank yourself later.

Tapered Lines

Photoshop provides two ways to create tapering lines that are reminiscent of brush strokes created using traditional techniques. You can specify the length over which a line fades by entering a value into the Fade option box, as described in the next section. Or, if you own a pressure-sensitive drawing tablet, you can draw brush strokes that fade in and out automatically according to the amount of pressure you apply to the stylus. Both techniques enable you to introduce an element of spontaneity into what otherwise seems at times like an absolute world of computer graphics.

Fading the paint

All three paint tools offer Fade check boxes in their respective Options panels that enable you to create lines that gradually fade away as you drag. Figure 7-27 shows the Fade option as it appears in the Paintbrush Options panel, along with some examples of the effect.

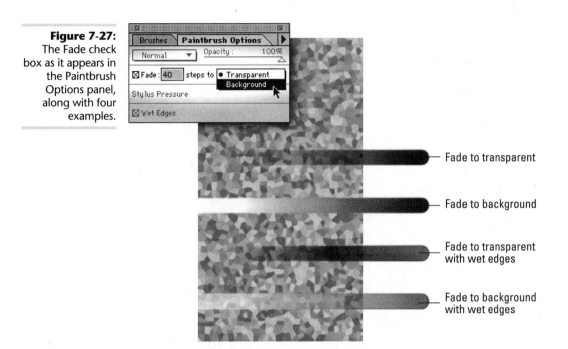

Figure 7-27:
The Fade check
box as it appears in
the Paintbrush
Options panel,
along with four
examples.

— Fade to transparent

— Fade to background

Fade to transparent
with wet edges

Fade to background
with wet edges

After selecting the Fade check box, enter a value into the option box to specify the distance over which the color fading should occur. The fading begins at the start of your drag and is measured in brush shapes.

For example, assume that the foreground color is black. If you enter 40 into the Fade option box — as in Figure 7-27 — Photoshop paints 40 brush shapes, the first in black and the remaining 39 in increasingly lighter shades of gray.

 In Photoshop, you can paint gradient lines by selecting the To Background radio button. Photoshop fades the line from the foreground color to the background color, much the same way that the gradient tool fades the interior of a selection. For more information on the gradient tool, see the "Applying Gradient Fills" section of Chapter 10.

Fading and spacing

The physical length of a fading line is dependent both on the Fade value and on the value entered into the Spacing option box in the Brush Options dialog box, discussed back in the "Editing a brush shape" section earlier in this chapter.

To recap, the Spacing value determines the frequency with which Photoshop lays down brush shapes, and the Fade value determines the number of brush shapes laid down. Therefore, as demonstrated in Figure 7-28, a high Fade value combined with a high Spacing value creates the longest line.

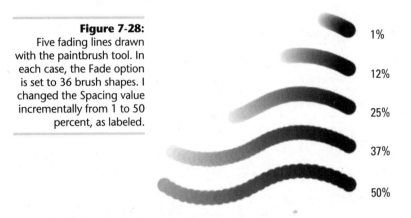

Figure 7-28:
Five fading lines drawn with the paintbrush tool. In each case, the Fade option is set to 36 brush shapes. I changed the Spacing value incrementally from 1 to 50 percent, as labeled.

1%

12%

25%

37%

50%

Creating sparkles and comets

Fading lines may strike you as pretty ho-hum, but they enable you to create some no-brainer, cool-mandoo effects, especially when combined with the Shift key techniques discussed earlier, in the "Drawing a straight line" section.

Figures 7-29 and 7-30 demonstrate two of the most obvious uses for fading straight lines: creating sparkles and comets. The top image in Figure 7-29 features two sets of sparkles, each made up of 16 straight lines emanating from the sparkle's center. To create the smaller sparkle on the right, I set the Fade value to 60 and drew each of the four perpendicular lines with the paintbrush tool. I changed the Fade value to 36 before drawing the four 45-degree diagonal lines. The eight very short lines that occur between the perpendicular and diagonal lines were drawn with a Fade value of 20. I likewise created the larger sparkle on the left by periodically adjusting the Fade value, this time from 90 to 60 to 42.

For comparison's sake, I used different techniques to add a few more sparkles to the bottom image in Figure 7-29. To achieve the reflection in the upper left corner of the image, I chose Filter⇨Stylize⇨Lens Flare and selected 50-300mm Zoom from the Lens Type options. I created the two tiny sparkles on the right edge of the bumper using a custom brush shape. I merely selected the custom brush, set the foreground color to white, and clicked once with the paintbrush tool in each location. So many sparkles make for a tremendously shiny image.

Figure 7-29:
I drew the sparkles in the top image using the paint-brush tool. The second image features a reflection applied with the Lens Flare filter (upper left corner) and two dabs of a custom brush shape (right edge of the bumper).

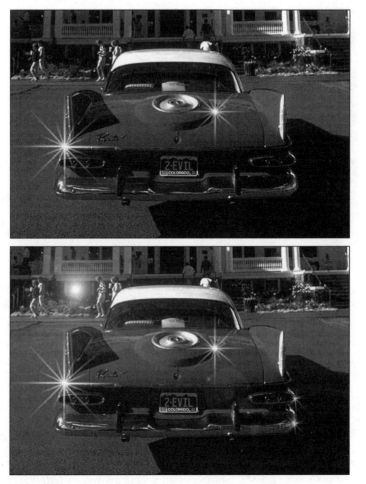

In Figure 7-30, I copied the car and pasted it on top of a NASA photograph of Jupiter. I then went nuts clicking and Shift-clicking with the paintbrush tool to create the comets — well, if you must know, they're actually cosmic rays — that you see shooting through and around the car.

After masking portions of the image (a process described at length in Chapter 9), I drew rays behind the car and even one ray that shoots up through the car and out the spare tire. The three bright lights in the image — above the left fin, above the roof, and next to the right turn signal — are more products of the Lens Flare filter.

Figure 7-30: Remember when gas was cheap and you all piled in the car to go for a drive in space? Unfortunately, you always had to worry about those cosmic rays. Luckily, they're a cinch to draw: Set the Fade option to 110 and then click and Shift-click on opposite sides of the image with the paintbrush tool.

I drew all the fading lines in Figures 7-29 and 7-30 with the paintbrush tool, using a variety of default brush shapes. Because I didn't edit any brush shape, the Spacing value for all lines was a constant 25 percent.

Lines created with pressure-sensitive tablets

The pressure-sensitive tablet has to be the single most useful piece of optional hardware available to computer artists. Not only can you draw with a pen-like *stylus* instead of a clunky mouse, you also can dynamically adjust the thickness of lines and the opacity of colors by changing the amount of pressure you apply to the stylus. As I write this, three vendors — Wacom, CalComp, and Kurta — manufacture pressure-sensitive tablets.

Of these, my favorite is Wacom's $400 ArtZ, a 6 × 8-inch tablet that plugs into your Mac's ADB port (or Window's serial port), which is the same port that accommodates the keyboard and mouse. The tablet offers 120 levels of pressure and a transparent overlay to hold pages you want to trace. It also has a cordless stylus that weighs less than an ounce and features both a pressure-sensitive nib and a side switch for double-clicking and choosing macros.

If your desk space is as limited as mine — I see a flat surface and I immediately stack 3-foot-high piles of papers, disks, CDs, manuals, and sodas on top of it — consider the new Wacom ArtPad. Measuring a diminutive 4×5 inches, this thing is smaller than a standard mouse pad. Its price is a mere $200 retail. You may not be crazy about the fact that it's a serial tablet, which means that it has to fight over the serial port with your modem. But because my Power Mac 7100 includes only one ADB port, I actually prefer it. I'd rather have to live without my modem for a little while than my mouse. I only got the thing last week, and it's already gained a place of honor in my cluttered office.

If you're an artist and you've never experimented with these or any other pressure-sensitive tablet, I recommend that you do so at your earliest convenience. You'll be amazed at how much it increases your range of artistic options. Minutes after I installed my first tablet, I was able draw the cartoon shown in Figure 7-31 (and in Color Plate 7-3) from scratch on a 13-inch monitor in about 30 minutes. Whether you like the image or not — I'll admit there is a certain troglodyte quality to the cut of his forehead, and that jaw could bust a coconut — it shows off the tablet's ability to paint tapering lines and accommodate artistic expression.

Figure 7-31:
Though I painted this caricature years ago, it embodies the range of artistic freedom provided by a Wacom tablet.

How to undo pressure-sensitive lines

Pressure-sensitive lines can be hard to undo. Because a Wacom or other stylus is so sensitive to gradual pressure, you can unwittingly let up and repress the stylus during what you think is a single drag. If, after doing so, you decide don't like the line and choose Edit⇨Undo, Photoshop deletes only the last portion of the line, because it detected a release midway through. As a result, you're stuck with half a line that you don't want or, worse, that visually mars your image.

Problems are even more likely to occur if you use a stylus with a side switch, such as the one included with Wacom's ArtZ or CalComp's DrawingPad. It's very easy to accidentally press your thumb or forefinger against the switch as you drag. If you have the switch set to some separate operation, such as double-clicking, you interrupt your line. This not only creates an obvious break but also makes the error impossible to undo.

To prepare for this eventuality — and believe me, it *will* happen — make sure to save your image at key points when you're content with its appearance. Then, if you find yourself stuck with half a line, you can remove the line by Option-dragging with the eraser tool, as discussed in the "Selectively Undoing Changes" section of Chapter 11.

Pressure-sensitive options

I'm happy to report that Photoshop 3.0 has gotten its act back together in the pressure-sensitivity department. Like its predecessor, it offers three options for interpreting pressure-sensitive input. But unlike Version 2.5, which was unable to properly taper lines (refer to page 255 of the previous edition of this book if you want the sordid details), Version 3.0 varies the thickness of a line every bit as well as Photoshop 2.0. Thanks, Adobe, for setting this one straight.

All paint and edit tools, as well as the eraser and rubber stamp, provide three check boxes for controlling Photoshop's reaction to stylus pressure (see Figure 7-32). Available from the Options panel only when a pressure-sensitive tablet is hooked up to your computer, these options include the following:

∞ **Size:** If you select the Size check box, Photoshop varies the thickness of the line. The more pressure you apply, the thicker the line. The Size check box is selected by default. Figure 7-33 shows three paintbrush lines drawn with the Size option selected. I drew the first line using a hard brush, the second with a soft brush, and the third with a hard brush and with the Wet Edges check box selected.

Figure 7-32:
Photoshop provides three check boxes for interpreting the signals from a pressure-sensitive tablet.

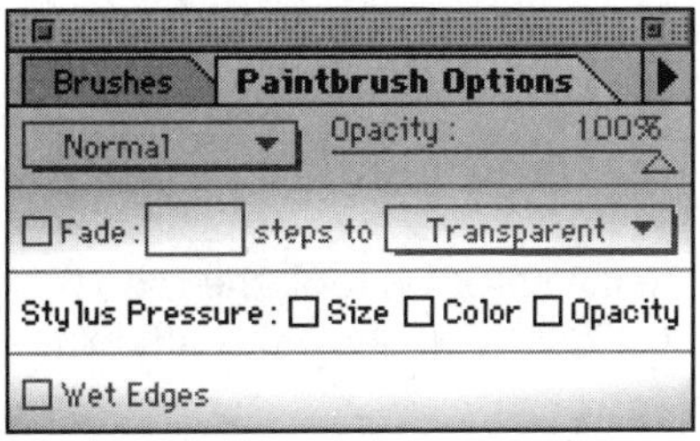

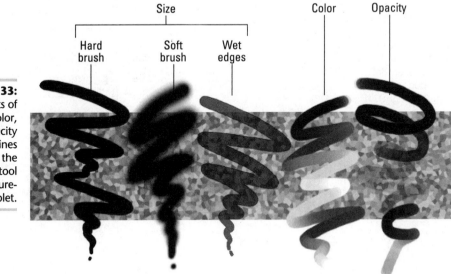

☞ **Color:** Select this option to create custom gradient lines. Full pressure paints in the foreground color; very slight pressure paints in the background color; medium pressure paints a mix of the two.

☞ **Opacity:** This option paints an opaque coat of foreground color at full pressure that dwindles to transparency at very slight pressure.

Because Photoshop presents its pressure options as check boxes, you can select more than one option at a time. For example, you can select both Size and Color to instruct Photoshop to change both the thickness and color of a line as you bear down or lift up on the stylus.

Figure 7-33:
The effects of the Size, Color, and Opacity options on lines drawn with the paintbrush tool and a pressure-sensitive tablet.

Brush Modes

The pop-up menu in the Options panel provides access to Photoshop's *brush modes*, which control how paint and edit tools affect existing colors in the image. Brush modes are not available when you use a navigation tool, the crop tool, the eyedropper, a selection tool, or the type tool. Figure 7-34 shows which brush modes are available when you select various tools.

 With the exception of the specialized brush modes provided for the dodge, burn, and sponge tools, brush modes and the overlay modes described in Chapter 17 are varieties of the same animal. Read this section to get a brief glimpse of brush modes; read Chapter 17 for a more detailed account that should appeal to brush-mode aficionados.

Figure 7-34:
The number of options in the brush modes pop-up menu varies depending on whether you select a paint tool (left), an edit tool (top right), the dodge or burn tool (middle right), or the sponge tool (bottom right).

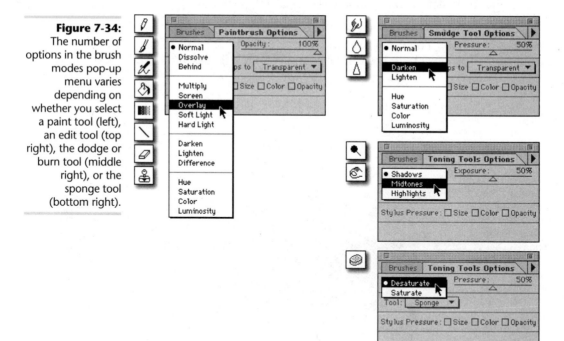

The 15 paint tool brush modes

Photoshop 3.0 provides a whopping 15 brush modes when you're using the pencil, paintbrush, airbrush, or any of the other tools shown on the left side of Figure 7-34. Just so that you can get an idea of what these various brush modes look like when applied to an image, Color Plate 7-4 shows each and every one of them. In each case, I painted a red stroke with the paintbrush tool. For maximum effect, I divided the underlying images into two halves. I simply washed out the colors in the right half, but in the left half, I shifted the colors toward blue-green, thus providing the maximum contrast to the red paint applied with the brush.

The 15 standard brush modes work as follows:

- ❧ **Normal:** Choose this mode to paint or edit an image normally. A paint tool coats the image with the foreground color and an edit tool manipulates the existing colors in an image according to the setting of the Opacity or Pressure slider bar.

- ❧ **Dissolve:** This mode and the six that follow are not applicable to the edit tools (though I wonder why — the Dissolve mode would be especially useful with the smudge tool). Dissolve scatters colors applied with a paint tool randomly throughout the course of your drag. The Dissolve mode produces the most pronounced effects when used with soft brushes and the airbrush tool.

- ❧ **Behind:** This one is applicable exclusively to layers with transparent backgrounds. When Behind is selected, the paint tool applies color behind the image on the layer, showing through only in the transparent and translucent areas. In Color Plate 7-4, for example, the brush stroke appears behind the image, but not in front of it. When you're working on an image without layers or on the background layer of a multilayered image, the Behind mode is dimmed.

- ❧ **Multiply:** The Multiply mode combines the foreground color with an existing color in an image to create a third color that is darker than the other two. Red times white is red, red times yellow is orange, red times green is brown, red times blue is violet, and so on. The effect is almost exactly like drawing with felt-tipped markers, except that the colors don't bleed. (This mode has no effect on the paintbrush when it's set to Wet Edges; the Wet Edges brush already multiplies.)

- **Screen:** The inverse of the Multiply mode, Screen combines the foreground color with an existing color in an image to create a third color that is lighter than the other two. Red times white is white, red times yellow is off-white, red times green is yellow, red times blue is pink, and so on. The effect is unlike any traditional painting technique; not even chalk lightens an image in this way. It's like some impossibly bright, radioactive Uranium-238 highlighter hitherto used only by G-Men to mark the pants cuffs of Communist sympathizers. (If the Wet Edges option always multiplies, combining it with the Screen mode must — you guessed it — render the brush invisible. If the paintbrush tool isn't working, this could be your problem.)

Overlay, Soft Light, and Hard Light are new to Photoshop 3.0. Because they are liable to give even seasoned Photoshop experts pause, I've created a separate full-color figure for these three modes (Color Plate 7-5). All three modes work by multiplying dark colors and screening light colors as you lay them down with a paint tool. The darkness and lightness of the existing colors in the image also enter the equation, but the ways in which these basic operations are applied and the manners in which the colors mix are unique. (In other words, you can't emulate the Soft Light mode by simply applying the Hard Light mode at 70 percent or some similar Opacity.)

- **Overlay:** Okay, here goes: Overlay is the kindest of the three new modes. It always enhances contrast and it always boosts the saturation of colors in an image. In fact, it works rather like a colored version of the sponge tool set to Saturate. But although it generously infuses an image with the foreground color, it is not the same as the Color brush mode (described shortly). Rather, it mixes the colors in the image with the foreground color to come up with a vivid blend that is almost always visually pleasing. This may be the most interesting and downright useful brush mode available in Photoshop 3.0.

- **Soft Light:** According to the Photoshop documentation, Soft Light casts a diffused spotlight on the image. It strikes me as more of a glazing. In fact, Soft Light is remarkably similar to applying a diluted wash of paint to a canvas. It never completely covers up the underlying detail — even black or white applied at 100 percent Opacity does no more than darken or lighten the image — but it does slightly diminish contrast.

- **Hard Light:** This mode might better be named *Obfuscate*. It's as if you were applying a thicker, more opaque wash to the image. Light colors screen the holy heck out of the image; dark colors multiply the image into obscurity. You might think of Hard Light as Normal with a whisper of underlying detail mixed in.

You want one more analogy? If Soft Light is like shining colored light onto the subject of the photograph, Hard Light is like shining the light directly onto the camera lens. (Of course, this analogy fails to account for dark colors — you can hardly make an image darker by casting light on it — but you get the idea.)

- **Darken:** Ah, back to the old familiars. If you choose the Darken mode, Photoshop applies a new color to a pixel only if that color is darker than the present color of the pixel. Otherwise, the pixel is left unchanged.

- **Lighten:** The opposite of the previous mode, Lighten ensures that Photoshop applies a new color to a pixel only if the color is lighter than the present color of the pixel. Otherwise, the pixel is left unchanged.

- **Difference:** While this operation is new to the brush modes, Photoshop has offered a Difference command since Version 1.0. When a paint tool is set to the Difference mode, Photoshop subtracts the brightness value of the foreground color from the brightness value of each affected pixel in the image — if the result is a negative number, Photoshop simply makes it positive — to create an inverted effect. Black has no effect on an image; white completely inverts it. Colors in between create psychedelic effects.

Because the Difference mode inverts an image, it results in an outline around the brush stroke. You can make this outline thicker by using a softer brush shape. For a really trippy effect, try combining the Difference mode with a soft brush shape and the paintbrush tool with Wet Edges turned on.

- **Hue:** Understanding the next few modes requires a color theory recap. Remember how the HSL color model calls for three color channels? One is for *hue,* the value that explains the colors in an image; the second is for *saturation,* which represents the intensity of the colors; and the third is for *luminosity,* which explains the lightness and darkness of colors. Therefore, if you choose the Hue brush mode, Photoshop applies the hue from the foreground color without changing any saturation or luminosity values in the existing image. This option has no effect when you work on a grayscale image.

- **Saturation:** If you choose this mode, Photoshop changes the intensity of the colors in an image without changing the colors themselves or the lightness and darkness of individual pixels. This option has no effect on a grayscale image.

- **Color:** This mode might be more appropriately titled *Hue and Saturation.* It enables you to change the colors in an image and the intensity of those colors without changing the lightness and darkness of individual pixels. This option has no effect on a grayscale image.

- **Luminosity:** The opposite of the Color mode, Luminosity changes the lightness and darkness of pixels but leaves the hue and saturation values unaffected. When you work on a grayscale image, this mode operates identically to the Normal mode.

The three dodge and burn modes

Phew, that takes care of the brush modes available to the paint tools, the smudge tool, and the two focus tools. I already explained the Desaturate and Saturate modes available to the sponge tool (back in the "Mopping up with the sponge tool" section of this chapter). That leaves us with the three brush modes available to the dodge and burn tools:

- **Shadows:** Along with the Midtones and Highlights modes (described next), Shadows is unique to the dodge and burn tools. When you select this mode, the dodge and burn tools affect dark pixels in an image more dramatically than they affect light pixels and shades in between.

- **Midtones:** Select this mode to apply the dodge or burn tools equally to all but the very lightest or darkest pixels in an image.

- **Highlights:** When you select this option, the dodge and burn tools affect light pixels in an image more dramatically than they affect dark pixels and shades in between.

Selecting Shadows when using the dodge tool or selecting Highlights when using the burn tool has an equalizing effect on an image. Figure 7-35 shows how using either of these functions and setting the Exposure slider bar to 100 percent lightens or darkens pixels in an image to very nearly identical brightness values.

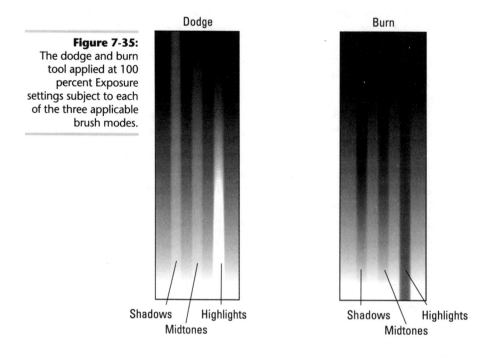

Figure 7-35:
The dodge and burn tool applied at 100 percent Exposure settings subject to each of the three applicable brush modes.

Dodge

Burn

Shadows   Highlights

Midtones

Shadows   Highlights

Midtones

Summary

➼ In Photoshop, you Option-click on the blur tool icon in the toolbox to replace it with the sharpen tool. Option-clicking a second time toggles back to the blur tool. You likewise can toggle between the burn tool and the dodge tool by Option-clicking on their icons.

➼ Click at one point and Shift-click at another with any paint or edit tool to draw a straight line between the two points. This technique is especially useful for controlling the behavior of an edit tool.

➼ Press Shift while dragging with any paint or edit tool to draw a perpendicular line.

➼ Option-drag with the smudge tool to dab on a bit of foreground color at the beginning of the drag. (This assumes that the Finger Painting check box is deselected.)

➼ Use the sponge tool to downplay the saturation of colors in an image or lessen the contrast of a grayscale image. You also have the option of boosting saturation and contrast levels in a washed-out image.

➼ Double-click on a brush shape in the Brushes palette to edit the size, hardness, roundness, and angle of the brush. Click on an empty brush slot to create a new brush shape.

➼ You can convert any selection into a custom brush shape.

➼ Press a number key to change the setting of the Opacity, Pressure, or Exposure slider bar in 10 percent increments.

➼ You can use the Fade option in combination with Shift-click techniques to create sparkles and comets.

➼ A pressure-sensitive tablet enables you to draw variable-weight lines that swell and taper based on how hard you bear down on the stylus.

➼ Photoshop 3.0 offers five new brush modes: Behind, which paints in back of existing colors in a layer; Difference, which inverts an image according to the brightness of the foreground color; and Overlay, Soft Light, and Hard Light, which alternatively multiply and screen an image to create unique color washes, similar to those available in traditional media.

Drawing Selection Outlines

CHAPTER 8

- -

In This Chapter

- ➠ Ways to switch between the rectangular and elliptical marquee tools
- ➠ How the magic wand's Tolerance setting works
- ➠ Manual and automatic methods for editing selection outlines
- ➠ How to move and clone selections and selection outlines
- ➠ The difference between antialiasing and feathering
- ➠ Ways to float a selection and convert it to an independent layer
- ➠ A discussion of Photoshop's path tools
- ➠ The hows and whys of painting along an open path
- ➠ How to export paths for use in Adobe Illustrator
- ➠ How to create partially transparent images for use in Illustrator or QuarkXPress

- -

Selection Fundamentals _____

Selections provide protection and automation. If it weren't for Photoshop's selection capabilities, you and I would be flinging paint on the canvas for all we were worth, like so many Jackson Pollock and Vasily Kandinsky wannabes, without any means to constrain, discriminate, or otherwise regulate the effects of our actions. Without selections, there'd be no filters, no color correction, no special effects. In fact, we'd all be dangerously close to real life, that dreaded environment we've spent so much time and money to avoid.

That's why this chapter and the one that follows are the most important chapters in this book.

Pretty cool, huh? You put a provocative sentence like that on a line by itself and everyone reads it. Granted, it's a little overstated, but can you blame me? I mean, I can't have a sentence like, "If you want my opinion, I think that these are some pretty doggone important chapters — at least, that's the way it seems to me; certainly, you might have a different opinion," on a line by itself. The other paragraphs would laugh at it.

At any rate, it's vital that you pay close attention to the selection concepts discussed in this chapter, because they're key to using Photoshop successfully. It's equally essential to understand how to apply masks in Photoshop, which is the subject of Chapter 9.

How selections work

Before you can edit a portion of an image, you must first *select* it — which is computerese for marking the boundaries of the area that you want to edit. To *select* part of an image in a painting program, you must surround it with a *selection outline* or *marquee*, which tells Photoshop where to apply your editing instructions. The selection outline appears as a moving pattern of dash marks, lovingly termed *marching ants* by doughheads who've been using the Mac too long. (See Figure 8-1 for the inside story.)

Figure 8-1:
A magnified view of a dash mark in a selection outline reveals a startling discovery.

Like its predecessors, Photoshop 3.0 provides five tools for drawing selection outlines, which are described in the following list. What's different in Version 3.0 is that you can now access the tools from the keyboard, as noted in the parentheses.

- **Rectangular marquee (M):** The rectangular marquee tool has been a staple of painting programs since the earliest MacPaint. It lets you select rectangular or square portions of an image.

- **Elliptical marquee (M):** Now relegated to an alternative tool in the upper left corner of the toolbox, the elliptical marquee tool works just like the rectangular marquee except that it selects elliptical or circular portions of an image.

- **Lasso (L):** Another hand-me-down from MacPaint 1.0, the lasso tool lets you select a free-form portion of an image. You simply drag with the lasso tool around the area you want to edit. However, unlike the lasso tools in most Macintosh painting programs, which shrink selection outlines to disqualify pixels in the background color, Photoshop's lasso tool selects the exact portion of the image you enclose in your drag.

- **Magic wand (W):** Originally introduced by Photoshop, this tool enables you to select a contiguous region of similarly colored pixels by clicking inside it. For example, you might click inside the boundaries of a face to isolate it from the hair and background elements. Novices tend to gravitate toward the magic wand because it seems like such a miracle tool, but in fact, it's the least predictable and ultimately least useful of the bunch.

When a marquee or lasso tool is selected, you can access the magic wand by pressing and holding the Control key. The wand remains active only as long as Control is pressed. This shortcut works only on the Mac.

- **Pen (T):** Available from the Paths panel in the Layers palette (which you can display by choosing Window⇨Palettes⇨Show Paths, the pen tool is both the most difficult to master and the most accurate and versatile of the selection tools. You use the pen tool to create a *path,* a special breed of selection outline. You click and drag to create individual points in the path. You can edit the path after the fact by moving, adding, and deleting points. You can even transfer a path via the Clipboard to or from Adobe Illustrator 5.5. For a discussion of the pen tool, read the "How to Draw and Edit Paths" section later in this chapter.

Technically, the type tool also is a selection tool, because Photoshop converts each character of type into its own floating selection boundary. However, the type tool automatically fills these boundaries with the foreground color and is otherwise sufficiently different from other selection tools to warrant its own chapter later in the book (Chapter 12, "Text Effects.")

If that's all there was to using the selection tools in Photoshop, the application would be on par with the average paint program. Part of what makes Photoshop exceptional, however, is that it provides literally hundreds of little tricks to increase the functionality of each and every selection tool.

Furthermore, all of Photoshop's selection tools work together in perfect harmony. You can exploit the specialized capabilities of all five tools to create a single selection boundary. After you come to understand which tool best serves which purpose, you'll be able to isolate any element in an image, no matter how complex or how delicate its outline.

Geometric selection outlines

The default tool in the upper left corner of the toolbox is the rectangular marquee tool. You can access the elliptical marquee tool by Option-clicking on the marquee tool icon or by pressing the M key when the rectangular marquee tool is already selected. Option-clicking or pressing M again takes you back to the rectangular marquee tool.

Both marquee tools are more versatile than they may appear at first glance. You can adjust the performance of each tool as follows:

- **Constraining to a square or circle:** Press and hold Shift *after* beginning your drag to draw a perfect square with the rectangular marquee tool or a perfect circle with the elliptical marquee tool. (Pressing Shift *before* dragging adds to a selection, as explained in the "Ways to Change Existing Selection Outlines" section later in this chapter.)

  In a popular on-line forum, I recently came across someone asking how to create a perfect circular marquee, and despite more than a month of helpful suggestions, no one managed to come up with the easiest one of them all. So remember to press Shift after you begin to drag and you'll be one step ahead of the game.

- **Drawing out from the center:** Option-drag to draw the marquee from the center outward instead of from corner to corner. This technique is especially useful when you draw an elliptical marquee. Frequently, it is easier to locate the center of the area you want to select than one of its corners — particularly because ellipses don't have corners.

- **Selecting a single-pixel line:** You can constrain the rectangular marquee tool so that it selects a single row or column of pixels. To do so, double-click on the tool's icon in the toolbox to display the Marquee Options panel of the Brushes palette, shown in Figure 8-2. Then choose the Single Row or Single Column option from the Shape pop-up menu. I use this option to fix screw-ups such as a missing line of pixels in a screen shot, to delete random pixels around the perimeter of an image, or to create perpendicular lines within a fixed space.

- **Constraining the aspect ratio:** If you know that you want to create an image that conforms to a certain height/width ratio — called an *aspect ratio* — you can constrain either marquee tool so that no matter how large or small a marquee you create, the ratio between height and width remains fixed. To accomplish this, double-click on the appropriate marquee tool icon in the toolbox and select Constrained Aspect Ratio from the Style pop-up menu. Then enter the desired ratio values into the Width and Height option boxes. For example, if you want to crop an image to the ratio of a 4 × 5-inch photograph, you double-click on the rectangular marquee tool icon, enter 4 and 5 respectively into the Width and Height option boxes, and press Return to confirm your changes. Then select the area of the image that you want to retain and choose Edit➪Crop.

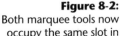

Figure 8-2:
Both marquee tools now occupy the same slot in the toolbox. On the right is the Marquee Options panel as it appears with the contents of the Shape and Style pop-up menus in full view.

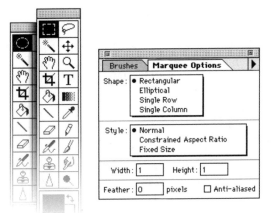

⊸ **Sizing the marquee numerically:** If you're editing a screen shot or some other form of regular or schematic image, you may find it helpful to specify the size of a marquee numerically. To do so, select the Fixed Size option from the Style pop-up menu and enter size values into the Width and Height option boxes. Suppose that you want to select a bunch of option boxes in a screen shot, like the three that appear in Figure 8-2. You select one of them and note its size — 36×16 pixels — which is displayed in the last item of the Info palette. You enter 36 and 16 respectively into the Width and Height option boxes. You then Shift-click in the upper left corner of each remaining option box to add it to the selection and perform the desired color manipulations.

The Info palette can be extremely useful for making precise selections and image adjustments. For more information on this feature, read the "Making precision movements" section later in this chapter.

⊸ **Drawing feathered selections:** A Feather option box is available when you use either of the marquee tools. To *feather* a selection is to soften its edges beyond the automatic antialiasing afforded to most tools. For more information on feathering, refer to the "Softening selection outlines" section later in this chapter.

⊸ **Creating jagged ellipses:** By default, elliptical selection outlines are antialiased. If you don't want antialiasing — you might prefer harsh edges when editing screen shots or designing screen interfaces — deselect the Anti-aliased check box. (This option is dimmed when you use the rectangular marquee because antialiasing is always off for this tool. Perpendicular lines are smooth without the help of antialiasing.)

Frequently, Photoshop's lack of geometric shape tools throws novices for a loop. In fact, such tools do exist — you just don't recognize them. To draw a rectangle or ellipse in Photoshop, draw the shape as desired using the rectangular or elliptical marquee tool. Then choose EditÍFill or EditÍStroke respectively to color the interior or outline of the selection. It's that easy.

Free-form outlines

In comparison to the rectangular and elliptical marquee tools, the lasso tool provides a rather limited range of options. Generally speaking, you just drag in a free-form path around the image you want to select. The few special considerations are as follows:

⌐ **Feathering and antialiasing:** To adjust the performance of the lasso tool, double-click on its icon in the toolbox (or press Return while the lasso tool is selected) to display the Lasso Options panel shown in Figure 8-3. Just as you can feather rectangular and elliptical marquees, you can feather selections drawn with the lasso tool. You can also soften the edges of a lasso outline by selecting the Anti-aliased check box (which is now the factory default setting).

You should be aware that although you can adjust the feathering of any selection after you draw it by choosing Select⇨Feather, you must specify antialiasing before you draw a selection. So unless you have a specific reason for doing otherwise, leave the Anti-aliased check box selected.

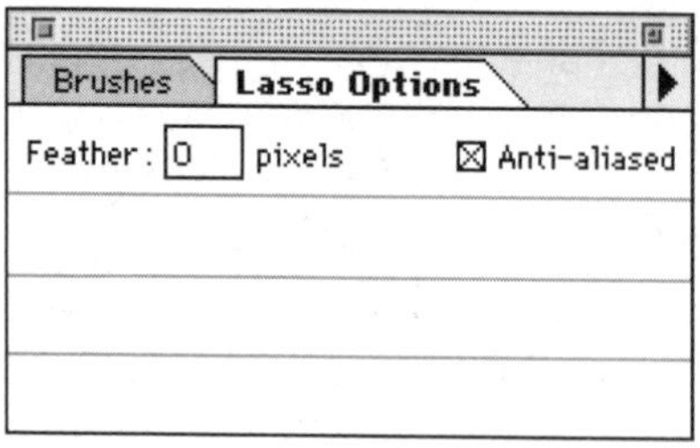

Figure 8-3:
Double-click on the lasso tool icon to access the veritable truckload of options shown here.

Brushes	Lasso Options	▶
Feather : 0 pixels	☒ Anti-aliased	

⌐ **Drawing polygons:** If you press and hold the Option key, the lasso tool works like a standard polygon tool. (*Polygon,* incidentally, just means a shape with multiple straight sides.) With the Option key down, you click to specify corners in a free-form polygon, as shown in Figure 8-4. If you want to add curves to the selection outline, just drag with the tool while still pressing the Option key. Photoshop closes the selection outline the moment you release both the Option key and the mouse button.

You can extend a polygon selection outline to the absolute top, right, or bottom edges of an image. To do so, Option-click with the lasso tool on the scroll bar or title bar of the image window, as illustrated by the gray lines and squares in Figure 8-4.

This technique does not work on the left side of an image because the left side lacks a scroll bar or title bar. To extend a selection to the absolute left edge of an image, drag out beyond the left edge of the image. Be sure to keep the mouse button down, and don't click outside the window, or you'll switch to some background application. (You Windows users are lucky; you don't have to worry about this one.)

Figure 8-4:
Option-click with the lasso tool to create corners in a selection outline, shown as black squares in the bottom image. Drag to create free-form curves. Surprisingly, you can Option-click on the scroll bar to add corners outside the boundaries of the image window.

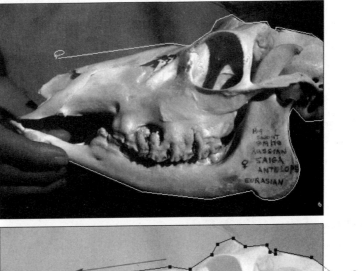

Option-click on scroll bar

End drag

Option-click   Begin drag

The world of the wand

Using the magic wand tool is a no-brainer, right? You just click with the tool and it selects all the neighboring colors that fall within a selected range. The problem, however, is getting the wand to recognize the same range of colors you recognize. For example, if you're editing a photo of a red plate against a pink tablecloth, how do you tell the magic wand to select the plate and leave the tablecloth alone?

Sadly, adjusting the performance of the wand is not that easy. If you double-click on the magic wand icon in the toolbox, you'll see three options inside the Magic Wand Options panel of the Brushes palette, as shown in Figure 8-5. The Anti-aliased option softens the selection, just as it does for the lasso tool described in the preceding section. The Tolerance value determines the range of colors the tool selects when you click with it in the image window. And the Sample Merged check box allows you to take all visible layers into account when defining a selection.

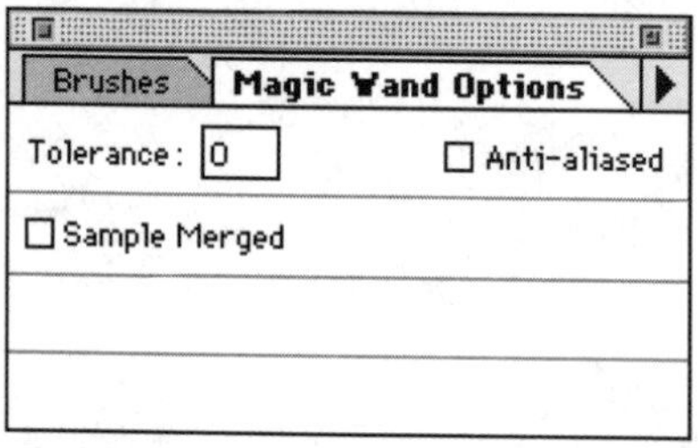

Figure 8-5:
Double-click on the magic wand icon to specify the range of colors you want to select the next time you use the tool.

Adjusting the tolerance

By now you already understand what's up with the Anti-aliased option, so I'll start with Tolerance. You may have heard the standard explanation for adjusting the Tolerance value: You can enter any number from 0 to 255 in the Tolerance option box. Enter a low number to select a small range of colors; increase the value to select a wider range of colors.

There's nothing wrong with that explanation — it's accurate in its own small way — but it doesn't provide one iota of information you couldn't glean on your own. The fact is, if you really want to understand this option, you must dig a little deeper.

When you click on a pixel with the magic wand tool, Photoshop first reads the brightness value assigned to that pixel by each of the color channels. If you're working with a grayscale image, Photoshop reads a single brightness value from the one channel only; if you're working with an RGB image, it reads three brightness values, one each from the red, green, and blue channels; and so on. Because each color channel permits 8 bits of data, brightness values range from 0 to 255.

Next, Photoshop applies the Tolerance value, or simply *tolerance,* to the pixel. The tolerance describes a range that extends in both directions — lighter and darker — from each brightness value.

Suppose that you're editing a standard RGB image. The tolerance is set to 32 (as it is by default), and you click with the magic wand on a turquoise pixel whose brightness values are 40 red, 210 green, and 170 blue. Photoshop adds and subtracts 32 from each brightness value to calculate the magic wand range, which in this case is 8 to 72 red, 178 to 242 green, and 138 to 202 blue. Photoshop selects any pixel that both falls inside this range *and* can be traced back to the original pixel via an uninterrupted line of other pixels that also fall within the range.

From this information, you can draw the following basic conclusions about the magic wand tool:

- **Creating a contiguous selection:** The magic wand selects a contiguous region of pixels emanating from the pixel on which you click. If you're trying to select land masses on a globe, for example, clicking on St. Louis selects everything from Juno to Mexico City, but it doesn't select London because the cities are separated by an ocean of water that doesn't fall within the tolerance range.

- **Clicking midtones maintains a higher range:** Because the tolerance range extends in two directions, you cut off the range when you click on a light or dark pixel. If the tolerance is 40 and you click on a grayscale pixel with a brightness value of 20, Photoshop calculates a range from 0 to 60. If you instead click on a pixel with a brightness value of 40, you increase your range to 0 to 80. Therefore, clicking on a medium-brightness pixel permits the most generous range.

- **Selecting brightness ranges:** Many people have the impression that the magic wand selects color ranges. In fact, it selects brightness ranges within color channels. So if you want to select a flesh-colored region — regardless of shade — set against an orange or red background that is roughly equivalent in terms of brightness values, you probably should use a different tool.

- **Selecting from a single channel:** If the magic wand repeatedly fails to select a region of color that appears to be unique from its background, try isolating that region on a single color channel. You probably will have the most luck isolating a color on the channel that least resembles it. For example, to select a yellow flower petal that's set against an azure sky filled with similar brightness values, go to the blue channel (by clicking on the Blue option in the Channels palette). Because yellow contains no blue and azure contains lots of blue, the magic wand can distinguish the two relatively easily. Experiment with this technique and it will prove more and more useful over time.

Making the wand see beyond a single layer

The final option, Sample Merged, is new to Version 3.0. Much like the identically named option available to the smudge and focus tools (see "Painting with the smudge tool" in Chapter 7), this option lets you take into account colors from different layers. In this particular case, Sample Merged allows the wand to draw selection outlines around similarly colored areas on different layers.

For example, returning to my earlier land mass example, suppose that you set Europe on one layer and North America on the layer behind it. (I explain how to establish layers in the "Sending a floating selection to its own layer" section later in this chapter.) The two countries overlap. Now normally, if you clicked inside Europe with the magic wand tool, the wand would select an area inside Europe without extending out into the area occupied by North America. This is because the wand doesn't even see the contents of other layers; anything outside of Europe is just an empty void of space. We're talking pre-Columbus Europe here.

However, if you select the Sample Merged option, things change. Suddenly, the wand can see all the layers that you can see. If you click on Europe, and North America and Europe contain similar colors, the wand selects across both shapes.

Mind you, the Sample Merged option does *not* permit the wand to select images on two separate layers. In fact, strange as it may sound, no selection tool can pull off this feat. You can only select, paint, and edit inside one layer at a time. (The one exception is the move tool, which lets you move multiple layers in their entirety, as explained in the upcoming "Sending a floating selection to its own layer" section.) Sample Merged merely allows the wand to draw selection outlines that appear to encompass colors on many layers. What good is that? Well, suppose that you want to apply an effect to both Europe and North America. With the help of Sample Merged, you can draw a selection outline that encompasses both countries. After you apply the effect to Europe, you can switch to the North America layer — the selection outline remains intact — and then reapply the effect.

Ways to Change Existing Selection Outlines

If you don't draw a selection outline correctly the first time, you have two options. You either can draw it again from scratch, which is a real bore, or change your botched selection outline, which is likely to prove the more gratifying solution. You can deselect a selection, add to a selection, subtract from a selection, and even select the stuff that's not selected and deselect the selected stuff. (If that sounds like a load of nonsense, keep reading.)

Quick changes

Some methods of adjusting a selection outline are automatic: You just choose a command and you're done. The following list explains how a few commands — all members of the Select menu — work:

- **Hide Edges (Command-H):** Get those marching ants out of my face! We're all grown ups, right? Do we really need these constant streams of marching ants to tell us what we've selected? We were there, we remember. My point is that although visible selection outlines can be helpful sometimes, they just as readily can impede your view of an image. When they annoy, press Command-H.

- **Deselect (Command-D):** You can deselect the selected portion of an image in three ways. You can select a different portion of the image; click anywhere in the image window with the rectangular marquee tool, the elliptical marquee tool, or the lasso tool; or choose Select⇨None. Remember, however, that when no part of an image is selected, the entire image is susceptible to your changes. If you apply a filter, choose a color-correction command, or use a paint tool, you affect every pixel of the foreground image.

- **Inverse:** Choose Select⇨Inverse to reverse the selection. Photoshop deselects the portion of the image that was previously selected and selects the portion of the image that was not selected. This way, you can start out a selection by outlining the portion of the image that you want to protect rather than the portion you want to affect.

Manually adding and subtracting

Ready for some riddles? When editing a portrait, how do you select both eyes without affecting any other portion of the face? Answer: By drawing one selection and then tacking on a second. How do you a select a doughnut and leave the hole behind? Answer: Encircle the doughnut with the elliptical marquee tool and then use that same tool to subtract the center.

Photoshop enables you to whittle away at a selection, add pieces back on, whittle away some more, ad infinitum, until you get it exactly right. Short of sheer laziness or frustration, there's no reason you can't eventually create the selection outline of your dreams.

- **Adding to a selection outline:** To increase the area enclosed in an existing selection outline, Shift-drag with the rectangular marquee, elliptical marquee, or lasso tool. You also can Shift-click with the magic wand tool or Shift-click with one of the marquee tools when the Fixed Size option is active (as described back in the "Geometric selection outlines" section earlier in this chapter).

- **Subtracting from a selection outline:** To take a bite out of an existing selection outline, press the Command key while using one of the selection tools.

 You can make Photoshop's lasso tool behave like lassos in other Macintosh painting programs by applying a simple subtraction technique. First drag with the lasso around the portion of the image that you want to select. Then double-click on the magic wand tool icon in the toolbox, change the Tolerance value to zero, and deselect the Anti-aliased check box. Press Return to tell Photoshop to accept your changes and then Command-click with the magic wand tool on a portion of the selection that appears in the background color. Photoshop deselects this portion, as other programs do automatically.

- **Intersecting one selection outline with another:** Another way to subtract from an existing selection outline is to Command-Shift-drag around the selection with the rectangular marquee, elliptical marquee, or lasso tool. You also can Command-Shift-click with the magic wand tool. Command-Shift-dragging instructs Photoshop to retain only that portion of an existing selection that also falls inside the new selection outline. I frequently use this technique to confine a selection within a rectangular or elliptical border.

Adding and subtracting by command

Photoshop provides several commands under the Select menu that automatically increase or decrease the number of selected pixels in an image according to numerical specifications. The commands in the Select⇨Modify submenu work as follows:

- **Border:** This command selects an area of a specified thickness around the perimeter of the current selection outline and deselects the rest of the selection. For example, to select a 6-point-thick border around the current selection, choose Select⇨Modify⇨Border, enter 6 into the Width option box, and press Return. But what's the point? After all, if you want to create an outline around a selection, you can accomplish this in fewer steps by choosing Edit⇨Stroke. The Border command, however, broadens your range of options. You can apply a special effect to the border, move the border to a new location, or even create a double outline effect by first applying Select⇨Modify⇨Border and then Edit⇨Stroke.

- **Smooth:** New to Photoshop 3.0, this command rounds off the sharp corners and weird anomalies in the outline of a selection. When you choose Select⇨Modify⇨ Smooth, the program asks you to enter a Sample Radius value. The first in about 6,000 Radius options available in Photoshop, this one represents the maximum distance that the Smooth command can move any point on the selection outline. So if you enter a value of 6 pixels, the smoothed selection outline can roam a maximum of 6 points in any direction from its current course, but no further. (Go ahead, give it a try. It won't bite.)

- **Expand and Contract:** Also new to Version 3.0, Select⇨Modify⇨Expand and Select⇨Modify⇨Contract perform much-needed services that were previously available only via a few rather challenging masking operations. Both commands do exactly what they say, either expanding or contracting the selected area by 1 to 16 pixels. For example, if you want an elliptical selection to grow by 8 pixels, choose Select⇨Modify⇨Expand, enter 8, and call it a day.

 Keep an eye out for the fact that both commands have a flattening effect on a selection. To round things off, apply the Smooth command with a Sample Radius value equal to the number you just entered into the Expand Selection or Contract Selection dialog box. You'll end up with a pretty vague selection outline, but what do you expect from automated commands?

In addition to the Expand command, Photoshop provides two older commands — Grow and Similar — that increase the area covered by a selection outline. Both commands resemble the magic wand tool in that they measure the range of eligible pixels by way of a Tolerance value. In fact, the commands rely on the very same Tolerance value found inside the Magic Wand Options panel. Therefore, if you want to adjust the impact of either command, you must first select the magic wand icon in the toolbox.

- **Grow (Command-G):** Choose Select⇨Grow to select all pixels that both neighbor an existing selection and resemble the colors included in the selection, in accordance with the Tolerance value. In other words, Select⇨Grow is the command equivalent of the magic wand tool. If you feel constrained by the fact you can click on only one pixel at a time with the wand tool, you may prefer to select a small group of representative pixels with a marquee tool and then choose Select⇨Grow to initiate the wand's magic.

- **Similar:** Another member of the Select menu, the Similar command works just like the Grow command except that the pixels don't have to be adjacent to one another. When you choose Select⇨Similar, Photoshop selects any pixel that falls within the tolerance range, regardless of its location in the foreground image.

One of the best applications for the Similar command is to isolate a complicated image that's set against a consistent background whose colors are significantly lighter or darker than the image. Consider Figure 8-6, which features a dark and ridiculously complex foreground image set against a continuous background of medium to light brightness values. Though the image features sufficient contrast to make it a candidate for the magic wand tool, I would never in a million years recommend that you use that tool, because so many of the colors in the foreground image are discontiguous. The following steps explain how to separate this image using the Similar command in combination with a few other techniques I've described thus far.

STEPS: Isolating a Complex Image Set Against a Plain Background

---

Step 1.   Use the rectangular marquee tool to select some representative portions of the background. In Figure 8-6, I selected the lightest and darkest portions of the background along with some representative shades in between. Remember, you make multiple selections by Shift-dragging with the tool.

Figure 8-6:
Before choosing Select⇔Similar, select a few sample portions of the background so that Photoshop has something on which to base its selection range.

Step 2.   Double-click on the magic wand tool icon to display the Tolerance option box. For my image, I entered a tolerance of 16, a relatively low value, in keeping with the consistency of the background. If your background is less homogenous, you may want to enter a higher value. Make sure that the Anti-aliased check box is turned on. Then press Return to exit the dialog box.

Step 3.   Choose Select⇔Similar. Photoshop should select the entire background. If it fails to select all of the background, choose Edit⇔Undo (Command-Z) and use the rectangular marquee tool to select more portions of the background. You may also want to increase the Tolerance value in the Magic Wand Options dialog box. If Photoshop's selection bleeds into the foreground image, try reducing the Tolerance value.

Step 4.   Choose Select⇔Inverse. Photoshop selects the foreground image and deselects the background.

Step 5. If the detail you want to select represents only a fraction of the entire image, Command-Shift-drag around the portion of the image that you want to retain using the lasso tool. In Figure 8-7, I Command-Shift-Option-dragged to draw a polygon with the lasso.

If the technique in Step 5 sounds tempting but you have problems keeping three fingers planted on the keyboard as you draw, here's a little hint. You only have to press Command-Shift at the beginning of the drag or until after you complete the first click. After the selection process is established, you can release the Command and Shift keys. The Option key, however, must remain pressed if you want to draw a polygon.

Figure 8-7:
Command-
Shift-Option-
drag with the
lasso tool to
intersect the
area that you
want to select
with a free-
form polygon.

Step 6. Congratulations, you've isolated your complex image. Now you can filter it, colorize it, or perform whatever operation inspired you to select this image in the first place. For myself, I wanted to superimpose the image onto a different background. To do so, I copied the image to the Clipboard (EditÍCopy), opened the desired background image, and then pasted the first image into place (EditÍPaste). The result, shown in Figure 8-8, still needs some touching up with the paint and edit tools, but it's not half bad for an automated selection process.

Figure 8-8: The completed selection superimposed onto a new background.

Although all the commands discussed in this section are applicable to any kind of selection outline, you should at least hesitate before modifying selections right after you paste or move them. Such selections are termed *floating*, because they hover independently in front of the rest of the image. If you apply Border, Smooth, Expand, Contract, Grow, or Similar to a floating selection, Photoshop adheres the selection to the image and then applies the automated changes. (The same goes for the Inverse command, described earlier, and the Feather command, described next.) Therefore, if you try to move the selection after choosing one of these commands, you'll take part of the image with you. For more information on floating and how it impacts your day-to-day life, see the upcoming section "Floating a selection."

Softening selection outlines

You can soften a selection in two ways. The first method is antialiasing, introduced in Chapter 3. Antialiasing is an intelligent and automatic softening algorithm that mimics the appearance of edges you'd expect to see in a sharply focused photograph. Where does the term *antialias* come from? Well, to *alias* an electronic signal is to dump essential data, thus degrading the quality of a sound or image. Antialiasing boosts the signal and smoothes out the rough spots in a way that preserves the overall quality.

When you draw an antialiased selection outline in Photoshop, the program calculates the hard-edged selection at twice its actual size. It then shrinks the selection in half using bicubic interpolation, as described in the "General environmental preferences" section of Chapter 2. The result is a crisp image with no visible jagged edges.

The second softening method, *feathering,* is less scientific. Feathering gradually dissipates the opacity of the pixels around the edge of a selection. You can specify the number of pixels affected — either before or after drawing a selection — by entering a value into the Feather Radius option box. To feather a selection before you draw it, double-click on the rectangular marquee, elliptical marquee, or lasso tool icon. To feather a selection after drawing it, choose Select⇨Feather.

The Feather Radius value determines the distance over which Photoshop fades a selection, measured in pixels in both directions from the original selection outline. Therefore, if you enter a radius of 4 pixels, Photoshop fades the selection over an 8-pixel stretch. Figure 8-9 shows three selections lifted from the image at the bottom of the figure. The first selection is antialiased only. I feathered the second and third selections, assigning Feather Radius values of 4 and 12, respectively. As you can see, a small feather radius makes a selection appear fuzzy; a larger radius makes it fade into view.

You can use feathering to remove an element from an image while leaving the background intact, a process described in the following steps. The image described in the steps, shown in Figure 8-10, is a NASA photo of a satellite with the earth in the background. I wanted to use this background with another image, but to do so I first had to get rid of that satellite. By Command-Option-dragging, feathering, and cloning, I covered the satellite with a patch so seamless you'd swear that the satellite was never there.

STEPS: Removing an Element from an Image

Step 1.   Draw a selection around the element using the lasso tool. The selection doesn't have to be an exact fit; in fact, you want it to be rather loose, allowing a buffer zone of at least six pixels between the edges of the image and the selection outline.

Step 2.   Now that you've specified the element you want to remove, you have to find some portion of the image that will cover the element in a manner that matches the surrounding background. In Figure 8-11, the best match seemed to be an area just below and to the right of the satellite. To select this area, move the selection outline independently of the image by Command-Option-dragging. Be sure to allow some space between the selection outline and the element you're trying to cover.

Figure 8-9: Three clones selected with the elliptical marquee tool. The top image is antialiased and not feathered; the next is feathered with a radius of 4 pixels; and the third is feathered with a radius of 12 pixels.

Step 3.   Choose Select⇨Feather. Enter a small value (8 or less) in the Feather Radius option box — just enough to make the edges fuzzy. I entered 3. Then press Return to initiate the operation.

Step 4.   Option-drag the feathered selection to clone and position the patch over the element you want to cover, as shown in Figure 8-12. To correctly align the patch, choose Select⇨Hide Edges (Command-H) to hide the marching ants and then nudge the patch into position with the arrow keys.

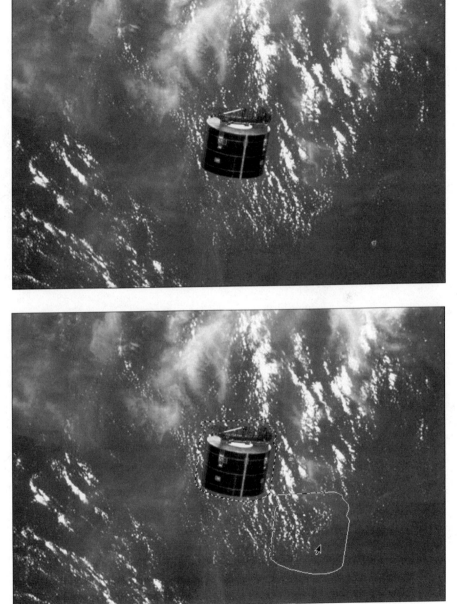

Figure 8-10:
The mission was to remove the satellite by covering it up with selections cloned from the background; the procedure is discussed in the section "STEPS: Removing an Element from an Image."

Figure 8-11:
After drawing a loose outline around the satellite with the lasso tool, I Command-Option-dragged the outline to select a portion of the background.

Figure 8-12:
Next, I Option-dragged the feathered selection over the satellite. The patch was imperfect and required further adjustments.

Step 5. My patch was only partially successful. The upper left corner of the selection matches clouds in the background, but the lower right corner is dark and cloudless, an obvious rift in the visual continuity of the image. The solution: Try again. With the lasso tool still active, I drew a loose outline around the dark portion of the image and Command-Option-dragged it up and to the left as shown in Figure 8-13.

Step 6. It's all déjà vu from here on out. I chose Select⇨Feather, entered 6 into the Feather radius option box — thus allowing the clouds a sufficient range to taper off — and pressed Return. I then Option-dragged the feathered patch over the dark, cloudless rift; nudged, nudged, nudged; and voilà! No more satellite. Figure 8-14 shows $200 million worth of hardware vaporized in less than five minutes.

Figure 8-13:
I drew a new outline around the dark, cloudless portion of the patch and Command-Option-dragged the outline to a different spot in the background.

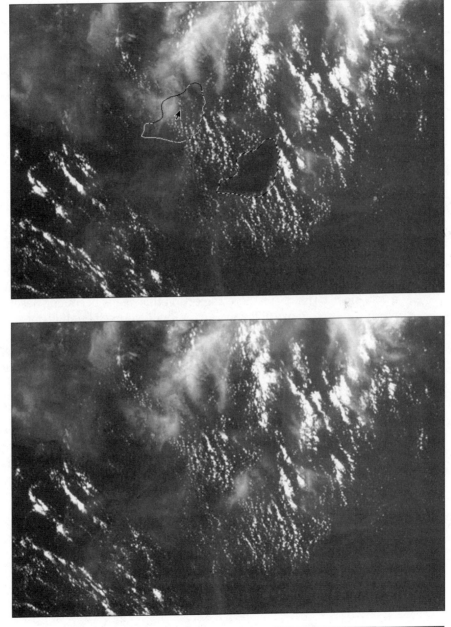

Figure 8-14:
I selected a new bit of cloudy sky and placed it over the formerly cloudless portion of the patch. Satellite? What satellite?

Moving, Duplicating, and Layering Selections

After you select a portion of an image, you can move either the selection or selection outline to a new location. To move a selection, just drag it while any one of the selection tools is active, regardless of which tool you used to select the image in the first place. For example, after selecting part of an image with the rectangular marquee tool, you can drag it to a new location using the elliptical marquee, lasso, or magic wand tool. You can even move a selection with the arrow tool found in the Paths panel of the Layers palette.

 As if you don't already have enough options, Version 3.0 provides a dedicated move tool just below the lasso in the toolbox. You can select it at any time by pressing the V key. This tool allows you to drag a selected area, whether or not you begin your drag on the selection. For example, if the lower right corner of an image is selected, you can drag in the upper left corner with the move tool and still grab the selection. This is especially useful when you're trying to move a very small or highly feathered selection that keeps becoming deselected when you try to move it. If you've ever found yourself hunting down the perfect place to drag a selection, waiting for that moment when the cursor becomes an arrow to show that you're finally over the selection and ready to drag it, the move tool is your saving grace. There's no chance of deselecting an image or messing up a path with this tool.

Normally, Photoshop displays the outline of the selected area during a move, as shown in the top image in Figure 8-15. But you can also preview the selected area in all its splendor as you move it, as shown in the bottom image in the figure. As you might expect, this significantly slows down the screen refresh speed. It also prevents you from viewing the portion of the image behind the selection. But there are times when this capability comes in extremely handy.

 To preview a selection as you move it, click and hold on the selection for a few moments before moving the mouse. The watch cursor appears. The moment the cursor changes back to the standard move cursor — which may happen very fast on some high-end computers — you can start dragging.

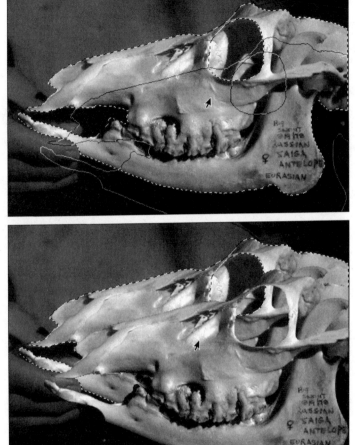

Figure 8-15:
You can drag a
selection right off
the bat to see
only its outline
(top) or you can
press and hold
the mouse button
for a moment
before beginning
your drag to
preview the
selection
(bottom).

Making precision movements

Photoshop provides three methods for moving selections in prescribed increments.
First, you can nudge a selection in one-pixel increments by pressing an arrow key on the
keyboard, or in 10-pixel increments by pressing Shift with an arrow key. This technique
is useful for making precise adjustments to the position of an image. Second, you can
press Shift during a drag to constrain a move to some 45-degree direction — that is,
horizontally, vertically, or diagonally. And third, you can use the Info palette to track
your movements and help locate a precise position in the image.

To display the Info palette, choose Window⇨Palettes⇨Show Info. Figure 8-16 shows the Info palette as it appears in Photoshop 3.0. The last four items in the palette monitor movement, as follows:

- ❧ **X, Y:** These values show the coordinate position of your cursor. The distance is measured from the upper left corner of the image in the current unit of measure. The unit of measure in Figure 8-16 is pixels.

- ❧ **ΔX, ΔY:** These values indicate the distance of your move as measured horizontally and vertically.

- ❧ **A, D:** The A and D values reflect the angle and direct distance of your drag.

- ❧ **W, H:** Not displayed in Photoshop 2.0, these values reflect the width and height of your selection.

Figure 8-16:
The Info palette provides a world of numerical feedback when you move a selection.

Info	
R:	218
G:	148
B:	140
C:	11%
M:	49%
Y:	33%
K:	1%
X:	289
Y:	271
ΔX:	4
ΔY:	-31
A:	82.6°
D:	31.26
W:	338
H:	267

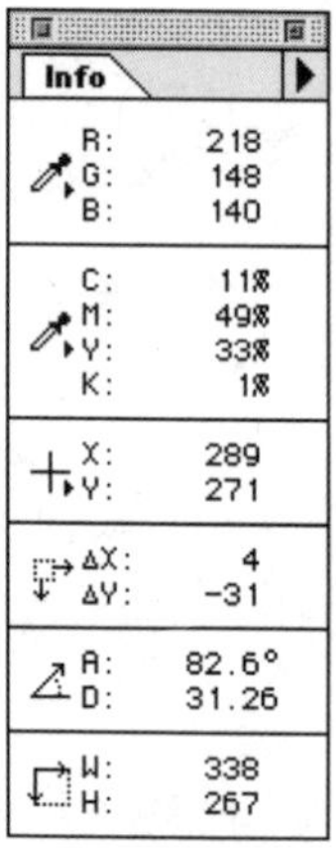

Cloning a selection

When you move a selection, you leave a hole in your image in the background color, as shown in the top half of Figure 8-17. If you prefer instead to leave the original in place during a move, you have to *clone* the selection — that is, create a copy of the selection without upsetting the contents of the Clipboard. Photoshop 3.0 now provides four different means for cloning a selection:

- ❧ **Option-dragging:** Press the Option key and drag a selection to clone it. The bottom half of Figure 8-17 shows a selection that I Option-dragged three times. (Between clonings, I changed the gray level of each selection to make them more identifiable.)

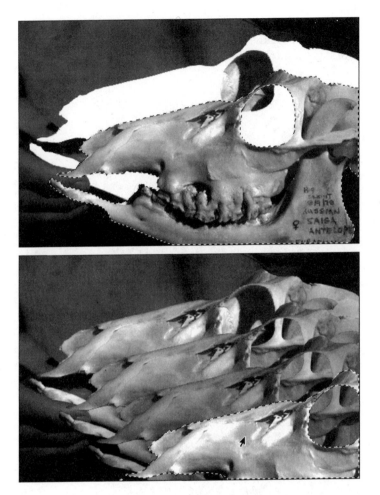

Figure 8-17:
When you move a selection, you leave a gaping hole in the selection's wake (top). When you clone an image, you leave a copy of the selection behind. (The selection in the bottom image was cloned several times.)

- **Option-arrowing:** Press Option in combination with one of the arrow keys to both clone the selection and nudge it one pixel away from the original. If you want to move the image multiple pixels, Option-arrow the first time only. Then just nudge the clone using the arrow key alone. Otherwise, you create a bunch of clones that you can't undo.

- **Floating:** Choose Select⇨Float (Command-J) to clone the selection in place. You then can move the clone to a new location as desired. (For more information about floating, read the upcoming "Floating a selection" section.)

- **Drag and drop:** Like just about every other program on the planet, Photoshop 3.0 now lets you clone a selection between documents by dragging it from one open window to another, as demonstrated in Figure 8-18. As long as you manage to drop into the second window, the original image remains intact and selected in the first window. My advice: Don't worry about exact positioning during a drag and drop; first get it into the second window and then worry about placement.

Figure 8-18:
Drag a
selection from
one open
window and
drop it into
another (top)
to create a
clone of
the selection in
the receiving
window
(bottom).

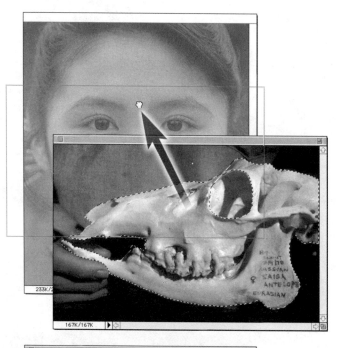

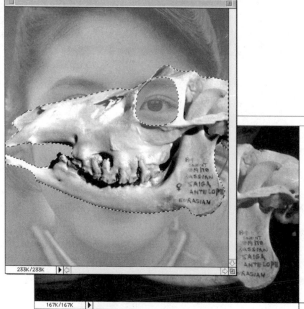

Figure 8-18: Drag a selection from one open window and drop it into another (top) to create a clone of the selection in the receiving window (bottom).

Moving a selection outline independently of its contents

If a selection outline surrounds the wrong portion of an image, you can move it independently of the image by Command-Option-dragging. This technique serves as yet another means for manipulating inaccurate selection outlines. It also enables you to mimic one portion of an image in another portion of the image.

In the top image in Figure 8-19, I Command-Option-dragged the skull outline down and to the right so that it still overlapped the skull. Note that the image itself remains unaltered. I then lightened the new selection, applied a couple of strokes to set it off from its background, and gave it stripes. For all I know, this is exactly what a female Russian Saiga Antelope looks like.

Figure 8-19: Command-Option-drag to move a selection outline independently of its image (top). The area to which you drag the selection outline becomes the new selection (bottom).

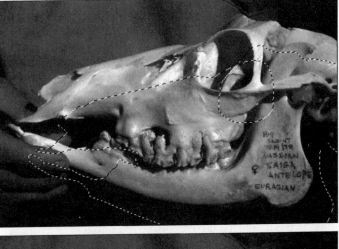

You can nudge a selection outline independently of its contents by pressing Command-Option-arrow key. Command-Shift-Option-arrow key moves the outline in 10-pixel increments.

Floating a selection

A *floating selection* is a selection that hovers above the surface of the image. The beauty of a floating selection is that you can manipulate it by painting inside it, applying filters, coloring the image, and so on, all without affecting the underlying image itself. Then you can mix the floating selection with the underlying image by adjusting the Opacity slider bar in the Layers palette or by selecting an overlay mode from the pop-up menu in the upper left corner of the Layers palette.

You can float a selection in any of the following ways:

- **Paste:** When you paste an image from the Clipboard into the image window, the pasted image floats inside a selection outline, waiting for your next instructions.

- **Move:** When you move a selection by dragging it or pressing an arrow key, Photoshop floats the selection at its new location.

- **Clone:** Whether you clone a selection by Option-dragging it or pressing Option in combination with an arrow key, Photoshop floats the cloned selection.

- **Select⇨Float:** As I mentioned a moment ago in the "Cloning a selection" discussion, you can clone a selection in place, which has the added effect of floating it, by choosing Select⇨Float (Command-J).

Conversely, any of the following techniques *defloat* a selection — that is, drop it in place — again making the image itself susceptible to changes:

- **Deselect:** Because a floating selection must remain selected to remain floating, choosing Select⇨None (Command-D) defloats a selection. Likewise, any operation that has the added effect of deselecting an image, such as selecting a different portion of the image, changing the canvas size, or choosing File⇨Revert, defloats the selection.

- **Add to the selection:** If you add to a selection outline by pressing Shift while using any of the selection tools (or adding a path to a selection outline from the Make Selection dialog box, as I'll describe shortly), Photoshop defloats the image. However, you can subtract from a selection outline and intersect it without defloating it.

- **Automatically adjusting the selection outline:** All the commands in the Select menu that affect the shape of a selection outline — including Inverse, Feather, Grow, Similar, and the commands in the Select⇨Modify submenu — set down the selection. Like Shift-dragging with a selection tool, these commands add pixels to the selection outline, which invariably requires a defloat.

- **Stroke the selection:** Photoshop automatically defloats a selection when you apply Edit⇨Stroke.

- **Editing a mask:** Photoshop retains selection outlines when you switch to a different color or mask channel. However, if you edit the selection in a different channel, you immediately defloat it. Furthermore, Photoshop automatically defloats a selection when you switch to the quick mask mode, whether you edit the mask or not. For more information on masks, read Chapter 9.

- **Select⇨Defloat:** You can drop a selection by choosing Select⇨Defloat (Command-J).

Setting down portions of a floating selection

While a selection is floating, you can chip away portions of it by Command-dragging with a marquee tool or the lasso tool or by Command-clicking with the magic wand. The area around which you Command-drag (or on which you Command-click) disappears. Similarly, you can Command-Shift-drag with a marquee or lasso tool or Command-Shift-click with the magic wand tool to specify the portion of the selection you want to retain. Anything not included inside the Command-Shift-drag or Command-Shift-click disappears.

 But what if rather than deleting a portion of a floating selection, you simply want to set it down? For example, perhaps you have pasted two eyes against a new background and you want to set one of them down and move the other one to a new position. The solution is to Command-drag or Command-Shift-drag with the type tool. (When you press the Command key, the I-beam cursor changes to a lasso cursor, but the tool doesn't work like the lasso tool.) Either Command-drag around the eye you want to set down or Command-Shift-drag around the eye that you want to leave floating. Either way, you'll still have both eyes, which is a must for decent depth perception.

Removing halos

When you move or clone an antialiased selection, you sometimes take with you a few pixels from the selection's previous background. These pixels can create a haloing effect if they clash with the selection's new background, as demonstrated in the top image in Figure 8-20.

You can instruct Photoshop to replace the fringe pixels with colors from neighboring pixels by choosing Select⇨Matting⇨Defringe. Enter the thickness of the perceived halo in the Width option box to tell Photoshop which pixels you want to replace. To create the image shown in the bottom half of Figure 8-20, I entered a Width value of 2. If you have to use a higher value than 2, you're probably better off redrawing your selection.

Figure 8-20:
To remove the halo around the cloned skull (top), I used the Defringe command to replace the pixels around the perimeter of the selection with colors borrowed from neighboring pixels (bottom).

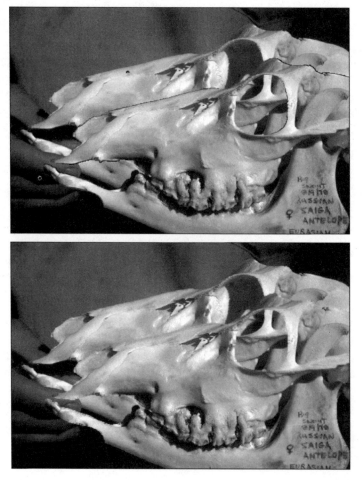

Photoshop 3.0 provides two additional commands under the Select⇨Matting submenu: Remove Black Matte and Remove White Matte. If you're familiar with Photoshop 2.5, these commands are identical to the Black Matte and White Matte overlay modes that used to be available from the Brushes palette pop-up menu. Just in case you never came to grips with how those options worked — frankly, it's unlikely that you'd have much call to use them — here's the scoop:

↝ **Remove Black Matte:** This command removes the residue around the perimeter of a floating selection that was copied from a black background. For example, consider the first example in Figure 8-21, which shows a feathered selection that I set down against a black background. When I floated the selection again and set it against a stucco background, I got a black ring around the image, as demonstrated in the top half of the second example in the figure. To eliminate the black ring, I chose Select⇨Matting⇨Remove Black Matte.

Figure 8-21:
If you drop a feathered selection onto a black background (top) and try to reuse it, you get a black ring (upper half, bottom example). Luckily, you can eliminate this ring with the Remove Black Matte command (lower half, bottom example).

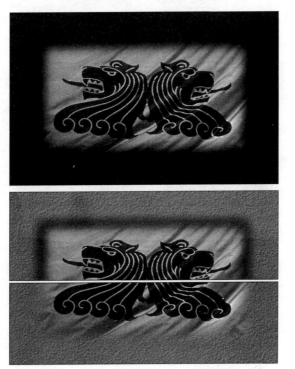

↝ **White Matte**: In the first example of Figure 8-22, I set the feathered selection onto a white background. When I later tried to apply the selection to the stucco texture, I got a white ring, as you can see in the top half of the bottom example. To eliminate the ring, I chose Select⇨Matting⇨Remove White Matte option.

Figure 8-22:
Conversely, if you drop a feathered selection onto a white background (top) and try to reuse it, you get a white ring (upper half, bottom example), which you can just as easily eliminate by choosing Remove White Matte (lower half, bottom example).

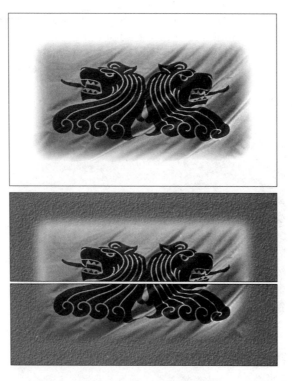

Sending a floating selection to its own layer

 Layers are easily the most powerful and amazing new feature added to Photoshop 3.0. Their impact is also wide ranging, which is why I'll be discussing them in bits and pieces. For a thorough overview of the subject, check out Chapter 17. In the meantime, however, I'll show you a preview of how layers work.

Do this: Select an area of an image, float it (Command-J), and then display the Layers palette (Window⇨Palettes⇨Show Layers). You'll see two items in the palette's scrolling list, Floating Selection and Background. The first item represents the floating selection. (Big surprise there.) The second is the underlying image. All standard images — that is, anything that hasn't been specially set up in Photoshop — contain a single Background layer. Throughout any layering you do, the Background represents the opaque base image; it is forever the rearmost layer in the image.

To send a floating selection to its own independent layer, choose the Make Layer command from the Layers palette pop-up menu, as in Figure 8-23. The Make Layer dialog box (also shown in the figure) appears, asking you to name the layer. You can also change the opacity and overlay mode or group the layer with the one in back of it. (That stuff is all discussed in Chapter 17; there's no need to worry about it now.) You can easily change any of these settings after the fact — at which time you can actually view the results of your changes — so it generally makes more sense to simply name the layer and press Return.

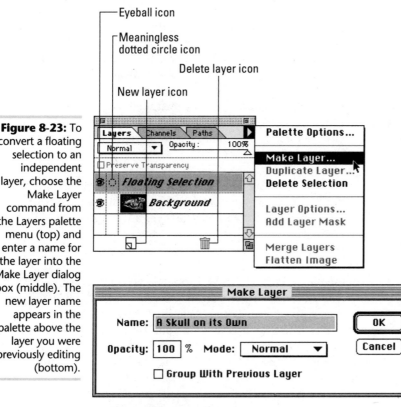

Figure 8-23: To convert a floating selection to an independent layer, choose the Make Layer command from the Layers palette menu (top) and enter a name for the layer into the Make Layer dialog box (middle). The new layer name appears in the palette above the layer you were previously editing (bottom).

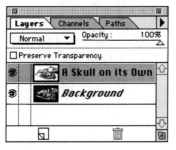

Rather than choosing Make Layer, you can simply drag the Floating Selection item onto the new layer icon at the bottom of the Layers palette (labeled in Figure 8-23). Or better yet, you can double-click on the Floating Selection item to bring up the Make Layer dialog box. To bypass the dialog box and let Photoshop name the new layer automatically — again, you can change the name later if you don't like it — Option-double-click on the Floating Selection item.

Although the contents of the image window change only slightly — the image suddenly appears deselected (which, incidentally, is no cause for alarm) — Photoshop shows you that the floating selection has been converted to a layer by the way it displays the item in the Layers palette (as in the bottom example in Figure 8-23). Instead of *Floating Selection* appearing in italic letters, your specified layer name now appears in upright type. This shows that the layer is independent and can be swapped with other layers later on down the line. A small preview of the layer appears to the left of the layer name. And that meaningless dotted circle icon in the column just to the right of the eyeball icon disappears.

 You don't have to float a selection to convert it to a new layer. That's simply the most convenient alternative. If you feel like working up a sweat, you can copy the selection, choose Edit⇨Paste Layers, name the layer and press Return. But this technique replaces the contents of the Clipboard and can be slow when you're working on very large images.

 Only one file format, the native Photoshop 3.0 format, saves images with layers. If you want to save a flattened version of your image — that is, with all layers fused together into a single image — in some other file format, choose File⇨Save a Copy and select the format you want from the Format pop-up menu. (If you select any format other than Photoshop 3.0, a Flatten Image check box appears in the lower left corner of the dialog box. The check box is automatically selected and dimmed so that you can't deselect it.)

Understanding transparency

Probably the most frightening thing about creating a new layer is watching the selection outline disappear. My first reaction was, "Hey, do you mind? I might want to do something with that!" But the truth is, it doesn't matter. Everything that was selected is now independent and ready for you to edit. Every little nuance of the selection outline — whether it's a jagged border, a little bit of antialiasing, or a feathered edge — is still 100 percent intact. Anything that wasn't selected is now transparent.

To see this transparency in action, click on the eyeball icon in front of the Background item in the Layers palette. This hides the Background layer and allows you to view the new layer by itself. As shown in Figure 8-24, the transparent areas are covered in a checkerboard pattern. Opaque areas look like the standard image, and translucent areas appear as a mix of image and checkerboard.

Figure 8-24:
The checker-
board pattern
represents
the transpar-
ent portions
of the layer.

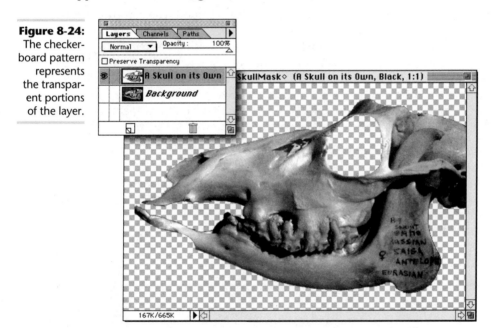

If the checkerboard pattern is hard to distinguish from the image, you can change the appearance of the pattern. Choose File⇨Preferences⇨Transparency to display the Transparency Options dialog box. Then edit away.

If you apply an effect to the layer while no portion of the layer is selected, Photoshop changes the opaque and translucent portions of the image but leaves the transparent background intact. For example, try choosing Image⇨Map⇨Invert (Command-I), which inverts the colors to create a photographic negative effect. The image inverts, and the checkerboard remains unchanged. If you click in the left column in front of the Background item to bring back the eyeball icon, you may notice a slight halo around the inverted image, but the edge pixels blend with the background image just as well as they ever did. In fact, it's exactly as if you applied the effect to a floating selection. The only difference is that this selection is permanently floating. You can do anything you want to it without running the risk of harming the underlying background.

Modifying the contents of a layer

Generally, editing a layer is just like editing a floating selection, except far more versatile. The following items document some of your new options and provide additional insights into the fantastic world of layers:

- **Activating layers:** When working with a floating selection, you can edit only the floating selection; you can't access the image behind the selection. With layers, you can edit any layer you want, whether it's the frontmost layer, the rearmost layer, or any layer in between. To select the layer you want to edit — called the *active* layer — simply click on that layer name in the Layers palette. The layer name becomes gray, showing that it is now active. Any edits now apply to this layer. (If an image from a different layer is preventing you from seeing all your edits, just hide it by clicking on the eyeball icon in front of the intrusive layer.)

- **Tightening selection outlines:** You may find it frustrating that Photoshop's selection tools — particularly the lasso tool — don't create selection outlines that automatically tighten around an image. Well, they do on layers. Try selecting an area of your image with the marquee or lasso tool. Make sure to select opaque and transparent areas alike. Now press Command-J to float the selection. The moment you float the image, the selection outline tightens to fit the exact contours of the image. The same holds true if you move the selection, clone it, or copy and paste it.

- **Selecting everything and tightening:** If you want to select everything on a layer as well as tighten the selection all at once, just press Command-Option-T. The contents of the layer are selected based on their degree of opacity. Opaque pixels are fully selected; transparent pixels are fully deselected; and transluscent pixels are partialy selected.

- **Transferring a selection outline:** As soon as you introduce multiple layers to an image, the selection outline becomes an independent creature. For example, take your tightened selection outline from the previous paragraph. You can use that same outline to select part of the Background layer. Simply click on the Background item in the Layers palette to make it active and then move the selection outline or apply some effect. You are now editing the Background layer using another layer's selection outline.

- **Importing a selection outline from the Clipboard:** One upshot of all this is that you can retain only the selection outline from an image copied to the Clipboard. Huh? Well, suppose that you copy part of a different image. You paste it into your new image but find that it's not exactly what you want. Eventually, you arrive at the conclusion that you'd like to use the selection outline from the floating pasted image, but you want to jettison the contents. In the old days, you had to turn the Opacity down to 1 percent and then defloat the selection to grab the underlying image. But this leaves a slight residue. (You might have to look hard to see it, but it's there.)

With layers, you have a more satisfactory solution: Send the floating selection to its own layer. Unfortunately, that deselects the image. To get the selection outline back, press Command-Option-T and drag the new layer name to the delete layer icon (the one that looks like a little trash can) at the bottom of the Layers palette. This deletes the contents of the selection but leaves the selection outline intact.

☞ **Using the move tool with layers:** When no portion of the image is selected, you can move an entire layer by dragging it with the move tool. If part of the layer disappears beyond the edge of the window, no problem. Photoshop still saves every bit of the hidden image (as long as you save the document in the native Photoshop 3.0 format).

☞ **Dragging multiple layers:** You can even move multiple layers — in their entirety — at one time. Just click in the second column on the left side of the Layers palette in front of any inactive layer that you want to move. Two little move icons appear in the column, one in front of the inactive layer and the other in front of the active layer, as in Figure 8-25. This shows that both layers will move in unison. Click in front of other layers to display and hide other move icons. Then drag with the move tool to move all layers together. (Note that this only works when nothing is selected. If a portion of the image is selected, the move tool moves only the selection on the active layer.)

☞ **Mixing a layer with the layer behind it:** To blend between layers with the smudge, blur, or sharpen tool, double-click on the tool icon in the toolbox and select the Sample Merged check box in the Options panel of the Brushes palette. You can also apply any of the commands in the Select⇨Matting submenu to a layer, whether selected or not.

☞ **Turning a layer back into a floating selection:** If you decide that you'd rather have a floating selection than a layer — you won't gain any options, but you may simply feel more comfortable working with a floating selection for a certain operation — press Command-A to select the entire layer and Command-C to copy it. Now delete the layer by dragging its name to the little trash can icon at the bottom of the Layers palette. Press Command-V to paste the image. The selection outline tightens around the floating image.

That's enough layers for now. If you haven't quite gotten your fix, you'll find more information about layers in Chapters 9 and 17. Chapter 9 shows how to mask layers, and Chapter 17 explains how to mix them with the background image.

Move icons

Figure 8-25:
Click in the second
column in the Layers
palette to display or hide
move icons (upper left).
All layers with move
icons move in unison
when you drag with the
move tool.

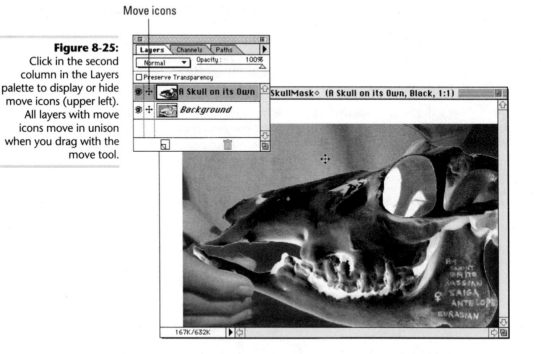

How to Draw and Edit Paths _____

Photoshop's path tools provide the most flexible and precise ways to define a selection
short of masking. But though a godsend to the experienced user, the path tools represent something of a chore to novices and intermediates. It takes most people quite a
while to become comfortable with the path tools because you have to draw a selection
outline one point at a time.

 If you're familiar with Illustrator's pen tool and other path-editing functions,
you'll find that Photoshop's tools are nearly identical. Photoshop doesn't
provide the breadth of options available in Illustrator — you can't transform
paths in Photoshop, for example — but the basic techniques are the same.

The following pages are designed to get you up and running with paths. I'll explain how
you approach drawing a path, how you edit it, how you convert it to a selection outline,
and how you stroke it with a paint or edit tool. All in all, you'll learn more about paths
than you ever wanted to know.

Paths overview

To access Photoshop's path tools, choose Window⇨Palettes⇨Show Paths to display the Paths panel of the Layers palette (which I'll simply call the Paths palette). Here you'll find five path tools, lots of commands, and an extensive panel of editing options, as shown in Figure 8-26. On the whole, this palette represents a fully functioning path-drawing environment that rivals similar features provided by Illustrator or FreeHand.

Figure 8-26:
The Paths palette provides access to every one of Photoshop's path-drawing and editing functions.

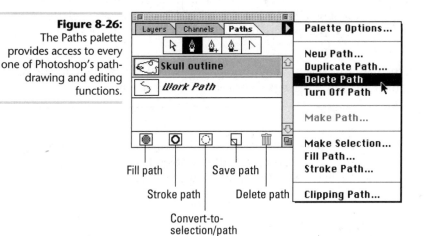

Fill path

Stroke path

Convert-to-selection/path

Save path

Delete path

How paths work

Paths differ from normal selections in that they exist on the equivalent of a distinct, object-oriented layer that sits in front of the bitmapped image. This setup enables you to edit a path with point-by-point precision after you draw it to make sure that it meets the exact requirements of your artwork. It also prevents you from accidentally messing up the image, as you can when you edit ordinary selection outlines. After creating the path, you convert it into a standard selection outline before using it to edit the contents of the image, as explained in the section "Converting and saving paths," later in this chapter.

The following steps explain the basic process of drawing a selection outline with the path tools.

STEPS: **Drawing a Selection with the Path Tools**

Step 1. Use the pen tool to draw the outline of your prospective selection.

Step 2. If the outline of the path requires some adjustment, reshape it using the other path tools.

Step 3. When you get the path exactly the way you want it, save the path in Photoshop by choosing the Save Path command from the Paths palette menu. (Alternatively, you can double-click on the Work Path item in the scrolling list.)

Step 4. Convert the path to a selection by choosing the Make Selection command or pressing the Enter key when a path or selection tool is active.

That's all there is to it. After you convert the path to a selection, it works just like any of the selection outlines described earlier. You can feather a selection, move it, copy it, clone it, or apply one of the special effects described in future chapters.

Using the Paths palette tools

Before I get into my long-winded description of how you draw and edit paths, here is a quick introduction to the tools available from the Paths palette:

Arrow: This tool lets you drag points and handles to reshape a path. You can access the arrow tool at any time by pressing and holding the Command key when a path, paint, or edit tool is selected.

Pen: Use the pen tool to draw paths in Photoshop one point at a time. I explain this tool in detail in the following section. Press the T key to select the tool.

Insert point: Click on an existing path to add a point to it. You can access this function when the arrow tool is selected by Command-Option-clicking on a segment in the path. When the pen tool is active, Control-click.

Remove point: Click on an existing point in a path to delete the point without creating a break in the path's outline. To accomplish this when the arrow tool is selected, Command-Option-click on a point in a path. When the pen tool is active, Control-click.

Convert point: Click or drag on a point to convert it to a corner or smooth point. You also can drag on a handle to convert the point. Press Control to access the convert point tool when the arrow tool is selected; press Command and Control when the pen is selected.

The terms *point, smooth point,* and others associated with drawing paths are explained in the upcoming section.

Drawing with the pen tool

When drawing with the pen tool, you build a path by creating individual points. Photoshop automatically connects the points with *segments* — which are simply straight or curved lines.

All paths in Photoshop are *Bézier* (pronounced *bay-zee-ay*) *paths,* meaning that they rely on the same mathematical curve definitions that make up the core of the PostScript printer language. The Bézier curve model allows for zero, one, or two levers to be associated with each point in a path. These levers, labeled in Figure 8-27, are called *Bézier control handles* or simply *handles.* You can move each handle in relation to a point, enabling you to bend and tug at a curved segment like a piece of soft wire.

Smooth points

Figure 8-27:
Drag with the pen tool to create a smooth point flanked by two Bézier control handles.

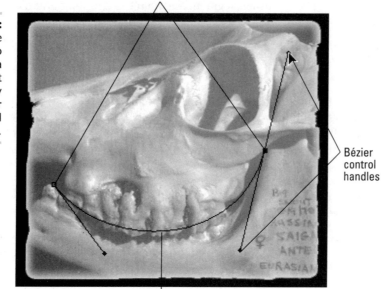

Bézier control handles

Curved segment

The following list summarizes how you can use the pen tool to build paths in Photoshop:

- ❧ **Adding segments:** To build a path, create one point after another until the path is the desired length and shape. Photoshop automatically draws a segment between each new point and its predecessor.

- ❧ **Closing the path:** If you plan on eventually converting the path to a selection outline, you need to complete the outline by clicking again on the first point in the path. Every point will then have one segment coming into it and another segment exiting it. Such a path is called a *closed path* because it forms one continuous outline.

- ❧ **Leaving the path open:** If you plan on applying the Stroke Path command (explained later), you may not want to close a path. To leave it open, so that it has a specific beginning and ending, deactivate the path by saving it (choose the Save Paths command from the Paths palette menu). After you complete the save operation, you can click in the image window to begin a new path.

- ❧ **Extending an open path:** To reactivate an open path, click or drag on one of its endpoints. Photoshop draws a segment between the endpoint and the next point you create.

- ❧ **Joining two open paths:** To join one open path with another open path, click or drag on an endpoint in the first path and then click or drag on an endpoint in the second.

Points in a Bézier path act as little road signs. Each point steers the path by specifying how a segment enters it and how another segment exits it. You specify the identity of each little road sign by clicking, dragging, or Option-dragging with the pen tool. The following items explain the specific kinds of points and segments you can create in Photoshop. See Figure 8-28 for examples.

- ❧ **Corner point:** Click with the pen tool to create a *corner point,* which represents the corner between two straight segments in a path.

- ❧ **Straight segment:** Click at two different locations to create a straight segment between two corner points. Shift-click to draw a 45-degree-angle segment between the new corner point and its predecessor.

- ❧ **Smooth point:** Drag to create a *smooth point* with two symmetrical Bézier control handles. A smooth point ensures that one segment meets with another in a continuous arc.

- ❧ **Curved segment:** Drag at two different locations to create a curved segment between two smooth points.

- ✐ **Curved segment followed by straight:** After drawing a curved segment, Option-click on the smooth point you just created to delete the forward Bézier control handle. This converts the smooth point to a corner point with one handle. Then click at a different location to append a straight segment to the end of the curved segment.

- ✐ **Straight segment followed by curved:** After drawing a straight segment, drag from the corner point you just created to add a Bézier control handle. Then drag again at a different location to append a curved segment to the end of the straight segment.

- ✐ **Cusp point:** After drawing a curved segment, Option-drag from the smooth point you just created to redirect the forward Bézier control handle, converting the smooth point to a corner point with two independent handles, sometimes known as a *cusp point.* Then drag again at a new location to append a curved segment that proceeds in a different direction than the previous curved segment.

Reshaping existing paths

As you become more familiar with the pen tool, you'll draw paths correctly the first time around more and more frequently. But you'll never get it right 100 percent of the time or even 50 percent of the time. From your first timid steps until you develop into a seasoned pro, you'll rely heavily on Photoshop's ability to *reshape* paths by moving points and handles, adding and deleting points, and converting points to change the curvature of segments. So don't worry if you don't draw a path correctly the first time. The paths tools provide all the second chances you'll ever need.

Using the arrow tool

The arrow tool represents the foremost path reshaping function in Photoshop. After selecting this tool, you can perform any of the following functions:

- ✐ **Selecting points:** Click on a point to select it independently of other points in a path. Shift-click to select an additional point, even if the point belongs to a different path than other selected points. Option-click on a path to select all its points in one fell swoop. You can even marquee points by dragging in a rectangle around them. You *cannot,* however, apply commands from the Select menu, such as All or None, to the selection of paths.

- ✐ **Drag selected points:** To move one or more points in a path, select the points you want to move and then drag one of the selected points. All selected points move the same distance and direction. When you move a point while a neighboring point remains stationary, the segment between the two points shrinks, stretches, and bends to accommodate the change in distance. Segments located between two selected or deselected points remain unchanged during a move.

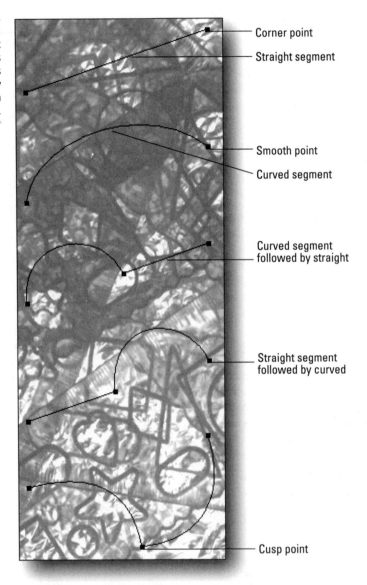

Figure 8-28:
The different kinds of points and segments you can draw with the pen tool.

Corner point

Straight segment

Smooth point

Curved segment

Curved segment followed by straight

Straight segment followed by curved

Cusp point

You can move selected points in one-pixel increments by pressing arrow keys. If both a portion of the image and points in a path are selected, the arrow keys move the point only. Because paths reside on a higher layer, they take precedence in all functions that might concern them.

Drag a segment directly: You also can reshape a path by dragging its segments. When you drag a straight segment, the two corner points on either side of the segment move as well. As illustrated in Figure 8-29, the neighboring segments stretch, shrink, or bend to accommodate the drag. When you drag a curved segment, however, you stretch, shrink, or bend that segment only, as demonstrated in Figure 8-30.

Figure 8-29:
Drag a straight segment to move the segment and change the length, direction, and curvature of the neighboring segments.

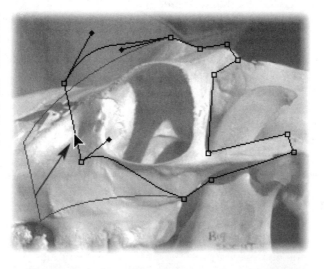

Figure 8-30:
Drag a curved segment to change the curvature of that segment only and leave the neighboring segments unchanged.

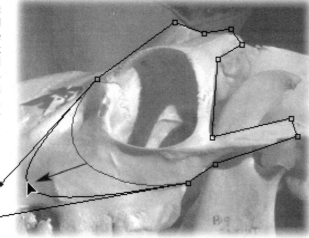

 When you drag a curved segment, drag from the middle of the segment, approximately equidistant from both its points. This method provides the best leverage and ensures that the segment doesn't go flying off in some weird direction you hadn't anticipated.

- **Drag a Bézier control handle:** Select a point and drag either of its Bézier control handles to change the curvature of the corresponding segment without moving any of the points in the path. If the point is a smooth point, moving one handle moves both handles in the path. If you want to be able to move a smooth handle independently of its partner, you must use the convert point tool, as discussed in the "Converting points" section later in this chapter.

- **Clone a path:** To make a duplicate of a selected path, Option-drag it to a new location in the image window. Photoshop automatically stores the new path under the same name as the original.

 Press and hold the Command key to temporarily access the arrow tool when the pen tool or any of the path or edit tools is selected. When you release the Command key, the cursor returns to the selected tool.

Adding and deleting points

The quantity of points and segments in a path is forever subject to change. Whether a path is closed or open, you can reshape it by adding and deleting points, which in turn forces the addition or deletion of a segment.

- **Appending a point to the end of an open path:** If an existing path is open, you can activate one of its endpoints by either clicking or dragging on it with the pen tool, depending on the identity of the endpoint and whether you want the next segment to be straight or curved. Photoshop is then prepared to draw a segment between the endpoint and the next point you create.

- **Closing an open path:** You also can use the technique I just described to close an open path. Just select one endpoint, click or drag on it with the pen tool to activate it, and then click or drag on the opposite endpoint. Photoshop draws a segment between the two endpoints, closing the path and eliminating both endpoints by converting them to *interior points,* which simply means that the points are bound on both sides by segments.

- **Joining two open paths:** You can join two open paths to create one longer open path. To do so, activate an endpoint of the first path and then click or drag with the pen tool on an endpoint of the second path.

- **Inserting a point in a segment:** Select the insert point tool and click anywhere along an open or closed path to insert a point and divide the segment on which you click into two segments. Photoshop automatically inserts a corner or smooth point, depending on its reading of the path. If the point does not exactly meet your needs, use the convert point tool to change it.

To access the insert or remove point tool, press Command and Option when using the arrow tool. Command-Option-click on an existing segment to insert a point; Command-Option-click on a point to remove it. If the pen tool is active, press the Control key instead.

↣ **Deleting a point and breaking the path:** The simplest way to delete a point is to select it with the arrow tool and press either the Delete or Clear key. (You also can choose Edit⇨Clear, though why you would want to expend so much effort is beyond me.) When you delete an interior point, you delete both segments associated with that point, resulting in a break in the path. If you delete an endpoint from an open path, you delete the single segment associated with the point.

↣ **Removing a point without breaking the path:** Select the remove point tool and click on a point in an open or closed path to delete the point and draw a new segment between the two points that neighbor it. The remove point tool ensures that no break occurs in a path.

↣ **Deleting a segment:** You can delete a single interior segment from a path without affecting any point. To do so, first click outside the path with the arrow tool to deselect the path. Then click on the segment you want to delete and press the Delete or Clear key. When you delete an interior segment, you create a break in your path.

↣ **Deleting a whole path:** To delete an entire path, select any portion of it and press the Delete or Clear key twice. The first time you press Delete, Photoshop deletes the selected point or segment and automatically selects all other points in the path. The second time you press Delete, Photoshop gets rid of everything it missed the first time around.

Converting points

Photoshop allows you to change the identity of an interior point. You can convert a corner point to a smooth point and vice versa. You perform all point conversions using the convert point tool as follows:

↣ **Smooth to corner:** Click on an existing smooth point to convert it to a corner point with no Bézier control handle.

↣ **Smooth to cusp:** Drag one of the handles of a smooth point to move it independently of the other handle, thus converting the smooth point to a cusp.

↣ **Corner to smooth:** Drag from a corner point to convert it to a smooth point with two symmetrical Bézier control handles.

↣ **Cusp to smooth:** Drag one of the handles of a cusp point to lock both handles back into alignment, thus converting the cusp to a smooth point.

Press the Control key to temporarily access the convert point tool when the arrow tool is selected. Press both Command and Control to access the convert point tool when the pen tool is active.

Painting along a path

After you finish drawing a path and getting it exactly the way you want it, you can convert it to a selection outline — as described in the next section — or you can paint it. You can either paint the interior of the path by choosing the Fill Path command from the Paths palette menu, or you can paint the outline of the path by choosing Stroke Path. The Fill Path command works very much like Edit⇨Fill. However, the Stroke Path command is altogether different than Edit⇨Stroke. Whereas Edit⇨Stroke creates outlines and arrowheads, the Stroke Path command allows you to paint a brush stroke along the contours of a path. It may not sound like a big deal at first, but this feature enables you to combine the spontaneity of the paint and edit tools with the structure and precision of a path.

Because the Fill Path command is very nearly identical to the standard fill options available to any selection — in fact, you can use selections and paths in tandem to specify a filled area — I discuss it in the "Filling paths" section of Chapter 10.

To paint a path, choose the Stroke Path command from the Paths palette menu to display the Stroke Path dialog box shown in Figure 8-31. In this dialog box, you can choose the paint or edit tool with which you want to *stroke* the path (which just means to paint a brush stroke along a path). Photoshop drags the chosen tool along the exact route of the path, retaining any tool or brush shape settings that were in force when you chose the tool.

Figure 8-31:
Photoshop displays this dialog box when you choose the Stroke Path command while a tool other than a paint or edit tool is selected.

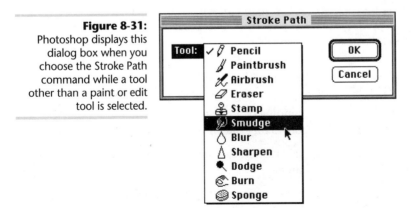

Color Plate 3-1:
This little warlock shows off the differences between the four different JPEG compression settings, from maximum quality, minimum compression (upper left) to minimum quality, maximum compression (lower right). Inspect the enlarged eye and sharpened staff for subtle erosions in detail.

Maximum   116K

High   66K

Medium   50K

Low   46K

Color Plate 3-2:
My personal 1,024 x 768-pixel startup screen features effects created with Kai's Power Tools, Xaos Paint Alchemy, Xaos Terrazzo, Aldus Gallery Effects, and Alien Skin.

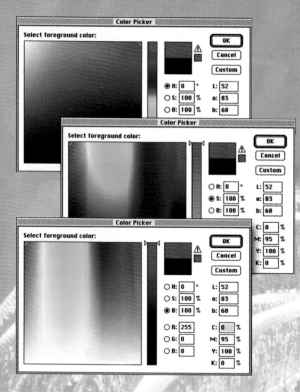

Color Plate 4-1:
The colors inside the field and slider in the Color Picker dialog box change to reflect the selection of the H (Hue), S (Saturation), and B (Brightness) radio buttons.

Color Plate 4-2:
I reduced a 24-bit color image (upper left) to the 8-bit System palette using three different Dither options: None (upper right), Pattern (lower right), and Diffusion (lower left). Of the three, Diffusion is almost always the best choice.

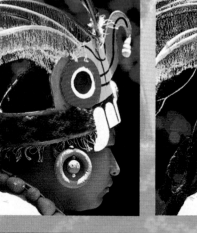

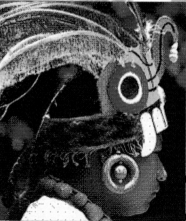

Color Plate 5-1:
The U. S. Capitol building (a.k.a. House of "What, Me Partisan?") on a peaceful evening. Look at those tax dollars glow.

Color Plate 5-2:
You can wreak some pretty interesting havoc on the colors in an image by copying the image from one channel and pasting it into another and by swapping images between color channels.

Replace red with blue

Replace blue with green

Replace green with red

Swap red and blue

© 1992 Mark Collen

SPALDING

Jim Thorpe

OKLAHOMA

The Greatest Athlete in the World

Color Plate 6-1:
A grayscale image printed as a quadtone using the colors navy blue, rose, teal, and dull orange. All colors were defined and printed using CMYK pigments.

Color Plate 7-1:
Starting with an image of typical saturation (upper left), I applied the sponge tool set to Desaturate to the inside of the pepper and the corn in the background (upper right). I then repeated the effect twice more to make the areas almost gray (lower right). Returning to the original image, I then selected the Saturate icon and again scrubbed inside the pepper and in the corn to boost the colors (lower left).

Color Plate 7-3:
I painted this image for *Macworld* magazine in 1990 using a Wacom SD-510 pressure-sensitive tablet and Photoshop 1.0.7. A pressure-sensitive tablet transforms Photoshop into a fully functioning artist's studio.

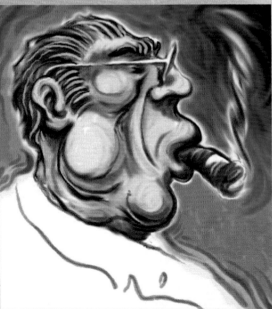

Color Plate 7-2:
To create this image, I traced an image from the PhotoDisc library using the paintbrush tool and a flat brush shape. Although Photoshop offers automated filters that you can use to create similar effects, nothing is so versatile and precise as a simple paintbrush.

Normal

Dissolve

Behind

Multiply

Screen

Overlay

Soft Light

Hard Light

Darken

Lighten

Difference

Hue

Saturation

Color

Luminosity

Color Plate 7-4:
Here I've painted red over an image with the paintbrush using each of the 15 brush modes available in Photoshop 3.0. The Hue brush mode shows up better in the blue half of the image because the right half already has a lot of red in it. Saturation shows up better on the right half because the saturation of the left half is already maxed out.

Color Plate 7-5:
Using the paintbrush tool, I've painted 12 lines in 12 evenly spaced hues — each exactly 20 degrees apart on the color wheel — in each of the three newest and most difficult to understand brush modes. Although all three brush modes mix the foreground color applied by the brush with the existing colors in the image, subtle but important differences distinguish one mode from the next.

Overlay   Soft Light   Hard Light

Color Plate 9-1:
Two inverted selections (top) and their equivalent masks (bottom). In this case, you can see both mask and image. Red-tinted areas are masked, representing deselected areas in the image; untinted areas are unmasked and represent selected areas.

Color Plate 9-2:
A colorized version of one of the parapets from the Great Wall created by converting the image itself to a mask. I drew the mask for the stylized sun using the elliptical marquee, paintbrush, and smudge tools.

Color Plate 10-1:
After filling my floating drop shadow with a reddish orange (top), I chose the Multiply option from the overlay modes pop-up menu in the Layers palette to mix the drop shadow with the underlying image (middle). Then I changed the Opacity setting to 70 percent (bottom) to create the finished colored drop shadow.

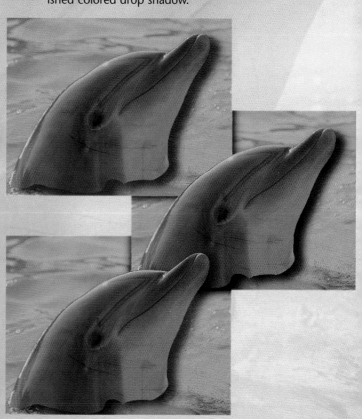

Color Plate 10-2:
The popular cartoon character Neutron Mammal — what, you've never heard of Neutron Mammal? — is the result of applying both the haloing and spotlighting effects described in Chapter 10 and then setting the whole thing against an inverted background.

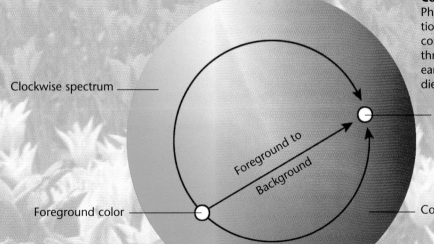

Color Plate 10-3:
Photoshop can assign colors to a gradation by roaming around the great HSB color wheel or by passing straight through it. Color Plate 10-4 shows linear examples of each of these three gradient styles.

Clockwise spectrum

Background color

Foreground to Background

Foreground color

Counterclockwise spectrum

Color Plate 10-4:
Three gradations between cyan and red created using each of three Style settings in the Gradient Tool Options panel.

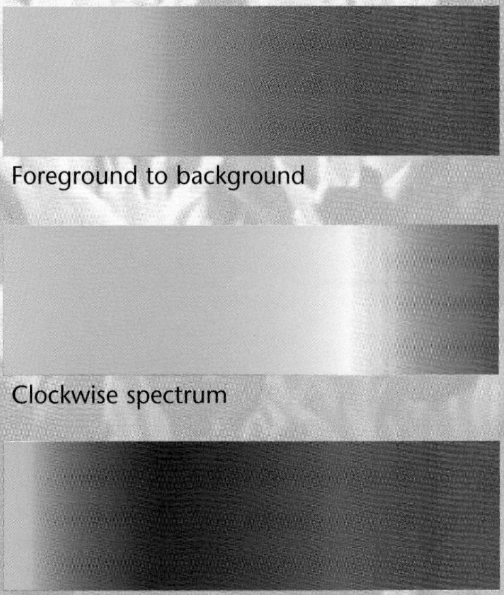

Foreground to background

Clockwise spectrum

Counterclockwise spectrum

Noise x 3

Blast, Motion Blur

Color Plate 10-5:
The results of filtering the three gradation styles from Color Plate 10-4 by applying the Add Noise filter three times in a row (top) and then blasting the gradations with the Wind filter and applying the Motion Blur filter (bottom).

Color Plate 13-1:
Clockwise from upper left, the effects of the Motion Blur, Sharpen Edges, Median, and High Pass corrective filters. Normally, the High Pass filter takes the saturation out of an image, leaving many areas gray, like an old, sun-bleached slide. To restore the colors, I pasted the original image in front of the filtered one and chose Color from the Brush ⮑Modes pop-up menu in the Brushes palette.

Color Plate 13-2:
Clockwise from upper left, the effects of the destructive filters Crystallize, Lens Flare, Color Halftone, and Twirl. The Lens Flare filter is applicable to color images only. Perhaps surprisingly, you can apply the Color Halftone filter to grayscale and color images alike.

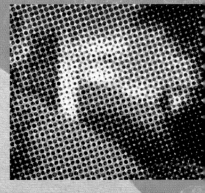

Color Plate 13-3:
The results of applying the Unsharp Mask filter to independent color channels in an RGB image. In each case, the Amount value was 300, the Radius value was 1.0, the Threshold was 0, and I applied the filter twice.

Color Plate 13-4:
Again, I applied Unsharp Mask to the independent color channels, but this time with an exaggerated Radius value, 10.0; a more moderate Amount value, 100; and the default Threshold, 0. Rather than pinpointing the sharpening effect, as in Color Plate 13-3, the high Radius value allows the colors to bleed as they are strengthened by the Amount value.

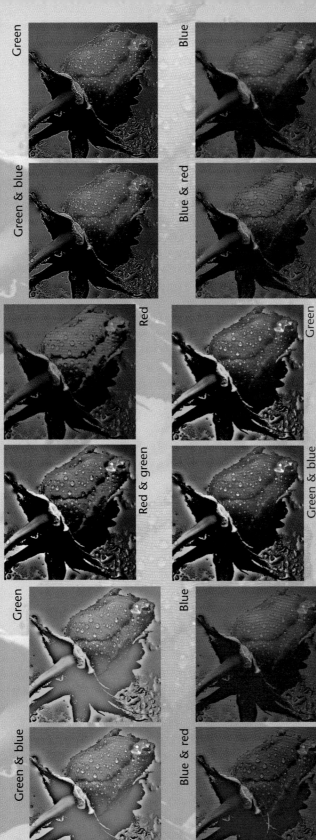

Color Plate 13-5:
The results of applying Image➪Other➪High Pass with a Radius value of 10.0 to each channel and pair of channels in an RGB image. To boost the color values in the images slightly, I applied the Levels command (Command-L) after each application of High Pass.

Color Plate 13-6:
After floating the image and applying the Gaussian Blur filter, I applied various Opacity and overlay mode settings. Clockwise from upper left, the overlay modes are Normal, Luminosity, Darken, and Lighten. I varied the Opacity value anywhere from 60 to 80 percent, depending on the image.

Color Plate 13-7:
After selecting the background using a very precise mask that I created using the High Pass, Threshold, Gaussian Blur, and Levels commands, I applied two variations on directional blurring effects. I applied the Wind and Motion Blur filters to make the background appear as if it were spinning around the woman (top). Starting over with the base image, I applied the Radial Blur filter set to Zoom to make the background appear to rush toward the viewer (bottom).

Noise, red

Noise, green

Noise, blue

Median, red

Median, green

Median, blue

Color Plate 13-8:
The top row shows the results of applying the Add Noise filter to each of the red, green, and blue channels with an Amount value of 75 and Gaussian selected. The bottom row shows the effects of the Median filter when applied to individual color channels when set to a Radius of 10.

Color Plate 13-9:
An image scanned from an old issue of *Macworld* magazine shown as it appears in the normal RGB mode (top right) and when each channel is viewed separately (top left). The middle images show the effects of the Dust & Scratches filter set to a Radius of 2 and a Threshold of 20. The bottom images show how the channels look after suppressing the moiré patterns with the Gaussian Blur, Median, and Unsharp Mask filters.

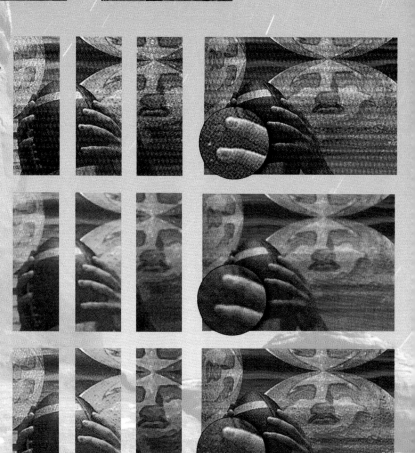

Color Plate 14-1:
The result of applying the Extrude filter to the lower left rose image from Color Plate 13-4. If you select the Blocks and Solid Front Faces options, the filter transforms the image into mosaic tiles and shoves the tiles out at you in 3-D space.

Color Plate 14-2:
After floating the image, I applied the Mezzotint filter set to the Long Strokes effect in each of the RGB, Lab, and CMYK color modes (top row). I then mixed the filtered image with the underlying original using the Overlay mode and an Opacity setting of 40 percent (bottom row).

RGB Lab CMYK

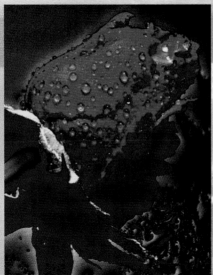

Color Plate 14-3:
Here I've taken a floating selection and applied the Emboss filter armed with an Angle of 135 degrees, a Height value of 2, and an Amount of 300 percent. To create the left image, I mixed the floater with the underlying original using the Luminosity overlay mode and an Opacity setting of 80 percent. To get the psychedelic effect on the right, I chose the Difference overlay mode and reduced the Opacity value to 40 percent.

Color Plate 14-4:
After selecting an image from the PhotoDisc library (left), I floated the image, Gaussian Blurred it with a 3.0 Radius, and applied the Find Edges filter. The effect was light, so I used the Levels command to darken it (middle). I then composited the image using the Overlay mode and an Opacity setting of 80 percent (right).

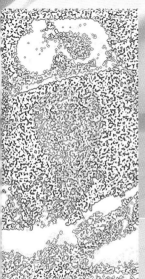

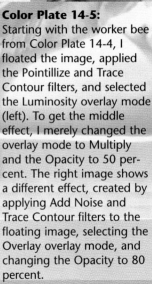

Color Plate 14-5:
Starting with the worker bee from Color Plate 14-4, I floated the image, applied the Pointillize and Trace Contour filters, and selected the Luminosity overlay mode (left). To get the middle effect, I merely changed the overlay mode to Multiply and the Opacity to 50 percent. The right image shows a different effect, created by applying Add Noise and Trace Contour filters to the floating image, selecting the Overlay overlay mode, and changing the Opacity to 80 percent.

Pinch　　　　　　　　　　　　　　　Spherize

Color Plate 14-6:
The results of using the Pinch (left column) and Spherize (right column) filters to create conical gradations. By the time I captured the first row of images, I had repeated each filter twice. By the second row, I had repeated each filter 12 times. I then mixed the Pinched gradation with the original image using the Soft Light overlay mode (bottom left). I cloned the Spherized gradation a few times and applied the Screen mode to each (bottom right).

x 2

x 12

Color Plate 14-7:
In this piece, titled *Knowing Risk,* Seattle-based artist Mark Collen combines a variety of distortion filtering effects to create a surrealistic landscape. The cat, the book, the mongoose, and the twigs are the only scanned images.

Clouds

Difference Clouds

x 10

Overlay

Screen

Hue

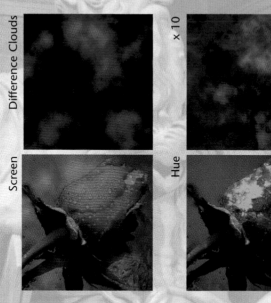

Color Plate 14-8:
The top row shows the results of Shift-choosing the Clouds filter (left), Shift-choosing Difference Clouds (middle), and pressing Command-Shift-F ten times in a row (right). I then took each of the images from the top row and mixed it with the rose using one of three overlay modes (labeled beside bottom row). You can create clouds, haze, and imaginative fill patterns with the Clouds filters.

Color Plate 14-9:
I used the Lighting Effects filter to assign three spotlights to a familiar image. The bumpy surfaces of the images are the results of texture maps. To create the left image, I used the red channel as the texture. In the right image, I used the repeating pattern of Lenins.

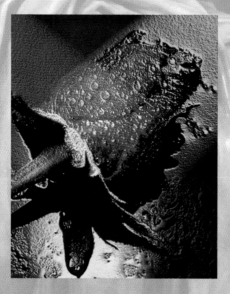

Color Plate 15-1:
Color versions of four Custom filter effects, including (clockwise from upper left) mild sharpening, offset sharpening, edge-detection, and full-color embossing.

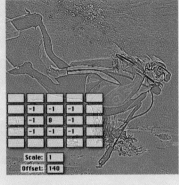

Color Plate 15-2:
Examples of applying four patterns from the Displacement Maps folder with the Displace filter, including (clockwise from upper left) Crumbles, Streaks pattern, Mezzo effect, and Twirl pattern.

Color Plate 15-3:
The top row shows three different applications of the Rotator filters with the Red, Green, and Blue slider bars set to various positions. The Distorto option was set to 0. In the bottom examples, I added a cranked up Distorto value to each of the rotations above.

R:1, G:2, B:3

R:80, G:85, B:90

R:240, G:230, B:250

Distort = 10

Distort = 40

Distort = 140

Channel Mixer

Color Creep

Crisscross

Color Plate 15-4:
Applications of six of the seven filters I created in Filter Factory that you'll find on the CD. Each filter has between 3 and 6 sliders, so you can create all sorts of variations.

Full Channel Press

Noise Blaster

SuperInvert

RGB | Lab | CMYK

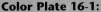

Color Plate 16-1:
The results of applying the Invert command to a single image in each of the three color modes. I inverted all channels in the RGB and Lab images and all but the black channel in the CMYK channel.

Color Plate 16-2:
Because the Equalize command finds different light and dark pixels throughout the channels in each of the three color modes, the mode has a tremendous effect on the performance of the command. The three images are identical, and the areas selected are identical, but the effects are different.

RGB | Lab | CMYK

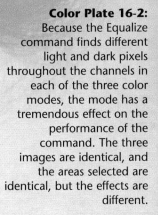

Luminosity | Overlay | Difference

  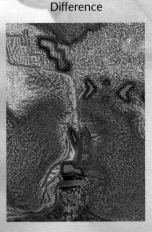

Color Plate 16-3:
After floating the image and applying the High Pass filter and the Posterize command, I mixed the floater and underlying original by choosing each of three overlay modes from the Layers palette. All effects were created with Opacity settings of 100 percent.

Color Plate 16-4:
You can downplay the colors in selected portions of an image by floating the selection and applying Desaturate to convert the pixels to grayscale (top left). Lessening the Opacity — say, to 50 percent — brings back some colors (top right). Alternatively, you can Invert the floating selection, choose the Color overlay mode, and change the Opacity to 50 percent (bottom left). Raising the Opacity increases the presence of inverted colors (bottom right).

Original

RGB

Color Plate 16-5:
Starting with the original pumpkin image (top left), I applied Image⇨Adjust⇨ Auto Levels in each of the three color modes. The command is really designed for RGB images and tends to mess up CMYK images (lower right). As you folks who live outside Love Canal are probably aware, few pumpkins are fire-engine red.

Lab

CMYK

Color Plate 16-6:
The results of choosing Image⇨Adjust⇨Hue/Saturation and applying various Hue values to an entire image (top row) and to only the red portions of the image (bottom row).

Master, –30°

Master, +15°

Master, +60°

Red only, –30°

Red only, +15°

Red only, +60°

Color Plate 16-7:
The results of applying various Saturation values to an entire image (top row) and to specified colors independently of others (bottom row). Because flesh tones reside primarily in the red tonal range — regardless of the skin pigment of the subject — you can almost always enhance or temper skin colors by selecting the R (Red) option and adjusting the Saturation value.

Master, -50

Master, +30

All But red, -100

Red, −100, All others, +50

Master, −50°

Master, +50°

Faces, −25°,
Background, 155°

Faces, 75°,
Background, −115°

Color Plate 16-8:
The results of applying various Hue values to an image when the Colorize option is inactive (top row) and active (bottom row). Note that while the top two images contain a rainbow of differently colored pixels, the bottom images contain only two apiece — pink and teal (bottom left), and chartreuse and violet (bottom right).

Color Plate 16-9:
You can change the hue and saturation and at the same time experiment with the affected area using the Replace Color command. The top row shows the results of clicking repeatedly on the pumpkin's face with one Fuzziness value (left) and clicking once in the background with another (right). The bottom examples show the results of adjusting the hues of predefined colors using the Selective Color command.

Fuzziness, 40

Fuzziness, 200

Red to violet, Relative

Red to violet and black to white, Absolute

More Green

Lighter

More Yellow

Color Plate 16-10:
The effects of applying each of the thumbnails offered in the Variations dialog box to the familiar pumpkin. In each case, the slider bar was set to its default setting, midway between Fine and Coarse, and the Midtones radio button was selected.

More Cyan

Original

More Red

More Blue

Darker

More Magenta

Color Plate 16-11:
The original scan of this 100-year-old poster required some color correction (top left). Although applying the Auto button from the Levels dialog box improved the image dramatically (bottom left), manually adjusting the Input Levels slider bars further enhanced the image by bringing out the medium gray values (right).

Color Plate 16-12:
The results of using the Curves command to lighten the colors in the red channel (left), increase the level of contrast in the green channel (middle), and apply an arbitrary color map to the blue channel (right).

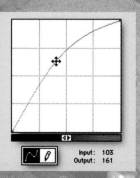

Input: 103
Output: 161

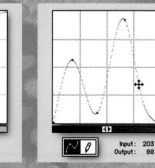

Input: 91
Output: 73

Input: 203
Output: 88

Normal	Overlay	Difference
Normal, 50%	Soft Light	Hue
Dissolve, 50%	Hard Light	Saturation
Multiply	Darken	Color
Screen	Lighten	Luminosity

Color Plate 17-1:
Examples of all 14 options available from the overlay modes pop-up menu in the Layers palette when you edit a layer or floating selection, represented here by the banner. Each overlay mode allows you to mix colors in a floating selection with colors in the underlying image in a unique way. Unless otherwise noted, the Opacity of each banner is set to 100 percent.

Color Plate 17-2:
Though frightening, these reckless combinations of bright colors are useful for demonstrating the effects of applying fuzziness ranges independently to the red (top row), green (middle), and blue (bottom) color channels using the This Layer (left column) and Underlying (right column) slider triangles. The banner in the upper right corner fades out because the underlying stucco texture is colored with a yellow-to-pink gradation, and the pink pixels are being forced through.

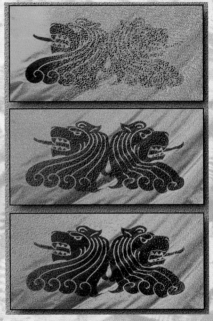

Color Plate 17-3:
For the purpose of comparison, the first image shows the result of compositing the RGB image from Color Plate 5-1 onto itself using the Hard Light mode. Other examples show the different effects you can achieve by duplicating the image, converting it to the Lab mode, and then mixing it with the original RGB image using the Apply Image command, again set to Hard Light.

RGB on RGB

Lab on RGB

Lightness on RGB

Inverted b on RGB

Mask Channel

Hard Light

Color Plate 17-4:
After creating a separate mask channel (top left), I used this mask to protect the sky in the target image. Though I used the Apply Image command to apply several compositing effects to the Capitol building, none affected the sky as long as the Mask check box was selected.

Screen

Inverted Difference

Color Plate 17-5:
The results of applying the Add (top left), Subtract (middle left) and Difference (bottom left) overlay modes, followed by the same images after swapping the red and blue color channels (right column).

Color Plate 18-1: To create this embossed text, I first used the Apply Image command set to the Screen overlay mode to composite the beach image with a white logo created in a mask channel (left.) I then used the Hard Light overlay mode to composite an embossed version of the logo. To keep the embossed edges from flowing out into the image, I used the original logo as a mask (right).

Color Plate 18-2: To create a punched effect (left), I inverted the embossed version of the logo and combined it with the last image from the Color Plate 18-1 using the Overlay mode. I also inverted the mask to protect the letters themselves, which already appear raised. I then inverted the logo using the Difference mode (right).

Color Plate 18-3: To prepare the logo, I selected a logo-shaped area of my image, applied the Add Noise and Filter commands, floated the selection, filled it with white, and changed the Opacity to 40 percent (left). After using masks based on the embossed logo to draw in the highlights and shadows, I inverted the logo to give it a marble-like texture (right).

Layer 1, filtered

Background copy

Background copy 2

Color Plate 18-4:
The first column shows the result of compositing a single filtered image (that looks much like the one in the upper left corner) onto the plain Capitol dome from Color Plate 5-1. In the second column, I duplicated the underlying dome to a layer above the filtered image and applied additional overlay modes. In the third column, I duplicated the dome again and heaped on still more overlay modes. Only the bottom right example had to be flattened for color correction.

Hard Light

Hard Light

Hard Light

Difference

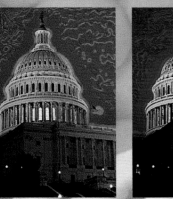

Color

Overlay

Hue

Hard Light

Difference with Auto Levels

Color Plate 18-5:
Starting with the last column of images from Color Plate 18-4, I applied various effects and overlay modes to the top layer while leaving the other layers untouched. In the left column, I inverted the top layer. In the middle column, I applied the Ripple command at its maximum setting and shifted the hues –90 degrees using the Hue/Saturation command. In the right column, I applied the Add Noise filter.

Invert

Ripple & Hue/Saturation

Add Noise

Color

Color

Overlay

Difference

Overlay

Screen

Overlay

Difference

Dissolve, 20%

You can also display the Stroke Path dialog box by Option-clicking on the stroke path icon at the bottom of the Paths palette (labeled back in Figure 8-26). If you prefer to bypass the dialog box, select a paint or edit tool and either click on the stroke path icon or simply press the Enter key on the numeric keypad. Instead of displaying the dialog box, Photoshop assumes that you want to use the selected tool and strokes away.

 If the path is selected, the Stroke Path command becomes a Stroke Subpath command. Photoshop then only strokes the selected path, rather than all paths saved under the current name.

The following steps walk you through a little project I created by stroking paths with the paintbrush and smudge tools. Figures 8-32 through 8-34 show the progression and eventual outcome of the image.

STEPS: Stroking Paths with the Paintbrush and Smudge Tools

Step 1.   After opening a low-resolution version of a hurricane image, I drew the zigzag path shown in Figure 8-32. As you can see, the path emits from the eye of the hurricane. I drew the path starting at the eye and working up-ward, which is very important because Photoshop strokes a path in the same direction in which you draw it.

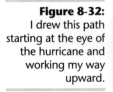
Figure 8-32:
I drew this path starting at the eye of the hurricane and working my way upward.

Step 2.   I saved the path by double-clicking on the Work Path name in the Paths palette, entering a name, and pressing Return.

Step 3.   I used the Brushes palette to specify three brush shapes, each with a Roundness value of 40. The largest brush had a diameter of 16, the next largest had a diameter of 10, and the smallest had a diameter of 4.

Step 4.   I double-clicked on the paintbrush tool and set the Fade-out value to 400. Then I selected the To Background radio button so that Photoshop would draw gradient strokes between the foreground and background colors.

Step 5.   I stroked the path with the paintbrush three times using the Stroke Path command, changing the foreground and background colors for each stroke. The first time, I used the largest brush shape and stroked the path from gray to white; the second time, I changed to the middle brush shape and stroked the path from black to white; and the final time, I used the smallest brush shape and stroked the path from white to black. The result of all this stroking is shown in Figure 8-33.

Step 6.   Next, I created two clones of the zigzag path by Option-dragging the path with the arrow tool. I pressed the Shift key while dragging to ensure that the paths aligned horizontally. I then clicked in an empty portion of the image window to deselect all paths so that they appeared as shown in Figure 8-33. This enabled me to stroke them all simultaneously in Step 9.

Figure 8-33:
After stroking the path three times with the paint-brush tool, I cloned the path twice.

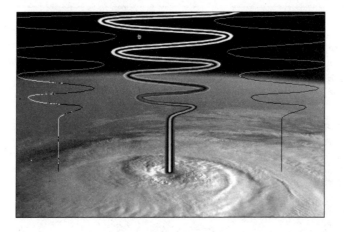

Step 7.   I created a 60-pixel version of my brush shape and reduced its Hardness value to 0 percent. I then painted a single white spot at the bottom of each of the new paths. I painted a black spot at the bottom of the original path.

Step 8.   I selected the smudge tool, moved the Pressure slider bar in the Brushes palette to 98 percent, and selected a brush shape with a radius of 16 pixels. At this setting, the tool has a tremendous range, but it eventually fades out.

Step 9.   I chose the Stroke Path command to apply the smudge tool to all three paths at once. The finished image appears in Figure 8-34.

Figure 8-34:
I stroked all three paths with the smudge tool set to 98 percent pressure to achieve this unusual extraterrestrial-departure effect. At least, I guess that's what it is. It could also be giant space slinkies probing the planet's surface. Hard to say.

If you're really feeling precise — I think they have a clinical term for that — you can specify the location of every single blob of paint laid down in an image. When the Spacing option in the Brush Options dialog box is deselected, Photoshop applies a single blob of paint for each point in a path. If that isn't sufficient control, I'm a monkey's uncle. (What a terrible thing to say about one's nephew!)

Converting and saving paths

Photoshop provides two commands to switch between paths and selections, both of which are located in the Paths palette menu. The Make Selection command converts a path to a selection outline; the Make Path command converts a selection to a path. And regardless of how you create a path, you can save it with the current image, which enables you not only to reuse the path but also to hide and display it at will.

After you choose the Make Selection command and establish the default settings, you can reapply the command by pressing the Enter key on the numeric keypad. As long as a path or selection tool is active, the Enter key converts the path to a selection. If some other tool is selected, you can click on the convert-to-selection/path icon at the bottom of the Paths palette (labeled back in Figure 8-26). To bring up the Make Selection dialog box, Option-click on the convert-to-selection/path icon.

Converting paths to selections

When you choose the Make Selection command or click on the convert-to-selection/ path icon when an area of your image is selected, Photoshop displays the dialog box shown in Figure 8-35. You can specify whether or not to antialias or feather the selection and to what degree. You also can instruct Photoshop to combine the prospective selection outline with any existing selection in the image. The Operation options correspond to the keyboard functions discussed in the "Manually adding and subtracting" section earlier in this chapter.

Figure 8-35:
When you choose the Make Selection command, you have the option of combining the path with an existing selection.

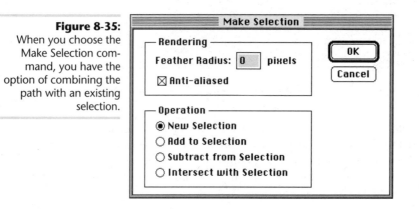

Make Selection

┌─ Rendering ─────────────────────
Feather Radius: [0] pixels

☒ Anti-aliased
└────────────────────────────────

┌─ Operation ─────────────────────
◉ New Selection
○ Add to Selection
○ Subtract from Selection
○ Intersect with Selection
└────────────────────────────────

[OK]
[Cancel]

If you haven't saved a path by the time you convert it, Photoshop leaves the path on-screen in front of the converted selection. If you try to copy, cut, delete, or nudge the selection, you perform the operation on the path instead. If, however, you save the path before converting it, Photoshop automatically hides the path and provides full access to the selection.

Converting selections to paths

When you choose the Make Paths command, Photoshop produces a single Tolerance option. Unlike the Tolerance options you've encountered so far, this one is accurate to $^1/_{10}$ pixel and has nothing to do with colors or brightness values. Rather, it permits you to specify Photoshop's sensitivity to twists and turns in a selection outline. The value you enter determines how far the path can vary from the original selection. The lowest possible value, 0.5, ensures that Photoshop retains every nuance of the selection, but it can also result in overly complicated paths with an abundance of points. If you enter the highest value, 10, Photoshop rounds out the path and uses very few points. If you plan on editing the path, you probably won't want to venture any lower than 2.0, the default setting.

Saving paths with an image

I mentioned at the beginning of the paths discussion that saving a path is an integral step in the path-creation process. You can store every path you draw and keep it on hand in case you decide later to select an area again. Because Photoshop defines paths as compact mathematical equations, they take up virtually no room when you save an image to disk.

You save one or more paths by choosing the Save Path command from the Paths palette menu or by simply double-clicking on the Work Path item in the scrolling list. After you perform the save operation, the path name appears in upright characters. A path name can include any number of separate paths. In fact, if you save a path and then set about drawing another one, Photoshop automatically adds that path in with the saved path. To start a new path under a new name, you first have to hide the existing path. You can hide and display a saved path by merely clicking on its name.

To hide all paths, click in the empty portion of the scrolling list below the last saved path name. You can even hide unsaved paths in this way. However, if you hide an unsaved path and then begin drawing a new one, the unsaved path is deleted, never to return again.

Swapping Paths with Illustrator __

Photoshop 3.0 can swap paths directly with Illustrator 5.5. All you have to do is copy a path to the Clipboard and paste it into the other program. This special cross-application compatibility feature expands and simplifies a variety of path-editing functions. For example, to scale, rotate, or flip a path — operations you can't perform inside Photoshop — you can simply copy a path, paste it into Illustrator, transform it as desired, copy it again, and paste it back into Photoshop.

On the Windows side, you can swap paths between Photoshop 3.0 and Illustrator 4.0 in the same manner.

When you copy a path in Illustrator and paste it into Photoshop, a dialog box appears offering you the option of rendering the path to pixels — just as you can render an Illustrator EPS document using File⇨Open — or keeping the path information intact. In other words, you can either turn the path into an image or bring it in as a path, which you can then use as a selection outline. If you want to save the path in the Paths palette, be sure to select the Paste As Paths option.

Things can get pretty muddled in the Clipboard, especially when you're switching applications. If you copy something from Illustrator, but the Paste command is dimmed inside Photoshop, you may be able to force the issue a little. Inside Illustrator, press the Option key and choose Edit⇨Copy. This supposedly copies a PICT version of the path, but it also seems to wake up the Clipboard to the fact that, yes indeed, there is something in here that Photoshop can use. (Computers are kind of slow sometimes. Every once in a while, you have to give them a kick in the pants.)

Exporting to Illustrator

If you don't have enough memory to run both Illustrator or Photoshop at the same time, you can export Photoshop paths to disk and then open them in Illustrator. To export all paths in the current image, choose File⇨Export⇨Paths to Illustrator. Photoshop saves the paths as a fully editable Illustrator document. This scheme allows you to exactly trace images with paths in Photoshop and then combine those paths as objects with the exported EPS version of the image inside Illustrator. Whereas tracing an image in Illustrator can prove a little tricky because of resolution differences and other previewing limitations, you can trace images in Photoshop as accurately as you like.

 Unfortunately, Illustrator provides no equivalent function for exporting paths for use in Photoshop, nor can Photoshop open Illustrator documents from disk and interpret them as paths. This means that the Clipboard is the only way to take a path created or edited in Illustrator and use it in Photoshop.

Retaining transparent areas in an image

Photoshop 3.0's transparency feature does not translate to other programs, not even Illustrator. (The PostScript language doesn't permit the same kind of transparency that Photoshop uses.) However, Illustrator, QuarkXPress, and other object-oriented applications enable you to mask away portions of an image that you want to appear transparent by using *clipping paths*. Elements that fall inside the clipping path are opaque; elements outside the clipping path are transparent. Photoshop lets you export an image in the EPS format with an object-oriented clipping path intact. When you import the image into the object-oriented program, it appears premasked with a perfectly smooth perimeter, as illustrated by the clipped image in Figure 8-36.

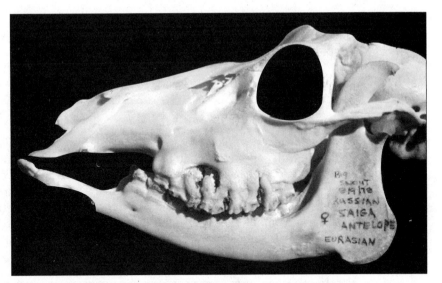

To following steps explain how to assign a set of saved paths as clipping paths.

STEPS: Saving an Image with Clipping Paths

Step 1.   Draw one or more paths around the portions of the image that you want to appear opaque. Areas outside the paths will be transparent.

Step 2.   Save the paths by double-clicking on the Work Path name in the Paths palette, entering a name, and pressing Return. (Try to use a name that will make sense three years from now when you have to revisit this document and figure out what the heck you did.) The path name appears in outline type in the Paths palette.

Step 3.   Choose the Clipping Path command from the Paths palette menu. Photoshop displays a dialog box that enables you to select the saved paths that you want to assign as the clipping path. (Actually, this step is optional. You can override your choice in the next step.)

If you like, enter a value into the Flatness option box. This option permits you to simplify the clipping paths by printing otherwise fluid curves as polygons. The Flatness value represents the distance — between 0.2 and 100 — in printer pixels that the polygon may vary from the true mathematical curve. A higher value leads to a polygon with fewer sides. Unless you experience a *limitcheck* error when printing the image from Illustrator, don't even bother to enter a value for this option. Even then, try simplifying your illustration first. Only use the Flatness value as a last resort.

Step 4.   Choose File⇨Save and select EPS from the Format menu. The EPS Format dialog box (shown back in Figure 3-5 of Chapter 3) now includes a Clipping Path pop-up menu. As long as the proper path name appears in the menu — it will if you followed the previous step — you can press the Return key. An EPS image with masked transparencies is saved to disk.

Figure 8-37 shows an enhanced version of the clipped skull from Figure 8-36. In addition to exporting the image with clipping paths in the EPS format, I saved the paths to disk by choosing File⇨Export⇨Paths to Illustrator. Inside Illustrator, I used the exported paths to create the outline around the clipped image. I also used them to create the shadow behind the image. The white of the eyeball is a reduced version of the eye socket, as are the iris and pupil. The background features a bunch of flipped and reduced versions of the paths. It may look like a lot of work, but the only drawing required was to create the two initial Photoshop paths.

Figure 8-37:
It's amazing what you can accomplish by combining scans edited in a painting program with smooth lines created in a drawing program.

Be prepared for your images to grow by leaps and bounds when imported into Illustrator. The EPS illustration shown in Figure 8-36 consumes a whopping 600K on disk. By contrast, the Photoshop image alone consumes only 100K when saved as an LZW-compressed TIFF file.

■ ■

Summary

- ➻ Option-click on the marquee tool icon to toggle between the rectangular and elliptical marquee tools. Or press the M key after the tool is selected.

- ➻ Option-drag with the rectangular or elliptical marquee tool to draw outward from the center of the shape. Press Shift after beginning your drag to constrain the shape to a square or circle.

- ➻ Option-click with the lasso tool to draw a selection outline with straight sides.

- ➻ It's a common misconception that the magic wand tool selects areas of similarly colored pixels. Rather, it distinguishes brightness values within color channels.

- ➻ Choose Select⇨Hide Edges to hide the marching ants and get an unobstructed view of your image.

- ➻ Shift-drag with a selection tool to add to a selection outline; Command-drag to subtract from a selection outline; Command-Shift-drag to intersect a selection.

- ➻ You can use the Similar and Inverse commands to automatically isolate a complex portion of an image.

- ➻ You can use feathering to hide an element in an image while leaving its background intact.

- ➻ Option-drag a selection to clone it. Command-Option-drag to move a selection outline independently of the image.

- ➻ You can float a selection by moving it, pasting it, cloning it, or simply pressing Command-J. To drop a floating selection, press Command-J again.

- ➻ To edit a floating selection entirely independently from the rest of an image — and likewise edit the rest of the image independently of the floating selection — convert the selection to a layer by double-clicking on the Floating Selection item in the Layers palette.

- ➻ You can move multiple layers at a time using the move tool.

- ➻ Photoshop's pen tool works identically to its counterpart in Adobe Illustrator, though Illustrator provides more options for editing a path.

- ➻ Be sure to save your path before hiding it or you'll end up replacing the path when you draw the next one.

- ➻ The pen tool lets you combine precise straight and curved segments in a single path. Click to create a corner with the pen tool; drag to create a seamless arc in a curve.

➡ Use the arrow, insert point, remove point, and convert point tools in the Paths palette to edit a path after you draw it with the pen tool.

➡ Use the Stroke Path command to apply a paint or edit tool along the route of a path. This is especially useful for creating duplicate versions of a single brush stroke.

➡ Use the Clipping Path command to import a partially transparent EPS image with mathematically precise edges into Illustrator or QuarkXPress.

Creating Masks

CHAPTER 9

![decorative dotted line]

In This Chapter

- ❖ Painting inside a selection outline
- ❖ Using the quick mask mode to create complex selection outlines
- ❖ Automating the creation of selection outlines using Select⇨Color Range
- ❖ Saving a selection outline to a mask channel
- ❖ Creating a mask based on the contours of the image itself
- ❖ Painting inside the opaque areas of a layer
- ❖ Creating a mask for a single layer
- ❖ Combining several layers into a clipping group

![decorative dotted line]

Selecting Via Masks

Most Photoshop users don't use masks. If my personal experience is any indication, it's not just that masks seem complicated, it's that they don't strike most folks as particularly useful. Like nearly everyone, when I first started using Photoshop, I couldn't even imagine any possible application for a mask. I've got my lasso tool, my magic wand, my pen tool; what more could I possibly want?

But in truth, masks are absolutely essential. They are, in fact, the most accurate method for defining selection outlines in Photoshop. Quite simply, masks allow you to devote every one of Photoshop's powerful capabilities to the task of creating a selection outline.

For those folks who aren't clear on what a Photoshop mask is — which is nearly everyone — let me take a moment to fill you in. A mask is an 8-bit representation of a selection outline that you can save to a separate channel. "Huh?" you might ask, all quizzical and curious-like. Well, here's another way to put it: A mask is a selection outline expressed as a grayscale image. Selected areas appear white, deselected areas appear black. Antialiased edges become gray pixels. Feathered edges are also expressed in shades of gray, from light gray near the selected area to dark gray near the deselected area.

Figure 9-1 shows two selection outlines and their equivalent masks. The top left example shows a rectangular selection that has been inverted (using Image⇨Map⇨Invert). Below it is the same selection expressed as a mask. Because the selection is hard-edged with no antialiasing or feathering, the mask appears hard-edged. The selected area is white and is said to be *unmasked*; the deselected area is black, or *masked*. The top right example shows a feathered selection outline. Again, I've inverted the selection so that you can better see the extent of the selection. (Marching ants can't accurately express softened edges, so the inversion helps show things off a little better.) The bottom right image is the equivalent mask. Here, the feathering effect is completely visible.

When you look at the masks in Figure 9-1, you may wonder where the heck the image went. One of the wonderful things about masks is that they can be viewed independently of an image, as in Figure 9-1, or with an image, as in Figure 9-2. Here, the mask is expressed as a color overlay. By default, the color of the overlay is a translucent red, like a conventional rubylith. (To see the overlay in its full, natural color, see Color Plate 9-1.) Areas covered with the rubylith are masked (deselected); areas that appear normal — without any red tint — are unmasked (selected). When you return to the marching ants mode, any changes you make to your image will not affect masked areas, only the unmasked portions.

Now that you know roughly what masks are (it will become progressively clearer throughout this chapter), the question remains, what good are they? Because a mask is essentially an independent grayscale image, you can edit the mask using any of the paint and edit tools discussed in Chapter 7, any of the filters discussed in Chapters 13 through 15, any of the color correction options discussed in Chapter 16, or just about any other function described in any other chapter. You can even use the selection tools, as discussed in the previous chapter. With all these features at your disposal, you can't help but create a more accurate selection outline and in a shorter period of time. All your changes affect the mask — and thus the shape and softness of the selection outline — only. The image itself remains inactive as you edit the mask.

For an example of using filters and color correction options to edit a mask, see the "Softening a selection outline" section of Chapter 13.

Figure 9-1:
Two selection outlines with inverted interiors (top) and their equivalent masks (bottom).

Figure 9-2:
The masks from Figure 9-1 shown as they appear when viewed along with an image.

Painting and Editing inside Selections

Before we immerse ourselves in 8-bit masking techniques, let's start with a warm-up topic, *selection masking*. When you were in grade school, perhaps you had a teacher who nagged you to color within the lines. (I didn't. My teachers were more concerned about preventing me from writing on the walls and coloring on the other kids.) At any rate, if you don't trust yourself to paint inside an image because you're afraid you'll screw it up, selection masking is the answer. Regardless of which tool you use to select an image — marquee, lasso, magic wand, or pen — you can paint or edit only the selected area. The paint can't enter the deselected (or *protected*) portions of the image, so you can't help but paint inside the lines. As a result, all selection outlines act as masks, hence the term *selection masking*.

Figures 9-3 through 9-6 show the familiar skull image subject to some pretty free-and-easy use of the paint and edit tools. (You think I ought to lay off the heavy metal or what?) The following steps describe how I created these images using a selection mask.

STEPS: Painting and Editing Inside a Selection Mask

Step 1.   Sometime while I was working on Chapter 8, I selected the slightly rotting skull of the enchanting Russian Saiga Antelope. You can see the selection outline in such golden oldies as Figures 8-15 and 8-17. If those figures are too remote, just look at the top example in Figure 9-3. For the record, I drew this selection outline using the pen tool.

Step 2.   I wanted to edit the area surrounding the skull, so I chose Select⇨Inverse to reverse which areas were selected and which were not. I then pressed the Delete key to fill the selected area with the background color — in this case, white — as shown in the bottom half of Figure 9-3.

Step 3.   The next step was to paint inside the selection mask. But before I began, I chose Select⇨Hide Edges (Command-H). This allowed me to paint without being distracted by those infernal marching ants. (In fact, this is one of the most essential uses for the Hide Edges command.)

Step 4.   I selected the paintbrush tool and the 21-pixel soft brush shape in the Brushes palette. The foreground color was black. I dragged with the paintbrush around the perimeter of the skull to set it apart from its white background, as shown in Figure 9-4. No matter how sloppily I painted, the skull remained unscathed.

Figure 9-3:
After drawing a selection outline around the antelope skull (top), I inversed the selection and deleted the background (bottom).

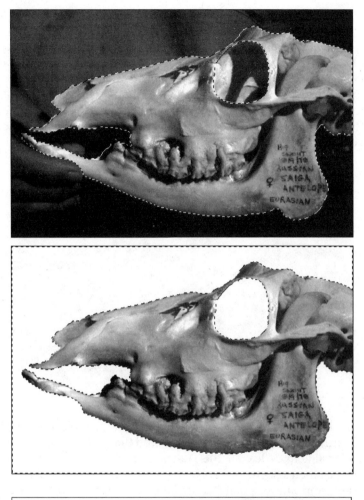

Figure 9-4:
I painted inside the selection mask with a 21-pixel soft brush shape.

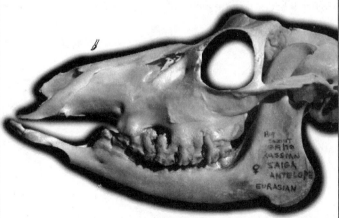

Step 5. I next selected the smudge tool and set the Pressure slider bar inside the Smudge Tool Options panel to 80 percent by pressing the 8 key. I dragged from inside the skull outward 20 or so times to create a series of curlicues. I also dragged from outside the skull inward to create white gaps between the curlicues. As shown in Figure 9-5, the smudge tool can smear colors from inside the protected area, but it does not apply these colors until you go inside the selection. This is an important point to keep in mind, because it demonstrates that although the protected area is safe from all changes, the selected area may be influenced by colors from protected pixels.

Figure 9-5:
Dragging with the smudge tool smeared colors from pixels outside the selection mask without changing the appearance of those pixels.

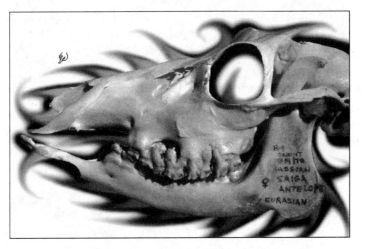

Step 6. I double-clicked on the airbrush tool icon in the toolbox to display the Airbrush Options panel. Then I selected the Fade check box and set the Fade value to 20, leaving the Transparent option selected in the pop-up menu. I then selected a 60-pixel soft brush shape and again dragged outward from various points along the perimeter of the skull. As demonstrated in Figure 9-6, combining airbrush and mask is as useful in Photoshop as it is in the real world.

Figure 9-6: I dragged around the skull with the airbrush to further distinguish it from its background. Pretty cool effect, huh? Well, if it's not your cup of tea, maybe you can track down a teenager who will appreciate it.

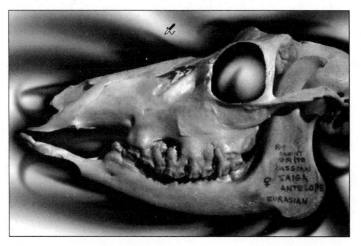

Temporary Masking Functions ____

Selection masks give you an idea of what masks are all about, but they only scrape the surface. The rest of the discussions in this chapter revolve around using masks to define complex selection outlines (which you can later use as selection masks or simply to select one image and move it, copy and paste it into another document, filter it, or whatever).

The most straightforward environment for creating a mask is the *quick mask mode.* To experience it for yourself, select some portion of an image and click on the quick mask mode icon in the toolbox, which is the righthand icon directly under the color controls. Or just press the Q key. All the deselected areas in your image appear covered in a translucent coat of red, and the selected areas appear without red coating, just as shown in Color Plate 9-1.

Another convenient method for creating a mask is the Color Range command under the Select menu. When you select this command, you use the eyedropper to specify areas of like color that you want to select, and other areas that you don't want to select. It's kind of like a magic wand tool on steroids, in that it allows you to change the tolerance of the selection on the fly.

Both options fall under the category of temporary masking functions because neither option allows you to retain the mask for later use. You have to use the selection outline immediately, just as if you had drawn it with the marquee, lasso, or magic wand. I'll describe a more permanent solution — that of saving masks to a separate mask channel — later in this chapter.

Using the quick mask mode

When I pressed the Q key to enter the quick mask mode after wreaking my most recent havoc on the extinct antelope skull, I got the image shown in Figure 9-7. The skull receives the mask because it was not selected. (In Figure 9-7, the mask appears as a light gray coating; on your color screen, the mask appears in red.) The area outside the skull looks just the same as it always did because it was selected and therefore not masked.

Figure 9-7:
Click on the quick mask mode icon (left) to instruct Photoshop to temporarily express the selection as a grayscale image.

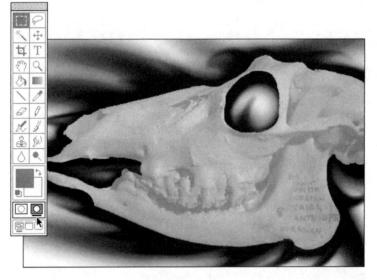

 Notice that the selection outline disappears when you enter the quick mask mode. That's because it temporarily ceases to exist. Any operations that you apply affect the mask itself and leave the underlying image untouched. When you click on the marching ants mode icon (to the left of the quick mask mode icon) or again press the Q key, Photoshop converts the mask back into a selection outline and again allows you to edit the image.

 Have you ever clicked on the quick mask mode icon without seeing anything change on-screen? Don't worry, your computer isn't broken. It just means that you didn't have anything selected before you entered the mode. When nothing is selected, Photoshop allows you to edit the entire image; in other words, everything's selected. (Only a few commands under the Edit menu, Image⇨Effects submenu, and Select menu require something to be selected before they work.) If everything is selected, the mask is white. Therefore, the quick mask overlay is transparent and you don't see any difference on-screen. Rest assured, however, that you are in the quick mask mode and you can apply any of the edits listed in this section.

Once in the quick mask mode, you can edit the mask in the following ways:

- ∞ **Subtracting from a selection:** Paint with black to add red coating and thus deselect areas of the image, as demonstrated in the top half of Figure 9-8. This means that you can selectively protect portions of your image by merely painting over them.

Figure 9-8:
After subtracting some of the selected area inside the eye socket by painting in black with the paintbrush tool (top), I feathered the outline by painting with white, using a soft 45-pixel brush shape (bottom).

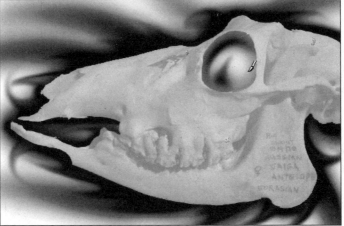

◌◈ **Adding to a selection:** Paint with white to remove red coating and thus add to the selection outline. You can use the eraser tool to whittle away at the masked area (assuming that the background color is set to white). Or you can swap the foreground and background colors so that you can paint in white with one of the painting tools.

◌◈ **Adding feathered selections:** If you paint with a shade of gray, you add feathered selections. You also can feather an outline by painting with black or white with a very soft brush shape, as shown in the bottom image in Figure 9-8.

◌◈ **Clone selection outlines:** You can clone a selection outline by selecting it with one of the standard selection tools and Option-dragging it to a new location in the image, as shown in Figure 9-9. Although I use the lasso tool in the figure, the magic wand tool also works well for this purpose. To select an antialiased selection outline with the wand tool, set the tolerance to about 10 and be sure that the Anti-aliased check box is active. Then click inside the selection. It's that easy.

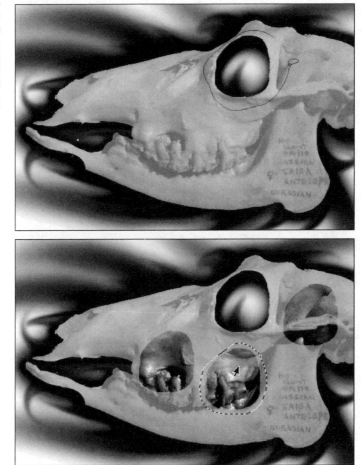

Figure 9-9:
To clone the eye socket selection, I lassoed around it (top) and Option-dragged it (bottom).

↬ **Transform selection outlines:** That's right, the quick mask mode provides a method for transforming a selection outline independently of its contents. Just enter the quick mask mode, select the mask using one of the standard selection tools, and transform it by choosing the desired command from the Image➪Flip, Image➪Rotate, or Image➪Effects submenu.

These are just a few of the unique effects you can achieve by editing a selection in the quick mask mode. Others involve tools and capabilities I haven't yet discussed, so expect to hear more about this feature in future chapters.

When you finish editing your selection outlines, click on the marching ants mode icon (just to the left of the quick mask mode icon) or just press the Q key again to return to the marching ants mode. Your selection outlines again appear flanked by marching ants, and all tools and commands return to their normal image-editing functions. Figure 9-10 shows the results of switching to the marching ants mode and deleting the contents of the selection outlines created in the last examples of the previous two figures.

Figure 9-10:
The results of deleting the regions selected in the final examples of Figures 9-8 (top) and 9-9 (bottom). Kind of makes me want to rent the video of *It's the Great Pumpkin, Charlie Brown.* I mean, who wouldn't give this antelope a rock?

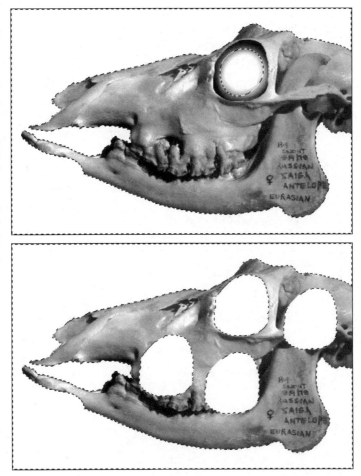

As demonstrated in the top example of Figure 9-10, the quick mask mode offers a splendid environment for feathering one selection outline while leaving another hard-edged or antialiased. Granted, because most selection tools offer built-in feathering options, you can accomplish this task without resorting to the quick mask mode. But the quick mask mode lets you change feathering selectively after drawing selection outlines. It also lets you see exactly what you're doing.

Changing the red coating

By default, the protected region of an image appears in translucent red in the quick mask mode, but you can change it to any color and any degree of opacity that you like. To do so, double-click on the quick mask icon in the toolbox (or double-click on the Quick Mask item in the Channels palette) to display the dialog box shown in Figure 9-11.

⌐⊸ **Color Indicates:** Select the Selected Areas option to reverse the color coating — that is, to cover the selected areas in a translucent coat of red and view the deselected areas normally. Select the Masked Areas option (the default setting) to cover the deselected areas in color.

You can reverse the color coating without ever entering the Quick Mask Options dialog box. Simply Option-click on the quick mask icon in the toolbox to toggle between coating the masked or selected portions of the image. The icon itself changes to reflect your choice.

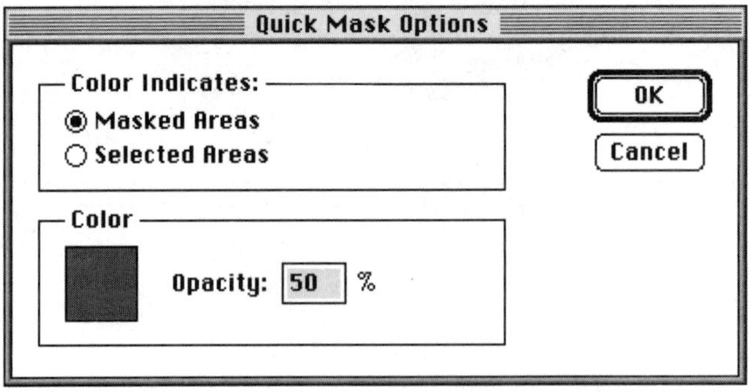

Figure 9-11:
Double-click on the quick mask mode icon to access the Quick Mask Options dialog box. You then can change the color and opacity of the protected or selected areas when viewed in the quick mask mode.

```
╔═══════════ Quick Mask Options ═══════════╗
║  ┌─ Color Indicates: ─────────┐           ║
║  │  ● Masked Areas            │   ┌─ OK ─┐ ║
║  │  ○ Selected Areas          │   └──────┘ ║
║  │                            │  ┌ Cancel ┐║
║  └────────────────────────────┘  └────────┘║
║  ┌─ Color ────────────────────┐           ║
║  │  ▓▓▓  Opacity: │ 50 │ %    │           ║
║  │  ▓▓▓                       │           ║
║  └────────────────────────────┘           ║
╚═══════════════════════════════════════════╝
```

∞ **Color:** Click on the Color icon to display the Adobe Color Picker dialog box and select a different color coating. For a detailed explanation of this dialog box, see the "Using the Color Picker" section of Chapter 4.

∞ **Opacity:** Enter a value to change the opacity of the translucent color that coats the image. A value of 100 percent is absolutely opaque.

Change the color coating to achieve the most acceptable balance between being able to view and edit your selection and being able to view your image. For example, the red coating shows up badly on grayscale screen shots, so I changed the color coating to light blue and the Opacity value to 65 percent before shooting the screens featured in Figures 9-7 through 9-9.

Generating masks automatically

Near the beginning of 1994, John Knoll released a free Photoshop plug-in called Xtract that automated the process of generating a mask. Unfortunately, the plug-in was never distributed with earlier versions of Photoshop and it didn't come out it time for inclusion in the previous edition of this book.

As luck would have it, however, Photoshop 3.0 has incorporated the Xtract plug-in, improved its design, and added to its capabilities. Adobe also changed the name. It's now the Color Range command, found under the Select menu.

When you choose Select⇨Color Range, Photoshop displays the Color Range dialog box shown in Figure 9-12. As I mentioned earlier, it's basically an enhanced version of the magic wand tool combined with the Similar command. It selects areas of related color, whether they're contiguous or not. However, instead of clicking with the magic wand to select colors, you click with an eyedropper tool. And rather than adjusting a Tolerance value before you use the tool, you adjust a Fuzziness option any old time you like. So why didn't the folks at Adobe merely enhance the functionality of the magic wand? Probably because the magic wand wouldn't let you load and save mask settings on disk the way the Color Range dialog box does. Also, the dialog box displays a preview of the mask, which is pretty essential for gauging the accuracy of your selection.

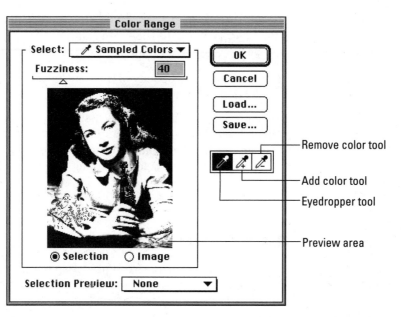

Figure 9-12:
The Color Range dialog box allows you to generate a mask by dragging with the eyedropper tool and adjusting the Fuzziness option.

Notice that when you move your cursor outside the Color Range dialog box, it changes to an eyedropper. Click with the eyedropper to specify the color on which you want to base the selection — which I call the *base color* — just as if you were using the magic wand. Alternatively, you can click inside the preview area, labeled in Figure 9-12. In either case, the preview area updates to show the resulting mask. You can also do the following:

- **Add colors to the selection:** To add base colors to the selection, select the add color tool inside the Color Range dialog box and click inside the image window or preview area. You can also access the tool while the standard eyedropper is selected by Shift-clicking (just as you Shift-click with the magic wand to add colors to a selection). You can Shift-drag with the eyedropper to add multiple colors in a single pass, which you can't do with the wand tool.

- **Remove colors from the selection:** To remove base colors from the selection, click with the remove color tool or Command-click with the eyedropper. You can also drag or Command-drag to remove many colors at a time.

↩ **Adjust the Fuzziness value:** This option resembles the Tolerance value in the Magic Wand Options panel in that it determines the range of colors that will be selected beyond the ones on which you click. Raise the Fuzziness value to expand the selected area; lower the value to contract the selection. A value of 0 selects the clicked-on color only. Unlike changes to Tolerance, however, changing the Fuzziness value adjusts the selection on the fly; no reclicking is required, as it is with the wand tool.

Another difference between Fuzziness and the less capable Tolerance option is the kind of selection outline each generates. Tolerance entirely selects all colors within the specified range and adds antialiased edges. If the selection were a mask, most of it would be white with a few gray pixels around the perimeter. By contrast, Fuzziness entirely selects only the colors on which you click and partially selects the other colors in the range (just as if the selection outline were feathered). That's why most of the mask is expressed in shades of gray. The light grays in the mask represent the most similar colors; the dark grays represent the least similar pixels that still fall within the Fuzziness range.

↩ **Toggle the preview area:** Use the two radio buttons below the preview area to control the preview's contents. If you select the first option, Selection, you see the mask that will be generated when you press Return. If you select the Image option, the preview shows a reduced version of the image. On the Mac, you can toggle between the two by pressing and holding the Control key. My advice is to leave the option set to Selection and press the Control key when you want to view the image.

↩ **Control the contents of the image window:** The Selection Preview pop-up menu at the bottom of the dialog box lets you change what you see in the image window. Select Grayscale to see the mask on its own. Select Quick Mask to see the mask and image together. Select Black Matte or White Matte to see what the selection would look like against a black or white background. Though they may sound weird, the Matte options allow you to get an accurate picture of how the selected image will mesh with a different background. Use the Fuzziness option in combination with Black Matte or White Matte to come up with a softness setting that will ensure a smooth transition. Leave this option set to None — the default setting — to view the image normally in the image window.

↩ **Select by predefined colors:** Choose an option from the Select pop-up menu at the top of the dialog box to specify the means of selecting a base color. If you choose any option besides Sampled Colors, the Fuzziness option and eyedropper tools become dimmed to show they are no longer operable. Rather, Photoshop selects colors based on their relationship to a predefined color. For example, if you select Red, the program entirely selects red and partially selects other colors based on the amount of red they contain. Colors composed exclusively of blue and green are not selected.

The most useful option in this pop-up menu is Out of Gamut, which selects all the colors in an RGB or Lab image that fall outside the CMYK color space. You can use this option to select and modify the out-of-gamut colors before converting an image to CMYK. Chapter 16 examines a use for this option.

  ∽ **Load and save settings:** Click on the Save button to save the current settings to disk. Click on Load to open a saved settings file.

When you define the mask to your satisfaction, click on the OK button or press Return to generate the selection outline. Although the Color Range command is more flexible than the magic wand, you can no more expect it to generate perfect selections than any other automated tool. Therefore, after Photoshop draws the selection outline, you'll probably want to switch to the quick mask mode and paint and edit the mask to taste.

If you learn nothing else about the Color Range dialog box, at least learn to use the Fuzziness option and the eyedropper tools. There are basically two ways to approach these options. If you want to create a diffused selection with gradual edges, set the Fuzziness option to a high value — 40 or more — and click and Shift-click only two or three times with the eyedropper. To create a more precise selection, enter a low Fuzziness value and Shift- and Command-drag with the eyedropper tool several times until you get the exact colors you want.

Figure 9-13 shows some sample results. To create the left images, I clicked with the eyedropper tool once on the bridge of the woman's nose and set the Fuzziness to 130. To create the right images, I lowered the Fuzziness value to 6; then I clicked, Shift-clicked, and Command-clicked with the eyedropper to lift exactly the colors I wanted. The top examples show special effects applied to the two images (Filter⇨Stylize⇨Find Edges). In the bottom example, I copied the selections and pasted them against an identical background of Cheerios. (Breakfast food suits this woman well.) In both examples, the higher Fuzziness value yields more generalized and softer results; the lower value results in a more exact but harsher selection.

 You can limit the portion of an image that Select⇨Color Range affects by selecting part of the image before choosing the command. When a selection exists, the Color Range command masks only those pixels that fall inside it. Even the preview area reflects your selection. Try it and see.

Fuzziness: 130   Fuzziness: 6

Figure 9-13:
After creating
two selections
with the
Color Range
command —
one with a high
Fuzziness value
(left) and one
with a low one
(right), I
alternately
applied the Find
Edges filter
(top) and
pasted the
selections
against a
different
background
(bottom).

 Goodie, another tip. If you get hopelessly lost when creating your selection and you can't figure out what to select and what to deselect, just click with the eyedropper tool to start over. This clears all the colors from the selection except the one you click on. Alternatively, you can press the Option key to change the Cancel button to a Reset button. Option-click on the button to return the settings inside the dialog box to those in force when you first chose Select⇔Color Range.

Creating an Independent Mask Channel

The problem with masks generated via the quick mask mode and Color Range command is that they're here one day and gone the next. Photoshop is no more prepared to remember them than it is a lasso or wand selection.

Most of the time, that's okay. You'll only use the selection once, so there's no reason to sweat it. But what if the selection takes you a long time to create? What if, after a quarter hour of Shift-clicking here and Command-dragging there, adding a few strokes in the quick mask mode, and getting the selection outline exactly right, a slight twitch pulses through your finger and you inadvertently double-click in the image window with the lasso tool? Good job — not only have you deselected the selection, you've eliminated your only chance to undo the deselection. To coin a euphemism from the world of women's lingerie, you're hosed.

For this reason, you'll probably want to back up your selection if you've spent any amount of time on it. Even if you're in the middle of creating the selection that you've been grinding at for quite a while, stop and take a moment to save it before all heck breaks loose. You wouldn't let a half an hour of image editing go by without saving, and the rules don't change just because you're working on a selection.

Saving a selection outline to a mask channel

The following steps describe a wonderful method for backing up a selection to an independent *mask channel*, which is any channel above and beyond those required to represent a grayscale or color image. Mask channels are saved along with the image itself, making it a safe and sturdy solution.

STEPS: Transferring a Selection to an Independent Channel

Step 1.   Choose Select⇨Save Selection, which allows you to save the selection as a mask. The dialog box shown in Figure 9-14 appears, asking you where you want to put the mask. In most cases, you'll want to save the mask to a separate channel inside the current image. To do so, make sure that the name of the current image appears in the Document pop-up menu and then select New from the Channel pop-up menu and press Return.

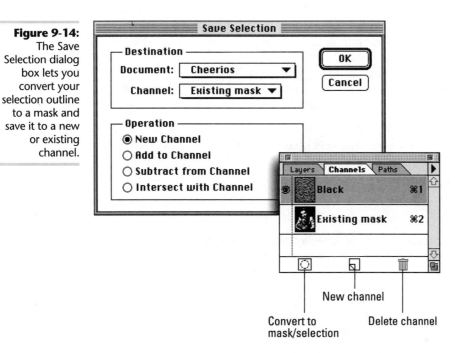

Figure 9-14:
The Save Selection dialog box lets you convert your selection outline to a mask and save it to a new or existing channel.

If you have an old channel that you want to replace, select the channel's name from the Channel pop-up menu. The radio buttons at the bottom of the dialog box become available, allowing you to add the mask to the channel, subtract it, or intersect it. These radio buttons work just like the equivalent options that appear when you make a path into a selection outline (see "Converting paths to selections" in Chapter 8), but they blend the masks together instead. The result is the same as if you were adding, subtracting, or intersecting selection outlines, except that it's expressed as a mask.

Alternatively, you can save the mask to a new document all its own. To do this, choose New from the Document pop-up menu and press Return.

Man, what a lot of options! If you just want to save the selection to a new channel and be done with it, don't bother with Select⇨Save Selection. Just click on the convert to mask/selection icon at the bottom of the Channels palette (labeled in Figure 9-14). Photoshop automatically creates a new channel, converts the selection to a mask, and places the mask in the channel. (Regardless of which of these methods you choose, your selection outline remains intact.)

Step 2. To view the saved selection in its new mask form, display the Channels palette by choosing Window⇨Palettes⇨Show Channels. Then click on the appropriate channel name in the Channels palette, presumably #2 if you're editing a grayscale image or #4 if you're working in the RGB or Lab mode. In Figure 9-14, I replaced the contents of an existing mask called — what else? — Existing Mask, so this is where my mask now resides.

Step 3. Return to the standard image-editing mode by clicking on the first channel name from the Channels palette. Better yet, press Command-1 if you're editing a grayscale image or Command-0 if the image is in color.

Step 4. Save the image to disk to store the selection permanently. Only the PICT, TIFF, and native Photoshop formats suffice for this purpose. Only the TIFF and native formats can handle more than four channels.

Step 5. To later retrieve your selection, choose Select⇨Load Selection. A dialog box nearly identical to the one shown in Figure 9-14 appears, except for the addition of an Invert check box. Select the document and channel that contains the mask you want to use. You can add it to a current selection, subtract it, or intersect it. Select the Invert option if you want to switch the selected and deselected portions of the mask. (Inverting a mask is the same as applying Select⇨Inverse to a selection outline because it makes the white areas black and the black areas white.)

Want to avoid the Load Selection command? Just Option-click on the channel name in the Channels palette that contains the mask you want to use. For example, if I Option-clicked on the Existing Mask item in Figure 9-14, Photoshop would load the equivalent selection outline into the image window. Or press Command-Option plus the channel number to convert the channel to a selection. For example, Command-Option-2 would convert the Existing Mask channel. (You can also drag the channel name onto the convert to mask/selection icon at the bottom of the Channels palette, but that takes so much more effort.)

You can also add to and subtract from a selection using keyboard shortcuts. Shift-Option-click on a channel to add it to the current selection outline; Command-Option-click to subtract the mask from the selection; and Command-Shift-Option-click to find the intersection. Cool stuff, eh?

Watch out, it's Tip City around here. Did you know that you can also save a quick mask to its own channel? It's true. When you enter the quick mask mode, the Channels palette displays an item called *Quick Mask*. The italic letters show that the channel is temporary and is not saved with the image. To clone it to a permanent channel, just drag the Quick Mask item onto the new channel icon at the bottom of the Channels palette (labeled in Figure 9-14). Now save the image to the PICT, TIFF, or Photoshop format, and you're backed up.

Viewing mask and image

Photoshop lets you view any mask channel along with an image, just as you can view mask and image together in the quick mask mode. To do so, click in the first column of the Channels palette to toggle the display of the eyeball icon. An eyeball in front of a channel name indicates that you can see that channel. If you are currently viewing the image, for example, click in front of the mask channel name to view the mask as a translucent color coating, again as in the quick mask mode. Alternatively, if the contents of the mask channel appear by themselves on-screen, click in front of the image name to display it as well.

Using a mask channel is different from using the quick mask mode in that you can edit either the image or mask channel when viewing the two together. You can even edit two or more masks at once. To decide which channel you want to edit, click on the channel name in the palette. To edit two channels at once, click on one and Shift-click on another. All active channel names appear gray.

You can change the color and opacity of each mask independently of other mask channels and the quick mask mode. Click on the mask channel name to select one channel only and then choose the Channel Options command from the Channels palette menu. Or just double-click on the mask channel name. (This is not an option when you're editing a standard color channel.) A dialog box similar to the one shown back in Figure 9-11 appears, the only difference being that this one contains a Name option box so that you can change the name of the mask channel. You can then edit the color overlay as described in the "Changing the red coating" section earlier in this chapter.

 If you ever need to edit a selection outline inside the mask channel using paint and edit tools, click on the quick mask mode icon in the toolbox. It may sound like a play within a play, but you can access the quick mask mode even when working in a mask channel. Just make sure that the mask channel color is different from the quick mask color so that you can tell what's going on.

Deriving selections from images

Here's your chance to see the mask channel in action. In the following steps, I start with the unadorned image of the Great Wall shown in Figure 9-15 and add the glow shown in Figure 9-18. Normally, this would be a fairly complex procedure. But when you employ a mask channel, it takes only minutes.

Rather than selecting a portion of the image and saving it to a channel, as described in the previous sections, I created the selection mask in the following steps by copying a portion of an image, pasting it into a mask channel, and editing it.

Figure 9-15:
A 1940s photograph of the Great Wall from the Bettmann Archive.

I have yet to cover a couple of the techniques I use in the following steps, specifically those of filling a selection and applying the Threshold command. For more information, read Chapter 10, "Filling and Stroking," and Chapter 16, "Mapping and Adjusting Colors."

STEPS: Using a Mask Channel to Enhance an Image

Step 1. I started by duplicating the image of the Great Wall to the mask channel. To do this, I dragged the Black item onto the new channel icon at the bottom of the Channels palette, thus cloning the channel.

 This is a grayscale image, so it only contains one channel, Black. If it were an RGB image, I would search through each of the Red, Green, and Blue channels to find the one with the most contrast. You could do the same in the Lab or CMYK modes. Then I would drag the high-contrast channel onto the new channel icon. (You cannot drag the color composite view — the one at the top of the Channels palette — onto the new channel icon, because you can only clone one channel at a time.)

Step 2. Photoshop automatically took me to the new mask channel, which it kindly labeled #2. To convert the image to a mask, I chose Image⇨Map⇨Threshold (Command-T), which changed all pixels in the mask channel to either white or black. This enabled me to isolate gray values in the image and create the reasonable beginnings of a selection outline.

Because I haven't described the Threshold command yet, let me take a moment to do so. Inside the Threshold dialog box, you move a slider bar to specify a brightness value. All pixels lighter than that value turn to white, and all pixels darker than that value change to black. I used the value 233 to arrive at the image shown in Figure 9-16.

Step 3. The black-and-white image from Figure 9-16 was far from perfect, but it was as good as it was going to get using Photoshop's automated color mapping. From here on, I had to rely on my tracing abilities. I used the pencil tool to fill in the gaps in the wall and the eraser tool to erase the black pixels from the sky. Notice that I did not use the paintbrush or airbrush tools; at this stage, I wanted hard edges.

Step 4. I softened portions of the boundaries between the black and white pixels using the blur tool at the default 50 percent pressure and with a small brush shape. (For a better way to accomplish this, read the "Softening a selection outline" section of Chapter 13.)

Step 5. To create the glow, I Option-dragged with the elliptical marquee tool to draw the marquee from the center outward. Before releasing, I pressed and held Shift (as well as Option) to constrain the marquee to a circle. After I finished drawing the marquee, I Command-Option-dragged it to position the selection outline exactly where I wanted it, as shown in the top half of Figure 9-17.

Figure 9-16:
After duplicating the
Black channel, I
changed all pixels to
white or black using
the Threshold com-
mand and set about
painting away the
imperfections.

Step 6.   I pressed Option-delete to fill the circular selection with black.

Step 7.   I double-clicked on the paintbrush tool icon and selected the Fade check box in the Paintbrush Options panel. Then I set the value to 40 pixels and drew several long rays about the perimeter of the circle.

Step 8.   Using the smudge tool set to 50 percent pressure, I dragged outward from the circle to create the tapering edges shown in the bottom half of Figure 9-17.

Step 9.   To apply the finished selection to the image, I pressed Command-1 to return to the standard image mode. (This is a grayscale image. If it had been color, I would have pressed Command-0.) I then chose Select⇨Load Selection to copy the selection from the mask channel.

Figure 9-17: I established the selection outline for the glow by Option-dragging with the elliptical marquee tool (top) and pressing Option-delete to fill the selection with black. I then used the paintbrush and smudge tools to paint in the rays (bottom).

Step 10. Because I only edited the upper third of the image in the mask channel, the lower two thirds of the document appeared selected. To deselect this region, I Command-dragged around it with the rectangular marquee tool.

Step 11. Because Photoshop selects the portions of the mask channel that are white, only that portion of the sky outside the glow was selected. The rest of the image was masked. I pressed Option-delete to fill the selection with black. Figure 9-18 shows the result.

Figure 9-18:
Returning back to the standard image mode, I loaded the selection outlines from the mask layer and pressed Option-delete to fill the selected area with black.

Color Plate 9-2 shows an alternative color scheme applied to Figure 9-18. Rather than filling the background with black, I filled it with a gradation from dark blue to light blue. I also filled the interior of the glow with yellow and applied a gradation from green to red across the Great Wall and hills. In less than an hour, I was able to convert an old grayscale stock photo into a full-color dazzler. For more information on applying colors to images using Photoshop's fill and gradient features, read the next chapter.

Masking and Layers _____

Layers offer special masking options unto themselves. You can paint inside the confines of a layer as if it were a selection mask, you can add a special mask for a single layer, or you can group multiple layers together and have the bottom layer in the group serve as the mask. Quite honestly, these are the kinds of thoughtful and useful functions that I've come to expect from Photoshop. Though they're fairly complicated — you really have to be on your toes once you start juggling layers (carnival music, please) — you'll discover a world of opportunity and flexibility once you come to terms with these amazing controls.

Preserving transparency

You may have already noticed a little check box near the top of the Layers palette called Preserve Transparency. If not, the option appears spotlighted in Figure 9-19. When checked, it prevents you from painting inside the transparent portions of the layer.

Figure 9-19:
An image composed of five layers and a background image. Arrows join the layer names to their contents. The numbers show the layering order of the faces, from 1 at the bottom to 5 at the top.

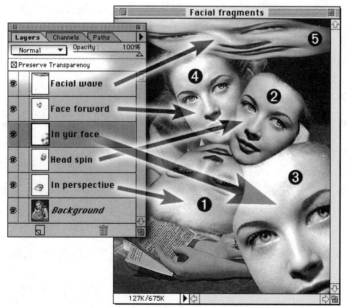

Consider the image shown in Figure 9-19. It comprises five layers in addition to the background image, each of which contains a modified version of the woman's head. (She's pining for her boyfriend overseas — that's what the letter in her hand is all about — so her head's all over the place. Literally, that is.) Arrows point from each of the layer names in the Layers palette to the contents of that layer in the image. Just to be safe, I've also included numbers — 1 is the lowest layer, 5 is the highest. Figure 9-19 is a masterpiece of over-annotation, if I do say so myself.

I'm happy with the transition between the large face in the lower right corner (numbered 3) and the two faces that border it (1 and 2). What I'd like to do is create a slight shadow around face 3 to distinguish it more clearly. If I just start in painting, however, I run the risk of getting paint all over faces 1 and 2, because both faces are behind face 3.

Everything making sense so far? If this were a flat, non-layered image, you'd have to carefully draw a selection outline between the borders of faces 1, 2, and 3 and then paint inside the resulting selection mask. But there's no need when you're using layers. Because all the faces are on separate layers, an implied selection mask exists between them. All opaque pixels are inside the selection; all transparent pixels are outside of it.

The first example in Figure 9-20 shows face 3 on its own. (I've hidden all the other layers by Option-clicking on the eyeball icon in front of the face 3 layer name.) The transparent and therefore implicitly deselected areas appear in the checkerboard pattern. When the Preserve Transparency option is turned off, you can paint anywhere inside the layer that you want. The implied selection mask is off. But with Preserve Transparency on, selection mask is on and the checkerboard area is off limits.

Figure 9-20:
The third layer as it appears on its own (left) and when airbrushed with the Preserve Transparency check box turned on (right).

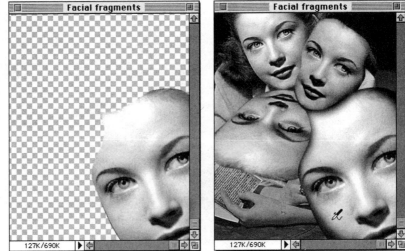

The right image in Figure 9-20 shows what happens when I select Preserve Transparency and paint inside the face with the airbrush. Notice that no matter how much paint I may apply, none of it leaks out onto the neighboring faces. As the old geezers at the Home for Retired Image Editors are always saying, good masks make good neighbors. How true it is.

 The setting of the Preserve Transparency check box applies to each layer independently. Therefore, if I select the option for the face 3 layer and then switch to face 2, the option turns off because it is not in effect for this layer. If I then switch back to face 3, the check box becomes selected again because the effect is still on for this layer.

Also worth noting: The Preserve Transparency option is dimmed when the Background layer is active, because this layer is entirely opaque. There's no transparency to preserve, eh? (That's my impression of a Canadian explaining layer theory. It needs a little work, but I think I'm getting close.)

Creating layer-specific masks

In addition to the implied selection mask that comes with every layer, you can add a mask to a layer to specify which portions of the layer are transparent or translucent and which parts are opaque. Won't simply erasing portions of a layer make those portions transparent? Yes, it will, but when you erase, you permanently delete them. By creating a layer mask, you instead make pixels temporarily transparent. You can come back later and bring those pixels back to life again simply by adjusting the mask. Therefore, layer masks add yet another level of flexibility to a program that's already a veritable image-editing contortionist.

To create a layer mask, select the layer that you want to mask and choose the Add Layer Mask command from the Layers palette pop-up menu. A second thumbnail preview appears to the left of the layer name, as labeled in Figure 9-21. A heavy outline around the preview shows that the layer mask is active.

To edit the mask, simply paint in the image window. Paint with black to make pixels transparent. (Because black represents deselected pixels in an image, it makes these pixels transparent in a layer.) Paint with white to make pixels opaque. The irony of this setup is that painting with the eraser tool when the background color is white — as is the default setting — actually makes pixels opaque. Strange but true.

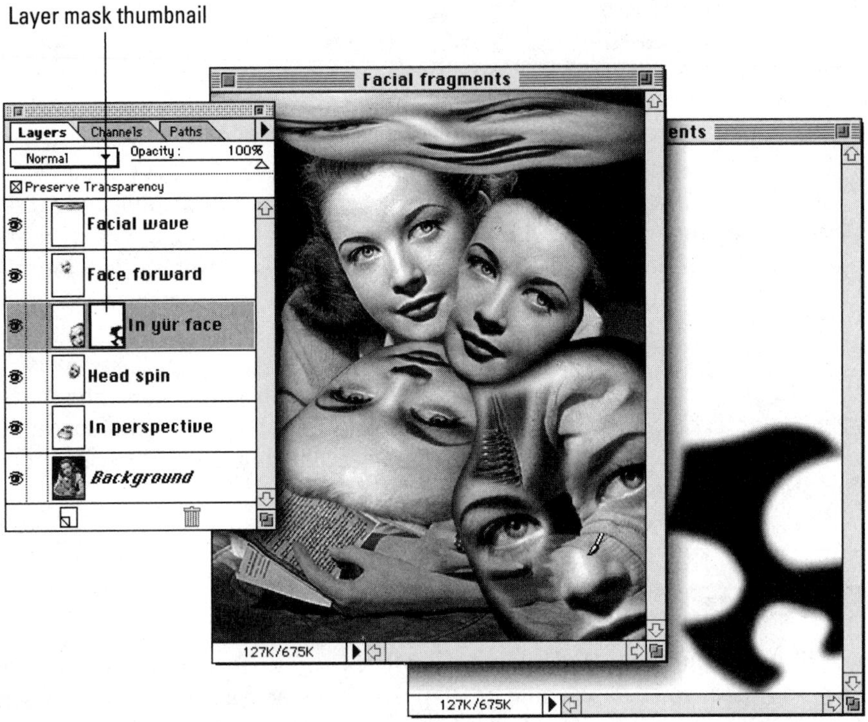

Layer mask thumbnail

Figure 9-21:
When the layer mask is active (as indicated by the heavy outline around the mask thumbnail in the Layers palette), paint with black to make pixels transparent and paint in white to make them opaque. The mask itself appears in the right window.

Facial fragments

Layers | Channels | Paths

Normal   Opacity: 100%

☒ Preserve Transparency

Facial wave

Face forward

In yür face

Head spin

In perspective

Background

127K/675K

127K/675K

The left image in Figure 9-21 finds me painting a soft hole into face 3 with the paintbrush. Notice that while the eyes, nose, mouth, and face outline remain at least opaque, other areas are translucent or altogether transparent. If I make a mistake — like accidentally lancing off the nose — no sweat. I just paint with white to bring it back again.

The right image in Figure 9-21 shows the mask by itself. A layer mask is actually a temporary channel. To view it with the image, go to the Channels panel of this same palette and click in the left column in front of the item that bears the name of the layer — in my case, *In yür face Mask*. To view the channel by itself, click on the eyeball icon in front of the composite view item.

Actually, you can do all this without ever leaving the Layers panel. To view the mask by itself, Option-click on the layer mask thumbnail. To see both mask and image together, Shift-click on the left layer thumbnail and then click again on the layer mask thumbnail to keep the mask active (so that you don't end up editing the image itself). You can also turn the mask on and off by Command-clicking on the mask thumbnail. A red X covers the thumbnail when it's inactive, and all masked pixels in the layer appear opaque.

You can also double-click on the layer mask thumbnail to view the Layer Mask Options dialog box. Mostly, these options are the same as those described in the earlier section "Changing the red coating," except the two Position Relative To radio buttons and the Do Not Apply to Layer check box. The latter simply turns off the layer, as when you Command-click on the mask thumbnail. The Position Relative To options specify whether the mask moves with the layer when you use the move tool. If you select Layer, you can move mask and layer at once. If you select Image, the layer moves independently of the mask. You can always move the mask independently of the layer with the move tool or move the layer independently by selecting it then moving it, so I recommend selecting the Layer radio button.

When and if you finish using the mask — you don't have to ever finish with it if you don't want to — you can choose Remove Layer Mask from the Layers palette menu. An alert box asks you if you want to discard the mask or permanently apply it to the layer. Click on the button of your choosing.

Masking groups of layers

This is about the point at which I grow a little fatigued with the topic of layering masking. But one more option requires discussion. You can group multiple layers into something called a *clipping group,* in which the lowest layer in the group determines the way all other layers in the group are masked. (Note that a clipping group has no practical similarities to a clipping path — that is, it doesn't allow you to prepare transparent areas for import into Illustrator or QuarkXPress.)

Creating a clipping group is easy. Just Option-click on the horizontal line between any two layers to group them into a single unit. Your cursor changes to the group layer icon shown in Figure 9-22 when you press Option; the horizontal line becomes dotted after you click. To break the layers apart again, just Option-click on the dotted line to make it solid.

All layers in the group remain discrete units. You can't select across layers or paint on two layers at once. (You can paint on one layer and have it flow out in front of other layers, but you can do that without grouping.) The move tool still moves the layers independently unless you specifically instruct it to do otherwise (as I explained in the previous chapter).

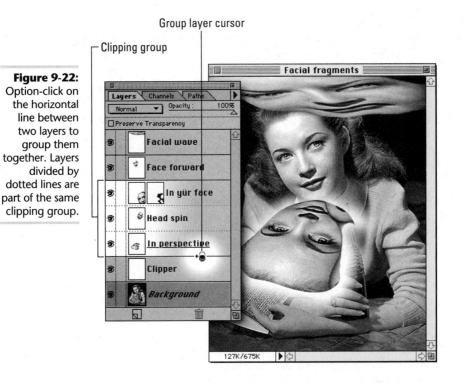

Figure 9-22:
Option-click on the horizontal line between two layers to group them together. Layers divided by dotted lines are part of the same clipping group.

The only thing that the layers in a clipping group share is a common selection mask. The lowest layer in the clipping group acts as a selection mask for the other layers in the group. Where the lowest layer is transparent, the other layers are hidden; where the lowest layer is opaque, the contents of the other layers are visible. In Figure 9-22, for example, face 1 — the upside-down face — is the lowest layer in the group. I've added a slight halo under the layer to show it off a little better. As you can see, just the base of the chin from face 2 and a sliver of the large face 3 — the other members of the clipping group — can be seen. It's not an effect you're likely to find much use for.

That's why it best to throw in a base layer whose only function is to serve as the selection mask. In the first example of Figure 9-23, I created a new empty layer called Clipper and made it the lowest layer in the clipping group. Because it's completely transparent, all the other layers in the group are invisible. I select a large oval area with the elliptical marquee tool and press Option-Delete to fill it with black. Actually, it doesn't matter which color I use, just as long as it's opaque. The selection mask immediately grows to fill the oval. As a result, all pixels in the other layers in the group that fit inside the opaque area become opaque as well, as shown in the bottom example of the figure. Now, faces 1 and 2 are completely visible because they fit entirely inside the oval; face 3 is half obscured.

Figure 9-23:
Starting with an entirely transparent bottom layer inside my clipping group (top), I select an oval area and fill it with opaque color, making the overlapping portions of the layers above the clipping group visible (bottom).

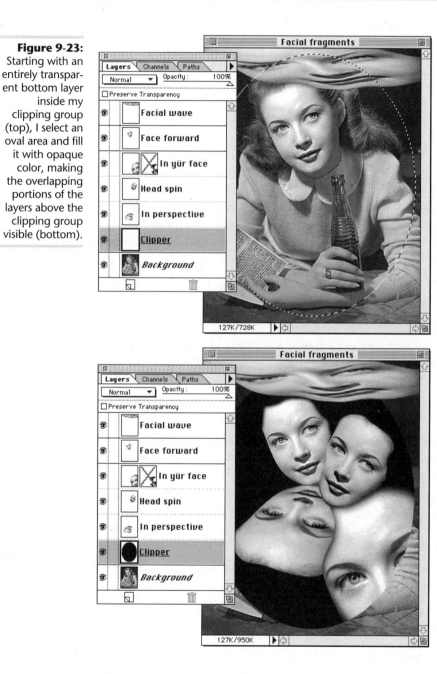

If you're familiar with Illustrator, you'll recognize this clipping group metaphor as a relative to Illustrator's clipping path. One object in the illustration acts as a mask for a collection of additional objects. In Illustrator 5.0 and 5.5, however, the topmost object in the collection is the mask, not the bottom one. So much for consistency.

Summary

- ⇨ Whether in the quick mask mode, a separate mask channel, or wherever, a mask is a grayscale representation of a selection outline. White represents selected areas, black represents deselected areas, and gray represents partial selections.

- ⇨ Every selection outline prevents you from painting outside the lines and therefore acts as a selection mask.

- ⇨ Press the Q key to enter and exit the quick mask mode.

- ⇨ Inside the quick mask mode, you can use paint tools, edit tools, special effects commands, color correction commands, selection tools, and any other Photoshop function to edit a selection outline.

- ⇨ Switch the color coating in the quick mask mode from the masked areas to the selected areas by Option-clicking on the quick mask mode icon in the toolbox.

- ⇨ While in the Color Range dialog box, Shift-click on a color to add it to the selection and Command-click to subtract it. Click to reset the colors and start over again. Or Option-click on the Reset button.

- ⇨ The Fuzziness value in the Color Range dialog box indicates the range of colors that will be selected from the base colors on which you click and Shift-click. Higher values create gradual selection outlines; low values result in more exact but more jagged selections.

- ⇨ By creating an independent mask channel, you can save a selection for re-peated use within an image.

- ⇨ Click on the convert to mask/selection icon at the bottom of the Channels palette to convert a selection outline into a mask channel. Drag the Quick Mask item in the palette onto the convert to mask/selection icon to save the quick mask for later use.

➥ Option-click on a mask channel name in the Channels palette to convert it into a selection outline.

➥ You can save as many mask channels as you like in the native Photoshop and TIFF formats.

➥ Select the Preserve Transparency check box in the Layers palette to paint or edit only inside the opaque areas of a layer.

➥ You can paint temporary holes into a layer by adding a layer mask and painting in black. Paint in white to make areas visible again.

➥ In a clipping group, the lowest layer serves as a selection mask for the layers above it. To create a clipping group, Option-click on the horizontal line between two layers in the Layers palette.

Filling and Stroking

CHAPTER 10

In This Chapter

➡ Applying color with the paint bucket tool, Fill command, or Delete key

➡ Creating an antique framing effect with the paint bucket

➡ Adding drop shadows, halos, and spotlights the new way, with layers and masks

➡ Adjusting settings in the Gradient Tool Options panel

➡ Using the gradient tool in combination with different brush modes

➡ Drawing gradient selection outlines in the quick mask mode

➡ Attaching arrowheads to any stroke

➡ Making translucent gradient arrowheads with halos

Filling Portions of an Image _____

No explanation of filling and stroking would be complete without a definition, so here goes: To *fill* a selection is to put color inside it; to *stroke* a selection is to put color around it. Simple stuff, actually. Lots of you already knew it and are getting plenty hot under the collar that you had to waste valuable seconds of your day reading such a flat-out obvious sentence. And you're getting even more steamed that you have to read sentences like these that don't add much to your overall understanding of Photoshop. And this sentence here, well, it's sufficient reason to write the publisher and burst a blood vessel.

In fact — he said, miraculously veering off the shoulder of the road and back onto the highway of the main story — Photoshop's fill and stroke functions are so straightforward that you may have long since dismissed them as wimpy little tools with remarkably limited potential. But in fact, you can do a world of stuff with them. In this chapter, for example, I'll show you how to create an antique framing effect, how to create drop shadows, halos, and spotlights, how to use gradations in masks, and how to create arrowheads that leap off the page, all in addition to the really basic stuff that you may already know. Actually, come to think of it, you might even want to read about the basic stuff on the off chance that you missed some golden nugget of information in your Photoshopic journeys thus far.

Filling an Area with Color

You can fill an area of an image with color in four ways:

- **The paint bucket tool:** You can apply the foreground color or a repeating pattern to areas of related color in an image by clicking in the image window with the paint bucket tool (known in some circles as the fill tool). For example, if you want to turn all midnight blue pixels in an image into red pixels, you just set the foreground color to red and then click on one of the blue pixels.

- **The Fill command:** Select the portion of the image that you want to color and then fill the entire selection with the foreground color or a repeating pattern by choosing Edit⇨Fill. To choose the command without so much as moving the mouse, press Shift-Delete.

- **Delete-key techniques:** Select part of an image and fill the selection with the background color by pressing the Delete key. To fill the selection with the foreground color, press Option-Delete.

- **The gradient tool:** Select an area and drag across it with the gradient tool to fill it with a multicolor gradation. Although it needs upgrading in order to match the power of gradient tools in some other programs, Photoshop's gradient tool is still so special and wide-ranging in its capabilities that I devote several pages to the topic in the section "Applying Gradient Fills" later in this chapter.

The following sections discuss each of these options in depth.

The paint bucket tool

Unlike remedial paint bucket tools in other painting programs, which apply paint exclusively within outlined areas or areas of solid color — thereby exhibiting all the subtlety of dumping paint out of a bucket — the Photoshop paint bucket tool offers several useful adjustment options. To explore them, double-click on the paint bucket icon in the toolbox to display the Paint Bucket Options panel of the Brushes palette, shown in Figure 10-1. (Alternatively, you can press the K key to select the paint bucket tool and then press Return to display the options panel.)

Figure 10-1:
The Paint Bucket Options panel governs the performance of the paint bucket tool.

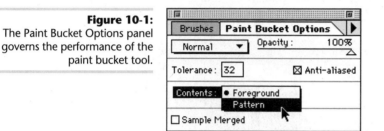

Three of the options — Tolerance, Anti-aliased, and Sample Merged — work exactly like their counterparts in the Magic Wand Options panel, which I explained in the "The world of the wand" section of Chapter 8. The brush modes pop-up menu and the Opacity slider bar work just like those in the Paintbrush Options panel, which I covered at extreme length in Chapter 7. But just in case you need a refresher, here's how these and the other options work, in the order they appear in the panel:

- ↪ **Brush modes:** Select an option from the brush modes pop-up menu to specify how and when color is applied. For example, if you select Darken, the paint bucket tool affects a pixel in the image only if the foreground color is darker than that pixel. If you select Color, the paint bucket colorizes the image without changing the brightness value of any pixel. For an in-depth look at brush modes, read the "The 15 paint tool brush modes" section back in Chapter 7.

- ↪ **Opacity:** Drag the Opacity slider or press a number key to change the translucency of a color applied with the paint bucket.

- ↪ **Tolerance:** Applying color with the paint bucket tool is a three-step process. Immediately after you click on a pixel with the tool, Photoshop reads the brightness value of that pixel from each color channel. Next, Photoshop calculates a tolerance range according to the value you enter in the Tolerance option box (you can enter any value from 0 to 255). It adds the Tolerance value to the brightness value of the pixel on which you click with the paint bucket tool to determine the top of the range; it subtracts the Tolerance value from the brightness value of the pixel to determine the bottom of the range. For example, if the pixel's brightness value is 100 and the Tolerance value is 32, the top of the range is 132 and the bottom is 68. After establishing a tolerance range, Photoshop applies the foreground color to any pixel that both falls inside the tolerance range and is contiguous to the pixel on which you clicked. A large Tolerance value causes the paint bucket to affect a greater number of pixels than a small Tolerance value. Figure 10-2 shows the result of clicking on the same pixel three times, each time using a lower Tolerance value.

Figure 10-2:
The results of applying the paint bucket tool to the exact same pixel after setting the Tolerance value to 32 (top), 16 (middle), and 8 (bottom). In each case, the foreground color is white.

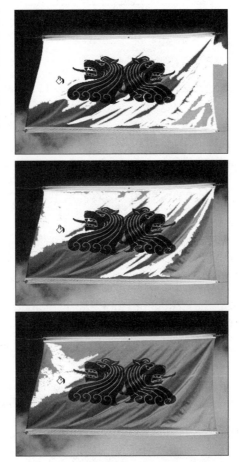

☞ **Anti-aliased:** Select this option to soften the effect of the paint bucket tool. As demonstrated in the top example of Figure 10-3, Photoshop creates a border of translucent color between the filled pixels and their unaffected neighbors. If you don't want to soften the transition, deselect the Anti-aliased check box. Photoshop then fills only those pixels that fall inside the tolerance range, as demonstrated in the bottom example of the figure.

Figure 10-3:
The results of selecting (top) and deselecting (bottom) the Anti-aliased check box prior to using the paint bucket tool. The inset rectangles show magnified pixels.

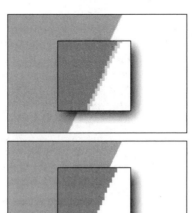

☞ **Contents:** You can either apply the foreground color or a repeating pattern created using Edit⇨Define Pattern. The Define Pattern command is covered in the "Applying Repeating Patterns" section of Chapter 11.

☞ **Sample Merged:** Select this option to make the paint bucket see beyond the current layer. When the option is selected, the tool takes all visible layers into account when calculating the area to be filled. Mind you, it only fills the active layer — as I've mentioned before, only the move tool can affect more than one layer at a time — but the way it fills an area is dictated by all layers. For example, suppose that you have an image of a dog on one layer and a fire hydrant on the other. The two images do not overlap. If you were to click on the fire hydrant when the dog layer was active *and* the Sample Merged option was turned off, you'd fill most of the image. The paint bucket can't see the hydrant; all it can see is the transparent area of the dog layer, so it tries to fill that. (This assumes that the Preserve Transparency option in the Layers palette is turned off.) However, if you were to select Sample Merged, the paint bucket would fill the portion of the hydrant on which you click. It would apply the paint to the dog layer, but the paint would follow the contours of the hydrant. In fact, as long as the dog layer was above the hydrant layer, it would look just as if you had filled the hydrant itself (but you would have the option of mixing hydrant fill and hydrant together, as discussed in Chapter 17, "The Fundamentals of Compositing").

To limit the area affected by the paint bucket, select a portion of the image before using the tool. As when you use any other tool, the region outside the selection outline is protected from the paint bucket.

The Fill command

The one problem with the paint bucket tool is its lack of precision. Though undeniably convenient, the paint bucket suffers the exact same limitations as the magic wand. The effects of the Tolerance value are so difficult to predict that you typically have to click with the tool, choose Edit⇨Undo when you don't like the result, adjust the Tolerance value, and reclick with the tool several times more before you fill the image as desired. For my part, I've almost given up using the paint bucket for any purpose other than filling same-colored areas. On my machine, the Tolerance option is nearly always set to 0 and Anti-alias is always off, which puts me right back in the all-the-subtlety-of-dumping-paint-out-of-a-bucket camp. (For an exception to this, see the upcoming "Creating Special Fill Effects" section.)

A better option is to select the area that you want to fill and choose Edit⇨Fill or press Shift-Delete. In this way, you can define the exact area of the image you want to color using the entire range of Photoshop's selection tools — including the path tools, quick mask mode, Color Range command, and so on — instead of limiting yourself to the equivalent of the magic wand. For example, instead of putting your faith in the paint bucket tool's Anti-aliased option, you can draw a selection outline that features hard edges in one area, antialiased edges elsewhere, and feathered edges in between.

When you choose the Fill command, Photoshop displays the Fill dialog box shown in Figure 10-4. In this dialog box, you can apply a translucent color or pattern by entering a value into the Opacity option box and you can choose a brush mode option from the Mode pop-up menu. In addition to its inherent precision, the Fill command maintains all the functionality of the paint bucket tool — and then some.

If you display the Contents pop-up menu, as shown in the lower example in Figure 10-4, you'll see a collection of things you can use to fill the selected area, many of which are new to Photoshop 3.0. Foreground Color and Pattern are in the menu, as with the paint bucket tool. So are Background Color and such monochrome options as Black, White, and 50% Gray. Black and White are useful if the foreground and background colors have been changed from their defaults; 50% Gray allows you to access the absolute medium color without having to mess around with the Color Picker dialog box or Picker palette. Saved and Snapshot allow you to revert the selected area to a previous appearance, as discussed in the "Reverting selected areas" section of Chapter 11.

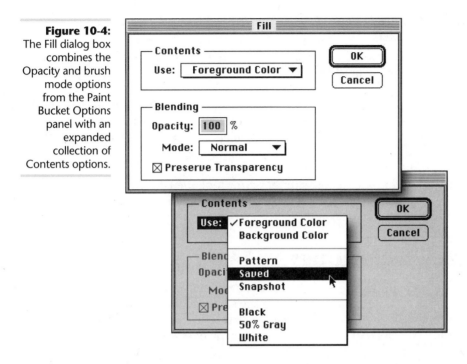

Figure 10-4:
The Fill dialog box combines the Opacity and brush mode options from the Paint Bucket Options panel with an expanded collection of Contents options.

The Preserve Transparency check box works exactly like the identically named option in the Layers palette (discussed in Chapter 9). When the option is turned on, you can't fill the transparent pixels in the current layer. Because you're already filling one selection mask, Photoshop gives you the option of considering the implied selection mask of the layer as well. When Preserve Transparency is turned off, you fill the selection outline uniformly. (The option is dimmed when you're working on the background layer or when the Preserve Transparency option in the Layers palette is checked for the current layer.)

Filling paths

Photoshop provides a variation on Edit⇨Fill that lets you fill paths that were created with the pen tool without first converting them to selections. After drawing a path, choose the Fill Path command from the Path palette pop-up menu or Option-click on the fill path icon in the lower left corner of the palette. Photoshop displays a slight variation of the Fill dialog box from Figure 10-4, the only difference being the inclusion of two Rendering options. Enter a value into the Feather Radius option box to blur the edges of the fill as if the path were a selection with a feathered outline. Select the Anti-aliased check box to slightly soften the outline of the filled area.

If one path falls inside another, Photoshop leaves the intersection of the two paths unfilled. Suppose that you draw two round paths, one fully inside the other. If you save the paths and then choose the Fill Path command, Photoshop fills only the area between the two paths, resulting in a letter *O*.

 If the Fill Path command fills only part or none of the path, it is very likely because the path falls outside the selection outline. Choose Select⇨None (Command-D) to deselect the image and then choose the Fill Path command again.

 If you select one or more paths with the arrow tool, the Fill Path command changes to Fill Subpaths, enabling you to fill the selected paths only.

Delete-key techniques

Of all the fill techniques, the Delete key is by far the most convenient and, in most respects, every bit as capable as the others. The key's only failing is that it can't fill a selection with a repeating pattern. But because you'll rarely *want* to fill a selection with a repeating pattern, you can rely on the Delete key for the overwhelming majority of your fill needs.

Here's how to get a ton of functionality out of the Delete key:

- ⤳ **Background color:** To fill a selection with solid background color, press Delete. The selection outline remains intact. Keep in mind that this technique works only when the selection is *not* floating. If you float the selection and then press Delete, you delete the selection entirely.

- ⤳ **Foreground color:** To fill a selection with solid foreground color, press Option-Delete. You can fill floating and nonfloating selections alike by pressing Option-Delete.

- ⤳ **Black or white:** To fill an area with black, press D to get the default foreground and background colors and then press Option-Delete. To fill it with white, press D for defaults, X to switch them, and then Option-Delete. This method works on both floating and nonfloating selections.

- ⤳ **Translucent color:** To fill a selection with a translucent coating of foreground color, choose Select⇨Float (Command-J) to float the selection. Then press Option-Delete, press the M key to make sure that a selection tool is active, and press a number key to change the setting of the Opacity slider bar in the Layers palette.

ᴄᴐ **Accessing brush modes:** To mix foreground color and original image using brush modes, float the selection, press Option-Delete, and select a mode from the pop-up menu on the left side of the Layers palette.

Creating Special Fill Effects

Ever seen *Sid and Nancy*? It's this movie where Gary Oldman plays Sid Vicious of the Sex Pistols. You know, the English punk band. No, really, it's a great movie, even if you don't like the Sex Pistols. With lyrics like, "God save the queen, she ain't no human being," I can't imagine what there is not to like. But the point is, in one scene in the movie, Sid and fellow band member Johnny Rotten climb onto the hood of a car that has this yappy poodle in it and kick in the windshield. (At least I think that's how it goes. I only saw the movie once and it was a long time ago, so I'm a little vague on the details. But really, it's a great picture.) Anyway, Sid and Johnny stand for a moment, staring down at what they've done, considering the damage. (Don't worry, the poodle's fine — it continues yapping away to prove it.) Then Sid and Johnny turn to each other and shout in unison, "Boring!" It's one of those classic movie moments that makes you feel tingly and weepy all over.

It's very possible that after reading the previous sections, you feel a bit like Sid. Oh, you're not going to spike your hair or take to wearing a dog collar — at least, not on a weekday — but, well, even Photoshop has its share of dull moments. Filling selections? Boring! Oh, sure, you were mesmerized by my entertaining text blended cleverly with comprehensive coverage, but in the background, I bet that you were lamenting your misspent youth. Face it, nowhere in the recipe for image-editing fun is there mention of a paint bucket, a Fill command, or a Delete key.

Ah ha, that's what *you* think. In reality, all three of these functions are capable of delivering some pretty wonderful results. Okay, so the paint bucket is a pitiful creature by anyone's standards — "*Pretty*, pretty *vacant*," as Johnny Rotten might say — but the Delete key alone is a cosmic and powerful force if you'll only take the time to unleash it correctly. So don't be so quick to dismiss a bunch of capable functions just because they're dull. I mean, I think that you really need to consider it carefully before you start looking to Sid and Johnny as your personal role models. Great lads at a party, just the blokes to call if you want to pierce something, but pinnacles of virtue? Very possibly not.

A use for the paint bucket discovered

So far, I've come up with two astounding generalizations: the paint bucket tool is mostly useless, and you can fill anything with the Delete key. Well, just to prove that you shouldn't believe everything I say — and certainly, there's a school of thought that you should dismiss *everything* I say — the following steps explain how to create an effect that you can perform only with the paint bucket tool. Doubtless, it's the only such example you'll ever discover using Photoshop — after all, the paint bucket *is* mostly useless and you *can* fill anything with the Delete key — but I'm man enough to eat my rules just this once.

The steps explain how to create an antique photographic frame effect like the one shown in Figure 10-5.

STEPS: Creating an Antique Photographic Frame

Step 1. Use the rectangular marquee tool to select the portion of the image that you want to frame. Make sure that the image extends at least 20 pixels outside the boundaries of the selection outline.

Step 2. Choose Select⇨Feather and specify a Radius value somewhere in the neighborhood of 6 to 12 pixels. I've found that these values work for just about any resolution of image. (If you enter too high a value, the color you'll add in a moment with the paint bucket will run out into the image.)

Step 3. Choose Select⇨Inverse to exchange the selected and deselected portions of the image.

Step 4. Press the D key to make sure that the background color is white. Then press the Delete key to fill the selected area with the background color.

Step 5. Double-click on the paint bucket tool icon in the toolbox to display the Paint Bucket Options panel. Enter 20 to 30 in the Tolerance option box and select the Anti-aliased check box. (You can also experiment with turning this option off.)

Step 6. Click inside the feathered selection to fill it with black (or whatever other foreground color you prefer). The result is an image fading into white and then into black, like the edges of a worn slide or photograph, as shown in Figure 10-5.

Figure 10-5:
I created this antique frame effect by filling a feathered selection with the paint bucket tool.

Figure 10-6 shows a variation on this effect that you can create using the Dissolve brush mode. Rather than setting the Tolerance value to 20, raise it to something in the neighborhood of 60. Then, after selecting the paint bucket tool, select the Dissolve option from the brush modes pop-up menu in the Paint Bucket Options panel. When you click inside the feathered selection with the paint bucket tool, you create a frame of random pixels, as illustrated in the figure.

Figure 10-6:
Select Dissolve from the Brushes palette pop-up menu to achieve a speckled frame effect.

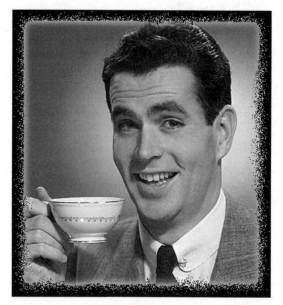

Creating drop shadows, halos, and spotlights

Okay, so there's one use for the paint bucket tool. Big whoop. In most cases, you don't need it. For example, you can create three of the most useful (and, some might argue, overused) of all image-editing enhancements — drop shadows, halos, and spotlights — using nothing but the selection tools and Option-Delete. Rather than throw a lot of in-depth analysis your way, I'll just jump right in and show you how.

In the first steps, I'll take the dolphin from Figure 10-7 and insert a drop shadow behind it. This might not be the exact subject to which you'll apply drop shadows — sea critters so rarely cast such shadows onto the water's surface — but it accurately demonstrates how the effect works.

Figure 10-7:
A dolphin in dire need of a drop shadow.

STEPS: **Creating a Drop Shadow**

Step 1.   Select the subject that you want to cast the shadow. In my case, I selected the dolphin by painting the mask shown in Figure 10-8 inside a separate mask channel. These days, I add a mask to nearly all my images that distinguishes the foreground image from its background. I converted the mask to a selection outline by Option-clicking on the mask name in the Channels palette and then pressing Command-0 to switch back to the composite view.

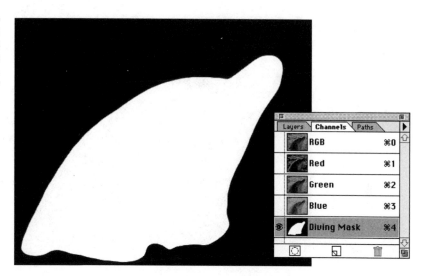

Figure 10-8:
This mask separates
the dolphin from its
watery home.

Step 2.   Float the selection by pressing Command-J. Then send the selection to its
own layer by switching to the Layers panel and Option-double-clicking on
the Floating Selection item in the scrolling list. Now that the selection is
elevated, you can slip the drop shadow underneath it.

Step 3.   In order to create the drop shadow, you need to retrieve the selection
outline and apply it to the background layer. To do this, press Command-
Option-T to select the layer and tighten the selection outline, and click on
the Background item in the Layers palette to apply the selection outline to
the original image. (If you saved the mask to a separate channel as I did, you
could alternatively Option-click on the Mask item in the Channels panel to
retrieve the selection.)

Step 4.   To create a softened drop shadow — indicative of a diffused light source —
choose Select⇨Feather. The Radius value you enter depends on the resolution of your image. I recommend dividing the resolution of your image by 20.
When working on a 200 ppi image, for example, enter a Radius value of 10.
My image is a mere 140 ppi, so I entered 7. Then press Return to soften the
image.

Step 5.   Press Command-J to float the selection and Command-H to hide the edges.
Then fill the selection with black (D, Option-Delete). A slight halo of dark
pixels forms around the edges of the image.

Step 6.   Use the arrow keys to nudge the shadow to the desired location. In Figure
10-9, I nudged the shadow 12 pixels to the right.

Figure 10-9:
A drop shadow nudged 12 pixels due right from the dolphin head, which is situated on the layer above it.

Step 7. If the shadow is too dark — black lacks a little subtlety — press M to make sure that a selection tool is active and then press a number key to change the opacity of the shadow. I typically press 7 for 70 percent. But I'm probably in a rut.

 If you don't like a black drop shadow, you can make a colored one with only slightly more effort. Instead of filling the shadow with black in Step 5, select a different foreground color and press Option-Delete. For the best result, select a color that is the complimentary opposite of the color of your background. In Color Plate 10-1, for example, the background is blue, so I selected a reddish orange as the foreground color. Next, choose Multiply from the overlay modes pop-up menu on the left side of the Layers palette. This burns the colors in the shadow into those in the image to create a darkened mix. Finally, press a number key to specify the opacity. (In the color plate, I again used 70 percent. I'm definitely in a rut.)

Creating a halo is very similar to creating a drop shadow. The only differences are that you have to expand the selection outline and that you fill the halo with white (or some other light color) instead of black. The following steps tell it all.

STEPS: Creating a Downright Angelic Halo

Step 1. Follow Steps 1 through 3 of the previous instructions. You'll end up with a version of the selected image on an independent layer and a matching selection outline applied to the Background image. (See, I told you that this was just like creating a drop shadow.)

Step 2. Unlike a drop shadow, which is offset slightly from an image, a halo fringes the perimeter of an image pretty evenly. Therefore, you need to expand the selection outline beyond the edges of the image so that you can see the halo clearly. To do this, choose Select⇨Modify⇨Expand. You'll be greeted by an Expand By option box. Generally speaking, you want the expansion to match the size of your feathering so that the softening occurs outward. Therefore, I entered 7. (The maximum permissible value is 16; if you want to expand more than 16 pixels, you have to apply the command twice.)

Step 3. Choose Select⇨Feather and enter the same value you entered in the Expand By option box. Again, you decide this value by dividing the resolution of your image by 20. Or not. Let experimentation be your guiding light.

Step 4. Float the selection. Change the foreground color to white (by pressing D and then X) and then press Option-Delete.

That's all there is to it. Figure 10-10 shows a particularly enlightened-looking dolphin set against a halo effect. I also drew a conventional halo above its head, added some sparklies, and even changed my finned friend's eye using the eyeball brush shape included in the Assorted Brushes document. I mean, if this aquatic mammal's not bound for glory, I don't know who is.

 Incidentally, you don't have to create a white halo any more than you have to create a black drop shadow. In Step 4, select some other foreground color than white. Then select the Screen option from the overlay modes pop-up menu in the Layers palette, thus mixing the colors and lightening them at the same time. If you don't like the effect, just select a different foreground color and press Option-Delete again. As long as the halo is floating, you can do just about anything you want and run no risk of harming the underlying original.

Figure 10-10:
Few dolphins reach this level of spiritual awareness, even if you do set them off from their backgrounds using the halo effect. He kind of looks like one of the cast members from *Cocoon,* don't you think?

Now, finally, for the spotlight effect. I use spotlights about a billion times in this book to highlight some special option that I want you to look at in a palette or dialog box. I've gotten so many questions (from fellow authors mostly) on how to perform this effect that I've decided I might as well write it down once in the book and be done with it. So here goes.

STEPS: Shining a Spotlight on Something Inside an Image

Step 1. Using the elliptical marquee tool, draw an oval selection inside your image. This represents the area where the spotlight will shine. If you don't like where the oval is located but you basically like its size and shape, Command-Option-drag it to a more satisfactory location.

Step 2. Choose Select⇨Feather and enter whatever Radius value you please. Again, you may want to follow the divide-the-resolution-by-20 rule, but feel free to use whatever value you like. (There's no such thing as a wrong Radius value.) To create Figure 10-11, I doubled my Radius value to 14 pixels to create a very soft effect.

Step 3. You really want to darken the area outside the spotlight, not lighten the spotlight itself. So choose Select⇨Inverse to swap what's selected and what's not.

Step 4. Float the selection, hide the outline, and fill it with black. That's Command-J, Command-H, D, Option-Delete. Then change the Opacity setting by pressing a number key. To get Figure 10-11, I pressed 6 for 60 percent.

Figure 10-11:
Create an elliptical
selection, feather it,
inverse it, float it, fill
it with black, and
lower the opacity to
create a spotlight
effect like this one.

Actually, the image in Figure 10-11 isn't all that convincing. Although the steps above are fine for spotlighting flat images such as screen shots, they tend to rob photographs of a little of their depth. After all, in real life, the spotlight wouldn't hit the water in the exact same way it hits the dolphin. But there is a way around this. You can combine the oval selection outline with the mask used to select the foreground image, thereby eliminating the background from the equation entirely.

Assuming that your image has a mask saved in a separate channel, do this: After Step 2, duplicate the mask channel so that you don't harm the original by selecting it in the Channels palette and choosing the Duplicate Channel command from the palette menu. Then choose Select⇨Save Selection. Inside the dialog box, select the duplicate mask channel from the Channel pop-up menu and then select the Intersect with Channel radio button. This creates a mask that retains only those selected areas that were selected both in the selection outline and the mask. Option-click on the revised mask channel in the Channels palette to convert it to a selection outline and switch to the composite view. Then inverse the selection, float it, fill it with black, and change the opacity as explained in Steps 3 and 4 above. Figure 10-12 shows this technique applied to a familiar character.

 Sometimes, the darkness of the area around the spotlight appears sufficiently dark that it starts bringing the spotlighted area down with it. To brighten the spotlight, inverse the selection (Select⇨Inverse) so that the spotlight is selected again. Then apply the Levels command (Image⇨Adjust⇨Levels) to brighten the spotlighted area. The Levels command is explained at length in Chapter 16.

Figure 10-12:
You can mix the feathered selection with the contents of a mask channel to limit the spotlighting effect to the foreground character only.

Just for fun — what other possible reason would there be? — Color Plate 10-2 shows one result of combining the spotlight effect with the halo effect. I filled the area outside the spotlight with a deep blue. (In this case, a similar color looked better than a complimentary one.) Then, using my original mask, I sent the dolphin to a separate layer and created a yellowish, pinkish halo behind it. Just to be safe, I sent the floating halo to its own layer as well. Then, I used Edit➪Fill to return the Background image to its original appearance (by selecting the Saved option from the Use pop-up menu in the Fill dialog box) and inverted the background by pressing Command-I. An interestingly lit dolphin in a radioactive bath is the result.

Applying Gradient Fills

Frankly, the gradient tool needs an upgrade. Although an image editor inherently provides a better environment for creating and editing gradations, Photoshop's gradient tool is fast becoming one of the least capable gradation generators available inside a high-end graphics application. Illustrator, Canvas, and Claris Draw — all object-oriented drawing programs — provide more versatile and more precise gradient tools than Photoshop.

But despite this middling tool, Photoshop still has the upper edge for two simple reasons: You can blur and mix colors in a gradation if they start banding — that is, if you can see a hard edge between one color and the next — and you'll never have problems printing gradations from Photoshop the way you will from Illustrator or some other drawing program. In a drawing program, each color is expressed as a separate shape, meaning that one gradation can contain hundreds or even thousands of objects. Gradations in Photoshop are just plain old colored pixels, the kind we've been editing for nine and a half chapters.

If you want a more comprehensive gradation generator, check out the Gradient Explorer module included with Kai's Power Tools (a set of filters sold separately by HSC Software). Otherwise, the next several pages explain how to use Photoshop's gradient tool to create standard gradations and special effects. You can even use the tool to edit selection outlines in the quick mask mode. Even though Photoshop's gradient tool isn't everything I wish it were, it nonetheless opens up a world of opportunities that you simply can't attain by pressing Option-Delete.

The gradient tool

First, the basics. A *gradation* (also called a *gradient fill*) is a progression of colors that fade gradually into one another, as demonstrated in Figure 10-13. The foreground color represents the first color in the gradation; the background color is the final color in the gradation. Photoshop automatically generates the hundred or so colors in between to create a smooth transition.

Figure 10-13:
Dragging with the gradient tool within a single selection (left) and across multiple selections (right).

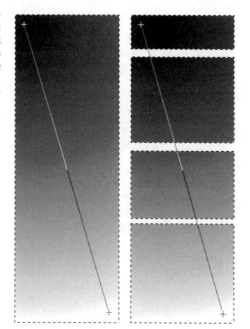

You create gradations using the *gradient tool* (just to the right of the paint bucket in the toolbox). Unlike the paint bucket tool, which fills areas of similar color whether or not they are selected, the gradient tool fills the confines of a selection. If you don't select a portion of your image, Photoshop applies the gradation to the entire image.

To select the gradient tool, press the G key. To use the tool, drag inside the selection, as shown in the left example of Figure 10-13. The point at which you begin dragging (upper left corner in the figure) defines the location of the foreground color in the gradation. The point at which you release (lower right corner) defines the location of the background color. (Alternatively, gradations in Photoshop 3.0 can fade to transparency.) If multiple portions of the image are selected, the gradation fills all selections continuously, as demonstrated by the right example of Figure 10-13.

Gradient tool options

To master the gradient tool, you have to fully understand how to modify its performance. Double-click on the gradient tool icon in the toolbox to display the Gradient Tool Options panel, shown in Figure 10-14. This panel allows you to specify the colors in a gradation as well as the arrangement of those colors by using the following options:

- ↪ **Brush mode and Opacity:** These options work the same as they do in the paint and edit tool Options panels, in the Paint Bucket Options panel, in the Fill dialog box, and everywhere else that they pop up. Select a different brush mode to change the way colors are applied; lower the Opacity value to make a gradation translucent. In both cases — as with all the other options in this panel — you have to adjust the options before using the gradient tool. They do not affect existing gradations.

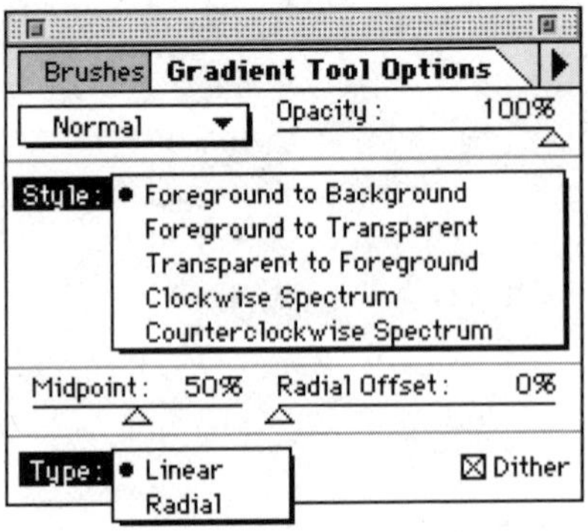

Figure 10-14:
The Gradient Tool Options panel as it appears with both the Style and Type pop-up menu open to scrutiny.

∞ **Style:** The five options in the Style pop-up menu determine how Photoshop selects colors in a gradation. The first option allows you to simply create a gradation from the foreground color to the background color. In Photoshop 3.0, you can also choose to fade the colors from the foreground color to transparency, or from transparency to the foreground color. (In the later case, the point at which you begin dragging determines the point of transparency, rather than the location of the foreground color.) When either of the Transparency options are selected, only the foreground color is treated as opaque; all other colors gradually fade through various levels of translucency until they reach absolute transparency.

The two Spectrum options are a little more complicated. Think of the foreground and background colors as points in the HSB color wheel featured in the Apple Color Picker dialog box, as illustrated in both Figure 10-15 and Color Plate 10-3. When you select the default Foreground to Background option, Photoshop selects colors in a beeline from the foreground color to the background color within the HSB color wheel. Such gradations typically travel through colors of low saturation (that is, gray) near the middle of the wheel. To maintain a high level of saturation, pick the Clockwise Spectrum option, which selects colors in a clockwise direction around the color wheel, or Counterclockwise Spectrum, which selects colors in a counterclockwise direction. Figure 10-15 illustrates all these options, as does Color Plate 10-3. Color Plate 10-4 shows linear examples of the three gradations created using cyan as the foreground color and red as the background color. The only difference between the gradations is the setting of the Style options.

Figure 10-15:
The Spectrum options determine the direction in which a gradation progresses with respect to the HSB color wheel.

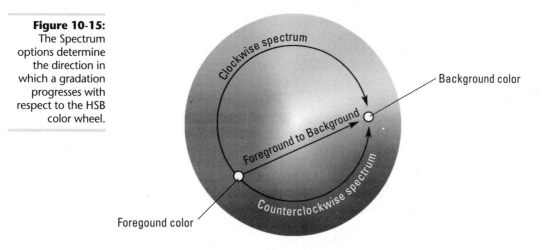

The two Spectrum options have no effect on grayscale gradations, nor do they influence gradations between any color and black, white, or any other shade of gray. To ensure the fastest gradations under these conditions, select the Foreground to Background option.

The two Transparency options are equally applicable to color or grayscale images; however, you cannot subject them to alternative Spectrum settings for the simple reason that they involve different opacities of one color only, this being the foreground color.

- **Type:** Though situated at the bottom of the Options panel, the Type pop-up menu is the next logical option to discuss. Select Linear or Radial to specify the variety of gradation you want to create. A *linear gradation* progresses in linear bands of color in a straight line between the beginning and end of your drag, like the gradation shown back in Figure 10-13. A *radial gradation* progresses outward from a central point in concentric circles, like those in Figures 10-16 and 10-17. The point at which you begin dragging defines the center of the gradation; the point at which you release defines the outermost circle. (Incidentally, I created the radial gradations in Figures 10-16 and 10-17 using white as the foreground color and black as the background color.)

- **Midpoint Skew:** This slider bar determines the location of the halfway point in the gradation. The default value of 50 percent sets the halfway point smack dab in the middle of your drag. If you lower the value, Photoshop arranges most of the colors in the gradation close to the beginning of your drag. This creates a gradation that progresses quickly at first and more slowly toward the end. If you raise the Midpoint Skew value above 50 percent, Photoshop arranges most of the colors toward the end of your drag, resulting in a gradation that progresses slowly at first and more quickly toward the end. Figure 10-16 shows four radial gradations subjected to different Midpoint Skew values, ranging from the minimum to maximum allowed values.

- **Radial Offset:** This slider is applicable exclusively to radial gradations. It defines the size of the central circle of foreground color as a percentage of the size of the entire gradation. A value of 0 percent results in a dab of foreground color in the center of the gradation; a value of 99 percent results in a huge circle of foreground color with a thin band of other colors around its perimeter. Figure 10-17 shows four examples of radial gradations subject to different Radial Offset values. Note that the foreground color is white and the background color is black.

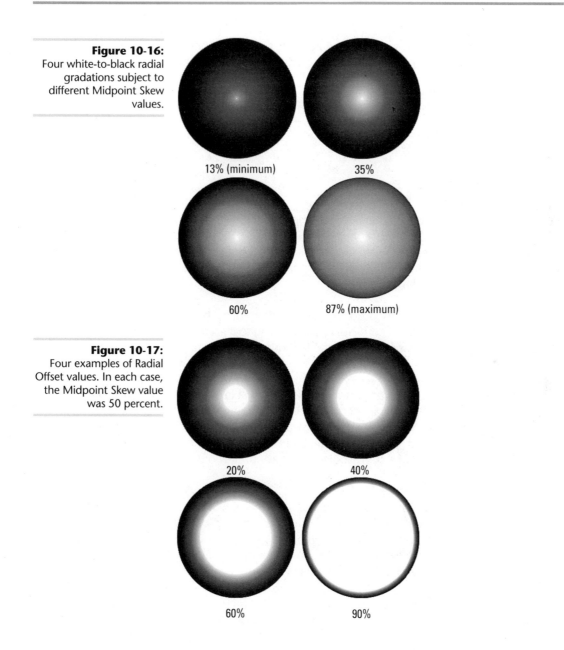

Figure 10-16:
Four white-to-black radial gradations subject to different Midpoint Skew values.

13% (minimum)   35%

60%   87% (maximum)

Figure 10-17:
Four examples of Radial Offset values. In each case, the Midpoint Skew value was 50 percent.

20%   40%

60%   90%

⊸ **Dither:** In the old days, Photoshop drew its gradients one band at a time. Each band was filled with an incrementally different shade of color. The potential result of this was an effect known as *banding*, which simply means that you can clearly distinguish the transition between two or more bands of color. Photoshop 3.0 offers a Dither option that mixes up the pixels a bit, thus helping to eliminate banding. (If selecting the Dither check box doesn't completely take care of the banding, see the next section.) I recommend that you leave this option on unless you want to use the banding to create a special effect.

How to eliminate banding

Thanks to the Dither check box in the Gradient Tool Options panel (which I just finished describing all of one paragraph ago), banding is less of a problem in Photoshop 3.0 than it was in earlier versions. But the problem is not necessarily eliminated completely. If you do experience banding, this section describes how to get rid of it.

As explained in Chapter 13, the Add Noise filter randomizes pixels in a selection. Therefore, when you apply Filter⇨Noise⇨Add Noise to a gradation, it randomly mixes the bands of color, very much like a variable dithering function. In fact, it allows you to out-dither the Dither check box.

The first column in Figure 10-18 shows linear and radial gradations. In the second column, I applied the Add Noise filter three times in a row to both gradations. To make the effect as subtle as possible — you don't want the noise to be obvious — I specified an Amount value of 8 and selected the Uniform radio button inside the Add Noise dialog box. Multiple repetitions of a subtle noise effect are preferable to a single application of a more radical effect.

If noise isn't enough or if the noise appears a little too obvious, you can further mix the colors in a gradation by applying a directional blur filter. To blur a linear gradation, apply the Motion Blur filter in the direction of the gradation. In the top right example of Figure 10-18, I applied Filter⇨Blur⇨Motion Blur with an Angle value of 90 degrees (straight up and down) and a Distance value of 3 pixels.

To blur a radial gradation, apply the Radial Blur filter (Filter⇨Blur⇨Radial Blur). To mix the noise around the center of the gradation, select the Spin option in the Radial Blur dialog box. To blend color in the bands, select the Zoom option. The lower right example in Figure 10-18 is divided into two halves. To create the top half, I applied the Spin option with an Amount value of 10; to create the bottom half, I applied Zoom with an Amount value of 20. (If you can barely see any difference between the two — that's the idea when it comes to gradations — look closely at the perimeter of the gradients. The top one, created with the Spin option, is smooth; the one created with the Zoom option is rougher.)

Figure 10-18:
The results of applying noise (middle column) and directional blur effects (right column) to linear and radial gradations.

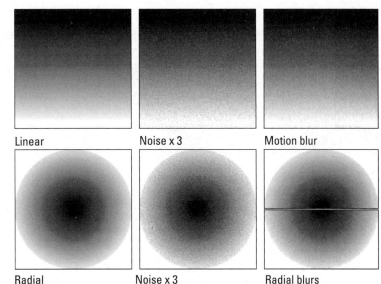

Linear   Noise x 3   Motion blur

Radial   Noise x 3   Radial blurs

To further de-emphasize color bands in a horizontal linear gradation, you can apply the Wind filter (Filter➪Stylize➪Wind). Color Plate 10-5 shows the three gradation styles from Color Plate 10-4 subject to the Add Noise, Wind, and Motion Blur filters. In each case, I applied the Add Noise filter three times (just as in Figure 10-18), the Blast option in the Wind dialog box twice (once in each direction), and the Motion Blur filter in a horizontal direction at 10 pixels.

 You can get a sense of what the Add Noise, Motion Blur, Radial Blur, and Wind filters do just by experimenting with them for a few minutes. If you want to learn even more, I discuss all four in Chapter 13, "Corrective Filtering."

Gradations and brush modes

As with any paint, edit, or fill tool, the brush mode and Opacity settings make a tremendous impression on the performance of the gradient tool. The following sections and steps examine a few ways to use brush modes to achieve special effects. These examples only scrape the surface of what's possible — despite its girth, this entire book only scrapes the surface of what's possible — but hopefully they'll inspire you to experiment and discover additional effects.

Randomized gradations

The following steps describe how to use one brush mode option, Dissolve, in combination with a radial gradation to create an effect not unlike a supernova. (At least, it looks like a supernova to me — not that I've ever seen one up close, mind you.) Figures 10-19 through 10-21 show the nova in progress. In addition to allowing you to experiment with a brush mode setting, the steps offer some general insight into creating radial gradations.

STEPS: **Creating a Gradient Supernova**

Step 1. Create a new image window — say, 500 × 500 pixels. A grayscale image is fine for this exercise.

Step 2. Click with the pencil tool at the apparent center of the image. Don't worry if it's not the exact center. This point is merely intended to serve as a guide. If a single point is not large enough for you to easily identify, draw a small cross.

Step 3. Option-drag from the point with the elliptical marquee tool to draw the marquee outward from the center. Before releasing the mouse button, press and hold the Shift key to constrain the marquee to a circle. Draw a marquee that fills about ³/₄ of the window.

Step 4. Choose Image⇨Map⇨Invert (Command-I) to fill the marquee with black and make the center point white.

Step 5. Choose Select⇨None (Command-D) to deselect the circle. Then Option-drag again from the center point with the elliptical marquee tool, again pressing Shift to constrain the shape to a circle, to create a marquee roughly 20 pixels larger than the black circle.

Step 6. Command-drag from the center point with the elliptical marquee tool and press and hold both Shift and Option midway into the drag to create a marquee roughly 20 pixels smaller than the black circle. The result is a doughnut-shaped selection — a large circle with a smaller circular hole — as shown in Figure 10-19.

Step 7. Choose Select⇨Feather and enter 10 for the Radius value. Then press Return to feather the section outline.

Step 8. Click on the default colors icon in the toolbox and then click on the switch colors icon to make the foreground color white and the background color black.

Step 9. Double-click on the gradient tool icon. Select the Radial option from the Type pop-up menu and set the Radial Offset value to 60 percent to increase the size of the central circle of foreground color to roughly the same size as the center marquee.

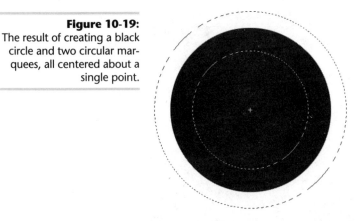

Figure 10-19:
The result of creating a black circle and two circular marquees, all centered about a single point.

Step 10. Select Dissolve from the brush modes pop-up menu on the left side of the Gradient Tool Options panel.

Step 11. Drag from the center point in the image window to anywhere along the outer rim of the largest marquee. The result is the fuzzy gradation shown in Figure 10-20.

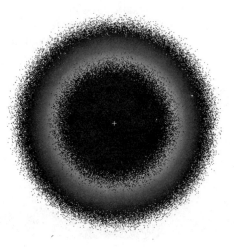

Figure 10-20:
The Dissolve brush mode option randomizes the pixels around the feathered edges of the selection outlines.

Step 12. Choose Select⇨None (Command-D) to deselect the image. Then choose Image⇨Map⇨Invert (Command-I) to invert the entire image.

Step 13. Click on the default colors icon to restore black and white as foreground and background colors respectively. Then use the eraser tool to erase the center point. The finished supernova appears in Figure 10-21.

Figure 10-21:
By inverting the image from the previous figure and erasing the center point, you create an expanding series of progressively lighter rings dissolving into the black void of space, an effect better known to its friends as a supernova.

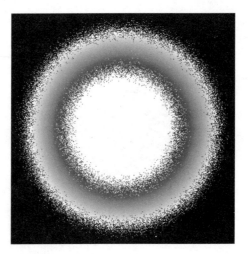

Amorphous gradient bubbles

Well-known image-editing expert Kai Krause came up with a way to mix radial gradations with the Lighten brush mode option to create soft bubbles like those shown in Figure 10-22. I call this the Larva Effect (talk about gall — naming other people's effects) because the darn thing looks like a goopy larva tail.

Figure 10-22:
I painted this larva tail by filling the image with black, selecting Lighten from the brush modes pop-up menu, and creating six radial gradations from white to black with the gradient tool.

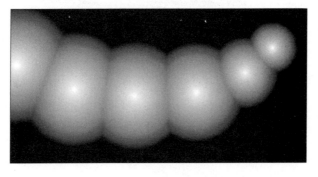

If you want to create this effect, press Command-A to select the entire image, press D to switch to the default colors, and then press Option-Delete to fill the image with black. Set the gradient tool to create radial gradations and select Lighten from the brush modes pop-up menu. Then drag with the tool in the image window to create one radial gradation after another. The Lighten option instructs Photoshop to apply a color to a pixel only if the color is lighter than the pixel's existing color. As a result, you only paint over part of a neighboring gradation when you create a new one, resulting in adjoining gradient bubbles like those shown in Figure 10-22.

To make the bubbles of larva flesh appear to emerge from a gradient pool, set the gradient tool to draw linear gradations and then drag upward from somewhere near the bottom of the image. The linear gradation starts out white at the bottom of the window and slowly fades to black, partially submerging the larva in gooey, glowing sludge. In Figure 10-23, I also dragged with the gradient tool from the top of the image to create a sort of larva cavern. Far out!

Figure 10-23:
To create the larva cavern, I added two linear gradations, one beginning in the upper right corner of the image and the other beginning in the lower left corner.

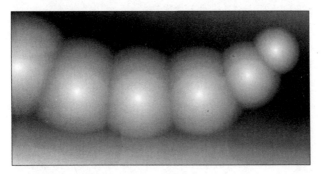

Sharpened amorphous bubbles

The problem with the Larva Effect is that it results in amorphous blobs that look great on-screen but offer too little contrast for most printing situations. Luckily, you can add definition to the blobs using the Unsharp Mask filter with a Radius value of 2.0 or higher.

 Like Add Noise, Motion Blur, and the other filters I mentioned earlier, the strangely named Unsharp Mask filter — which merely sharpens the focus of an image — is covered in greater detail than you probably bargained for in Chapter 13, "Corrective Filtering."

For example, Figure 10-24 shows the results of applying Unsharp Mask with an Amount value of 500 percent, a Radius of 2.0, and a Threshold of 0. The high Radius value helps the filter find the extremely soft edges in the image. (A lower Radius value would just heighten the contrast between individual pixels, creating a grainy effect — if any effect whatsoever.) I applied the filter once to achieve the top example in the figure. I applied the filter a second time to create the bottom example.

As demonstrated in the magnified inset in Figure 10-24, crystalline snowflake patterns begin to emerge with the second application of Unsharp Mask. There's no doubt that the snowflakes are way cool, doubly so because I stumbled on them completely by accident. However, if you would rather skip the snowflakes and further reinforce the edges, you're better off applying higher Radius values from the get-go. The top example in Figure 10-25 shows the result of applying the Unsharp Mask filter with a Radius value of 10.0; the bottom example shows the result of a 20.0 Radius value applied twice. What was once a larva tail is now a bony dinosaur tail.

Figure 10-24:
I sharpened the edges of the larva by applying the Unsharp Mask filter with a 2.0 Radius value once (top) and twice (bottom). Snowflake patterns begin to emerge with the second application of the filter (magnified inset).

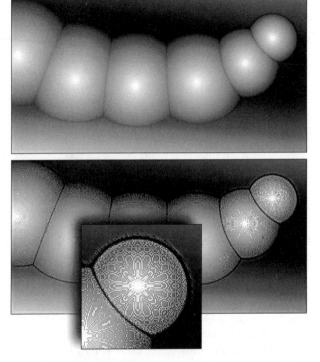

Figure 10-25:
The results of applying Unsharp Mask once with a 10.0 radius (top) and twice with a 20.0 radius (bottom).

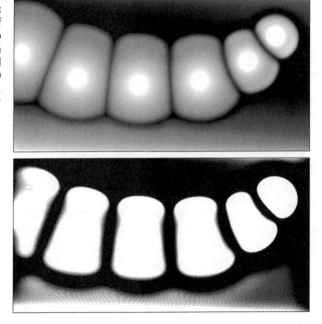

If you're more interested in snowflakes than in sharpening, try applying an edge-detection effect with the Custom filter (Filter⇨Other⇨Custom). This filter requires you to enter numbers into a matrix of option boxes. Figure 10-26 shows some interesting crystals along with the Custom matrix values I used to create them. Now, I'll warn you, some folks go nuts over these effects; some folks break into a cold sweat and have nightmares about their algebra teachers for weeks. Whatever your reaction may be, consider Figure 10-26 the smallest of all possible enticements for reading Chapter 15, "Constructing Homemade Effects."

Figure 10-26:
I filtered this image by entering some pretty extreme edge-detection values into the Custom dialog box (inset lower left). Edge-detection snowflakes (magnified inset) tend to be more spectacular than their Unsharp Mask equivalents.

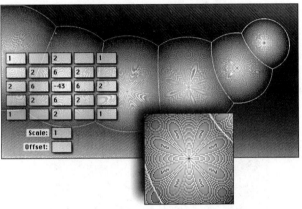

Gradations as masks

If you think that the Feather command is a hot tool for creating softened selection outlines, wait until you get a load of gradations in the quick mask mode. There's simply no better way to create fading effects than selecting an image with the gradient tool.

Fading an image

Consider the Moses set against a white background in Figure 10-27. He's high art, he's got a beard that just won't quit, and he's got muscles bulging out of every corner of his body, including his neck, for heaven's sake. (Is this guy the pumping-iron poster boy for the Benedictine set or what?) Now suppose that you decide that maybe Moses could be even more impressive if he were to fade into view. You're in luck, because that is one of the easiest effects to pull off in Photoshop.

Switch to the quick mask mode by pressing the Q key. Then use the gradient tool to draw a linear gradation from black to white. The white portion of the gradation represents the portion of the image that you want to select. I wanted to select and delete the bottom portion of Moses, so I drew the gradation from top to bottom, as shown in the first example of Figure 10-28.

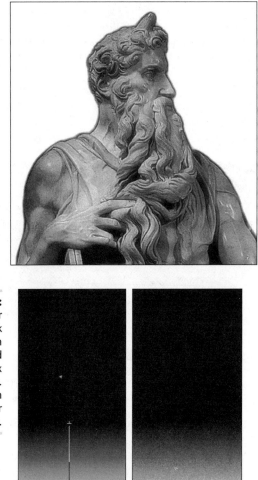

Figure 10-27:
Michelangelo's muscle-bound Moses set against a plain white background.

Figure 10-28:
After drawing a linear gradation in the quick mask mode from top to bottom (left), I applied the Add Noise filter six times to mix up the colors a bit (right). Both images are shown narrower than their actual size.

Banding is typically even more noticeable when you use a gradation as a selection outline. Therefore, to eliminate the banding effect, apply the Add Noise filter at a low setting several times. To create the right example in Figure 10-28, I applied Add Noise six times using an Amount value of 8 and the Uniform distribution option.

To apply the gradation as a selection, return to the marching ants mode by again pressing Q. Press Command-H so that you can see what you're doing. With white as the background color, press Delete to fill the selected portion of the image with white, creating a fading effect. In Figure 10-29, I combined a faded Moses with a traditional gradient background created in the marching ants mode.

Figure 10-29:
The result of selecting the
bottom portion of the
image with a gradation
and pressing Delete to fill it
with white. I also added a
gradient background to
make the image more
powerful.

Applying special effects gradually

You also can use gradations in the quick mask mode to taper the outcomes of filters
and other automated special effects. For example, I wanted to apply a filter around the
edges of the banner image that appears in Figure 10-30. I began by switching to the
quick mask mode, choosing Select⇨All (Command-A), and pressing Option-Delete to
fill the entire mask with black. Then I double-clicked on the gradient tool icon in the
toolbox and selected Linear from the Type pop-up menu inside the Gradient Tool
Options panel. I also selected Lighten from the brush modes pop-up menu in the upper
left corner. (The default option, Foreground to Background, was selected in the Style
pop-up menu.)

Figure 10-30:
I wanted to
highlight the
background
around the
banner by
applying a
gradual
filtering effect.

I pressed the X key to make the foreground color white and the background color black. Then I dragged with the gradient tool from each of the four edges of the image inward to create a series of short gradations that trace the boundaries of the banner, as shown in Figure 10-31. The white areas of the figure represent the portions of the image that I wanted to select.

Figure 10-31: Inside the quick mask mode, I dragged from each of the four edges with the gradient tool (as indicated by the arrows). The Lighten brush mode was active; white and black were the foreground and background colors, respectively.

After taking the above steps, I switched back to the marching ants mode and applied the desired effect, which in this case was the Color Halftone filter from the Filter⇨Stylize submenu. The result appears in Figure 10-32.

Figure 10-32: After switching back to the marching ants mode, I chose Filter⇨Stylize⇨ Color Halftone to create the halftoning effect shown here.

Notice the harsh corners in the mask in Figure 10-31? To create the effect in Figure 10-32, I wanted these corners, but you may not. To bevel the corners, either select the Foreground to Transparent option from the Style pop-up menu or select the Screen option from the brush modes pop-up menu. For a really unusual corner treatment, leave the Style option set to Foreground to Background and choose Difference from the brush modes menu.

Applying Strokes and Arrowheads

In the "Painting along a path" section of Chapter 8, I discussed how to use one of the paint or edit tools to trace along a path created with the pen tool. The following sections discuss the more mundane aspects of stroking, namely how to apply a border around a selection outline — which isn't particularly interesting — and create arrowheads — which can yield more interesting results than you might think.

Stroking a selection outline

Stroking is useful for creating frames and outlines. Generally speaking, you can stroke an image in Photoshop in three ways:

➭ **Using the Stroke command:** Select the portion of the image that you want to stroke and choose Edit⇨Stroke to display the Stroke dialog box shown in Figure 10-33. Enter the thickness of the stroke in pixels into the Width option box. Select a Location radio button to specify the position of the stroke with respect to the selection outline. The Stroke dialog box also includes Opacity, Mode, and Preserve Transparency options that work just like those in the Fill dialog box.

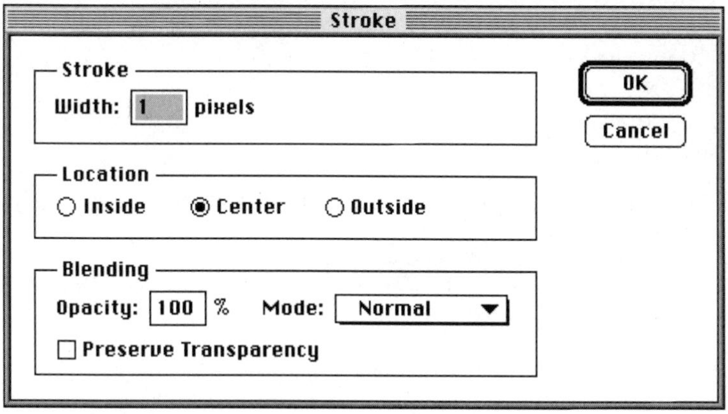

Figure 10-33:
Use the options in the Stroke dialog box to specify the thickness of a stroke and its location with respect to the selection outline.

```
┌──────────────────── Stroke ────────────────────┐
│  ┌─ Stroke ──────────────────────┐   ┌────────┐ │
│  │  Width: [1    ] pixels        │   │   OK   │ │
│  │                               │   └────────┘ │
│  └───────────────────────────────┘   ┌────────┐ │
│                                       │ Cancel │ │
│  ┌─ Location ────────────────────┐   └────────┘ │
│  │  ○ Inside   ● Center  ○ Outside│             │
│  └───────────────────────────────┘             │
│                                                 │
│  ┌─ Blending ────────────────────┐             │
│  │ Opacity: [100] %  Mode: [Normal  ▼]│         │
│  │ □ Preserve Transparency        │             │
│  └───────────────────────────────┘             │
└─────────────────────────────────────────────────┘
```

When in doubt, select Inside from the Location radio buttons. This ensures that the stroke is entirely inside the selection outline in case you decide to move the selection. If you select Center or Outside, Photoshop applies part or all of the stroke to the deselected area around the selection outline.

- **Using the Border command:** Don't forget about Select⇨Modify⇨Border, described back in Chapter 8. Select a portion of the image and choose the Border command to retain only the outline of the selection. Specify the size of the border by entering a value in pixels into the Width option box and press Return. To fill the border with the background color, press Delete. To fill the border with the foreground color, press Option-Delete. To apply a repeating pattern to the border, choose Edit⇨Fill and select the Pattern option from the Use pop-up menu. You can even apply a command under the Filter menu or some other special effect.

- **Framing the image:** Okay, so this is a throwaway, but it's pretty useful just the same. To create an outline around the entire image, change the background color to the color that you want to apply to the outline. Then choose Image⇨Canvas Size and add twice the desired border thickness to the Width and Height options in pixels. For example, to create a 1-pixel border, add 2 pixels to the Width value (1 for the left side and 1 for the right) and 2 pixels to the Height value (1 for the top edge and 1 for the bottom). When you press Return, Photoshop enlarges the canvas size according to your specifications and fills the new pixels around the perimeter of the image with the background color. Simplicity at its best.

Applying arrowheads

The one function missing from all the operations in the previous list is applying arrowheads. The fact is, in Photoshop, you can only apply arrowheads to straight lines drawn with the line tool. To create an arrowhead, double-click on the line tool icon in the toolbox (or press N to select the line tool and then Return) to display the Line Tool Options panel shown in Figure 10-34. Enter a value into the Line Width option box to specify the thickness of the line — better known as the line's *weight* — and then use the Arrowheads options as follows:

- **Start:** Select this check box to append an arrowhead to the beginning of a line drawn with the line tool.

- **End:** Select this check box to append an arrowhead to the end of a line. (Like you needed me to tell you *that*.)

- **Shape:** Click on the Shape button to display the Arrowhead Shape dialog box, which also appears in Figure 10-34.

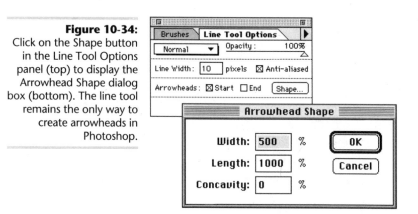

Figure 10-34:
Click on the Shape button in the Line Tool Options panel (top) to display the Arrowhead Shape dialog box (bottom). The line tool remains the only way to create arrowheads in Photoshop.

The Arrowhead Shape dialog box contains three options that let you specify the size and shape of the arrowhead as a function of the line weight:

- **Width:** Enter the width of the arrowhead in pixels into this option box. The width of the arrowhead is completely independent of line weight.

- **Length:** Enter the length of the arrowhead, measured from the base of the arrowhead to its tip, into this option box. Again, length is measured in pixels and is independent of line weight.

- **Concavity:** You can specify the shape of the arrowhead by entering a value between negative and positive 50 percent into the Concavity option box. Figure 10-35 shows examples of a few Concavity settings applied to an arrowhead 50 pixels wide and 100 pixels long.

Figure 10-35:
Examples of a 50 × 100-pixel arrowhead subject to five different Concavity values.

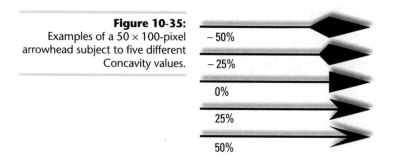

Appending arrowheads onto curved lines

Applying arrowheads to straight lines is a simple matter. Double-click on the line tool icon, select a few choice options, and draw a line with the line tool. Applying an arrowhead to a stroked selection outline is a little trickier, but still possible. The following steps explain the process.

STEPS: **Adding an Arrowhead to a Free-form Stroke**

Step 1. You revert your image later in these steps, so save your image to disk now by choosing File⇨Save.

Step 2. Draw any selection outline you desire and stroke it by choosing Edit⇨Stroke and applying whatever settings strike your fancy. Remember the value you enter into the Width option. In Figure 10-36, I applied a 2-point stroke to a circular marquee.

Step 3. Choose Select⇨None (Command-D) to deselect all portions of the image.

Step 4. As you'll discover in the next chapter, the eraser tool allows you to revert portions of an image to their previous appearance. Select the eraser tool by pressing the E key and Option-click anywhere in the image window to instruct Photoshop to load the saved image into memory. When the cursor returns to its eraser-like appearance, Option-drag to revert the portions of the stroke at which you want to add arrowheads. I wanted to add arrowheads around the lions' tongues, so I Option-dragged around each tongue as demonstrated in Figure 10-36.

Figure 10-36:
Stroke a selection, deselect it, and Option-drag with the eraser tool to create gaps in the stroke for the arrowheads.

Step 5. Double-click on the line tool icon. Enter the line weight that you used when stroking the selection outline (Step 2) into the Line Width option box. Select the Start check box and deselect the End check box if necessary. Then click on the Shape button and specify the width, length, and concavity of the arrowhead as desired.

Step 6.   Zoom in on the point in the image at which you want to add the arrowhead. Draw a very short line exactly the length of the arrowhead at the tip of the stroke, as demonstrated in Figure 10-37. This may take some practice to accomplish. Make sure to start the line a few pixels away from the end of the stroke, because the tip of the arrowhead is narrower than the line weight. If you mess up the first time, choose Edit⇨Undo (Command-Z) and try again.

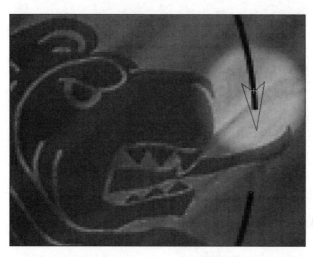

Figure 10-37: Draw a line no longer than the arrowhead with the line tool to append the arrow-head to the end of the stroke. The view size of this image is magnified 400 percent.

That's all there is to it. From there on, you just keep attaching as many arrowheads as you like. In Figure 10-38, I attached four arrowheads to the circular stroke, one above and one below each of the two tongues. Notice that I also reverted the area of the stroke that overlapped the lions' manes. I then created a circular feather marquee inside the circular stroke and drew six large arrowheads inside the selection mask. Finally, I inversed the selection and applied the Tiles and Radial Blur filters.

The old translucent-gradient-arrowheads-with-halos trick

The exercise in the following set of steps takes advantage of several things you've learned throughout the chapter. Back in Figure 9-19 in the previous chapter, I created a bunch of arrowheads that joined a bunch of layers to the images that resided on those layers inside the document. I could have created those arrowheads in a drawing program to get nice sharp points and smooth outlines. But I chose to create them in Photoshop because I could take advantage of two options that drawing programs don't offer: gradient lines and halos.

Figure 10-38:
The finished image contains four arrowheads at the end of free-form strokes as well as six additional arrows inside a feathered selection.

Now you might be thinking to yourself, "Gee wizickers, Deke, you can't create gradient lines in Photoshop either." Of course, you can. You think I'd introduce the topic if you couldn't do it? Just quit interrupting for a moment and you'll find out how.

(Sorry about that little interchange. After several hours of sitting in an office by myself whacking away at the keyboard until my fingerprints start to wear off, it helps to pretend that you, the reader, are talking to me. Even if I have to make you sound like a Shirley Temple imitator. Just write it off as a mental defect. I'm sure it will get better the second I stop working on this book.)

The following steps explain how to add cool fading arrows like those shown in Figure 10-40. The steps involve the quick mask mode, the gradient tool, the Fill command, and good old Delete.

STEPS: Creating Fading Arrows with Halos

Step 1. Save your image (Command-S), deselect everything (Command-D), and switch to the quick mask mode (Q). The image should appear absolutely normal.

Step 2. Double-click on the line tool icon in the toolbox and adjust the line weight and arrowhead settings in the Line tool Option panel to fit your needs. To create my first arrows (the ones that come inward from the corners in Figure 10-40), I set the Line Width value to 20 and the Width, Length, and Concavity values in the Arrowhead Shape dialog box to 400, 600, and 20 respectively.

Step 3. Press D to switch to the default colors. Then draw your line, which will show up in red. (If you don't get it right the first time — as is often the case with this tool — just press Command-Z and try again.) The beauty of drawing a line in the quick mask mode is that you can edit it after the fact without damaging the image. (You could also do the same on a separate layer, but the quick mask mode affords you a little more flexibility in this specific exercise.)

Step 4. Double-click on the gradient tool icon in the toolbox and make sure that the Style option is set to Foreground to Background, the Type option is set to Linear, and the Opacity slider is set to 100 percent. Then choose Lighten from the brush modes pop-up menu.

Step 5. You can now use the gradient tool to fade the base of the line. Drag with the gradient tool from the point at which you want the line to begin to fade down to the base of the line. Try to make the direction of your drag parallel to the line itself, thus ensuring a smooth fade. The first example in Figure 10-39 shows me in the progress of dragging along one of my arrows with the gradient tool. The small white arrow shows the direction of my drag. (The black line shows the actual cursor that you see on-screen.) The second example shows the result of the drag.

Figure 10-39:
Drag from the point at which you want the arrow to begin fading to the base of the line (left) parallel to the line itself (indicated here by the white arrow) to fade the line out (right).

Step 6. Choose Image⇨Map⇨Invert (Command-I) to invert the quick mask, thus making the arrow the selected area.

Step 7. Drag the quick mask item in the Channels palette onto the new channel icon at the bottom of the palette to copy the quick mask to a permanent mask channel. You'll need it again.

Step 8.   Time now to create the halo. Press Q to switch back to the marching ants mode. Choose Select⇨Modify⇨Expand and enter the desired value. As described in the "Creating drop shadows, halos, and spotlights" section earlier in this chapter, base the value on the resolution of your image. I entered 6.

Step 9.   Choose Select⇨Feather, enter the same value, and press Return.

Step 10.   Make sure that the default colors are in force. (Just because they are in force in the quick mask mode doesn't mean that they are in the marching ants mode, so you may want to press D to be sure.) Then press the Delete key to fill the selected areas with white.

Step 11.   Option-click on the Quick Mask Copy item in the Channels palette to regain your original arrow selection outlines.

Step 12.   Choose Select⇨Fill to bring up the Fill dialog box. Then select Saved from the Use pop-up menu to revert the portion of the image inside the arrows and press Return.

Step 13.   Float the selection outlines by pressing Command-J. Change the foreground color to your favorite color and press Option-Delete to fill the selection.

Step 14.   Press the M key to activate a selection tool. Then choose Multiply from the overlay modes pop-up menu in the upper left corner of the Layers palette and press a number key to change the Opacity setting. I used 4 for 40 percent.

After that, I just kept adding more and more arrows by repeating the process. Every once in a while I saved the image so that I could create arrows on top of arrows. Most notably, I saved the image before adding the last, big arrow that shoots up from the bottom. Then when I filled the arrow with the saved version, I brought back bits and pieces of a couple of the other arrows. (Had I not first saved the image, the arrow fragments behind the big arrow would have disappeared.)

Figure 10-40:
I don't know whether this guy's in store for a cold front or what, but if you ever need to annotate an image with arrows, this translucent-gradient-arrowheads-with-halos trick is certainly the way to do it.

Summary

- To limit the area affected by the paint bucket tool, apply the tool inside the confines of a selection outline.

- Press Delete to fill a selection with the background color. Press Option-Delete to fill it with the foreground color.

- If you float a selection before pressing Option-Delete, you can make the color translucent easily by pressing a number key. (Pressing Delete when a selection is floating deletes the selection rather than filling it with the background color.)

- To create a drop shadow behind a floating selection, send the selection to its own layer, send the selection back to the Background image, feather the selection outline, float it, fill it with black, and nudge it into position. You can even change the Opacity setting in the Layers palette if you care to.

➥ To create a colored shadow, fill the floating feathered selection with color and then choose Multiply from the overlay modes pop-up menu in the Layers palette.

➥ Use the Style options inside the Gradient Tool Options panel to specify the way Photoshop selects colors for a gradation. The two Spectrum options have no effect on grayscale gradations.

➥ The new Dither check box in the Gradient Tool Options panel helps to eliminate banding. If it doesn't work, you can mix the colors up some more by applying the Add Noise filter in combination with the Motion Blur and Radial Blur commands.

➥ You can paint amorphous bubbles and planes with the gradient tool by filling the image window with black, setting the brush mode to Lighten, and creating gradations from white to black.

➥ When sharpening gradations, set the Radius value inside the Unsharp Mask dialog box to 2.0 or higher. You also can use the Unsharp Mask and Custom filters to derive crystal structures from radial gradations.

➥ In the quick mask mode, you can apply gradations to create soft transitions between selected and deselected regions of an image.

➥ The Select➪Border command can be a more versatile solution for stroking a selection outline than Edit➪Stroke because it allows you to stroke with the background color, a repeating pattern, or a filter.

➥ Use the line tool to add arrowheads to the end of strokes.

➥ The trick to creating gradient arrowheads with halos is to draw the lines in the quick mask mode. Then you can edit the lines before applying them as selection outlines.

Duplicating and Reverting

In This Chapter

➥ A complete description of the rubber stamp tool and its many settings

➥ How to clone portions of an image to touch up blemishes and eliminate elements from an image

➥ How to use the rubber stamp to paint with a repeating pattern

➥ A step-by-step guide to creating seamless patterns and textures

➥ Descriptions of the Undo and Revert commands

➥ Lots of kudos for the newly enhanced eraser tool

➥ Ways to use the magic eraser and rubber stamp tools to selectively revert portions of an image

➥ An explanation of the Take Snapshot command

Introducing the Amalgamated Rubber Stamp

This chapter is primarily about just one tool: the rubber stamp tool. Although the eraser figures into the reversion discussion in this chapter, and I even include a small reference to the pencil tool, the main ingredient — after you boil it down at your local editorial content refinery — is the rubber stamp tool. This tool provides four loosely related but distinct capabilities, every one of which deserves to be split off into a tool of its own.

The name *rubber stamp* is pretty misleading because this particular tool has nothing to do with rubber stamps. First of all, no tree sap is involved — let's get that sticky issue resolved right off the bat. Secondly, you don't use it to stamp an image. When I think of rubber stamps, I think of those things you see in stationery stores that plunk down laudatory exclamations and smiley faces and Pooh bears. Elementary school teachers and little girls use rubber stamps. I've never seen a professional image editor walking around with a rubber stamp in my life.

So put rubber stamps entirely out of your mind for the moment. To discover exactly what the stamp tool does, you must double-click on its icon in the toolbox. Photoshop then displays the Rubber Stamp Options panel of the Brushes palette, shown in Figure 11-1. In addition to the standard brush modes pop-up menu, Opacity slider, Stylus Pressure options, and Sample Merged check box provided with half a dozen paint and edit tools (see Chapter 7 if your memory's getting a tad fuzzy), the Rubber Stamp Options panel includes an Option pop-up menu. The real heart of the tool, this pop-up menu includes the following options:

↪ **Cloning:** Select one of the two Clone options to duplicate portions of an image by dragging over it. Option-click with the tool to specify a point of reference and then drag in a different area of the image to begin cloning. (Don't worry, I cover the difference between the two Clone options in the upcoming "Aligned and non-aligned cloning" section.)

Figure 11-1:
Select an option from the Options pop-up menu to define the way the rubber stamp tool works.

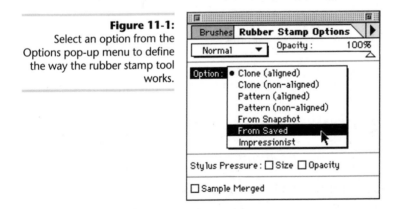

↪ **Pattern application:** Select one of the two Pattern options to paint an image with a repeating pattern rather than the standard foreground color. Before using this option, you must establish a pattern by selecting a portion of the image and choosing Edit⇨Define Pattern.

⚬ **Reversion:** The From Snapshot option lets you use the rubber stamp tool to revert portions of your image to the way they appeared when you last chose Edit⇨Take Snapshot. From Saved enables you to revert portions of an image to the way they appeared when you last saved the image.

⚬ **Impressionist:** The last option, Impressionist, retrieves the last saved version of the image and sort of smears it around to create a gooey, unfocused effect. You can achieve some mildly interesting and halfway useful effects — and I'm being generous here — by combining this function with the Overlay, Hard Light, or Soft Light brush modes, but it wouldn't be my first choice for any job. This is my nomination for the least useful of the rubber stamp settings, and this is the last time I'll mention it.

 If there is a tie that binds the rubber stamp's various capabilities, it is the fact that most enable you to paint with images. When you clone with the rubber stamp tool, for example, you paint with a displaced version of the image itself. When you paint a pattern, you paint with an image fragment. When you revert, you paint with the saved version of the image. Even Impressionist paints with the saved image in its own skewed sort of way. (Ah, man, I wasn't going to mention that option again.)

As you can see, a better name for the rubber stamp tool might be the *clone/pattern/ revert/stupid effects tool* or maybe the junk-drawer tool. Then again, *the mother of all mixed-up tools* has a certain ring to it. In any case, the remainder of this chapter explores every one of the rubber stamp's capabilities.

Cloning Image Elements

So far, my take on the rubber stamp tool may sound a bit derogatory. But in truth, most of its capabilities can come in very handy. All except that dumb Impressionist option — which I swear, really, I'm going to stop mentioning.

Take cloning, for example. As any died-in-the-wool Photoshop user will tell you, the rubber stamp is an invaluable tool for touching up images, whether you want to remove dust fragments, hairs, and other blotches scanned with a photo or to eliminate portions of an image (as described in the "Softening selection outlines" section of Chapter 8).

You also can use the rubber stamp to duplicate specific elements in an image, like flowers and umbrellas, as described in the Photoshop manual. But by all accounts, this is an inefficient use of the tool. If you want to duplicate an element, you'll have better luck if you select it and clone it by Option-dragging the selection. By taking that approach, you can specify the exact boundaries of the element, the softness of its edges, and the precise location of the clone. Cloning an element with the rubber stamp is more of an ordeal, because it's easy to accidentally clone areas around the element and to begin a clone in the wrong location.

The cloning process

To clone part of an image, double-click on the rubber stamp tool icon and select either the Clone (Aligned) or Clone (Non-aligned) option. (The upcoming section explains the difference between the two.) Option-click in the image window to specify a point of reference in the portion of the image you want to clone. Then click or drag with the tool in some other region of the image to paint a cloned spot or line.

In Figure 11-2, for example, I Option-clicked just above and to the right of the bird's head, as demonstrated by the appearance of the stamp pickup cursor. I then painted the line shown inside the white rectangle. The rubber stamp cursor shows the end of my drag; the cross-shaped clone reference cursor shows the corresponding point in the original image.

Figure 11-2:
After Option-clicking at the point indicated by the stamp pickup cursor, I dragged with the rubber stamp tool to paint with the image. (The only reason I painted inside the white rectangle was to set off the line so that you can see it better.)

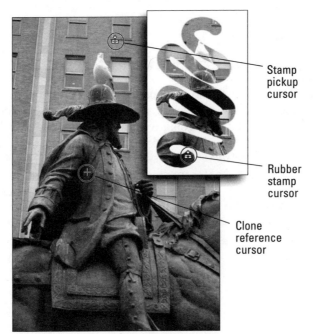

Stamp pickup cursor

Rubber stamp cursor

Clone reference cursor

Photoshop lets you clone not only from within the image you're working on, but also from an entirely separate image window. This technique enables you to merge two different images together, as demonstrated in Figure 11-3. To achieve this effect, Option-click in one image, bring a second image to the foreground, and then drag with the rubber stamp tool to clone from the first image.

Figure 11-3:
I merged the area around horse and rider with a water image from another open window (see the upcoming Figure 11-6). The translucent effects were created by periodically adjusting the Opacity slider bar to settings ranging from 50 to 80 percent.

Aligned and nonaligned cloning

Now that I've explained how to use the tool, I'll return to the options in the Rubber Stamp Options panel:

- **Clone (Aligned):** To understand how this option works, think of the locations where you Option-click and begin dragging with the rubber stamp tool as opposite ends of an imaginary straight line, as illustrated in the top half of Figure 11-4. The length and angle of that imaginary line remains fixed until you Option-click a second time. As you drag, Photoshop moves the line, cloning pixels from one end of the line and laying them down at the other. Regardless of how many times you start and stop dragging with the stamp tool, all lines match up as seamlessly as pieces in a puzzle.

- **Clone (Non-aligned):** If you want to repeatedly clone from a single portion of an image, select this option. The second example in Figure 11-4 shows how the length and angle of the imaginary line change every time you paint a new line with the rubber stamp tool.

Figure 11-4:
Select the Clone (Aligned) option to instruct Photoshop to clone an image continuously, no matter how many lines you paint (top). If you select Clone (Non-aligned), Photoshop clones each new line from the point at which you Option-click.

Stamp differences

When cloning, the Photoshop 3.0 rubber stamp tool works just like the Version 2.5 rubber stamp, which is different than the Version 2.0 stamp. Between you and me, I like the Version 2.0 setup best. In Version 2.0, the rubber stamp clones the image as it exists before you start using the tool. Even when you drag over an area that contains a clone, the tool references the original appearance of the image to prevent recloning. This keeps you from creating more than one clone during a single drag, as witnessed in the first example of Figure 11-5.

In Photoshop 3.0, however, any changes you make to the image affect the tool as you use it, which can resuit in the repeating patterns like those shown in the second example of the figure. Although you can create some interesting effects, avoid cloning and recloning areas when retouching, because it can result in obvious patterns that betray your adjustments.

To avoid recloning areas in Photoshop 3.0, clone from a duplicate of the image. Begin by choosing Image➪Duplicate to create a copy of the current image (as explained back in Chapter 3). Option-click with the rubber stamp tool somewhere in the duplicate window. Then switch to the original image and drag freely with the tool to clone from the duplicate. Because your changes don't affect the duplicate image, there's no chance of recloning.

Figure 11-5:
Photoshop 2.0's rubber stamp tool clones the image as it exists before you start using the tool (top). In Version 3.0, the tool clones and reclones images during a single drag (bottom).

Touching up blemishes

One of the best uses for the rubber stamp tool is to touch up a scanned photo. Figure 11-6 shows a Photo CD image that desperately needs the stamp tool's attention. Normally, Kodak's Photo CD process delivers some of the best consumer-quality scans money can buy. But this particular medium-resolution image looks like the folks at the lab got together and blew their respective noses on it. It's a little late to go back to the service bureau and demand that they rescan the photo, so my only choice is to touch it up myself.

The best way to fix this image — or any image like it — is to use the rubber stamp over and over again, repeatedly Option-clicking at one location and then clicking at another. Begin by selecting a brush shape that's a little larger than the largest blotch. Of the default brushes, the hard-edged varieties with diameters of 5 and 9 pixels generally work best. (The soft-edged brush shapes have a tendency to incompletely cover the blemishes.)

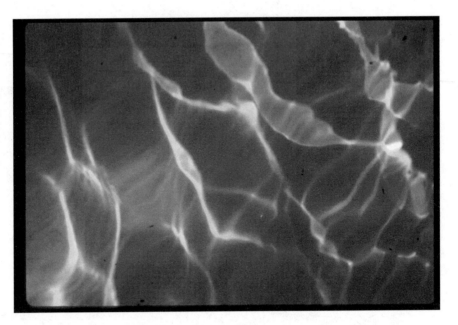

Option-click with the stamp tool at a location that is very close to the blemish and features similarly colored pixels. Then click — do not drag — directly on the blemish. The idea is to change as few pixels as possible.

If the retouched area doesn't look quite right, choose Edit➪Undo (Command-Z), Option-click at a different location, and try again. If your touch-up appears seamless — *absolutely* seamless — move on to the next blemish, repeating the Option-click and click routine for every dust mark on the photo.

This process isn't necessarily time-consuming, but it does require patience. For example, although it took more than 40 Option-click and click combinations (not counting 10 or so undos) to arrive at the image shown in Figure 11-7, the process itself took less than 15 minutes. Boring, but fast.

(Could be a beer commercial, eh? Sid Vicious says, "Boring." Then Johnny Rotten replies, "Yeah, well, that's your worthless opinion, isn't it Sid? I say it's fast." Sid: "Boring!" Johnny: "Fast!" And so on. Can't imagine why some New York ad exec hasn't latched onto that one yet.)

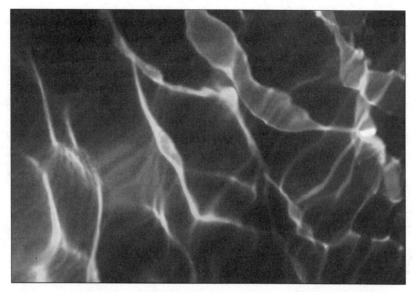

Figure 11-7:
The result of Option-
clicking and clicking
more than 40 times
on the photo shown
in Figure 11-6. Notice
that I also cropped
the image and added
a border. Now I can
use the image as a
background, as I did
in Figure 11-3.

It's a little trickier to retouch hairs than dust and other blobs. That's because a hair, although very thin, can be surprisingly long. However, the retouching process is the same. Rather than dragging over the entire length of the hair, Option-click and click your way through it, bit by little bit. The one difference is brush shape. Because you'll be clicking so many times in succession and because the hair is so thin, you'll probably achieve the least conspicuous effects if you use a soft brush shape, such as the default 9-pixel model in the second row of the Brushes palette.

Before going to the effort with the rubber stamp tool, you might want to first check how well the new Dust & Scratches filter (Filter⇨Noise⇨Dust & Scratches) remedies your problems. It performed remarkably poorly where Figure 11-6 was concerned, but if your image isn't quite so bad, it may help a good deal. To find out more information on this and other corrective filters, read Chapter 13.

Personally, I find the rubber stamp cursor to be the most intrusive of all Photoshop's cursors. After all, when you're cloning an element, you need to see exactly what you're doing. You don't need to see a blocky icon that has nothing to do with the current operation. To get rid of this eyesore and view a simple crosshair cursor instead, press the Caps Lock key. You can also go into the General Preferences dialog box (Command-K) and select the Brush Size radio button, but this does not affect the appearance of the stamp cursor when you press the Option key.

Eliminating distracting background elements

Another way to apply the stamp tool's cloning capabilities is to eliminate background action that competes with the central elements in an image. Figure 11-8, for example, shows a one-in-a-million news photo from the Reuters image library. Although the image is well-photographed and historic in its implications — in case you missed the last decade, that's Comrade V. I. Lenin (Vlad to his mom) — that rear workman doesn't contribute anything to the scene and in fact draws your attention away from the foreground drama. I mean, hail to the worker and everything, but the image would be better off without him. The following steps explain how I eradicated the offending workman from the scene.

Keep in mind as you read the following steps that deleting an image element with the rubber stamp tool is something of an inexact science; it requires some trial and error. So regard the following steps as an example of how to approach the process of editing your image rather than a specific procedure that works for all images. You may need to adapt the process slightly depending upon your image.

Figure 11-8:
You have to love that old Soviet state-endorsed art. So bold, so angular, so politically intolerant. But you also have to lose that rear workman.

STEPS: **Eliminating Distracting Elements from an Image**

Step 1. I began by cloning the area around the neck of the statue with a soft brush shape. Abandoning the controlled clicks I recommended in the last section, I allowed myself to drag with the tool because I needed to cover relatively large portions of the image. The apartment building (or whatever that structure is) behind the floating head is magnificently out of focus, just the thing for hiding any incongruous transitions I might create with the rubber stamp. So I warmed up to the image by retouching this area first. Figure 11-9 shows my progress.

Notice that I covered the workman's body by cloning pixels from both his left and right sides. I also added a vertical bar where the workman's right arm used to be to maintain the rhythm of the building. Remember that variety is the key to using the rubber stamp tool: If you consistently clone from one portion of the image, you create an obvious repetition that the viewer can't help but notice.

Figure 11-9:
Cloning over the background worker's upper torso was fairly easy because the background building is so regular and out of focus, providing a wealth of material from which to clone.

Step 2. The next step was to eliminate the workman's head. This was a little tricky because it involved rubbing up against the focused perimeter of Lenin's neck. I had to clone some of the more intricate areas using a hard-edged brush. I also ended up duplicating some of the neck edges to maintain continuity. In addition, I touched up the left side of the neck (your left, not Lenin's) and removed a few of the white spots from his face. You see my progress in Figure 11-10.

Figure 11-10: I eliminated the workman's head and touched up details around the perimeter of the neck.

Step 3. Now for the hard part: eliminating the worker's legs and lower torso. See that fragment of metal that the foreground worker is holding? What a pain. Its edges were so irregular that there was no way I could restore it with the rubber stamp tool if I messed up while trying to eradicate the background worker's limbs. So I lassoed around the fragment to select it and chose Select⇨Inverse to protect it. I also chose Select⇨Feather and gave it a Radius value of 1 to slightly soften its edges. This prevented me from messing up the metal no matter what edits I made to the background worker's remaining body parts.

Step 4. From here on out, it was just more cloning. Unfortunately, I barely had anything to clone from. See that little bit of black edging between the two "legs" of the metal fragment? That's it. That's all I had to draw the strip of edging to the right of the fragment that eventually appears in Figure 11-11. To pull off this feat, I double-clicked on the rubber stamp tool icon in the toolbox and chose the Clone (Non-aligned) option. Then I Option-clicked on the tiny bit of edging and click, click, clicked my way down the street.

Step 5. Unfortunately, the strip that I laid down in Step 4 appeared noticeably blobular — it looked for all the world like I clicked a bunch of times. Darn. To fix this problem, I clicked and Shift-clicked with the smudge tool set to about 30 percent pressure. This smeared the blobs into a continuous strip, but again, the effect was noticeable. It looked as if I had smeared the strip. So I went back and cloned some more, this time with the Opacity slider bar set to 50 percent.

Step 6. To polish the image off, I chose Select⇨None (Command-D) and ran the sharpen tool along the edges of the metal fragment. This helped to hide the fact that I retouched around it and further distinguished the fragment from the unfocused background. I also cropped away 20 or so pixels from the right side of the image to correct the balance of the image.

What I hope I demonstrated in this section is that cloning with the rubber stamp tool requires that you alternate between patching and whittling away. There are no rights and wrongs, no hard and fast rules. Anything you can find to clone is fair game. As long as you avoid mucking up the foreground image, you can't go wrong (so I guess there is *one* hard and fast rule). If you're careful and diligent, no one but you is going to notice your alterations.

Figure 11-11:
After about 45 minutes worth of monkeying around with the rubber stamp tool — a practice declared illegal during Stalin's reign — the rear workman is gone, leaving us with an unfettered view of the dubious one himself.

Any time you edit the contents of a photograph, you tread on very sensitive ground. Though some have convincingly argued that electronically retouching an image is theoretically no different than cropping a photograph, a technique that has been available and in use since the first daguerreotype, photographers have certain rights under copyright law that cannot be ignored. A photographer may have a reason for including an element that you wish to eliminate. So before you edit any photograph, be sure to get permission either from the original photographer or from the copyright holder.

Applying Repeating Patterns _____

Before you can use the rubber stamp tool to paint with a pattern, you must define a pattern by selecting a portion of the image with the rectangular marquee tool and choosing Edit⇨Define Pattern. For the Define Pattern command to work, you must use the rectangular marquee — no other selection tool will do. In addition, the selection cannot be feathered, smoothed, expanded, or in any other way altered. If it is, the command is dimmed.

Figure 11-12 shows an example of how you can apply repeating patterns. I selected the single apartment window (surrounded by marching ants) and chose Edit⇨Define Pattern. I then applied the pattern with the rubber stamp tool at 80 percent opacity over the horse and rider statue.

Figure 11-12:
After marqueeing a single window (top) and choosing Edit⇨Define Pattern, I painted a translucent coat of the pattern over the statue with the rubber stamp tool (bottom).

Like the Clipboard, Photoshop can retain only one pattern at a time and remembers the pattern throughout a single session. Any time you choose Edit➪Define Pattern, you delete the previous pattern as you create a new one. Photoshop also deletes the pattern when you quit the program. Therefore, each time you launch Photoshop, you must define the pattern from scratch.

Pattern options

To paint with a pattern, double-click on the rubber stamp tool icon and select either the Pattern (Aligned) or Pattern (Non-aligned) option from the Option pop-up menu in the Rubber Stamp Options panel. These options work as follows:

- **Pattern (Aligned):** Select this option to align all patterns you apply with the stamp tool, regardless of how many times you start and stop dragging. The two left examples in Figure 11-13 show the effects of selecting this option. The elements in the pattern remain exactly aligned throughout all the lines. I painted the top image with the Opacity slider bar set to 50 percent, which is why the lines darken when they meet.

- **Pattern (Non-aligned):** To allow patterns in different lines to align randomly, select this option. The positioning of the pattern within each line is determined by the point at which you begin dragging. I dragged from right to left to paint the horizontal lines and from top to bottom to paint the vertical lines. The two right examples in Figure 11-13 show how nonaligned patterns overlap.

Figure 11-13:
Select the Pattern (Aligned) option to align the patterns in all brush strokes painted with the stamp tool (left). If you select Pattern (Non-aligned), Photoshop aligns each pattern with the beginning of the line (right).

After you select Pattern (Aligned) or Pattern (Non-aligned), you're free to start dragging with the stamp tool. You don't need to Option-click or make any other special provisions, as you do when cloning.

 As discussed in Chapter 10, you can also apply a pattern to a selected portion of an image by choosing Edit⇨Fill and selecting the Pattern option from the Use pop-up menu. The problem with this technique is that it involves choosing Edit⇨Define Pattern to establish the pattern in the first place. Photoshop 3.0 offers a new function that lets you load an image from disk and apply it as a repeating pattern throughout the selection. Choose Filter⇨Render⇨Texture Fill to open any image saved in the native Photoshop format and then repeat it as many times as the selection will permit.

How to create patterns

The biggest difficulty with painting patterns is not figuring out the rubber stamp tool, but creating the patterns in the first place. Ideally, your pattern should repeat continuously, without vertical and horizontal seams. Here are some ways to create repeating, continuous patterns:

- ○→ **Load a displacement map:** Photoshop offers a Displacement Maps folder inside the Plug-ins folder. This folder contains several images, each of which represents a different repeating pattern, as illustrated in Figure 11-14. To use one of these patterns, open the image, choose Select⇨All (Command-A), and choose Edit⇨ Define Pattern. (For more information on displacement maps, see Chapter 15.)

- ○→ **Illustrator patterns:** Sunk deep inside the PostScript Patterns folder inside the Brushes & Patterns folder in the Goodies folder are 22 Illustrator EPS files that contain repeating object patterns. The patterns, some of which appear in Figure 11-15, are all seamless repeaters. You can open them and rasterize them to any size you like. Then press Command-A, choose Edit⇨Define Pattern, and you have your pattern.

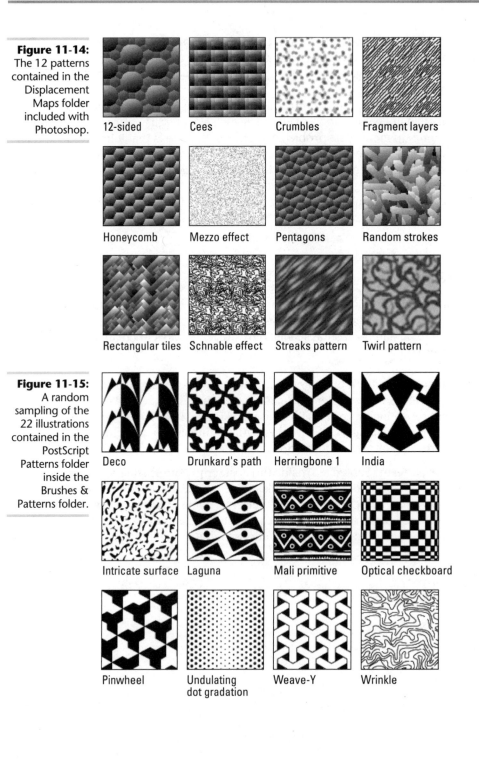

Figure 11-14:
The 12 patterns
contained in the
Displacement
Maps folder
included with
Photoshop.

12-sided   Cees   Crumbles   Fragment layers

Honeycomb   Mezzo effect   Pentagons   Random strokes

Rectangular tiles   Schnable effect   Streaks pattern   Twirl pattern

Figure 11-15:
A random
sampling of the
22 illustrations
contained in the
PostScript
Patterns folder
inside the
Brushes &
Patterns folder.

Deco   Drunkard's path   Herringbone 1   India

Intricate surface   Laguna   Mali primitive   Optical checkboard

Pinwheel   Undulating dot gradation   Weave-Y   Wrinkle

⌒⊗ **Using filters:** As luck would have it, you can create your own custom textures without painting a single line. In fact, you can create a nearly infinite variety of textures by applying several filters to a blank document. To create the texture shown in the bottom right box in Figure 11-16, for example, I began by selecting a 128 × 128-pixel area. I then chose Filter⇨Noise⇨Add Noise, entered a value of 32, and selected the Gaussian radio button. I pressed Command-F twice to apply the noise filter two more times. Finally, I chose Filter⇨Stylize⇨Emboss and entered 135 into the Angle option box, 1 into the Height option box, and 100 percent into the Amount option box. The result is a bumpy surface that looks like stucco. This is merely one example of the myriad possibilities filters afford. There's no end to what you can do, so experiment away. (For more information on using Add Noise, see Chapter 13, "Corrective Filtering." For info about Emboss and other filter commands, see Chapter 14, "Full-Court Filtering.")

Figure 11-16:
To create a stucco texture, apply Filter⇨Noise⇨Add Noise three times in a row (upper left, upper right, lower left). Then choose Filter⇨Stylize⇨Emboss and enter a Height value of 1 (lower right).

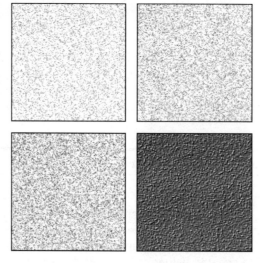

⌒⊗ **Marquee and clone:** You can use the rectangular marquee and rubber stamp tools to transform a scanned image into a custom pattern. Because this technique is more complicated as well as more rewarding than the others, I explain it in the upcoming section, "STEPS: Building a Repeating Pattern from a Scanned Image."

⌒⊗ **Texture collections:** If you don't have the time or energy to create your own custom patterns but you do have some extra cash lying around, all sorts of texture libraries are available on CD-ROM. My favorite is the Wraptures collection from Form and Function, because all patterns on these discs repeat seamlessly. The Folio collection from D'pix provides a wide range of images, but these do not repeat and are therefore more conducive to backgrounds than patterns. Figure 11-17 shows examples from both collections.

Figure 11-17:
A repeating texture from
Form and Function's
Wraptures collection (top)
and a nonrepeating back-
ground image from D'pix's
Folio collection (bottom).

The following steps describe how to change a scanned image into a seamless, repeating pattern. To illustrate how this process works, Figures 11-18 through 11-21 show various stages in a project I completed. You need only two tools to carry out these steps: the rectangular marquee tool and the rubber stamp tool with the Clone (Aligned) option active.

STEPS: Building a Repeating Pattern from a Scanned Image

Step 1.   Begin by marqueeing a portion of your scanned image and copying it to the Clipboard. For best results, specify the exact size of your marquee by double-clicking on the rectangular marquee icon in the toolbox, selecting Fixed Size from the Style pop-up menu (in the Marquee Options panel), and entering specific values into the Width and Height option boxes. This way, you can easily reselect a portion of the pattern in the steps that follow and use the fixed-size marquee to define the pattern when you are finished. To create the patterns shown in the example, I set the marquee to 128×128 pixels.

Step 2.   Choose File⇨New (Command-N) and triple the values Photoshop offers as the default image dimensions. In my case, Photoshop offered 128×128 pixels because that was the size of the image I copied to the Clipboard. Therefore, I changed the image size to 384×384 pixels.

Step 3.   Paste the marqueed image into the new image window. It appears smack dab in the center of the window, which is exactly where you want it. This image will serve as the central tile of your repeating pattern. Clone the selection by Option-dragging it eight times to create a 3×3-tile grid, as shown in Figure 11-18.

Figure 11-18:
To build the repeating pattern shown in Figure 11-21, I started by creating a grid of nine image tiles. As you can see, the seams between the tiles in this grid are harsh and unacceptable.

Step 4. Drag the title bar of the new image window to position it so that you can see the portion of the image you copied in the original image window. If necessary, Command-drag the title bar of the original image window to reposition it as well. This way, you can clone from the original image without switching back and forth between windows.

Step 5. Double-click on the rubber stamp tool icon in the toolbox, select the Clone (Aligned) option, and press Return to exit the dialog box.

Step 6. To specify the image you want to clone, Option-click with the stamp tool in the original image window — no need to switch out of the new window — on an easily identifiable pixel that belongs to the portion of the image you copied. The *exact* pixel you click is very important. If you press the Caps Lock key, you get the crosshair cursor, which allows you to narrow in on a pixel. In my case, I clicked on the center of Lenin's right eye.

Step 7. Now click with the stamp tool on the matching pixel in the central tile of the new window. If you've clicked on the correct pixel, the tile should not change one iota. (If it does, choose Edit⇨Undo and repeat Steps 6 and 7.)

Step 8. Now that you've aligned the cloned image within the new window, use the stamp tool to fill in portions of the central tile. For example, in Figure 11-19, I extended the chin down into the lower row of tiles, I extended the central face to meet the Lenin on the left, and I extended the head upward into the jawline of the top-row Lenin.

Step 9. After you establish one continuous transition between two tiles in any direction — up, down, left, or right — select a portion of the image with the rectangular marquee tool and clone the selection repeatedly to fill out a single row or column. In my case, I managed to create a smooth transition between the central and left-hand tiles. Therefore, I selected a region that includes half of the left tile and half of the central tile. Because I fixed the rectangular marquee to a 128×128-pixel square, I only had to click on an area to select it. (Drag to position the marquee exactly where you want it.) I then cloned that selection along the entire length of the middle row.

Figure 11-19:
I used the rubber stamp's cloning capability to extend the features in the central face toward the left and downward.

Step 10. If you started by creating a horizontal transition, use the rubber stamp tool to now create a vertical transition. (Likewise, if you started vertically, now go horizontally.) You may very well need to Option-click again on that special pixel in the original window. By Option-clicking, you allow yourself to build onto one of the perimeter tiles. In my case, I Option-clicked again in the original right eye. Next, I clicked on the matching pixel in the left tile and dragged around to build out the left Lenin's chin. To complete the vertical transition, I Option-clicked a third time and clicked on the matching pixel in the lower center tile, building a transition between the lower Lenin's head and the central Lenin's neck, as shown in Figure 11-20.

Figure 11-20:
After completing a smooth
transition between the
central tile and the tiles
below and to the left of it, I
selected a portion of the
image and choose
Edit⇨Define Pattern.

Step 11. After you build up one set of both horizontal and vertical transitions, you
can select a portion of the image and choose Edit⇨Define Pattern. Figure
11-20 shows where I positioned my 128×128-pixel selection boundary. It
included both halves of the chin along with a smooth transition between
head, jaw, and left side of the face (Lenin's left, that is). Don't worry that the
image doesn't appear centered inside the selection outline. What counts is
that the selection repeats seamlessly when placed beside itself.

Step 12. To confirm that the pattern is indeed seamless and every bit as lovely as
you had hoped, double-click on the rubber stamp icon in the toolbox and
select the Pattern (Aligned) option. After closing the Rubber Stamp
Options dialog box, drag around inside the current image with the
rubber stamp tool and a large brush shape. Figure 11-21 shows the seamless
results of my dragging.

Step 13. Be sure to save your completed image. You don't want to go to all this
trouble for nothing.

Figure 11-21:
This Big Brother montage is the result of applying the Lenin pattern. I half expect him to say something about how the Great and Powerful Wizard of Oz has spoken, but I don't think that movie got out much in Russia.

Selectively Undoing Changes

Welcome to the second act of this chapter. It's a short act — more like a scene, really — so you'll have to forgo the intermission.

Now that I've explained the cloning and related patterning attributes of the rubber stamp tool, it's time to turn your attention — come on, turn, turn, just a little more, there you go — to a new topic. The rest of this chapter deals with *reversion,* which is a fancy word for returning your image to the way it looked before you went and made an unholy mess of it.

Using the traditional undo functions

Before I dive into the rubber stamp's reversion capabilities, allow me to introduce the more traditional reversion functions that are found in nearly all paint applications, including Photoshop:

➣ **Undo:** To restore an image to the way it looked before the last operation, choose Edit⇨Undo (Command-Z). You can undo the effect of a paint or edit tool, a change made to a selection outline, or a special-effect or color-correction command. You can't undo disk operations, such as opening or saving. However, Photoshop does let you undo an edit after printing an image. You can test out an effect, print it, and then undo it if you think it looks awful.

- **Revert:** Choose File⇨Revert to reload an image from disk. Most folks think of this as the last-resort function, the command you choose after everything else has failed. But really, it's quite useful as a stop-gap measure. Suppose that you're about to embark on a series of filtering operations that may or may not result in the desired effect. You're going to perform multiple operations, so you can't undo them if they don't work. Before choosing your first filter, choose File⇨Save. Now you're ready for anything. You can wreak a degree of havoc on your image that no user in his or her right mind would dare. If everything doesn't go exactly as you planned or hoped, you can simply choose File⇨Revert and you're back in business.

- **The eraser tool:** Drag with the eraser tool to paint in white or some other background color. This allows you to revert portions of your image back to bare canvas.

In Photoshop 3.0, the eraser is no longer hard-edged. If you double-click on the eraser — go ahead, it doesn't erase the entire image any more — you'll display the Eraser Options panel. As shown in Figure 11-22, the panel offers a pop-up menu of eraser styles. Block is the old 16×16-pixel square eraser that's great for hard-edged touch-ups. The other options work exactly like the tools for which they're named. And you don't even have to go to the trouble of selecting the options from the pop-up menu. When the eraser is selected, pressing the E key cycles through the different eraser styles. (Coincidentally, you can also select the eraser tool by pressing E.)

As if that weren't enough, the eraser is now pressure-sensitive, it responds to Opacity settings, and you can create fading eraser strokes. For cryin' in a bucket, you even have access to the Wet Edges check box described back in Chapter 7. The only thing missing is the brush modes menu, which I'm afraid you'll just have to live without. (Of course, if you really need to access a brush mode, you can just switch the foreground and background colors and paint with the paintbrush, airbrush, or pencil.)

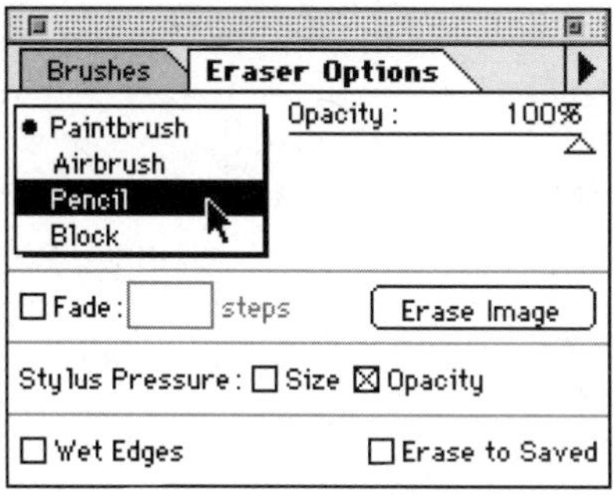

Figure 11-22:
The eraser tool can now paint like the paintbrush, the airbrush, the pencil, or the old eraser (Block). The only question is, why didn't Adobe do this a long time ago?

- **Erasing on a layer:** By now, some of you are probably thinking, "You know, why does Photoshop even have an eraser? If all it does is paint in the background color, who needs it? You can do that with any paint tool just by pressing the X key." You're right. And if you had asked that question about Version 2.5 or earlier, I would have had no answer for you. What makes Photoshop 3.0's eraser tool unique is layers. When working on a layer with the Preserve Transparency check box turned off, the eraser tool actually removes paint and exposes portions of the underlying image. Suddenly, the eraser tool performs like a *real* eraser. (If the Preserve Transparency option is on, however, Photoshop won't let the eraser bore holes in the layer and instead paints in the background color.)

Change the Opacity setting in the Eraser Options panel to make portions of the layer translucent in inverse proportion to the Opacity value. For example, if you set the Opacity to 90 percent, you remove 90 percent of the opacity from the layer and therefore leave 10 percent of the opacity behind. The result is a nearly transparent stroke through the layer.

- **The eraser compared with layer masks:** As described in the "Creating layer-specific masks" section of Chapter 9, you can also erase holes in a layer using a layer mask. But although a layer mask doesn't do any permanent damage to an image, erasing actually gets rid of pixels for good. On the other hand, using the eraser tool doesn't increase the size of your image, as a layer mask does. It's a trade-off.

- **Erasing everything:** In case you're curious, you now restore the entire image window to the background color by clicking on the Erase Image button in the Eraser Options panel. When you're working on a layer, the button changes to Erase Layer and erases the current layer only. Considering how often most folks need to start over at square one — that is, almost never — this seems a much more sensible way to handle the function.

- **Erasing with the pencil:** If you double-click on the pencil icon in the toolbox and select the Auto Erase check box in the Pencil Options panel, the pencil draws in the background color any time you click or drag on a pixel colored in the foreground color. This can be very useful when you're drawing a line against a plain background. Set the foreground color to the color of the line; set the background color to the color of the background. Then use the pencil tool to draw and erase the line until you get it just right. (Unlike the eraser, the pencil always draws either in the foreground or background color, even when used on a layer.)

Reverting to the last saved image

The traditional reversion functions just described are all very well and good. But they don't hold a candle to Photoshop's *selective reversion* functions, which allow you to restore specific portions of an image to the way they looked when you last saved the image to disk.

The most convenient selective reversion function is the magic eraser tool. To access the magic eraser, press the Option key while using the standard eraser tool. (You can also select the Erase to Saved check box in the Eraser Options panel, in which case dragging with the eraser reverts and Option-dragging paints in the background color.) A tiny page icon appears behind the eraser cursor. Option-drag with the magic eraser to paint with the last saved image or, if you prefer to think of it in a different way, to scrape away paint laid down since the last time you saved the image to disk. The process is demonstrated in Figure 11-23.

Figure 11-23:
After making a dreadful mistake (top), I Option-dragged with the eraser tool to restore the image to the way it looked when I last saved it (bottom).

Before Photoshop can begin to selectively revert an image, it must load the last saved version of the image into memory. This operation takes a little time — the same amount of time, in fact, that it took Photoshop to open the image in the first place. You probably won't want to hold the mouse button down for the entire time. Therefore, if this is the first time you've selectively reverted inside the current image, Option-click with the eraser tool and then wait for Photoshop to load the image. Your click won't effect the image in the slightest. After the load operation is completed, Option-drag with the eraser as described earlier.

Reverting with the rubber stamp tool

Thanks to the improved performance of the eraser tool in Photoshop 3.0, the rubber stamp tool offers only two advantages over the magic eraser. The first is that you can take advantage of brush modes. By choosing a different brush mode from the pop-up menu in the upper left corner of the Rubber Stamp Options panel, you can mix pixels from the changed and saved images to achieve interesting and sometimes surprising effects.

The other advantage is that you can revert to one of two different images. Either choose From Saved from the Options pop-up menu in the Rubber Stamp Options panel to revert to the last image saved to disk, or choose From Snapshot to revert to the last image stored in memory as a *snapshot.*

To store the current version of an image in memory, choose Edit⇨Take Snapshot. The operation takes no time to complete because the image is already in memory. By choosing the Take Snapshot command, you merely instruct Photoshop not to get rid of this image.

There's no waiting when you use the tool either. When you drag with the rubber stamp tool set to From Snapshot, you don't have to wait for the image to load into memory as you do when reverting to a saved version, because it's already there. The function works instantaneously.

Photoshop can remember only one snapshot at a time. Therefore, when you choose the Take Snapshot command, you not only capture the current image, you abandon any snapshot previously stored in memory. You cannot undo the Take Snapshot command, so be careful how you use it.

Reverting selected areas

As I explained briefly in the previous chapter, you can also revert selected areas of an image. After selecting the portion of the image you want to revert, choose Edit⇨Fill to display the Fill dialog box. Then select the Saved or Snapshot option from the Use pop-up menu and press the Return key. The selected area reverts to the saved image or snapshot, according to your choice.

Because you're actually filling the selected area with the saved image or snapshot, all the operations I mentioned in Chapter 8 are equally applicable to reversions. You can revert a feathered or antialiased selection; you can revert an area selected with the pen tool; you can even revert a floating selection and apply overlay modes from the layers palette. (The Fill dialog box offers its own Mode pop-up menu, but it's easier to apply the overlay modes to a floating selection from the Layers palette because you can preview the results as they occur.) This capability was late in coming — Adobe introduced it in Version 2.5.1 — but Photoshop's implementation is first-rate.

Reversion limitations

Photoshop doesn't allow you to selectively revert from disk if you have in any way changed the number of pixels in the image since it was last saved. The process won't work if you have chosen Image⇨Image Size or Image⇨Canvas Size or if you have used the crop tool or Edit⇨Crop command.

Photoshop also can't revert an image if you haven't yet saved the image or if it can't read the document from disk (as when the image is saved in a format that requires conversion or can only be opened by means of a plug-in module).

You can, however, work around the image size problem by taking the following steps.

STEPS: Selectively Reverting a Resized Image

Step 1. Select the entire image and copy it to the Clipboard.

Step 2. Option-click on the preview box in the lower left corner of the window to view the size of the document in pixels. Write this information down or assign it to memory (the memory in your head, that is).

Step 3. Choose File⇨Revert to load the last-saved version of the image into the image window.

Step 4. Choose Image⇨Canvas Size to resize the image to the dimensions you noted when Option-clicking the preview box in Step 2.

Step 5. After completing the resize operation, save the image to disk.

Step 6. Paste the copied changes back into the image window and use the rubber stamp or magic eraser to selectively revert the image.

That's all there is to it. In fact, it's so simple that Photoshop should be able to revert from a resized image without your help. Hopefully, Adobe will remedy this problem in the future as well as they remedied so many other functions covered in this chapter.

Summary

- The rubber stamp tool acts like four tools in one. It can clone images, paint in repeating patterns, revert portions of an image to their previous appearance, and apply goofy special effects.

- No matter how you use the tool, the rubber stamp reacts to the settings in the Brushes palette.

- To use the rubber stamp as a cloning tool, Option-click on the point in the image at which you want to begin cloning. Then drag to paint with the clone.

- The Clone (Aligned) and Pattern (Aligned) options ensure that images laid down with the rubber stamp tool match up with each other regardless of how many times you press and release the mouse button.

- Press the Caps Lock key to replace the bulky rubber stamp cursor with a more serviceable crosshair.

- The rubber stamp is an ideal tool for touching up dust and hair scanned with an image and for eliminating distracting or nonessential elements.

- You can create repeating patterns by loading a displacement map, applying filters to an empty portion of an image (starting with Filter⇨Noise⇨Add Noise), marqueeing and cloning portions of a scan, or purchasing texture collections.

- When working on a layer, you can use the eraser tool to erase holes in the layer or fix rough edges by deselecting the Preserve Transparency check box in the Layers palette.

➥ You can selectively revert portions of an image to the way they appeared when you last saved the image to disk by Option-dragging with the eraser tool or using the rubber stamp tool. The rubber stamp lets you erase to the last saved image or the last snapshot.

➥ Choose Edit➪Fill and select Saved or Snapshot from the Use pop-up menu to revert a selected area of an image. This is frequently a lot easier than scrubbing with either the eraser or rubber stamp.

■ ■

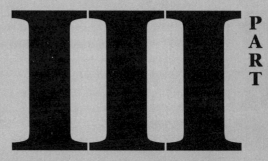

Special Effects

PART III

Special effects comprise a tremendous variety of automated functions that can change an image slightly or completely alter it beyond recognition. Photoshop's type tool, for example, provides one of the great means for applying special effects to an image. Each character is a predefined graphic that you can edit using any of the techniques described in previous and future chapters. If you're thinking that type effects probably aren't Photoshop's forte — after all, type created in a painting program is pretty jagged, right? — a quick browse through Chapter 12 should change your mind.

All the special-effect commands discussed in Chapters 13 through 15 reside under the Filter menu, but that doesn't mean that they produce even vaguely similar effects. Chapter 13 deals primarily with Photoshop's most subtle filters, those that affect the focus of an image. After you become familiar with commands such as Unsharp Mask and Gaussian Blur, chances are you'll use one or the other at least once every time you edit an image in Photoshop.

Chapter 14 delves into the world of special-effects filters. These commands wreak a variety of havoc on images that Louis Daguerre and Ansel Adams — had they had a moment to discuss the matter — would have judged impossible. In addition to covering the usual crowd of destructive filters that cluster images into geometric patterns, trace outlines, and distort an image by poking it, twisting it, and generally putting it through the ringer, I explain Photoshop's new lighting filters, which let you diffuse brightness values and add light to a textured surface.

Chapter 15 shows you how to create your own special effects using the Custom and Displace filters, both of which provide access to all kinds of effects that you simply can't accomplish using any other Photoshop function. And if you're really feeling ambitious, I show you how to program your own interactive filter using the new Filter Factory. The CD includes seven filters that I created with this command; Chapter 15 describes how to create one more on your own.

Text Effects

In This Chapter

- ➥ Understanding the advantages and disadvantages of using bitmapped type

- ➥ Entering and editing type inside the Type Tool dialog box

- ➥ Specifying and measuring type size, leading, and spacing

- ➥ Kerning the space between two specific characters of type

- ➥ Selecting a portion of an image using character outlines

- ➥ Creating raised type and drop shadows

- ➥ Creating logos and other custom letterforms by using path tools to edit character outlines

- ➥ Building an image out of a page of type using the corrective filters discussed in the next chapter

Type Basics

What I'm about to say is going to shake you to the very core. I'm warning you — this is a biggie. You may want to sit down before you read any further. In fact, after you sit down, you may want to strap yourself in. Maybe go ahead and soundproof the room so that no one's alarmed when you scream, "Oh, no, it can't be true!" and "Say it ain't so!"

(Ahem.) Type and graphics are the same thing.

There, there now. I understand. I reacted the same way when I heard the news. Dry your eyes while I explain. You see, your computer treats each character in a word as a little picture. The letter *O*, for example, is a big black oval with a smaller transparent oval set inside it. The only difference between a character of type and a standard graphic is that you don't have to draw type; every letter is already drawn for you. A font, therefore, is like a library of clip art you can access from the keyboard.

Qualities of bitmapped type

Now that you understand the realities of type, it should come as no surprise to learn that Photoshop treats type just like any other collection of pixels in an image. Type legibility is dependent upon the size and resolution of your image.

Figure 12-1, for example, shows four lines of type printed at equal sizes but at different resolutions. If these lines were printed at equal resolutions, each line would be twice as large as the line that precedes it. Hence, big type printed at a high resolution yields smooth, legible output, just as a big image printed at a high resolution yields smooth, detailed output. In fact, everything that you can say about an image is true of bitmapped type.

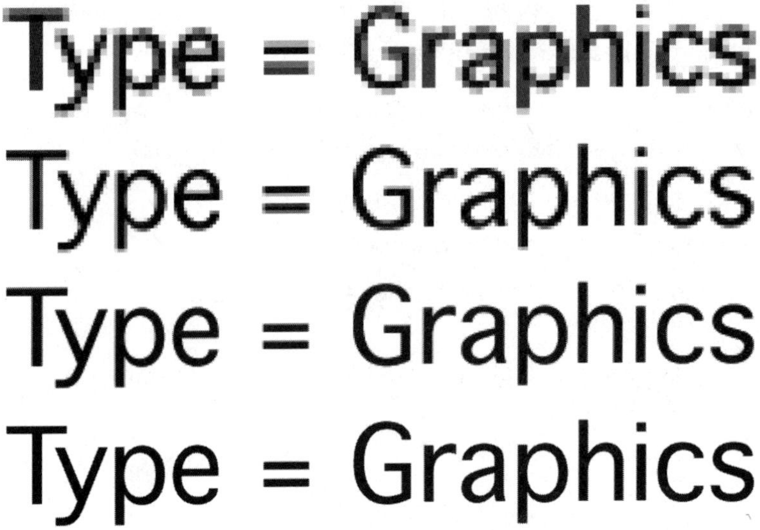

Figure 12-1:
Four lines of type set in the TrueType font Geneva and printed at different resolutions.

Type = Graphics

Type = Graphics

Type = Graphics

Type = Graphics

 You can create smooth, legible type in Photoshop only if you use TrueType fonts in combination with System 7 or Windows 3.1 or if you use PostScript fonts with ATM (Adobe Type Manager) installed. To use a PostScript font, both the screen and printer version of the font must be installed on your machine. For a detailed introduction to the world of type on the Mac, see the "Using Fonts" section of Chapter A on the CD. (You Windows folks probably already know this stuff.)

The disadvantages of working with type in a painting program are obvious. First, the resolution of the type is fixed. Rather than matching the resolution of printed text to that of your printer — a function provided by drawing, word processing, and desktop publishing programs, just to name a few — Photoshop prints type at the same resolution it prints the rest of the image.

In addition, after you add a line of type to an image, you can't go back and add and delete characters from the keyboard as you can in an object-oriented program. If you misspell a word or just want to rephrase some text, you must erase the offending characters or words and start over again. In terms of entering type, Photoshop is more likely to remind you of a typewriter and a bottle of correction fluid than a typical computer program.

But although the disadvantages of creating type in a painting program may initially hamper your progress, the advantages are tremendous. You can do all of the following:

∞ **Create translucent type:** Photoshop enables you to change the translucency of type using the Opacity slider bar in the Layers palette. By using this technique, you can merge type and images to create subtle overlay effects, as illustrated in the top example in Figure 12-2.

Figure 12-2:
Examples of translucent white type (top), type used as a selection (middle), and type enhanced with painting and editing tools (bottom). On the whole, these effects are beyond the means of object-oriented programs.

- ↪ **Use type as a selection:** As I mentioned in Chapter 8, text is just another variety of selection outline. You can mask portions of an image and even select elements and move, copy, or otherwise manipulate them using character outlines, as demonstrated in the middle example in Figure 12-2. I explore this option in detail in the upcoming "Character Masks" section.

- ↪ **Customize characters:** You also can customize a character of type by converting it to a path, editing the path using the tools in the Paths palette, and converting it back to a selection outline. Only high-end drawing programs such as Illustrator, FreeHand, and Canvas match this capability.

- ↪ **Edit type as part of the image:** You can erase type, paint over type, smear type, fill type with a gradation, draw highlights and shadows, and create a range of special text effects that fall well outside the capabilities of an object-oriented program. The last example in Figure 12-2 is just one of the bazillion possibilities.

- ↪ **Trade images freely:** If you've ever traded documents over a network or otherwise tried to share a file created in a word processor or desktop publishing program with associates and coworkers, you know what a nightmare fonts can be. If other people's machines aren't equipped with the fonts you used in your document — which seems to be the case more often than not — your document looks awful on their screens. "What's wrong with this file you gave me?" "Why did you use *this* font?" And "I liked what you wrote in your report, but it is sure ugly!" are only a few of the responses you can expect.

  When you work with images, however, your font worries are over, because type in an image is bitmapped. Other users don't need special screen or printer fonts to view your images exactly as you created them. Mind you, I don't recommend that you use Photoshop as a word processor, but it's great for creating headlines and short missives that you want to fling about the office.

The type tool

In a drawing or desktop publishing program, the type tool typically serves two purposes. You can create text with the tool or you can edit the characters of existing text by highlighting them and either replacing characters or applying formatting commands. However, Photoshop doesn't allow you to reword or reformat text after you add it to an image.

To create text, click with the type tool in the image window (or just press the Y key). Instead of producing a blinking insertion marker in the window, as other graphics programs do, Photoshop displays the Type Tool dialog box shown in Figure 12-3.

Expect to wait a few minutes before you use the type tool for the first time in Photoshop 3.0. You'll see a message saying, "Building a font menu. This may take a minute or so. . ." Unlike Photoshop 2.5, which automatically built its library during the startup cycle, Photoshop 3.0 does so only if you use the type tool, thus saving time for folks who don't use the type tool. If you do use the tool, Photoshop has to build the library only once per session. On my Power Mac, it takes a little less than 20 seconds to load nearly 300 fonts. If you're using a slower machine, it will take longer (probably a minute or so).

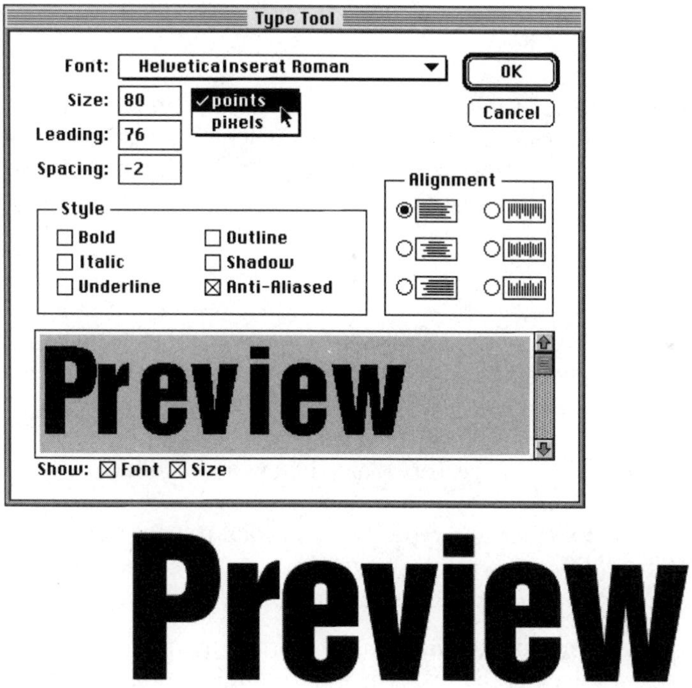

Figure 12-3:
To create type in Photoshop, enter it into the Type Tool dialog box, which appears after you click with the type tool. The bottom example shows the type as it appears in the image window.

Entering and editing type

At the bottom of the Type Tool dialog box is the text-entry box. You enter and edit the text you want to add to the current image into this box.

You can edit text up to the moment you add it to the image. To make your edits, first select the characters you want to change by dragging over them with the cursor. Then enter new text from the keyboard. To select a whole word, double-click on it. You can also cut, copy, and paste text by choosing commands from the Edit menu or using keyboard equivalents.

If the text you are typing reaches the right edge of the text-entry box, the word in progress automatically drops down to the next line. However, when you click on the OK button or press Enter on the keypad to exit the dialog box, all text appears on the same line unless you specifically entered carriage returns between lines (by pressing Return). Each carriage return indicates the end of one line and the beginning of the next, just as it does when you use a typewriter.

Get in the habit of pressing Enter rather than Return to exit the Type Tool dialog box. You can press Return to exit the dialog box when the Size, Leading, or Spacing option box is active, but the key inserts a carriage return when the text-entry box is active.

If your text doesn't look the way you anticipated after you exit the Type Tool dialog box, choose Edit➪Undo (Command-Z) or simply press Delete. Then start the process over again by clicking with the type tool. When the Type Tool dialog box appears, your previous text is displayed in the text-entry box.

Formatting type

Photoshop formats *all* text entered into the text-entry box identically according to the specifications in the Type Tool dialog box. You can't select a single character or word in the text-entry box and format it differently than its deselected neighbors.

The formatting options in the Type Tool dialog box work as follows:

- **Font:** Select the typeface and type style you want to use from the Font pop-up menu. Alternatively, you can just select the plain version of the font, such as Times Roman or Helvetica Regular, and apply styles using the Style options.

- **Size:** Type size is measured either in points (one point equals $\frac{1}{72}$ inch) or pixels. You can select the desired measurement from the pop-up menu to the right of the Size option box, as shown in Figure 12-3. If the resolution of your image is 72 ppi, points and pixels are equal. However, if the resolution is higher, a single point may include many pixels. The resolution of Figure 12-3, for example, is 140 ppi, which is why the final text in the image (shown at bottom) is almost twice as large as the 72 ppi text in the dialog box. The moral? Select the points option when you want to scale text independently of image resolution; select pixels when you want to map text to an exact number of pixels in an image.

Type is measured from the top of its *ascenders* — letters like *b, d,* and *h* that rise above the level of most lowercase characters — to the bottom of its *descenders* — letters like *g, p,* and *q* that sink below the baseline. That's the way it's supposed to work, anyway. Characters from fonts in the Adobe Type Library, including those built into all PostScript laser printers and image setters, measure only 92 percent as tall as the specified type size.

The top two lines in Figure 12-4 contain 120-pixel type set in the Adobe versions of Times and Helvetica. All characters easily fit inside rectangular outlines that measure exactly 120 pixels tall. By contrast, the third and fourth lines of type are set in the TrueType fonts New York and Geneva. These characters are bursting their 120-point rectangular outlines at the seams.

Figure 12-4:
From top to bottom, I formatted these lines of type in the PostScript versions of Times and Helvetica and the TrueType versions of New York and Geneva. The PostScript characters fit inside their 120-point rectangular outlines with room to spare; the TrueType characters slightly overlap their outlines.

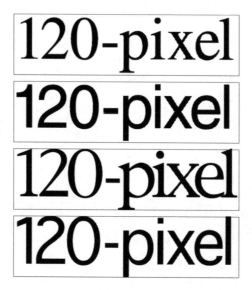

⇥ **Leading:** Also called line spacing, *leading* is the vertical distance between the baseline of one line of type and the baseline of the next line of type within a single paragraph, as illustrated in Figure 12-5. (You must separate lines of type manually by pressing the Return key in the text-entry box.) Leading is measured in the unit you selected from the Size pop-up menu. If you don't specify a leading value, Photoshop automatically inserts leading equal to 125 percent of the type size.

Figure 12-5:
Leading is the distance between any two baselines in a single paragraph of text created with the type tool. Here, the type size is 120 pixels and the leading is 150 pixels.

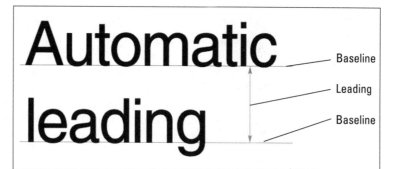

- **Spacing:** Each character in a font carries with it a predetermined amount of *side bearing* that separates it from its immediate neighbors. Although you can't change the amount of side bearing, you can insert and delete the overall amount of space between characters by entering a value into the Spacing option box. Enter a positive value to insert space; enter a negative value to delete space. The value is measured in the unit you selected from the Size pop-up menu.

- **Style:** Select one or more Style check boxes to specify the type styles you want to apply to your text. If you choose the plain version of a font, the Bold and Italic options call up the bold and italic PostScript or TrueType font definitions. If you apply the Bold option to a font that is already bold, such as Helvetica Bold or Helvetica Black (both shown in Figure 12-6), Photoshop makes the characters slightly heavier. If you apply the Italic option to a font that is already italicized, such as Helvetica Oblique (again, see Figure 12-6), Photoshop slants the characters even more.

Figure 12-6: The Style options affect fonts that are already bold or italic. Bolding a plain font produces the same result as choosing the bold version of the font (second and third lines), just as italicizing the plain style is the same as choosing an italicized font (seventh and eighth lines). But you can achieve unique results by applying styles to already stylized fonts (fourth, sixth, and ninth examples).

Helvetica Regular

Helvetica Regular Bold

Helvetica Bold

Helvetica Bold Bold

Helvetica Black

Helvetica Black Bold

Helvetica Regular Italic

Helvetica Oblique

Helvetica Oblique Italic

The Outline option produces unspeakably ugly results, as demonstrated by the top two examples in Figure 12-7. You can create a better outline style using Edit⇨Stroke. First, create your text using the Type Tool dialog box as usual. (Don't you dare select the Outline option.) Press Enter to exit the dialog box. With the foreground color set to black, choose Image⇨Map⇨Invert (Command-I) to change the selected text to white. Finally, choose Edit⇨Stroke and enter the outline thickness of your choice. Figure 12-7 shows two stroked examples, one with a 1-pixel outline and the other with a 2-pixel outline.

The Shadow option produces equally unattractive results. To create attractive shadowed type, try out one of the techniques discussed in the "Character Masks" section of this chapter.

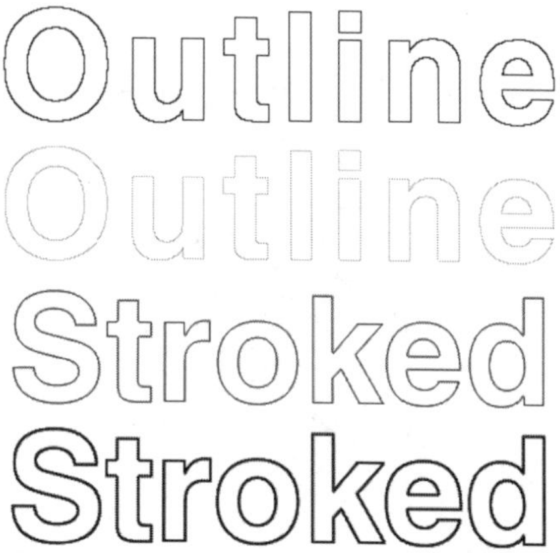

Figure 12-7:
Photoshop's automated outline style, shown here when jagged (top) and antialiased (second), is nothing short of hideous. You can get better results by stroking the characters with 1-pixel or 2-pixel outlines (third and bottom).

Outline

Outline

Stroked

Stroked

- ✑ **Anti-aliased:** This Style option is special enough to mention separately. When you select Anti-aliased, Photoshop softens characters by slightly blurring pixels around the perimeter, as shown in Figure 12-8. Unless you want to create very small type or intend to match the resolution of your output device — printing a 300 ppi image to a 300 dpi printer, for example — select this check box. Photoshop takes longer to produce antialiased type, but it's worth it. Unless otherwise indicated, I created all figures in this chapter with the Anti-aliased check box selected.

Figure 12-8:
The difference between 120-pixel type when the Anti-aliased option is selected (top line) versus deselected (bottom). Both examples were printed at 190 ppi.

Antialiased
Jagged as
all get out

- ✑ **Alignment:** Select one of these radio buttons to specify the way lines of type in a single paragraph align to the point at which you originally clicked with the type tool. Photoshop 3.0 offers three additional options for creating vertically aligned text. In my opinion, every one of them is a waste of time, particularly because you have no control over how the text aligns horizontally within the vertical columns. In Figure 12-9, for example, you can see how the characters in each vertical line are always aligned along their left edges. (Incidentally, I used capital letters to show off the vertical alignment options because vertically aligned lowercase letters always look bad, regardless of the program that creates them.

Figure 12-9:
A single paragraph of
type shown as it appears
if you select each of the
six Alignment radio
buttons. The I-beam
cursor shows the point
at which I clicked to
display the Type Tool
dialog box.

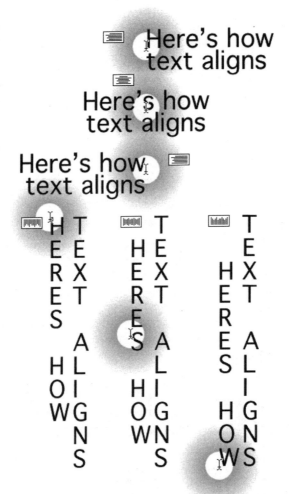

Figure 12-9:
A single paragraph of type shown as it appears if you select each of the six Alignment radio buttons. The I-beam cursor shows the point at which I clicked to display the Type Tool dialog box.

✐ **Show:** Photoshop 3.0's Type Tool dialog box can preview your settings for the Font, Size, and Style options. Select the Font check box at the bottom of the dialog box to preview font and type style; select the Size check box to preview type size. The size preview is always at 72 ppi, so the size is accurate only if you selected Pixels from the Size pop-up menu. That's why the text outside the dialog box back in Figure 12-3 is larger than the text inside the text entry area. Your settings for the Leading, Spacing, and Alignment options as well as the Anti-aliased check box are not reflected in the preview.

Manipulating type in the image window

After you confirm the contents of the Type Tool dialog box by clicking on the OK button or pressing Enter, the type appears selected in the image window. You can move it, clone it, copy it to the Clipboard, transform it by applying commands from the Image⇨Flip, Image⇨Rotate, or Image⇨Effects submenus, or perform any other operation that's applicable to a floating selection.

If you want to hide the marching ants that surround selected characters, choose Select⇨Hide Edges (Command-H). To make the selected text transparent, adjust the Opacity slider bar in the Layers palette while the type tool, one of the four selection tools, or one of the tools in the Paths palette is active. You also can select a brush mode from the pop-up menu on the left side of the Layers palette.

Pressing the Option key when the type tool is selected brings up the eyedropper cursor. Therefore, to clone selected text, you either have to switch to one of the selection tools (rectangular marquee, elliptical marquee, lasso, or magic wand) and Option-drag the text or press Option with an arrow key.

In addition, you can move characters of text independently of each other by Command-dragging with the type tool. When you press and hold the Command key, the standard I-beam cursor changes to a lasso cursor. Command-drag around the portions of the floating selection that you want to deselect and set in place. The rest of the text remains selected and floating.

This technique is ideal for *kerning* — that is, adjusting the amount of space between two neighboring characters. Suppose that you want to adjust the distance between the *P* and *a* in the last line of the novel-turned-top-40-song title shown in Figure 12-10. First, you position the paragraph in your image. You then Command-drag around the portion of the paragraph that you want to set down, as shown in the top example in the figure. To kern the text that remains floating, you Shift-drag it into place, as shown in the bottom half of the figure. Or you can just as easily nudge the selected text with the left and right arrow keys.

Want an even better method of kerning? Create your text directly in the quick mask mode. This way, you can adjust the location of individual characters without deselecting any of them. Just switch to the quick mask mode, create your text, and then select individual characters and adjust their positioning as desired. When you finish, choose Image⇨Map⇨Invert (Command-I) to make the text white so that it will serve as the selection. Then switch back to the marching ants mode. Your text is both kerned and 100 percent selected.

You also can Command-drag around a portion of a floating selection with the rectangular marquee, elliptical marquee, or lasso tool. However, if you do so, you don't just deselect the portion of the selection around which you drag, you delete it. Try it out

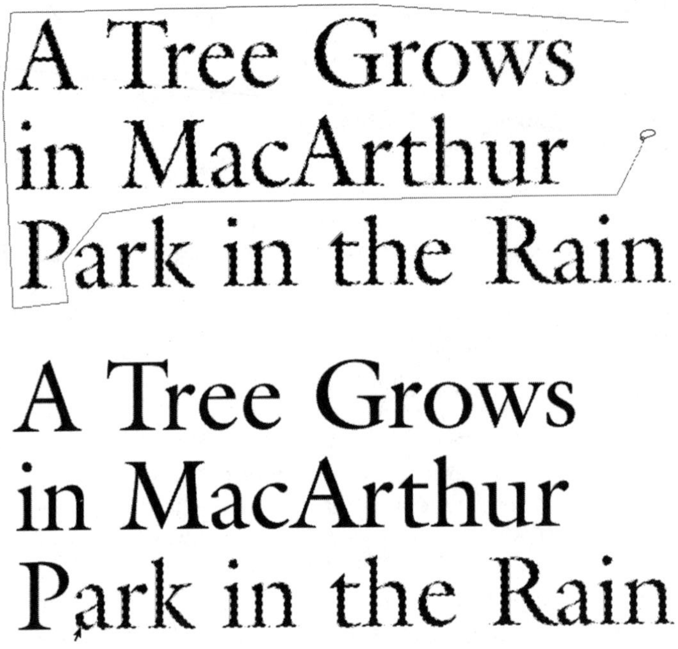

Figure 12-10:
After Command-dragging with the type tool around the text that I wanted to set down (top), I Shift-dragged the text that remained selected to close the gap between the *P* and *a* in *Park* (bottom).

A Tree Grows in MacArthur Park in the Rain

A Tree Grows in MacArthur Park in the Rain

and you'll see what I mean. Click with the type tool, enter the word *Park,* and then press Enter. While the text remains floating, select the lasso tool and Command-drag around the *P.* The *P* disappears, leaving you stranded with an *ark.* After choosing Edit⇨Undo (Command-Z) to reinstate the *P,* select the type tool and Command-drag around the *P.* This time you deselect the *P* and make it part of your image, enabling you to nudge the *ark* into a better location.

 I mentioned this tip in Chapter 8, but folks always ooh and ah over it when I tell them about it, so I figure that the message isn't getting out there. Repetition might help. You can Command-drag with the type tool to set down portions of any floating selection, not just text. You can also Command-Option-drag to draw a polygon around an area, as demonstrated in the first example of Figure 12-10, or Command-Shift-drag to intersect the portion of the floating selection that you want to remain selected and set down the portion outside your drag.

Character Masks

Recapping today's news: Type outlines are selections. Except for the fact that they arrive on the scene already filled with the foreground color, they act like any other selection outline. With that in mind, you can create an inexhaustible supply of special type effects.

The following sections demonstrate a few examples. Armed with these ideas, you should be able to invent enough additional type effects to keep you busy into the next millennia. Honestly, you won't believe the number of effects you can invent by screwing around with type outlines.

Filling type with an image

One of the most impressive and straightforward applications for text in Photoshop is to use the character outlines to mask a portion of an image. In fact, the only trick is getting rid of the foreground fill. You can accomplish this in a matter of a few straightforward steps.

STEPS: **Selecting Part of an Image Using Character Outlines**

Step 1. Begin by opening the image you want to mask. Then create your text by clicking with the type tool, entering the text you want to use as a mask, formatting it as desired, and pressing Enter to display the type in the image window. Large, bold characters work best. In Figure 12-11, I used the PostScript font Eras Ultra — an extremely bold type style — with a Size value of 260 and a Spacing value of negative 10.

Figure 12-11:
When you use type to mask an image, bold and blocky characters produce the best results because they enable you to see large chunks of unobstructed image.

Step 2.   Choose Edit⇨Cut (Command-X) to delete the text from the image and transfer it to the Clipboard.

Step 3.   Choose Select⇨All (Command-A) to marquee the entire image. Then press the Option key and choose Edit⇨Paste Into to paste the text in back of the image. The result is that you can see the character outlines without seeing the foreground fill, as demonstrated in Figure 12-12.

Figure 12-12:
By pasting the text behind the image, you can use the selection outlines without worrying about the fore-ground fill of the characters.

 If you choose Edit⇨Paste Into, Photoshop pastes the contents of the Clipboard inside the current selection. The selection therefore masks the pasted image. Photoshop 2.5 used to have a Paste Behind command that pasted the contents of the Clipboard behind the selected area of the image. But in Version 3.0, Paste Behind has disappeared. You now access this function by Option-choosing Edit⇨Paste Into.

Step 4.   Using the type tool, drag the character outlines into position. Because the selection is in back of the image, you move only the outlines without affecting the image itself. When you get the outlines where you want them, choose Select⇨Defloat (Command-J) to set the selection down so that it is no longer floating behind the image.

Step 5.   Selection and image are no longer separate entities. You now can clone the selected portion of the image and drag it to a new location, as demonstrated in Figure 12-13, or copy it to a new image.

Figure 12-13:
The result of Option-dragging the selected image to an empty part of the image window using one of the selection tools.

Painting raised type

Instead of moving the selected image or copying it to a different window, as suggested in Step 5 of the preceding section, you can paint around the character outlines to create a raised text effect, as illustrated in Figure 12-14.

Figure 12-14:
Raised type created by painting with the dodge and airbrush tools around the perimeter of the character outlines.

To create this image, I carried out the first four steps described in the preceding section. I then prepared the characters by dragging inside them with the dodge tool. I used a 65-pixel soft brush shape and selected Shadows from the brush modes pop-up menu (on the left side of the Brushes palette) to concentrate the lightening effect on the very dark areas in the image.

As shown in the top image in Figure 12-15, this helps set the letters apart from the rest of the image. To give the letters depth, I set the foreground color to black and used the airbrush tool with a 35-pixel soft brush shape to apply shadows around the lower and right portions of each character, as shown in the middle row of Figure 12-15.

Figure 12-15:
After using the dodge tool to lighten the darkest pixels inside the letters (top), I painted in the shadows by airbrushing in black around the right and bottom edges of the letters (middle). Finally, I painted in the highlights by airbrushing in white around the left and top edges of the letters (bottom).

I next switched the foreground color to white and applied highlights around the upper and left portions of characters, which results in the image shown in the bottom row of Figure 12-15.

If you don't consider yourself an artist, you may find the prospect of painting around the edges of characters a little intimidating. But bear in mind that it's next to impossible to make a mistake. Because you're painting inside the selection, there's no danger of harming any portion of the image outside the character outlines. And if you mess up inside the selection, the problem is easily resolved.

If you look closely at the last image in Figure 12-15, for example, you can see that in applying white to the arch of the *a,* I accidentally got some on the right corner of the *e.* Hey, nobody's perfect. To fix the problem, all I need to do is select a smaller brush shape and paint over that area of the *e* with black.

So if you make a mistake, choose Edit⇨Undo or just keep painting. Give it a try. The process takes less than an hour and I bet you'll be pleasantly surprised with your results.

Feathering effects

You can feather text outlines just as you can feather other kinds of selections. However, in doing so, you modify the shape of the selection and therefore set the characters down in the image area.

If you want to combine feathered text with an image, take care to paste the text behind the image by Option-choosing Edit⇨Paste Into, as explained in Steps 2 and 3 in the recent section "Filling type with an image." (You don't have to perform Step 4, choosing Select⇨Defloat, because feathering automatically defloats the selection.) Otherwise, you leave behind deselected remnants of the foreground color that used to fill the characters.

For example, the top image in Figure 12-16 shows the result of creating a line of type, feathering it with an 8-pixel radius, and deleting the feathered selection. You can plainly see that Photoshop leaves behind a harsh black outline after the deletion. If, on the other hand, you create the type, cut it to the Clipboard, select the image, paste the type in back of the image, and *then* feather it and delete it, you eliminate any chance that some of the type will be left behind, as demonstrated in the bottom image in Figure 12-16.

The following steps describe how to create a backlighting effect using Photoshop's feathering capability. Figure 12-17 shows the finished image. To simplify the process, the text appears in front of a plain black background. But you can just as easily apply this technique to an image as long as you take care to paste the text behind the image before choosing Select⇨Feather.

Figure 12-16: The results of feathering and deleting text positioned in front of an image (top) and in back of an image (bottom).

STEPS: Using Feathering to Backlight Text

Step 1. Create a new image window large enough to accommodate a single line of large text. I created an image 800 pixels wide by 300 pixels tall.

Step 2. Choose Select⇨All (Command-A) and press Option-Delete to fill the entire image with black. (I'm assuming here that black is the foreground color and white is the background color. If this is not the case, press D to make it so.)

Step 3. Create your text using the type tool and the Type Tool dialog box. The text in the figure is set in 240-pixel Helvetica Inserat, a member of the Adobe Type Library.

Step 4. Copy the text to the Clipboard (Command-C).

Step 5. Choose Select⇨Feather, enter a number that's about equal to $1/20$ the resolution of your image into the Radius option box, and press Return. My resolution is about 180 ppi, so I entered 9. (Dividing by 20 isn't a hard and fast rule — you can use any Radius value that works for your image.)

Step 6. Press the Delete key to fill the feathered selection with white.

Step 7. Choose Edit⇨Paste (Command-V) to reintroduce the copied line of text to the image. As long as you don't select the feathered area, the black letters will appear in same spot from which they were copied. Use the down arrow key to nudge the selection 3 to 5 pixels. The result is shown in the top half of Figure 12-17.

Figure 12-17:
You can create backlit text — also known as the movie-of-the-week effect — by deleting a feathered version of a line of type and then pasting the original, unfeathered type in front (top). A slash of the airbrush takes away some of the flatness of the image (bottom).

Step 8. For extra credit, set the foreground color to 50 percent black and then use the airbrush tool with the 100-pixel soft brush shape to paint a single line across the text. This creates the effect of light seeping through a slightly open door, as shown in the bottom half of the figure.

If you read Chapter 10, you'll recognize this as a close cousin — *very* close, more like a Siamese twin — of the haloing technique described in the "Creating drop shadows, halos, and spotlights" section. In this example, you don't have to resort to layers because the letters and background are the same color — black. But if you wanted to set green letters against a red background — like, maybe to create a really scary Christmas card — you would need to send the letters to their own layer in Step 3, skip Step 4, sink the selection to the background layer and then feather it in Step 5, skip Step 6, and finally go back to the layer and paint inside the letters with the Preserve Transparency check box selected. Go back to Chapter 10 if you need a refresher. If you do, don't forget that any text block works exactly like a filled selection outline.

Creating drop shadows

That same section of Chapter 10 also covered how to create drop shadows. And again, the process is a little easier when you're working with text because you don't have to fool around with layers. This section examines two methods for adding drop shadows: one that involves changing the translucency of type (demonstrated in Figure 12-18); and another that relies on feathering (Figure 12-19).

 The first steps work only if text and drop shadow are the same color. In the second set of steps, the text and background can be any colors.

STEPS: Creating Quick and Easy Hard-edged Drop Shadows

Step 1.   Create your text. In Figure 12-18, I used an unusual typeface called Remedy Single from Emigre Graphics. It's about the wildest font I've ever come across — it looks like something The Cure might use on its album covers — so it lends itself well to this technique, which is by contrast quite simple.

Step 2.   Select any selection tool and clone the selected type by Option-dragging it a few pixels down and to the right.

Step 3.   Press 4 on the keyboard to lower the opacity of the cloned selection to 40 percent. The translucent clone serves as the drop shadow.

Figure 12-18:
I took two lines of type set in the font Remedy (yes, those lower characters are part of the font), cloned the paragraph, and changed the opacity of the clone to 40 percent.

The benefit of this technique is that is takes about six seconds to complete. The downside is that it only works with text that is set in a solid color. You can't paint inside the text or fill it with an image because the drop shadow actually lies in front of the text.

The next steps describe a more functional, albeit slightly more complicated, drop shadow technique. The effect is illustrated in Figure 12-19.

STEPS: **Creating a Feathered Drop Shadow**

Step 1.   Create your type. Use any foreground and background colors you want. Figure 12-19 features that old standby, 240-pixel Helvetica Inserat, in that old standby color, black.

Figure 12-19:
Feather the text and fill it with black to create the drop shadow (top). Then paste the copied version of the text in front of the drop shadow (middle) and paint inside the characters as desired (bottom).

Step 2.   Cut the text to the Clipboard (Command-X). Then select the entire image (Command-A) and Option-choose Edit⇨Paste Into to paste the letters behind the selected image.

Step 3.   Choose Select⇨Feather, enter whatever value you like into the Radius option box, and press Return. I entered 8 because it looks like a snowman with its head knocked off and also because it was roughly ¹/₂₀ of the resolution of the image. The selection is now feathered.

Step 4.   Press Option-Delete to fill the feathered text with black, as shown in the first example of Figure 12-19. If black is not your foreground color, float the feathered selection (Command-J) before filling it (Option-Delete). Then choose Multiply from the overlay modes pop-up menu in the Layers palette and change the Opacity if you so desire. Whatever color you use, the feathered text will serve as the drop shadow.

Step 5.   Paste another copy of the text in front of the drop shadow (Command-V) and nudge it slightly off center from the shadow, as demonstrated in the second row of Figure 12-19. (I've made the text white so that you can see it clearly against the black shadow.)

Step 6.   From here on, what you do with the text is up to you. You can fill the selected type with a different color or gradation. I chose to paint inside my characters with the rubber stamp and airbrush tools. After defining a pattern from a small selection in the familiar ColorBytes gears image (Figures 12-11 through 12-16), I selected the rubber stamp tool and chose Pattern (Aligned) from the Options pop-up menu in the Rubber Stamp Options panel. Then I painted inside my text with a 65-pixel brush shape, taking care to leave some white spaces showing. To finish things off, I dragged with the airbrush tool and a 35-pixel brush shape. The result is the bottom image shown in Figure 12-19.

Converting characters to paths

You can create your own letterforms by editing selection outlines using the tools in the Paths palette. After creating the text you want to edit, choose the Make Path command from the Paths palette menu, edit the selection outlines as desired, and choose the Make Selection command. This technique is perfectly suited to designing logos and other elements that call for custom characters. The following steps explain the technique in greater detail and describe how I created the type shown in Figure 12-22. (Figures 12-20 and 12-21 illustrate steps in the process.)

STEPS: **Editing a Character Outline Using the Path Tools**

Step 1. Begin by creating your text, as always. When inside the Type Tool dialog box, select a font that best matches the eventual letterforms you want to create. I selected Avant Garde Gothic because of its perfectly circular letterforms, which go well with the circular shapes in the ColorBytes gears image (see Figure 12-20).

Step 2. After creating your text, place it in back of your image so that you don't leave any deselected characters sitting around. Choose Edit⇨Cut (Command-X) to send the text to the Clipboard. Then choose Select⇨All (Command-A) and then Option-choose Edit⇨Paste Into.

Step 3. Applying one of Photoshop's transformation effects to alter the text is sometimes a good first step in creating custom letterforms. It enables you to prepare outlines for future edits by minimizing the number of point-by-point edits you have to perform later. In my case, I wanted to rotate my single character — a circular letter *e* — to a different angle. I chose Image⇨Rotate⇨Free and dragged the corner handles until the angle of the horizontal bar in the *e* matched the angle of the rod protruding from one of the gears, as demonstrated in Figure 12-20. Then I clicked inside the character with the gavel cursor to exit the transformation mode.

Figure 12-20:
I rotated the angle of my character outline to match the angle of the rod coming out of the central gear.

Step 4. Choose the Make Path command from the Paths palette menu (or click on that little convert-to-selection/path icon at the bottom of the palette) and press Return to accept the default Tolerance setting. Photoshop converts the character outline to a Bézier path, as shown in the left example in Figure 12-21.

Figure 12-21:
After converting the
letter to a path (left), I
edited the outline by
moving and deleting
points (right).

Step 5.   Edit the Bézier path as desired using the tools in the Paths palette. I reduced the thickness of the circular perimeter of my *e* by dragging the inside edges of the paths outward with the arrow tool, as illustrated in the second example of Figure 12-21. I also simplified the structure of the paths by deleting some points with the remove point tool. Finally, I shortened the length of the *e*'s lip — that loose part that swings around to the right and makes the letter look like it's smiling.

Step 6.   When you finish editing the character outlines, save them by choosing Save Path from the Paths palette menu. Then choose the Make Selection command and press Return to accept the default settings. Or just press the Enter key to avoid both command and dialog box altogether. The letters are again selection outlines.

Step 7.   What you do from this point on is up to you. Want to know what I did? Sure you do. I copied the selection, created a new image window measuring about 500×500 pixels, and pasted the *e* into the window's center. I then clicked the switch colors icon in the toolbox to make white the foreground color and black the background color. I wanted to create a drop shadow for my character, so I pressed Option-delete to fill the selection with white and then chose Select⇨Feather and set the Radius value to 8. (Who can say why I'm so stuck on this value? I guess I'm in a rut.) To complete the drop shadow, I pressed the Delete key to fill the feathered selection with black. Next, I pasted the character again and nudged it a few pixels up and to the left to offset it in relation to the shadow. Then, with the type tool still active, I selected the Dissolve option from the brush modes pop-up menu in the Brushes palette to rough up the edges of the floating character. The finished character appears in Figure 12-22.

Figure 12-22:
I used the Dissolve option in the brush modes pop-up menu to randomize the pixels along the edges of the character.

Where Text and Filters Meet

The other chapters in this part of the book revolve around using Photoshop's filters. Now, there must be close to a bazillion ways to combine text outlines and filters (I'm only estimating, of course), but before you leave this chapter, I want to show you just two. Both techniques permit you to actually build an image inside Photoshop using text. You vary the brightness and boldness of each letter to create a pattern of characters that suggest an image. It's sort of like the custom halftoning effect that Photoshop can apply automatically to black-and-white images (as shown in Figure 4-14 back in Chapter 4), except that instead of using a repeating image pattern, the individual color cells are made up of characters of text. If you're still not quite sure what I'm talking about, Figures 12-24 and 12-25 show one possible result of each technique.

To start with, you need a high-resolution, grayscale image, 200 ppi or better. The high resolution will make your text more legible and permit more letters to fit inside smaller areas in your image, hence increasing image detail. In Figure 12-23, I selected the grumpy baby image from PhotoDisc's "Retro Americana" collection that I featured in Chapter 6, except that this time the nose ring and anarchy tattoo are absent. The resolution of the image is 240 ppi. I masked off the image and removed the background to make the baby stand out as much as possible. I also used the Levels command to increase the contrast in the image, as described in Chapter 16.

When you have your image in hand, you're ready to take on the following steps:

STEPS: The Easy Way to Build an Image Out of Text

Step 1.   Start by saving your image. In the next few steps, you're going to destroy it.

Step 2.   Display the Channels palette and drag the Black channel onto the duplicate channel icon at the bottom of the palette. This creates a new mask channel filled with a clone of your image.

Step 3. Press Command-1 to return to the Black channel. This technique relies on white text against a black background. Prepare the foreground and background colors by pressing D and then X. Now white is the foreground color, and black is the background color.

Step 4. Select the entire image (Command-A) and press the Delete key. The window turns black. (Don't worry. The original image is still safe in the mask channel.)

Step 5. Use the text tool to fill the screen with text. Enter anything you want. I recommend using a bold font that's very easy to read. I used 36-point Helvetica Bold, the plainest font in town. Insofar as filling the image window is concerned, you might want to take measurements. Create a very long line and see how much will fit across the screen. Then insert paragraph returns inside the Type Tool dialog box accordingly. You'll probably have to create your text in a few passes. I created the text shown in Figure 12-23 one line at a time.

Figure 12-23: A screen full of white text against a black background (top) and the image that served as the mask (bottom). Together, I used these two images to create the text/image montages shown in Figures 12-24 and 12-25.

Don't worry, this is the hardest step. Well, at least it's the most tedious. After you're finished, you may want to save your image under a different name (using File⇨Save a Copy, in the Photoshop or TIFF format) so that you don't have to redo all this work if you decide to attempt the next set of steps.

Step 6. Now, make the text shrink where the image is dark and make it grow where the image is light. Option-click on the mask channel name (presumably Black Copy) in the Channels palette to convert it to a selection outline. This outline represents the lightest portions of the image. But I suggest that you start by thinning the letters inside the darkest areas. So choose Select⇨Inverse to draw the selection around the darkest portions of the image.

Step 7. Choose Filter⇨Other⇨Minimum. This filter increases the size of the black areas in your image. For my 240 ppi image, I entered a value of 2 to instruct Photoshop to expand the black areas by two pixels. If the resolution of your image is higher, you may want to enter a higher value. Then press Return. Notice that the selected letters have lost weight in direct proportion to the darkness of the original image. Cool, huh? (If you want to experiment with different values, just press Command-Z to undo the effect and press Command-Option-F to again display the Minimum dialog box.)

Step 8. That's it for the dark areas; now for the light ones. Choose Select⇨Inverse to select the light areas. Then choose Filter⇨Other⇨Maximum. The exact opposite of the Minimum filter, Maximum expands the white areas of your image. Figure 12-24 shows the result of entering 3 in the Maximum dialog box and pressing Return. I know, it's a higher value than I entered into the Minimum dialog box, and here's the reason: A Minimum value of more than 2 would have completely eliminated a large amount of my text, whereas a Maximum value of 3 still leaves a few distinguishing holes — inside the *o*'s and *d*'s — in the fattest of the expanded characters.

Figure 12-24:
The result of applying the grumpy baby image as a mask and using the Minimum and Maximum filters to shrink and expand the letters, respectively.

Using the Minimum and Maximum filters has the advantage of being remarkably straightforward. But it's not the best method. Most of the letters are barely legible, and all of the letterforms are pretty well ruined. The next steps show a better but more difficult method for shrinking and expanding type that results in much more legible text. You'll be using the Gaussian Blur and Unsharp Mask filters, both discussed in great depth in the next chapter, and the Levels command, discussed in Chapter 16.

STEPS: The Harder but Better Way to Build an Image out of Text

Step 1. Perform Steps 1 through 5 from the previous technique. (If you saved your image as I advised in Step 5, you can just open it and start from there.)

Step 2. Before you select anything, choose Filter⇨Blur⇨Gaussian Blur. This filter instructs Photoshop to examine your image one pixel at a time and mix up pixels within a specified Radius. For my 240 ppi image, I entered a value of 2 and pressed Return. I might raise it as high as 3 for a 300 ppi image; otherwise, 2 is fine. The image was once composed almost exclusively of black and white pixels; you have now introduced a whole host of gray pixels via the Gaussian Blur filter. In future steps, you nudge these gray pixels toward black or white to shrink or expand the letters.

Step 3.   Option-click on the Black Copy mask channel in the Channels palette to select the light portion of your image. Choose Select⇨Inverse to switch and select the dark portions instead.

Step 4.   Choose Image⇨Adjust⇨Levels or just press Command-L. I don't have room to offer a complete explanation of the Levels dialog box here, so let me just say this: You enter values in the three Input option boxes at the top of the dialog box to specify the brightness of the pixels that will change to black, medium gray, and white, respectively. For now, you only need to be concerned with the first option box, which represents black, and the third option box, which represents white.

Step 5.   Enter 130 into the first option box and press Return. This instructs Photoshop to send every selected pixel that's darker than a brightness value of 130 — roughly medium gray — to black. Partially selected pixels become only partially black. Lighter pixels become darker; only white remains white. The upshot is that the selected letters shrink.

Step 6.   You're done with the dark areas; now go to work on the light ones. Choose Select⇨Inverse to deselect the stuff you just edited and select the stuff you haven't had a chance to mess up.

Step 7.   Choose the Levels command again (Command-L). This time, you want to lighten the selected area instead of darkening it. To do this, change the value of the third Input option box at the top of the Levels dialog box. Enter 90 and press Return. This tells Photoshop to send all selected pixels that are lighter than a brightness value of 90 — which, judging by the fact that 255 is white, is on the dark side of medium gray — to white. All darker grays are lightened to incrementally lighter colors except black, which remains black.

Step 8.   That's it. The last step is to firm things up by applying the Unsharp Mask filter, which sharpens the focus of the image. So choose Filter⇨Sharpen⇨Unsharp Mask. I recommend some pretty radical values in this dialog box. Enter 300 percent into the Amount option box. Because you blurred the image so aggressively before, enter 8 into the Radius option box (a very high value). Then press Return. Figure 12-25 shows the result.

Figure 12-25:
This time I bagged
the Minimum and
Maximum filters
and relied instead
on the Gaussian
Blur filter to insert
gray values into
the letterforms and
the Levels
command to send
those gray values
to either black or
white.

You can make out the baby face in Figures 12-24 and 12-25 about equally well. But the text in Figure 12-25 is decidedly more legible. Unlike Minimum and Maximum, the Gaussian Blur filter doesn't entirely eliminate detail, it merely smoothes it out. The Levels and Unsharp Mask commands helped to reestablish the detail.

And I don't know if you noticed it, but there's no way you could have pulled this off with Illustrator or FreeHand. Photoshop rules, dude. (Heh heh.)

Summary

➻ In Photoshop, the only way to fix typos or otherwise alter text after you add it to an image is to choose Edit⇨Undo and start over again.

➻ When entering text, you must press Return to specify the end of one line of type and the beginning of the next. Press Enter to confirm your text and exit the dialog box.

➻ To create outline type, choose Edit⇨Stroke after creating your text; don't rely on Photoshop's automatic Outline style.

➻ To clone text, click on one of the selection tools in the toolbox and Option-drag the text to a new location in the image window.

➻ To deselect part of a floating selection without deleting it, Command-drag around that part of the selection with the type tool. This technique allows you to adjust the distance between characters — or *kern* them — by setting the characters down one at a time.

➻ To select part of an image using character outlines, cut the outline to the Clipboard, select the image, paste the outlines behind the image by Option-choosing Edit⇨Paste Into, and then set the outlines down by choosing Select⇨Defloat.

➻ You can use the Feather command to create backlighting effects and drop shadows.

➻ If you want to edit a character outline, first convert it to a Bézier path. Then reshape the path using the tools from the Paths palette and convert the finished product back to a selection.

➻ The filters discussed in the upcoming chapters can be instrumental in turning text into something very unlike what you may have previously envisioned text to be. Text becomes just another image to edit, just another selection outline with which to mask. (And all this time you thought you were supposed to *read* the stuff.)

Corrective Filtering

In This Chapter

- ➥ How to dissipate the effects of filters using floating selections

- ➥ Comprehensive explanations of Photoshop's focus filters, including Unsharp Mask and Gaussian Blur

- ➥ Analyses of the most important corrective filters applied to individual color channels

- ➥ How to establish a selection outline using the High Pass filter

- ➥ Ways to antialias jagged images and masks

- ➥ Creative uses for the Motion Blur, Wind, and Radial Blur filters

- ➥ Adding manual motion effects

- ➥ Feathering a selection using Minimum and Gaussian Blur

- ➥ A complete guide to the filters in the Noise submenu

- ➥ Reducing moiré patterns in scanned images

Filter Basics

In Photoshop, *filters* enable you to apply automated effects to an image. Though named after photographer's filters, which typically allow you to correct lighting and perspective fluctuations, Photoshop's filters can accomplish a great deal more. You can slightly increase the focus of an image, introduce random pixels, add depth to an image, or completely rip it apart and reassemble it into a hurky pile of goo. Any number of special effects are made available via filters.

At this point, a little bell should be ringing in your head, telling you to beware standardized special effects. Why? Because everyone has access to the same filters that you do.

If you rely on filters to edit your images for you, your audience will quickly recognize your work as poor or at least unremarkable art.

Think of it this way: You're watching MTV. You should be watching VH1 with the rest of the old folks, but when you were flipping through the channels you got stuck on Peter Gabriel's "Sledgehammer" video. Outrageous effects, right? He rides an imaginary roller coaster, bumper cars crash playfully into his face, fish leap over his head. You couldn't be more amused or impressed.

As the video fades, you're so busy basking in the glow that you neglect for a split second to whack the channel-changer. Before you know it, you're midway through an advertisement for a monster truck rally. Like the video, the ad is riddled with special effects — spinning letters, a reverberating voice-over slowed down to an octave below the narrator's normal pitch, and lots of big machines filled with little men filled with single brain cells working overtime.

In and of themselves, these special effects aren't bad. There was probably even a time when you thought that spinning letters and reverberating voice-overs were hot stuff. But ever since you grew out of preadolescence, your taste has become, well, more refined. In truth, you're probably the same as you always were; you've simply grown tired of these particular effects. You've come to associate them with raunchy, local car-oriented commercials. Certainly, these effects are devoid of substance, but more importantly, they're devoid of creativity.

This chapter and the two that follow, therefore, are about the creative application of special effects. Rather than trying to show an image subject to every single filter — a service already performed quite adequately by the manual included with your software — these chapters explain exactly how the most important filters work and offer some concrete ways to use them.

You'll also learn how to apply several filters in tandem and how to use filters to edit images and selection outlines. My goal is not so much to teach you what filters are available — you can find that out by tugging on the Filter menu — but how and when to use filters.

A first look at filters

You access Photoshop's special-effects filters by choosing commands from the Filter menu. These commands fall into two general camps: corrective and destructive.

Corrective filters, which are the subject of this chapter, comprise limited functions that you use to modify scanned images and prepare an image for printing or screen display. In most cases, the effects are subtle enough that a viewer won't even notice that you applied a corrective filter. As demonstrated in Figure 13-1 and Color Plate 13-1, these filters include those that change the focus of an image (Blur, Sharpen), enhance color transitions (High Pass), and randomize pixels (Add Noise).

Figure 13-1:
Michelangelo's Moses from *Saint Peter in Chains* subject to four corrective filters, including (clockwise from upper left) Blur, Sharpen More, High Pass, and Add Noise. You have to love those old, uncopyrighted masterpieces, not to mention those explicit basilica names.

Many corrective filters have direct opposites. Blur is the opposite of Sharpen, Despeckle is the opposite of Add Noise, and so on. This is not to say that one filter entirely removes the effect of the other; only reversion functions such as the Undo command provide that capability. Instead, two opposite filters produce contrasting effects.

Destructive filters — found under the Filter⇨Distort, Pixelate, Stylize, and, to a lesser extent, Render submenus — produce effects so dramatic that they can, if used improperly, completely overwhelm your artwork, making the filter more important than the image itself. A few examples of overwhelmed images appear in Figure 13-2 and Color Plate 13-2.

Destructive filters produce way-cool effects, and many people gravitate toward them when first experimenting with Photoshop. But the filters invariably destroy the original clarity and composition of the image. Yes, every Photoshop function is destructive to a certain extent, but destructive filters change your image so extensively that you can't easily disguise the changes later by applying other filters or editing techniques.

Figure 13-2:
The effects of applying four destructive filters (clockwise from upper left): Facet, Find Edges, Ripple, and Pointillize. These filters produce such dramatic effects that they are best used in moderation.

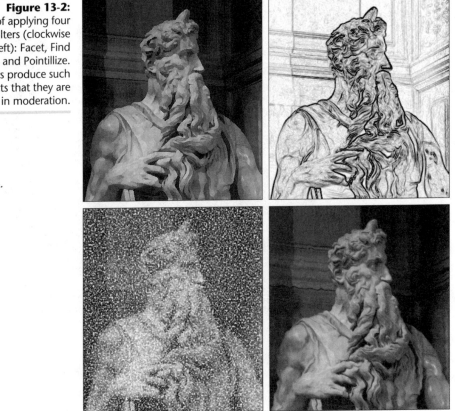

To get the best results from these filters, apply them to selected portions of an image rather than to the entire image. In addition, apply them partially, as described in the upcoming "Float before filtering" section. And make sure to save your image to disk before applying a destructive filter so that you can revert to the saved image if your changes don't turn out the way you hoped.

Corrective filters are the subject of this chapter. Although they number fewer than their destructive counterparts, they represent the functions you're most likely to use on a day-to-day basis, so I spend more time on them. I devote fewer words to destructive filters, as you can read in Chapter 14. (The homemade effects explained in Chapter 15 fall into both camps.)

General filtering techniques

When you choose a command from the Filter menu, Photoshop applies the filter to the selected portion of the image. If no portion of the image is selected, Photoshop applies the filter to the entire image. Therefore, if you want to filter every nook and cranny of an image, choose Select⇨None (Command-D) and then choose the desired command.

External plug-ins

Some filters are built into the Photoshop application. Others reside externally inside the Plug-ins folder. This allows you to add filters from third-party collections, such as Kai's Power Tools, Paint Alchemy, and the Andromeda Series.

If you open the Plug-ins folder inside the Photoshop folder, you'll see that Adobe has divided it up into several subfolders, one of which is labeled *Filters*. But guess what? It doesn't matter where you put your plug-ins, as long as they reside somewhere — anywhere — inside the Plug-ins folder. Even if you create a new folder inside the Plug-ins folder and call it *No Filters Here*, create another folder inside that called *Honest, Fresh Out of Filters*, toss in one more folder called *Carpet Beetles Only* for good measure, and put every plug-in you own inside this latest folder, Photoshop sees through your clever ruse and displays the exact same filters you always see under their same submenus in the Filter menu. The Filter subfolder, therefore, is provided purely for organizational purposes so that you don't have to look through a list of 6,000 files inside a single Plug-ins folder.

Previewing filters

For years, the biggest problem with Photoshop's filters was that none offered previews to help you predict the outcome of an effect. You just had to tweak your 15,000 meaningless settings and hope for the best. Meanwhile, third-party filters such as Aldus Gallery Effects offered previews right inside the dialog box. In Photoshop 2.5, John Knoll made it possible to access previews when you used a filter from the Filter⇨Distortion submenu. But in order to see them, you had to press the Option key while choosing one of several commands from the Apple⇨About Plug-in submenu and then . . . well, let's just say that the logic in this case seemed to have been twisted by a distortion filter.

In Photoshop 3.0, things are finally as they should be. Nearly every filter that displays a dialog box includes two previewing capabilities. As shown in Figure 13-3, the first is a 100 × 100-pixel preview box inside the dialog box. Drag inside the preview box to scroll the portion of the image you want to preview. Move the cursor outside the dialog box to get the square preview cursor (labeled in the figure). Click with the cursor to center the contents of the preview box at the clicked position in the image. Click on the zoom buttons (+ and –) to reduce the image inside the preview box.

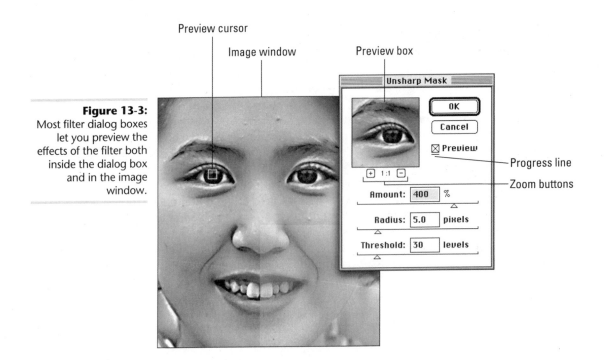

Preview cursor

Image window

Preview box

Figure 13-3:
Most filter dialog boxes let you preview the effects of the filter both inside the dialog box and in the image window.

Progress line

Zoom buttons

In addition to clicking on the zoom buttons, you can access the zoom tool inside the preview box by pressing Command-spacebar or Option-spacebar, depending on whether you want to zoom in or out.

Many dialog boxes also preview effects in the full image window. Just select the Preview check box to activate this function. While the effect is previewing, a blinking progress line appears under the check box. (You may also notice a blinking line under the Zoom Ratio numbers when the contents of the preview box are updating.) In Figure 13-3, for example, you can see that the lower right quadrant of the image still hasn't finished previewing, so the progress line strobes away. If you're working on a relatively poky computer, like a 68030 Mac or a 386 PC, you'll probably want to turn this check box off to speed up the pace at which the filter functions. Even on my Power Mac, I frequently become impatient waiting for the image window preview to complete. (Incidentally, the Preview check box does not affect the contents of the preview box; the latter always displays, whether you like it or not.)

 Use the Preview check box to compare the before and after effects of a filter in the image window. Turn it on to see the effect; turn it off to see the original image. You can also compare the image in the preview box by clicking on the box. Mouse down to see the old image; release to see the filtered image. It's like an electronic, high-priced, adult version of peek-a-boo. But not nearly as likely to induce giggles.

More tips, more tips: Even though a dialog box is on-screen and active, you can zoom and scroll the contents of the image window. Command-spacebar-click to zoom in, Option-spacebar-click to zoom out, and spacebar-drag to scroll.

And one more: When you press the Option key, the Cancel button changes to a Reset button. Option-click on this button to restore the settings that appeared when you first opened the dialog box. (These are not necessarily the factory default settings; they are the settings you last applied to an image.)

Only a few, very time-consuming filters can't preview in the image window. These include all filters under the Filter⇨Distort and Render submenus, all filters under the Filter⇨Pixelate submenu except Mosaic, and the Wind and Filter Factory filters. Six filters leave you completely blind, previewing neither in the image window nor inside the dialog box: Radial Blur, Displace, Color Halftone, Extrude, Tiles, and De-Interlace. Of course, single-shot filters — the ones that don't bring up dialog boxes — don't need previews because there aren't any settings to adjust.

Reapplying the last filter

 To reapply the last filter used in the current Photoshop session, choose the first command from the Filter menu or simply press Command-F. If you want to reapply the filter subject to different settings, Option-choose the first Filter command or press Command-Option-F to redisplay that filter's dialog box.

Both techniques work even if you undo the last application of a filter. However, if you cancel a filter while in progress, pressing Command-F or Command-Option-F applies the last uncanceled filter.

Float before filtering

In many cases, you apply filters to a selection or image at full intensity, meaning that you marquee an area using a selection tool, choose a filter command, enter whatever settings you deem appropriate if a dialog box appears, and sit back and watch the fireworks.

What's so "full intensity" about that? Sounds normal, right? Well, the fact is, you can dissipate the intensity of a filter by floating the selection and then mixing it with the original, underlying image by using the Opacity slider bar and overlay modes pop-up menu in the Layers palette.

For example, Figure 13-4 shows a series of applications of the Emboss filter (from the Filter⇨Stylize submenu). The original image appears in the upper left corner; the full-intensity effect of the filter appears in the lower right corner. To create the images in between, I floated the selection, applied the filter, and then changed the Opacity setting in the Layers palette to the value that appears in the figure.

An alternative method is to select the image, enter the quick mask mode (or a separate mask channel), and fill the area that you want to select with a percentage of black equal to the opposite of the Opacity value. An 80 percent black results in the 20 percent filtering effect, a 60 percent black results in the 40 percent effect, and so on. This technique works because — as you may recall from Chapter 9 — white in the quick mask mode equates to a full-intensity selection and 100 percent black equates to no selection. After filling the selection, you return to the marching ants mode and apply the filter.

Figure 13-4:
You can dissipate the effect of a filter by overlaying a translucent filtered image over the unfiltered original or by editing the selection in the quick mask mode.

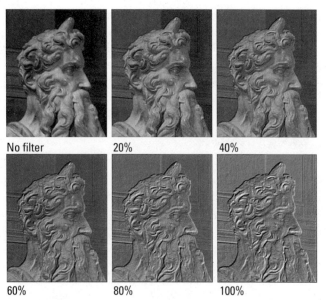

No filter   20%   40%

60%   80%   100%

Although floating is more straightforward and offers the added advantage of allowing you to see the results of Opacity settings and overlay modes on the fly, the quick mask method offers its own advantages. You can paint partial selections in the quick mask mode that are either exceedingly complex or impossible to duplicate in the marching ants mode. Figure 13-5 shows a row of selections as they appear in the quick mask mode followed by the result of applying the Emboss filter to each of these selections in the marching ants mode.

Figure 13-5:
After creating a selection in the quick mask mode (top row), I applied the Emboss filter to each selection in the marching ants mode (bottom row).

And certainly, there's nothing to prevent you from combining these two powerful options. You can achieve the best of both worlds by painting a selection outline in the quick mask mode, switching to the marching ants mode, floating the image, filtering it, and then experimenting with the Opacity and overlay mode settings. In fact, I personally never filter an image without first floating it, regardless of how I drew the selection outline.

Floating inside a border

Here's another reason to float before you filter: If your image has a border around it — like the ones shown in Figure 13-6 — and you don't want the border to be considered in the filtering operation, be sure to float the image before applying the filter. The reason is that most filters take neighboring pixels into consideration even if they are not selected. By contrast, when a selection floats, it has no neighboring pixels, and therefore the filter affects the selected pixels only.

Figure 13-6 shows the results of applying two filters discussed early on in this chapter — High Pass and Unsharp Mask — when the image is anchored in place and when it's floating. In all cases, the 3-pixel border was not selected. In the left examples, the High Pass filter leaves a black residue around the edge and the Unsharp Mark filter leaves a white residue. Both residues vanish when the filters are applied to floating selections, as seen on right.

Even if the area outside the selection is not a border per se — perhaps it's just a comparatively dark or light area that serves as a visual frame — floating comes in handy. You should always float the selection unless you specifically want edge pixels to be calculated by the filter.

Reverting a floating image

Okay, here's one more reason to float before you filter, and that's it. If you're not convinced after this argument, you must be the sort of hard-headed rascal that thinks, "If God meant for images to float, he would've given them little helicopter propellers, or hummingbird wings, or one of them darn fool devices. But he didn't, so they shouldn't." I mean, you sure like to keep your virtual feet on the ground, boy. *Fft, ptang.* (That's the sound of some chaw hitting a spittoon, by the way.)

Not floating   Floating

Figure 13-6:
The results of applying High Pass (top) and Unsharp Mask (bottom) to images surrounded by borders. In each case, only the image was selected; the border was not. You can see how floating the right examples prevented the borders from affecting the performance of the filters.

High pass

Unsharp mask

Floating protects the underlying image. You may have noticed that despite its many enhancements, Photoshop still offers only one Undo command, which reverses the last action performed. You also have a Revert command and various revert-to-snapshot options (as discussed in Chapter 11). But what if you don't want to save your image, nor do you want to bother with a snapshot? If you just want to experiment a little, floating is your solution. After applying 40 or 50 filtering effects to a floating image, you can undo all that automated abuse by simply pressing the Delete key.

By the way, every single argument I've made in favor of floating images also applies to floating's more permanent cousin, layering. Layers offer even more flexibility, in fact, because you can revisit them several times throughout the editing process without worrying about the image defloating. You can even conduct many experiments on a single image, each on a different layer, and then compare the results and select the one you like best.

Heightening Focus and Contrast

If you've experimented at all with Photoshop, you've no doubt had your way with many of the commands in the Filter⇨Sharpen submenu. By increasing the contrast between neighboring pixels, the sharpening filters enable you to compensate for image elements that were photographed or scanned slightly out of focus.

The Sharpen, Sharpen More, and Sharpen Edges commands are easy to use and immediate in their effect. However, you can achieve better results and widen your range of sharpening options if you learn how to use the Unsharp Mask and High Pass commands, which are discussed at length in the following pages.

Using the Unsharp Mask filter

The first thing you need to know about the Unsharp Mask filter is that it has a weird name. The filter has nothing to do with "unsharpening" — whatever that is — nor has it anything to do with Photoshop's masking capabilities. It's named after a traditional film compositing technique (which is also oddly named) that highlights the edges in an image by combining a blurred film negative with the original film positive.

That's all very well and good, but the fact is most Photoshop artists have never touched a stat camera (an expensive piece of machinery, roughly twice the size of a washing machine, used by image editors of the late Jurassic, pre-Photoshop epoch). Even folks like me who used to operate stat cameras professionally never had the time to delve into the world of unsharp masking. In addition — and much to the filter's credit — Unsharp Mask goes beyond traditional camera techniques.

To understand Unsharp Mask — or Photoshop's other sharpening filters, for that matter — you first need to understand some basic terminology. When you apply one of the sharpening filters, Photoshop increases the contrast between neighboring pixels. The effect is similar to what you see when you adjust a camera to bring a scene into sharper focus.

Two of Photoshop's sharpening filters, Sharpen and Sharpen More, affect whatever area of your image is selected. The Sharpen Edges filter, however, performs its sharpening operations only on the *edges* in the image — those areas that feature the highest amount of contrast.

Unsharp Mask gives you both sharpening options. It can sharpen only the edges in an image or it can sharpen any portion of an image according to your exact specifications, whether it finds an edge or not. It fulfills the exact same purposes as the Sharpen, Sharpen Edges, and Sharpen More commands, but it's much more versatile. Simply put, the Unsharp Mask tool is the only sharpening filter you'll ever need.

When you choose Filter⇨Sharpen⇨Unsharp Mask, Photoshop displays the Unsharp Mask dialog box, shown in Figure 13-7, which offers these options:

• **Amount:** Enter a value between 1 and 500 percent to specify the degree to which you want to sharpen the selected image. Higher values produce more pronounced effects.

Figure 13-7:
Despite any conclusions you may glean from its bizarre name, the Unsharp Mask filter sharpens images according to your specifications in this dialog box.

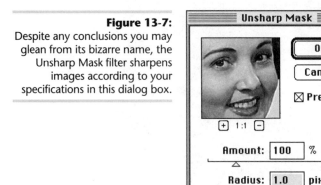

• **Radius:** This option enables you to distribute the effect of the filter by applying it over a range of 0.1 to 250.0 pixels at a time. Low values produce crisp images. High values produce softer, higher contrast effects.

• **Threshold:** Enter a value between 0 and 255 to control how Photoshop recognizes edges in an image. The value indicates the numerical difference between the brightness values of two neighboring pixels that must occur if Photoshop is to sharpen those pixels. A low value sharpens lots of pixels; a high value excludes most pixels from the running.

The preview options offered by the Unsharp Mask dialog box are absolutely essential visual aids that you're likely to find tremendously useful throughout your Photoshop career. Just the same, you'll be better prepared to experiment with the Amount, Radius, and Threshold options and less surprised by the results if you read the following sections, which explain these options in detail and demonstrate the effects of each.

Specifying the amount of sharpening

If Amount were the only Unsharp Mask option, no one would have any problems understanding this filter. If you want to sharpen an image ever so slightly, enter a low percentage value. Values between 25 and 50 percent are ideal for producing subtle effects. If you want to sharpen an image beyond the point of good taste, enter a value somewhere in the 300 to 500 percent range. And if you're looking for moderate sharpening, try out some value between 50 and 300 percent. Figure 13-8 shows the results of applying different Amount values while leaving the Radius and Threshold values at their default settings of 1.0 and 0 respectively.

Figure 13-8: The results of sharpening an image with the Unsharp Mask filter using eight different Amount values. The Radius and Threshold values used for all images were 1.0 and 0, respectively (the default settings).

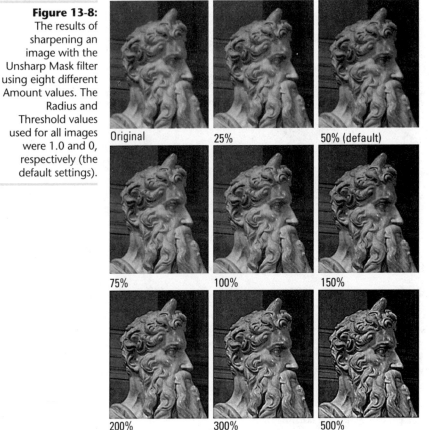

If you're not sure how much you want to sharpen an image, try out a small value, in the 25 to 50 percent range. Then reapply that setting repeatedly by pressing Command-F. As you can see in Figure 13-9, repeatedly applying the filter at a low setting produces a nearly identical result to applying the filter once at a higher setting. For example, you can achieve the effect shown in the middle image in the figure by applying the Unsharp Mask filter three times at 50 percent or once at 250 percent.

The benefit of using small values is that they allow you to experiment with sharpening incrementally. As the figure demonstrates, you can add sharpening bit by bit to increase the focus of an image. You can't, however, reduce sharpening incrementally if you apply too high a value; you must choose Edit⇨Undo and start again.

Figure 13-9: Repeatedly applying the Unsharp Mask filter at 50 percent (top row) is nearly equivalent on a pixel-by-pixel basis to applying the filter once at higher settings (bottom). The top row results were created using a constant Radius value of 1.0. In the second row, I lowered the Radius progressively from 1.0 (left) to 0.8 (middle) to 0.6 (right).

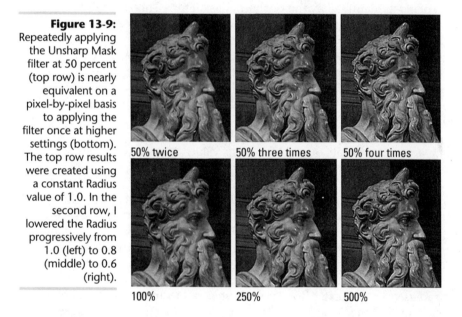

50% twice 50% three times 50% four times

100% 250% 500%

Just for fun, Color Plate 13-3 shows the results of applying the Unsharp Mask filter to each of the color channels in an RGB image independently. In each case, the Amount value was set to 300 percent, and the Radius and Threshold values were set to their defaults (1.0 and 0). To heighten the effect, I applied the filter twice to each channel. The top row shows the results of applying the filter to a single channel; in the second row, I applied the filter to two of the three channels (leaving only one channel unfiltered). You can see how the filter creates a crisp halo of color around the rose. Sharpening the red channel creates a red halo, sharpening the red and green channels together creates a yellow halo, and so on. Applying the filter to the red and green channels produced the most noticeable effects because these channels contain the lion's share of the image detail. The blue channel contained the least detail — as is typical — so sharpening it produced the least dramatic results.

If you're a little foggy on how to access individual color channels, read Chapter 5. Incidentally, you can achieve similar effects by sharpening the individual channels in a Lab or CMYK image.

Distributing the effect

Understanding the Amount value is a piece of cake. It's a little more difficult to wrap the old noodle around the Radius value.

Here's the scoop: For each and every pixel Photoshop decides to sharpen, it distributes the effect according to the value you specify in the Radius option box. It's as if you selected the range of pixels identified by the Unsharp Mask filter's Threshold option, applied the Select⇨Feather command to them, and then applied the Amount value.

In fact, the Radius values offered by the Unsharp Mask and Feather dialog boxes operate on the exact same principle. The result is that lower values concentrate the impact of the Unsharp Mask filter. Higher values distribute the impact and, in doing so, lighten the lightest pixels and darken the darkest pixels, almost as if the image had been photocopied too many times.

Figure 13-10 demonstrates the results of specific Radius values. In each case, the Amount and Threshold values remain constant at 100 percent and 0, respectively.

 Most softening effects in Photoshop — including feathering, softened brush shapes, and the radius of the Unsharp Mask filter — work according to a bell-shaped *Gaussian distribution curve*. The curve slopes gradually in the beginning, radically in the middle, and gradually at the end, thus softening the effect without altogether destroying its impact. The Unsharp Mask filter, however, conforms to the Gaussian curve only at Radius values of 2.0 and less. If you specify a radius greater than 2.0, the curve flattens out to accelerate the speed of the filter. The filter then destroys edges instead of working to retain edges as it does when the normal Gaussian curve is in effect. For this reason, I recommend that you use Radius values less than 2.0 to accomplish most of your sharpening effects.

Figure 13-10:
The results of applying eight different Radius values, ranging from precisely concentrated to overly generalized.

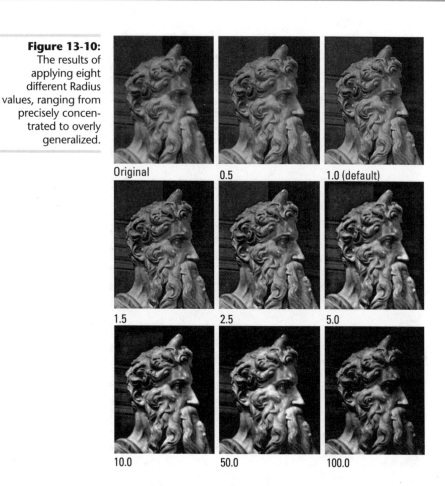

Original 0.5 1.0 (default)

1.5 2.5 5.0

10.0 50.0 100.0

Figure 13-11 shows the results of combining different Amount and Radius values. You can see that a large Amount value helps to offset the softening of a high Radius value. For example, when the Amount is set to 200 percent, as in the first row, the Radius value appears to mainly enhance contrast when raised from 0.5 to 2.0. However, when the Amount value is lowered to 50 percent, the higher Radius value does more to distribute the effect than boost contrast.

Figure 13-11:
The effects of combining different Amount (first value) and Radius (second value) settings. Relatively high Amount and Radius values bring out the deep curls in the hair, as you can see in the top middle image. The Threshold value for each image was set to 0, the default setting.

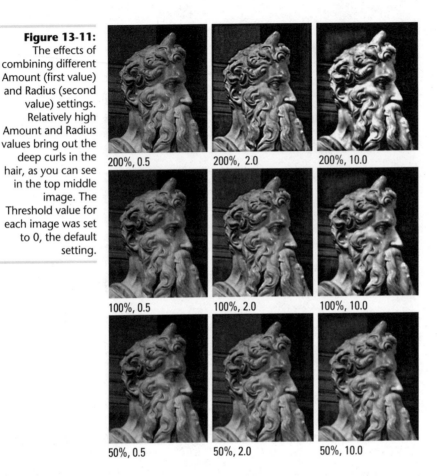

200%, 0.5   200%, 2.0   200%, 10.0

100%, 0.5   100%, 2.0   100%, 10.0

50%, 0.5   50%, 2.0   50%, 10.0

By the way, in case you're wondering how Moses got that huge bump on his head — from this angle the growth looks rather like a finger — it wasn't because someone whacked him one. Ostensibly, the Hebrew word for *shaft of light* and *horn* are one and the same. Naturally confused, Michelangelo opted for the latter interpretation. Great sculptor, that Michelangelo, but a poor translator of the world's languages.

For those few folks who are thinking, "By gum, I wonder what would happen if you applied an unusually high Radius value to each color channel independently," you have only to gaze upon the wondrous Color Plate 13-4. In this figure, I again applied the Unsharp Mask filter to each channel and each pair of channels in the RGB rose image independently. But I changed the Amount value to 100 percent, the Radius value to a relatively whopping 10.0 pixels, and left the Threshold at 0. To make the splash more apparent, I applied the filter twice to each image. The colors now bound out from the rose, bleeding into the gray background by as much as 10 pixels, the Radius value. Notice how the color fades away from the rose, just as if I had feathered it? Is this beginning to make sense? A high Radius value spreads the sharpening effect and, in doing so, allows colors to bleed. Because you normally apply the filter to all channels simultaneously, the colors bleed uniformly to create high-contrast effects.

Recognizing edges

By default, the Unsharp Mask filter sharpens every pixel in a selection. However, you can instruct the filter to sharpen only the edges in an image by raising the Threshold value from zero to some other number. The Threshold value represents the difference between two neighboring pixels — as measured in brightness levels — that must occur for Photoshop to recognize them as an edge.

Suppose that the brightness values of neighboring pixels A and B are 10 and 20. If you set the Threshold value to 5, Photoshop reads both pixels, notes that the difference between their brightness values is more than 5, and treats them as an edge. If you set the Threshold value to 20, however, Photoshop passes them by. A low Threshold value, therefore, causes the Unsharp Filter to affect a high number of pixels, and vice versa.

In the upper left image in Figure 13-12, the carved curls in the ravishing Moses hairdo stand out in stark contrast against the light gray of the poofier portions of the coiffure. I can sharpen the edges of the curls exclusively of other portions of the image by raising the Threshold value to 50 or even 30, as demonstrated in the second and third examples of the figure.

Figure 13-12:
The results of applying eight different Threshold values. High Threshold values limit the effect of the Unsharp Mask filter to high-contrast regions; low values apply the filter more evenly. To best show off the differences between each image, I set the Amount and Radius values to 500 percent and 0.5 respectively.

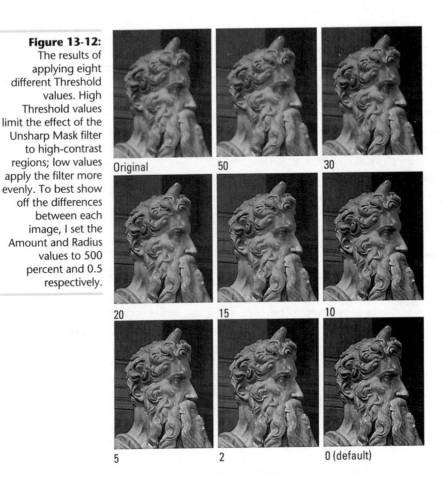

Using the preset sharpening filters

So how do the Sharpen, Sharpen Edges, and Sharpen More commands compare with the Unsharp Mask filter? First of all, none of the preset commands can distribute a sharpening effect, a function provided by the Unsharp Mask filter's Radius option. Secondly, only the Sharpen Edges command can recognize high-contrast areas in an image. And third, all three commands are set in stone — you can't adjust their effects in any way. Figure 13-13 shows the effect of each preset command and the nearly equivalent effect created with the Unsharp Mask filter.

Figure 13-13:
The effects of the three preset sharpening filters (top row) compared with their Unsharp Mask equivalents (bottom row). Unsharp Mask values are listed in the following order: Amount, Radius, Threshold.

Sharpen   Sharpen Edges   Sharpen More

100%, 0.5, 0   100%, 0.5, 5   300%, 0.5, 0

Using the High Pass filter

The High Pass filter falls more or less in the same camp as the sharpening filters but is not located under the Filter⇨Sharpen submenu. This frequently overlooked gem enables you to isolate high-contrast image areas from their low-contrast counterparts.

When you choose Filter⇨Other⇨High Pass, Photoshop offers a single option: the familiar Radius value, which can vary from 0.1 to 250.0. As demonstrated in Figure 13-14, high Radius values distinguish areas of high and low contrast only slightly. Low values change all high-contrast areas to dark gray and low-contrast areas to a slightly lighter gray. A value of 0.1, not shown in the figure, changes all pixels in an image to a single gray value and is therefore useless.

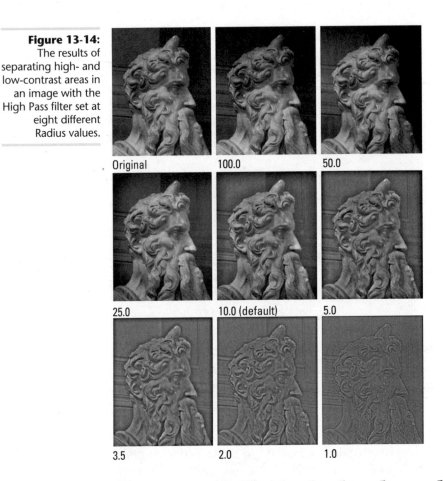

Figure 13-14:
The results of separating high- and low-contrast areas in an image with the High Pass filter set at eight different Radius values.

Original · 100.0 · 50.0

25.0 · 10.0 (default) · 5.0

3.5 · 2.0 · 1.0

Applying High Pass to individual color channels

In my continuing series of color plates devoted to taking the simple beauty of a rose and abusing it but good, Color Plate 13-5 shows the results of applying the High Pass filter set to a Radius value of 10.0 to the various color channels. This application is actually a pretty interesting use for this filter. When applied to all channels at once, High Pass has an irritating habit of robbing the image of color in the low-contrast areas, just where the color is needed most. But when applied to a single channel, there's no color to steal. In fact, the filter adds color. For example, because there is almost no contrast in the black shadow of the rose, High Pass elevates the black to gray in each of the affected color channels. The gray in the red channel appears red, the gray in the red channel mixed with the gray in the green channel appears yellow, and so on. As a result, the filter imbues each image with a chalky glow.

I enhanced the High Pass effect slightly in Color Plate 13-5 by increasing the contrast of each affected color channel using the Levels command. Using the three Input option boxes at the top of the Levels dialog box, I changed the first value to 65 and the third value to 190, thereby compressing the color space equally on both the black and white sides. Had I not done this, the images would appear a little more washed out. (Not a lot, but I figure that you deserve the best color I can deliver.) For more information on the Levels command, read Chapter 16.

Combining High Pass with Threshold

The High Pass filter is especially useful as a precursor to choosing Image⇨Map⇨ Threshold (Command-T), which converts all pixels in an image to black and white. As illustrated in Figure 13-15, the Threshold command produces entirely different effects on images before and after you alter them with the High Pass filter. Applying the High Pass filter with a Radius value of 1.0 and then issuing the Threshold command converts your image into a line drawing. The effect is similar to choosing Filter⇨Stylize⇨Find Edges, but the lines are crisper and, obviously, black and white. (An image filtered with the Find Edges command remains in color.)

Figure 13-15:
The original image and two counterparts edited with the High Pass command (top row) followed by the same images subject to the Threshold command set to 124 (bottom).

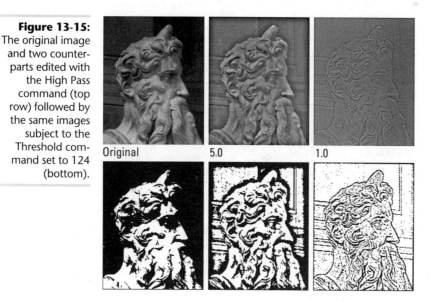

Original   5.0   1.0

Why change your image to a bunch of slightly different gray values and then apply Image⇨Map⇨Threshold? Why, to select portions of an image using a mask channel, of course. Because the High Pass filter sees an image in terms of contrast levels, which is one of the ways your eyes perceive images in real life, it can be a useful first step in selecting an image element that is clearly visually unique but has proved difficult to isolate.

I introduced the idea of employing the Threshold command as a selection tool in the "Deriving selections from images" section of Chapter 9. The following steps explain how you can use the High Pass filter to help distinguish an image element from a busy background. The image in the top half of Figure 13-16 is used as an example.

STEPS: **Selecting an Image Element Set Against a Busy Background**

Step 1. Compare the red, green, and blue channels in your image to determine which one features the most contrast. At first, the channels may appear relatively similar, but with a little patience and effort, you can locate edge detail that — however slight — distinguishes the foreground image from its background.

Step 2. After you decide on a channel — when in doubt, go with green — drag the channel name in the Channels palette onto the new channel icon at the bottom of the palette, thus duplicating the image to a separate mask channel.

Step 3. Choose Filter⇨Other⇨High Pass and enter the desired Radius value. To create the image shown in the bottom half of Figure 13-16, I entered a Radius value of 3.0, which isolates most of the high-contrast portions of the image while retaining some thick outlines of solid color that will prove useful during the editing process. If your image is more highly focused than mine, enter a lower value. If less focused, raise the value. Don't go any lower than 1.0 or any higher than 6.0 or 7.0. (Resolution, incidentally, isn't a consideration.) Press Return to filter the image.

Step 4. Choose Image⇨Map⇨Threshold (Command-T). I found the best balance of black and white pixels by setting the slider bar in the Threshold dialog box to 124. The resulting image appears in the top half of Figure 13-17.

Figure 13-16:
A busy image before (top) and after (bottom) applying the High Pass filter with a Radius value of 3.0.

Step 5.   You should now be able to eliminate the background elements fairly easily by dragging with the eraser tool. Because you're editing black and white pixels, it's best to set the eraser to its Pencil or Block mode, either of which offers hard edges. (Soft-edged cursors will introduce grays.) Next, use the pencil tool to close the gaps in the outline of the foreground elements and click with the paint bucket tool (set to a Tolerance of 0 and with Anti-aliased off) to fill the elements with black, as demonstrated in the second example of Figure 13-17. You'll probably have to fill in some remaining gaps by painting with the pencil tool with a large brush shape.

Figure 13-17:
The result of applying the Threshold command set to 124 (top) and editing the black and white image with the eraser, pencil, and paint bucket tools (bottom).

Step 6.   To apply the mask to the image, simply Option-click on the mask channel in the Channels palette to convert the mask to a selection outline and press Command-0 to return to your image (Command-1 if you're working in grayscale). If you prefer to select the foreground elements, choose Select⇨Inverse.

Blurring an Image

The commands under the Filter⇨Blur submenu produce the opposite effects of their counterparts under the Filter⇨Sharpen submenu, or, for that matter, the High Pass command. Rather than enhancing the amount of contrast between neighboring pixels, the Blur filters diminish contrast to create softening effects.

Gaussian blur

The preeminent Blur filter, Gaussian Blur, blends a specified number of pixels incrementally, following the bell-shaped Gaussian distribution curve I touched on earlier. When you choose Filter⇨Blur⇨Gaussian Blur, Photoshop produces a single Radius option box, in which you can enter any value from 0.1 to 250.0. (Beginning to sound familiar?) As demonstrated in Figure 13-18, Radius values of 1.0 and smaller blur an image slightly; moderate values, between 1.0 and 5.0, turn an image into a rude approximation of life without my glasses on; and higher values blur the image beyond recognition.

Figure 13-18:
The results of blurring an image with the Gaussian Blur filter using eight different Radius values, ranging from slightly out of focus to Bad Day at the Ophthalmologist's Office.

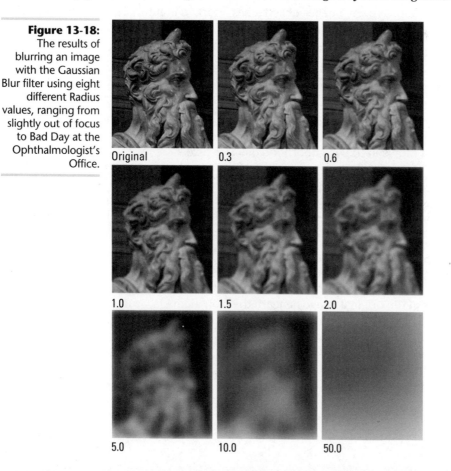

Original   0.3   0.6

1.0   1.5   2.0

5.0   10.0   50.0

Applying the Gaussian Blur filter to a selection in the quick mask mode is almost the exact equivalent of feathering the selection in the marching ants mode. The only difference is that the Radius option in the Gaussian Blur dialog box is accurate to $1/10$ pixel, while its counterpart in the Feather dialog box accepts whole numbers only. To see this tip in action, read the "Softening a selection outline" section later in this chapter.

Moderate to high Radius values can be especially useful for creating that hugely amusing "Star Trek" Iridescent Female effect. This is the old "Star Trek," of course. Captain Kirk meets some bewitching ambassador or scientist who has just beamed on board. He takes her hand in sincere welcome as he gives out with a lecherous grin and explains how truly honored he is to have such a renowned guest in his transporter room, and so charming to boot. Then we see it — the close-up of the fetching actress shrouded in a kind of gleaming halo that prevents us from discerning if her lips are chapped or perhaps she's hiding an old acne scar, because some cockeyed cinematographer smeared Vaseline all over the camera lens. I mean, what *wouldn't* you give to be able to recreate this effect in Photoshop?

Unfortunately, I don't have any images of actresses adorned in futuristic go-go boots, so Moses will have to do in a pinch. The following steps explain how to make Moses glow as demonstrated in Figure 13-19.

STEPS: The Wondrous Iridescent Effect

Step 1. Choose Select⇨All (Command-A) to select the entire image. If you only want to apply the effect to a portion of the image, be sure to feather the selection with a radius in the neighborhood of 5 to 8 pixels.

Step 2. Choose Select⇨Float (Command-J) to clone the image in place.

Step 3. Choose Filter⇨Blur⇨Gaussian Blur, enter some unusually large value into the Radius option box — say, 5.0 — and press Return. This blurs the cloned image only; the original image remains unchanged.

Step 4. Press M to make sure that a selection tool is active. Then press the 7 key to change the Opacity slider bar in the Layers palette to 70 percent, making the blurred image slightly translucent. This setting enables you to see the hard edges of the original image beneath the cloned image, as demonstrated in the first example of Figure 13-19.

Step 5. You can achieve additional effects by selecting options from the overlay modes pop-up menu on the left side of the Layers palette. For example, I created the image in the upper right corner of Figure 13-19 by selecting the Screen option, which combines colors in the original and floating images to create a lightening effect. I created the two bottom examples in the figure by choosing the Lighten and Darken options.

Figure 13-19:
After floating the selection, blurring it, and changing the Opacity slider bar to 70 percent, I applied overlay modes to alter the image further. Clockwise from upper left, the overlay modes used were Normal, Screen, Darken, and Lighten.

Color Plate 13-6 shows an image that's more likely to interest Captain Kirk. It shows a young agrarian woman subject to most of the same settings I applied earlier to Moses. Again, I floated the image and applied the Gaussian Blur filter with a Radius of 5.0. The upper left image shows the Normal overlay mode, but the upper right image shows the Luminosity mode. In this case, the Screen mode resulted in a washed-out effect, whereas Luminosity yielded an image with crisp color detail and fuzzy brightness values. As a result, there are some interesting places where the colors leap off her checkered dress. As in Figure 13-19, the bottom two images show the effects of the Lighten and Darken modes.

You know, though, as I look at this woman, I'm beginning to have my doubts about her and Captain Kirk. I mean, she has Scotty written all over her.

The preset blurring filters

Neither of the two preset commands in the Filter⇨Blur submenu, Blur and Blur More, can distribute its blurring effect over a bell-shaped Gaussian curve. For that reason, these two commands are less functional than the Gaussian Blur filter. However, just so you know where they stand in the grand Photoshop focusing scheme, Figure 13-20 shows the effect of each preset command and the nearly equivalent effect created with the Gaussian Blur filter.

Figure 13-20:
The effects of the two preset blurring filters (top row) compared with their Gaussian Blur equivalents (bottom row), which are labeled according to Radius values.

Blur   Blur More

0.3   0.7

Antialiasing an image

If you have a particularly jagged image, such as a black-and-white MacPaint file or a 256-color GIF file, there's a better way to soften the rough edges than applying the Gaussian Blur filter. The best solution is to antialias the image. How? After all, Photoshop doesn't offer an Antialias filter. Well, think about it. Back in Chapter 8, I described how Photoshop antialiases a brushstroke or selection outline at twice its normal size and then reduces it by 50 percent and applies bicubic interpolation. You can do the same thing with an image.

First, go into the General Preferences dialog box (Command-K) and make sure that Bicubic is selected from the Interpolation pop-up menu. (You can also experiment with Bilinear for a slightly different effect, but don't use Nearest Neighbor.) Next, choose Image⇔Image Size and enlarge the image to 200 percent of its present size. Finally, turn right around and choose Image⇔Image Size again, but this time shrink the image by 50 percent.

The top left example in Figure 13-21 shows a jagged image subject to this effect. I used Image⇔Map⇔Posterize to reduce Moses to four colors. It's ugly, but it's not unlike the kind of images you may encounter, particularly if you have access to an aging image library. To the right is the same image subject to Gaussian Blur with a very low Radius value of 0.5. Rather than appearing softened, the result is just plain fuzzy.

However, if I instead enlarge and reduce the image with the Image Size command, I achieve a true softening effect, as shown in the lower left example in the figure, commensurate with Photoshop's antialiasing options. Even after enlarging and reducing the image four times in a row — as in the bottom right example — I don't make the image blurry, I simply make it softer.

Directional blurring

In addition to its everyday blurring functions, Photoshop provides two *directional blurring* filters, Motion Blur and Radial Blur. Instead of blurring pixels in feathered clusters like the Gaussian Blur filter, the Motion Blur filter blurs pixels in straight lines over a specified distance. The Radial Blur filter blurs pixels in varying degrees depending on their distance from the center of the blur. The following pages explain both of these filters in detail.

Figure 13-21:
A particularly jagged image (top left) followed by the image blurred using a filter (top right). By enlarging and reducing the image one or more times (bottom left and right), I can soften the pixels without making them appear blurry. The enlarged details show each operation's effect on the individual pixels.

Jagged original   Gaussian Blur, 0.5

Antialiased   Antialiased x 4

Motion blurring

The Motion Blur filter makes an image appear as if either the image or camera was moving when you shot the photo. When you choose Filter⇨Blur⇨Motion Blur, Photoshop displays the dialog box shown in Figure 13-22. You enter the angle of move-ment into the Angle option box. Alternatively, you can indicate the angle by dragging the straight line inside the circle on the right side of the dialog box, as shown in the figure. (You'll notice that the arrow cursor actually appears outside the circle. Once you begin dragging on the line, you can move the cursor anywhere you want and still affect the angle.)

Figure 13-22:
Drag the line inside the circle to change the angle of the blur.

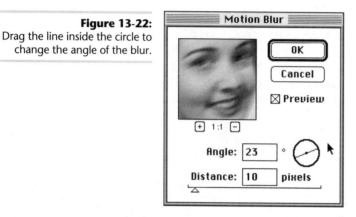

You then enter the distance of the movement in the Distance option box. Photoshop permits any value between 1 and 999 pixels. The filter distributes the effect of the blur over the course of the Distance value, as illustrated by the examples in Figure 13-23.

Figure 13-23:
A single black rectangle followed by five different applications of the Motion Blur filter. Only the Distance value varied, as labeled. A 0-degree Angle value was used in all five examples.

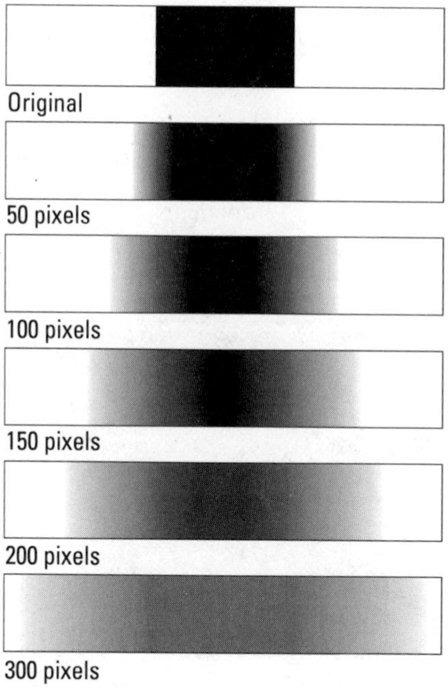

Original

50 pixels

100 pixels

150 pixels

200 pixels

300 pixels

Mathematically speaking, Motion Blur is one of Photoshop's simpler filters. Rather than distributing the effect over a Gaussian curve — which one might argue would produce a more believable effect — Photoshop creates a simple linear distribution, peaking in the center and fading at either end. It's as if the program took the value you specified in the Distance option, created that many clones of the image, offset half the clones in one direction and half the clones in the other — all spaced 1 pixel apart — and then varied the opacity of each.

Using the Wind filter

The problem with the Motion Blur filter is that it blurs pixels in two directions. If you want to distribute pixels in one absolute direction or the other, try out the Wind filter, which you can use either on its own or in tandem with Motion Blur.

When you choose Filter⇨Stylize⇨Wind, Photoshop displays the Wind dialog box shown in Figure 13-24. You can select from three methods and two directions to distribute the selected pixels. Figure 13-25 compares the effect of the Motion Blur filter to each of the three methods offered by the Wind filter. Notice that the Wind filter does not blur pixels. Rather, it evaluates a selection in 1-pixel-tall horizontal strips and offsets the strips randomly inside the image.

Figure 13-24:
Use the Wind filter to randomly distribute a selection in 1-pixel horizontal strips in one of two directions.

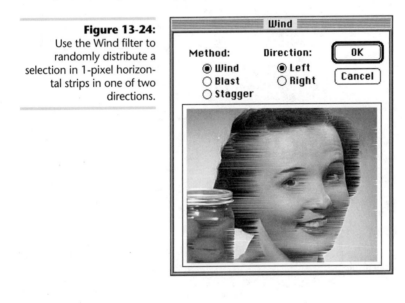

Figure 13-25:
The difference between the effects of the Motion Blur filter (top left) and the Wind filter. Clockwise from upper right, I applied the Wind filter using the Method options Wind, Blast, and Stagger.

To get the best results, try combining the Motion Blur and Wind filters with a translucent selection. For example, to create Figure 13-26, I floated the entire image and applied the Wind command twice, first selecting the Stagger option and then selecting Blast. Next, I applied the Motion Blur command with a 0-degree angle and a Distance value of 30. I then set the Opacity slider bar to 50 percent and selected Lighten from the brush modes pop-up menu. Unlike the example in Figure 13-25, the motion lines in the image in Figure 13-26 no longer completely obliterate the original image.

Figure 13-26:
The result of
combining the Wind
and Motion Blur
filters with a
translucent selection.

Directional smudging

If you have problems creating an acceptable motion effect because the results of the filters are either too random or too generalized, you can create very precise motion lines using the smudge tool inside a translucent selection, as demonstrated in Figure 13-27. The following steps explain how to achieve this effect. The process has nothing to do with filters — I just thought I'd throw them in as an alternative to the Motion Blur and Wind commands.

STEPS: **Painting Motion Lines with the Smudge Tool**

Step 1. Begin by using the rectangular marquee tool to select the area in which you want the motion lines to appear. Be sure to select all of the background area that will contain the motion lines as well as at least part of the foreground element that's responsible for the motion lines. Don't worry if you select too much of the image; you remedy that problem in the next step.

Step 2.   Press Q to enter the quick mask mode. Use the paintbrush tool and a soft
brush shape to trace along the edge of the foreground element, giving it a
feathered selection outline. Then go ahead and fill in the rest of the foreground element so that only the background remains selected, as demonstrated in the top image in Figure 13-27.

Figure 13-27:
I edited and
softened the
selection outline so
that it followed the
contours of the
foreground image
(top). Then I floated
the selection,
changed its Opacity
setting to 70
percent, and
dragged inside the
selection in a
consistent direction
with the smudge
tool (bottom).

Step 3.   Press Q again to return to the marching ants mode. Then clone the selection
by choosing Select⇨Float (Command-J).

Step 4. Select the marquee tool or some other selection tool and press 7 to change the opacity of the floating selection to 70 percent.

Step 5. Create a new, flat, vertical brush shape. You can specify any diameter with which you're comfortable. Enter 100 percent for the Hardness value, 1 percent for Spacing, and 0 percent for Roundness. Angle the brush perpendicularly to the prospective motion lines. When creating the image in Figure 13-27, I wanted to paint horizontal lines, so I made my brush vertical by entering an Angle value of 90 degrees.

Step 6. Select the smudge tool and set the Pressure slider bar in the Smudge Tool Options panel to 95 percent.

Step 7. Apply the smudge tool repeatedly inside the floating selection. Be sure to drag in a consistent direction. In my case, I dragged from right to left, pressing the Shift key to constrain the drag so that it was perfectly horizontal. Drag as many times as you deem necessary. The result of my efforts appears in the bottom example in Figure 13-27.

Floating and mixing 175 clones

A few months after the first edition of this book came out, one reader asked whether there was any way to automate this omnidirectional blurring technique so that you didn't have to use the smudge tool. At the time, I considered the question for a few fractions of a second and dutifully answered, "Nope." No way such a method existed, it was flat out impossible, forget it. Needless to say, I was wrong. In fact, the next set of steps documents exactly such a process. Now, I'm not sure that I would call these steps easier — they involve the layering and mixing of no fewer than 175 clones (no joke) — but if you simply don't like the idea of scrubbing on an image with the smudge tool, you might want to give this method a try. As Figure 13-28 shows, the steps offer the added advantage of producing extremely accurate, flexible, and believable results.

STEPS: **Creating a Motion Effect by Cloning a Translucent Selection**

Step 1. Create 175 clones.

Step 2. Ha ha, just joking. I only threw in that step to freak you out. What I really want you to do first is select your foreground image. You should try to follow the lines — use the quick mask mode if you want — but you don't have to be super precise.

Step 3. Choose Select⇨Feather and enter a Radius value equal to about $1/20$ the resolution of your image. Actually, the resolution of Figure 13-28 is 180 ppi, and I entered a value of 6 — $1/30$ the resolution — so I guess you can be pretty free and easy with your values. Just soften it so that you don't have any hard edges. That's all we're looking for here.

Step 4. Float the image and send it to its own layer. (Command-J to float, display the Layers palette, and Option-double-click on the Floating Selection item in the scrolling list to convert the selection to a layer.) This way, you can blur the background image as much as you want and keep the foreground image in its original, pristine form.

Step 5. Oops, your selection outline is gone. (In Chapter 8, I said that it was no biggie that you lose the selection when creating a layer. But frankly, it's beginning to irritate me now.) To regain the darn thing and apply it to the Background layer, press Command-Option-T and click on the Background item in the Layers palette.

Step 6. Press Command-J to float the selected area of the Background layer. You'll use this single selection — and its 175 clones — to create the entire directional blur.

Step 7. Press the arrow key that corresponds to the direction in which you want the blur to occur. To create the images in Figure 13-28, for example, I pressed the left arrow key because the blur fades off toward the left.

(Actually, you could have skipped Step 6 by pressing Option-arrow key, which would have cloned and floated the image simultaneously. I only wrote it out this way so that I could explain things a little more thoroughly.)

Step 8. Choose the Soft Light option from the overlay modes pop-up menu on the left side of the Layers palette. Assuming that a selection tool is active, press 4 to change the Opacity setting to 40 percent.

Step 9. Press Option-arrow key (the same arrow key you pressed last time) 10 times in a row. You don't have to wait for Photoshop to catch up with you. Just press and hold Option and wail on that arrow key. Then sit back and watch Photoshop sweat. The result is a 10-pixel trail of translucent image.

Step 10. Press 3 to lower the Opacity value to 30 percent. Then press and hold Option and whack the arrow key 15 times.

Step 11. Press 2 to change the Opacity to 20 percent. Then Option-arrow key 20 times. Notice how the number of arrow-key whacks keeps getting larger? This results in a tapering effect, consistent with real movement.

Figure 13-28:
After mixing the original image on Layer 1 with the underlying blur pattern using the Hard Light overlay mode (top), I cloned the layer and mixed the clone with the rest of the image using the Normal overlay mode and a 60 percent Opacity setting (bottom).

Step 12. Press 1 for 10 percent opacity. Press and hold Option and smack the arrow key 30 times. Bad arrow key, bad!

Step 13. Change the Opacity slider to 5 percent. I'm afraid you'll have to do this manually; there's no keyboard equivalent. Then Option-arrow key 40 times. Oh, and by the way, I'll need you to sign this waiver. It says that you won't sue me for any repetitive stress injury caused by these steps.

Step 14. Tired of abusing your arrow key? I don't blame you. But if you want to do things right, you'll change the Opacity slider to 2 percent and Option-arrow key a whopping 60 times.

Step 15. That's 175 clones. You can stop now. I just hope that I haven't started any compulsive arrow-key whackers down a path they'll later regret. In any case, the drudgery is over. Now it's time to mix the independent layer that you created in Step 4 with the underlying blur. To do this, click on the layer name in the Layers palette — probably *Layer 1* — and choose the Hard Light option from the overlay modes pop-up menu. You get the effect shown in the top example of Figure 13-28.

Step 16. Clone the layer by dragging the layer name onto the new layer icon at the bottom of the Layers palette. A new layer called *Layer 1 Copy* appears above Layer 1. Photoshop automatically makes this the active layer.

Step 17. To create the effect shown in the second example of Figure 13-28, choose Normal from the overlay modes pop-up menu and change the Opacity setting to 60 percent.

If I ever see that reader again, he'll probably explain, "Uh, perhaps you and I don't share the same interpretation of the word *automated*. Pounding on the arrow key 175 times doesn't strike me as any particular form of automation." True, true, there's a lot of grunt work involved. But just think of all the options you have. There's nothing that says you have to create 175 clones, for example. You could create 40 clones to get a shorter blur, or 300 clones to get a longer one. You could use a different overlay mode. In Step 8, experiment with the Lighten overlay mode or even Overlay. You can also try out different overlay modes and Opacity settings in Steps 15 through 17, and you can clone and mix Layer 1 as many times as you like. Though monotonous, this technique is surprisingly versatile. (If you need to bone up on your key-whacking skills, just borrow your kid's Sega. One thing you can say for video games: They give you tendons of steel.)

Radial blurring

Choosing Filter⇨Blur⇨Radial Blur displays the Radial Blur dialog box shown in Figure 13-29. The dialog box offers two Blur Method options: Spin and Zoom.

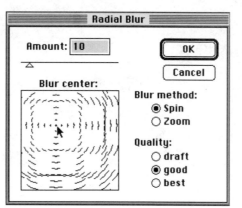

Figure 13-29: Drag inside the Blur Center grid to change the point about which the Radial Blur filter spins or zooms the image.

If you select Spin, the image appears to be rotating about a central point. You specify that point by dragging in the grid inside the Blur Center box (as demonstrated in the figure). If you select Zoom, the image appears to rush away from you, as if you were zooming the camera while shooting the photograph. Again, you specify the central point of the Zoom by dragging in the Blur Center box. Figures 13-30 and 13-31 feature examples of both settings.

After selecting a Blur Method option, you can enter any value between 1 and 100 in the Amount option box to specify the maximum distance over which the filter blurs pixels. (You can enter a value of 0, but doing so merely causes the filter to waste time without producing an effect.) Pixels farthest away from the center point move the most; pixels close to the center point barely move at all. Keep in mind that large values take more time to apply than small values. The Radial Blur filter, incidentally, qualifies as one of Photoshop's most time-consuming operations.

Select a Quality option to specify your favorite time/quality compromise. The Good and Best Quality options ensure smooth results by respectively applying bilinear and bicubic interpolation (as explained in the "General environmental preferences" section of Chapter 2). However, they also prolong the amount of time the filter spends calculating pixels in your image.

The Draft option *diffuses* an image, which leaves a trail of loose and randomized pixels but takes less time to complete. I used the Draft setting to create the left images in Figures 13-30 and 13-31; I selected the Best option to create the images on the right.

Figure 13-30: Two versions of the Radial Blur filter set to Spin, using the Draft option (left) and Best option (right). In both cases, I specified Amount values of 5 pixels. Each effect is centered about Moses's eye.

Figure 13-31:
Two versions of Radial Blur set to Zoom, using the Draft (left) and Best (right) options. I entered an Amount value of 20 because Zoom produces less-pronounced blurs than Spin. Again, the effects are centered about the eyes.

Blurring a background

One of the best ways to combine commands from the Filter⇨Sharpen and Filter⇨Blur submenus is to differentiate foreground elements from their backgrounds. The foreground elements get the sharpening, the background gets the blur.

For example, consider the image in Figure 13-32. On its own, it's not what I would call an inspirational image — just your standard everyday lady talking on the phone surrounded by your standard everyday urban landscape. Sure, the photo was shot in Japan, so it might stir up that world travel feeling in those of us who go in for that kind of thing. But I wouldn't call it exciting or provocative. In fact, it's a real snoozer.

Figure 13-32:
This photo is a yawner, but it has potential that can be drawn to the surface using sharpening and blurring filters.

The image does have one thing going for it, however. It features a distinct pair of foreground elements — the woman and the telephone — set against a clearly independent background, which includes everything else. This composition means that I can differentiate the two using sharpening and blurring effects.

To create the image in Figure 13-33, I selected the foreground elements and applied the Unsharp Mask filter. I used an Amount value of 75 percent, a Radius of 0.5, and a Threshold of 3. Then, just for laughs, I chose Select⇨Inverse and applied the Wind filter, selecting the Blast and Right radio buttons. Finally, I applied the Motion Blur filter, entering a Distance value of 20 pixels and a 0-degree angle.

Figure 13-33: The world swirls around this woman after liberal applications of the Wind and Motion Blur filters. Yet she remains calm and collected, thanks to the use of Unsharp Mask.

The Wind and Motion Blur filters produce the effect of moving the camera from right to left. By applying the Unsharp Mask filter, I kept the camera focused on the foreground elements throughout the move. This effect is extremely difficult to pull off in real life, but it's a simple matter in Photoshop.

Actually, I saw this technique applied once with great success to a photo of a baseball player preparing to bat in a big stadium. The crowds were swirling around him. But he looked cool, cocky, and above all, completely stationary. Sadly, I didn't have any baseball photos lying around, so I picked the next best thing, a woman on the phone. I mean, hey, maybe her world's falling apart, you know. Maybe she's on the phone with the mob, and they're telling her that they've kidnapped her youngest child. She feels the city spinning around her, closing in. Well, she looks a little calm for that, huh? Okay, maybe she's trying to get her watch repaired, and the store's about to close. Or maybe she's trying to order a pizza, but the clerk is being kind of surly, or at least unhelpful. Use your imagination.

Figure 13-34 shows a different take on the same scene. Again, I sharpened the foreground elements. But this time, instead of applying the Wind and Motion Blur filters to the background, I chose Filter⇨Blur⇨Radial Blur. I selected the Zoom option and raised the Amount value to 50. I also selected Draft from the Quality settings — not to save time, but to give the background a grainy appearance.

This image imitates the appearance of zooming the camera to a lower magnification while moving it forward, thus maintaining a constant focal distance between camera and foreground elements. You may remember that Hitchcock used this effect to make the background appear as if it were moving independently of the acrophobic Jimmy Stewart in *Vertigo*. The effect looks a little different when applied to a still photo, but it nevertheless lends a dynamic quality to the image.

Figure 13-34:
You can use the Radial Blur filter to zoom out from the background while retaining a constant focal distance between viewer and foreground elements.

Softening a selection outline

In Figures 13-33 and 13-34, the blurring filters had no effect on the foreground elements because those elements were not selected when the filters were applied. But rather than having the blurring start at the exact boundaries between the foreground and background elements, which would produce the highly unrealistic effect of drawing colors from the foreground elements into the background, the blurring becomes more pronounced a few pixels away from the foreground elements. This is because the foreground is protected by a feathered buffer zone.

If I had simply applied Select⇨Feather to my original selection boundary, displayed in progress back in Figure 13-17, the command would have feathered the selection in both directions — that is, inward and outward. In that case, the blurring would slightly affect the edges of the foreground elements, again producing an unrealistic effect. So instead, I edited the selection outline in the quick mask mode using two filters: Gaussian Blur, which I discussed earlier in this chapter; and Minimum, which you learn about in the next section.

Minimum and Maximum

The Minimum filter enhances the dark portions of an image, spreading them outward into other pixels. Its opposite, the Maximum filter, enhances the light portions of an image. In traditional stat photography, these techniques are known as *spread* and *choke*, respectively.

When you are working in the quick mask mode or an independent mask channel, applying the Minimum filter has the effect of incrementally increasing the size of black areas, which deselects pixels evenly around the edges of a selection. The Radius value that you enter into the Minimum dialog box tells Photoshop how many edge pixels to deselect. Just the opposite, the Maximum filter incrementally increases the size of white areas, which adds pixels evenly around the edges of a selection.

Feathering outward from a selection outline

The following steps describe how to use the Minimum and Gaussian Blur filters to feather an existing selection outline outward only. These steps start where "STEPS: Selecting an Image Element Against a Busy Background," earlier in this chapter, left off.

STEPS: Adding a Soft Edge in the Quick Mask Mode

Step 1.   Start with a selection outline that exactly follows the boundaries of one or more foreground elements. Then press Q to switch to the quick mask mode. In Figure 13-35, the background is selected and the foreground is deselected.

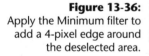

Figure 13-35:
Begin in the quick mask mode with a selection that clearly distinguishes foreground and background elements.

Step 2.   Choose Filter➪Other➪Minimum. Enter a Radius value of 4 to push back the boundaries of the selection outline 4 pixels and then press Return. (If you prefer to add 4 pixels to the selection outline, choose Filter➪Other➪ Maximum.) The result appears in Figure 13-36.

Figure 13-36:
Apply the Minimum filter to add a 4-pixel edge around the deselected area.

Step 3. Choose Filter⇨Blur⇨Gaussian Blur and enter 3.9 to soften nearly all of the edge you added to your selection outline. The unaffected $^1/_{10}$ pixel serves as a tiny insurance policy, so that any effect you apply later doesn't harm the foreground elements. The Gaussian Blur filter feathers the selection outline, as shown in Figure 13-37.

Figure 13-37:
Use the Gaussian Blur filter to soften the 4-pixel edge, thus feathering the selection outline.

Step 4. Switch back to the marching ants mode (by pressing Q again) and apply your effect. In Figure 13-38, I deleted the selected area to demonstrate how the foreground elements remain entirely protected, with a feathered buffer zone to spare.

Figure 13-38:
I deleted the selected background in the marching ants mode. The foreground elements remain intact and are surrounded by a soft halo of residual image data.

Antialiasing a selection outline

Ah, yes, but what if you want a more subtle effect? A jagged selection is nearly always too hard, but a feathered selection is frequently too soft. You know what Goldilocks would say, don't you? "Antialiasing is just right."

If you read the "Antialiasing an image" section earlier in this chapter, you may be tempted to enlarge the mask to twice its normal size and then reduce it to 50 percent. The problem is, this would affect the image as well as the mask, and you don't want that. Luckily, there's a better way that involves the Gaussian Blur filter and the Levels command.

STEPS:	**Antialiasing a Selection Outline in the Quick Mask Mode**

Step 1. Starting with a selection outline that exactly follows the boundaries of the foreground image, press Q to switch to the quick mask mode. Figure 13-39 shows how the mask looks when the image itself is hidden (which you accomplish by clicking on the eyeball icon in front of the composite view name in the Channels palette).

Step 2. Choose Filter⇨Blur⇨Gaussian Blur and enter a Radius value of 1.0 for a 300 ppi image. When working on a lower resolution image, scale the Radius value in kind. (A 150 ppi image, for example, calls for a Radius of 0.5. Don't go any lower than 0.5.)

Step 3. The result is a fuzzy mask. To firm it up a bit, choose Image⇨Adjust⇨Levels (Command-L). Then enter 65 in the first Input option box and 190 in the third option box. (The second value should remain 1.00.) Then press Return. By making most of the gray values either black or white, you give the mask an antialiased appearance, as in the second example of Figure 13-39.

You may have noticed that this is the third time I've referred to these exact same Input values — 65 and 190 — in the Levels dialog box. It's not that these are some kind of magic numbers. It's just that they lend themselves to many situations, and as long as I haven't formally discussed the Levels dialog box, I want us to remain on vaguely familiar footing. If you already understand how the dialog box works, feel free to experiment with your own values.

Step 4. Now switch back to the matching ants mode (by pressing Q) and apply the desired effect. In Color Plate 13-7, I floated the selection and applied the exact same directional blur effects shown back in Figures 13-33 and 13-34. As you can see, these more precise selection outlines result in more precise effects.

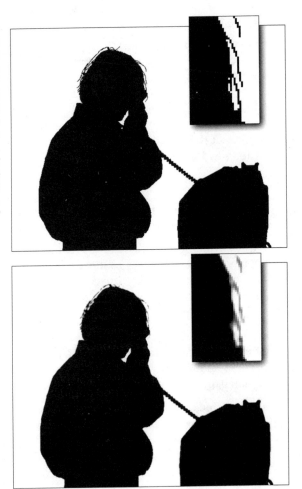

Figure 13-39:
The final jagged mask created with the High Pass and Threshold commands (top) and the same image antialiased using the Gaussian Blur and Levels commands (bottom). Enlarged details show the effects of these operations on individual pixels.

Noise Factors

Photoshop offers four loosely associated filters in its Filter⇨Noise submenu. One filter adds random pixels — known as *noise* — to an image. The other two, Despeckle and Median, blur an image in ways that theoretically remove noise from poorly scanned images. In fact, they function nearly as well at removing essential detail as they do at removing extraneous noise. The only tried and true way to fix a badly scanned image is to chuck it and rescan. Garbage in, garbage out, as the lava lamp manufacturers used to say.

In the following sections, I show you how the Noise filters work, demonstrate a few of my favorite applications, and leave you to draw your own conclusions.

Adding noise

Noise adds grit and texture to an image. You can find examples of noise in grainy album covers, perfume commercials, Levi's 501 Blues ads . . . in short, anything that's trying to appeal to a hip, young, no-marbles-in-their-heads audience.

Noise makes an image look like you shot it in New York on the Lower East Side and were lucky to get the photo at all because someone was throwing sand in your face as you sped away in your chauffeur-driven, jet-black Maserati Bora, hammering away at the shutter release. In reality, of course, a guy over at Sears shot the photo while you toodled around in your minivan trying to find a store that sold day-old bread. But, hey, if there's a moral to this book — which there most certainly is *not* — it's that impressions talk, reality walks.

You add noise by choosing Filter⇨Noise⇨Add Noise. Shown in Figure 13-40, the Add Noise dialog box features the following options:

- **Amount:** Enter any value between 1 and 999 to specify the amount that pixels in the image can stray from their current colors. The value itself represents a color range rather than a brightness range. For example, if you enter a value of 10, Photoshop can apply any color that is 10 shades more or less green, more or less blue, *and* more or less red than the current color. Any value over 255 allows Photoshop to select random colors from the entire 16-million color spectrum. The higher you go above 255, the more likely Photoshop is to pick colors at opposite ends of the spectrum — that is, white and black.

Figure 13-40:
The Add Noise dialog box enables you to specify the amount and variety of noise you want to add to the selection.

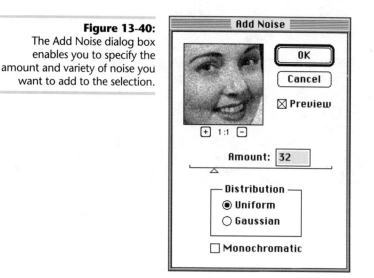

- **Uniform:** Select this option to apply colors absolutely randomly within the specified range. Photoshop is no more likely to apply one color within the range than another, thus resulting in an even color distribution.

- **Gaussian:** When you select this option, you instruct Photoshop to prioritize colors along the Gaussian distribution curve. The effect is that most colors added by the filter either closely resemble the original colors or push the boundaries of the specified range. In other words, this option results in more light and dark pixels, thus producing a more pronounced effect.

- **Monochromatic:** When working on a full-color image, the Add Noise filter distributes pixels randomly throughout the different color channels. However, when you select the Monochrome check box, Photoshop distributes the noise in the same manner in all channels. The result is grayscale noise. (This option does not affect grayscale images; the noise can't get any more grayscale than it already is.)

Figure 13-41 compares three applications of Gaussian noise to identical amounts of Uniform noise. Figure 13-42 features magnified views of the noise so that you can compare the colors of individual pixels.

Figure 13-41:
The Gaussian option produces more pronounced effects than the Uniform option at identical Amount values.

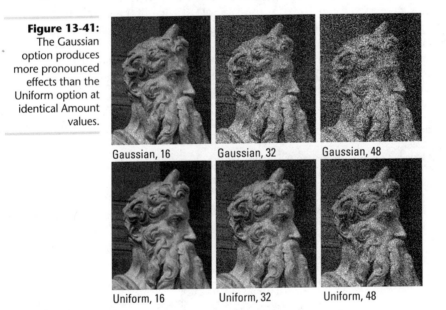

Gaussian, 16   Gaussian, 32   Gaussian, 48

Uniform, 16   Uniform, 32   Uniform, 48

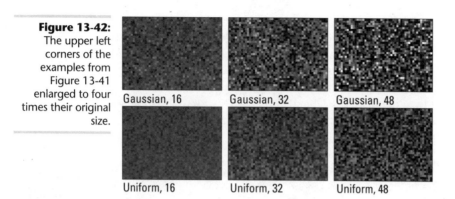

Figure 13-42:
The upper left
corners of the
examples from
Figure 13-41
enlarged to four
times their original
size.

Gaussian, 16 Gaussian, 32 Gaussian, 48

Uniform, 16 Uniform, 32 Uniform, 48

Noise variations

Normally, the Add Noise filter adds both lighter and darker pixels to an image. If you prefer, however, you can limit the effect of the filter to strictly lighter or darker pixels. To do so, float the selection before applying the filter and then select the Lighten or Darken overlay mode.

Figure 13-43 shows sample applications of lighter and darker noise. I began each example by selecting the entire image and choosing Select⇨Float (Command-J). I then chose Filter⇨Noise⇨Add Noise, entered an Amount value of 500, and selected Uniform. To create the left example in the figure, I changed the Opacity setting in the Layers palette to 20 percent and selected Lighten from the overlay modes pop-up menu. To create the right example, I changed the Opacity to 40 percent and selected Darken from the pop-up menu. In each case, I added a layer of strictly lighter or darker noise while at the same time retaining the clarity of the original image.

Figure 13-43:
You can limit the
Add Noise filter to
strictly lighter
(left) or darker
(right) noise by
applying the filter
to a floating,
translucent
selection.

You can achieve a softened noise effect by applying one of the Blur filters to the floating selection before setting it down onto the original image. Figure 13-44, for example, shows images subject to the same amount of noise as those in Figure 13-43. But in this case, immediately following the application of the Add Noise filter, I chose Filter⇨Blur⇨Motion Blur, changed the angle to 30 degrees, and entered a Distance value of 3 pixels. I then changed the Opacity and overlay mode settings as described in the preceding paragraph. In this way, I applied softened grains that are strictly lighter or darker than the original pixels in the image.

Figure 13-44:
To create these rainy and scraped effects, I applied motion blurring to the noise in the floating selections from Figure 13-43.

Applying noise to individual color channels

A few paragraphs ago, I explained that Photoshop 3.0 provides a Monochrome option that allows you to apply grayscale noise to a color image. You can just as easily generate noise that is strictly red, green, or blue by applying the Add Noise filter exclusively to the red, green, or blue color channel, as demonstrated in the top half of Color Plate 13-8. (Because you're only editing one channel, it doesn't matter whether Monochrome is turned on or not.) You can likewise make yellow noise by editing both the red and green channels, cyan noise by editing the green and blue channels, or magenta noise by editing the blue and red channels. (In these cases, Monochrome should be turned off.)

When editing a Lab image, applying noise to the luminosity channel produces the same effect as selecting the Monochrome check box. Apply the filter to the *a* channel to get green and pink noise; apply it to the *b* channel to get blue and orange noise.

Randomizing selections

As with any other filter, you can apply Add Noise to a selection in the quick mask mode. For example, I wanted to again edit the background of the woman-on-the-phone image, this time creating a static effect, as demonstrated in the top example in Figure 13-45.

I entered the quick mask mode and drew the selection outline shown back in Figure 13-36. I only wanted to randomize the pixels within the selected background, so I used the magic wand tool to select the transparent areas of the mask that surround the woman and phone unit.

To soften the selection, I chose Select⇨Feather and entered a Radius value of 2. Next, I chose the Add Noise filter and entered a value of 500 to heavily randomize the selection. When I switched back to the marching ants mode, only random pixels in the background were selected. By pressing the Delete key, I achieved the effect shown in the top example of Figure 13-45.

Figure 13-45:
You can create a static effect (top) by randomizing pixels of a selection in the quick mask mode. To achieve a snow effect (bottom), apply the Gaussian Blur filter to the randomized selection.

The bottom example in Figure 13-45 features a blurred version of the static effect that looks vaguely like snow. (More like a blizzard, really.) After applying the Add Noise command in the quick mask mode — before switching to the marching ants mode and pressing Delete — I chose Filter⇨Blur⇨Gaussian Blur and entered a Radius value of 0.5. This softened the transition between random pixels in the selected region. I then switched back to the marching ants mode and pressed Delete to create the snow shown in the figure.

Chunky noise

My biggest frustration with the Add Noise filter is that you can't specify the size of individual specks of noise. No matter how you cut it, noise only comes in 1-pixel squares. It may occur to you that you can enlarge the noise dots in a floating selection by applying the Minimum filter. But in practice, doing so simply fills in the selection, because there isn't sufficient space between the dark noise pixels to accommodate the larger dot sizes.

Luckily, Photoshop provides a Pointillize filter, which adds variable-sized dots and then colors those dots in keeping with the original colors in the image. Though Pointillize lacks the random quality of the Add Noise filter, you can use it to add texture to an image.

To create the left image in Figure 13-46, I selected the entire image and chose Select⇨Float. I then chose Filter⇨Pixelate⇨Pointillize and entered 3 into the Cell Size option box. After pressing Return to apply the filter (for your information, it's a slow one), I changed the Opacity slider bar in the Layers palette to 20 percent. The effect is rather like applying chunky bits of noise.

The problem with this technique is that it has the added effect of softening an image. To preserve image detail and create the right-hand image in Figure 13-46, I transferred the floating selection to its own layer by Option-double-clicking on the Floating Selection item in the Layers palette. I then returned to the Background layer, selected the entire image, and applied the Unsharp Mask filter. Because the Pointillized image contains its own color detail, I could sharpen with impunity by entering 500 percent for the Amount value, 0.5 for Radius, and 5 for Threshold. After pressing Return, I chose Filter⇨Other⇨ High Pass and applied a Radius value of 20.0. I then switched to the Pointillized layer and pressed 4 to change the Opacity slider bar value to 40 percent. The resulting image is crisp, clear, and chunky. Yes, friends, it's Cream of Moses soup, so hearty you can eat it with a fork.

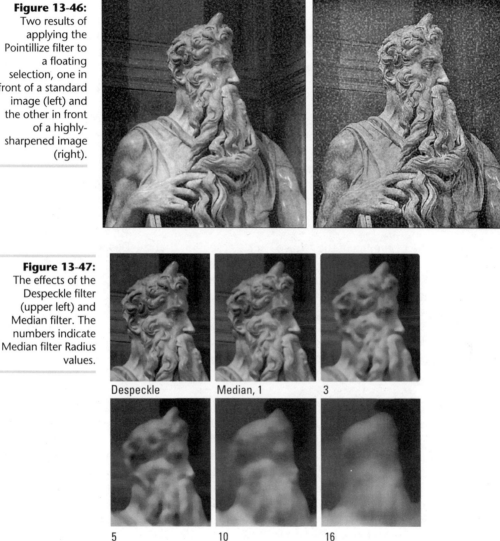

Figure 13-46:
Two results of applying the Pointillize filter to a floating selection, one in front of a standard image (left) and the other in front of a highly-sharpened image (right).

Figure 13-47:
The effects of the Despeckle filter (upper left) and Median filter. The numbers indicate Median filter Radius values.

Despeckle Median, 1 3

5 10 16

Removing noise

Now for the noise removal filters. Strictly speaking, the Despeckle command belongs in the Filter➪Blur submenu. It blurs a selection while at the same time preserving its edges — the idea being that unwanted noise is most noticeable in the continuous regions of an image. In practice, this filter is nearly the exact opposite of the Sharpen Edges filter.

The Despeckle command searches an image for edges using the equivalent of an Unsharp Mask Threshold value of 5. It then ignores the edges in the image and blurs everything else with the force of the Blur More filter, as shown in the upper left image in Figure 13-47.

Using the Median filter

Another command in the Filter⇨Noise submenu, Median, removes noise by averaging the colors in an image, one pixel at a time. When you choose Filter⇨Noise⇨Median, Photoshop produces a Radius option box, into which you can enter any value between 1 and 16. For every pixel in a selection, the filter averages the colors of the neighboring pixels that fall inside the specified radius — ignoring any pixels that are so different that they might skew the average — and applies the average color to the central pixel. As verified by Figure 13-47, large values produce the most destructive effects.

I mentioned at the beginning of the "Noise Factors" section that the Despeckle and Median filters are something of a wash for removing noise because they eliminate too much detail. However, you can apply the Median filter to a floating selection to mute an image and give it a plastic, molded quality, as demonstrated by the examples in Figure 13-48.

To create the left example, I cloned the image by selecting it and choosing Select⇨Float. I then chose Filter⇨Noise⇨Median and entered a Radius value of 3. After pressing Return, I pressed 6 to change the Opacity slider bar to 60 percent.

When used in this manner, the Median filter over-softens the image, even when constrained to a floating selection. To remedy this problem, I used the same tactics I used to fix the over-softening produced by the Pointillize filter in Figure 13-46. After applying Median, I cut the floating selection to the Clipboard, applied the Unsharp Mask filter to the original image at 500 percent, applied the High Pass filter with a 20-pixel radius, and pasted the floating selection back into place. To achieve the effect shown in the right example of Figure 13-48, I pressed 8 to raise the opacity of the floating selection to 80 percent. The result is a gradually contoured image unlike anything you could accomplish using traditional techniques.

Figure 13-48:
Two results of applying the Median filter to a floating selection, one in front of a standard image (left) and the other in front of a highly-sharpened image (right).

Applying Median to individual color channels

What explanation of any corrective filter would be complete without showing how it affects individual color channels? The bottom row in Color Plate 13-8 does just that. In this figure, I've applied the Median filter with a Radius value of 10 to the red, green, and blue channel. But notice that rather than adding red when I edited the red channel, the filter added red's opposite, cyan. Likewise, the filter added magenta when applied to the green channel and yellow when applied to the blue channel. How is this possible? What really happened is that the Median filter expanded the black shadow in the edited channel, thereby deleting color from the red, green, or blue channel. What remains from the unedited channels combines to form a darker area of contrasting color.

Another interesting observation about the color plate: Compare the focus of the three images in the bottom row. The first example is a little soft; the second example is even softer. But the third example is as crisp as it was before I applied the filter. As I've noted a few times through the book, the red and green channels typically contain the majority of edge detail in an image; the blue channel contains color information, but the detail is sometimes a mess (a design function of many medium-priced scanners). So when you apply Gaussian Blur or Median to the blue channel, you're less likely to impact edge detail.

Cleaning up Scanned Halftones

 Photoshop 3.0 offers a new filter in the Filter⇨Noise submenu called Dust & Scratches. The purpose of this filter is to remove dust particles, hairs, scratches, and other imperfections that may accompany a scan. The filter offers two options, Radius and Threshold. As long as the offending imperfection is smaller or thinner than the Radius value and different enough from its neighbors to satisfy the Threshold value, the filter deletes the spot or line and interpolates between the pixels around the perimeter.

But like so many automated tools, this one works only when conditions are favorable. I'm not saying that you shouldn't ever use it — in fact, you may always want to give this filter the first crack at a dusty image. But if it doesn't work, don't get your nose out of joint. Just hunker down and eliminate the imperfections manually using the rubber stamp tool, as explained in the "Touching up blemishes" section of Chapter 11.

Now, as I say, Dust & Scratches was designed to get rid of gunk on a dirty scanner. But another problem that the filter may be able to eliminate is moiré patterns. These patterns appear when scanning halftoned images from books and magazines. See, any time you scan a printed image, you're actually scanning a collection of halftone dots rather than a continuous-tone photograph. In most cases, the halftone pattern clashes with the resolution of the scanned image to produce rhythmic and distracting moirés.

 When scanning published photographs or artwork, take a moment to find out if what you're doing is legal. It's up to you to make sure that the image you scan is no longer protected by copyright — most, but not all, works over 75 years old are considered free game — or that your noncommercial application of the image falls under the fair-use umbrella of commentary or criticism. To find out more information on this topic, check out Jim Martin's "Are You Breaking the Law" article included as an Acrobat PDF file on the CD.

The Dust & Scratches filter can be pretty useful for eliminating moirés, particularly if you reduce the Threshold value below 40. But this also goes a long way toward eliminating the actual image detail, as shown in Color Plate 13-9. This figure features an image scanned from a previous issue of *Macworld* magazine. (Because I created the original image, *Macworld* probably won't sue me, but you shouldn't try it.)

The left half of Color Plate 13-9 shows the individual color channels in the image; the right half shows the full-color image. I've blown up a detail in each image so that you can better see the pixels in the moiré pattern.

The top example in the color plate shows the original scanned image with its awful moirés. (Actually, I've slightly exaggerated the moirés to account for any printing anomalies; but believe me, with or without enhancement, the image is a mess on-screen.) The middle example shows the same image subject to the Dust & Scratches filter with a Radius of 2 and a Threshold value of 20. The moirés are gone, but the edges have all but disappeared as well. I'm tempted to describe this artwork using adjectives like *soft* and *doughy*. Them are fightin' words in the world of image editing.

But what about that bottom example? How did I managed to eliminate the moirés *and* preserve the detail that are shown here? Why, by applying the Gaussian Blur, Median, and Unsharp Mask filters to individual color channels.

The first step is to examine the channels independently (by pressing Command-1, Command-2, and Command-3). You'll likely find that each one is affected by the moiré pattern to a different extent. In the case of this scan, all three channels need work, but the blue channel — the usual culprit — is the worst. The trick, therefore, is to eliminate the patterns in the blue channel and draw detail from the red and green channels.

To fix the blue channel, I applied both the Gaussian Blur and Median commands in fairly hefty doses. I chose Filter⇨Blur⇨Gaussian Blur and specified a Radius value of 1.5 pixels, rather high considering that the image measures only about 300 pixels tall. Then I chose Filter⇨Noise⇨Median and specified a Radius of 2.

The result was a thickly modeled image with no moirés but little detail. To firm things up a bit, I chose Filter⇨Sharpen⇨Unsharp Mask and entered 200 percent for the Amount option and 1.5 for the Radius. I opted for this Radius value because it matches the Radius that I used to blur the image. When correcting moirés, a Threshold value of 0 is almost always the best choice. A higher Threshold value not only prevents the sharpening of moiré pattern edges but also ignores real edges, which are already fragile enough as it is.

The green and red channels required incrementally less attention. After switching to the green channel, I applied the Gaussian Blur filter with a Radius of 1.0. Then I sharpened the image with the Unsharp Mask filter set to 200 percent and a Radius value of 0.5. In the red channel (Command-1), I applied Gaussian Blur with a Radius value of 0.5. The gradual effect wasn't enough to warrant sharpening.

When you're finished, switch back to the RGB view (Command-0) to see the combined result of your labors. (Or keep an RGB view of the image up on-screen by choosing Window⇨New Window.) The focus of the image will undoubtedly be softer than it was when you started. You can cure this to a limited extent by applying very discreet passes of the Unsharp Mask filter, say, with an Amount value of 100 percent and a low Radius value. Keep in mind that oversharpening may bring the patterns back to life or even uncover new ones.

 One last tip: Always scan halftoned images at the highest resolution available to your scanner. Then resample the scan down to the desired resolution using Image⇨Image Size. This step by itself goes a long way toward eliminating moirés.

Summary

- Press Command-F to reapply the most recently used filter. Press Command-Option-F to display the dialog box for that filter.

- If you apply a filter to a floating selection, you can dissipate its effect by adjusting the translucency of the selection or changing the overlay mode. Floating also eliminates artifacts caused by image borders.

- Use the Unsharp Mask filter to gain control over the sharpening process. The filter is exponentially more functional than the preset Sharpen, Sharpen Edges, and Sharpen More crowd.

- Use the High Pass filter in combination with Image⇨Map⇨Threshold to select the exact boundaries of a foreground element set against a busy background.

- The Gaussian Blur filter distributes the blurring effect along a bell-shaped curve, thus blending neighboring pixels while retaining the greatest amount of detail.

- Enlarge and reduce a jagged image with the Image Size command (when the Interpolation option in the General Preferences dialog box is set to Bicubic) to antialias the edges.

- Use the Wind filter in combination with Motion Blur to point the blur in one direction or the other. Use the smudge tools for even better control.

- The Minimum and Maximum filters are ideal for reducing and enlarging the area of a selection outline inside the quick mask mode or inside an independent mask channel.

- To antialias a selection outline, apply the Gaussian Blur filter to the outline in the quick mask mode. Then use the Levels command to reduce the bluriness of the edges.

- The Despeckle command blurs all but the edges in an image; Median averages the colors of neighboring pixels. Neither removes noise that well, but each can be useful for creating special effects.

- The new Dust & Scratches filter can be useful for eliminating moiré patterns, but it also eliminates an excessive amount of detail.

Full-Court Filtering

In This Chapter

- The seven Photoshop filters you'll use only once every blue moon

- Clever ways to use the filters under the Filter⇨Pixelate submenu

- An introduction to the new Mezzotint filter

- In-depth analysis of the three edge-enhancement filters — Emboss, Find Edges, and Trace Contour

- Everything you ever wanted to know about distortion filters (including what the heck to do with them)

- How to change a picture's atmosphere using Clouds, Difference Clouds, and Lighting Effects

Destructive Filters

Corrective filters allow you to both eliminate flaws in an image and apply special effects. Destructive filters, on the other hand, are devoted solely to special effects. That's why this chapter is actually shorter than its predecessor, even though Photoshop offers nearly twice as many destructive filters as corrective counterparts. Quite simply, destructive filters are less frequently used and ultimately less useful.

Don't get me wrong — these filters are a superb bunch. But because of their more limited appeal, I don't explain each and every one of them. Rather, I concentrate on the ones that I think you'll use most often, describe in detail the very few that are new to Photoshop 3.0, breeze over a handful of others, and let you discover on your own the seven that I ignore.

The also-rans

Oh, heck, I guess I can't just go and ignore seven destructive filters — they're not completely useless, after all. It's just that you aren't likely to use them more than once every lunar eclipse. So here is the briefest of all possible descriptions of these seven filters:

- ➷ **Color Halftone:** Located under the Filter⇨Pixelate submenu, this command turns an image into a piece of Roy Lichtenstein artwork, with big, comic-book halftone dots. The filter is fun and it takes about a year and a half to apply. I even include a sample effect in Color Plate 13-2. But if you depend on it on a regular basis, you're as devoid of original ideas as — dare I say it? — Lichtenstein himself.

- ➷ **Fragment:** Ooh, it's an earthquake! This lame filter repeats an image four times in a square formation and lowers the opacity of each to create a sort of jiggly effect. You don't even have any options to control it. I guess I'm just missing the genius behind Filter⇨Pixelate⇨Fragment.

- ➷ **Lens Flare:** This filter adds sparkles and halos to an image to suggest light bouncing off the camera lens. Even though photographers work their behinds off trying to make sure that these sorts of reflections don't occur, you can go and add them after the fact. You can select from one of three Lens Type options, adjust the Brightness slider between 10 and 300 percent (though somewhere around 100 is bound to deliver the best results), and move the center of the reflection by dragging a point around inside the Flare Center box. It's a novelty filter that you'll probably want to use sparingly. One small tip: If you want to add a flare to a grayscale image, first convert it to the RGB mode. Then apply the filter and convert back to grayscale. The Lens Flare filter is applicable to RGB images only.

- ➷ **Diffuse:** This single-shot filter under the Filter⇨Stylize submenu dithers the edges of color, much like the Dissolve brush mode dithers the edges of a soft brush. It's moderately useful, but not likely to gain a place among your treasured few.

- ➷ **Solarize:** Located in the Stylize submenu — as are the two filters that follow — Solarize is easily Photoshop's worst filter. It's really just a color-correction effect that changes all medium grays in the image to white, all blacks and whites to black, and remaps the other colors to shades in between. (If you're familiar with the Curves command, the map for Solarize looks like a pyramid.) It really belongs in the Image⇨Map submenu, or better yet, on the cutting room floor.

↬ **Tiles:** This filter breaks an image up into a bunch of regularly sized but randomly spaced rectangular tiles. You specify how many tiles fit across the width and height of the image — a value of 10, for example, creates 100 tiles — and the maximum distance each tile can shift. You can fill the gaps between tiles with foreground color, background color, or an inverted or normal version of the original image. A highly intrusive and not particularly stimulating effect.

↬ **Extrude:** The more capable cousin of the Tiles filter, Extrude breaks an image into tiles and forces them toward the viewer in three-dimensional space. The Pyramid option is a lot of fun, devolving an image into a collection of spikes. When using the Blocks option, you can select a Solid Front Faces option that renders the image as a true 3-D mosaic. The Mask Incomplete Blocks option simply leaves the image untouched around the perimeter of the selection where the filter can't draw complete tiles.

Actually, I kind of like the Extrude command. For the pure and simple heck of it, Color Plate 14-1 shows an example of Extrude applied to one of the sharpened rose images from Color Plate 13-4 (the bottom left one, to be exact). I set the Type to Blocks, the Size to 10, the Depth to 30 and Random, with both the Solid Front Faces and Mask Incomplete Blocks radio buttons selected. Pretty great, huh? I only wish that the filter would generate a selection outline around the masked areas of the image so that I could get rid of anything that hadn't been extruded. It's a wonderful effect, but it's not one that lends itself to many occasions.

What about the others?

Some filters don't really belong in either the corrective or destructive camp. Take Filter⇨Video⇨NTSC Colors and Filter⇨Other⇨Offset, for example. Both are examples of commands that have no business being under the filter menu, and both could have been handled much better than they are.

NTSC Colors modifies the colors in your RGB or Lab image for transfer to videotape. Vivid reds and blues that might otherwise prove very unstable and bleed into their neighbors are curtailed. The problem with this function is that it's not an independent color space; it's a single shot filter that changes your colors and is done with it. If you edit the colors after choosing the command, you may very well reintroduce colors that are incompatible with NTSC devices and therefore warrant a second application of the filter. Conversion to NTSC — another light-based system — isn't as fraught with potential disaster as conversion to CMYK pigments, but it still deserves better treatment than this.

The Offset command moves an image a specified number of pixels. Why didn't I cover it in Chapter 8 with the other movement options? Because the command actually moves the image inside the selection outline while keeping the selection outline itself stationary. It's as if you had pasted the entire image into the selection outline and were now moving it around. The command is a favorite among fans of channel operations, a topic I cover in Chapters 17 and 18. You can duplicate an image, offset the entire thing a few pixels, and then mix the duplicate and original to create highlight or shadow effects. But I much prefer the more interactive control of floating and nudging with the arrow keys. In fact, to be perfectly blunt, channel operations are vastly overrated. See Chapter 17 for an earful on the subject.

Among the filters I've omitted from this chapter is Filter⇨Stylize⇨Wind, which is technically a destructive filter but is covered along with the blur and noise filters in Chapter 13. For complete information about Filter⇨Other⇨Custom, Filter⇨Distort⇨Displace, and Filter⇨Synthetic⇨Filter Factory, read the following chapter, "Constructing Homemade Effects." Filter⇨Video⇨De-Interlace is covered in Chapter C on the CD, and Filter⇨Render⇨Texture Fill is covered in Chapter 11.

As for the other filters in the Filter⇨Distort, Pixelate, Render, and Stylize submenus, read on to discover all the latest and greatest details.

Third-party filters

In addition to the filters provided by Photoshop, you can purchase all sorts of plug-in filters from other companies. In fact, Photoshop supports its own flourishing cottage industry of third-party solutions.

The CD at the back of this book includes sample versions of some of my favorite filters, including the awesome Gradient Designer and several others from Kai's Power Tools; Drop Shadow and The Boss from independent Alien Skin; 3-D and cMulti from Andromeda; DPA's Intellihance (Mac only); and Xaos Tools' Terrazzo and a few Paint Alchemy brushes (Mac only). Kai's Power Tools and the Alien Skin and Andromeda filters are provided in both Mac and Windows versions. Intellihance and Terrazzo are for the Mac only. Many of these filters are exclusive to this CD. A few filters are demo versions of the shipping products, which means that you can see what they do but you can't actually apply the effects. I know, it's a drag, but these folks claim that they like to make money every once in a while, and I can't say that I blame them.

Also included on the CD is a feature article called "Special Effects in Photoshop," which I wrote for the November 1994 edition of *Macworld* magazine. The article sums up nine commercial filter packages from five different vendors and lists my favorites. It's provided as a PDF file, so you can open it up and read it on-screen or print it. Better still, it's full of all sorts of full-color artwork that shows off the various tools.

The Pixelate Filters

The new Filter⇨Pixelate submenu features a handful of commands that rearrange your image into clumps of solid color:

- **Crystallize:** This filter organizes an image into irregularly shaped nuggets. You specify the size of the nuggets by entering a value from 3 to 300 pixels in the Cell Size option.

- **Facet:** Facet fuses areas of similarly colored pixels to create a sort of hand-painted effect.

- **Mosaic:** The Mosaic filter blends pixels together into larger squares. You specify the height and width of the squares by entering a value into the Cell Size option box.

- **Pointillize:** This filter is similar to Crystallize, except that it separates an image into disconnected nuggets set against the background color. As usual, you specify the size of the nuggets by changing the Cell Size value.

The Crystal Halo effect

By applying one of these filters to a feathered selection, you can create what I call a Crystal Halo effect, named after the Crystallize filter, which tends to deliver the most successful results. (For a preview of these effects, sneak a peek at Figure 14-2.) The following steps explain how to create a Crystal Halo, using the images in Figures 14-1 and 14-2 as an example.

STEPS:	Creating the Crystal Halo Effect

Step 1. Begin by selecting the foreground element around which you want to create the halo. Then choose Select⇨Inverse to deselect the foreground element and select the background.

Step 2. Enter the quick mask mode. Choose Filter⇨Other⇨Minimum to increase the size of the deselected area around the foreground element. The size of the Radius value depends on the size of the halo you want to create. For my part, I wanted a 15-pixel halo. Unfortunately, the Radius option box in the Minimum dialog box can't accommodate a value larger than 10. So I entered 10 the first time. When Photoshop finished applying the filter, I pressed Command-Option-F to bring up the Minimum dialog box again and entered 5.

Step 3. Choose Filter⇨Blur⇨Gaussian Blur and enter a Radius value 0.1 less than the amount by which you increased the size of the deselected area. In my case, I entered 14.9. The result appears in the left image in Figure 14-1.

Figure 14-1:
Create a heavily feathered selection outline (left) and then apply the Crystallize filter to refract the feathered edges (right).

Step 4. Choose Filter⇨Pixelate⇨Crystallize and enter a moderate value into the Cell Size option box. I opted for the value 12, just slightly larger than the default value. After pressing Return, you get something along the lines of the selection outline shown in the right image in Figure 14-1. The filter refracts the softened edges, as if you were viewing them through textured glass.

Step 5. Switch back to the marching ants mode and use the selection as desired. I merely deleted the selection to produce the effect shown in the top left image in Figure 14-2. You may find this technique particularly useful for combining images. You can copy the selection and paste it against a different background or copy a background from a different image and choose Edit⇨Paste Into to paste it inside the crystal halo's selection outline.

Figure 14-2 shows several variations on the Crystal Halo effect. To create the upper right image, I substituted Filter⇨Pixelate⇨Facet for Filter⇨Pixelate⇨Crystallize in Step 4. I also sharpened the result to increase the effect of the filter (which nevertheless remains subtle). To create the lower right image, I applied the Mosaic filter in place of Crystallize, using a Cell Size value of 8. Finally, to create the lower left image, I applied the Pointillize filter. Because Pointillize creates gaps in a selection, I had to paint inside Moses to fill in the gaps and isolate the halo effect to the background before returning to the marching ants mode.

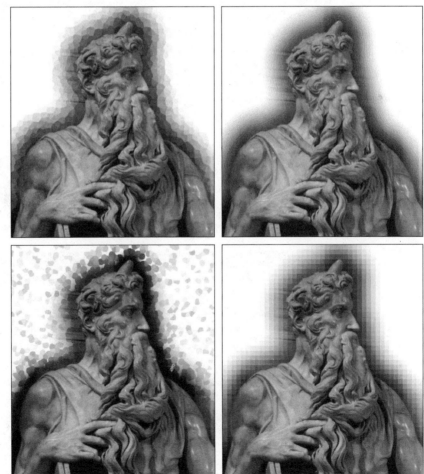

Figure 14-2:
Which aura will Moses don today? The images illustrate the effects of applying each of four filters to a heavily feathered selection in the quick mask mode and pressing the Delete key. Clockwise from upper left, the filters used were Crystallize, Facet, Mosaic, and Pointillize.

Creating a mezzotint

A *mezzotint* is a special halftone pattern that replaces dots with a random pattern of swirling lines and worm holes. Photoshop 3.0's Mezzotint filter is an attempt to emulate this effect. Although not entirely successful — true mezzotinting options can only be properly implemented as PostScript printing functions, not as filtering functions — they do lend themselves to some pretty interesting interpretations.

The filter itself is straightforward. You choose Filter⇨Pixelate⇨Mezzotint, select an effect from the Type submenu, and hit the Return key. A preview box allows you to see what each of the ten Type options looks like. Figure 14-3 shows off four of the effects at 230 ppi.

Figure 14-3: The results of applying the Mezzotint filter set to each of four representative effects. These line patterns are on par with the halftoning options offered when you select Mode⇨Bitmap, as discussed back in Chapter 4 (see Figure 4-12).

Medium dots

Coarse dots

Short lines

Long strokes

To create Figure 14-4, I floated Moses before applying the Mezzotint filter set to the Long Lines effect. I then mixed floating image and underlying original by selecting options from the overlay modes pop-up menu in the Layers palette. In this case, I applied the Overlay option and set the Opacity slider to 40 percent. The result is a scraped image. (I've decreased the resolution of the image to 180 ppi so that you can see the effect a little more clearly.)

Figure 14-4:
To get this effect, I floated the great work of marble before applying the Mezzotint filter. Then I selected the Overlay mode and set the Opacity slider to 40 percent.

When applied to grayscale artwork, the Mezzotint filter always results in a black-and-white image. When applied to a color image, the filter automatically applies the selected effect independently to each of the color channels. Though all pixels in each channel are changed to either black or white, you can see a total of eight colors — black, red, green, blue, yellow, cyan, magenta, and white — in the RGB composite view. The upper left example of Color Plate 14-2 shows an image subject to the Mezzotint filter in the RGB mode.

If the Mezzotint filter affects each channel independently, then it follows that the color mode in which you work directly and dramatically affects the performance of the filter. For example, if you apply Mezzotint in the Lab mode, you again whittle the colors down to eight, but a very different eight — black, cyan, magenta, green, red, two muddy blues and a muddy rose — as shown in the top middle example of Color Plate 14-2. If you're looking for bright happy colors, don't apply Mezzotint in the Lab mode.

In CMYK, the filter produces roughly the same eight colors that you get in RGB — white, cyan, magenta, yellow, violet-blue, red, deep green, and black. However, as shown in the top right example of the color plate, the distribution of the colors is much different. The image appears much lighter and more colorful than its RGB counterpart. This happens because the filter has a lot of black to work with in the RGB mode but very little — just that in the black channel — in the CMYK mode.

The bottom row of Color Plate 14-2 shows the effects of the Mezzotint filter when I first floated each image and then mixed it with the original. As in Figure 14-4, I chose Overlay from the overlay modes pop-up menu in the Layers palette and set the Opacity value to 40 percent. (It's gotten kind of confusing since Photoshop named one of the overlay modes Overlay, but hang in there.) These three very different images were all created using the same filter set to the same effect. Absolutely the only difference is color mode.

Edge-Enhancement Filters

The Filter⇨Stylize submenu offers access to a triad of filters that enhance the edges in an image. The most popular of these is undoubtedly Emboss, which adds dimension to an image by making it look as if it were carved in relief. The other two, Find Edges and Trace Contour, are less commonly applied, but every bit as capable and deserving of your attention.

Embossing an image

The Emboss filter works by searching for high-contrast edges (just like the Sharpen Edge and High Pass filters), highlighting the edges with black or white pixels, and then coloring the low-contrast portions with medium gray. When you choose Filter⇨Stylize⇨Emboss, Photoshop displays the Emboss dialog box shown in Figure 14-5. The dialog box offers three options:

⌦ **Angle:** The value in this option box determines the angle at which Photoshop lights the image in relief. For example, if you enter a value of 90 degrees, you light the relief from the bottom straight upward. The white pixels therefore appear on the bottom sides of the edges, and the black pixels appear on the top sides. Figure 14-6 shows eight reliefs lit from different angles. I positioned the images so that they appear lit from a single source.

Figure 14-5:
The Emboss dialog box enables you to control the depth of the filtered image and the angle from which it is lit.

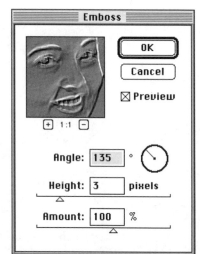

Figure 14-6:
Reliefs lighted from eight different angles, in 45-degree increments. In all cases, the central sun image indicates the location of the light source. Height and Amount values of 1 pixel and 250 percent were used for all images.

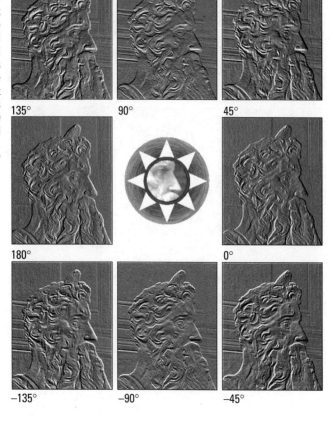

⧉ **Height:** The Emboss filter accomplishes its highlighting effect by displacing one copy of an image relative to another. You specify the distance between the copies using the Height option, which can vary from 1 to 10 pixels. Lower values produce crisp effects, as demonstrated in Figure 14-7. Values above 3 goop things up pretty good unless you also enter a high Amount value. Together, the Height and Amount values determine the depth of the image in relief.

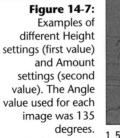

Figure 14-7:
Examples of different Height settings (first value) and Amount settings (second value). The Angle value used for each image was 135 degrees.

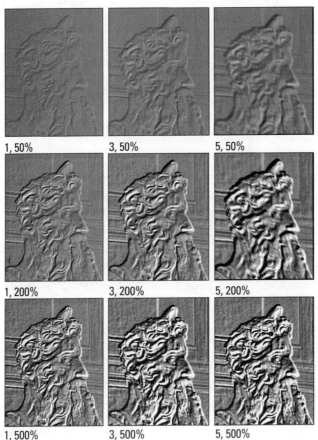

⧉ **Amount:** Enter a value between 1 and 500 percent to determine the amount of black and white assigned to pixels along the edges. Values of 50 percent and lower produce almost entirely gray images, as you can see in the top row of Figure 14-7. Higher values produce sharper edges, as if the relief were carved more deeply.

As a stand-alone effect, Emboss is something of a dud. It's one of those filters that makes you gasp with delight the first time you see it but never quite lends itself to any practical application after you become acquainted with Photoshop. But if you think of Emboss as an extension of the High Pass filter, it takes on new meaning. You can use it to edit selection outlines in the quick mask mode, just as you might use the High Pass filter. You also can use it to draw out detail in an image.

Figure 14-8 shows Emboss applied to floating selections. To create the left example, I selected Darken from the overlay modes pop-up menu in the Layers palette to add shadows to the edges of the image, thus boosting the texture without unduly upsetting the original brightness values. I selected Lighten from the overlay modes pop-up menu to create the right example. In both cases, I applied the Emboss filter at an Angle of 135 degrees, a Height of 2 pixels, and an Amount of 250 percent. I also set the Opacity slider bar to 70 percent.

Figure 14-8:
I limited the effect of the Emboss filter to darkening the image (left) and then to lightening the image (right) by applying the filter to a floating, translucent selection.

 To create a color relief effect, apply the Emboss filter to a floating selection and then select the Luminosity option from the overlay modes pop-up menu in the Layers palette. This retains the colors from the original image while applying the lightness and darkness of the pixels from the floating selection. The effect looks something like an inked lithographic plate, with steel grays and vivid colors mixing together. An example of this effect at 80 percent Opacity is shown in the first example of Color Plate 14-3.

The second example in that same color plate shows a more impressive — if less practical — technique. Rather than applying the Luminosity overlay mode, I chose the Difference option. With its hard edges and vivid colors, this image looks like some impossible frame from an educational film on genetic engineering. I can just hear the narrator commenting, "Prom dates across America have perked up significantly since scientists discovered how to splice the red rose with a poppy."

Tracing around edges

I love these next two filters. Find Edges and Trace Contour — also located in the Filter⇨Stylize submenu — trace around pixels in your image to accentuate the edges. As shown in the top left example of Figure 14-9, Find Edges detects edges similarly to High Pass. Low-contrast areas become white, medium-contrast edges become gray, and high-contrast edges become black. Hard edges become thin lines; soft edges become fat ones. The result is a thick, organic outline that you can overlay onto an image to give it a waxy appearance. In the top right example of Figure 14-9, I applied the command to a floating image and mixed it with the underlying original using the Overlay mode and a 50 percent Opacity setting. She'll never get her hand off that canning jar as long as she lives.

Trace Contour, also illustrated in Figure 14-9, is a little more involved and slightly less interesting. When you choose Filter⇨Stylize⇨Trace Contour, you're presented with a dialog box containing three options: Level, Upper, and Lower. The filter traces a series of single-pixel lines along the border between light and dark pixels. The Level value indicates the lightness value above which pixels are considered to be light and below which they are dark. For example, if you enter 128 — medium gray, as by default — Trace Contour draws a line at every spot where an area of color lighter than medium gray meets an area of color darker than medium gray. Upper and Lower just tell the filter where to position the line — inside the lighter color's territory (Upper) or inside the space occupied by the darker color (Lower). Get it wrong, and you'll start a turf war. (Not true, actually. Colors are very docile creatures, quite accustomed to being pushed and smeared around by the powers that be.)

Like Mezzotint, Trace Contour applies itself to each color channel independently and renders each channel as a 1-bit image. A collection of black lines surrounds the areas of color in each channel; the RGB, Lab, or CMYK composite view shows these lines in the colors associated with the channels. When you work in RGB, a cyan line indicates a black line in the red channel (no red plus full intensity green and blue becomes cyan). A yellow line indicates a black line in the blue channel, and so on. You get a single black line when working in the grayscale mode.

Figure 14-9:
After applying Find Edges to a floating selection (top left), I blended the floater with the underlying original using the Overlay mode and 80 percent Opacity (top right). The bottom examples show the results of applying Trace Contour to a floater (left) and using the Multiply mode to mix it with the original (right).

Creating a metallic coating

The question becomes, what the heck do you do with two such edge-finding filters? Unlike High Pass, Find Edges and Trace Contour are not particularly suited to defining masks. Rather, they're primarily geared toward the creation of special effects.

The metallic coating effect is a case in point. Have you ever seen that Chrome filter that's included with Aldus Gallery Effects, the third-party filter collection? I don't like it — never have — not because it's without merit, but because Photoshop already offers this capability via the Gaussian Blur and Find Edges commands, which together do a better job. The Chrome filter always produces grayscale results and offers poor edge antialiasing. The duo of Gaussian Blur and Find Edges works in color and looks smooth as silk.

To create this effect, float your image (Command-J, in case you're rusty) and apply Filter⇨Blur⇨Gaussian Blur. A Radius value between 1.0 and 4.0 produces the best results, depending on how gooey you want your edges to be. My favorite setting is 3.0, as in the first example of Figure 14-10. Then apply Filter⇨Stylize⇨Find Edges, which results in the effect shown in the top right corner of the figure. In the bottom left example, I mixed the floater with the underlying original using the Overlay mode and an Opacity of 70 percent. But the result is a little washed out. So I defloated the image, chose the Levels command, and raised the first Input value to 50, thereby increasing the number of dark colors in the image (as shown in the final example).

Figure 14-10:
After applying the Gaussian Blur filter with a Radius of 3.0 (top left), I chose the Find Edges filter (top right). I then composited the filtered image with the original using the Overlay mode (bottom left) and used the Levels command to darken the image and give it strength (bottom right).

Color Plate 14-4 shows the same effect in color. Starting with an unedited construction worker, I went through the usual calisthenics of selecting and floating the image. Next, I applied Gaussian Blur (3.0 Radius) and Find Edges. The effect was too light, so I chose Image⇨Adjust⇨Levels and entered 128 into the first option box. (You may notice that I worked in a slightly different order than before, but you can apply color corrections before or after you mix the images.) Everything darker than medium gray went to black, uniformly strengthening the effect. The result is the full-color metallic coating shown in the second example in Color Plate 14-4. To get the last image, I merely chose the Overlay option from the overlay modes pop-up menu in the Layers palette and changed the Opacity to 80 percent.

Tracing noise

One of my favorite uses for the Trace Contour filter is to trace around noise. Check out Color Plate 14-5, for example. I started by floating the image — no surprise there — and applying the Pointillize filter with a Cell Size of 6. Then I chose Trace Contour, set the Levels slider to 128, and let her rip. Photoshop traced around each and every chunk of Pointillized noise to create the mottled effect shown on the left side of the figure. I also chose the Luminosity option from the Layers palette to borrow the colors from the underlying image. That image struck me as a little too flimsy, however, so I switched the overlay mode to Multiply and lowered the Opacity setting to 50 percent, which resulted in the second example of Color Plate 14-5.

If Trace Contour creates a mottled effect when applied to a Pointillized image, what does it do to real noise? The right example of Color Plate 14-5 shows all. Here I applied the Add Noise command to the floating image with an Amount value of 100 and Gaussian turned on. After completing the noise, I traced it with Trace Contour. To get the maximum effect, I had to lower the Levels value in the Trace Contour dialog box to 90. I then applied the Overlay mode and set the Opacity to 80 percent, as I've done about 100 times now. The image took on a downright grainy appearance, an effect that noise — whether regular or chunky — can't accomplish on its own.

Distortion Filters

For the most part, commands in the Distort submenu are related by the fact that they move colors in an image to achieve unusual stretching, swirling, and vibrating effects. They're rather like the transformation commands from the Image⇨Effects submenu in that they perform their magic by relocating and interpolating colors rather than by altering brightness and color values.

The distinction, of course, is that while the transformation commands let you scale and distort images by manipulating four control points, the Distort filters provide the equivalent of hundreds of control points, all of which you can use to affect different portions of an image. In some cases, you're projecting an image into a fun-house mirror; other times, it's a reflective pool. You can fan images, wiggle them, and change them in ways that have no correlation to real life, as illustrated in Figure 14-11.

Figure 14-11:
This is your image (left); this is your image on distortion filters (right). Three filters, in fact: Spherize, Ripple, and Polar Coordinates.

Distortion filters are very powerful tools. Although they are easy to apply, they are extremely difficult to use well. Here are some rules to keep in mind:

- **Practice makes practical:** Distortion filters are like complex vocabulary words. You don't want to use them without practicing a little first. Experiment with a distortion filter several times before trying to use it in a real project. You may even want to write down the steps you take so that you can remember how you created an effect.

- **Use caution during tight deadlines:** Distortion filters are enormous time-wasters. Unless you know exactly how you want to proceed, you may want to avoid using them when time is short. The last thing you need when you're working under the gun is to get trapped trying to pull off a weird effect.

- **Apply selectively:** The effects of distortion filters are too severe to inflict all at once. You can achieve marvelous, subtle effects by distorting feathered and floating selections. Although I wouldn't call the image in Figure 14-11 subtle, no effect was applied to the entire image. I applied the Spherize filter to a feathered elliptical marquee that included most of the image. I then reapplied Spherize to the eye. I selected the hair and beard and applied the Ripple filter twice. Finally, after establishing two heavily feathered vertical columns on either side of the image in the quick mask mode, I applied the Polar Coordinates filter, which reflected the front and back of the head. Turn the book upside down and you'll see a second face.

- ☞ **Combine creatively:** Don't expect a single distortion to achieve the desired effect. If one application isn't enough, apply the filter again. Experiment with combining different distortions.

- ☞ **Save your original:** Never distort an image until you save it. After you start down Distortion Boulevard, the only way to go back is File⇨Revert. And, as always, it's a good idea to float the image before applying the filter so that you can delete it if you don't like the effect.

Distortion filters interpolate between pixels to create their fantastic effects. This means that the quality of your filtered images is dependent on the setting of the Interpolation option in the General Preferences dialog box. If a filter is producing jagged effects, the Nearest Neighbor option is probably selected. Try selecting the Bicubic or Bilinear option instead.

Reflecting an image in a spoon

Most folks take their first ventures into distortion filters by using Pinch and Spherize. Pinch maps an image onto the inside of a sphere or similarly curved surface; Spherize maps it onto the outside of a sphere. It's sort of like looking at your reflection on the inside or outside of a spoon.

You can apply Pinch to a scanned face to squish the features toward the center or apply Spherize to accentuate the girth of the nose. Figure 14-12 illustrates both effects. It's a laugh, and you pretty much feel as though you're onto something that no one else ever thought of before. (At least that's how I felt — but I'm easily amazed.)

Figure 14-12:
The stereotypical rookie applications for the Pinch (left) and Spherize (right) filters.

You can pinch or spherize an image using either the Pinch or Spherize command. As shown in Figure 14-13, a positive value in the Pinch dialog box produces a similar effect to a negative value in the Spherize dialog box. There is a slight difference between the spatial curvature of the 3-D calculations: Pinch pokes the image inward or outward using a rounded cone — we're talking bell-shaped, much like a Gaussian model. Spherize wraps the image on the outside or inside of a true sphere. As a result, the two filters yield subtly different results. Pinch produces a soft transition around the perimeter of a selection; Spherize produces an abrupt transition. If this doesn't quite make sense to you, just play with one, try out the same effect with the other, and see which you like better.

Another difference between the two filters is that Spherize provides the additional options of allowing you to wrap an image onto the inside or outside of a horizontal or vertical cylinder. To try out these effects, select the Horizontal Only or Vertical Only radio button in the lower left corner of the Spherize dialog box.

Figure 14-13:
Both the Pinch and Spherize dialog boxes enable you to pinch or spherize an image. Pinch wraps on a rounded cone; Spherize wraps onto a sphere.

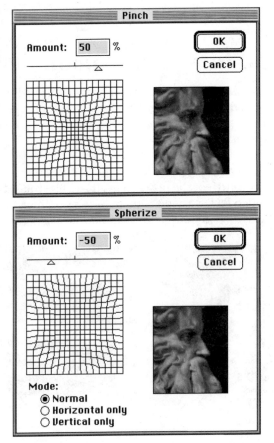

Both the Pinch and Spherize filters are applicable only to elliptical regions of an image. If a selection outline is not elliptical in shape, Photoshop applies the filter to the largest ellipse that fits inside the selection. As a result, the filter may leave behind a noticeable elliptical boundary between the affected and unaffected portions of the selection. To avoid this effect, select the region you want to edit with the elliptical marquee tool and then feather the selection before filtering it. This softens the effect of the filter and provides a more gradual transition (even more so than Pinch already affords).

One of the more remarkable properties of the Pinch filter is that it lets you turn any image into a conical gradation. Figure 14-14 illustrates how the process works.

First, blur the image to eliminate any harsh edges between color transitions. Then apply the Pinch filter at full strength (100 percent). Reapply the filter several more times. Each time you press Command-F, the center portion of the image recedes farther and farther into the distance, as shown in Figure 14-14. After 10 repetitions, the face in the example all but disappeared.

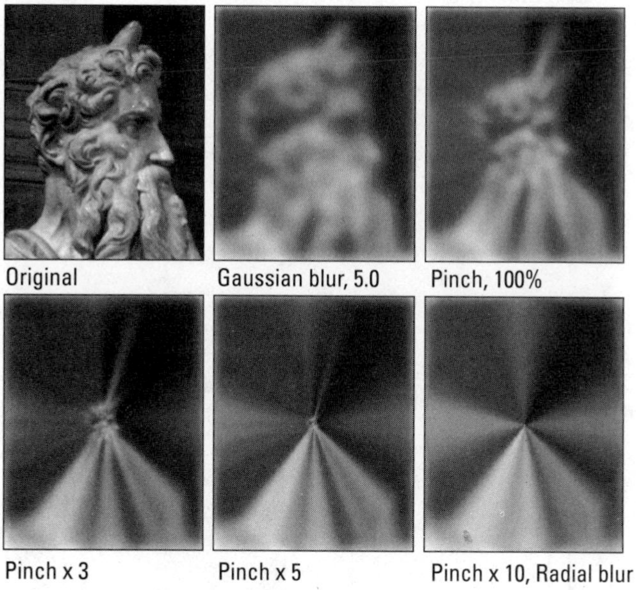

Figure 14-14:
After applying the Gaussian Blur filter, I pinched the image 10 times and applied the Radial Blur filter to create a conical gradation.

Original	Gaussian blur, 5.0	Pinch, 100%
Pinch x 3	Pinch x 5	Pinch x 10, Radial blur

Next, apply the Radial Blur filter set to Spin 10 pixels or so to mix the color boundaries a bit. The result is a type of gradation that you can't create using Photoshop's gradient tool.

You can also use the Spherize tool set to a negative Amount value to create a conical gradation. Color Plate 14-6 shows off the subtle differences between using the Pinch and Spherize filters for this purpose. The left examples were created with Pinch; the right examples with Spherize. The first row shows the effect of applying each filter twice set to 100 and –100 percent, respectively. The Spherized face is larger, showing that the Spherize filter works more slowly. But it also grabs more edge detail. The second row shows the results of 12 repetitions of each filter. Though the two gradations are very similar, the Spherized one contains a hundred or so extra streaks. In the last row, I mixed the gradation with the underlying image using different overlay modes. The Soft Light mode was responsible for the alarming conical-sunburn effect on the left. I repeated the filter four times using the Screen mode to get the right image. "Look, ma, I had a sprinkler system installed on my helmet!"

Twirling spirals

The Twirl filter rotates the center of a selection while leaving the sides fixed in place. The result is a spiral of colors that looks for all the world as if you poured the image into a blender set to a very slow speed.

When you choose Filter⇨Distort⇨Twirl, Photoshop displays the Twirl dialog box, shown in Figure 14-15. Enter a positive value from 1 to 999 degrees to spiral the image in a clockwise direction. Enter a negative value to spiral the image in a counterclockwise direction. As you are probably already aware, 360 degrees make a full circle, so the maximum 999-degree value equates to a spiral that circles around approximately three times, as shown in the bottom right example in Figure 14-16.

Figure 14-15:
The Twirl dialog box lets you create spiraling images.

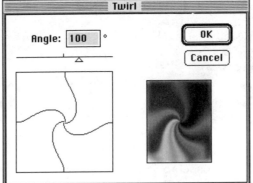

The Twirl filter produces smoother effects when you use lower Angle values. Therefore, you're better off applying a 100-degree spiral 10 times rather than applying a 999-degree spiral once, as verified by Figure 14-16.

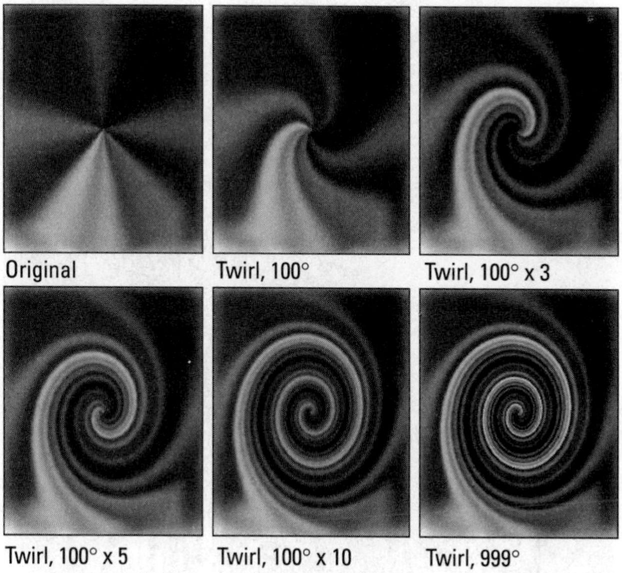

Figure 14-16:
The effects of applying the Twirl filter. Repeatedly applying the Twirl filter at a moderate value (bottom middle) produces a smoother effect than applying the filter once at a high value (bottom right).

Original	Twirl, 100°	Twirl, 100° x 3
Twirl, 100° x 5	Twirl, 100° x 10	Twirl, 999°

In addition to creating ice-cream swirls like those shown in Figure 14-16, you can use the Twirl filter to create organic images virtually from scratch, as witnessed by Figures 14-17 and 14-18.

To create the images shown in Figure 14-17, I used the Spherize filter to flex the conical gradation vertically by entering 100 percent in the Amount option box and selecting Vertical Only from the Mode radio buttons. After repeating this filter several times, I eventually achieved a stalactite-stalagmite effect, as shown in the center example of the figure. I then repeatedly applied the Twirl filter to curl the flexed gradations like two symmetrical hairs. The result merges the simplicity of pure math with the beauty of bitmapped imagery.

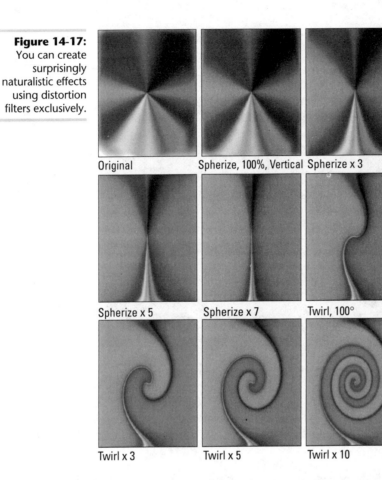

Original   Spherize, 100%, Vertical Spherize x 3

Spherize x 5   Spherize x 7   Twirl, 100°

Twirl x 3   Twirl x 5   Twirl x 10

Figure 14-18 illustrates a droplet technique designed by Mark Collen. I took the liberty of breaking down the technique into the following steps.

STEPS: Creating a Thick-liquid Droplet

Step 1.   Click on the default colors icon to restore black as the foreground color and white as the background color. Select a square portion of an image by dragging with the rectangular marquee tool while pressing the Shift key.

Step 2.   Drag inside the selection outline with the gradient tool. Drag a short distance near the center of the selection from upper left to lower right, creating the gradation shown in the top left box in Figure 14-18.

Figure 14-18:
If you know your way around Photoshop, you may at first misinterpret the bottom two images as the result of the Zigzag filter, discussed in the next section. In fact, they were created entirely by using the gradient tool and Twirl filter and then applying a couple of transformations to a floating selection.

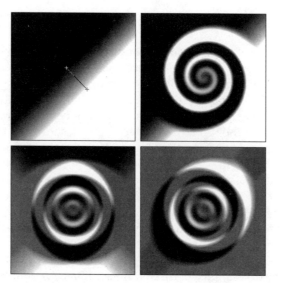

Step 3. Choose the Twirl filter and apply it at –360 degrees so that the spiral moves counterclockwise. To create the top right image in the figure, I applied the Twirl filter three times. Each repetition of the filter adds another ring of ripples.

Step 4. Choose Select⇨Float (Command-J) to clone the image. Then choose Image⇨Flip⇨Horizontal.

Step 5. Select the rectangular marquee tool. Press 5 to change the Opacity slider bar in the Brushes palette to 50 percent. The result is shown in the lower left image in Figure 14-18.

Step 6. Choose Image⇨Rotate⇨90° CW to rotate the image a quarter turn, thus creating the last image in the figure. You can achieve other interesting effects by choosing Lighten, Darken, and others from the brush modes pop-up menu.

Creating concentric pond ripples

I don't know about you, but when I think of zigzags, I think of cartoon lighting bolts, wriggling snakes, scribbles — anything that alternately changes directions along an axis, like the letter *Z*. The Zigzag filter does arrange colors into zigzag patterns, but it does so in a radial fashion, meaning that the zigzags emanate from the center of the image like spokes in a wheel. The result is a series of concentric ripples. If you want parallel zigzags, check out the Ripple and Wave filters, described in the next section. (The Zigzag filter creates ripples and the Ripple filter creates zigzags. Go figure.)

When you choose Filter⇨Distort⇨Zigzag, Photoshop displays the Zigzag dialog box shown in Figure 14-19. The dialog box offers the following options:

➥ **Amount:** Enter an amount between negative and positive 100 in whole-number increments to specify the depth of the ripples. If you enter a negative value, the ripples descend below the surface. If you enter a positive value, the ripples protrude upward. Examples of three representative Amount values appear in Figure 14-20.

Figure 14-19:
The Zigzag dialog box lets you add concentric ripples to an image, as if the image were reflected in a pond into which you dropped a pebble.

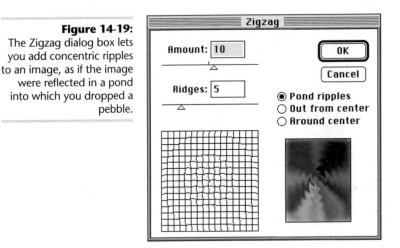

Figure 14-20:
The effects of the Zigzag filter subject to three Amount values and the Pond Ripples, Out From Center, and Around Center settings. In all cases, the Ridges value was 5.

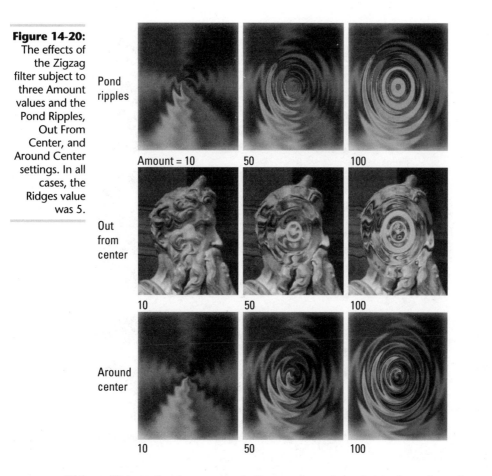

Pond ripples

Amount = 10   50   100

Out from center

10   50   100

Around center

10   50   100

- **Ridges:** This option box controls the number of ripples in the selected area and accepts any value from 1 to 20. Figure 14-21 demonstrates the effect of three Ridges values.

- **Pond Ripples:** This option is really a cross between the two that follow. It moves pixels outward and rotates them around the center of the selection to create circular patterns. As demonstrated in the top rows of Figures 14-20 and 14-21, this option truly results in a pond ripple effect.

- **Out From Center:** When you select this option, Photoshop moves pixels outward in rhythmic bursts according to the value in the Ridges option box. Because the gradation image I created in Figure 14-14 was already arranged in a radial pattern, I brought in Moses to demonstrate the effect of the Out From Center option, as shown in the second rows of Figures 14-20 and 14-21.

Figure 14-21:
The effects of the Zigzag filter using three Ridges values and each of the three radio button settings. In all cases, the Amount value was 20.

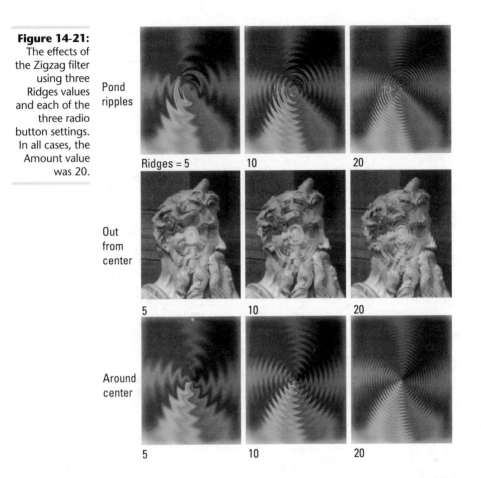

Pond ripples

Ridges = 5   10   20

Out from center

5   10   20

Around center

5   10   20

    ✑ **Around Center:** Select this option to rotate pixels in alternating directions around the circle without moving them outward. This is the only option that produces what I would term a zigzag effect. The last rows of Figures 14-20 and 14-21 show the effects of the Around Center option.

Creating parallel ripples and waves

Photoshop provides two means to distort an image in parallel waves, as if the image were lying on the bottom of a shimmering or undulating pool. Of the two, the Ripple filter is less sophisticated, but it's also straightforward and easy to apply. The Wave filter affords you greater control, but its options are among the most complex Photoshop has to offer.

To use the Ripple filter, choose Filter⇨Distort⇨Ripple. Photoshop displays the Ripple dialog box shown in Figure 14-22. You have the following options:

⊶ **Amount:** Enter an amount between negative and positive 999 in whole-number increments to specify the width of the ripples from side to side. Negative and positive values change the direction of the ripples, but visually speaking, they produce identical effects. The ripples are measured as a ratio of the Size value and the dimensions of the selection — all of which translates to, "Experiment and see what happens." You can count on getting ragged effects from any value over 300, as illustrated in Figure 14-23.

Figure 14-22:
The Ripple filter makes an image appear as if it were refracted through flowing water.

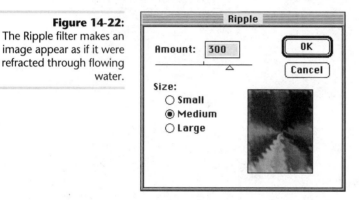

⊶ **Size:** Select one of the three radio buttons to change the length of the ripples. The Small option results in the shortest ripples and therefore the most ripples. As shown in the upper right corner of Figure 14-23, you can create a textured glass effect by combining the Small option with a high Amount value. The Large option results in the longest and fewest ripples.

You can create a blistered effect by overlaying a negative ripple onto a positive ripple. Try this: First, copy the selection. Then apply the Ripple filter with a positive Amount value — say, 300. Next, paste the copied selection and apply the Ripple filter at the exact opposite Amount value, in this case, –300. Press 5 to change the Opacity slider bar to 50 percent. The result is a series of diametrically opposed ripples that cross each other to create teardrop blisters.

Now that you're familiar with the Ripple filter, it's on to the Wave filter. I could write a book on this filter alone. It wouldn't be very big, nobody would buy it, and I'd hate every minute of it, but you never know what a free-lancer will do next. Keep an eye out at your local bookstore. In the meantime, I'm going to breeze though this filter like a little dog on the Oz-bound Kansas Express.

Figure 14-23:
The effects of
combining three
different Ripple filter
Amount values with
three different Size
settings.

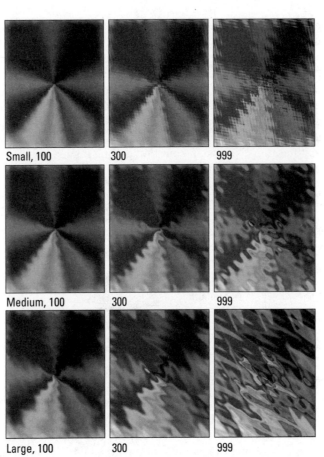

Small, 100   300   999

Medium, 100   300   999

Large, 100   300   999

Here goes: Choose Filter⇨Distort⇨Wave (that's the easy part) to display the Wave
dialog box shown in Figure 14-24. Photoshop presents you with the following options,
which makes applying a distortion almost every bit as fun as operating an oscilloscope:

- **Number of Generators:** Right off the bat, the Wave dialog box boggles the brain.
  A friend of mine likened this option to the number of rocks you throw in the
  water to start it rippling. One generator means that you throw in one rock to
  create one set of waves, as demonstrated in Figure 14-25. You can throw in two
  rocks to create two sets of waves (see Figure 14-26), three rocks to create three
  sets of waves, and all the way up to a quarry-full of 999 rocks to create, well, you
  get the idea. If you enter a high value, however, be prepared to wait a few years
  for the preview to update. If you can't wait, press Command-period, which turns
  off the preview until the next time you enter the dialog box.

Figure 14-24:
The Wave dialog box enables you to wreak scientific havoc on an image. Put on your pocket protector, take out your slide rule, and give it a whirl.

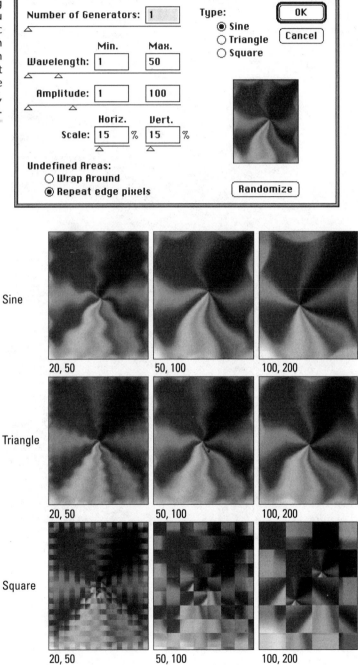

Figure 14-25:
The effect of three sets of Maximum Wavelength (first value) and Amplitude (second value) settings when combined with each of the three Type settings. The Number of Generators value was 1 in all cases.

Sine
20, 50   50, 100   100, 200

Triangle
20, 50   50, 100   100, 200

Square
20, 50   50, 100   100, 200

↪ **Wavelength and Amplitude:** Beginning to feel like you're playing with a HAM radio? The Wave filter produces random results by varying the number and length of waves (Wavelength) as well as the width of the waves (Amplitude) between minimum and maximum values, which can range anywhere from 1 to 999. (The Wavelength and Amplitude options, therefore, correspond in theory to the Size and Amount options in the Ripple dialog box.) Figures 14-25 and 14-26 show examples of representative Wavelength and Amplitude values.

Figure 14-26:
The only difference between these images and their counterparts in Figure 14-25 is that the Number of Generators value used for all images was 2.

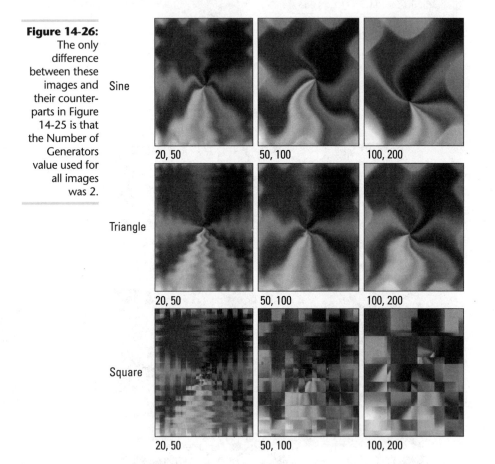

Sine

20, 50   50, 100   100, 200

Triangle

20, 50   50, 100   100, 200

Square

20, 50   50, 100   100, 200

⊕ **Scale:** You can scale the effects of the Wave filter between 1 and 100 percent horizontally and vertically. All the effects featured in Figures 14-25 and 14-26 were created by setting both Scale options to 15 percent.

⊕ **Undefined Areas:** The Wave filter distorts a selection to the extent that gaps may appear around the edges. You can either fill those gaps by repeating pixels along the edge of the selection, as in the figures, or by wrapping pixels from the left side of the selection onto the right side and pixels from the top edge of the selection onto the bottom.

⊕ **Type:** You can select from three kinds of waves. The Sine option produces standard sine waves that rise and fall smoothly in bell-shaped curves, just like real waves. The Triangle option creates zigzags that rise and fall in straight lines, like the edge of a piece of fabric cut with pinking shears. The Square option has nothing to do with waves at all, but rather organizes an image into a series of rectangular groupings, reminiscent of Cubism. You might think of this option as an extension of the Mosaic filter. All three options are demonstrated in Figures 14-25 and 14-26.

⊕ **Randomize:** The Wave filter is random by nature. If you don't like the effect you see in the preview box, click on the Randomize button to stir things up a bit. You can keep clicking on the button until you get an effect you like.

Distorting an image along a curve

The Distort command, which isn't discussed elsewhere in this book, creates four corner handles around an image. You drag each corner handle to distort the selected image in that direction. Unfortunately, you can't add other points around the edges to create additional distortions, which can be very frustrating if you're trying to achieve a specific effect. If you can't achieve a certain kind of distortion using Image⇨Effects⇨Distort, the Shear filter may be your answer.

Shear distorts an image along a path. When you choose Filter⇨Distort⇨Shear, you get the dialog box shown in Figure 14-27. Initially, a single line that has two points at either end appears in the grid at the top of the box. When you drag the points, you slant the image in the preview. This plus the fact that the filter is named Shear — Adobe's strange term for skewing (it appears in Illustrator as well) — leads many users to dismiss the filter as nothing more than a slanting tool. But in truth, it's more versatile than that.

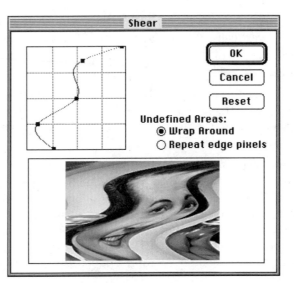

Figure 14-27:
Click on the grid line in the left corner of the Shear dialog box to add points to the line. Drag these points to distort the image along the curve.

You can add points to the grid line by simply clicking on it. A point springs up every time you click on an empty space in the line. Drag the point to change the curvature of the line and distort the image along the new curve. To delete a point, drag it off the left or right side of the grid. To delete all points and return the line to its original vertical orientation, click on the Reset button.

The Undefined Area options work just as they do in the Wave dialog box (described in the preceding section). You can either fill the gaps on one side of the image with pixels shoved off the opposite side by selecting Wrap Around or you can repeat pixels along the edge of the selection by selecting Repeat Edge Pixels.

Changing to polar coordinates

The Polar Coordinates filter is another one of those gems that a lot of folks shy away from because it doesn't make much sense at first glance. When you choose Filter⇨Distort⇨Polar Coordinates, Photoshop presents two radio buttons, as shown in Figure 14-28. You can either map an image from rectangular to polar coordinates or from polar to rectangular coordinates.

All right, time for some global theory. The top image in Figure 14-29 shows a stretched detail of the world map included in the default System 7 Scrapbook file. Though a tad simplistic, this map falls under the heading of a *Mercator projection,* meaning that Greenland is all stretched out of proportion, looking as big as the United States and Mexico combined.

Figure 14-28:
In effect, the Polar Coordinates dialog box lets you map an image onto a globe and view the globe from above.

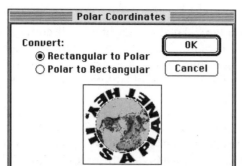

Figure 14-29:
The world from the equator up expressed in rectangular (top) and polar (bottom) coordinates.

The reason for this has to do with the way different mapping systems handle longitude and latitude lines. On a spherical globe, lines of latitude converge at the poles. On a Mercator map, they run absolutely parallel. Because the Mercator map exaggerates the distance between longitude lines as you progress away from the equator, it likewise exaggerates the distance between lines of latitude. The result is a map that becomes infinitely enormous at each of the poles.

When you convert the map to polar coordinates (by selecting the Rectangular to Polar radio button in the Polar Coordinates dialog box), you look down on it from the extreme north or south pole. This means that the entire length of the top edge of the Mercator map becomes a single dot in the exact center of the polar projection. The length of the bottom edge of the map wraps around the entire perimeter of the circle. The bottom example in Figure 14-29 shows the result. As you can see, the Rectangular to Polar option is just the thing for wrapping text around a circle.

If you select the Polar to Rectangular option, the Polar Coordinates filter produces the opposite effect. Imagine for a moment that the conical gradation shown in the upper left corner of Figure 14-30 is a fan spread out into a full circle. Now imagine closing the fan, breaking the hinge at the top, and spreading out the rectangular fabric of the fan. The center of the fan unfolds to form the top edge of the fabric, and what was once the perimeter of the circle is now the bottom edge of the fabric. Figure 14-30 shows two examples of what happens when you convert circular images from polar to rectangular coordinates.

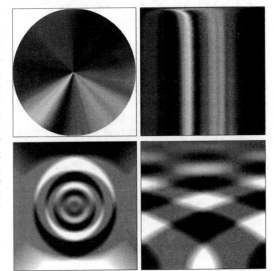

Figure 14-30:
Two familiar circular images (left) converted from polar to rectangular coordinates (right). The top example is simple enough that you can probably predict the results of the conversion in your head. The lower example looks cool, but you'd need a brain extension to predict the outcome.

The Polar Coordinates filter is a great way to edit gradations. After drawing a linear gradation with the gradient tool (as discussed in Chapter 10), try applying Filter⇨Distort⇨Polar Coordinates with the Polar to Rectangular option selected. (Rectangular to Polar just turns it into a radial gradation, sometimes with pretty undesirable results.) You get a redrawn gradation with highlights at the bottom of the selection. Press Command-F to reapply the filter to achieve another effect. You can keep repeating this technique until jagged edges start to appear. Then press Command-Z to go back to the last smooth effect.

Distorting an image inside out

The following exercise describes how to achieve a sizzling Parting of the Red Sea effect. Though it incorporates several distortion filters, the star of the effect is the Polar Coordinates filter, which is used to turn the image inside out and then convert it back to polar coordinates after flipping it upside down. No scanned image or artistic talent is required. Rumor has it that Moses puts in a guest appearance in the final image.

This effect is the brainchild of Mark Collen, easily the most authoritative filtering expert I've had the pleasure of knowing. I already mentioned his name in this chapter, in connection with the "Creating a Thick-liquid Droplet" steps. To be perfectly honest, I probably should have mentioned him more than that, because many of the ideas conveyed in this chapter were based on long, expensive telephone conversations with the guy.

At any rate, Figures 14-31 through 14-36 show the progression of the image through the following steps, starting with a simplistic throwback to Dada (the art movement, not the family member) and continuing to the fabled sea rising in billowing streams. Color Plate 14-7 shows one of Mark's most vivid images, which was created in part using many of the techniques from the steps below. Obviously, a lot of other filtering and nonfiltering techniques were used to create that image, but gee whiz folks, you can't expect the guy to share everything he knows in one fell swoop. He has to make a living, after all.

STEPS: The Parting of the Red Sea Effect

Step 1.   Draw some random shapes in whatever colors you like. My shapes appear against a black background in Figure 14-31, but you can use any shapes and any colors you like. To create each shape, I used the lasso tool to draw the outline of the shape and pressed Option-Delete to fill the lassoed selection with the foreground color. The effect works best if there's a lot of contrast between your colors.

Figure 14-31:
Draw several meaningless shapes with the lasso tool and fill each with a different color.

Step 2.   In Step 3, you apply the Wind Filter to add streaks to the shapes you just created, as shown in Figure 14-32. Because the Wind filter creates horizontal streaks only, and your goal is to add vertical streaks, you must temporarily reorient your image before applying the filter. To do so, choose Image⇨Rotate⇨90° CCW, which rotates the entire image a quarter turn counterclockwise.

Figure 14-32:
The result of rotating the image a quarter turn, blasting it in both directions with the Wind filter, rotating it back into place, and applying the Motion Blur filter vertically.

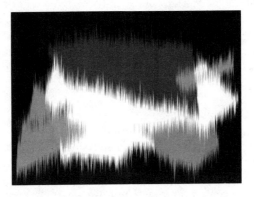

Step 3.   Choose Filter⇨Stylize⇨Wind. Select Blast and Left and press Return. To randomize the image in both directions, choose the Wind filter again and select Blast and Right.

Step 4.   Choose Image⇨Rotate⇨90° CW to return the image to its original orientation.

Step 5.   Choose Filter⇨Blur⇨Motion Blur. Enter 90 degrees into the Angle option and use 20 pixels for the Distance option. This blurs the image vertically to soften the blast lines, as demonstrated in Figure 14-32.

Step 6. Choose Filter⇨Distort⇨Wave and enter the values shown in Figure 14-33 into the Wave option box. Most of these values are approximate. You can experiment with other settings if you like. The only essential value is 0 percent in the Vert. option box, which ensures that the filter waves the image in a horizontal direction only.

Figure 14-33:
Apply these
settings from the
Wave dialog box
to wave the
image in a
vertical direction
only.

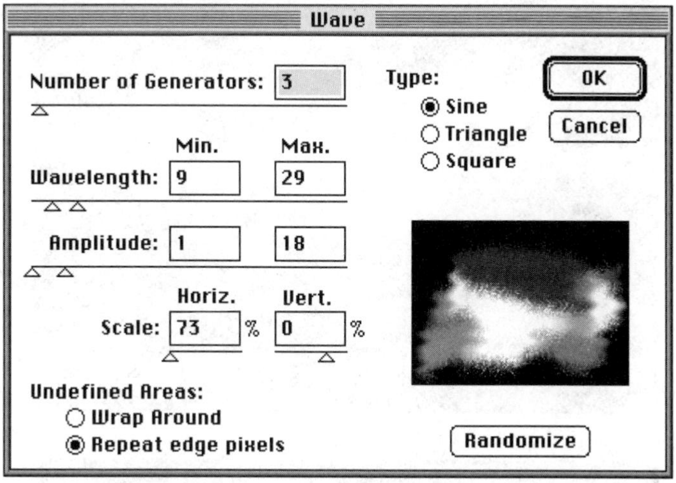

Step 7. Choose Filter⇨Distort⇨Ripple. I entered 300 for the Amount value and selected the Medium radio button.

Step 8. To perform the next step, the Polar Coordinates filter needs lots of empty room in which to maneuver. If you filled up your canvas like I did, choose Image⇨Canvas size and add 200 pixels both vertically and horizontally. The new canvas size, offering generous borders, appears in Figure 14-34.

Step 9. So far, you've probably been a little disappointed by your image. I mean, it's just this disgusting little hairy thing that looks like a bad rug or something. Well, now's your chance to turn it into something special. Choose Filter⇨Distort⇨Polar Coordinates and select the Polar to Rectangular radio button. Photoshop in effect turns the image inside out, sending all the hairy edges to the bottom of the screen. Finally, an image worth waiting for.

Step 10. Choose Image⇨Flip⇨Vertical to turn the image upside down. The hair now rises, as shown in Figure 14-35. This step prepares the image for the next polar conversion.

Figure 14-34:
After applying the
Ripple filter, use the
Canvas Size
command to add a
generous amount
of empty space
around the image.

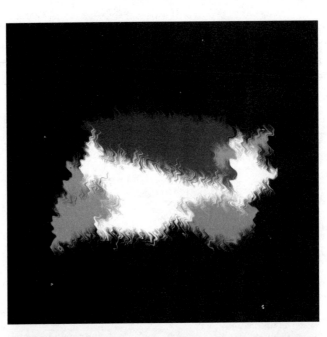

Figure 14-35:
Convert the image
from polar to
rectangular
coordinates to turn
it inside out. Then
flip it vertically to
prepare it for the
next polar
conversion.

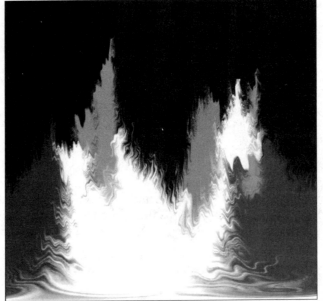

Step 11.   Use the rectangular marquee tool to select the central portion of the image. Leave deselected about 50 pixels along the top and bottom of the image and 100 pixels along both sides. Then feather the selection with a 15-pixel radius.

Step 12.   Press Command-F to reapply the Polar Coordinates filter just as before. The pixels inside the selection now billow into a fountain.

Step 13.   Add Moses to taste. The finished image appears in Figure 14-36.

Figure 14-36:
Marquee the central portion of the image with a heavily feathered selection outline, convert the selection from rectangular to polar coordinates, and put Moses into the scene. My, doesn't he look natural in his new environment?

Adding Clouds and Spotlights ____

In a way, you can think of all five filters in the Filter⇨Render submenu as lighting filters. You can use Clouds and Difference Clouds to create a layer of haze over an image. Lens Flare creates light flashes and reflections (as I mentioned earlier). Lighting Effects lights an image as if it were hanging on a gallery wall. You can even use the unremarkable Texture Fill command to add an embossed texture to a piece lighted with the Lighting Effects filter. Together, these five suggest a new category called *creative filters*, but it's really too early to tell.

Creating clouds

If you've played with the Clouds filters at all, you probably thought, "Hmf," and gave them up for a screwy feature that Adobe's programmers decided to add in lieu of some meatier functions. Certainly these filters don't qualify as ground-breaking, but they're not at all bad and can yield some pretty entertaining results.

Clouds create an abstract and random haze of color between the foreground and background colors. Difference Clouds works exactly like floating the image, applying the Clouds filter, and choosing the Difference overlay mode from the Layers palette. Why on earth should this filter make special provisions for a single overlay mode? Because you can create cumulative effects. Try this: Select blue as the foreground color and then choose Filter⇨Render⇨Clouds. Ah, just like a real sky, huh? Now choose Filter⇨Render⇨Difference Clouds. It's like some kind of weird Halloween motif, all blacks and oranges. Press Command-F to repeat the filter. Back to the blue sky. Keep pressing Command-F over and over and notice the results. A pink cancer starts invading the blue sky; a green cancer invades the orange one. Multiple applications of the Difference Clouds filter generate organic oil-on-water effects.

 To strengthen the colors created by the Clouds filter, press Shift when choosing the command. This same technique works when using the Difference Clouds filter as well. In fact, I don't know of any reason *not* to Shift-choose these commands, unless you have some specific need for washed-out effects. Oh, by the way, you can repeat a filter, such as Difference Clouds, at this high-intensity setting by pressing Command-Shift-F (as long as you haven't gone and assigned the key combination to something different, as I suggested back in Chapter 2).

Color Plate 14-8 shows some pretty entertaining applications of the Clouds filters. With the foreground and background colors set to blue and orange respectively, I applied the Clouds filter to a floating version of the rose image. For maximum effect, I Shift-chose the filter to create the top left image in the color plate. I then Shift-chose the Difference Clouds filter to create the purple montage in the figure, and pressed Command-Shift-F ten times to achieve the top right image. Looks to me like I definitely have something growing in my Petri dish.

Yeah, so really groovy stuff, right? Shades of "Purple Haze" and all that. 'Scuze me while I kiss that filter. But now that I've created this murky mess, what the heck do I do with it? Composite it, of course. The bottom row of Color Plate 14-8 shows examples of mixing each of the images from the top row with the original rose. In the left example, I chose the Overlay option from the overlay modes pop-up menu in the Layers palette. In the middle example, I chose the Screen option. And in the last example, I chose Hue. This last one is particularly exciting, completely transforming the colors in the rose while leaving the gray (and therefore unsaturated) background untouched. Without a mask, without anything but a rectangular marquee, I've managed to precisely color the interior of the rose.

Lighting an image

Photoshop 3.0 is definitely venturing into 3-D drawing territory with the Lighting Effects filter. This very complex function allows you to shine lights on an image, color the lights, position them, focus them, specify the reflectivity of the surface, and even create a surface map. In many ways, it's a direct lift from Fractal Design Painter. But whereas Painter provides predefined paper textures and light refraction effects that bolster the capabilities of its excellent tool, Photoshop offers better controls and more lighting options.

When you choose Filter⇨Render⇨Lighting Effect, Photoshop displays what is easily its most complex dialog box, as shown in Figure 14-37. The dialog box has two halves, one in which you actually position light with respect to a thumbnail of the selected image, and one that contains about a billion intimidating options. Between you and me, I think Adobe could have done a better job, but the dialog box is functional.

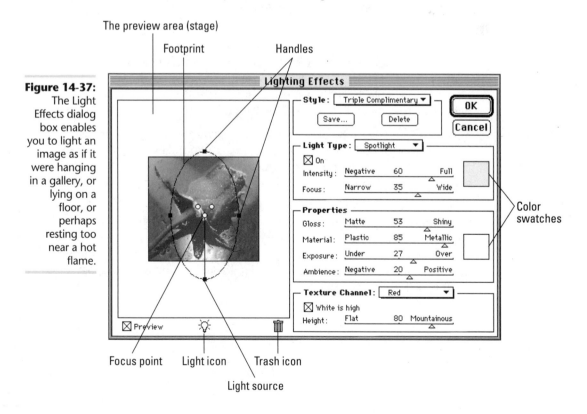

Figure 14-37:
The Light Effects dialog box enables you to light an image as if it were hanging in a gallery, or lying on a floor, or perhaps resting too near a hot flame.

No bones about it, this dialog box is a bear. The easiest way to apply the filter is to choose one of the predefined lighting effects from the Style pop-up menu at the top of the right side of the dialog box, see how it looks in the preview area, and — if you like it — press Return to apply the effect.

But if you want to create your own effects, you'll have to work a little harder. Here are the basic steps involved in creating a custom effect.

STEPS: **Lighting an Image**

Step 1. Drag from the light icon at the bottom of the dialog box into the preview area to create a new light source. I call this area the *stage* because it's as if the image is painted on the floor of a stage and the lights are hanging above it.

Step 2. Select the kind of light you want from the Light Type pop-up menu (just below the Style pop-up menu). You can select from Directional, Omni, and Spotlight. Directional works like the sun, being a general, unfocused light that hits a target from an angle. Omni is a bare light bulb hanging in the middle of the room, shining in all directions from a center point. And Spotlight is a focused beam that is brightest at the source and tapers off gradually.

Step 3. Specify the color of the light by clicking on the top color swatch (labeled in Figure 14-37). You can also muck about with the Intensity slider bar to control the brightness of the light. If Spotlight is selected, the Focus slider becomes available. Drag the slider toward Narrow to create a bright laser of light; drag toward Wide to diffuse the light and spread it over a larger area.

Step 4. Move the light source by dragging at the *focus point*, which appears as a colored circle in the stage. When Directional or Spotlight is selected, the focus point represents the spot at which the light is pointing. When Omni is active, the focus point is the actual bulb. (Don't burn yourself.)

Step 5. If Directional or Spotlight is active, you can change the angle of the light by dragging at the *light source*. When you use a Directional light, the source appears as a black square at the end of a line joined to the focus point. The same holds true when you edit a Spotlight; the confusing thing is that there are four black squares altogether. The light source is joined to the focus point by a line, the three *handles* are not.

Step 6. When Omni is in force, a circle surrounds the focus point. When editing a Spotlight, you see an ellipse. Either way, this shape represents the *footprint* of the light, which is the approximate area of the image affected by the light. You can change the size of the light by dragging the handles around the footprint. Enlarging the shape is like raising the light source. When the footprint is small, the light is close to the image, so it's concentrated and very bright. When the footprint is large, the light is high above the image, so it's more generalized.

Step 7. Introduce more lights as you see fit by repeating the steps thus far. To delete a light, drag the focus point onto the trash can icon at the bottom of the dialog box.

Step 8. Change the Properties and Texture Channel options as you see fit. (I explain these in detail in a moment.)

Step 9. If you want to save your settings for future use, click on the Save button. Photoshop invites you to name the setup, which then appears as an option in the Style pop-up menu. If you want to get rid of one of the presets, select it from the pop-up menu and click on the Delete button.

Step 10. Press Return to apply your settings to the image.

That's almost everything. The only parts I left out are the Properties and Texture Channel options. The Properties slider bars control how light reflects off the surface of your image:

- **Gloss:** Is the surface dull or shiny? Drag the slider toward Matte to make the surface flat and nonreflective, like dull enamel paint. Drag the slider toward Shiny to make it glossy, as if you had slapped on a coat of lacquer.

- **Material:** This option determines the color of the light that reflects back off the image. According to the logic employed by this option, Plastic reflects back the color of the light; Metallic reflects the color of the object itself. If only I had a bright, shiny plastic thing and a bright, shiny metal thing, I could check to see if this logic holds true in real life (like maybe that matters).

- **Exposure:** I'd like this option better if you could vary it between Sun Block 65 and Melanoma. Unfortunately, the more prosaic titles are Under and Over — exposed, that is. This option controls the brightness of all lights like a big dimmer switch. You can control a single selected light using the Intensity slider, but the Exposure slider offers the added control of changing all lights in the stage area and the ambient light (described next) together.

✎ **Ambience:** The last slider allows you to add *ambient light,* which is a general, diffused light that hits all surfaces evenly. First, select the color of the light by clicking on the color swatch to the right. Then drag the slider to cast a subtle hue over the stage. Drag toward Positive to tint the image with the color in the swatch; drag toward Negative to tint the stage with the swatch's opposite. Keep the slider set to 0 — dead in the center — to cast no hue.

The Texture Channel options let you treat one channel in the image as a *texture map,* which is a grayscale surface in which white indicates peaks and black indicates valleys. (As long as White is High is selected, that is. If you deselect that option, everything flips, and black becomes the peak.) It's as if one channel has a surface to it. By selecting a channel from the pop-up menu, you create an emboss effect, much like that created with the Emboss filter, except much better because you can light the surface from many angles at once, and it's in color to boot.

Choose a channel to serve as the embossed surface from the pop-up menu. Then change the Height slider to indicate more or less Flat terrain or huge Mountainous cliffs of surface texture.

Color Plate 14-9 shows the rose lit with three colored spotlights. In the first example, I selected the red channel as the surface map. In the second example, I filled a separate mask channel with my seamlessly repeating Lenin pattern from Chapter 11 (using Filter➪Render➪Texture Fill) and then selected that channel from the Texture Channel pop-up menu in the Lighting Effects dialog box. It's as if I took my Lenin pattern, stamped into the surface of the rose, and then shined a bunch of spotlights on it. What fun!

Summary

- You can create unusual halo effects by applying the Crystallize or Mosaic filter to a heavily feathered selection.

- The Mezzotint and Trace Contour filters convert every color channel to a black-and-white image, leaving eight vivid primary colors in their wake. You'll almost always want to composite the results with the unfiltered original.

- To retain the colors in an embossed image, first float the image, then apply the Emboss filter, and finally choose the Luminosity option from the overlay modes pop-up menu in the Layers palette.

- To add a metallic coating to an image, float the image, Gaussian Blur it, and apply the Find Edges filter. Then composite floater and underlying original using Overlay or some other overlay mode.

- Apply the Trace Contour filter after Add Noise or one of the filters in the Pixelate submenu to infest your image with a network of fine lines, suggesting thousands of hairline cracks in a window pane (or some such thing).

- Get to know the distortion filters before trying to use them in a real project, especially if you're under a mean, grueling deadline.

- Apply the Pinch filter 10 times in succession at 100 percent to turn any image into a conical gradation. Use the Spherize filter set to –100 percent to get a very similar effect.

- The Twirl filter results in spirals; the Zigzag filter results in concentric pond ripples; the Ripple filter results in smooth waves; and the Wave filter results in smooth waves, abrupt zigzags, and mosaic patterns.

- Use the Polar Coordinates filter to create text on a curve. The filter folds and unfolds images like they were patterns on a Japanese fan.

- Press the Shift key while choosing the Clouds or Difference Clouds filter to intensify the colors of the haze. Apply the Difference Clouds command over and over to get some decidedly uncloud-like effects.

- Successfully using the Lighting Effects filter is mostly a matter of experimenting with positioning and editing the lights inside the preview area. You can also simply select predefined settings from the Style pop-up menu.

Constructing Homemade Effects

In This Chapter

- The mathematics behind the Custom filter
- Demonstrations of more than 70 custom sharpening, blurring, edge-detection, and embossing effects
- An in-depth analysis of the Displace filter
- A look at Photoshop's predefined displacement maps
- How to apply custom gradations and textures as displacement maps
- A relatively brief tour of the immensely powerful but complicated Filter Factory
- Create your own fully-functioning filter that rotates channels independently and distorts their centers

Creating a Custom Effect

If my wife were here right now, she might be tempted to say something diplomatic like, "Deke, dear, I think that our guests are growing a teeny bit tired of the subject of filters. Perhaps this would be a good time to move on to a new subject." To which I would respond, "Nonsense! Folks love to listen to me drone on and on about filters. I can't imagine anything more intriguing, can you? Speaking of which, is there any beer left in this house? (Urp.)" Whether you share my fascination with filters or not, don't get up and go home just yet, because I've yet to tell you about three very important filters: Custom, Displace, and the Filter Factory, a plug-in that's new to Photoshop 3.0. With these three filters, you can create your own, custom-tailored special effects.

Fully understanding the Custom and Displace filters requires some mathematical reasoning skills — and even if you're a math whiz, you'll probably have occasional difficulty predicting the outcomes of these filters. Using the Filter Factory requires flat-out programming skills. If math isn't your bag, if number theory clogs up your synapses to the extent that you feel like a worthless math wimp, by all means don't put yourself through the torture. Skip all the mathematical background in this chapter and read the "Applying Custom Values" and "Using Displacement Maps" sections to try out some specific, no-brainer effects.

If you have no desire to learn the Filter Factory, you can experiment with some filters that I programmed using this plug-in. On the CD, you'll find seven fully functioning filters, all of which include interactive slider bars and previews. If you copy the filters to your Plug-ins folder and launch Photoshop, you'll see my filters in the Filter➪Tormentia submenu. (These filters torment your image in a demented way, hence *Tormentia*. I also considered *Tormento*, but that sounds like something you'd put on your pizza.) I explain what the filters do and how they work in a text file included on the CD.

The Tormentia filters are for the Mac only; a Windows version of Filter Factory is not available as I write this.

On the other hand, if you're not scared silly of math and you want to understand how to eventually create effects of your own, read on, you hearty soul.

The Custom filter

The Custom command enables you to design your own *convolution kernel*, which is a variety of filter in which neighboring pixels get mixed together. The kernel can be a variation on sharpening, blurring, embossing, or half a dozen other effects. You create your filter by entering numerical values into a matrix of options.

When you choose Filter➪Other➪Custom, Photoshop displays the dialog box shown in Figure 15-1. It sports a 5 × 5 matrix of option boxes followed by two additional options, Scale and Offset. The matrix options can accept values from negative to positive 999. The Scale value can range from 1 to 9,999, and the Offset value can range from negative to positive 9,999. The dialog box includes Load and Save buttons so that you can load settings from disk and save the current settings for future use.

Figure 15-1:
The Custom dialog box lets you design your own convolution kernel by multiplying the brightness values of pixels.

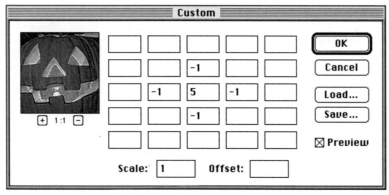

The new incarnation of the filter also includes a constantly updating preview box, which you'll have lots of time to appreciate if you decide to try your hand at designing your own effects. Select the Preview check box to view the effect of the kernel in the image window as well.

Here's how the filter works: When you press the Return key to apply the values in the Custom dialog box to a selection, the filter passes over every pixel in the selection one at a time. For each pixel being evaluated — which I'll call the PBE, for short — the filter multiplies the PBE's current brightness value by the number in the center option box (the one that contains a 5 in Figure 15-1). To help keep things straight, I'll call this value the CMV, for *central matrix value.*

The filter then multiplies the brightness values of the surrounding pixels by the surrounding values in the matrix. For example, Photoshop multiplies the value in the option box just above the CMV by the brightness value of the pixel just above the PBE. It ignores any empty matrix option boxes and the pixels they represent.

Finally, the filter totals the products of the multiplied pixels, divides the sum by the value in the Scale option, and adds the Offset value to calculate the new brightness of the PBE. It then moves on to the next pixel in the selection and performs the calculation all over again. Figure 15-2 shows a schematic drawing of the process.

Perhaps seeing all of this spelled out in an equation will help you understand the process. Then again, perhaps not — but here it comes anyway. In the following equation, NP stands for *neighboring pixel* and MV stands for the corresponding matrix value in the Custom dialog box.

New brightness value = (((PBE × CMV) + (NP1 × MV1) + (NP2 × MV2) + . . .) ÷ Scale) + Offset

Luckily, Photoshop calculates the equation without any help from you. All you have to do is punch in the values and see what happens.

Figure 15-2:
The Custom filter multiplies each matrix value by the brightness value of the corresponding pixel, adds the products together, divides the sum by the Scale value, adds the Offset value, and applies the result to the pixel being evaluated.

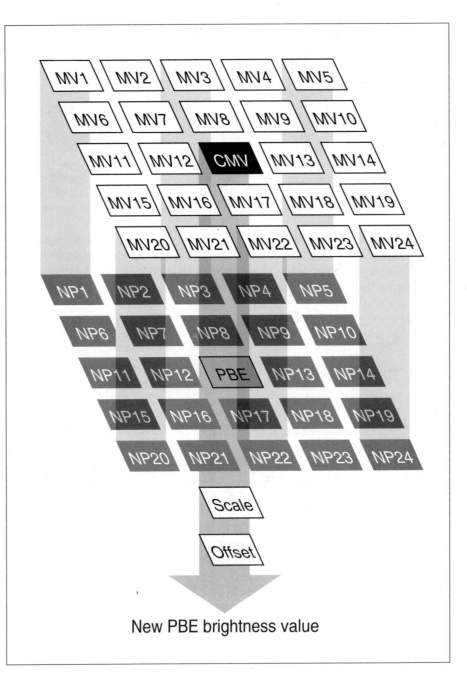

Custom filter advice

Now obviously, if you go around multiplying the brightness value of a pixel too much, you end up making it white. And a filter that turns an image white is pretty darn useless. The key, then, is to filter an image and at the same time maintain the original balance of brightness values. To achieve this, just be sure that the sum of all values in the matrix is 1. For example, the default values in the matrix shown back in Figure 15-1 are 5, –1, –1, –1, and –1, which add up to 1.

If the sum is greater than 1, use the Scale value to divide the sum down to 1. Figures 15-3 and 15-4 show the results of increasing the CMV from 5 to 6 and then 7. This raises the sum of the values in the matrix from 1 to 2 and then 3.

In Figure 15-3, I entered the sum into the Scale option to divide the sum back down to 1 (any value divided by itself is 1, after all). The result is that Photoshop maintains the original color balance of the image while at the same time filtering it slightly differently. When I did not raise the Scale value, the image became progressively lighter, as illustrated in Figure 15-4.

If the sum is less than 1, increase the CMV until the sum reaches the magic number. For example, in Figure 15-5, I lowered the values to the left of the CMV and then above the CMV by 1 apiece to increase the sharpening effect. To ensure that the image did not darken, I also raised the CMV to compensate. When I did not raise the CMV, the image turned black, as shown in Figure 15-6.

Figure 15-3:
Raising the Scale value to reflect the sum of the values in the matrix maintains the color balance of the image.

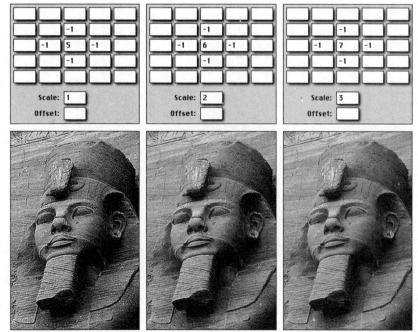

Figure 15-4:
Raising the sum of the matrix values without counterbalancing it in the Scale option lightens the image.

First matrix:

		-1		
	-1	5	-1	
		-1		

Scale: 1
Offset:

Second matrix:

		-1		
	-1	6	-1	
		-1		

Scale: 1
Offset:

Third matrix:

		-1		
	-1	7	-1	
		-1		

Scale: 1
Offset:

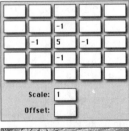
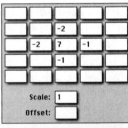

Figure 15-5:
Raising the CMV to compensate for the lowered values in the matrix maintains the color balance of the image.

First matrix:

		-1		
	-1	5	-1	
		-1		

Scale: 1
Offset:

Second matrix:

		-1		
	-2	6	-1	
		-1		

Scale: 1
Offset:

Third matrix:

		-2		
	-2	7	-1	
		-1		

Scale: 1
Offset:

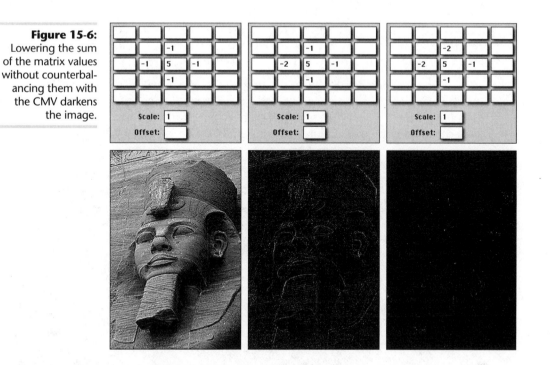

Figure 15-6:
Lowering the sum of the matrix values without counterbalancing them with the CMV darkens the image.

Though a sum of 1 provides the safest and most predictable filtering effects, you can use different sums, such as 0 and 2, to try out more destructive filtering effects. If you do, be sure to raise or lower the Offset value to compensate. For some examples, see the "Non-one variations" section.

Applying Custom Values

The following sections show you ways to sharpen, blur, and otherwise filter an image using specific matrix, Scale, and Offset values. It is my sincere hope that by the end of the Custom filter discussions, you not only will know how to repeat my examples, but also how to apply what you've learned to design special effects of your own.

Symmetrical effects

Values that are symmetrical both horizontally and vertically about the central matrix value produce sharpen and blur effects:

- **Sharpening:** A positive CMV surrounded by symmetrical negative values sharpens an image, as demonstrated in the first example of Figure 15-7. Figures 15-3 through 15-6 also demonstrate varying degrees of sharpening effects.

☞ **Blurring:** A positive CMV surrounded by symmetrical positive numbers — balanced, of course, by a Scale value as explained in the preceding section — blurs an image, as demonstrated in the second example of Figure 15-7.

☞ **Blurring with edge-detection:** A negative CMV surrounded by symmetrical positive values blurs an image and adds an element of edge-detection, as illustrated in the last example of the figure. These effects are unlike anything provided by Photoshop's standard collection of filters.

Figure 15-7:
Symmetrical values can result in sharpening (left), blurring (middle), and edge-detection (right) effects.

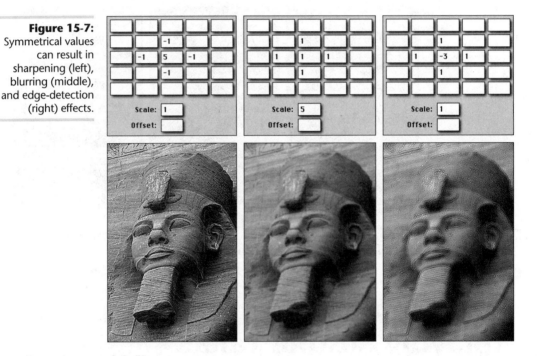

Sharpening

The Custom command provides as many variations on the sharpening theme as the Unsharp Mask filter. In a sense, it provides even more, for whereas the Unsharp Mask filter requires you to sharpen an image inside a Gaussian radius, you get to specify exactly which pixels are taken into account when you use the Custom filter.

To create Unsharp Mask-like effects, enter a large number in the CMV and small values in the surrounding option boxes, as demonstrated in Figure 15-8. To go beyond Unsharp Mask, you can violate the radius of the filter by entering values around the perimeter of the matrix and ignoring options closer to the CMV, as demonstrated in Figure 15-9.

You can sharpen an image using the Custom dialog box in two basic ways. First, you can enter lots of negative values into the neighboring options in the matrix and then enter a CMV just large enough to yield a sum of 1. This results in radical sharpening effects, as demonstrated throughout the examples in Figures 15-8 and 15-9.

Figure 15-8:
To create severe
sharpening effects,
enter a CMV just
large enough to
compensate for the
negative values in
the matrix.

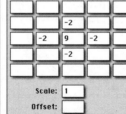

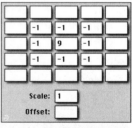

Scale: 1
Offset:

Scale: 1
Offset:

Scale: 1
Offset:

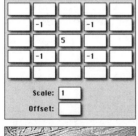

Figure 15-9:
To heighten the
sharpening effect
even further, enter
negative values
around the
perimeter of the
matrix.

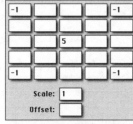

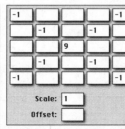

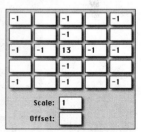

Scale: 1
Offset:

Scale: 1
Offset:

Scale: 1
Offset:

Second, you can tone down the sharpening by raising the CMV and using the Scale value to divide the sum down to 1. Figures 15-10 and 15-11 show the results of raising the CMV to lessen the impact of the sharpening effects performed in Figures 15-8 and 15-9.

Figure 15-10:
To sharpen more subtly, increase the central matrix value and then enter the sum into the Scale value.

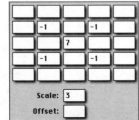
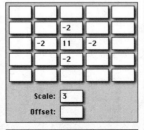
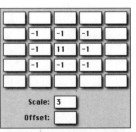

Figure 15-11:
When you soften the effect of radical sharpening, you create a thicker, higher contrast effect, much as when raising the Radius value in the Unsharp Mask dialog box.

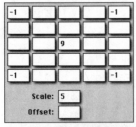
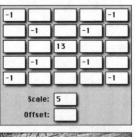
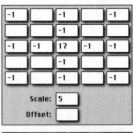

Blurring

The philosophy behind blurring is very much the same as that behind sharpening. To produce extreme blurring effects, enter lots of values or high values into the neighboring options in the matrix, enter 1 into the CMV, and then enter the sum into the Scale option. Examples appear in Figure 15-12. To downplay the blurring, raise the CMV and the Scale value by equal amounts. In Figure 15-13, I used the same neighboring values as in Figure 15-12, but I increased the CMV and the Scale value by 3 apiece.

Figure 15-12: To create severe blurring effects, enter 1 for the CMV and fill the neighboring options with 1s and 2s.

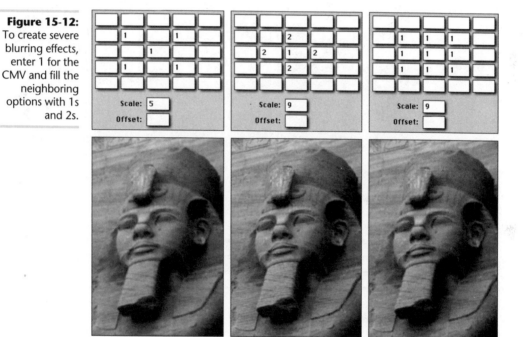

Edge-detection

Many of you are probably beginning to get the idea by now, but just in case you're the kind of person who believes that friends don't let friends do math, I'll breeze through it one more time in the venue of edge-detection. If you really want to see those edges, enter 1s and 2s into the neighboring options in the matrix and then enter a CMV just *small* enough — it's a negative value, after all — to make the sum 1. Examples appear in Figure 15-14 for your viewing pleasure.

To lighten the edges and bring out the blur, raise the CMV and enter the resulting sum into the Scale option box. The first example in Figure 15-15 pushes the boundaries between edge-detection and a straight blur.

Figure 15-13:
To blur more subtly, increase the central matrix value and the Scale value by equal amounts.

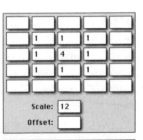

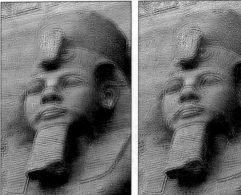
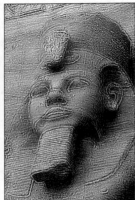

Figure 15-14:
To create severe edge-detection effects, enter a negative CMV just small enough to compensate for the positive values in the matrix.

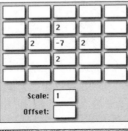
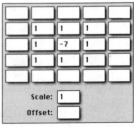

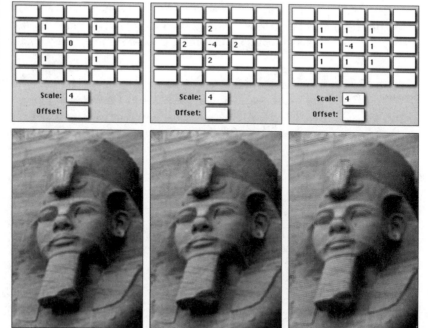

Figure 15-15:
To blur the edges, increase the central matrix value and then enter the sum into the Scale value.

Non-1 variations

Every image shown in Figures 15-7 through 15-15 is the result of manipulating matrix values and using the Scale option to produce a sum total of 1. Earlier in this chapter, I showed you what can happen if you go below 1 (black images) or above 1 (white images). But I haven't shown you how you can use non-1 totals to produce interesting, if somewhat washed-out, effects.

The key is to raise the Offset value, thereby adding a specified brightness value to each pixel in the image. By doing this, you can offset the lightening or darkening caused by the matrix values to create an image that has half a chance of printing.

Lightening overly dark effects

The first image in Figure 15-16 uses nearly the exact same values used to create the extreme sharpening effect in the last image of Figure 15-8. The only difference is that the CMV is 1 lower (8, down from 9), which in turn lowers the sum total from 1 to 0.

The result is an extremely dark image with hints of brightness at points of high contrast. The image looks okay on-screen — actually, it looks pretty cool because of all those little star-like sprinkles in it — but it's likely to fill in during the printing process. If the first image in Figure 15-16 looks like anything but a vague blob of blackness, it's a credit to the printer of this book. Most printers who didn't have a giant publisher breathing down their necks would have kissed this image good-bye, and rightly so. It's too darn dark.

Figure 15-16:
Three examples of sharpening effects with sum totals of 0. I lightened the images incrementally by entering positive values into the Offset option box.

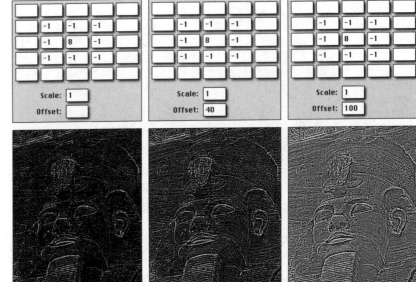

To prevent the image from filling in and to help head off any disputes with your printer, lighten the image using the Offset value. Photoshop adds the value to the brightness level of each selected pixel. A brightness value of 255 equals solid white, so you don't need to go too high. As shown in the last example of Figure 15-16, an Offset value of 100 is enough to raise most pixels in the image to a medium gray. Figure 15-17 shows the results of lightening an overly dark edge-detection effect using the Offset value.

Darkening overly light effects

You also can use the Offset value to darken filtering effects with sum totals greater than 1. The images in Figures 15-18 and 15-19 show sharpening and edge-detection effects whose matrix totals amount to 2. On their own, these filters produce effects that are too light. However, as demonstrated in the middle and right examples in the figures, you can darken the effects of the Custom filter to create high-contrast images by entering a negative value into the Offset option box.

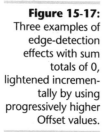

Figure 15-17:
Three examples of
edge-detection
effects with sum
totals of 0,
lightened incremen-
tally by using
progressively higher
Offset values.

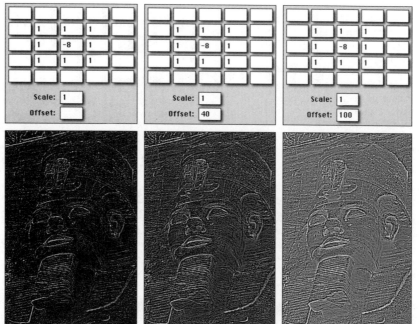

Using extreme offsets

If a brightness value of 255 produces solid white and a brightness value of 0 is solid
black, why in blue blazes does the Offset value permit any number between negative
and positive 9,999, a number 40 times greater than solid white? The answer lies in the
fact that the matrix options can force the Custom filter to calculate brightness values
much darker than black and much lighter than white. Therefore, you can use a very
high or very low Offset value to boost the brightness of an image in which all pixels are
well below black or diminish the brightness when all pixels are way beyond white.

Figure 15-20 shows exaggerated versions of the sharpening, blurring, and edge-
detection effects. The sum totals of the matrixes are –42, 54, and 42, respectively.
Without some help from the Offset value, each of these filters would turn every pixel
in the image black (in the case of the sharpening effect) or white (blurring and edge-
detection). But as demonstrated in the figure, using enormous Offset numbers brings
out those few brightness values that remain. The images are so polarized that there's
hardly any difference between the three effects, except that the first image is an inverted version of the other two. The difference is even less noticeable if you apply the
effect to a translucent floating selection, as demonstrated in the second row of examples in Figure 15-20.

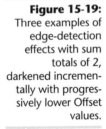

Figure 15-18: Three examples of sharpening effects with sum totals of 2. I darkened the images incrementally by entering negative values into the Offset option box.

Figure 15-19: Three examples of edge-detection effects with sum totals of 2, darkened incrementally with progressively lower Offset values.

Figure 15-20: You can create high-contrast effects by exaggerating all values in the matrix and then compensating by entering a very high or very low Offset value (top row). When applied to translucent floating selections (bottom row), the sharpening, blurring, and edge-detection effects are barely discernible.

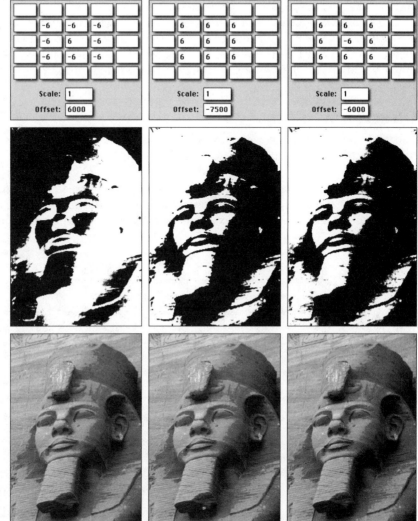

Other custom effects

By now, I hope that you understand what an absolute trip the Custom filter can be, provided that you immerse yourself in the old adventurous spirit. Quite honestly, I could keep showing you ways to use the Custom filter for another 20 or 30 pages. But then my publisher would come unglued because I'd never finish the book, and you'd miss the pleasure of discovering variations on your own.

Nonetheless, you're probably wondering what happens if you just go absolutely berserk, in a computer-geek sort of way, and start entering matrix values in unusual or even arbitrary arrangements. The answer is that as long as you maintain a sum total of 1, you achieve some pretty interesting and even usable effects. Many of these effects will be simple variations on sharpening, blurring, and edge-detection.

Directional blurs

Figure 15-21 shows examples of entering positive matrix values all in one row, all in a column, or in opposite quadrants. As you can see, as long as you maintain uniformly positive values, you get a blurring effect. However, by keeping the values lowest in the center and highest toward the edges and corners, you can create directional blurs. The first example resembles a slight horizontal motion blur, the second looks like a slight vertical motion blur, and the last example looks like it's vibrating horizontally and vertically.

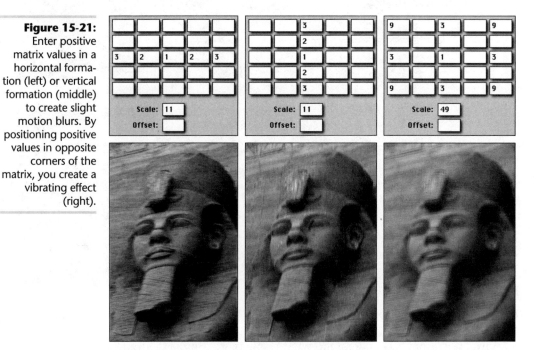

Figure 15-21: Enter positive matrix values in a horizontal formation (left) or vertical formation (middle) to create slight motion blurs. By positioning positive values in opposite corners of the matrix, you create a vibrating effect (right).

Directional sharpening

To selectively sharpen edges in an image based on the angles of the edges, you can organize negative and positive matrix values into rows or columns. For example, to sharpen only the horizontal edges in an image, fill the middle row of matrix options with positive values and the rows immediately above and below with negative values, as demonstrated in the left example in Figure 15-22. Similarly, you can sharpen only the vertical edges by entering positive values in the middle column and flanking the column on left and right with negative values, as shown in the middle example in the figure. In the last example, I arranged the positive values along a diagonal axis to sharpen only the diagonal edges.

Figure 15-22:
Arrange positive values in a row (left), column (middle), or along a diagonal axis (right) to sharpen horizontal, vertical, and diagonal edges exclusively.

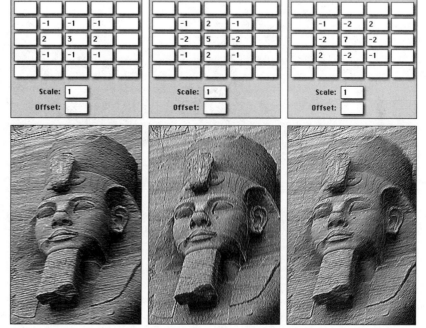

You even can combine directional sharpening with directional blurring. Figure 15-23 shows the first example from Figure 15-22 blurred both horizontally and vertically. To blur the image horizontally, as in the middle example of Figure 15-23, I added positive values to the extreme ends of the middle row, thereby extending the range of the filter and creating a sort of horizontal jumbling effect. To blur the image vertically, as in the final example of the figure, I added positive values to the ends of the middle column.

Embossing

So far, we aren't going very nuts, are we? Despite their unusual formations, the matrix values in Figures 15-21 through 15-23 still manage to maintain symmetry. Well, now it's time to lose the symmetry, which typically results in an embossing effect.

Figure 15-24 shows three variations on embossing, all of which involve positive and negative matrix values positioned on opposite sides of the CMV. (The CMV happens to be positive merely to maintain a sum total of 1.)

Figure 15-23:
The image from Figure 15-22 (left) blurred horizontally (middle) and vertically (right).

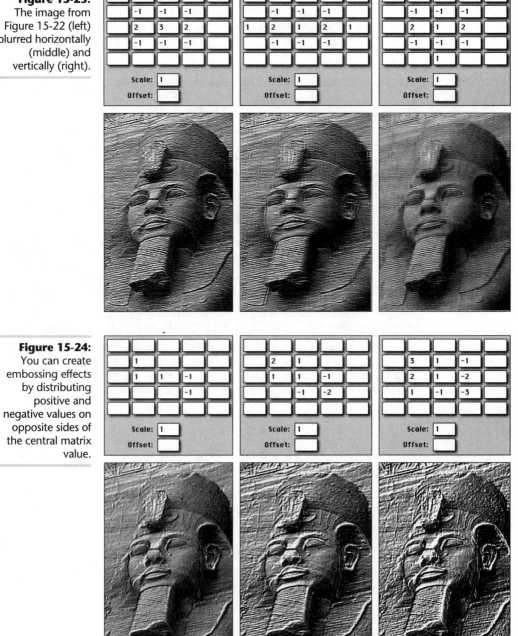

Figure 15-24:
You can create embossing effects by distributing positive and negative values on opposite sides of the central matrix value.

This type of embossing has no hard and fast light source, but you might imagine that the light comes from the general direction of the positive values. Therefore, when I swapped the positive and negative values throughout the matrix (all except the CMV), I approximated an underlighting effect, as demonstrated by the images in Figure 15-25.

In truth, it's not so much a lighting difference as a difference in edge enhancement. White pixels collect on the side of an edge represented by positive values in the matrix; black pixels collect on the negative-value side. So when I swapped the locations of positive and negative values between Figures 15-24 and 15-25, I changed the distribution of white and black pixels in the filtered images.

Embossing is the loosest of the Custom filter effects. As long as you position positive and negative values on opposite sides of the CMV, you can distribute the values in almost any way you see fit. Figure 15-26 demonstrates three entirely arbitrary arrangements of values in the Custom matrix. Figure 15-27 shows those same effects downplayed by raising the CMV and entering the sum of the matrix values into the Scale option box.

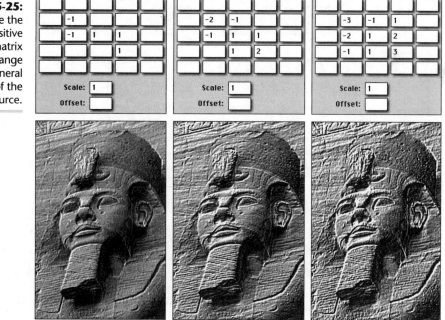

Figure 15-25:
Change the location of positive and negative matrix values to change the general direction of the light source.

Figure 15-26:
You can create whole libraries of embossing effects by experimenting with different combinations of positive and negative values.

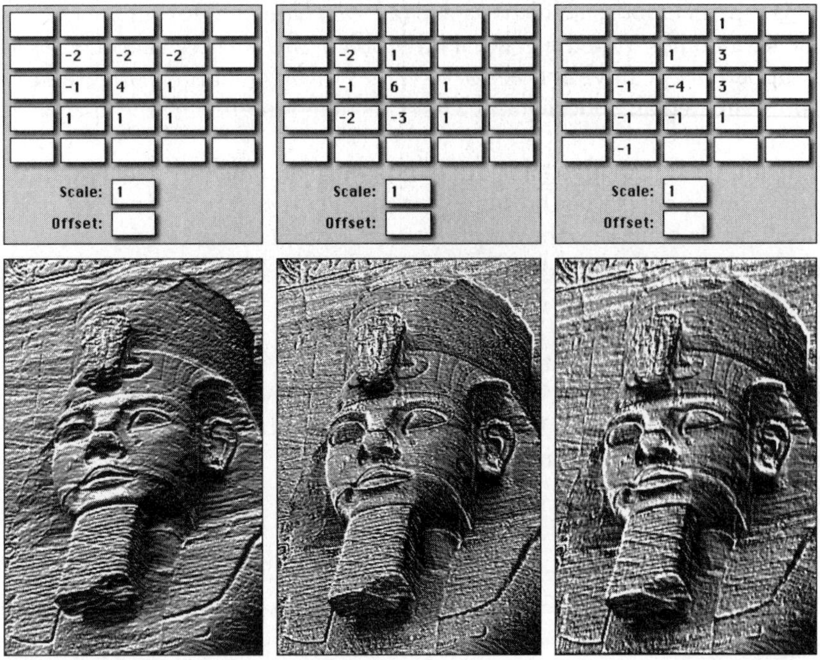

Figure 15-27:
To emboss more subtly, increase the central matrix value and the Scale values by equal amounts.

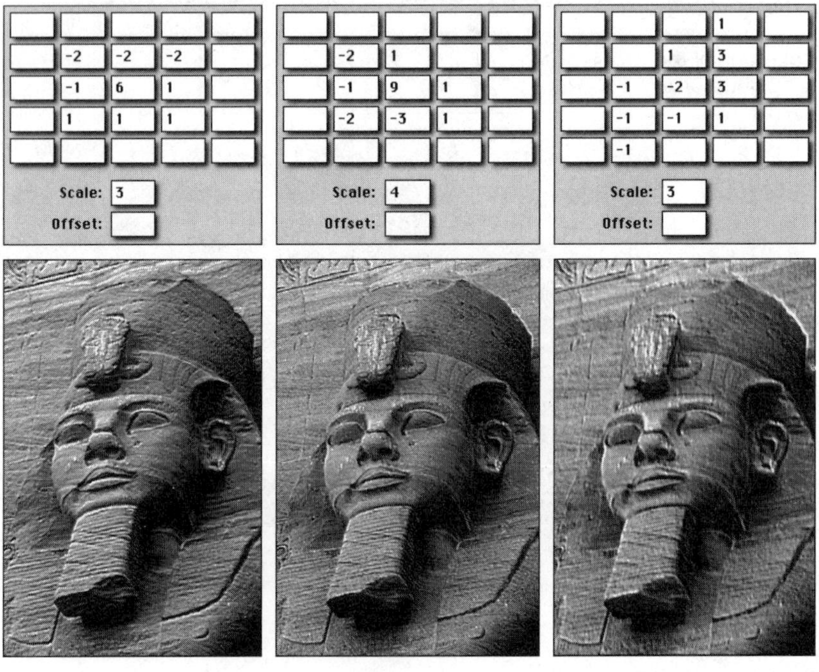

Incidentally, the main advantage of using the Custom filter rather than using Filter⇨Stylize⇨Emboss to produce embossing effects is that Custom preserves the colors in an image while Emboss sacrifices color and changes low-contrast portions of an image to gray. Color Plate 15-1 shows the matrix values from the first example of Figure 15-26 applied to a color image. It also shows examples of other Custom effects, including variations on sharpening and edge-detection.

Displacing Pixels in an Image _____

Photoshop's second custom-effects filter is Filter⇨Distort⇨Displace, which enables you to distort and add texture to an image by moving the colors of certain pixels in a selection. You specify the direction and distance that the Displace filter moves colors by creating a second image called a *displacement map,* or *dmap* (pronounced *dee-map*) for short. The brightness values in the displacement map tell Photoshop which pixels to affect and how far to move the colors of those pixels:

- **Black:** The black areas of the displacement map move the colors of corresponding pixels in the selection a maximum prescribed distance to the right and/or down. Lighter values between black and medium gray move colors a shorter distance in the same direction.

- **White:** The white areas move the colors of corresponding pixels a maximum distance to the left and/or up. Darker values between white and medium gray move colors a shorter distance in the same direction.

- **Medium gray:** A 50 percent brightness value, such as medium gray, ensures that the colors of corresponding pixels remain unmoved.

Suppose that I create a new image window the same size as the scan of the Egyptian temple carving that I've used about 60 times now in this chapter. This new image will serve as the displacement map. I divide the image into four quadrants. As shown in the middle example of Figure 15-28, I fill the upper left quadrant with black, the lower right quadrant with white, and the other two quadrants with medium gray. (The arrows indicate the direction in which the quadrants will move colors in the affected image. They do not actually appear in the dmap.)

When finished, I save the dmap to disk in the native Photoshop format so that the Displace filter can access it. I then return to the Egyptian carving image, choose Filter⇨Distort⇨Displace, edit the settings as desired, and open the dmap from disk. The result is the image shown in the last example of Figure 15-28. In keeping with the distribution of brightness values in the dmap, the colors of the pixels in the upper left quadrant of the carving image move rightward, the colors of the pixels in the lower right quadrant move to the left, and the colors in the upper right and lower left quadrant remain intact.

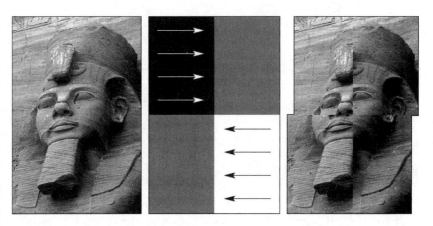

Figure 15-28:
The Displace filter
enables you to
move colors in an
image (left)
according to the
brightness values in
a separate image,
known as a
displacement map
(middle). The
arrows indicate the
direction in which
the brightness
values will move
colors in the
original image, as
verified by the
image on the right.

A dmap must be a color or grayscale image, and you must save the dmap in the native Photoshop file format. The Displace command does not recognize PICT, TIFF, or any of the other non-native (albeit common) file formats. Who knows why? Those programmers move in mysterious ways.

At this point, you likely have two questions: How do you use the Displace filter, and why in the name of all that is good would you possibly want to? The hows of the Displace filter are covered in the following section. To discover some whys — which should in turn help you dream up some whys of your own — read the "Using Displacement Maps" section later in this chapter.

Displacement theory

Like any custom filtering effect worth its weight in table salt — an asset that has taken something of a nose dive in the recent millennium — you need a certain degree of mathematical reasoning skills to predict the outcome of the Displace filter. Though I was a math major in college (well, actually, I double-majored in math and fine arts, and I must admit to paying the lion's share of attention to the latter), I frankly was befuddled by the results of my first few experiments with the Displace command. Don't be surprised if you are as well. With some time and a modicum of effort, however, you can learn to anticipate the approximate effects of this filter.

Direction of displacement

Earlier, I mentioned — and I quote — "The black areas of the displacement map move . . . colors . . . to the right and/or down . . . the white areas move . . . colors . . . to the left and/or up." Yikes, talk about your fragmented quotations. I think I'll sue! Anyway, the point is, you may have wondered to yourself what all this "and/or" guff was all about. "Is it right or is it down?" you may have puzzled, and rightly so.

The truth is that the direction of a displacement can go either way. It's up to you. If you like right, go with it. If you like down, don't let me stop you. If you like both together, by all means, have at it.

Beginning to understand? No? Well, it works like this: A dmap can contain one or more color channels. If the dmap is a grayscale image with one color channel only, the Displace filter moves colors that correspond to black areas in the dmap both to the right *and* down, depending on your specifications in the Displace dialog box. The filter moves colors that correspond to white areas in the dmap both to the left and up.

Figure 15-29 shows two examples of an image displaced using a single-channel dmap, which appears on the left side of the figure. (Again, the arrows illustrate the directions in which different brightness values move colors in the affected image. They are not part of the dmap file.) I displaced the middle image at 10 percent and the right image at 20 percent. Therefore, the colors in the right image travel twice the distance as those in the middle image, but all colors travel the same direction. (The upcoming section "The Displace dialog box" explains exactly how the percentage values work.)

Figure 15-29:
The results of applying a single-channel displacement map (left) to an image at 10 percent (middle) and 20 percent (right).

However, if the dmap contains more than one channel — whether it's a color image or a grayscale image with an independent mask channel — the first channel indicates horizontal displacement, and the second channel indicates vertical displacement. All other channels are ignored. Therefore, the Displace filter moves colors that correspond to black areas in the first channel of the dmap to the right and colors that correspond to white areas to the left. (Again, this depends on your specifications in the Displace dialog box.) The filter then moves colors that correspond to the black areas in the second channel downward and colors that correspond to white areas upward.

Figure 15-30 shows the effect of a two-channel dmap on our friend the pharaoh. The top row shows the appearance and effect of the first channel on the image at 10 percent and 20 percent. The bottom row shows the appearance and effect of the second channel.

Brightness value transitions

If you study Figure 15-30 for any length of time, you'll notice a marked stretching effect around the edges of the image, particularly around the two right images. This is an effect you want to avoid.

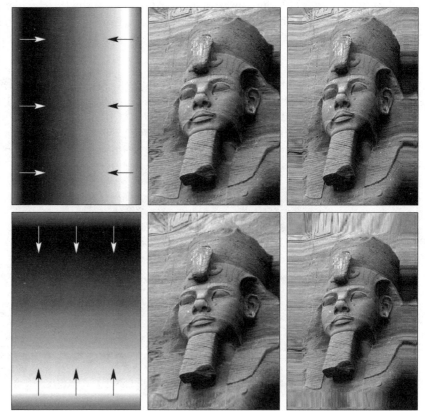

Figure 15-30:
The horizontal (top row) and vertical (bottom row) results of applying a two-channel displacement map (left column) to an image at 10 percent (middle) and 20 percent (right).

The cause of the effect is twofold: First, the transition from gray to black and gray to white pixels around the perimeter of the dmap is relatively quick, especially compared with the gradual transitions in the central portion of the image. Second, transitions — reading from left to right, or top to bottom — produce a more noticeable effect when they progress from light to dark than from dark to light. The reason for this is that these transitions follow the direction of Photoshop's displacement algorithm. (I know, when I throw in a word like *algorithm,* everybody's eyes glaze over, but try to stick with me.)

For example, in the light-to-dark transition on the left side of the first-channel dmap in Figure 15-30, one gray value nudges selected colors slightly to the right, the next darker value nudges them an extra pixel, the next darker value another pixel, and so on, resulting in a machine-gun displacement effect that creates a continuous stream of the same colors over and over again. Hence, the big stretch.

Get it? Well, if not, the important part is this: To avoid stretching an image, make your dmap transitions slow when progressing from light to dark and quick when progressing from dark to light. For example, in the revised dmap channels shown in the left column of Figure 15-31, the gray values progress slowly from gray to black, abruptly from black to gray to white, and then slowly again from white to gray. Slow light to dark, fast dark to light. The results are smoother image distortions, as demonstrated in the middle and right columns of the figure.

Figure 15-31:
Changing the speeds of color transitions in the two-channel displacement map (left column) created smoother image distortions at both the 10 percent (middle) and 20 percent (right) settings.

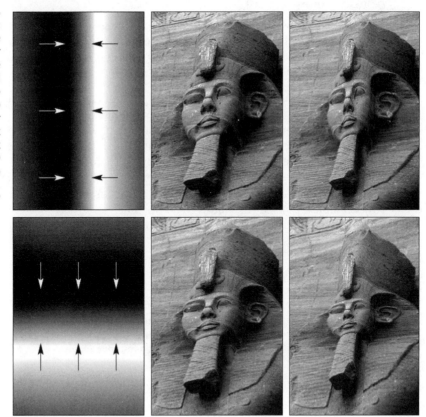

The Displace dialog box

When you choose Filter⮞Distort⮞Displace, Photoshop displays the Displace dialog box. ("Displays the Displace" is the modern equivalent of "Begin the Beguine," don't you know.) As shown in Figure 15-32, the Displace dialog box provides the following options:

⮞ **Scale:** You can specify the degree to which the Displace filter moves colors in an image by entering percentage values into the Horizontal Scale and Vertical Scale option boxes. At 100 percent, black and white areas in the dmap each have the effect of moving colors 128 pixels. That's 1 pixel per each brightness value over or under medium gray. You can isolate the effect of a single-channel dmap vertically or horizontally — or ignore the first or second channel of a two-channel dmap — by entering 0 percent into the Horizontal or Vertical option box respectively.

Figure 15-33 shows the effect of distorting an image exclusively horizontally (top row) and vertically (bottom row) at each of three percentage values: 5 percent, 15 percent, and 30 percent. In each case, I used the two-channel dmap from Figure 15-31.

⮞ **Displacement Map:** If the dmap contains fewer pixels than the image, you can either scale it to match the size of the selected image by selecting the Stretch to Fit radio button or repeat the dmap over and over within the image by selecting Tile. Figure 15-34 shows a small two-channel dmap that contains radial gradations. In the first column, I stretched the dmap to fit the image. In the second column, I tiled the dmap. To create both examples in the top row, I set the Horizontal Scale and Vertical Scale values to 10 percent. To create the bottom-row examples, I raised the values to 50 percent.

Figure 15-32:
Use the options in the Displace dialog box to specify the degree to which the filter distorts the selection, how the filter matches the displacement map to the image, and how it colors the pixels around the perimeter of the selection.

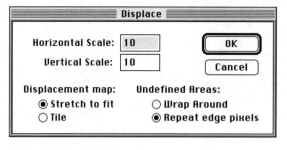

Figure 15-33:
The results of
applying the Distort
filter exclusively
horizontally (top
row) and exclusively
vertically (bottom
row) at 5 percent
(left column), 15
percent (middle),
and 30 percent
(right).

- ⌖ **Undefined Areas:** These radio buttons let you tell Photoshop how to color pixels around the outskirts of the selection that are otherwise undefined. By default, the Repeat Edge Pixels radio button is selected, which repeats the colors of pixels around the perimeter of the selection. This can result in extreme stretching effects, as shown in the middle example of Figure 15-35. To instead repeat the image inside the undefined areas, as demonstrated in the final example of the figure, select the Wrap Around option.

 The Repeat Edge Pixels setting was active in all displacement map figures prior to Figure 15-35. In these cases, I frequently avoided stretching effects by coloring the edges of the dmap with medium gray and gradually lightening or darkening the brightness values toward the center.

After you finish specifying options in the Displace dialog box, click on the OK button or press Return to display the Open dialog box, which allows you to select the displacement map saved to disk. Only native Photoshop documents show up in the scrolling list.

Figure 15-34:
Using a small, two-channel dmap (offset top left), I stretched the dmap to fit (left column) and tiled it (right column) at 10 percent (top row) and 50 percent (bottom row).

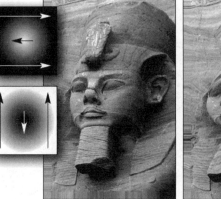

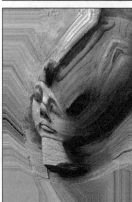

Figure 15-35:
After creating a straightforward, single-channel displacement map (left), I applied the filter subject to two different Undefined Areas settings, Repeat Edge Pixels (middle) and Wrap Around (right).

Using Displacement Maps

So far, all the displacement maps demonstrated involve gradations of one form of another. Gradient dmaps distort the image over the contours of a fluid surface, like a reflection in a fun-house mirror. In this respect, the effects of the Displace filter closely resemble those of the Pinch and Spherize filters described in the last chapter. But the more functional and straightforward application of the Displace filter is to add texture to an image.

Creating texture effects

Figure 15-36 shows the results of using the Displace filter to apply nine of the patterns from the Displacement Maps folder inside the Plug-ins folder. Color Plate 15-2 shows the effects of applying four of the patterns to color images. Introduced in the "How to create patterns" section of Chapter 11, this folder contains repeating patterns that Adobe Systems designed especially with the Displace filter in mind.

As shown in the figure and color plate, most of these patterns produce the effect of viewing the image through textured glass — an effect known in high-end graphics circles as *glass refraction.* Those few patterns that contain too much contrast to pass off as textured glass — including Fragment layers, Mezzo effect, and Schnable effect — can be employed to create images that appear as if they were printed on coarse paper or even textured metal.

 To view each of the textures from the Displacement Maps folder on its own, see Figure 11-14 in the "How to create patterns" section of Chapter 11. Like Figure 15-36, Figure 11-14 is labeled so that you can easily match texture and effect.

When using a repeating pattern — including any of the images inside the Displacement Maps folder — as a dmap, be sure to select the Tile radio button inside the Displace dialog box. This repeats the dmap rather than stretching it out of proportion.

I also explained in Chapter 11 that you can create your own textures from scratch using filtering effects. I specifically described how to create a stucco texture by applying the Add Noise filter three times in a row to an empty image and then using the Emboss filter to give it depth. (See the "Using filters" item in the "How to create patterns" section.) This texture appears in the first example of Figure 15-37. I applied the texture at 2 percent and 10 percent to create the windblown middle and right examples in the figure.

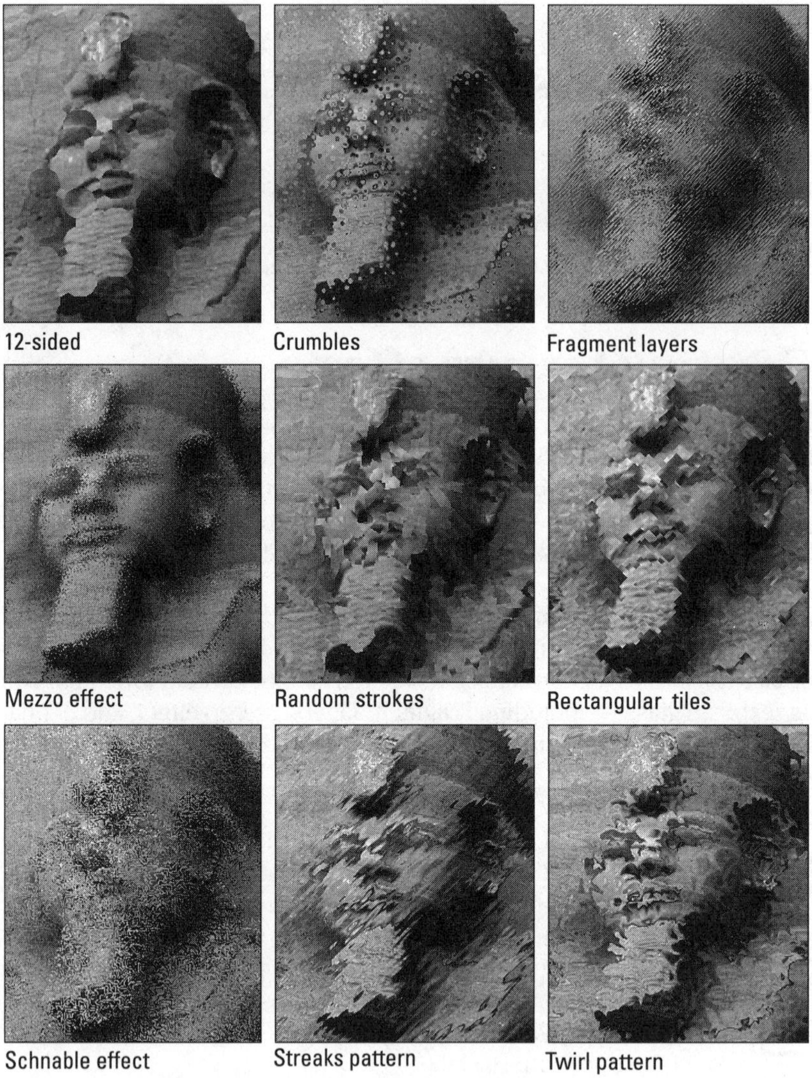

12-sided
Crumbles
Fragment layers
Mezzo effect
Random strokes
Rectangular tiles
Schnable effect
Streaks pattern
Twirl pattern

Figure 15-36: Examples of applying nine patterns from the Displacement Maps folder with the Displace filter at 10 percent horizontally and vertically.

The stucco pattern is only one of an infinite number of textures that you can create using filters. In fact, stucco is a great base texture on which to build. For example, to create the wavy texture that starts off the first row of Figure 15-38, I softened the stucco texture by applying the Gaussian Blur filter with a 0.3-pixel radius. I then applied the Ripple filter twice with the Large option selected and an Amount value of 100. That's all there was to it.

Figure 15-37:
After creating a stucco texture with the Add Noise and Emboss filters (left), I applied the texture as a displacement map at 2 percent (middle) and 10 percent (right).

To create the second texture in the figure, I applied the Crystallize filter at its default Cell Size value of 10. Believe me, I could go on creating textures like this forever, and more importantly, so could you. The images in the second and third columns of Figure 15-38 show the results of applying the textures with the Displace filter at 2 percent and 10 percent respectively.

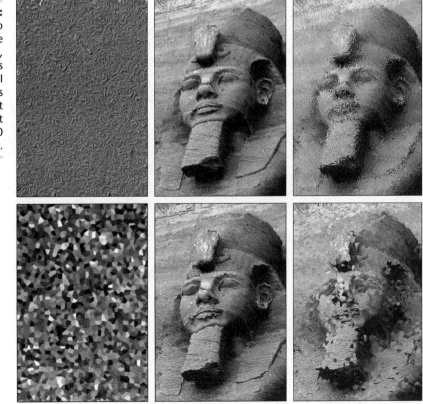

Figure 15-38:
After creating two textures with the Add Noise, Emboss, and Ripple filters (first column), I applied the textures as displacement maps at 2 percent (middle) and 10 percent (right).

In the final analysis, any pattern you design for use with the rubber stamp tool is equally applicable for use with the Displace filter. Furthermore, of the two options — rubber stamp and Displace — the latter is more likely to yield the kind of textured effects that will leave your audience begging, pleading, and scraping for more.

Displacing an image onto itself

I throw this technique in just for laughs. Personally, I can't get enough of *Dr. Strangelove.* That's why I call this the *Make My Day at the Atomic Café* effect. Warning: This effect features simulated melting Egyptian carvings. If you find them unnerving, you have a very soft stomach.

The Make My Day at the Atomic Café effect involves nothing more than using an image as its own displacement map. First, make sure that the image you want to distort is saved to disk in the native Photoshop format. Then choose Filter⇨Distort⇨Displace, specify the desired settings, and select the version of the image saved to disk. Figure 15-39 shows three applications of this effect, once applied at 10 percent exclusively horizontally, the next at 10 percent vertically, and the last at 10 percent in both directions.

Figure 15-39: See Egypt, have a blast. Here I applied the pharaoh image as a displacement map onto itself at 10 percent horizontally (left), 10 percent vertically (middle), and 10 percent in both directions.

As a variation, save the image in its original form. Then choose Image⇨Map⇨Invert (Command-I) and save the inverted image to disk under a different name. Open the original image and use the Displace filter to apply the inverted image as a displacement map. Figure 15-40 shows some results.

If you really want to blow an image apart, apply Horizontal Scale and Vertical Scale values of 50 percent or greater. The first row of Figure 15-41 shows a series of 50 percent applications of the Displace filter. I took the liberty of sharpening each image to heighten the effect. In the second row, I applied the filter to floating selections and changed the translucency of each filtered image to 10 percent. In this way, I retained the detail of the original image while still managing to impart a smidgen of sandblasting.

Figure 15-40:
The results of applying an inverted version of the pharaoh as a displacement map onto the original image at 10 percent horizontally (left), 10 percent vertically (middle), and 10 percent in both directions.

Figure 15-41:
The results of displacing the pharaoh image with itself at 50 percent horizontally, 50 percent vertically, and 50 percent in both directions (top row), followed by the same effects applied to highly translucent floating selections (bottom row).

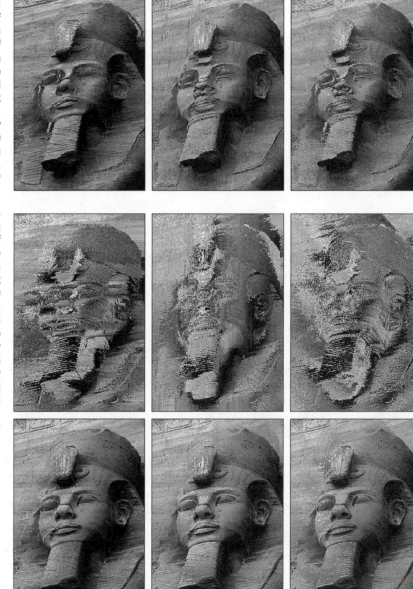

Using the Filter Factory _____

If you've made it this far through the chapter, I just want to say one thing about the Filter Factory: It's incredibly powerful and capable of doing far, far more than any filter I've described so far. But it's also difficult to use — so difficult, in fact, that it makes everything I've discussed in the previous pages look incredibly easy and transparently obvious. The Filter Factory tests the capabilities of the most experienced Photoshop user.

Before you can use Filter Factory, you must install the Filter Factory plug-in in your Plug-ins folder. The Filter Factory is included only on the Photoshop CD and does not install during the normal installation process. See Appendix A for more information.

Choose Filter⇨Synthetic⇨Filter Factory to display the Filter Factory dialog box, shown in Figure 15-42. By any account, I think this has to be the scariest dialog box ever put before a Photoshop user. Yours is probably even more scary. The R option box contains a little *r*, the G option box contains a little *g*, and the B option box contains a little *b*. Throw in a few arbitrarily named slider bars, and you have the perfect formula for striking terror in the unsuspecting image-editor's heart.

Figure 15-42:
The Filter Factory dialog box containing the formulas for adding a series of grid lines to an image. The formula in the R option box is partially cut off because it's too long to fit on two lines.

Filter Factory

Map 0:   238 / 238

Map 1:   128 / 0

Map 2:   0 / 0

Map 3:   0 / 0

R: `put(val(0,X,0),0), put(val(1,Y,0),1),`
`put((((ctl(4)*ctl(2))+(r*(255-ctl(2))))/255),3), put((X%get(0))?r:get(3),2),`

G: `put((((ctl(5)*ctl(2))+(g*(255-ctl(2))))/255),4),`
`put((X%get(0))?g:get(4),2), (y%get(1))?get(2):get(4)`

B: `put((((ctl(6)*ctl(2))+(b*(255-ctl(2))))/255),5),`
`put((X%get(0))?b:get(5),2), (y%get(1))?get(2):get(5)`

[Load...] [Save...] [Make...]   [Cancel] [OK]

If the command is dimmed, it's because you're not in the RGB mode. Like the Light Flare and Lighting Effects filters, Filter Factory is applicable to RGB images only.

Now I need to make something perfectly clear: There's no way I can describe every nuance of programming a custom filter with the Filter Factory in less than 100 pages. So to keep the story short and sweet, I'll explain the most important functions and variables, walk you through the process of creating a moderately amusing effect, and show you how to save your work as a fully-functioning filter. If you're serious about using the Filter Factory, I suggest that you also read the sparse PDF documentation that Adobe includes on the CD. It isn't the kind of thing you simply read through and ingest immediately, and some of the formulas are inaccurate (in my version, anyway), but it at least lists all the variables, operators, and functions permitted in the programming language. You may also want to load the settings that I've included on my CD and study my work. If you find a useful operation, feel free to copy it and paste it into a filter of your own. It's not stealing; it's research.

How the Factory works

To use this filter, you enter formulaic *expressions* into the R, G, and B option boxes. Each option box represents what you're doing to the red, green, or blue color channel. You can also integrate the slider bars at the top of the dialog box into your formulas. When you convert the formulas into a filter, you can specify which slider bars to include in the filter's own dialog box, enabling the user to modify the settings. You don't have to use the slider bars, but without them you get a single-shot filter like Photoshop's Sharpen More or Facet effects.

 The Load and Save buttons enable you to load formulas from disk or save them for later use or editing. If you've had a long hard day and it's time to go home — or you're already home and you want to go to bed — don't forget to save the formulas to disk. Every time you restart Photoshop, the Filter Factory reverts to its original useless values of *r, g,* and *b.*

The Make button creates a filter (as I'll discuss more later). The problem is, you can't open a filter with the Filter Factory once you've created it. So if you ever want to modify a setting or two — and believe me, you will — be sure to save the settings separately using the Save button. I recommend saving filter and settings under the same name in different folders to eliminate as much confusion as possible.

The expressions

Like the Custom filter, the Filter Factory evaluates each pixel in each channel one at a time and then finishes up by sending a new brightness value to that pixel. So in the following discussions, I'll take advantage of that same acronym I used earlier in this chapter — PBE, to indicate the *pixel being evaluated.*

You change the brightness of the PBE using three kinds of expressions — *variables*, *operators*, and *functions*. Here's the scoop on each.

Variables

There are two kinds of values that you can enter into a Filter Factory option box — hard and fast numbers, such as 3 and 17, and *variables*. The latter are single letters that represent values that are forever changing. The *r* that first appears in the R option box, for example, represents the brightness value that currently occupies the PBE in the red channel. So by entering *r* in the R option box, you tell Photoshop to change the red PBE to its current color, which is no change whatsoever. It's just Adobe's way of creating a clean slate for you to work in.

All variables reset to a new value every time the filter advances from one pixel to the next. The most important variables are as follows:

- **r, g, and b:** The brightness value currently assigned to the PBE in the red channel is *r*. The green value of the PBE is *g*; the blue value is *b*. Why the heck would you want access to any of these values? Why, to mix them, of course. For example, if you enter $(r*g)/255$ in the R option box — that's all you have to enter — you multiply the red value by the green value, divide the result by 255, and put the result in the filtered red channel. The final product is identical to copying the contents of the green channel, pasting it onto the red channel, and choosing the Multiply overlay mode. Try it out and see.

- **c:** This variable represents the brightness value of the PBE in the current channel, whatever that may be. In the R option box, *c* is identical to *r*. So the equation $(c*g/255)$ means $(r*g/255)$ in the R channel and $(b*g/255)$ in the B channel.

- **x and y:** The horizontal coordinate of the PBE is saved to *x*. This value is measured in pixels from the left edge of the image. The vertical coordinate is *y*, as measured from the top of the image. These values are useful for shifting pixels around or mixing neighboring pixels together (as you can with the Custom command).

- **X and Y:** The total width of the image is *X*, the total height is *Y*. So $X-x$ calculates the distance from the PBE to the right edge.

You can also use other variables: The letter *m,* for example, measures the distance from the PBE to the exact center of the image, and *d* is the angle from the PBE to the center pixel (measured from 0 to 1,024, so that 255 is equivalent to 90 degrees). But *r, g, b, c, x, y, X,* and *Y* are the ones you'll use most often.

Operators

Operators include arithmetic signs, such as plus and minus, as well as relational symbols, such as < and >. They also include logical operations. For example, *?* tells the Filter Factory to complete the following operation only if the previous expression holds true, and if it is false, complete the operation after the colon (:). For example, the expression $x<(X/2)?r:g$ means that if the PBE is inside the left side of the image, color it with the red channel value. If not, color it with the green value. The following are the most important operators.

- **+, −, *, and /:** These symbols stand for plus, minus, multiply, and divide. The Filter Factory always handles multiply and divide operations before plus and minus operations. So the equation *4+8/2* equals 8, not 6.

- **%:** Use the percentage sign to retain the remainder from a division equation. For example, *11%4* equals 3.

- **(and):** Parentheses tell the Filter Factory to complete the equation inside the parentheses before completing others. The equation *(4+8)/2* equals 6 because 4 and 8 are added before dividing by 2.

- **<, >, <=, and >=:** These symbols mean less than, greater than, less than or equal to, and greater than or equal to. All four are used primarily within conditional operations like the one I mentioned at the beginning of this section.

- **==, =!:** Two equal signs in a row mean "equal to." An equal sign and an exclamation point mean "not equal to." Again, use these inside conditional operations.

- **?:** Here's the conditional operation, as I explained earlier.

Again, these aren't all the possible operators, just the best of. But I should mention one additional operator: The comma separates phrases in an expression, sort of like a period separates sentences. The phrase after the final comma is the one that the Filter Factory applies to the PBE. All previous phrases are used for calculation purposes only. You can see how this works in the step-by-step example that's coming up right after the discussion of functions.

Functions

All functions are composed of three letters followed by numbers, variables, and equations inside parentheses. For example, $abs(x-X)$ finds the absolute value of the equations inside the parentheses, which means that you get a positive result whether the answer to the equation is positive or negative. (Because negative brightness values simply become black, this can be useful.)

Rather than simply listing the functions, I'll explain them in groups. First, there are the two functions that use holding cells. In typical programming, you store the results of incremental equations in variables, but in the Filter Factory, variables are used by the filter only. You get ten numbered cells, ranging from 0 to 9. The two functions that work with cells are *put*, to place a number inside a cell, and *get*, to retrieve it. It's sort of like copying and pasting with ten tiny Clipboards. The expression *put(r+b,0)* puts the result of the equation *r+b* into cell 0. Conversely, *put(r+b,1)* puts it in cell 1, and so on. The expression *get(0)/2* would retrieve the result of *r+b* and divide it by 2.

The function *src* retrieves information about a specific pixel in your image. For example, *src(x+5,y+5,0)* returns the brightness of the pixel five pixels to the right and five pixels down from the PBE. What is that last *0* for? That tells the function to get the value from the red channel. The green channel is *1*, the blue channel is *2*, mask channels are *3* through *9*.

Similar to *src, rad* finds out the brightness value of a pixel in a certain channel based on its distance and direction from the center of the image. For example, if you enter *rad(d–16,m–16,0)* into the red channel, you rotate the contents of the channel 16 increments (about 6 degrees) counterclockwise and distort its center outward. The upcoming step-by-step example uses this function.

The function *rnd* generates a random number between two extremes, which is great for creating noise. The expression *rnd(r,g)* generates a random value between the red brightness value of the PBE and the green brightness of the PBE.

Evaluating the sliders

These next functions — *ctl* and *val* — get their own headline because they're so important. They evaluate how a user of your filter sets the slider bars. The function *ctl* simply retrieves the setting of a specified slider bar. There are eight slider bars in all, numbered 0 to 7 from top to bottom. (The sliders labeled Map 0 are therefore sliders 0 and 1; Map 1 includes sliders 2 and 3; and so on.) Each slider can be adjusted from 0 to 255. So if the first slider bar is set to 128, the function *ctl(0)* retrieves the number 128. You can then change the impact of your filter by moving the slider in real time. For example, if you enter *r*ctl(0)/255* in the R option box, you multiply the red value of the PBE by the setting of the top slider divided by 255. This makes the red channel black when the slider is set to 0, normal when the slider is set to 255, and darker shades when set to any increment in between.

The *val* function evaluates the setting of a slider bar within a specified range. For example, *val(0,15,–15)* takes the setting of the top slider, translates it to 15 when it's at 0, and translates it to –15 when it's at 255. As you can see, this function lets you translate the data within any specified range, even making the low values high and vice versa. This is useful when you don't want the entire range of data from 0 to 255 to mess up the results of your equations.

Touring the factory

Okay, now for a little hands-on action. The steps will be short and straightforward, but the results are both useful and interesting. I encourage you to try these steps out. Even if you've been sitting there with your jaw hanging open throughout the entire chapter, even if you haven't the slightest idea what you're doing, you'll be able to create a fully functioning filter that is not included on the CD. Talk about your incentives.

STEPS: **Creating a Filter inside the Factory**

Step 1. Open an RGB image or convert some other image to the RGB mode. (This filter yields interesting results even when applied to grayscale images converted to RGB.)

Step 2. Choose Filter➪Synthetic➪Factory and set all the slider bars back to 0 (just in case somebody's been fooling around with them).

Step 3. Enter *rad(d–(4*ctl(0)),m,0)* into the R option box. The first argument in the expression — *d–(4*ctl(0))* — subtracts four times the value of the top slider bar from the angle variable *d*. Why four times? Because the slider only offers 256 increments, and the filter measures a full circle in 1,024 increments — 256 times 4 equals 1,024, thus allowing you to translate the slider values to a full circle.

Meanwhile, *d* is the angle of the current pixel from the center and *m* is the distance from the pixel to the center. So *rad(d–(4*ctl(0)),m,0)* tells the filter to lift the brightness from the pixel in a counterclockwise direction from the PBE. The result is that the red channel rotates in the opposite direction, clockwise. Drag the slider bar and you'll see that this is true.

Step 4. Now, you'll use the second and third slider bars — *ctl(1)* and *ctl(2)* — for rotating the other two channels. But I think that I'd like to use the fifth slider bar for distorting the image. Why not the fourth channel? Well, because the first three sliders are going to be devoted to rotation. The distortion slider will be logically different, so it might be nice to create a blank space between the rotation and distortion sliders. Not using slider four is the way to do it.

Now that I've told you why you're doing what you're doing, go ahead and do it: Insert the phrase *–ctl(4)/2* after the *m* so that the expression reads *rad(d–(4*ctl(0)),m–ctl(4)/2,0)*. This subtracts half the value from the fourth slider from the distance-from-center variable, thus shoving the pixels outward as you drag the fifth slider bar (the top of the two labeled Map 2). Give it a try.

Step 5. Select the entire expression in the R option box, copy it by pressing Command-C, tab to the G option box, and press Command-V to paste. Then change the *ctl(0)* function to *ctl(1)* and the final number after the comma from a *0* to a *1*, so that it reads *rad(d–(4*ctl(1)),m–ctl(4)/2,1)*. Now the expression takes rotation data from the second slider bar and lifts its colors from the green channel. The result is a rotating green channel.

Step 6. Tab to the B option box and press Command-V again. Change *ctl(0)* to *ctl(2)* and change the final *0* to a *2*. The result is *rad(d–(4*ctl(2)),m–ctl(4)/2,2)*. Just to make sure that you haven't fallen behind, Figure 15-43 shows all three expressions exactly as they should appear.

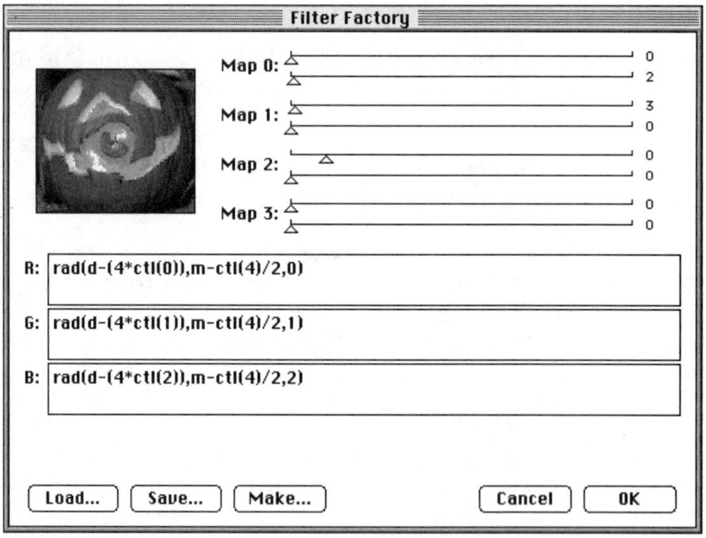

Figure 15-43:
These three
expressions let
you rotate the
three color
channels
independently
using the first
three slider bars
and distort the
image using
the fifth slider.

Step 7. Click on the Save button and save your settings to disk. You may want to use the name *Rotator.afs* to show that it's a Filter Factory file. (For some reason, *afs* is the accepted suffix for settings files.)

Step 8. Now it's time to turn this sucker into its own filter. But before you do, be sure that the sliders are set how you want them to appear by default. Every time you open the new filter for the first time during a Photoshop session, these slider values will appear as they do now. You may want to set all sliders to 0 so that the user starts from square one, but it's completely up to you.

Step 9. Click on the Make button to display the dialog box shown in Figure 15-44. Enter the submenu in which you want the filter to appear in the Category option box. If you want it to appear with the rest of the *Photoshop Bible* filters, enter Tormentia. Enter the name of the filter, Rotator, in the Title option box. Then enter copyright and author info in the next two option boxes. (Go ahead, give yourself credit. You've earned it.)

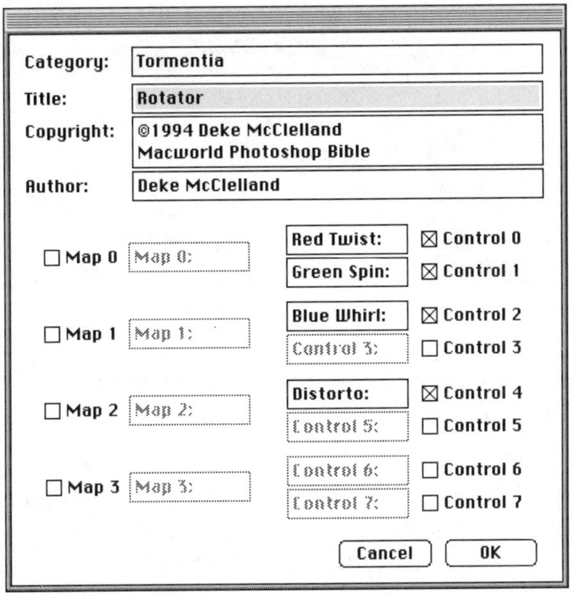

Figure 15-44:
Click on the Make button to display this dialog box, which lets you name your filter, assign it to a submenu, and select the slider bars that you want to appear in the final dialog box.

Category:	Tormentia
Title:	Rotator
Copyright:	©1994 Deke McClelland Macworld Photoshop Bible
Author:	Deke McClelland

☐ Map 0 Map 0: Red Twist: ☒ Control 0

Green Spin: ☒ Control 1

☐ Map 1 Map 1: Blue Whirl: ☒ Control 2

Control 3: ☐ Control 3

☐ Map 2 Map 2: Distorto: ☒ Control 4

Control 5: ☐ Control 5

Control 6: ☐ Control 6

☐ Map 3 Map 3: Control 7: ☐ Control 7

[Cancel] [OK]

Step 10. The Control check boxes along the right side represent the slider bars inside the Filter Factory dialog box. Select the check box for every slider you want to appear in your final filter. This means Control 0, Control 1, Control 2, and Control 4. Then name them appropriately. My suggested names appear in Figure 15-44, but they may be a little too clever for your tastes.

Watch out: The Filter Factory allows you to select any of the slider check boxes, whether they were used in your formulas or not. If you're not careful, you can activate a slider bar that has no function.

Step 11. When you're finished, click on OK or press Return. You're asked to specify the location of the filter. To keep things tidy, you'll probably want to put it in the Filters folder inside the Plug-ins folder, but anywhere in the Plug-ins folder is okay. Click on the Cancel button to escape the Filter Factory dialog box.

Step 12.   Quit Photoshop and relaunch it. Open an RGB image — like the Filter Factory itself, any filter you create in the factory is applicable to RGB images only — and choose your newest command, Filter⇨Tormentia⇨Rotator. The dialog box should look something like the one shown in Figure 15-45. Notice the gaps between the Blue Whirl and Distorto sliders. Nice logical grouping, huh? Feel free to drag the controls and apply the filter as much as you want. It's alive!

Figure 15-45:
The new
Rotator filter
complete with
its four slider
bars.

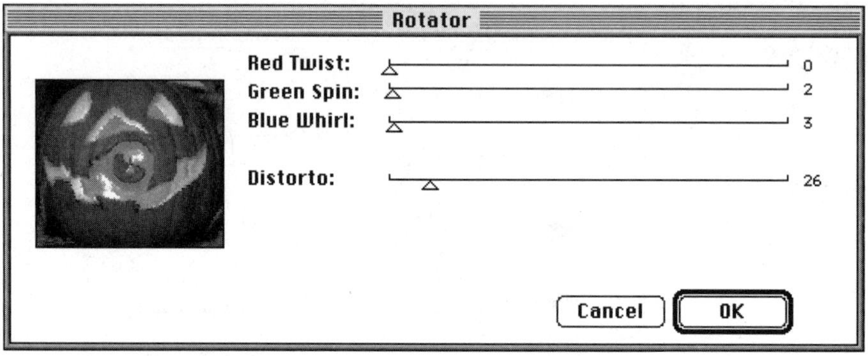

Rotator	
Red Twist:	0
Green Spin:	2
Blue Whirl:	3
Distorto:	26
Cancel	OK

To see a demonstration of your powerful new filter, check out Color Plate 15-3, in which I applied the filter six times at various settings. The top row shows the effect of rotating the channels to different degrees with the Distorto option set to 0. The bottom row shows the same rotation values, but with the Distorto slider turned up to various volumes. It's not the most practical filter on earth, but it's diverting. You might even find something to do with it.

By the way, those sliders have a tendency to move around after you finish dragging them. It's very irritating. If you're interested in achieving an exact value, click at the location where you want to move the slider triangle. The triangle jumps in place. Then click, click, click to get it right where you want it.

If you want practical filters, check out the ones I've included on the CD. Most are much more complicated than the one you created in the steps, but they all use the variables, operators, and functions described in this chapter. Open the settings files to take a look at my code. (Just click on the Load button inside the Filter Factory dialog box.) To whet your appetite, take a look at Color Plate 15-4, which shows all but one of the filters applied to the pumpkin. (The one that wouldn't fit is Ripping Pixels, which creates a random value between the brightness of the pixel in one channel and that of one of the other channels, creating a highly customizable noise effect.) These are only sample applications, most of them using the default slider bar settings. Obviously, jillions of other variations are possible. Have loads of fun.

Summary

- The Custom filter multiplies the brightness values of pixels by the corresponding numbers in the matrix, adds them up, divides the sum by the Scale value, and adds the Offset value to compute the new brightness value for a single pixel.

- As long as the sum of the matrix values divided by the Scale value is equal to 1, the Custom filter maintains the original color balance of an image.

- A positive central matrix value surrounded by negative values results in a sharpening effect; a positive CMV surrounded by positive values results in blurring; and a negative CMV surrounded by positive values results in edge-detection.

- Use the Offset value to compensate for overly dark or overly light custom effects.

- Non-symmetrical matrix values in which positive and negative numbers are arranged on opposite sides of the CMV result in embossing effects.

- The Displace filter works by moving colors in a selection according to the brightness values in a separate image saved to disk. This image is called a *displacement map.*

- If a displacement map features a single color channel, black regions in the dmap move colors down and to the right, and white regions move colors up and to the left. If a dmap contains more than one color channel, the first channel moves colors horizontally; the second channel moves them vertically.

- Use gradient dmaps to distort an image. Use repeating patterns such as those in the Displacement Maps folder to add texture to an image.

- Apply an image as a displacement map onto itself to melt the faces off those you love to hate.

- Use the Filter Factory to generate complete filters with customizable slider bars that can be used to correct focus, edit colors, add noise, distort images, and just about anything else you'd want to do.

Corrections and Composites

Whether you're working on a full-color or grayscale image, color correction is an essential part of the image-editing process. In fact, commands such as Hue/ Saturation, Levels, and Curves are as important to correcting the appearance of a scanned image as Unsharp Mask and Gaussian Blur. Discussed in Chapter 16, these commands enable you to shift the colors in an image to better resemble real life, increase or decrease saturation, and adjust the amount of contrast between light and dark pixels. You can even introduce color to a grayscale image, prepare an RGB image for conversion to the CMYK color space, or restore a badly scanned image.

The last two chapters address the complex issue of *compositing,* which enables you to combine different images and mix the colors of their corresponding pixels in literally thousands of ways. Taking a foreground element from one image and pasting it against a different background is a simple example of compositing. But that's just the beginning of the fun. Do you want to merge the two images using overlay modes? Do you want to position the foreground element on its own layer, where you can edit it independently? Do you want to fade the shadows of the foreground into the highlights of the background? And why would you want to experiment with any of these options in the first place? Chapter 17 answers these questions and more, examining the myriad ways to composite images, from the very powerful Layer Options dialog box to the very complex Apply Image and Calculations commands. Chapter 18 includes several sample projects so that you can get a feel for why these functions are so useful.

Mapping and Adjusting Colors

CHAPTER 16

In This Chapter

- Using commands in the Image➪Map submenu
- Using Threshold and Posterize in combination with the High Pass filter
- Converting a selection to gray values using the Desaturate command
- Rotating colors in an image around the color wheel using the Hue/Saturation command
- Editing saturation levels to prepare an RGB image for conversion to the smaller CMYK color space
- Colorizing grayscale images
- Color correcting with the Replace Color, Selective Color, and Variations commands
- Using the Levels and Curves commands
- Boosting brightness and contrast levels
- Drawing arbitrary color maps that lead to psychedelic effects

Mapping Colors

Color mapping is just a fancy name for shuffling colors around. For example, to map Color A to Color B simply means to take all the A-colored pixels and convert them to B-colored pixels. Although many painting programs require you to map colors one color at a time, Photoshop provides several commands that enable you to map entire ranges of colors based on their hues, saturation levels, and, most frequently, brightness values.

Color effects and corrections

Why would you want to change colors around? For one reason, to achieve special effects. You know those psychedelic videos that show some guy's hair turning blue while his face turns purple and the palms of his hands glow a sort of cornflower yellow? Although not the most attractive effect by modern standards — you may be able to harvest more tasteful results if you put your shoulder to the color wheel — psychedelia qualifies as color mapping for the simple reason that each color shifts incrementally to a new color.

The more common reason to use color mapping is to enhance the appearance of a scanned image. In this case, you're not creating special effects, just making straightforward color adjustments, known in the biz as *color corrections*. Scans are never perfect, no matter how much money you spend on a scanning device or a service bureau. They can always benefit from tweaking and subtle adjustments, if not outright overhauls, in the color department.

Keep in mind, however, that Photoshop can't make something from nothing. In creating the illusion of more and better colors, every color-adjustment operation that you perform actually takes some small amount of color *away* from the image. Invariably, two pixels that were two different colors before you started the correction change to the same color. The image may look 10 times better, but it will in fact be less colorful than when you started.

It's important to keep this principle in mind because it demonstrates that color mapping is a balancing act. The first nine operations you perform may make an image look progressively better, but the tenth may send it into decline. There's no magic formula, unfortunately. The amount of color mapping you need to apply varies from image to image. For the moment, the only advice I can offer is that you use moderation, know when to stop, and — as always — save your image to disk before launching into the color mapping process.

This whole bit about how color mapping sucks color out of an image to produce the illusion of a more colorful image probably sounds strange on the face of it. But if you think about it, it has to be true. Photoshop maps colors by applying one or more complex equations to a pixel and then rounding off the results of those equations to the nearest brightness value, hue, what have you. Because entire communities of pixels in an image are very close in color — say, only a brightness value or two apart — the equations frequently convert two slightly different colors to the same color. By contrast, the equations never, *ever* change a single color into two different colors. So when it comes to color correction, colors don't procreate, they die like flies for the good cause — the illusion of better color.

Photoshop's color correction functions fall into three categories: those that produce immediate and useful effects, such as Invert and Threshold; those that require significantly more work but are nonetheless designed to be understood by novices, such as the Brightness/Contrast and Color Balance commands; and those that are still more complicated but provide better control and better functionality, such as Hue/Saturation, Replace Color, Levels, and Curves.

This chapter contains no information about the second category of commands for the simple reason that they are inadequate and ultimately a big waste of time. I know because I spent my first year with Photoshop relying exclusively on Brightness/Contrast and Color Balance, all the while wondering why I never achieved the effects I wanted. Then, one happy day, after spending about a half an hour learning Levels and Curves, the quality of my images skyrocketed and the amount of time I spent on them plummeted. So wouldn't you just rather learn it right in the first place? (I hope so, because you're stuck with it.) To this end, I discuss the supposedly more complicated and indisputably more capable high-end commands as if they were the only ones available.

Color mapping commands

Before we get into all the high-end gunk, however, I'll take a moment to explain the first category of commands, all of which happen to reside in the Image⇨Map submenu. These commands produce immediate effects that are either difficult to duplicate or not worth attempting with the more full-featured commands.

Invert

When you choose Image⇨Map⇨Invert (Command-I), Photoshop converts every color in your image to its exact opposite, just as in a photographic negative. As demonstrated in Figure 16-1, black becomes white, white becomes black, fire becomes water, good becomes evil, Imelda Marcos goes barefoot, and the brightness value of every primary color component changes to 255 minus the original brightness value. The only color that doesn't change is medium gray, because it is its own opposite. (Ooh, I saw a movie like that once.)

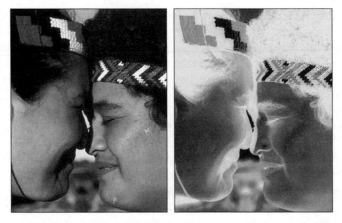

Figure 16-1:
An image before the advent of the Invert command (left) and after (right).

Image⇨Map⇨Invert is just about the only color mapping command that retains every single drop of color in an image. (The Hue/Saturation command also retains colors under specific conditions.) If you apply the Invert command twice in a row, you arrive at your original image.

When you're working on a full-color image, the Invert command simply inverts the contents of each color channel. This means that the command produces very different results when applied to RGB, Lab, and especially CMYK images. Color Plate 16-1 shows the results of inverting a single image in each of these modes. The RGB and Lab images share some similarities, but you'll find all kinds of subtle differences if you study the backgrounds and the basic colors of the faces.

Inverting in CMYK is much different. Typically, the Invert command changes much of a CMYK image to black. Except in very rare instances — such as in night scenes — the black channel contains lots of light shades and very few dark shades. So when you invert the channel, it becomes extremely dark. To reverse this effect, I inverted only the cyan, magenta, and yellow channels in the right example of Color Plate 16-1. (I did this by inverting the entire image and then going to the black channel — Command-4 — and pressing Command-I again.) Though this approach is preferable to inverting the black channel, it prevents the blacks in the hair and shadows from turning white (which would be the only portions even remotely light had I inverted the black channel as well).

Just so you know, when I refer to applying color corrections in the CMYK mode, I mean applying them after choosing Mode⇨CMYK Color. Applying corrections in the RGB mode when Mode⇨CMYK Preview is active produces the same effect as when CMYK Preview is not selected; the only difference is that the on-screen colors are curtailed slightly to fit inside the CMYK color space. You're still editing inside the same old red, green, and blue color channels, so the effects are the same.

As I mentioned back in Chapter 9, inverting the contents of the mask channel is the same as applying Select⇨Inverse to a selection outline in the marching ants mode. In fact, this is one of the most useful applications of the filter. If you're considering inverting a color image, however, I strongly urge you to try out the SuperInvert filter that I created for the CD. It permits you to invert each channel independently and incrementally. Any setting under 128 lessens the contrast of the channel; 128 makes it completely gray; and any value over 128 inverts it to some degree.

Equalize

Equalize is the smartest and at the same time least useful of the Image⇨Map pack. When you invoke this command, Photoshop searches for the lightest and darkest color values in a selection. Then it maps the lightest color in all the color channels to white, maps the darkest color in the channels to black, and distributes the remaining colors to other brightness levels in an effort to evenly distribute pixels over the entire brightness spectrum. This doesn't mean that any one pixel will actually appear white or black after you apply Equalize; rather, that one pixel in at least one channel will be white and another pixel in at least one channel will be black. In an RGB image, for example, the red, green, or blue component of one pixel would be white, but the other two components of that same pixel might be black. The result is a higher contrast image with white and black pixels scattered throughout the color channels.

If no portion of the image is selected when you choose Image⇨Map⇨Equalize (Command-E), Photoshop automatically maps out the entire image across the brightness spectrum, as shown in the upper right example of Figure 16-2. However, if you select a portion of the image before choosing the Equalize command, Photoshop displays a dialog box containing the following two radio buttons:

- **Selected Area Only:** Select this option to apply the Equalize command strictly within the confines of the selection. The lightest pixel in the selection becomes white, the darkest pixel becomes black, and so on.

- **Entire Image Based on Area:** If you select the second radio button, which is the default setting, Photoshop applies the Equalize command to the entire image based on the lightest and darkest colors in the selection. All colors in the image that are lighter than the lightest color in the selection become white, and all colors darker than the darkest color in the selection become black.

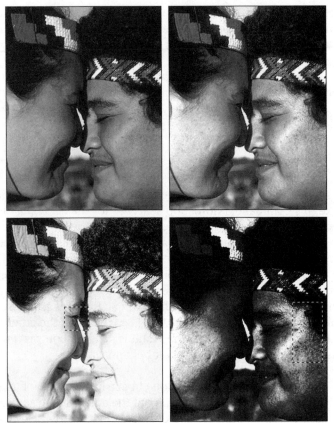

Figure 16-2:
An image before (top left) and after (top right) applying the Equalize command when no portion of the image is selected. You also can use the brightness values in a selected region as the basis for equalizing an entire image (bottom left and right).

The bottom two examples in Figure 16-2 show the effects of selecting different parts of the image when the Entire Image Based on Area option is in force. In the left example, I selected a very dark portion of the image, which resulted in over-lightening of the entire image. In the right example, I selected an area with both light and dark values, which boosted the amount of contrast between highlights and shadows in the image.

As when you use the Invert command, the color mode in which you work has a profound effect on the Equalize command. Although the command does not apply itself to each color channel independently, as does Invert, it does evaluate the lightest and darkest values throughout all channels. The distribution of brightness values changes significantly when you switch color modes — for example, light blue is represented in the RGB mode as light pixels in the blue channel, while it's represented in the CMYK mode as dark pixels in the cyan channel — which changes the command's reading of the image in kind. Color Plate 16-2 shows how the command affects the same image with the same detail selected in each of the three color modes. The differences are striking.

The problem with the Equalize command is that it relies too heavily on some pretty bizarre automation to be of much use as a color correction tool. Certainly, you can create some interesting special effects. But if you'd prefer to automatically adjust the colors in an image from black to white regardless of the color mode and composition of the individual channels, choose Image⇨Adjust⇨Auto Levels (new to Photoshop 3.0). If you want to adjust the tonal balance manually and therefore with a higher degree of accuracy, the Levels and Curves commands are tops. I explain all of these commands at length later in this chapter.

Threshold

I touched on the Threshold command a couple of times in previous chapters. As you may recall, Threshold converts all colors to either black or white based on their brightness values. When you choose Image⇨Map⇨Threshold (Command-T), Photoshop displays the Threshold dialog box shown in Figure 16-3. The dialog box offers a single option box and a slider bar, either of which you can use to specify the medium brightness value in the image. Photoshop changes any color lighter than the value in the Threshold option box to white and any color darker than the value to black.

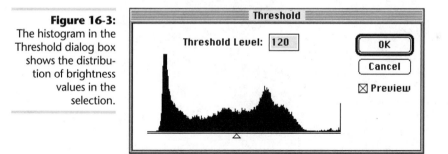

Figure 16-3:
The histogram in the Threshold dialog box shows the distribution of brightness values in the selection.

Situated directly above the slider bar is a graph of the colors in the selection (or in the entire image if no portion of the image is selected). The width of the graph represents all 256 possible brightness values, starting at black on the left and progressing through white on the right. The height of each vertical line in the graph demonstrates the number of pixels in the image currently associated with that brightness value. Such a graph is called a *histogram*. (You can see a more detailed version of the graph in the Levels dialog box.)

Generally speaking, you achieve the best effects if you change an equal number of pixels to black as you change to white (and vice versa). So rather than moving the slider bar to 128, which is the medium brightness value, move it to the point at which the area of the vertical lines to the left of the slider triangle looks roughly equivalent to the area of the vertical lines to the right of the slider triangle.

The upper right example in Figure 16-4 shows the result of applying the Threshold command with a Threshold Level value of 120 (as in Figure 16-3). Although this value more or less evenly distributes black and white pixels, I lost a lot of detail in the dark areas.

Figure 16-4:
An image before applying the Threshold command (top left) and after (top right). You can retain more detail in the image by applying the High Pass filter before applying Threshold (bottom left and right).

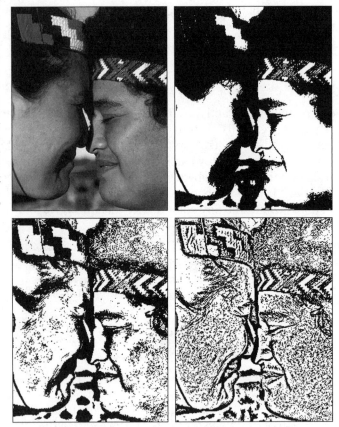

As you may recall from my discussion in "Using the High Pass filter" section of Chapter 13, you can use Filter⇨Other⇨High Pass in advance of the Threshold command to retain areas of contrast. For example, in the lower left image in Figure 16-4, I applied the High Pass filter with a radius of 10.0 pixels, followed by the Threshold command with a value of 124. In the lower right example, I applied High Pass with a radius of 3.0 pixels and then applied Threshold with a value of 126.

Higher High Pass radiuses combined with higher Threshold values result in more detail, which is the good news, as well as more random artifacts, which can detract from an image. So it's a mixed bag. Isn't everything? If you're looking for a real-life application of the Threshold command, Figure 16-5 shows all the effects from Figure 16-4 applied to floating selections set to 15 percent opacity. In each example, the translucent selection helps to add contrast and reinforce details in the original image.

Figure 16-5:
The Threshold and High Pass operations from Figure 16-4 applied to floating selections set to 15 percent opacity, thus permitting the underlying original to show through.

You can compare the before and after effects of any color correction command that includes a Preview check box in its dialog box by turning the check box off and then mousing down on the title bar. When you turn the Preview check box off, the settings in the dialog box apply not only to the selection but to the entire screen (provided that the Video LUT Animation option in the General Preferences dialog box is turned on, as by default). Mousing down on the title bar temporarily nullifies the effects of the command so that you can see the original image. Release the mouse button to apply the settings to the entire screen again.

Ooh, I hate that tip. I purposely left it out of the previous edition of the book, but I've since noticed that every time someone shows it off at a conference, the audience practically weeps with excitement and gratitude. So I thought that I'd better throw it in and then criticize it, as I'm doing now. The fact is, the screen animation feature that enables this tip to work is not always accurate. Try out the tip with the Threshold command, for example, and you'll see just how inaccurate it can be. Rather than black and white, you get eight colors, because the animation affects each channel independently. The difference with other color correction commands is most evident when you work on a Lab or CMYK image, because the screen animation always works within the RGB color space. Also, you have no idea how the selection that you're editing compares with unedited areas outside the selection when Preview is off.

So it's up to you. Use the tip if you find it helpful; avoid the tip like the plague if you value an accurate preview. I don't want to bias you one way or another. Hey, it's your funeral, man.

Posterize

The Posterize command is Threshold's rich cousin. Whereas Threshold boils down an image into two colors only, Posterize can retain as many colors as you like. However, you can't control how colors are mapped, as you can when you use Threshold. The Posterize dialog box provides no histogram or slider bar. Instead, Posterize automatically divides the full range of 256 brightness values into a specified number of equal increments.

To use this command, choose Image⇨Map⇨Posterize and enter a value into the Levels option box. The Levels value represents the number of brightness values that the Posterize command retains. Higher values result in subtle color adjustments; lower values produce more dramatic effects. The upper right example in Figure 16-6 shows an image subject to a Levels value of 8.

By now, you may be thinking, "By golly, if Posterize is so similar to Threshold, I wonder how it works when applied after the High Pass filter?" Well, if you *were* thinking that, you're in luck, because this is exactly the purpose of the two bottom examples in Figure 16-6. As in Figure 16-4, I applied the High Pass filter with Radius values of 10.0 and 3.0, respectively, to the left and right examples. I then applied the Posterize filter with the same Levels value as before (8) to achieve some unusual, high-contrast effects.

Just in case you've tried this same effect on your full-color image and thought, "Yech, this looks terrible — half the color just disappeared," the key is to apply High Pass and Posterize to a floating version of the image and then mix the effect with the underlying original. Color Plate 16-3 shows the results of applying the High Pass filter with a Radius of 3 and the Posterize command with a setting of 8 to the floating selection and then compositing floater and underlying original using each of three overlay modes from the Layers palette. The Luminosity option applies only the lights and darks in the floating selection, allowing the colors in the underlying image to show through; Overlay strengthens the light and dark shades; and Difference selectively inverts the image. (Note that I lightened the Difference example slightly using Image⇨Adjust⇨Levels after defloating the image. The Levels command is explained later in this chapter.) You may also want to try out the Soft Light and Hard Light options for variations on the Overlay effect. And don't forget to experiment with the ever-important Opacity slider bar.

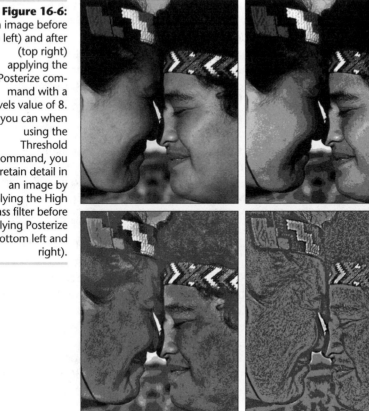

Figure 16-6:
An image before (top left) and after (top right) applying the Posterize command with a Levels value of 8. As you can when using the Threshold command, you can retain detail in an image by applying the High Pass filter before applying Posterize (bottom left and right).

Quick adjustments

Photoshop 3.0 offers two new commands under the Image⇨Adjust submenu that I want to discuss before entering the larger world of advanced color correction. Both are single-shot commands that alter your image without any dialog boxes or special options. The first, Desaturate, sucks the saturation out of a selection and leaves it looking like a grayscale image. The second, Auto Levels, automatically increases the contrast of an image according to what Photoshop deems to be the ideal brightness values.

Desaturate

There's little reason to apply the Desaturate command to an entire image; you can just as easily choose Mode⇨Grayscale to accomplish the same thing and dispose of the extra channels that would otherwise consume room in memory and on disk. But Desaturate is useful when applied to selected portions of an image or to floating selections.

For example, in Color Plate 16-4, I used Select⇨Color Range to select all of the pumpkin except the eyes and mouth and a few speckly bits here and there. (I would have gone into the quick mask mode to make the selection just right — as explained in Chapter 9 — but it didn't strike me as particularly important in this case.) I then floated the selection and applied Image⇨Adjust⇨Desaturate to achieve the first example. In the top right example, I changed the Opacity of the floating selection to 50 percent, bringing back some of the original colors from the underlying original and achieving an only slightly desaturated pumpkin.

The bottom row shows the results of using a different color correction command — Image⇨Map⇨Invert — to suck the saturation out of the selection. In this example, I floated the same selection outline I created with the Color Range command and applied Invert (Command-I). I then chose the Color overlay mode from the Layers palette and changed the Opacity setting to 50 percent to get the bottom left example. Note that the result is slightly different than the desaturated image above it. When set to the Color overlay mode, the colors in the inverted image should theoretically cancel out the colors in the underlying original. However, the Invert command doesn't change the saturation of the floating image, so the saturation of the floating and underlying pixels are the same. As a result, some colors from the underlying image are allowed to show through, as the bottom left image shows.

The bottom right example shows what happened when I changed the Opacity to 70 percent, thus favoring the inverted colors. Had I lowered the setting to 30 percent, I would have achieved nearly the same effect shown in the top right example.

Auto Levels

Image⇨Adjust⇨Auto Levels goes through each color channel and changes the lightest pixel to white, changes the darkest pixel to black, and stretches out all the shades of gray to fill out the spectrum. Unlike the Equalize command, which considers all color channels as a whole, Auto Levels looks at each channel independently. So once again, the active color mode makes quite a difference to this command. Color Plate 16-5 shows a stock image prior to color corrections, followed by the same image corrected with Auto Levels in the RGB, Lab, and CMYK modes. The RGB image offers highlights that the Lab image lacks, but both are acceptable. The CMYK image is absolutely unacceptable. Again, that black channel is a culprit, becoming much darker than it ought to. But the cyan channel has also darkened dramatically, turning the pumpkin a bright red that verges on violet — a remarkably unpumpkin-like hue. Like Invert and Equalize, Auto Levels is designed specifically for use in the RGB mode. If you use it in CMYK, you're more likely to achieve special effects than color correction.

The Auto Levels command serves the same purpose and produces the same effect as the Auto button in the Levels dialog box. You should only occasionally rely on either. What you *should* do is read the rest of this chapter and learn about the bigger and better color correction commands.

Hue Shifting and Colorizing _____

The commands I've discussed so far skirt the border between the worlds of utility and futility. I use the Invert and Threshold commands on a regular basis, and the Posterize, Desaturate, and Auto Levels commands are nice to have around. Equalize is a big stinker.

The rest of the commands covered in this chapter — all of which reside in the Image⇨Adjust submenu — are both more powerful and more complex. As I stated before, I ignore two commands — Brightness/Contrast and Color Balance — because they're a complete waste of time. The others enable you to adjust colors both selectively and with absolute precision.

The sections that follow cover the commands that are specifically designed to change the distribution of colors in an image. You can rotate the hues around the color spectrum, change the saturation of colors, adjust highlights and shadows, and even tint an image. Two of these commands — Hue/Saturation and Selective Color — are applicable exclusively to color images. The other two — Replace Color and Variations — can be applied to grayscale images, but are not the best solutions. Although both permit you to select specific ranges of brightness values that you want to edit, they apply their corrections with less finesse than either the Levels or Curves commands, both of which are discussed toward the end of the chapter.

 Before I go any further, I should mention one awesome little bit of advice. Remember that Command-Option-F redisplays the last filter dialog box so that you can tweak the effect? Well, a similar shortcut is available when you're applying color corrections. Press the Option key when choosing any command under the Image⇨Adjust submenu that has an ellipsis to display that command's dialog box with the settings last applied to the image. If the command has a keyboard equivalent, just add Option to reapply the last settings. Command-Option-U, for example, brings up the Hue/Saturation dialog box with the last settings applied.

Using the Hue/Saturation command

The Hue/Saturation command provides two functions. First, it enables you to adjust colors in an image according to their hues and saturation levels. You can apply the changes to individual color channels or affect all colors equally across the spectrum. And second, the command lets you colorize images by applying new hue and saturation values while retaining the core brightness information from the original image.

This command is perfect for colorizing grayscale images. I know, I know, Woody Allen wouldn't approve, but with some effort, you can make Ted Turner green with envy. Just scan him and change the Hue value to 140 degrees. (It's a joke, son.)

When you choose Image⇨Adjust⇨Hue/Saturation (Command-U), Photoshop displays the Hue/Saturation dialog box, shown in Figure 16-7. Before I explain how to use this dialog box to produce specific effects, let me briefly introduce the options:

- **Master:** Select the Master option to adjust all colors in an image to the same degree. If you prefer to adjust some colors in the image differently than others, select one of the color radio buttons along the left side of the dialog box. In the RGB and CMYK modes, the dialog box offers the R (Red), Y (Yellow), G (Green), C (Cyan), B (Blue), and M (Magenta) options, as shown in Figure 16-7. In the Lab mode, two radio buttons bite the dust, leaving Y (Yellow), G (Green), B (Blue), and M (Magenta), each of which represents an extreme end of the *a* or *b* spectrum. You can specify different slider bar settings for every one of the color ranges. For example, you might select R (Red) and move the Hue slider triangle to +50 and then select Y (Yellow) and move the Hue triangle to –30. All radio buttons are dimmed when you select the Colorize check box.

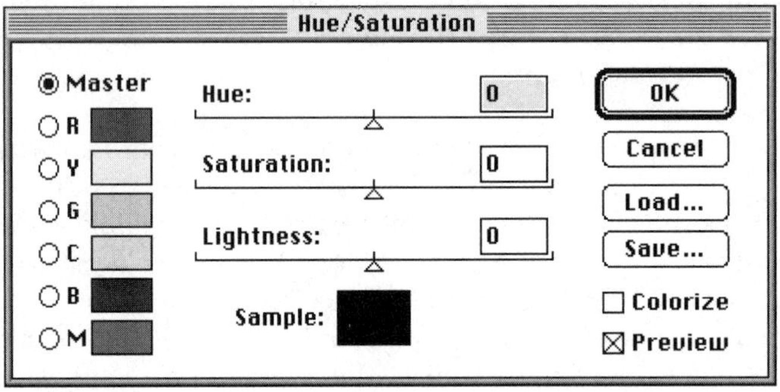

Figure 16-7:
The Hue/ Saturation dialog box enables you to adjust the hues and saturation values in a color image or colorize a grayscale image.

- **Hue:** The Hue slider bar measures colors on the 360-degree color circle, familiar from the Apple Color Picker dialog box. When Master is selected, you can adjust the Hue value from negative to positive 180 degrees. When one of the other color radio buttons is active in the RGB or CMYK mode, the Hue value can vary from negative to positive 60 degrees, because each of the colors is 60 degrees from either of its neighbors in the color wheel. (Red is 60 degrees from yellow, which is 60 degrees from green, and so on.)

  When a color radio button is active in the Lab mode, the Hue value can vary from negative to positive 90 degrees, thanks to Lab's specialized color organization. Regardless of mode, letters appears at either end of the Hue slider when any option except Master is selected. The letters indicate the effect of moving the slider triangle in either direction. For example, if you select R (Red), the letters *M* and *Y* flank the slider, indicating that a negative value maps red pixels toward magenta, while a positive value maps red pixels toward yellow.

⊛ **Saturation:** Normally, the Saturation value can vary from negative to positive 100. The only exception occurs when the Colorize check box is active, in which case saturation becomes an absolute value. In other words, you can't subtract saturation from a colorized image, so the range becomes 0 to 100.

Photoshop precedes positive values in the Hue, Saturation, and Lightness option boxes with plus signs (+) to show that you are adding to the current color attributes of the pixels. When you select Colorize, the plus signs disappear from all but the Lightness value because hue and saturation become absolute values that you apply to pixels rather than adding to or subtracting from existing pixel colors.

⊛ **Lightness:** You can darken or lighten an image by varying the Lightness value from negative to positive 100. However, because this value invariably changes *all* brightness levels in an image to an equal extent — whether or not Colorize is selected — it permanently dulls highlights and shadows. Therefore, you'll most likely want to avoid this option like the plague and rely instead on the Levels or Curves command to edit brightness and contrast.

⊛ **Sample:** This color swatch serves as a guidepost. Really, it's pretty redundant, because you can monitor the effects that your settings have on an image by selecting the Preview check box. But if you want to see the impact of your settings on one color in particular, you can isolate it by clicking on that color in the image window with the eyedropper cursor. (The cursor automatically changes to an eyedropper when you move it outside the Hue/Saturation dialog box and into the image window.)

⊛ **Load/Save:** As in all the best color correction dialog boxes (including Levels and Curves, naturally), you can load and save settings to disk in case you want to reapply the options to other images. These options are especially useful if you find a magic combination of color-correction settings that accounts for most of the color mistakes produced by your scanner.

⊛ **Colorize:** Select this check box to apply a single hue and a single saturation level to the entire selection, regardless of how it was previously colored. All brightness levels remain intact, though you can adjust them incrementally using the Lightness slider bar (a practice that I do *not* recommend, as I mentioned earlier).

⊛ **Preview:** Select the Preview check box to continually update the image every time you adjust a setting.

You can restore the options in the Hue/Saturation, Levels, and Curves dialog boxes to their original settings by Option-clicking on the Reset button (the Cancel button changes to Reset when you press the Option key) or by simply pressing Command-Option-period.

Adjusting hue and saturation

All right, now that you know how the options work, it's time to give them a whirl. One caveat before I launch into things: Grayscale figures won't help you one whit in understanding the Hue/Saturation options, so I refer you a few times to three color plates. You may want to take a moment to slap a Post-it note in the general area of Color Plates 16-6, 16-7, and 16-8 before you begin reading so that you can easily flip back and forth between text and color plates.

Changing hues

When the Colorize check box is inactive, the Hue slider bar shifts colors in an image around the color wheel. It's as if the pixels were playing a colorful game of musical chairs, except that none of the chairs disappear. If you select the Master radio button and enter a value of +60 degrees, for example, all pixels stand up, march one sixth of the way around the color wheel, and sit down, assuming the colors of their new chairs. A pixel that was red becomes yellow, a pixel that was yellow becomes green, and so on. The top row of Color Plate 16-6 shows the result of applying various Hue values to a single image. Note that in each case, all colors in the image change to an equal degree.

As long as you select only the Master option and edit only the Hue value, Photoshop retains all colors in an image. In other words, after shifting the hues in an image +60 degrees, you can later choose Hue/Saturation and shift the hues –60 degrees to restore the original colors.

If you select any radio button other than Master, the musical chairs metaphor breaks down a little. All pixels that correspond to the color you select move to the exclusion of other pixels in the image. The pixels that move must, well, sit on the non-moving pixels' laps, meaning that you sacrifice colors in the image.

For example, I edited the images in the second row of Color Plate 16-6 by applying Hue values while the R (Red) radio button only was selected. (In other words, I didn't apply Hue changes in combination with any other radio button.) All pixels that included some amount of red shifted to new hues according to the amount of red that the pixels

---

STEPS: **Eliminating Out-of-Gamut Colors**

Step 1. Press the Option key and choose Image⇨Duplicate to create a second copy of your image on-screen. Choose Mode⇨CMYK Preview. This image represents what Photoshop will do with your image if you don't make any corrections whatsoever. It's good to have around for comparative purposes.

Step 2. Return to your original image and choose Select⇨Color Range. Then select the Out Of Gamut option from the Select pop-up menu and press Return. You have now selected all the nonconformist Pinko pixels throughout your image. Eugene McCarthy would have loved this option and bemoaned its absence in the film industry.

Step 3. To monitor your progress, choose Mode⇨Gamut Warning to display the gray pixels. Oh, and don't forget to press Command-H to get rid of those pesky ants.

Step 4. Press Command-U to display the Hue/Saturation dialog box. Don't change any settings while Master is selected; it's not exacting enough. Rather, experiment with selecting individual color radio buttons and lowering the Saturation value. The Hue slider can sometimes be useful as well. Every time you see one of the pixels change from gray to color, it means that another happy pixel has joined the CMYK pod. You may want to shout, "It's pointless to resist!" and laugh with evil delight just to make your work more entertaining.

 Keep an eye on the duplicate image in the CMYK preview mode. If you edit a color in your original image and render it less colorful than the previewed image, it means that you're doing damage you could avoid by simply choosing Mode⇨CMYK Color. So if you drag the Saturation slider down to –35 for Y (Yellow) and notice that the revived pixels in the original image have become noticeably less colorful than their counterparts in the duplicate, nudge the slider back up to brighten the colors. If you can't seem to find an equitable solution, try selecting a different color radio button and editing it. Or try nudging the Hue slider and see what happens. Be patient, it takes a little time.

Step 5. When only a few hundred sporadic gray spots remain on-screen, click on the OK button to return to the image window. Bellow imperiously, "You may think you have won, you little gray pixels, but I have a secret weapon!" Then choose Mode⇨CMYK Color and watch as Photoshop forcibly thrusts them into the gamut. (Don't worry, automatically changing a few pixels here and there isn't going to hurt anything.)

Mind you, the differences between your duplicate image and the one you manually turned away from the evil empire of RGB excess will be subtle, but they may prove enough to produce a better looking image with a wider range of colors.

 If the Hue/Saturation command doesn't seem to be working out, try using the Variations command or the Levels and Curves commands, as explained later in this chapter. The Variations command goes so far as to display the out-of-gamut gray pixels inside its previews and even hide the gray as the colors come into the fold.

 The one thing I don't like about the previous steps is that the Color Range command selects only the out-of-gamut pixels without even partially selecting their neighbors. As a result, you desaturate out-of-gamut colors while leaving very similar colors fully saturated, an effect that can produce visual edges in an image. One solution is to insert a step between Steps 2 and 3 in which you do the following: Double-click on the magic wand tool to display the Magic Wand Options panel and then change the Tolerance value to, say, 12. Next, choose Select⇨Similar, which expands the selected area to all pixels that fall within the Tolerance range of the previously selected pixels. Finally, choose Select⇨Feather and enter a value that's about a quarter of the Tolerance value — in this case, 3. This solution isn't perfect — ideally, the Color Range option box wouldn't dim the Fuzziness slider when you choose Out Of Gamut — but it does succeed in partially selecting a few neighboring pixels without sacrificing too many of the out-of-gamut bunch.

Colorizing images

When you select the Colorize check box in the Hue/Saturation dialog box, the options in the dialog box perform differently. Returning to that wonderful musical chairs analogy, the pixels no longer walk around a circle of chairs; they all get up and go sit in the same chair. Every pixel in the selection receives the same hue and the same level of saturation. Only the brightness values remain intact to ensure that the image remains recognizable.

The top row of Color Plate 16-8 shows the results of shifting the hues in an image in two different directions around the color wheel. In each case, the Colorize option is inactive. The second row shows similar colors applied separately to the faces and background of the image using the Colorize option. The colors look approximately the same within each column in the color plate. However, the Hue values are different in the shifted images than those in the colorized images because the shifted colors are based on flesh tones in the orange (25 degree) range as well as a variety of other colors in the original image, while all the colorized colors are based on absolute 0 degree, which is red.

In most cases, you'll only want to colorize grayscale images or bad color scans, because colorizing ruins the original color composition of an image. You'll probably also want to lower the Saturation value to somewhere in the neighborhood of 50 to 75 degrees. All the colors in the second-row images in Color Plate 16-8 are the result of entering Saturation values of 60 degrees.

 To touch up areas in a colorized image, change the foreground color to match the Hue and Saturation values that you used in the Hue/Saturation dialog box. The B (Brightness) value in the Color Picker dialog box — which you display by clicking on a color swatch in the toolbox — should be 100 percent. Select the paintbrush tool and change the brush mode in the Paintbrush Options panel to Color. Then paint away.

Shifting selected colors

The Replace Color command allows you to select an area of related colors and adjust the hue and saturation of that area. When you select Image⇨Adjust⇨Replace Color, you get a dialog box much like the Color Range dialog box. Shown in Figure 16-8, the Replace Color dialog box varies in only a few respects: It's missing the Select and Selection Preview pop-up menus and it offers three slider bars, taken right out of the Hue/Saturation dialog box. In fact, this dialog box works exactly as if you were selecting a portion of an image using Select⇨Color Range and editing it with the Hue/Saturation command. There is no functional difference whatsoever. The Replace Color and Color Range dialog boxes even share the same default settings. If you change the Fuzziness value in one, the default Fuzziness value of the other changes as well. It's like they're identical twins or something.

So why does the Replace Color command even exist? Because it allows you to change the selection outline and apply different colors without affecting the image in any way. Just select the Preview check box to see the results of your changes on-screen, and you're in business.

The top row of Color Plate 16-9 shows two effects created by selecting an area and changing the Hue value to +148 and the Saturation value to –12 (as in Figure 16-8). In the first example, I selected the pumpkin face by setting the Fuzziness value to 40 and clicking and Shift-clicking a few times with the eyedropper tool. In the right example, I clicked just once in the area behind the pumpkin and changed the Fuzziness to 200, the maximum setting. I was able to experiment freely without once leaving the dialog box or redrawing the selection outline.

Figure 16-8:
The Replace Color
dialog box works like
the Color Range dialog
box described back in
Chapter 9, with a few
Hue/Saturation options
thrown in.

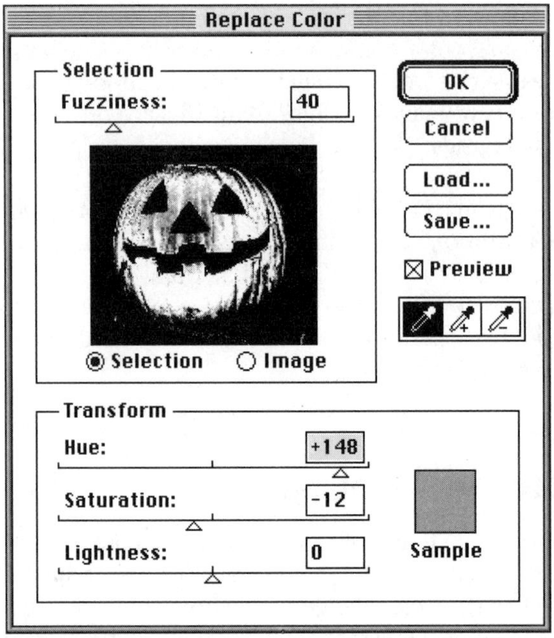

Replace Color

Selection
Fuzziness: `40`

OK
Cancel
Load...
Save...

☒ Preview

◉ Selection   ○ Image

Transform
Hue: `+148`
Saturation: `-12`
Lightness: `0`

Sample

If you're not clear on how to use all the options in the Replace Color dialog box, read the "Generating masks automatically" section in Chapter 9. It tells you all about the eyedropper tools and the Fuzziness option.

Shifting predefined colors

I really think that Adobe got these command names mixed up: The Replace Color command should be called Selective Color — because you select color (duh) — and Selective Color should be called Replace Color, because that's one of the things you can actually do with the command.

But naming problems aside, choosing Image⇨Adjust⇨Selective Color brings up the dialog box shown in Figure 16-9. To use the dialog box, choose the predefined color that you want to edit from the Colors pop-up menu and then adjust the four process-color slider bars to change the predefined color. When the Relative radio button is selected, you add or subtract color, much as if you were moving the color around the musical chairs using the Hue slider bar. When you select Absolute, you change the predefined color to the exact value entered into the Cyan, Magenta, Yellow, and Black option boxes. The Absolute option is therefore very much like the Colorize check box in the Hue/Saturation dialog box.

Figure 16-9:
Select a predefined
color from the
Colors pop-up menu
and adjust the slider
bars to change that
color.

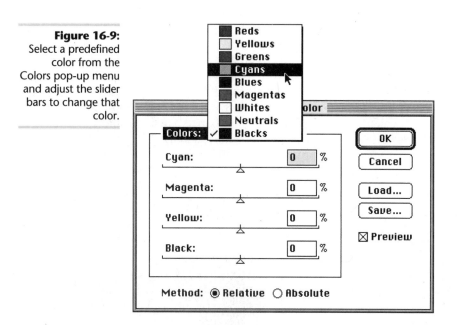

If you examine it closely, you'll notice that the Selective Color dialog box is very much
like the Hue/Saturation dialog box. You have access to predefined colors in the form of
a pop-up menu instead of radio buttons, and you can adjust slider bars to alter the
color. The key differences are that the pop-up menu lets you adjust whites, medium
grays (Neutrals), and blacks — options missing from Hue/Saturation — and the slider
bars are always measured in CMYK color space. But I think that the Selective Color
options would have made a lot more sense had Adobe brought them into the Variations
dialog box. As I explain in the next section, Variations offers the equivalent of a Colors
pop-up menu and a series of slider bars; but, inexplicably, it provides fewer Colors
options and more slider bars. If you were to simply combine these two functions, you'd
have a very strong command that would rival and possibly surpass the capabilities of
the Hue/Saturation dialog box. Alas, Adobe still hasn't offered to put me on the payroll
and buy all my swell ideas, so I guess I'll just have to settle for grumbling, gnashing my
teeth, and cursing like Fred Flintstone. (*Rassam, grassam, frassam* — ever notice that the
guy's expletives rhyme?)

Anyway, just so that you can see how this dialog box works, the bottom row of Color
Plate 16-9 shows two examples. To create the first, I chose Red from the Colors pop-up
menu and dragged the Cyan slider bar all the way up to +100 percent and the yellow
slider all the way to –100 percent. I also selected the Relative radio button, which
retains a lot of pink in the pumpkin's face. To create the second example, I reapplied the
same colors but selected the Absolute radio button, making the entire pumpkin purple.
I also chose Black from the Colors pop-up menu and dragged the Black slider to –100
percent.

The Selective Color command produces the most predictable results when you're working inside the CMYK color space. When you drag the Cyan slider triangle to the right, for example, you're actually transferring brightness values to the cyan color channel. However, you have to keep an eye out for a few anomalies, particularly when editing Black. In the CMYK mode, black areas include not only black, but also shades of cyan, magenta, and yellow, resulting in what printers call a *rich black*. Therefore, to change black to white, as I did in the lower right example of Color Plate 16-9, you have to set the Black slider to –100 percent and also set the Cyan, Magenta, and Yellow sliders to the same value.

Using the Variations command

In the previous section, I mentioned that the Variations command offers the equivalent of the Colors pop-up menu and slider bars found in the Selective Color dialog box. If you've ever used this command, you may be wondering what the heck I'm talking about. But it's true. Choose Image⇨Adjust⇨Variations and you'll see them all plain as day. It's just that the Colors pop-up menu options appear as four radio buttons, and the slider bars are presented as thumbnails, as shown in Figure 16-10.

Here's how it works: To infuse color into the selected image, click on one of the thumbnails in the central portion of the dialog box. The thumbnail labeled More Cyan, for example, shifts the colors toward cyan. The thumbnail even shows how the additional cyan will look when added to the image. In case you're interested in seeing how these thumbnails actually affect a final printed image, check out Color Plate 16-10.

Now notice that each thumbnail is positioned directly opposite its complimentary color. More Cyan is across from More Red, More Blue is across from More Yellow, and so on. In fact, clicking on a thumbnail not only shifts colors toward the named color but away from the opposite color. For example, if you click on More Cyan and then click on its opposite, More Red, you arrive at the original image. Although this isn't exactly how the colors in the additive and subtractive color worlds work — cyan is not the empirical opposite of red — the colors are theoretical opposites, and the Variations command makes the theory a practicality. After all, you haven't yet applied the color to the image, so the dialog box can calculate its adjustments in a pure and perfect world. Cyan and red ought to be opposites, so for the moment, they are.

To control the amount of color shifting that occurs when you click on a thumbnail, move the slider triangle in the upper right corner of the dialog box. Fine produces very minute changes; Coarse creates massive changes. Just to give you an idea of the difference between the two, you have to click on a thumbnail about 40 times when the slider is set to Fine to equal one click when it's set to Coarse.

Figure 16-10:
Click on the thumbnails to shift the colors in an image; adjust the slider bar in the upper right corner to change the sensitivity of the thumbnails; and use the radio buttons to determine which part of an image is selected.

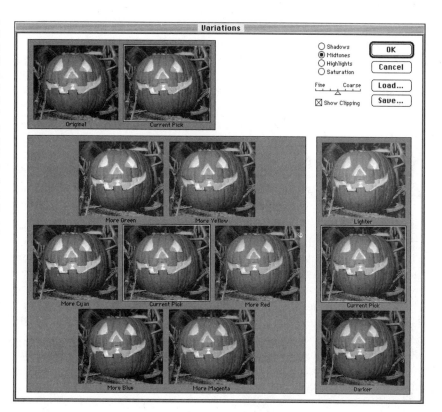

As you click, you may notice that weird colors begin to appear inside the thumbnails. These bits of inverted image represent colors that exceed the boundaries of the current color space. Though the colors won't actually appear inverted as they do in the dialog box, it's not a good idea to exceed the color space because it results in areas of flat color, just as when you convert between the RGB and CMYK spaces. (To prevent the inverted color areas from appearing inside the dialog box, deselect the Show Clipping check box. Incidentally, this use of the word *clipping* — Photoshop's third, in case you're counting — has nothing to do with masks.)

Finally, the radio buttons at the top control which colors in the image are affected. Select Shadows to change the darkest colors, Highlights to change the lightest colors, and Midtones to change everything in between. (In fact, if you're familiar with the Levels dialog box — as you will be if you read the next section — the first three radio buttons have direct counterparts in the slider triangles in the Levels dialog box. For example, when you click on the Lighter thumbnail when the Highlights option is selected in the Variations dialog box, you perform the same action as moving the white triangle in the Levels dialog box to the left — that is, you lighten the lightest colors in the image to white.)

The Saturation radio button lets you increase or decrease the saturation of colors in an image. Only one thumbnail appears on either side of the Current Pick image — one that decreases the saturation, and another that increases it. These options are more sensitive than the Saturation slider bar in the Hue/Saturation dialog box, affecting only the midtones in the image and leaving the lightest and darkest colors unaffected.

Making Custom Brightness Adjustments

The Lighter and Darker options in the Variations dialog box are preferable to the Lightness slider bar inside the Hue/Saturation dialog box because you can specify whether to edit the darkest, lightest, or medium colors in an image. However, this is just the tip of the iceberg where Photoshop is concerned. The program provides two expert-level commands for adjusting the brightness levels in both grayscale and color images. The Levels command is ideal for most color corrections, enabling you to adjust the darkest values, lightest values, and midrange colors for the entire selection or independently within each color channel. The Curves command is great for creating special effects and correcting images that are beyond the help of the Levels command. Using the Curves command, you can map every brightness value in every color channel to an entirely different brightness value.

The Levels command

When you choose Image⇨Adjust⇨Levels (Command-L), Photoshop displays the Levels dialog box shown in Figure 16-11. The dialog box offers a histogram, as explained in the "Threshold" section earlier in this chapter, as well as two sets of slider bars with corresponding option boxes and a few automated eyedropper options in the lower right corner. You can compress and expand the range of brightness values in an image by manipulating the Input Levels options and then map those brightness values to new brightness values by adjusting the Output Levels options.

Figure 16-11:
Use the Levels dialog box to map brightness values in the image (Input Levels) to new brightness values (Output Levels).

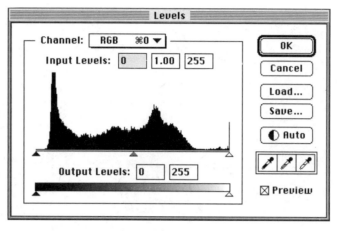

The options in the Levels dialog box work as follows:

- ☞ **Channel:** Select the color channel that you want to edit from this pop-up menu. You can apply different Input Levels and Output Levels values to each color channel. However, the options along the right side of the dialog box affect all colors in the selected portion of an image regardless of which Channel option is active.

- ☞ **Input Levels:** Use these options to select the darkest and lightest colors in the selected portion of an image, which is useful when the selection is washed out, offering insufficient shadows or highlights. The Input Levels option boxes correspond to the slider bar immediately below the histogram. You map pixels to black (or the darkest Output Levels value) by entering a number from 0 to 255 into the first option box or by dragging the black slider triangle. For example, if you raise the value to 55, all colors with brightness values of 55 or less in the original image become black, darkening the image as shown in the first example of Figure 16-12.

  You can map pixels at the opposite end of the brightness scale to white (or the lightest Output Levels value) by entering a number from 0 to 255 into the last option box or by dragging the white slider triangle. If you lower the value to 200, all colors with brightness values of 200 or greater become white, lightening the image as shown in the second example of Figure 16-12. In the last example of the figure, I raised the first value and lowered the last value, thereby increasing the amount of contrast in the image.

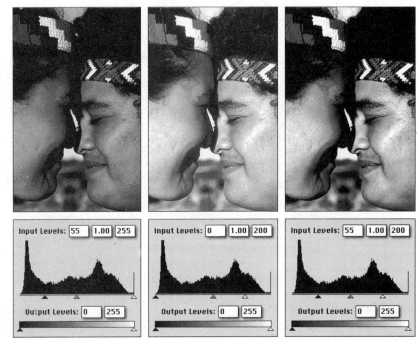

Figure 16-12:
The results of raising the first Input Levels value to 55 (left), lowering the last value to 200 (middle), and combining the two (right).

❀ **Gamma:** The middle Input Levels option box and the corresponding gray triangle in the slider bar (shown highlighted in Figure 16-13) represent the *gamma* value, which is the brightness level of the medium gray value in the image. The gamma value can range from 0.10 to 9.99, with 1.00 being dead-on medium gray. Any change to the gamma value has the effect of decreasing the amount of contrast in the image by lightening or darkening grays without changing shadows and highlights. Increase the gamma value or drag the gray slider triangle to the left to lighten the medium grays (also called *midtones*), as in the first and second examples of Figure 16-14. Lower the gamma value or drag the gray triangle to the right to darken the medium grays, as in the last example in the figure.

❀ **Output Levels:** Use these options to curtail the range of brightness levels in an image by lightening the darkest pixels and darkening the lightest pixels. You adjust the brightness of the darkest pixels — those that correspond to the black Input Levels slider triangle — by entering a number from 0 to 255 into the first option box or by dragging the black slider triangle. For example, if you raise the value to 55, no color can be darker than that brightness level (roughly 80 percent black), which lightens the image as shown in the first example of Figure 16-15. You adjust the brightness of the lightest pixels — those that correspond to the white Input Levels slider triangle — by entering a number from 0 to 255 into the second option box or by dragging the white slider triangle. If you lower the value to 200, no color can be lighter than that brightness level (roughly 20 percent

Figure 16-13:
I highlighted the gamma options by selecting everything but the highlighted areas and applying the values shown above.

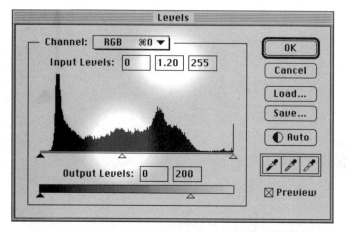

Figure 16-14:
The results of raising (left and middle) and lowering (right) the gamma value to lighten and darken the midtones in an image.

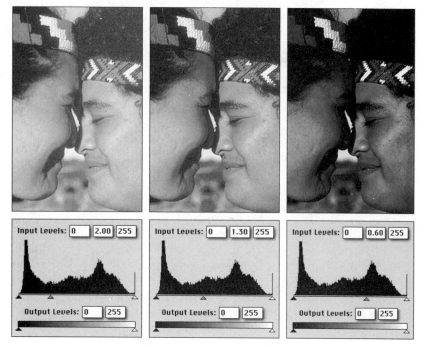

black), darkening the image as shown in the second example of Figure 16-15. In the last example of the figure, I raised the first value and lowered the second value, thereby dramatically decreasing the amount of contrast in the image.

You can fully or partially invert an image using the Output Levels slider triangles. Just drag the black triangle to the right and drag the white triangle to the left past the black triangle. The colors flip, whites mapping to dark colors and blacks mapping to light colors.

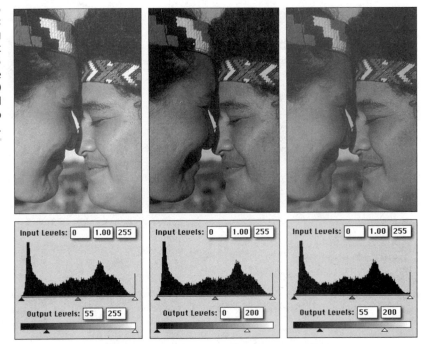

Figure 16-15:
The result of raising the first Output Levels value to 55 (left), lowering the second value to 200 (middle), and combining the two (right).

- **Load/Save:** You can load and save settings to disk using these buttons.

- **Auto:** Click on the Auto button to automatically map the darkest pixel in your selection to black and the lightest pixel to white, just like Image⇨Adjust⇨Auto Levels. Photoshop actually darkens and lightens the image by an extra half a percent to account for the fact that the darkest and lightest pixels may be anomalies. To enter a percentage of your own, Option-click on the Auto button (the button name changes to Options) to display the Auto Range Options dialog box shown in Figure 16-16. Enter higher values to increase the number of pixels mapped to black and white; decrease the values to lessen the effect. The first two examples in Figure 16-17 compare the effect of the default 0.50 percent values to higher values of 5.00 percent. (Strictly for comparison purposes, the last image in the figure demonstrates the effect of the Equalize command applied to the entire image.)

Figure 16-16:
Option-click on the Auto button to change the extent to which Photoshop closes the range of black and white pixels.

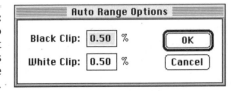

Figure 16-17:
The default effect of
the Auto button
(left), the effect of
the Auto button
after raising the Clip
values (middle), and
the effect of the
Equalize filter
(right).

0.50% Clips   5.00% Clips   Equalize

Any changes made inside the Auto Range Options dialog box also affect the performance of the Auto Levels command. At all times, the effects of the Auto button and Auto Levels command are absolutely identical.

↬ **Eyedroppers:** Select one of the eyedropper tools in the Levels dialog box and click on a pixel in the image window to automatically adjust the color of that pixel. If you click on a pixel with the black eyedropper tool (the first of the three), Photoshop maps the color of the pixel and all darker colors to black. If you click on a pixel with the white eyedropper tool (last of the three), Photoshop maps it and all lighter colors to white. Use the gray eyedropper tool (middle) to change the exact color on which you click to medium gray and adjust all other colors in accordance. For example, if you click on a white pixel, all white pixels change to medium gray and all other pixels change to even darker colors.

One way to use the eyedropper tools is to color-correct scans without a lot of messing around. Include a neutral swatch of gray with the photograph you want to scan. (If you own a Pantone swatch book, Cool Gray 5 or 6 is your best bet.) After opening the scan in Photoshop, choose the Levels command, select the gray eyedropper tool, and click on the neutral gray swatch in the image window. This technique won't perform miracles, but it will help you to more evenly distribute lights and darks in the image. You then can fine-tune the image using the Input Levels and Output Levels options.

↬ **Preview:** Select this option to preview the effects of your settings in the image window.

When the Preview check box is inactive — yes, you read that right, *in*active — you can preview the exact pixels that will turn to black or white in the image window by Option-dragging the black or white triangle in the Input Levels slider bar.

To give you a sense of how this command works, the following steps describe how to improve the appearance of a washed-out, faded, overly dark, scanned image using the options in the Levels dialog box. In fact, the very image I'll be using is included on the CD. From the Planet Art "French Posters" collection, this image is a scan of a well-known advertisement created by 19th-century poster artist Henri de Toulouse-Lautrec for the seedy Moulin Rouge. Though the piece itself it a masterwork, the Photo CD scan can be improved dramatically using the Levels command.

STEPS: Giving the Moulin Rouge a Much-Needed Face Lift

Step 1. Okay, here's the deal. You're a restorer of priceless artwork. You begin by opening up the Moulin Rouge image on the CD inside the Planet Art folder. The Photo CD dialog box comes up, asking you what resolution you want to open. Select the size that's most likely to work smoothly on your machine. (If you have problems with this dialog box, consult the "Photo CD YCC images" section of Chapter 3.)

Step 2. Press Command-L to display the Levels dialog box. Just to check it out, click on the Auto button. (Make sure that the Preview check box is on so that you can accurately see the results of your changes.) Just one click of the button results in a remarkable difference. In case you're not following along with the exercise, the first example in Color Plate 6-11 shows the difference between the original image (at the top) and the image subject to the Auto button (bottom).

Step 3. You could stop right here if you wanted to. It's good enough for government work. But I suggest that you pursue things a little further; although it's better, the image still has some problems. Too many of the pixels have turned black and too many have turned white. Meanwhile, the majority of the medium colors still appear very dark. So press the Option key and click on the Reset button to restore the original image.

Step 4. The best way to approach a color image is one channel at a time. So press Command-1 to switch to the red channel. Notice the histogram. It's all the way over to the left side, indicating a preponderance of dark colors. To lighten things up, drag the white triangle to the left. The third Input Levels value changes to keep up with you. Drag the triangle until it lines up with the lightest of the histogram bars, somewhere around 165 (as indicated in the third option box). This means that everything lighter than 165 — which is only slightly lighter than medium gray — will turn white.

Step 5.   Now drag the black triangle slightly to the right, until the first Input Levels value is 6. This blackens the darkest colors and keeps them from appearing washed out. By now, the image in the window will appear overly red. Don't worry, you'll equalize the colors in the next step.

Step 6.   So much for the red channel; now to repeat the process for the green and blue channels. Press Command-2 to switch to the green channel. Again, the pixels are all bunched up toward the dark end of the spectrum. Drag the white triangle to about 150 and drag the black triangle to 10. Next, press Command-3 to switch to the blue channel. Drag the white triangle left to 160, the black triangle right to 12. Keep in mind that these values are my suggestions only. I encourage you to experiment with other values to see if you find something that works better.

Step 7.   Now press Command-0 to return to the RGB view. See how the histogram bars are now spread out all the way from black to white? Notice the gaps between bars? These gaps indicate brightness values that are associated with no pixels — and I mean none in the red channel, none in the green channel, and none in the blue channel. Few images are quite this bad off.

Step 8.   The grays in the image are still too dark. So it's time to adjust the gamma. Drag the middle slider triangle to the right to lighten the medium colors. I suggest dragging until the middle Input Levels value reads 1.40. This brings out the color in that snobbish man in the foreground of the image — you know, that guy who's indicating, "None of this uncivilized behavior for me. In fact, I don't know what made me come into this place. Nonetheless, I must admit, that woman wears some nice undies." Anyway, you can start to see some purples and browns inside the gent where once there were only sooty grays.

Step 9.   Now that you elevated the grays, the blacks are starting to weaken again. So raise the black slider triangle to 10. Now the blacks look black.

Step 10.   Click on the OK button or press Return. Photoshop applies your changes to the image. Just for fun, press Command-Z a few times to see the before and after shots. Quite the transformation, what?

The second image in Color Plate 16-11 shows the color-corrected image. I also firmed up the detail a bit by applying the Unsharp Mask filter with an Amount value of 200 percent and a Radius of 0.5. There are still some rough spots in the image, but come on, it's right at a hundred years old. I mean, it's not even a painting, it's printed on paper. You should look so good. You can go in and retouch away some of those problems using the 5,000 techniques discussed in Part II of this book, but the color correction phase of the project is complete.

The Curves command

If you want to be able to map any brightness value in an image to absolutely any other brightness value — no holds barred, as they say at the drive-in movies — you want the Curves command. When you choose Image⇨Adjust⇨Curves (Command-M), Photoshop displays the Curves dialog box, shown in Figure 16-18, which must be the most functional collection of color correction options on the planet.

Figure 16-18:
The Curves dialog box lets you distribute brightness values by drawing curves on a graph.

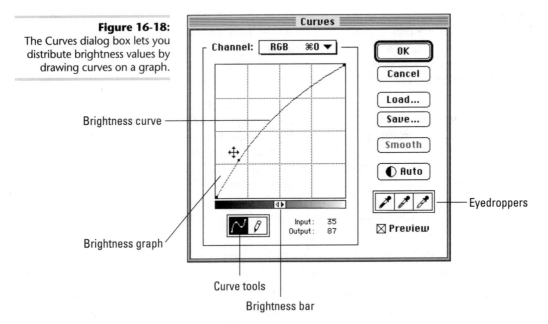

Brightness curve

Brightness graph

Curve tools

Brightness bar

Eyedroppers

Quickly, here's how the options work:

  ↪ **Channel:** Surely you know how this option works by now. You select the color channel that you want to edit from this pop-up menu. You can apply different mapping functions to different channels by drawing in the graph below the pop-up menu. But, as is always the case, the options along the right side of the dialog box affect all colors in the selected portion of an image regardless of which Channel option is active.

◦ **Brightness graph:** The brightness graph is where you map brightness values in the original image to new brightness values. The horizontal axis of the graph represents input levels; the vertical axis represents output levels. The *brightness curve* charts the relationship between input and output levels. The lower left corner is the origin of the graph (the point at which both input and output values are 0). Move right in the graph for higher input values, up for higher output values. Because the brightness graph is the core of this dialog box, upcoming sections explain it in more detail.

◦ **Brightness bar:** The brightness bar shows the direction of light and dark values in the graph. By default, colors are measured in terms of brightness values, in which case the colors in the brightness bar proceed from black to white (reading left to right), as demonstrated in the left example of Figure 16-19. Therefore, higher values produce lighter colors. However, if you click on the brightness bar, white and black switch places, as shown in the second example of the figure. The result is that Photoshop measures the colors in terms of ink coverage, from 0 percent of the primary color to 100 percent of the primary color. Higher values now produce darker colors. If you click on the brightness bar in the process of drawing a curve, the curve automatically flips so as to retain any changes you made, as the figure illustrates.

Figure 16-19:
Click on the brightness bar to change the way in which the graph measures color: by brightness values (left) or by ink coverage (right).

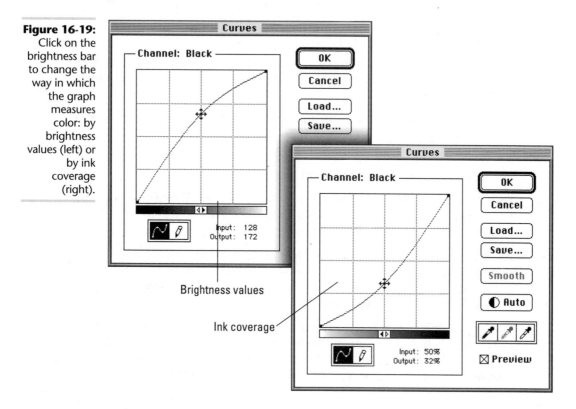

Brightness values

Ink coverage

○→ **Curve tools:** Use the curve tools to draw the curve inside the brightness graph. Click in the graph with the point tool (on the left, selected by default) to add a point to the curve. Drag a point to move it. To delete a point, drag it outside the boundaries of the graph. The pencil tool (on the right) enables you to draw free-form curves simply by dragging inside the graph, as shown in Figure 16-20.

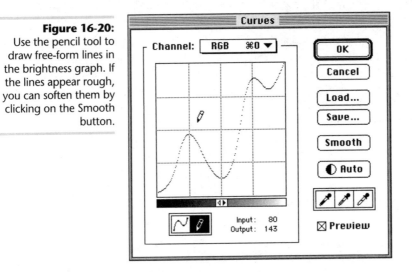

Figure 16-20:
Use the pencil tool to draw free-form lines in the brightness graph. If the lines appear rough, you can soften them by clicking on the Smooth button.

You can draw straight lines with the pencil tool by clicking at one location in the graph and Shift-clicking at a different point, just as you can when using the real pencil tool in the image window.

○→ **Input/Output numbers:** The input and output numbers monitor the location of your cursor in the graph according to brightness values or ink coverage, depending on the setting of the brightness bar.

○→ **Load/Save:** Use these buttons to load and save settings to disk.

○→ **Smooth:** Click on the Smooth button to smooth out curves drawn with the pencil tool. Doing so leads to smoother color transitions in the image window. This button is dimmed except when you use the pencil tool.

○→ **Auto:** Click on this button to automatically map the darkest pixel in your selection to black and the lightest pixel to white. Photoshop throws in some additional darkening and lightening according to the Clip percentages, which you can edit by Option-clicking on the button.

○→ **Eyedroppers:** Photoshop actually permits you to use a fourth eyedropper from the Curves dialog box. If you don't select any eyedropper tool (or you click in the graph to deselect the current eyedropper) and move the cursor out of the dialog box into the image window, you get the standard eyedropper cursor. Click on a pixel in the image to locate the brightness value of that pixel in the graph. A circle appears in the graph, and the input and output numbers list the value for as long as you hold down the mouse button, as shown in the first example in Figure 16-21.

The other eyedroppers work as they do in the Levels dialog box, mapping pixels to black, medium gray, or white. For example, the second image in Figure 16-21 shows the white eyedropper tool clicking on a light pixel, thereby mapping that value to white, as shown in highlighted portion of the graph below the image. You can further adjust the brightness value of that pixel by dragging the corresponding point in the graph, as demonstrated in the last example of the figure.

↪ **Preview:** Select this option to preview your settings in the image window.

Figure 16-21:
Use the standard eyedropper cursor to locate a color in the brightness graph (left). Click with one of the eyedropper tools from the Curves dialog box to map the color of that pixel in the graph (middle). You then can edit the location of the point in the graph by dragging it (right).

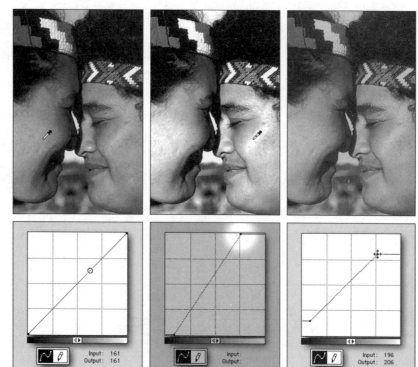

Continuous curves

All discussions in the few remaining pages of this chapter assume that the brightness bar is set to edit brightness values (in which case the gradation in the bar lightens from left to right). If you set the bar to edit ink coverage (the bar darkens from left to right), you can still achieve the effects I describe, but you must drag in the opposite direction. For example, if I tell you to lighten colors by dragging upward, you drag downward. In a backward world live the ink coverage people.

When you first enter the Curves dialog box, the brightness curve appears as a straight line strung between two points, as shown in the first example of Figure 16-22, mapping every input level from white (the lower left point) to black (the upper right point) to an identical output level. If you want to perform seamless color corrections, the point tool is your best bet because it enables you to edit the levels in the brightness graph while maintaining a continuous curve.

To lighten the colors in the selected portion of the image, click near the middle of the curve with the point tool to create a new point and then drag the point upward, as demonstrated in the second example of Figure 16-22. To darken the image, drag the point downward, as in the third example.

Figure 16-22: Create a single point in the curve with the point tool (left) and then drag it upward (middle) or downward (right) to lighten or darken the image evenly.

Create two points in the curve to boost or lessen the contrast between colors in the image. In the first example of Figure 16-23, I created one point very near the white point in the curve and another point very close to the black point. I then dragged down on the left point and up on the right point to make the dark pixels darker and the light pixels lighter, which translates to higher contrast.

In the second example of the figure, I did just the opposite, dragging up on the left point to lighten the dark pixels and down on the right point to darken the light pixels. As you can see in the second image, this lessens the contrast between colors, making the image more gray.

In the last example in Figure 16-23, I bolstered the contrast with a vengeance by dragging the right point down and to the left. This has the effect of springing the right half of the curve farther upward, thus increasing the brightness of the light pixels in the image.

Figure 16-23:
Create two points in the curve to change the appearance of contrast in an image, whether by increasing it mildly (left), decreasing it (middle), or boosting it dramatically (right).

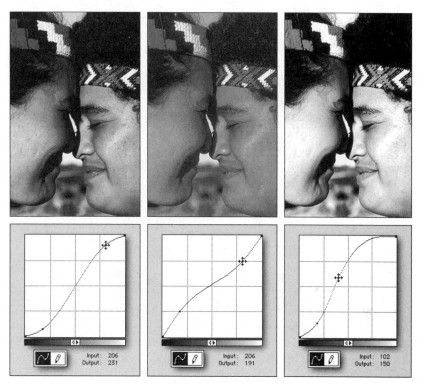

Arbitrary curves

You can create some mind-numbing color variations by adjusting the brightness curve arbitrarily, mapping light pixels to dark, dark pixels to light, and in-between pixels all over the place. In the first example of Figure 16-24, I used the point tool to achieve an arbitrary curve. By dragging the left point severely upward and the right point severely downward, I caused dark and light pixels alike to soar across the spectrum.

If you're interested in something a little more subtle, try applying an arbitrary curve to a single channel in a color image. Color Plate 16-12, for example, shows an image subject to relatively basic color manipulations in the red and green channels, followed by an arbitrary adjustment to the blue channel.

Although you can certainly achieve arbitrary effects using the point tool, the pencil tool is more versatile and less inhibiting. As shown in the second example of Figure 16-24, I created an effect that would alarm Carlos Castaneda just by zigzagging my way across the graph and clicking on the Smooth button.

Figure 16-24:
Arbitrary brightness
curves created using the
point tool (left) and the
pencil tool (right).

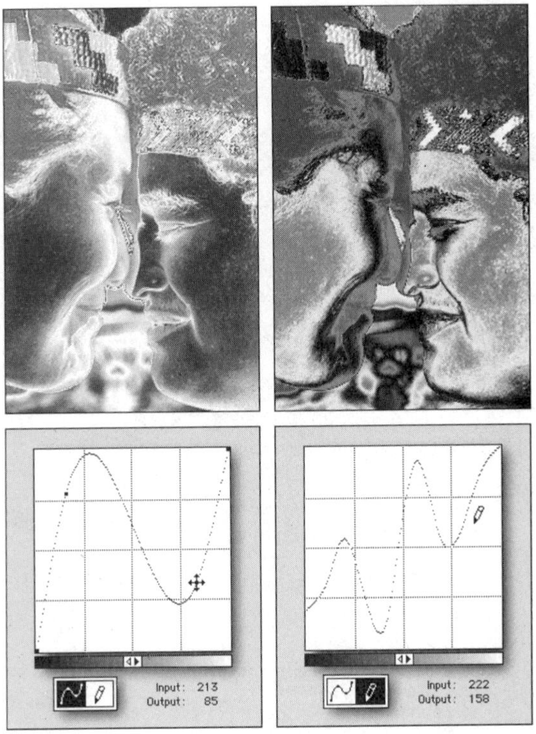

In fact, the Smooth button is an integral part of using the pencil tool. Try this little experiment: Draw a bunch of completely random lines and squiggles with the pencil tool in the brightness graph. As shown in the first example of Figure 16-25, your efforts will most likely yield an unspeakably hideous and utterly unrecognizable effect.

Next, click on the Smooth button. Photoshop automatically connects all portions of the curve, miraculously smoothing out the color-mapping effect and rescuing some semblance of your image, as shown in the second example of the figure. If the effect is still too radical, you can continue to smooth it out by clicking additional times on the Smooth button. I clicked on the button twice more to create the right image in Figure 16-25. Eventually, the Smooth button restores the curve to a straight line.

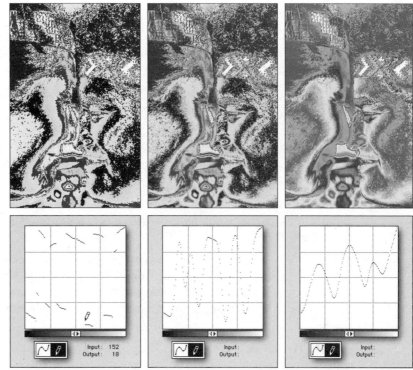

Figure 16-25:
After drawing a series of completely random lines with the pencil tool (left), I clicked on the Smooth button once to connect the lines into a frenetic curve (middle) and then twice more to even out the curve, thus preserving more of the original image (right).

Summary

➜ Color mapping is useful for creating special effects and correcting and balancing colors in an image.

➜ The Invert command and hue changes applied to all colors from the Hue/Saturation dialog box are the only color-mapping functions that do not destroy so much as a single color in an image.

➜ The Equalize command automatically redistributes colors in an entire image according to the colors in a selected portion of the image. It is the only Photoshop command that can affect pixels outside a selection.

➜ Use the Desaturate command to suck the colors out of a selection. For best results, float the selection before applying the command so that you have the option of reintroducing some colors by changing the Opacity setting.

➜ Image↪Adjust↪Auto Levels works exactly like the Auto button in the Levels dialog box, adjusting all color channels so that the lightest color in the channel becomes white and the darkest color becomes black.

➥ The Hue/Saturation command lets you rotate colors in an image around the color wheel, an effect called *color shifting.*

➥ To reset all options in the Hue/Saturation, Levels, and Curves dialog boxes, press Command-Option-period.

➥ If you were to attempt color mapping on a television, you would change the hue with the Tint knob, manipulate saturation levels with the Color knob, and edit lightness values with the Brightness knob.

➥ The Colorize option in the Hue/Saturation dialog box applies an absolute hue and saturation level to an image while retaining the image's original brightness values.

➥ The Replace Color command provides the same automated selection options as Select⇨Color Range and mixes in the color-shifting options in the Hue/Saturation dialog box.

➥ Selective Color and Variations would be better if they were combined into a single dialog box, but as they stand, they both allow you to edit predefined areas of color by adding or subtracting other colors. The Variations dialog box offers the added advantage of thumbnails that preview the effects of each option.

➥ The Levels and Curves commands work by changing brightness levels inside one or more color channels in an image.

➥ Use the Auto button and eyedropper tool to apply automated color corrections to an image.

➥ Draw a curve in the brightness graph in the Curves dialog box to map any brightness value in an image to any other brightness value.

➥ The Smooth button smoothes out curves drawn with the pencil tool, regardless of how erratic.

The Fundamentals of Compositing

17

In This Chapter

- ◗ Continuing information about working with layers

- ◗ Using overlay modes to mix active layers and floating selections with underlying images

- ◗ Using the options in the Layer Options dialog box

- ◗ Exploring the advantages and disadvantages of channel operations

- ◗ Mixing same-sized images with the Apply Image command

- ◗ Masking images combined with channel operations

- ◗ Using the Add and Subtract overlay modes

- ◗ Modifying selection outlines, masks, and layer transparencies like a pro using the Calculations command

---

Mixing Images Together _____

In earlier chapters, I demonstrated many examples of *compositing,* which is the sometimes straightforward, sometimes extremely complex process of mixing two or more images together. But however straightforward or complex, Photoshop's compositing capabilities fall into three categories:

↪ **Floating selections:** The simple act of floating a selection, applying a filter to it, and using the Opacity slider bar to mix the floater with the underlying original is the quickest and most direct method of compositing available inside Photoshop. Whether you float an image by moving it, choosing Select➪Float, copying and pasting it, or dragging and dropping it from another image window, you can apply any of the overlay mode options from the Layers palette as well as adjust the Opacity slider bar to mix the floating selection with the fixed image behind it.

- **Layers:** When an image is on a separate layer, you can take advantage of the overlay modes pop-up menu and the Opacity slider bar, just as you can when working with a floating selection. But you also have access to two additional features, both of which are unique to layers. You can bring up the Layers Options dialog box, which allows you to drop colors out of the active layer and force colors to show through from background layers. You also have the option of compositing more than two images at a time. Combining floating selections with layers provides even more options.

- **Channel operations:** The so-called channel operations enable you to combine two open images of identical size (or one image with itself) using two commands, Image⇨Apply Image and Image⇨Calculations. Unusually complex and completely lacking in sizing and placement functions, these commands provide access to only two unique options, the Add and Subtract overlay modes. Simply put, unless a technique involves the Add or Subtract mode or you're specifically interested in combining individual channels from different images, you can composite with greater ease, flexibility, and feedback using floating selections or layers. For more on this lively topic, see the "Using Channel Operation Commands" section later in this chapter.

This chapter contains explanations of the various compositing options, including complete information on the Layers palette and the Apply Image and Calculations commands. The following chapter, "Compositing on the March," offer a series of step-by-step methods for taking advantage of these options. Together, these chapters should provide a complete picture of how compositing works and how you can integrate it into your daily image-editing regimen. (A little Slim-Fast here, a few composites there, and you'll be shipshape in no time.)

Compositing with Layers _____

I've already discussed the layering feature in some detail in Chapters 8 and 9, so I'll concentrate now on the handful of layering functions that I've so far breezed over or ignored.

Figure 17-1 shows the Layers palette as it appears with pop-up menu exposed. By now, you're probably already familiar with the overlay modes pop-up menu and the Opacity slider bar, but just in case, both appear labeled in the figure.

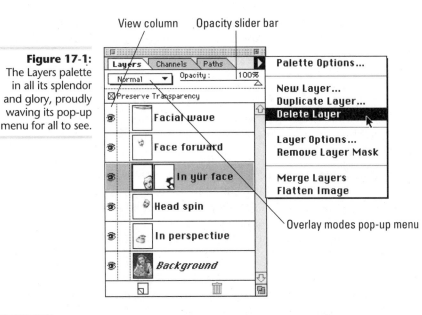

Figure 17-1:
The Layers palette in all its splendor and glory, proudly waving its pop-up menu for all to see.

 For information about establishing layers, read the "Sending a floating selection to its own layer" section of Chapter 8. This section also explains the basic concepts behind layering.

The items in the Layers palette that are integral to the subject of compositing include the following:

- **The Opacity slider bar:** Drag the slider triangle or press a number on the keyboard to change the opacity of the active layer or floating selection. Remember that one of the first eight tools in the toolbox or one of the path tools must be active for the keyboard shortcuts to work, so press the M key to get the marquee tool before starting in on the number keys. (If one of the painting or editing tools is selected, pressing a number key changes the opacity of that tool.)

- **The overlay modes pop-up menu:** Also available to floating selections, the overlay modes pop-up menu mixes every pixel in the active layer with the pixel directly behind it according to one of several mathematical equations. For example, when you choose Multiply, Photoshop really does multiply the brightness values of the two pixels and then divides the result by 255, the maximum brightness value. If you're more concerned with the effects of the overlay modes than their equations, see the upcoming "Overlay modes" section.

↪ **Layer Options:** Choose the Layer Options command or double-click on a layer to display the Layer Options dialog box. Applicable exclusively to layers, this dialog box duplicates the two options described above as well as adding a few functions. For example, using the slider bars, you can specify which colors are visible in the active layer and which colors show through from the ones behind it. You can also mix the colors using special fuzziness controls and change the slider bar settings for each individual color channel. For a complete description of the Layer Options dialog box, read the "Blending layers with supreme control" section later in this chapter.

↪ **Keyboard navigation:** Switch to the next layer up by pressing Command-right bracket. Move down a layer by pressing Command-left bracket. You can also go from the top layer to the Background layer by pressing Command-right bracket or vice versa by pressing Command-left bracket. To go to a layer that contains a specific image, press V to select the move tool and then Command-click on the image.

↪ **Layer order:** Drag a layer name up or down in the scrolling list to move it forward or backward in layering order. The only trick is to make sure that the black bar appears at the point where you want to move the layer before you release the mouse button, as demonstrated in Figure 17-2. You can even move floating selections by dragging them up and down in the palette. The floating selection neither loses its contents nor stops floating; it simply hovers above a different layer. But don't miss that black bar, or Photoshop won't move a darn thing.

The all-important black bar

Figure 17-2:
Drag the layer between two other layers to make the all-important black bar appear (left) to change the hierarchy of the layer (right).

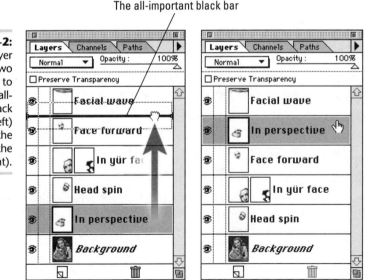

☞ **View column:** You know that you can hide layers and display them by clicking in the view column — the one with all the eyeballs. But did you know that you can Option-click in front of a layer to display only that layer and hide all others? When you view a single layer out of context, Photoshop disregards any overlay mode and Opacity setting applied to the layer and shows it fully opaque so that you can more carefully examine its pixels. Option-click in front of the layer again to bring all the layers back into view and reinstate the overlay mode and translucency.

☞ **Palette Options:** I only mention this command because I've thus far ignored it. When you choose Palette Options from the Layers palette menu, you can select from one of three sizes at which to display the thumbnail preview to the left of the layer name in the palette, or you can hide the thumbnail. You could have easily figured that out without me, but I just don't want anyone out there thinking, "What in the Sam Peckinpah-Hill does this command do?"

☞ **Flatten Image and Merge Layers:** Choose the Merge Layers command to merge all visible layers into a single layer. If the layer is not visible — that is, no eyeball icon appears in front of the layer name — Photoshop doesn't get rid of it; the layer simply remains independent. The Flatten Image command, on the other hand, merges all visible layers and throws away the invisible ones. Be wary of commands that want to flatten the image for you. For example, Photoshop has to flatten an image in order to switch color modes. So be sure to display all layers that you want to retain before choosing any of the first eight commands from the Mode menu.

Overlay modes

The overlay modes options available from the Layers palette include the same bunch that I discussed at the end of Chapter 7, in "The 15 paint tool brush modes" section. When manipulating the active layer, you see only 14 brush modes, all of which are found in the brush modes pop-up menu in the Paintbrush Options panel. Only the Behind mode is missing — you can't apply the active layer behind itself.

Behind and Clear

If you float a selection on the active layer, however, you gain access not only to the Behind mode, but also to a 16th overlay mode, Clear. Just like the Behind mode available for brushes, this Behind mode lets you tuck the floating selection behind the opaque portions of the active layer. In other words, the floating selection is allowed to fill the transparent and translucent areas of the active layer only.

The Clear mode uses the floating selection to cut a hole in the active layer. It's like having a little hole that you can move around independently of the pixels, without danger of harming them. You know that scene in *Yellow Submarine* where the Fab Four are making fun of that poor little marsupial dude with the long, mustard-colored nose? After they finish labeling him a "Nowhere Man" — hey, give him a break, guys, maybe his priorities are just different — the creature announces that he has a hole in his pocket. He then takes it out, puts it on the floor, and it becomes a hole in the floor. (Well, it's not really a floor. They're all in this nebulous white space that represents nowhere, I guess — either that or the band's last album.) Later, the holes multiply — can't remember why — and all the guys sail through the holes while singing some other song that has nothing to do with the plot, which was already in awfully short supply. Granted, it's a pointless movie — not nearly so great as *Sid and Nancy* — but the concept is absolutely the same as Photoshop's Clear mode. Clear turns a floating selection into a portable hole in the active layer.

This feature is especially useful for clipping holes into a layer using character outlines. Create some text, convert it to a bunch of holes by choosing the Clear mode, defloat the selection outline, and see what lies below. If you suddenly become concerned that you've lost part of the layer, don't panic. Just choose the Normal mode, and all will be forgotten.

Both the Behind and Clear modes are dimmed when you edit the Background layer (or an image without layers), because you can't scoot the floater under the background, and you can't cut a hole in the background because there's nothing underneath. (Well, I know some metaphysical types who say there might be something underneath, but you don't want to know what it is.)

The 14 universal overlay modes

The remaining overlay modes are available whether you're editing a layer or a floating selection and, in principle, they work the same as the brush modes I covered in Chapter 7. But some functional differences come into play when you're compositing layers or floating selections, so I include the following list just to be safe.

In case you're curious, the old Black Matte and White Matte overlay modes are now available from the Select➪Matting submenu in the form of the Remove Black Matte and Remove White Matte commands. Applicable to floating selections and layers alike, these commands are discussed in the "Removing halos" section of Chapter 8.

As I said, these overlay modes are applicable to both the active layer or a floating selection. But it seems like a lot of excess verbiage to keep saying "active layer or floating selection" over and over again. So any time I say "active layer" in the following list, you'll know that I mean both. (Wink, wink.)

Also, when I allude to something called a *composite pixel*, I mean the pixel color that results from all the mixing that's going on in back of the active layer or floating selection. For example, your document may have hoards of layers with all sorts of overlay modes in effect, but as long as you work on, say, layer 17, Photoshop treats the image formed by layers 1 through 16 as if it were one flattened image filled with a bunch of static composite pixels.

- **Normal:** In combination with an Opacity setting of 100 percent, this option displays every pixel in the active layer normally regardless of the colors of the underlying image. Figure 17-3 shows a banner that has been positioned on a single layer composited in front of a stucco texture created on the Background layer. The overlay mode in force is Normal. (The drop shadow, incidentally, is merely an artistic embellishment that exists on the background layer.)

  When you use an Opacity of less than 100 percent, the color of each pixel in the active layer is averaged with the composite pixel in the layers behind it according to the Opacity value. The first two examples of Color Plate 17-1 compare color versions of the banner set against a stucco background at 100 percent and 50 percent Opacity.

Figure 17-3:
An active layer containing the banner image and drop shadow subject to the Normal overlay mode and an Opacity setting of 100 percent.

↪ **Dissolve:** This option specifically affects feathered or softened edges. If the active layer is entirely opaque with hard edges, this option has no effect. If the selection is antialiased, the effect is generally too subtle to be of much use. The Dissolve option randomizes the pixels in the feathered portion of an active layer, as shown in the top example of Figure 17-4. It also randomizes pixels of hard- or soft-edged selections when the Opacity value is set below 100 percent, as witnessed by the second example in the figure and the third example in Color Plate 17-1.

Figure 17-4:
The Dissolve option applied to an opaque floating selection with heavily feathered edges (top) and to a second selection set to 40 percent opacity (bottom).

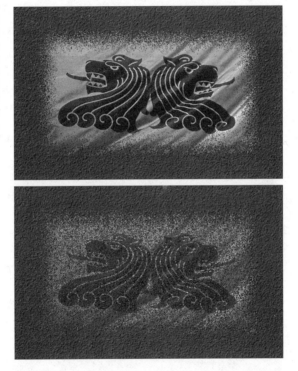

↪ **Multiply:** To understand the Multiply and Screen modes, you have to use a little imagination. So here goes: Imagine that the active layer and the underlying image are both photos on transparent slides. The Multiply mode produces the same effect as holding those slides up to the light, one slide in front of the other. Because the light has to travel through two slides, the outcome is invariably a darker image that contains elements from both images. Examples of the Multiply overlay mode appear in Figure 17-5 and Color Plate 17-1.

Figure 17-5:
The Multiply overlay mode produces the same effect as holding two overlapping transparencies up to the light. It always results in a darker image.

⌦ **Screen:** Still have those transparent slides from the Multiply analogy? Well, place them both in separate projectors and point them at the same screen and you'll get the same effect as Screen. Rather than creating a darker image, as you do with Multiply, you create a lighter image, as demonstrated in Figure 17-6 and Color Plate 17-1.

You can use the Screen overlay mode to emulate film that has been exposed multiple times. Ever seen Thomas Eakin's pioneering *Jumping Figure*, which shows rapid-fire exposures of a naked man jumping from one location to another? Each shot is effectively screened onto the other, lightening the film with each and every exposure. The photographer was smart enough to limit the exposure time so as not to overexpose the film; likewise, you should only apply Screen when working with images that are sufficiently dark so that you avoid overlightening.

Figure 17-6:
The Screen mode produces the same effect as shining two projectors at the same screen. It always results in a lighter image.

∽ **Overlay, Soft Light, and Hard Light:** You just can't separate these guys. All three multiply the dark colors in the active layer and screen the light colors into the composite pixels in the background layers, creating a heightened contrast effect. In fact, these three options are a little like the three bears of compositing. (I know, two Goldilocks analogies in one book is two too many, but bear with me for a moment.) The Hard Light overlay mode is papa bear, because it's too blunt; Soft Light is mama bear, because it's too subtle; and Overlay is baby bear, because it's just right.

Of course, that's something of an oversimplification. (A fairy tale analogy applied to a complex overlay mode qualifies as oversimplification? Never!) But it's frequently true. Figure 17-7 shows all three overlay modes — from top to bottom, Overlay, Soft Light, and Hard Light — applied to a single banner image on the left and to two layers of banner images on the right. Color Plate 17-1 shows the effect applied once only. As these examples demonstrate, the modes effectively tattoo one image onto the image in back of it. Notice, for example, that even after multiple repetitions of the banners in the figure, the stucco texture still shows through, as if the banner were actually appliquéd on.

I recommend starting with the Overlay mode any time you want to mix both active layer and the composite image behind it to create a reciprocal blend. By this I mean that it mixes the colors evenly without eliminating any of the detail in either image — unlike the Normal mode at 50 percent Opacity or any of the other modes, for that matter. After you apply Overlay, vary the Opacity to favor one image or the other. If you can't quite get the effect you want at lower Opacity settings, switch to the Soft Light mode and give that a try. If the Overlay mode at 100 percent seems too faint, switch to Hard Light. You can even copy the image, paste it onto another layer, and apply Hard Light a second time to darn well brand the layered image onto its background (as in the bottom right example of Figure 17-7).

∽ **Darken:** When you select this option, Photoshop applies colors in the active layer only if they are darker than the corresponding composite pixels formed by the underlying layers. Keep in mind that Photoshop compares the brightness levels of pixels in a full-color image on a channel-by-channel basis. So although the red component of a pixel in the active layer in an RGB image may be darker than the red component of the corresponding pixel in the underlying image, the green and blue components may be lighter. Photoshop would then assign the red component of the pixel in the layer, but not the green or blue component, thereby subtracting some red and making the pixel slightly more turquoise. Compare the predictable grayscale example of the Darken overlay mode in Figure 17-8 to its more challenging color counterpart in Color Plate 17-1.

Figure 17-7:
The results of the Overlay (top), Soft Light (middle), and Hard Light (bottom) overlay modes as they appear when applied to a single floating banner image (left) and a second layer of the banner image (right).

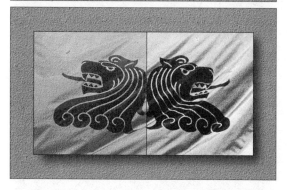

Figure 17-8:
The same active layer subject to the Darken overlay mode. Only those pixels in the selection that are darker than the pixels in the underlying stucco texture remain visible.

- **Lighten:** If you select this option, Photoshop applies colors in the active layer only if they are lighter than the corresponding pixels in the underlying image. Again, Photoshop compares the brightness levels in all channels of a full-color image. Examples of the Lighten overlay mode appear in Figure 17-9 and Color Plate 17-1.

Figure 17-9:
Our friend the active layer subject to the Lighten overlay mode. Only those pixels in the selection that are lighter than the pixels in the underlying stucco texture remain visible.

- **Difference:** This overlay mode simply inverts the background image according to the brightness value of the pixels in the active layer. At 100 percent Opacity, white inverts the background absolutely, black inverts it not at all, and all the other brightness values invert it to some degree in between. As a result, the stucco shows through the black areas of the lion heads in Figure 17-10, while the light areas of the banner have inverted the texture nearly to black. As with the other overlay modes, Difference applies its changes on a channel-by-channel basis. Therefore, the light green-blue of the banner inverted the contents of the green channel to black (because the yellow stucco contains lots of green) and the blue channel to white (because the stucco contains very little blue), while leaving the contents of the red channel nearly untouched. This elimination of green and the addition of blue results in a magenta shade across the banner.

Figure 17-10:
When you apply the Difference mode, the white pixels in the active layer invert the composite pixels beneath them, while the black pixels — such as those inside the silhouettes — leave the background untouched.

- **Hue:** The Hue mode and the following three overlay modes make use of the HSL color model to mix colors between active layer and underlying image. When you select Hue, Photoshop retains the hue values from the active layer and mixes them with the saturation and luminosity values from the underlying image. An example of this mode appears in the right column of Color Plate 17-1.

> I don't include grayscale figures for the Hue, Saturation, Color, and Luminosity overlay modes for the simple reason that those modes produce no effect on grayscale images. Actually, I shouldn't say *no* effect. In fact, they produce the exact same effect as the Normal option. After all, grayscale images don't include hue or saturation values; they only have luminosity.

- **Saturation:** When you select this option, Photoshop retains the saturation values from the active layer and mixes them with the hue and luminosity values from the underlying image. This mode rarely results in anything but very subtle effects, as demonstrated in Color Plate 17-1. You'll usually want to apply it in combination with some other overlay mode. For example, after applying some other overlay mode to a layer, you might duplicate the layer and then apply the saturation mode to either boost or downplay the saturation, much like printing a gloss or matte coating over the image.

- **Color:** This option combines hue and saturation. Photoshop retains both the hue and saturation values from the active layer and mixes them with the luminosity values from the underlying image. Because the saturation portion of the Color mode has such a slight effect, Color frequently produces an almost identical effect to Hue. In Color Plate 17-1, for instance, the Color example is actually less bright than the Hue example because the colors in the banner image are less saturated than their counterparts in the stucco texture.

- **Luminosity:** The Luminosity overlay mode retains the lightness values from the active layer and mixes them with the hue and saturation values from the underlying image. An example of this mode appears in the lower right corner in Color Plate 17-1. As you can see, this is the only example other than Normal that completely eliminated the bump in the stucco texture. This happened because the texture is composed entirely of abrupt brightness-value variations that are smoothed over by the more continuous brightness values in the banner.

Blending layers with supreme control

When you double-click on a layer other than the Background layer, Photoshop displays the Layer Options dialog box shown in Figure 17-11. With the exception of a couple of layer-specific options, this dialog box is identical to the old Composite Controls dialog box available in Photoshop 2.5. In fact, the primary functional difference between this feature and its elder counterpart is that you can no longer apply it to floating selections; it's now applicable exclusively to layers. To me, this is Photoshop 3.0's biggest disappointment. No more quick compositing with the brightness value slider bars; now you have to convert the floater to an independent layer even for the most minute compositing operations.

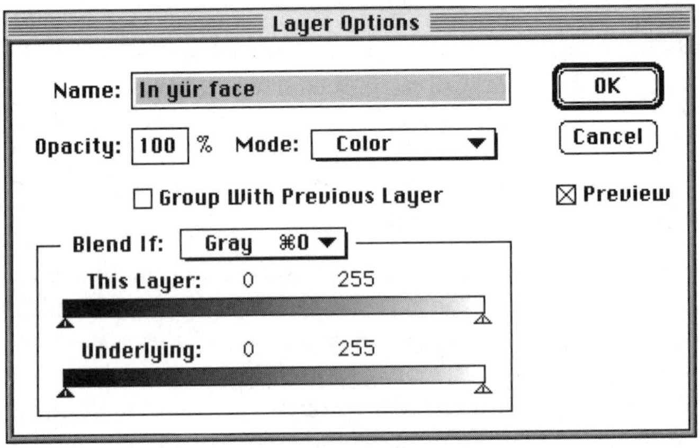

Figure 17-11:
When editing a layer, you can access a dialog box of options for selectively mixing the colors in the active layer with the colors in the image below.

```
┌─────────────────────── Layer Options ───────────────────────┐
│                                                              │
│   Name: │In yür face                      │      ┌────────┐  │
│                                                  │   OK   │  │
│   Opacity: │100│ %  Mode: │   Color      ▼│      └────────┘  │
│                                                  ┌────────┐  │
│              ☐ Group With Previous Layer         │ Cancel │  │
│                                                  └────────┘  │
│         ┌ Blend If: │ Gray   ⌘0 ▼│ ──────        ☒ Preview   │
│           This Layer:    0      255                          │
│           ▣▔▔▔▔▔▔▔▔▔▔▔▔▔▔▔▔▔▔▔▔▔▔▣                           │
│           ▲                     ▲                            │
│           Underlying:    0      255                          │
│           ▣▔▔▔▔▔▔▔▔▔▔▔▔▔▔▔▔▔▔▔▔▔▔▣                           │
│           ▲                     ▲                            │
└──────────────────────────────────────────────────────────────┘
```

But such is life. One is born, one grows up, one learns that even amazingly powerful applications such as Photoshop can wrench one's tiny heart to pieces. (Sniff.) I mean, it's a sad law of nature that we live in the kind of world where precious dialog boxes are ripped from the arms of innocents like myself just when we've come to rely on them. It's just (sniff), well, it's just not fair.

Having pretty thoroughly summed up my feelings on that subject, let me take this opportunity to announce that the Layer Options dialog box offers the following eight options:

↪ **Name:** Use this option box to change the layer name that appears in the Layers palette. I would have gladly sacrificed this option to be able to once again access the Composite Controls dialog box for floating selections.

☞ **Opacity:** The Opacity option box enables you to specify the translucency of the active layer. This option works identically to the Opacity slider bar in the Layers palette. I would have thrown this option in as well and considered myself better off for the bargain.

☞ **Mode:** Here's where you select one of the 14 overlay modes you could already access in the Layers palette pop-up menu. I don't mean to belabor a point, but this duplicate option isn't worth a plug nickel — whatever that is — compared with the wonders of being able to apply the once proud Composite Controls command to a free-range floating selection.

☞ **Group with Previous Layer:** Select this option to combine the active layer and the one below it into a clipping group, as discussed in the "Masking groups of layers" section of Chapter 9. I ignored this option in Chapter 9 because it's easier to simply Option-click on the horizontal line between the two layers to convert them to a clipping group.

☞ **Blend If:** Select a color channel from the Blend If pop-up menu to apply the effects of the slider bars beneath the menu to one color channel independently of the others. When the Gray option is active, as it is by default, your changes affect all color channels equally. (To my knowledge, this is the only instance where Gray means all color channels; elsewhere, Gray means a gray composite, just like Gray ought to mean. Boy, I'm starting to get steamed.) Just for the record, the Opacity value and Mode option affect all channels regardless of the color channel you select from Blend If.

☞ **This Layer:** This slider bar lets you exclude ranges of colors according to brightness values in the active layer. When you exclude colors by dragging the black triangle to the right or the white triangle to the left, the colors disappear from view.

☞ **Underlying:** This slider forces colors from the underlying layers to poke through the active layer. Any colors not included in the range set by the black and white triangles cannot be covered and are therefore visible regardless of the colors in the active layer.

☞ **Preview:** Select the Preview check box to continually update the image window every time you adjust a setting.

The slider bars are far too complicated to explain in a bulleted list. To find out more about these options as well as the Blend If pop-up menu, read the following sections.

You can restore all options in the Layer Options dialog box to their original settings by Option-clicking on the Reset button (the Cancel button changes to Reset when you press the Option key) or by simply pressing Command-Option-period.

Color exclusion sliders

Drag the triangles along the This Layer slider bar to abandon those pixels in the active layer whose colors fall within a specified range of brightness values. You can abandon dark pixels by dragging the left slider triangle or light pixels by dragging the right slider triangle. Figure 17-12 shows examples of each. To create the top example, I dragged the left slider bar until the value immediately to the right of the *This Layer* label read 50, thereby deleting pixels whose brightness values were 50 or less. To create the bottom example, I dragged the right slider triangle until the second value read 180, deleting pixels with brightness values of 180 or higher.

Figure 17-12:
The results of moving the left This Layer slider triangle to 50 (top) and, after Option-clicking on the Reset button, dragging the right slider triangle to 180 (bottom).

Drag the triangles along the Underlying slider bar to force pixels in the underlying image to show through if they fall within a specified brightness range. To force dark pixels in the underlying image to show through, drag the left slider triangle; to force light pixels to show through, drag the right slider triangle.

To achieve the effect in the top example in Figure 17-13, I dragged the left slider triangle until the value immediately to the right of the *Underlying* label read 120, forcing the pixels in the stucco pattern that had brightness values of 120 or lower to show through. In the second example, I dragged the right slider triangle until the second value read 180, uncovering pixels at the bright end of the spectrum.

Figure 17-13:
The results of moving the left Underlying slider triangle to 120 (top) and then resetting the left triangle back to 0 and moving the right triangle to 180 (bottom).

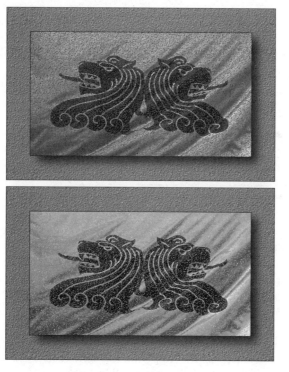

Fuzziness

The problem with abandoning and forcing colors with the slider bars is that you achieve some pretty harsh color transitions. Both Figures 17-12 and 17-13 bear witness to this fact. Talk about your jagged edges! Luckily, you can soften the color transitions by abandoning and forcing pixels gradually over a fuzziness range, which works much like the Fuzziness value in the Color range dialog box, leaving some pixels opaque and tapering others off into transparency.

To taper off the opacity of pixels in either the active layers or the underlying image, Option-drag one of the triangles in the appropriate slider bar. The triangle splits into two halves, and the corresponding value above the slider bar splits into two values separated by a slash, as demonstrated in Figure 17-14.

The left triangle half represents the beginning of the fuzziness range — that is, the brightness values at which the pixels begin to fade into or away from view. The right half represents the end of the range — that is, the point at which the pixels are fully visible or invisible.

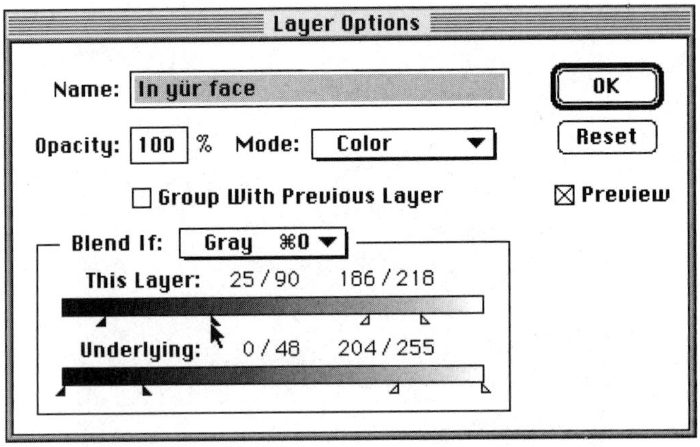

Figure 17-14: Option-drag a slider triangle to split it in half. You can then specify a fuzziness range across which brightness values will gradually fade into transparency.

Figures 17-15 and 17-16 show softened versions of the effects from Figures 17-12 and 17-13. In the top example of Figure 17-15, for example, I adjusted the range of the left This Layer slider triangle so that the value immediately to the right of the *This Layer* label read 30/70. The result is a much smoother effect than achieved in the top example in Figure 17-12. In the bottom example of Figure 17-15, I changed the range of the right This Layer slider triangle so that the second value read 120/230.

In Figure 17-16, I applied fuzziness ranges with the Underlying slider. In fact, both examples in the figure are the result of applying the same value, 120/180, to opposite Underlying slider triangles. In the top example, all brightness values under 120 gradually extending to values up to 180 show through the active layer. In the second example, all brightness values above 180 gradually extending down to 120 show through. The resulting two images look very much like sand art. (The next thing you know, I'll be showing you how to create string art and black velvet Elvises.)

Figure 17-15:
The results of adjusting the fuzziness range of the left This Layer slider triangle to 30/70 (top) and that of the right This Layer slider triangle to 120/230 (bottom).

Figure 17-16:
The results of adjusting the fuzziness range of both the left (top) and right (bottom) Underlying slider triangles to 120/180.

Color channel options

The options in the Blend If pop-up menu are applicable exclusively to the settings you apply using the This Layer and Underlying slider bars. When you work with a grayscale image, the Blend If pop-up menu offers one option only — Black — meaning that the Blend If option has no effect on grayscale editing. However, when you work in the RGB, CMYK, or Lab mode, the Layer Options dialog box enables you to abandon and force ranges of pixels independently within each color channel.

To do so, select a color channel from the Blend If pop-up menu and then set the slider triangles as desired. Each time you select a different Blend If option, the slider triangles retract to the positions at which you last set them for that color channel. Color Plate 17-2 demonstrates the effect of manipulating the This Layer and Underlying slider triangles independently for the red, green, and blue color channels.

Using Channel Operation Commands _____

Image⇨Apply Image and Image⇨Calculations provide access to Photoshop's *channel operations*, which composite one or more channels with others according to predefined mathematical calculations. Once found in the Image⇨Calculate submenu, channel operations have been hailed by some Photoshop users as the program's most powerful capabilities. I emphatically disagree. Though the commands have been improved in Photoshop 3.0, they remain less powerful and less flexible than their options in the Layers palette.

But before I hurl myself into the whys, wherefores, and what-have-yous, let me explain how the commands work. The Apply Image and Calculations commands composite one or two images in their entirety using nine of the 14 overlay modes discussed earlier plus two additional modes, Add and Subtract. In a nutshell, the commands automate the process of selecting one image, dragging and dropping it onto another, and using the overlay mode and Opacity settings in the Layers palette to mix the images. (When you're compositing a single image onto itself, the process is like floating the image and then using the Layers palette to mix floater and underlying original.)

The Apply Image command takes an open image and composites it onto the foreground image (or takes the foreground image and composites it onto itself). You can apply the command to either the full-color image or one or more of the individual channels inside the image. The Calculations command, on the other hand, works on individual channels only. It takes a channel from one image, mixes it with a channel from another (or the same) image, and puts the result inside an open image or in a new image window.

What is the purpose of these commands? Their primary advantage over earlier compositing methods is that they allow you to access and composite the contents of individual color channels without a lot of selecting, copying and pasting, cloning, floating, and layering.

But it's the commands' secondary advantage that has led to their romanticizing. Because you apply changes to an image using dialog box options, it's an easy matter to keep track of the way in which you achieve a particular special effect, should you choose to do so. You choose this command, select this option, enter this value, and so on. All you have to do is scribble down a few notes or, if you're sufficiently organized, use a macro utility such as QuicKeys or Tempo to record your actions. This way, you can try out an effect on a low-resolution image and then later repeat the operations on a high-resolution image, thus speeding up the experimentation process.

The mythic status of channel operations began when folks started sharing their techniques. If you can track and replicate your techniques, you can pass them along to your friends and neighbors. In a relatively small period of time, folks were creating all sorts of unusual effects by replaying a few channel operations.

This is all very well and good. Threads of information weave the fabric of an educated and productive nation. I'm all for it. The only problem is that while repeating someone else's technique is easy stuff, coming up with one of your own is both difficult and limiting. Simply put, channel operations do not lend themselves particularly well to the all-important task of experimentation. Here are a few areas in where they go awry:

- **No scaling or cropping:** If you want to mix two images using Apply Image or Calculations, both images must be exactly the same size, down to the pixel. Unlike PixelPaint Professional 3.0, Photoshop is unable to scale or crop images to match each other. As a result, nearly all channel operation techniques begin by compositing one image onto itself; this way, there's no chance of the images being different sizes.

- **No placement control:** One image is centered onto the other. If you want to offset one image from the other, you have to offset the image in advance, either by selecting the image and nudging it with the arrow keys or by applying Filter⇨Other⇨Offset. This is fine for creating drop shadows and other effects that involve mixing a single image with itself, but it makes it nearly impossible to position two different images with respect to each other with any degree of accuracy.

- **No brightness value control:** Unlike the Layer Options command, Apply Image and Calculations don't let you exclude colors from an image. The only way to prevent a channel operation from affecting every single pixel in an image is to draw a selection outline or include a mask channel.

⮑ **No tweaking the results:** If you don't like the result of a channel operation, you have to undo the operation and try it again. Meanwhile, when compositing floating selections or independent layers, you can experiment with slightly different overlay modes and Opacity settings till the cows come home (though what those truant cows are up to is anyone's guess).

 The good news is that the Apply Image and Calculations commands now provide previewing options. By selecting the Preview option in either dialog box, you can see how an effect will look in the image window. This essential capability makes channel operations more usable, but it doesn't quite make up for the remaining problems mentioned in the previous list.

So when should you use channel operations? When you want to mix specific channels in an image or combine masks and layer transparencies to create exact selection outlines, the Calculations command is a handy — though complex — solution (as explained in "The Calculations command" section later in this chapter). Meanwhile, the Apply Image command is good for compositing images in different color models, such as RGB and Lab (as I explain in the "Mixing images in different color modes" section).

But otherwise, use Apply Image and Calculations only when you want to mix entire images or selected portions of those images or when performing some cool technique that a friend of yours passed along. But keep in mind that even in these last two cases, you may be better off using the controls offered by the Layers palette. (If you're interested, the following chapter compares a standard compositing operation performed first using channel operations and then with Layers controls.)

 In Photoshop 2.5 and earlier, channel operations offered the advantage of speed. Copying a very high resolution image from one document and pasting it into another can take a long time because it involves transferring data to the Clipboard. By contrast, channel operations merely write data directly from one image to another and therefore involve no use of the Clipboard whatsoever. But now that you can assign floating images to layers and drag and drop selections between image windows — both operations that likewise bypass the Clipboard — the speed advantage of channel operations has dried up. It's not that channel operations have slowed down, mind you, it's just that other compositing operations have come up to speed.

The Apply Image command

Channel operations work by taking one or more channels from an image, called the *source*, and duplicating them to another image, called the *target*. When you use the Apply Image command, the foreground image is always the target, and you can select only one source image. Photoshop then takes the source and target, mixes them together, and puts the result in the target image. Therefore, the target image is the only image that the command actually changes. The source image remains unaffected.

When you choose Image⇨Apply Image, Photoshop displays the dialog box shown in Figure 17-17. Notice that you can select from a pop-up menu of images to specify the Source, but the Target item — listed just above the Blending box — is fixed. This is the active layer in the foreground image.

Figure 17-17:
The Apply Image command lets you mix one source image with a target image and make the result the new target.

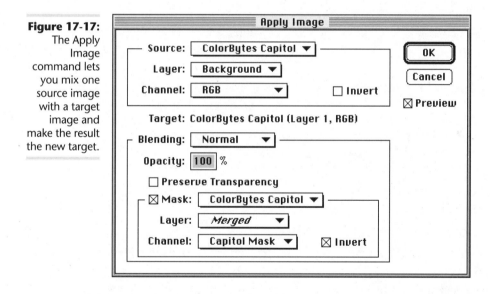

If this sounds a little dense, just think of it this way: The source image is the floating selection and the target is the underlying original. Meanwhile, the Blending options are the overlay modes pop-up menu and Opacity slider in the Layers palette.

Using the Apply Image command is a five-step process. You can always simply choose the command and hope for the best, but you'll get the most use out of it if you do the following:

STEPS: **Applying the Apply Image Command**

Step 1. First, open the two images that you want to mix. If you want to mix the image with itself to create some effect, just open the one image.

Step 2. Make sure that the two images are exactly the same size, down to the pixel. Use the crop tool and Image Size command as necessary. (You don't have to worry about this step when mixing an image with itself because the image is always the same size as itself — except, of course, when it's having a bad hair day.)

Step 3. Inside the target image, switch to the channel and layer that you want to edit. If you want to edit all channels, press Command-0 to remain in the composite view.

 When you're editing a single channel, I strongly advise you to display all channels on-screen. For example, after pressing Command-1 to switch to the RGB channel, click in front of the RGB item in the Channels palette to display the eyeball icon and show all channels. Only one channel is active, but all are visible. This way, you can see how your edits inside the Apply Image dialog box will affect the entire image, not just the one channel.

Step 4. Select the portion of the target image that you want to edit. If you want to affect the entire image, don't select anything.

Step 5. Choose Image⇨Apply Image and have at it.

Obviously, that last step is a little more difficult than it sounds. That's why I've put together the following list to explain how all those options in the Apply Image dialog box work:

- **Source:** The Source pop-up menu contains the name of the foreground image as well as any other images that are both open and exactly the same size as the foreground image. If the image you want to merge is not available, you must not have been paying much attention to Step 2. Press Command-period to cancel, resize and crop as needed, choose Image⇨Apply Image, and try again.

- **Layer:** This pop-up menu lists all layers in the selected source image. If the image doesn't have any layers, Background is your only option. Otherwise, select the layer that contains the prospective source image. Select Merged to mix all visible layers in the source image with the target image.

↪ **Channel:** Select the channels that you want to mix from this pop-up menu. Both composite views and individual color and mask channels are included. Keep in mind that you'll be mixing these channels with the channels that you made available in the target image before choosing the command. For example, if the target image is an RGB image shown in the full-color composite view, and you choose RGB from the Channel pop-up menu in the Apply Image dialog box, Photoshop mixes the red, green, and blue channels in the source image with the corresponding red, green, and blue channels in the target image. However, if you switched to the red channel before choosing Apply Image and then selected the RGB option, the program mixes a composite grayscale version of the RGB source image with the red channel in the target and leaves the other target channels unaffected. Conversely, if you are working in the composite view in the target image and you select red from the Channel pop-up menu, the red channel from the source image is mixed in with all three channels in the target. I could come up with about 50 other combinations, but hopefully you get the idea.

↪ **Selection, Transparency, and Layer Mask:** If a portion of the source image is selected, the pop-up menu offers a Selection option, which lets you apply the selection outline as if it were a grayscale image, just like a selection viewed in the quick mask mode. If you selected a specific layer from the Layer pop-up menu, you'll find a Transparency option. If the layer includes its own mask, as explained in the "Creating layer-specific masks" section of Chapter 9, a Layer Mask option also appears. These options also create grayscale images in which the opaque portions of the layer are represented as white and the transparent portions are black. None of the three options is particularly useful when you work in the composite view of the target image; you'll usually want to apply the Selection, Transparency, or Layer Mask option only to a single channel, as described in "The Calculations command" section toward the end of this chapter. (For an exception, see the upcoming tip.)

↪ **Invert:** Select this check box to invert the contents of the source image before compositing it with the target image. This option allows you to experiment with different effects. The last example in Color Plate 17-3, for example, shows one use for the Invert check box. I inverted the *b* channel before compositing it with the RGB image to create an early dawn effect.

↪ **Target:** You can't change this item. It merely shows which image, which channels, and which layers are being affected by the command.

↪ **Blending:** This pop-up menu offers access to nine of the overlay modes I discussed in the "The 14 universal overlay modes" section earlier in this chapter. The Dissolve, Hue, Saturation, Color, and Luminosity options are missing. (Darken and Lighten have inexplicably been renamed Darker and Lighter, though they work just the same.) Two additional options, Add and Subtract, are discussed in the "Add and Subtract" section later in this chapter.

- **Opacity:** You know how this one works. The source image works just like a floating selection, so the Opacity setting lets you set the translucency of the source.

- **Preserve Transparency:** When you're editing a layer in the target image — that is, you activated a specific layer before choosing Image⇨Apply Image — the Preserve Transparency check box becomes available. Select it to protect transparent portions of the layer from any compositing, much as if the transparent portions were not selected and are therefore masked.

- **Mask:** Select this option to mask off a portion of the source image. I already mentioned that you can specify the exact portion of the target image you want to edit by selecting that portion before choosing the Apply Image command. But you can also control which portion of the source image is composited on top of the target through the use of a mask. When you select the Mask check box, three new pop-up menus and an Invert check box appear at the bottom of the Apply Image dialog box. For complete information on these options, see the upcoming "Compositing with a mask" section.

- **Result:** If you press the Option key when choosing Image⇨Apply Image, Photoshop appends one additional option — the Result pop-up menu — at the end of the Apply Image dialog box. This option lets you send the result of the operation to a separate image window, layer, or channel. This can be useful if you don't want to upset the contents of the foreground window, if you want to send the result to a separate layer for further compositing, or if you just want to edit a mask. (This last operation is generally made easier by the Calculations command, as described in the "Combining masks" section near the end of this chapter.)

One of my favorite reasons to Option-choose Apply Image, however, is to transfer selection outlines from one image to another of equal size. Inside the image to which you want to transfer the selection, Option-choose Apply Image. (Be sure that nothing in the image is already selected, or the Result pop-up menu will not appear.) Select the identically sized image that contains the selection from the Source pop-up menu, choose Selection from the Channel pop-up, and choose Normal from the Blending menu. Then choose Selection from the Result pop-up menu and press Return. Then say, "Welcome, Mr. Selection Outline, to your brand new image."

Mixing images in different color modes

 Throughout my laborious explanations of all those options in the Apply Image dialog box, I've been eagerly waiting to share with you the command's one truly unique capability. Image⇨Apply Image is the only way to composite RGB and Lab images while leaving them set to their separate color modes. For example, you could mix the lightness channel from the Lab image with the red channel from the RGB image, the *a* channel with the green channel, and the *b* channel with the blue channel. By contrast, you'd have to composite the channels one at a time if there were no Apply Image command. (If you were to simply drag and drop a Lab image into an RGB image, Photoshop would automatically convert the image to the RGB color space, which results in a very different effect.)

To help make things a little more clear, Color Plate 17-3 shows four examples of an image composited onto itself using the Hard Light overlay mode (which you select from the Blending pop-up menu, as I'll cover shortly). The first example shows the result of selecting the RGB image as both source and target. As always, this exaggerates the colors in the image and enhances contrast, but retains the same basic color composition as before.

The other examples in the color plate show what happened when I duplicated the image by choosing Image⇨Duplicate, converted the duplicate to the Lab mode (Mode⇨Lab Color), and then composited the Lab duplicate with the RGB original. To do this, I switched to the RGB image, chose Image⇨Apply Image, and selected the Lab image from the Source pop-up menu. In the top right example, I chose Lab from the Channel pop-up menu to blend each of the Lab channels with one of the RGB channels — lightness with red, and so on. Though I stuck with the Hard Light overlay mode, you can see that the effect is very different. In the bottom left example, I chose Lightness from the Channel pop-up, which mixed the lightness channel with all three RGB channels. And in the bottom right image, I chose *b* from the Channel pop-up menu and selected the Invert check box, which inverted the *b* channel before applying it.

 You cannot mix an entire CMYK image with an RGB or Lab image, because the images contain different numbers of channels. In other words, while you can mix individual channels from CMYK, RGB, and Lab images, you can't intermix the channels — cyan with red, magenta with green, and so on. In other words, CMYK does not appear as an option inside the Channel pop-up menu when you edit an RGB image. In other words . . . oh, nuts, that's enough of that.

Compositing with a mask

I said that I'd go into a little more depth about the Mask option in this section, and here I am being true to my word. (I really think that I deserve some kind of badge for this.) All the Mask option does is provide a method for you to import only a selected portion of the source image into the target image. Select the Mask check box and choose the image that contains the mask from the pop-up menu on the immediate right. As with the Source pop-up menu, the Mask menu lists only those images that are open and happen to be the exact same size as the target image. If necessary, select the layer on which the mask appears from the Layer pop-up menu. Then select the specific mask channel from the final pop-up menu. This doesn't have to be a mask channel; you can use any color channel as a mask.

After you select all the necessary options, the mask works like so: Where the mask is white, the source image shows through and mixes in with the target image, just as if it were a selected portion of the floating image. Where the mask is black, the source image is absent, as if you had Command-dragged around that portion of the floating selection with the lasso or some other selection tool, leaving the target entirely protected. Gray values in the mask mix the source and target with progressive emphasis on the target as the grays darken.

If you prefer to swap the masked and unmasked areas of the source image, select the Invert check box at the bottom of the dialog box. Now, where the mask is black, you see the source image; where the mask is white, you don't.

The first example in Color Plate 17-4 shows a mask that I used to select the Capitol dome while protecting the sky. I prepared this mask and put it in a separate mask channel. In the other examples in the color plate, I again composited the RGB and Lab versions of the image — as in the previous section — using various overlay modes. No matter how dramatically the Apply Image command affected the dome, the sky remained unscathed, thanks to the mask. If the Mask option had not been turned on, for example, the top right image in Color Plate 17-4 would have looked exactly like the corresponding image in Color Plate 17-3.

You can even use a selection outline or layer as a mask. If you select some portion of the source image before switching to the target image and choosing Image⇨Apply Image, you can access the selection by choosing — what else? — Selection from the Channel pop-up menu at the very bottom of the dialog box. Those pixels from the source image that fall inside the selection remain visible; those that do not are transparent. Use the Invert check box to inverse the selection outline. To use the boundaries of a layer selected from the Layer pop-up menu as a mask, choose the Transparency option from the Channel menu. Where the layer is opaque, the source image is opaque (assuming that the Opacity option is set to 100 percent, of course); where the layer is transparent, so too is the source image.

If you're familiar with Photoshop 2.5, this new Mask option corresponds to the old Composite channel operation (Image⇨Calculate⇨Composite). I mention this because I've heard rumors lately that the function of the Composite command vanished in Version 3.0. Not only is this rumor untrue, the function has actually been enhanced. You can now mask images as well as apply overlay modes, whereas the old channel operations let you either mask or apply overlay modes, but not both. (Likewise, the Opacity option takes the place and improves on the old Image⇨Calculate⇨Blend operation.)

Add and Subtract

The Add and Subtract overlay modes found in the Apply Image dialog box (and also in the Calculations dialog box) work a bit like the Custom filter discussed in Chapter 15. However, instead of multiplying brightness values by matrix numbers and calculating a sum, as the Custom filter does, these modes add and subtract the brightness values of pixels in different channels.

The Add option adds the brightness value of each pixel in the source image to that of its corresponding pixel in the target image. The Subtract option takes the brightness value of each pixel in the target image and subtracts the brightness value of its corresponding pixel in the source image. When you select either Add or Subtract, the Apply Image dialog box offers two additional option boxes, Scale and Offset. Photoshop divides the sum or difference of the Add or Subtract mode by the Scale value (from 1.000 to 2.000) and then adds the Offset value (from negative to positive 255).

If equations will help, here's the equation for the Add overlay mode:

Resulting brightness value = (Target + Source) ÷ Scale + Offset

And here's the equation for the Subtract mode:

Resulting brightness value = (Target − Source) ÷ Scale + Offset

If equations only confuse you, just remember this: The Add option results in a destination image that is lighter than either source; the Subtract option results in a destination image that is darker than either source. If you want to darken the image further, raise the Scale value. To darken each pixel in the target image by a constant amount, which is useful when applying the Add option, enter a negative Offset value. If you want to lighten each pixel, as when applying the Subtract option, enter a positive Offset value.

Applying the Add command

The best way to demonstrate how these commands work is to offer an example. To create the effects shown in Figures 17-19 and 17-20, I began with the two images shown in Figure 17-18. The first image, Capitol Gray, is merely a grayscale composite of the image from Color Plate 5-1. The second image, Capitol Blur, took a little more work. I duplicated the original RGB image, converted it to the CMYK color mode, and jettisoned all but the yellow channel because that channel does a good job of separating building and sky. I then applied the Minimum filter to enlarge the dark regions of the image by a radius of 3 pixels and applied the Gaussian Blur filter with a radius of 6.0 pixels. I next chose Image➪Adjust➪Levels (Command-L) and changed the lighter of the two Output Levels values to 140, thus uniformly darkening the image. (The Add and Subtract commands work best when neither target nor source contains large areas of white.) Finally, just for the sheer heck of it, I drew in some clouds and lightning bolts with the airbrush and smudge tools.

Figure 17-18:
The target (left) and source (right) used to create the effects shown in Figures 17-19 and 17-20.

After switching to the Capitol Gray image and choosing Image➪Apply Image, I selected the Capitol Blur image from the Source pop-up menu. I was working with flat, grayscale images, so I didn't have to worry about the Layer and Channel options. I selected the Add option from the Blending pop-up menu and accepted the default Scale and Offset values of 1 and 0, respectively, to achieve the first example in Figure 17-19. Because the skies in both the target and source images were medium gray, they added up to white in the resulting image. The black areas in the source image helped prevent the colors inside the building from becoming overly light.

Unfortunately, the image I created was a bit washed out. To improve the quality and detail of the image, I changed the Scale value to 1.2 to slightly downplay the brightness values and entered an Offset value of –60 to darken the colors uniformly. The result of this operation is the more satisfactory image shown in the second example of Figure 17-19.

Figure 17-19: Two applications of the Add overlay mode on the images from Figure 17-18, one subject to Scale and Offset values of 1 and 0 (left) and the other subject to values of 1.2 and –60 (right).

Applying the Subtract command

To create the first example in Figure 17-20, I selected the Subtract option from the Blending pop-up menu, once again accepting the default Scale and Offset values of 1 and 0, respectively. This time, the sky turns pitch black because I subtracted the medium gray of the Capitol Blur image from the medium gray of the Capitol Gray image, leaving no brightness value at all. The building, however, remains a sparkling white because most of that area in the Capitol Blur image is black. Subtracting black from a color is like subtracting 0 from a number — it leaves the value unchanged.

Figure 17-20: Two applications of the Subtract command on the images from Figure 17-18, one subject to Scale and Offset values of 1 and 0 (left) and the other subject to values of 1.2 and 60 (right).

The image seemed overly dark, so I lightened it by raising the Scale and Offset values. To create the second image in Figure 17-20, I upped the Scale value to 1.2, just as in the second Add example, which actually darkened the image slightly. Then I changed the Offset value to 60, thus adding 60 points of brightness value to each pixel. This second image is more likely to survive reproduction with all detail intact.

The difference between Subtract and Difference

I've already shown examples of how the Difference mode inverts one image using the brightness values in another. But the math behind Difference is actually very similar to that behind Subtract. Like Subtract, the Difference option subtracts the brightness values in the source image from those in the target image. However, instead of treating negative values as black, as Subtract does, or allowing you to compensate for overly dark colors with the Scale and Offset options, Difference changes all calculations to positive values.

If the brightness value of a pixel in the target image is 20 and the brightness value of the corresponding pixel in the source image is 65, the Difference option performs the following equation: $20 - 65 = -35$. It then takes the *absolute value* of -35 (or, in layman's terms, hacks off the minus sign) to achieve a brightness value of 35. Pretty easy stuff, huh?

Any divergence between the Subtract and Difference options becomes more noticeable on repeated applications. The top row of Figure 17-21, for example, shows the effect of applying the Subtract mode (left) versus the Difference mode (right). As before, I applied these commands to the Capitol Gray and Capitol Blur images from Figure 17-18.

As far as perceptible differences between the two images are concerned, the pixels that make up the bushes in the lower left corner of each image and those of the clouds along each image's right side are on the rebound in the Difference example. In effect, they became so dark that they are again lightening up. But that's about the extent of it.

In the second row of Figure 17-21, I applied the Subtract and Difference options a second time. Using the top left example in the figure as the target and the Capitol Blur image as the source, I achieved two very different results. When calculating the colors of the pixels in the sky, the Difference overlay mode apparently encountered sufficiently low negative values that removing the minus signs left the sky ablaze with light. Everything dark is light again.

Just for fun, the left column of examples in Color Plate 17-5 features full-color versions of the right image from Figure 17-19 and the bottom two images in Figure 17-21. In each case, I used the full-color Capitol Dome image from Color Plate 5-1 instead of the Capital Gray image as the target image and used the grayscale Capitol Blur as the source. As if that weren't enough fun already, the right column of examples in Color Plate 17-5 shows the same images after swapping the red and blue color channels in each. The results look like something out of *The War of the Worlds*. The only difference is that instead of being scary, they look like just the thing to convince Earthlings that Martian rule wouldn't be so bad. "You guys are attacking the Senate? Oh, that's different. Why sure, count me in. Maybe then we'll get some gun control around here."

Figure 17-21:
Repeated applications of the Subtract (left column) and Difference (right column) commands.

The Calculations command

Though its options are nearly identical, the Calculations command performs a slightly different function than Apply Image. Rather than compositing a source image on top of the current target image, Image➪Calculations combines two source channels and puts the result in a target channel. You can use a single image for both sources, a source and the target, or all three. The target doesn't have to be the foreground image (although Photoshop previews the effect in the foreground image window). And the target can even be a new image. But the biggest difference is that instead of affecting entire full-color images, the Calculations command affects individual color channels only. Only one channel changes as a result of this command.

Choosing Image➪Calculations displays the dialog box shown in Figure 17-22. Rather than explaining this dialog box option by option — I'd just end up wasting 35 pages and repeating myself every other sentence — I'll attack the topic in a little less structured fashion.

When you arrive inside the dialog box, you select your source images from the Source 1 and Source 2 pop-up menus. As with Apply Image, the images have to be exactly the same size. You can composite individual layers using the Layer menus. Select the channels you want to mix together from the Channel options. In place of the full-color options — RGB, Lab, CMYK — each Channel menu offers a Gray option, which represents the grayscale composite of all channels in an image.

Figure 17-22:
Use the Calculations command to mix two source channels and place them inside a new or existing target channel.

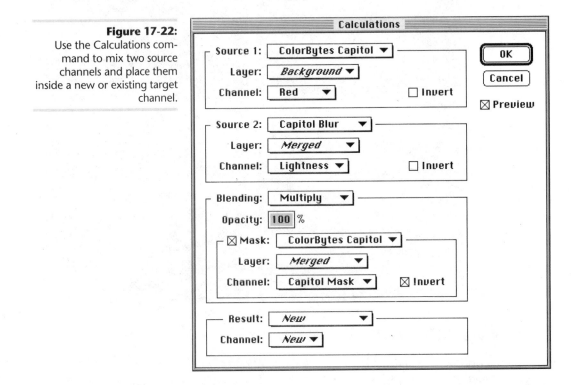

The Blending pop-up menu offers the same 11 overlay modes — including Add and Subtract — that are found in the Apply Image dialog box. But it's important to keep in mind how the Calculations dialog box organizes the source images when working with overlay modes. The Source 1 image is equivalent to the source when using the Apply Image command (or the floating selection when compositing conventionally); the Source 2 image is equivalent to the target (or the underlying original). Therefore, choosing the Normal overlay mode displays the Source 1 image. The Subtract command subtracts the Source 1 image from the Source 2 image.

Half of the overlay modes perform identically regardless of which of the two images is Source 1 and which is Source 2. The other half — including Normal, Overlay, Soft Light, and Hard Light — produce different results based on the image you assign to each spot. But as long as you keep in mind that Source 1 is the floater — hey, it's at the top of the dialog box, right? — you should be okay.

The only one that throws me off is Subtract, because I see Source 1 at the top of the dialog box and naturally assume that Photoshop will subtract Source 2, which is underneath it. Unfortunately, this is exactly opposite to the way it really works. If you find yourself similarly confused and set up the equation backwards, you can reverse it by selecting both Invert options. Source 2 minus Source 1 results in the exact same effect as an inverted Source 1 minus an inverted Source 2. (After all, the equation *(255 – Source 1) – (255 – Source 2)*, which represents an inverted Source 1 minus an inverted Source 2, simplifies down to *Source 2 – Source 1*. If math isn't your strong point, don't worry. I was just showing my work.)

As you can in the Apply Image dialog box, you can specify a mask using the Mask options in the Calculations dialog box. The difference here is that the mask applies to the first source image and protects the second one. So where the mask is white, the two sources mix together normally. Where the mask is black, you see the second source image only.

The Result options determine the target for the composited channels. If you select New from the Result pop-up menu, as in Figure 17-22, Photoshop creates a new grayscale image. Alternatively, you can stick the result of the composited channels in any channel inside any image that is the same size as the source images.

If a dialog box full of 12-point Chicago type is too crowded and clunky for you, you can Option-choose Image⇨Calculations to display the text in 9-point Geneva. It's not the most exciting or useful function, but you may find it helpful.

Converting layers to selections

As described for the Apply Image command, Selection, Transparency, and Layer Mask may be available as options from any of the Channels pop-up menus. But here they have more purpose. You can composite layer masks to form selection outlines, selection outlines to form masks, and all sorts of other pragmatic combinations.

Figure 17-23 shows the multilayered-layered image from Figure 9-19 minus a few layers. In fact, I've hidden all but two — the wavy face at the top and the close-up in the lower right corner. Now suppose that I want to select the exact area occupied by these two layers and apply that selection to the Background layer. I could screw around with the magic wand tool or try to create a mask, but both of those options would be big time-wasters. I could use the Command-Option-T trick I described in the "Modifying the contents of a layer" section of Chapter 8, but that only works for one layer, not two. The better solution is to use Image⇨Calculations. The following steps describe how this intricate operation works.

STEPS: Selecting the Area Occupied by Two Layers

Step 1.   After choosing the Calculations command, I selected my layered faces image from the Source 1, Source 2, and Result pop-up menus. All my layers resided in this image, and I wanted to apply the selection outline to this image, so this is the only image that the Calculations command needed to worry about.

Step 2.   I next selected the wavy face layer from the first Layer pop-up menu and the close-up face from the second. To consider the space occupied by the layers (as opposed to the contents of the layers), I chose Transparency from both of the two top Channel pop-up menus.

Figure 17-23: I used the Calculations command to convert the area occupied by the wavy face and close-up face layers (left) into a selection outline. I then hid the layers and used the selection outline to edit the Back-ground layer (right).

Step 3. Now that I had assembled the layers I wanted to use, the question became how to combine them. The Screen overlay mode was the answer. Because the opaque areas of the layer are white and the transparent areas black, I wanted the white to show through the black, which is a job for Screen. Therefore, I chose Screen from the Blending pop-up menu. (Though I could have also used Lighter or Add in this specific example, Screen is the more flexible choice, as I explain in the next section.) The grayscale representation of the transparent areas previewed in the foreground window.

Step 4. Finally, I needed to convert the grayscale representation to a selection outline. To accomplish this, I chose the Selection option from the Channel pop-up menu at the bottom of the dialog box. This told Photoshop to convert the mask into a selection outline.

Step 5. Pressing Return initiated the conversion. I then switched to the Background layers, Option-clicked on the eyeball in front of the Background item to hide the wavy face and close-up layers, and used the selection outline to edit the image. The right image in Figure 17-23 shows the result of a simple application of the Invert command (Command-I).

Ah, but that's just where the fun begins. Unlike the Apply Image command, which only offers a couple of unique options that you might want to use every blue moon, Calculations is a practical tool for combining selection outlines and mixing masks. The next section tells it all.

Combining masks

Figure 17-24 shows how the Calculations command sees selected areas. Whether you're working with masks, selection outlines, layer transparencies, or layer masks, the Calculations command sees the area as a grayscale image. So in Figure 17-24, the white areas are selected or opaque, and the black areas are deselected or transparent.

Figure 17-24:
Two selections expressed as grayscale images (a.k.a. masks). The left image is the first source, and the right image is the second.

Source 1   Source 2

If these were traditional selection outlines, I could add one to the other by pressing the Shift key, subtract one from the other by pressing Command, and retain only the intersecting area by pressing Command and Shift. (On the off chance this doesn't sound familiar, leave this chapter immediately and check out Chapter 8.) The problem is, these techniques only apply when you're creating selection outlines. In my case, the outlines already exist. So the best way to combine them is to use Calculations.

Assuming that I've chosen Image⇨Calculations and selected the images using the Source 1 and Source 2 options, the only remaining step is to select the proper overlay mode from the Blending pop-up menu. Screen, Multiply, and Difference are the best solutions. The top row in Figure 17-25 shows the common methods for combining selection outlines. In the first example, I added the two together using the Screen mode, just as in the previous steps. In fact, Screening masks and adding selection outlines are exact equivalents. To subtract the Source 1 selection from Source 2, I inverted the former (by selecting the Invert check box in the Source 1 area) and applied the Multiply overlay mode. To find the intersection of the two masks, I simply applied Multiply without inverting.

Figure 17-25:
Starting with the masks shown in Figure 17-25, I combined them in traditional (top row) and nontraditional (bottom row) ways using the Calculations command.

Screen (add)

Invert + Multiply (subtract)

Multiply (intersect)

Invert + Screen

Difference

Invert + Difference

But the Calculations command doesn't stop at the standard three — add, subtract, and intersect. The bottom row of Figure 17-25 shows three methods of combining selection outlines that are not possible using keyboard shortcuts. For example, if I invert the Source 1 mask and combine it with the Screen mode, I add the inverse of the elliptical selection and add it to the polygonal one. The Difference mode adds the portion of the elliptical selection that doesn't intersect the polygonal one and subtracts the intersection. And inverting Source 1 and then applying Difference retains the intersection, subtracts the portion of the polygonal selection that is not intersected, and inverts the elliptical selection where it does not intersect. These may not be options you use every day, but they are extremely powerful if you can manage to wrap your brain around them.

Depending on how well you've been keeping up with this discussion, you may be asking yourself, "Why not apply Lighter or Add in place of Screen, or Darker or Subtract in place of Multiply?" The reason becomes evident when you combine two soft selections. Suppose that I blurred the Source 2 mask to give it a feathered edge. Figure 17-26 shows the results of combining the newly blurred polygonal mask with the elliptical mask using a series of overlay modes. In the top row, I added the two selection outlines together using the Lighter, Add, and Screen modes. Lighter results in harsh corner transitions, while Add cuts off the interior edges. Only Screen does it just right. The bottom row of the figure shows the results of subtracting the elliptical mask from the polygonal one by occasionally inverting the elliptical mask and applying Darker, Subtract, and Multiply. Again, Darker results in sharp corners. The Subtract mode eliminates the need to invert the elliptical marquee, but it brings the black area too far into the blurred edges, resulting in an overly abrupt interior cusp. Multiply ensures that all transitions remain smooth as silk.

The reason for the success of the Screen and Multiply modes is that they mix colors together. Lighter and Darker simply settle on the color of one source image or the other — no mixing occurs — hence the harsh transitions. Add and Subtract rely on overly simplistic arithmetic equations — as I explained earlier, they really just add and subtract brightness values — which result in steep fall-off and build-up rates; in other words, there are cliffs of color transition where there ought to be rolling hills. Both Screen and Multiply soften the transitions using variations on color averaging that makes colors incrementally lighter or darker.

Figure 17-26: When adding softened selections (top row) and subtracting them (bottom row), the Screen and Multiply modes provide the most even and continuous transitions.

Lighter

Add

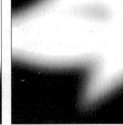

Screen

Invert + Darker

Subtract

Invert + Multiply

Summary

-∞ The overlay modes and Opacity slider bar in the Layers palette are applicable to both floating selections and active layers.

-∞ Hide all but one layer by Option-clicking on the eyeball icon in front of a layer name in the Layers palette. Option-click again to redisplay the layers.

-∞ The Clear overlay mode turns a floating selection into a hole though a layer (other than the Background layer).

-∞ The Multiply and Screen overlay modes let you combine images as if they were photographic transparencies.

-∞ Use the Overlay mode to tattoo a layer onto the underlying image. If the effect is too light, try the Hard Light option. If it's too wimpy at low Opacity settings, bump the Opacity back up to 100 percent and try out Soft Light instead.

•• The Hue, Saturation, Color, and Luminosity overlay modes are applicable exclusively to full-color images.

•• Taking the place of the old Composite Controls dialog box, the new layer Options dialog box is applicable only to layers, not floating selections.

•• Option-drag the slider triangles in the Layer Options dialog box to soften the exclusion of colors in the floating selection or the forcing of colors in the underlying image.

•• Channel operations — represented by Image⇨Apply Image and Image⇨Calculations — are limiting in that they offer no sizing, cropping, or placement options. But you can now preview your settings as well as mask or change the opacity of any effect, all significant improvements over previous versions of Photoshop.

•• You use the Apply Image command to mix RGB and Lab images without converting modes.

•• The Add and Subtract options add and subtract brightness values in two images. Generally speaking, they are rudimentary overlay modes that may come in handy for creating the occasional special effect.

•• While the Subtract command reduces brightness values well below black, Difference finds the absolute values of the brightness values, thus bringing very dark values back into the light.

•• Use the Selection, Transparency, and Layer Mask options in combination with the Calculations command to mix masks and layer transparencies to create combined selection outlines. Basically, everything in your image is a selection outline waiting to happen.

Compositing on the March

. . . .

In This Chapter

- ➬ Practical applications of channel operations, masks, and overlay modes
- ➬ A method for creating embossed type using the Apply Image command
- ➬ An even better method for embossing text using floating selections
- ➬ Opposite overlay modes: Color and Luminosity, Overlay and Hard Light
- ➬ Sandwiching a heavily filtered image between two unfiltered originals
- ➬ Compositing multiple filtered images from different layers

. . . .

Putting Compositing to Work ____

Now that I've explained all the nitty-gritty details about layering, overlay modes, and the Apply Image and Calculations commands, it's time to demonstrate a few practical applications. Obviously, I can't show you every possible approach to compositing, but I can run through a few inspirational and even unusual scenarios and leave you to discover the hundred zillion or so others on your own. (I mean, come on, if this book gets much fatter, I'll have to call it the *Encyclopedia Photoshopia* and start hawking it door to door.)

Creating an embossing effect with Apply Image

In the preceding chapter, I alluded to the fact that you can perform most compositing effects without the aid of Apply Image and Calculations. The following two sets of steps offer proof of that statement. The first set explains a typical method for burning embossed text into a background image using the Apply Image command. The second set shows you how you can accomplish the same thing with a greater degree of flexibility by relying exclusively on masks and floating selections.

STEPS: **Creating an Embossed Text Effect, Method #1**

Step 1.   I started off with a tropical image shown in Figure 18-1. This image is mostly scenery with just a hint of foreground information here and there — such as that vacationer in the lower right corner — making it ideally suited to some textual abuse.

Figure 18-1:
This alluring beach image was shot by my buddy Russell McDougal while he was cruising about in the Caribbean. Although he was really selfish not to bring me along, the image is ideally suited as a background for large text.

Step 2.   As I mentioned in Chapter 12, it's always a good idea to create complex text in the quick mask mode or in a separate mask channel so that you can kern and embellish the text without harming the original image. I used a mask channel because doing so allowed me to save the text with the image. After I clicked on the new channel icon at the bottom of the Channels palette and naming the channel *Logo*, the image window filled with black. Photoshop 3.0 always fills new mask channels with black, which suited my purposes to a tee. I wanted to create white text against a black background so that I could later screen it against the beach image.

Step 3.   I pressed D and then X to make the foreground color white and the background color black. I then used the type tool to enter the word *Tropical* in 300-point bold, condensed letters. I kerned the letters close together by selecting them one at a time with the lasso and nudging them with the arrow keys. To make the characters overlap, I chose the Screen option from the overlay modes pop-up menu in the Layers palette. This option retained the white area and made the black ridge around each letter invisible. I then extended the stem of the *p* and drew in the palm fronds with the pen tool. Figure 18-2 shows the finished result. Notice that I created the logo specifically so that it wouldn't cover the vacationer in the foreground.

Figure 18-2: My completed logo as it appears in the Logo mask channel when the mask is viewed by itself (top) and in combination with the beach image (bottom).

Step 4. To create the embossing effect, I first duplicated my mask channel to protect my painstaking logo and retain it for later use. I accomplished this by dragging the mask channel item in the Channels palette onto the new channel icon. I then double-clicked on the new mask item in the palette and changed its name from *Logo copy* to *Embossed Logo*.

Step 5. Because this was a grayscale mask channel, the standard Emboss command was the most straightforward tool. I chose Filter⇨Stylize⇨Emboss and entered an Angle value of 135 degrees, a Height of 10 pixels, and an Amount of 100 percent. The only important value was the Height, for which I entered the maximum value. If you're working along with these steps, you can change the Angle and Amount values to anything you like.

If a Height of 10 isn't sufficient for your purposes, you can use the patented Kai Krause technique for creating a custom embossing effect as follows: Select the entire channel, float it, invert it, change the Opacity to 50 percent, and nudge it as desired using the arrow keys. That's Command-A, Command-J, Command-I, 5, arrow, arrow, arrow. The distance of the nudge determines the amount of the emboss, so you can create as radical an effect as you like. Just be sure to fill in the gaps around the edges of the image using 50 percent gray. You'll also want to center the effect. For example, if you scoot the text 10 pixels up and 10 to the right, you should then select the entire channel and scoot it 5 pixels back down and 5 to the left.

(If the text violates the edge of the image, the best solution is to send the floated text to its own layer. Then you can nudge the layered text 5 pixels up and to the right and nudge the underlying text 5 pixels down and to the left. This way, the text won't appear cut off around the edges.)

Step 6. I blurred the embossing effect by applying Filter⇨Blur⇨Gaussian Blur with a Radius of 3.0. Figure 18-3 shows the result, which includes black rims along the tops of the letters, white rims along the bottoms, and medium gray everywhere else.

Figure 18-3: After duplicating the logo to a second mask channel called *Embossed Logo,* I applied the Emboss filter with the maximum Height value of 10 pixels and applied the Gaussian Blur filter with a Radius of 3.

Step 7. Now for the actual channel operations. After switching back to the full-color composite view of the beach by pressing Command-0, I chose Image⇨Apply Image to display the Apply Image dialog box. I wanted to accomplish two things here: I wanted to apply the white logo against the beach without affecting the area outside the logo and I wanted to burn in the embossing effect. To accomplish the first objective, I chose the Logo mask channel from the Channel pop-up menu. Then I chose the Screen option from the Blending pop-up menu and changed the Opacity value to 40 percent. As you can see in the first example of Figure 18-4, this mixed in the white text while making the black background invisible. I pressed Return to apply the effect.

Figure 18-4:
With the Apply Image command, I composited the Logo channel onto the beach image using the Screen overlay mode at 40 percent Opacity (top). Then, in two additional passes of the command, I applied the Embossed Logo channel using the Hard Light mode with the Logo channel as a mask, and composited the Logo channel again using the Multiply mode and an Opacity of 20 percent.

Step 8. To emboss the text, I turned right around and choose the Apply Image command again. I chose the Embossed Logo mask channel from the Channel pop-up menu and the Hard Light option from the Blending menu. Then I entered 100 percent into the Opacity option box. The black portions of the embossing effect darkened the image, the white portions lightened it, and the medium gray portions produced no effect.

Step 9.   The problem is that the embossing effect got outside the character outlines and leaked all over the scenery. Still inside the Apply Image dialog box, I remedied the situation with a mask. I selected the Mask check box and then selected the Logo mask channel from the lower Channel pop-up menu. Where the mask was white — inside the letters — the embossing showed through. This kept the effect from spilling out onto the beach, as demonstrated in the last example in Figure 18-4. I pressed Return to apply the effect.

Step 10.   To make the text stand out just a little more, I chose the Apply Image command a third time. I chose the Logo channel from the Channel pop-up menu, Multiply from the Blending menu, lowered the Opacity to 20 percent, and deselected the Mask check box. The black background around the logo slightly darkened the beach image without affecting the embossed text.

The bottom example of Figure 18-4 shows the result of the steps. Color Plate 18-1 shows a full-color version of Figure 18-4. The text has a soft, organic appearance and appears naturally lit, almost as if the light were bouncing off the beach and hitting the letters.

I didn't have to stop here, of course. I could have kept on compositing those same two mask channels until my hair fell out and my hands became arthritic. (It's in my will that whatever old-age home they stick me in has to include Photoshop.) The first example of Color Plate 18-2, for example, shows what happened when I chose Apply Image a fourth time, selected the Embossed Logo from the Channel pop-up menu, chose Overlay from the Blending pop-up menu, changed the Opacity value to 100 percent, and again selected the Mask check box and assigned the Logo channel as the mask. But this time, I inverted both the Embossed Logo and the Logo mask (by selecting both Invert check boxes). Inverting the Embossed Logo channel switched the light and dark colors, resulting in highlights above and to the left of the letters and shadows below and to the right. Inverting the mask protected the letters instead of the area outside the letters.

To create the second image in Color Plate 18-2, I merely inverted the logo. I could have Option-clicked on the Logo channel name in the Channels palette to convert the white letters to a selection outline and then pressed Command-I. Or I could have chosen Apply Image for the fifth time, selected Logo from the first Channel pop-up menu and Difference from the Blending menu, and deselected the Mask check box. (Actually, it doesn't matter if the mask is off or on; it just isn't needed, so I would turn it off.)

Creating a better effect via floating selections

The Apply Image command is certainly powerful, and if you made it through that last exercise, you may very well be busily playing with other options and testing out additional ideas. For many users, channel operations become addictive, but I prefer floating selections. You can still take advantage of specially constructed mask channels, as in the previous steps, but rather than flopping them all over each other as with Apply Image, you can convert the masks into selection outlines and apply them discretely. You can even introduce manual retouching and filtering effects, features that the Apply Image command fails to integrate.

With this premise in mind, the following steps show an embossing effect created entirely without the Apply Image or Calculations commands. No doubt, somebody somewhere could come up with a convoluted series of channel operations that enable you to accomplish the same thing. But my method provides real-time feedback and a degree of flexibility absolutely unmatched by Apply Image.

STEPS: **Creating an Embossed Text Effect, Method #2**

Step 1. After creating the Logo and Embossed Logo masks described in Steps 1 through 6 of the preceding section, I suddenly had the notion that I might be able to avoid the Apply Image command and open up a whole world of additional options. To kick off my newfound philosophy, I returned to the full-color composite view of the beach image by pressing Command-0. Then I Option-clicked on the Logo channel in the Channels palette to convert the character outlines to a selection.

Step 2. To add some texture to the letters, I chose Filter➪Noise➪Add Noise, entered 32 for the Amount, and selected the Uniform radio button. After pressing Return, I pressed Command-F to reapply the filter.

Step 3. Next, I decided to create a refraction effect using the Ripple filter. After choosing Filter➪Distort➪Ripple, I maxed out the Amount value to 999, selected Medium from the Size radio buttons, and pressed Return.

Step 4. Now that the basic texture for the logo looked the way I wanted it, I was ready to lighten it. I pressed Command-J to float the logo, D and then X to make white the foreground color, and Option-Delete to fill the text with white. Then I pressed the M key to activate a selection tool and the 4 key to change the Opacity setting to 40 percent. The result of all this activity appears in the first example of Color Plate 18-3. The effect is subtle, but it will become more apparent by the time I finish the steps.

By working with a selection outline instead of a channel operation, I was able to accomplish in a series of quick and familiar keystrokes — Command-J, D, X, Option-Delete, M, 4 — what required a bit of manual labor back in Step 7 of the previous section. Heck, I didn't even have to select the Screen overlay mode because there was no black background to make invisible.

Step 5. I wanted more control over the highlights and shadows that I would apply to the letters, so I decided to create a couple of additional mask channels. In preparation, I dragged the Emboss Logo item onto the new channel icon in the Channels palette to duplicate it. I double-clicked on the new channel name and changed it from *Emboss Logo copy* to *Highlights*. (Then I checked out the hidden picture puzzle and read "Gufus and Gallant." Oops, wrong *Highlights*.) To create the second new mask channel, I again dragged the Emboss Logo item onto the new channel icon, double-clicked on it, and changed its name to *Shadows*.

Step 6. Returning to the Highlights channel (Command-6), I pressed Command-L to bring up the Levels dialog box. I then changed the first Input Levels value to 128 to send all grays to black and leave only the highlights white. I then pressed Return to accept my changes.

Step 7. To clean up the highlights so that they fell inside the logo only, I Option-clicked on the Logo channel name in the Channels palette to convert the logo to a selection outline. I chose Select⇨Inverse to select the area surrounding the letters and pressed Delete to fill the selection with black (because black was still the background color). The result appears in the first example of Figure 18-5.

Step 8. I pressed Command-D to deselect the image, followed by Command-7 to switch to the Shadows channel and Command-L to display the Levels dialog box. This time, I wanted to make the shadows white and everything else black. So I changed the third Input Levels value to 128, which made the shadows black and everything else white. To invert this image, I changed the first Output Levels value to 255 and the second one to 0. Then I pressed Return to exit the dialog box.

Step 9. I could no more permit the shadows to exceed the boundaries of the logo than the highlights, so I again Option-clicked on the Logo channel to convert it to a selection outline, chose Select⇨Inverse to select the area outside the logo, and pressed the Delete key to fill the selection with the background color, black.

Step 10. Command-0 took me back to the full-color view. I Option-clicked on the Highlights item in the Channels palette to select the areas I wanted to highlight. I then filled the selection outlines with white by pressing Option-Delete. (White is still the foreground color.) The result was a white highlight around the right and bottom edges of the letters.

Figure 18-5:
The Highlights
(top) and
Shadows
(bottom)
channels after I
finished adjusting
their contents
with the Levels
command and
cleaning them up
with the help of
the Logo mask.

Step 11. I wanted to temper the highlight a little by tracing a shadow along its edge. So I floated the selection (Command-J) and nudged it two pixels up and two pixels to the left, away from the edge of the letters and toward their centers. Then I pressed D to make black the foreground color and pressed Option-Delete, filling the selection with black.

Step 12. Now for the shadows. I Option-clicked on the Shadow item in the Channels palette to convert the mask to a selection outline. I then pressed Option-Delete to fill the selection with black, creating a shadow along the top and left sides of the letters. As in Step 11, I wanted to temper the shadow by tracing it with a highlight, so I floated the selection, nudged it two pixels down and two to the right, pressed the X key to make white the foreground color, and pressed Option-Delete to fill the selection with white.

The first example in Figure 18-6 shows how the text looked up to this point. You can see how the outlines of the letters are double-traced, once with white and once with black. The bottom and right sides are traced first with white and then with black. The top and left sides are traced first with black and then with white. The effect is one of a raised edge running around the letters.

Figure 18-6: The result of applying the raised-edge effect described in Steps 10 through 12 (top), and the same image after compositing the Emboss Logo channel using the Hard Light mode (bottom).

Step 13. Creeping carefully down the pitch-black corridor, I felt my way past the open door. The room was likewise dark except for the fading glow of a dying street lamp. Suddenly, the light was interrupted by a figure. As the figure turned, I heard the unmistakable click of a pistol hammer. I groped for my gun, but I was too late. A light flashed, and my ears rang with the roar of flying lead. "Aaaugh, I've been shot!" cried the prime minister. As the body slumped at my feet, I knew that the bullet had been meant for me (though what the prime minister is doing in this story, I haven't the vaguest idea). It struck me that my mother was right when she told me to steer clear of . . . *Step 13!* (Blood-curdling scream followed by musical embellishments.)

Step 14. See, now you know why I normally skip that step. It's very distracting, besides which it makes the other steps look very boring by comparison. Anyway, as you may recall, I had just finished tracing an edge around the perimeter of my logo. After that, I figured that I might as well add some highlights and shadows around the letters to offset them from the image. This meant retrieving the contents of the Emboss Logo channel and compositing it with the image, which meant that I had to copy and paste.

Therefore, I pressed Command-5 to go to the Emboss Logo channel. I then Option-clicked on the Logo channel name in the Channels palette to select the letters and chose Select⇨Inverse to switch the selection to the area around the letters. This represented the portion of the channel that I wanted to copy, so I pressed Command-C.

Step 15. After pressing Command-0 to return to the RGB view, I pressed Command-V to paste the embossed image copied in the preceding step. I then switched to the Layers panel and chose the Hard Light option from the overlay modes pop-up menu to mix floating selection and underlying image. The resulting highlights and shadows appear in the bottom example of Figure 18-6.

Step 16. To emphasize the logo for once and for all, I chose Select⇨Inverse to return the selection outline to the logo. Then I pressed Command-I to invert the logo and give its rippled texture a marble-like appearance. The finished image appears at the bottom of Color Plate 18-3.

Sure, this section involved more steps than the preceding one — not to mention an exciting novella — but let's face it, I accomplished a heck of a lot more this time as well. The edges in Color Plate 18-3 are cleaner than their counterparts in Color Plate 18-2, and I was able to easily add filtering details that would have taken all kinds of preparation to pull off using the Apply Image command.

In truth, you'll probably have the best success if you mix channel operations with floating and layering techniques as you work. For example, I could have avoided the copying and pasting in Steps 14 and 15 by choosing the Apply Image command, selecting the Embossed Logo channel from the Channel pop-up menu, using an inverted version of the Logo channel as a mask, and selecting Hard Light from the Blending pop-up menu. This technique would eliminate any delay that might occur as a result of using Clipboard functions on a very large image.

So the moral is, use whatever compositing method makes you most comfortable. But don't think that using the Apply Image and Calculations commands somehow miraculously transforms you into a power user. As the previous steps demonstrate, floating and filtering can prove much more capable than Apply Image, and when you add layers into the recipe, you get a combination of compositing options that can't be beat.

More Compositing Madness

Remember that scene in *Amadeus* where Mozart is talking to the king about some opera or other he's writing — "Marriage of Franz Joseph Haydn" or something like that — and he's bragging about how many folks he has singing on stage at the same time? Remember that scene? Oh, you're not even trying. Anyway, you can do that same thing with Photoshop. Not with melody or recitative or anything like that, but with imagery. Just as Mozart might juggle several different melodies and harmonies at once, you can juggle layers upon layers of images, each filtered differently and mixed differently with the images below it. Predicting the outcome of these monumental composites takes a brain the magnitude of Mozart's. But screwing around with different settings takes no intelligence at all, which is where I come in.

The hierarchy of overlay modes

The most direct method for juggling multiple images is *sandwiching*. By this I mean placing a heavily filtered version of an image between two originals. This technique is based on the principal that many overlay modes — Normal, Overlay, Soft Light, Hard Light, Hue, Saturation, Color, and Luminosity — change depending on which of two images is on top. For example, I created a document comprising two layers. One layer contained the plain old, unembellished Capitol dome image; the other contained a heavily filtered version of the image. Following the basic guidelines laid out in the "Creating a metallic coating" section of Chapter 14, I applied the Gaussian Blur filter with a Radius of 3.0, chose Filter⇨Stylize⇨Find Edges, and used the Unsharp Mask filter to bring out the detail, using an Amount value of 500 percent and a Radius of 10.0. The plain and filtered images appear in the first two examples of Figure 18-7.

Figure 18-7:
The Overlay mode is the exact opposite of the Hard Light mode, as demonstrated here. When the filtered image is on top, I achieved the same effect using the Overlay mode (top row) as I did when the plain dome was on top and I used the Hard Light mode (bottom row).

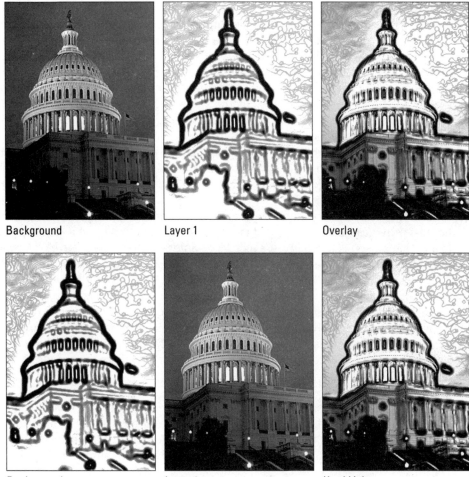

Background   Layer 1   Overlay

Background   Layer 1   Hard Light

Obviously, if you use the Normal overlay mode, whichever image is on top is the one that you see. However, if you change the Opacity, you reveal the underlying image. At 50 percent Opacity, it doesn't matter which image is on top. The color of every pair of pixels in both images is merely averaged. So an inverse relationship exists. If the filtered image is on top, an Opacity setting of 25 percent produces the same effect as if you reversed the order of the images and changed the Opacity to 75 percent.

The Normal overlay mode, then, is its own opposite. Multiply, Screen, Darken, and Lighten work the same regardless of who's on top. (There are definitely some jokes begging to be told here, but I'm trying to retain that Rated G status.) But a few of the others have their opposites in fellow overlay modes. Color, for example, is the opposite of Luminosity. So positioning the filtered image on top and selecting Luminosity produces the exact same effect as positioning the plain image on top and selecting Color.

That was easy, but here's one I bet you didn't know: Hard Light is the opposite of Overlay. It's true. Positioning the filtered image on top and choosing Hard Light produces an identical effect to positioning the plain image on top and choosing Overlay, and vice versa. In fact, this very vice versa is demonstrated in Figure 18-7. In the top example, the plain dome is situated on the Background layer and the filtered image is on Layer 1. The top right image shows the result of choosing Overlay from the overlay modes pop-up menu in the Layers palette. In the bottom row, I've reversed the order. Now the filtered image is on the Background layer and the plain dome is on Layer 1. To achieve the same effect as before, I had to choose Hard Light. Therefore, if the Overlay option reinforces the brightness values in an underlying image using colors from a floating image, the opposite must be true for Hard Light, which uses the underlying image to reinforce the floating one.

If Color is the opposite of Luminosity, and Overlay is the opposite of Hard Light, why not just provide one of each — that is, Color and Overlay, or Luminosity and Hard Light? One reason is flexibility. It's nice to be able to pull off the same effect regardless of how you organize your layers. But the bigger reason is that all four overlay modes offer their own unique effects when you adjust the Opacity slider bar. As you already know, any Opacity value less than 100 percent favors the underlying image. Therefore, you achieve very different effects when applying the Overlay mode at 50 percent Opacity than when applying the Hard Light mode at the same setting. Figure 18-8 shows examples of various Opacity settings applied in combination with each overlay mode. Keep in mind that the right two examples in Figure 18-7 showed the modes as they appear at 100 percent.

 For what it's worth, the Soft Light overlay mode is structured differently and does not have a direct opposite. Hue and Saturation likewise have no opposites. (The opposite of Hue would be a combination of Saturation and Luminosity; the opposite of Saturation would involve both Hue and Luminosity.)

Sandwiching a filtered image

When you sandwich a filtered image between two originals — which, as you may recall, is what all this is supposed to be leading up to — you can dissipate the effect of the filtered image without lowering the Opacity setting and at the same time achieve a variety of different effects. You at once mix the floating filtered image with the underlying original and mix a floating original with the underlying filtered image. Back in Photoshop 2.5, you could only achieve these sorts of effects on a very limited basis using channel operations. Layers give you the flexibility to experiment as much as you want and for as long as you please.

Figure 18-8:
The effects of
progressively
smaller
Opacity
settings on
the Overlay
and Hard
Light overlay
modes. As in
Figure 18-7,
the filtered
image is on
top in the top
row, and the
plain dome is
on top in the
bottom row.

Overlay, 75%   Overlay, 50%   Overlay, 25%

Hard Light, 75%   Hard Light, 50%   Hard Light, 25%

Color Plate 18-4 shows several different examples of the sandwiching technique. The first column of examples shows what happened when I positioned the metallic filtered image on Layer 1 and the original dome on the Background layer. No sandwiching has yet occurred. Each example in the column is labeled according to the overlay mode I used.

To create the second column, I dragged the Background item onto the new layer icon at the bottom of the Layers palette to create a duplicate layer (which Photoshop automatically names *Background Copy*). I then dragged the layer above the other two to make it the top layer in the document. The examples in the column show the results of applying different overlay modes to the Background Copy layer while leaving Layer 1 unchanged. For example, the first example in the second column is the result of setting both Layer 1 and Background Copy to the Hard Light mode. In the second example, I set Layer 1 to the Difference mode and Background Copy to the Color mode.

In the third column, I duplicated the Background Copy layer to create — you guessed it — Background Copy 2 and made that the top layer. Then I chose the overlay modes listed below each example. The bottom right example is a special case. After applying the Difference mode, I recognized some major stuff happening in the image, but it was way too dark. After flattening the layers by choosing the Flatten Image command from the Layers palette menu, I applied Image⇨Adjust⇨Auto Levels to bring the glowing worms to life. (Can you believe that you can create an image like this without painting a single brush stroke? It's amazing.) Except for this last image, all the examples can be achieved without upsetting the layers, making it possible to experiment to your heart's content.

Adding effects to the sandwich

In addition to sandwiching an effect, you can composite multiple effects. Color Plate 18-5 shows examples of different effects and overlay modes applied to the top layer of my document, Background Copy 2. To make things crystal clear, I changed the name of this layer to Effects. Just to recap:

- **Background:** The bottom layer contains the plain dome image.

- **Layer 1:** The first layer contains the metallic dome effect.

- **Background Copy:** The next layer up contains a second copy of the plain dome image.

- **Effects:** Yet another copy of the plain dome image subject to the various effects I explain in this section.

Everybody with me? Most groovy. Now then, to create the first column of Color Plate 18-5, all I did was invert the Effects layer by pressing Command-I. I then assigned each of the overlay modes labeled in the color plate. The Difference mode combined with an inverted image — as in the second example — is nearly guaranteed to produce interesting effects. Note that the Layer 1 and Background Copy layers are still assigned the same overlay modes I selected in the preceding section (and labeled in Color Plate 18-4). In the top image, for example, both Layer 1 and Background Copy are assigned the Hard Light mode. In the second image, Layer 1 is assigned the Difference mode and Background Copy is assigned Color. In the final example, Layer 1 gets Hue, and Background Copy gets Hard Light.

In the second column of Color Plate 18-5, I again inverted the Effects layer to return it to its original appearance and then applied the Ripple filter with an Amount value of 999 and Medium selected. I then used the Hue/Saturation command to shift the Hue –90 degrees, making the sky green and the dome purple, just as it is on Mars. Then I applied the overlay modes listed below each example.

In the final column, I pasted in a new version of the dome and applied the Add Noise filter with an Amount value of 100 and with Gaussian selected. In the first example, I achieved a grainy effect using the Overlay mode. In the next example, it's Christmas at the Capitol with the Screen mode. And in the bottom example, I chose the Dissolve mode and set the Opacity to 20 percent. Rather than making the noise pixels translucent, this made 80 percent of the pixels invisible and the other 20 percent opaque. I believe that if you count those points of light, they'll tally 1,000.

Keep in mind that I came up with the results shown in Color Plates 18-4 and 18-5 purely through experimentation. In fact, those figures show only a representative handful of the hundreds of combinations I put together, most of which were too ugly to print. Just consider these as examples of the kinds of effects you can achieve if you take the time to experiment.

Summary

- If you take the time to create your text in a mask channel, you can assign all sorts of effects to the text using channel operations and modified selection outlines.

- To emboss an image on the fly, select it, float it, invert it, change the Opacity setting to 50 percent, and nudge it around using the arrow tools. You can achieve other interesting effects by changing the overlay mode.

- Keep your original text and any preparatory effects applied to the text in separate mask channels. This way, you can turn around and use the original text as a mask to prevent the effect from bleeding outside the lines.

- By converting masks to selection outlines instead of or in addition to compositing them with channel operations, you can easily assign filters and color corrections to the affected areas.

- Compositing two images with the Color overlay mode produces the same effect as flipping the images and applying the Luminosity mode. The same holds true for overlay mode opposites Overlay and Hard Light.

- To dissipate a filtering effect and at the same time take advantage of multiple overlay modes, sandwich the filtered image between two versions of the original, one in a lower layer and one in a higher layer.

- The prime minister lived through Step 13 and is currently recuperating in the recovery ward of Sweet Mercy Hospital. Experts still aren't certain how the head of state wandered into the story or, for that matter, how the story got inside this chapter.

Appendixes

How to Install Photoshop

The process of installing Photoshop is well documented in the user manual, and it's remarkably straightforward. So rather than waste valuable pages slogging through a step-by-step discussion, I'll just touch on the few areas that may prove helpful.

 Sorry, this appendix is geared toward Mac users. The Windows version of Photoshop 3.0 is in a very early beta cycle as I write this, so the installation process is not yet set in stone. No doubt, however, the process will remain similarly straightforward. Inside the Windows Program Manager — the main window — choose File⇨Run. Enter **A:\Setup** into the Command Line option box and press the Enter key. Then follow the instructions more or less as laid out in this chapter.

One special note: If you have a CD-ROM drive, be sure to copy the file ESPRESSO.8BF from the CD included with Photoshop into the PLUGINS folder (C:\PHOTOSHP\PLUGINS). At least, it's currently called ESPRESSO. Word has it, it was once known as CAPUCINO. By the time you read this, it may be some other caffeinated beverage. JOLT.8BF perhaps? At any rate, this represents the Filter Factory (so it may actually be called FACTORY.8BF), which lets you program your own custom filters as described in Chapter 15.

You install Photoshop 3.0 by running the Install Adobe Photoshop utility found on Disk 1 of your Photoshop disks. (Most folks already know this, but just to eliminate any confusion, I do *not* provide the Photoshop software on the CD included with this book. This book is intended to teach you how to use the software; you have to purchase the program itself from a software reseller. It costs roughly 15 times as much as this book, so you can see how it might be tough for us to include it.)

After you run the Install program, a splash screen appears. Press Return to continue, and up pops the Install Adobe Photoshop dialog box. You can now simply click on the Install button to install the 20MB of programs, plug-ins, and extensions that Adobe thinks you need to get the most out of Photoshop. However, I prefer to be in a little more control over the prospective contents of my hard drive. Therefore, I recommend that you choose the Custom Install option from the pop-up menu in the upper left corner of the dialog box. A scrolling list of check box options then fills the central portion of the dialog box. These options work as follows:

- **Adobe Photoshop 3.0:** Select just one of the first three check boxes to decide which version of Photoshop gets installed. If you own a Power Mac, select the Power Macintosh option. Otherwise, select the 68K option. Only select the Universal option if you want to install the "fat" version of Photoshop, which is compatible with both kinds of Macs but consumes more space on the hard drive.

- **Plug-ins:** This installs the many external filters, acquire modules, and export modules used by Photoshop. If you don't install this stuff, you miss out on half the program.

- **Kodak Photo CD Support:** Select this option to enable Photoshop to open Photo CD images. I heartily recommend it.

- **Tutorial:** We don't need no stinking tutorials. That's why you bought this book, right?

- **Brushes & Patterns:** This installs a folder filled with custom brush shapes that you can load into the Brushes palette. I say install.

- **Calibration:** Select this option to install the Gamma control panel, which lets you calibrate your monitor and includes three images that you may want to display on-screen when performing the calibration. The operation is well documented in the manual. If hard disk space is limited and your screen seems to be displaying colors just fine, don't worry about it. You can always come back and install it later.

- **Color Palettes:** Select this option to install the custom color palettes from Pantone, Trumatch, and other companies discussed in Chapter 4. They're a must for creating duotones and can be helpful in everyday image editing as well. Besides, they take up barely more than 100K. Go for it.

- **Command Sets:** This option installs predefined keyboard equivalents that you can load into the Commands palette. Personally, I think that my recommendations in Chapter 2 pretty much take care of all your keyboard equivalent needs, but if you'd like to be able to switch from one set to another, select this option.

- **Duotone Curves:** This option installs a whopping 2MB of files for creating duotones, tritones, and quadtones. If you don't anticipate creating such images — all covered in Chapter 6 — don't waste the disk space. If you do work with duotones, you'll find these predefined curve settings useful but not essential. (If you select this option, make sure that the Color Palettes option is selected as well.)

- **Adobe Type Manager:** Unlike the automated teller machines that spew money from your bank account, this ATM makes typefaces smooth on-screen and is essential for creating text in Photoshop (as explained in Chapter A on the CD).

Select this option to install ATM 3.8, which supports Power Mac acceleration, System 7.5, QuickDraw GX, and everything else on earth. Unless you already have ATM 3.8 on your hard drive, install away.

⌖ **QuickTime:** Ouch, this sucker is getting big. To install the QuickTime 2.0 system extension, the QuickTime PowerPlug, and the Musical Instruments extension takes 2MB. Unfortunately, you need QuickTime to view thumbnails inside the Open dialog box and to apply JPEG compression to PICT files. Bite the bullet and install.

⌖ **Adobe Type Reunion:** This little system extension automatically organizes fonts into families inside all program menus and speeds up Photoshop's font loading process. Definitely install it.

⌖ **SimpleText:** You probably already have SimpleText or TeachText — the former is an update to the latter — installed on your hard drive. If you're like most folks, you have several copies floating around. In fact, the darn thing is installed with your system software. Be smart: Don't waste another 83K of space on your hard drive. Just say no to SimpleText.

 If you forget to install something, don't worry. You can always reinstall a single item later on. Just rerun the Install Adobe Photoshop utility, choose the Custom Install option from the upper left pop-up menu, and select the items that you want to install from the scrolling list. Then choose the Select Folder option from the pop-up menu in the Install Location area at the bottom of the dialog box. An Open dialog box appears, enabling you to select the folder in which you previously installed Photoshop 3.0.

After you select the desired options, press the Return key to send the installation process on its merry way. You'll be instructed to swap disks every so often. Do the computer's bidding like a mindless automaton. Remember, you work for the computer now.

When the installation process is complete, the utility displays an alert box with three buttons: Restart, Quit, and Continue. You must restart the machine to load Adobe Type Manager, QuickTime, and Type Reunion. But I recommend that instead of restarting at this point, you click on the Quit button so that you can change things around slightly.

After you quit the Install program, search around for the new Adobe Photoshop 3.0 folder, which should be in the root directory of your primary hard drive. (In other words, just double-click on the hard drive icon in the upper left corner of your screen, and you'll find it.) Move the folder as desired — inside an Applications folder, for example. Then open the folder and take a look at its contents. Most notably, you'll see two subfolders, Plug-ins and Goodies. The former contains the plug-in files that you installed by selecting the Plug-Ins and Kodak Photo CD Support items in the Install

Adobe Photoshop dialog box. The Goodies folder contains the Tutorial, Brushes & Patterns, and other items in the third grouping of check boxes (depending on which items you chose to install). Each folder contains several subfolders of its own, purely for organizational purposes. You can move things around if you like, as long as you don't move the files in the Plug-ins folder out of that folder. (In other words, you can move a file from the Filters folder in the Plug-ins folder to the Extensions folder inside that same folder, but you don't want to move the file outside the Plug-ins folder.) If you do, you'll prevent that file from loading when you start up Photoshop, which in turn makes that feature unavailable.

Now open the Goodies folder and open the Calibration folder inside that. It contains two items, the Separation Sources folder and the Gamma control panel. Drag Gamma onto your System Folder. When you do, System 7 displays an alert box that requests permission to place Gamma in the Control Panels folder automatically. Click on the OK button. Optionally, you may want to drag the Separation Sources folder out of the Calibration folder and into the Goodies folder. Then drag the empty Calibration folder to the Trash. After all, there's no sense in having a folder like Calibration that contains nothing but another folder.

The Install utility doesn't necessarily install everything you may need to use Photoshop. For example, stick Disk 1 back into your computer, open it up, and you'll discover a folder called Optional Extensions. Contained herein are several extensions that you may or may not want to add to your Plug-ins folder, each of which modify the program's behavior ever so slightly. The folder contains read-me files that describe each extension, but because I'm such a chic type — that's *sheik teep*, French for heckuva nice guy — I'm going to tell you how they work:

- **Even Odd to Winding Rule:** As described at the end of Chapter 8, Photoshop lets you define clipping paths to mask off portions of an image before importing it into Illustrator, QuarkXPress, or some other program. If you have problems printing clipping paths, install this little extension and see if that doesn't solve your problems. It converts Photoshop's default path structure to a different structure that's easier to print.

- **Piggy Plug-ins Patch:** If you use Gallery Effects — a mediocre collection of third-party filters from Aldus, the company that was recently gobbled up by Adobe — and you assign more than 36MB of RAM to Photoshop (as explained in Chapter A on the CD), install this extension. The name of the extension refers to the fact that Gallery Effects and some other third-party filters are memory pigs. Under some conditions, they want more than the 12MB of maximum RAM Photoshop is willing to allocate to them. In fact, Gallery Effects wants a full third of whatever memory you have assigned to Photoshop. This extension gives the little piggy plug-in what it wants.

◌➙ **Don't Tag RGB PostScript:** Don't you love these crystal-clear extension names? "Pardon me, I was hoping we could all speak English?" First of all, you only need this extension if you'll be working with a PostScript Level 2 device. (Ask your service bureau if you aren't sure.) When printing or exporting to the EPS format, Photoshop explains how your monitor is set up so that it can better match the colors you see on-screen. If the program's attempts at color matching make the colors worse instead of better, install this extension to tell Photoshop to cease and desist.

◌➙ **XL7700 Patch:** Though it sounds like something R2D2 might wear if it were trying to stop smoking, this extension actually enables Photoshop 3.0 to support old, inaccurately programmed export modules, such as the one for the Kodak 7700. Unfortunately, it slows down the program, so my advice is to update your plug-ins rather than force the new Photoshop to support them.

◌➙ **Disable Scratch Compression:** When you have a small but highly irritating itch, you need a compressed scratch. Oops, wrong extension. In truth, this one speeds up Photoshop's performance when using state-of-the-art, high-speed hard disks. See, in order to speed up the performance of slower drives, Photoshop compresses data on the fly before writing it to virtual memory (also known as the scratch disk, as described in Chapter B on the CD). This reduces the amount of time spent writing to the disk, but it also entails some additional time compressing the image in memory. The question is, which takes more time — writing the additional data or compressing the image in RAM. On fast drives, the compression does more harm than good. Installing this extension eliminates the compression. (Incidentally, this extension doesn't require Photoshop to create a larger scratch disk and therefore consume more hard disk space. The size of the virtual memory allocation is not affected by this extension.)

◌➙ **Disable Clipboard Size Limit:** If you like to copy large images to the Clipboard and paste them into other programs — not a super common practice unless you're switching between two bitmapped applications — go ahead and install this extension. It allows Photoshop to write images larger than 4MB to the generic Clipboard (the one used by all applications) when you switch out of Photoshop. This can make the system slightly unstable, but what the hey. If you need the big Clipboard space, you have no other choice. (This extension has no effect on images copied and pasted inside Photoshop, which can be as big as you like. Of course, dragging and dropping takes less time, as described in Chapter 8.)

To use one of these extensions, drag it into Photoshop's Plug-ins folder on your hard drive. For organizational purposes, you may want to put it inside the Extensions folder, but anywhere in the Plug-ins folder is acceptable.

Only one thing left: If you have a CD-ROM drive, put the CD included with Photoshop — not the one included with this book — into your drive. Then locate the Filter Factory folder inside the Other Goodies folder. As described in Chapter 15, the Filter Factory allows you to program your own custom filters. Drag the Filter Factory folder into the Plug-ins folder on your hard drive to copy it.

Now open the Extensions folder inside your System Folder. Inside, you'll find two QuickTime files — QuickTime and QuickTime Musical Instruments. If you're using a Power Mac, you'll also see a third file, QuickTime PowerPlug. The 650K Musical Instruments file contains all kinds of instrument sounds that you can play using a MIDI file, but has nothing whatsoever to do with Photoshop. If multimedia isn't your bag, you can save 650K by deleting it.

Restart your computer to load QuickTime, ATM, Type Reunion, and Gamma into RAM. Then double-click on the Photoshop application to start using it. You'll be asked for a password. Enter PSW251R . . . ooh, you almost had me going there.

That's it. Now you're ready to start using the program, as described throughout the 18 chapters in this book.

Photograph Credits

The images used in this book came from all kinds of sources. The following list cites the figures or color plates in which a photograph appears. Following the figure number is the name of the photographer and the company from which the photo was licensed. In each case, the photographer holds the copyright. If the photograph comes from a CD collection, the product name appears in italics along with or instead of a photographer, and the company holds the copyright. If no company is listed, the photo was licensed from the photographer directly.

To all who contributed their photography, my heartfelt thanks.

Images	Photographer/Product	Company
Figures A-13 through A-15, A-17, and A-18	Russell McDougal	
Figure A-23	Denise McClelland	
Figure B-3	*V. 5, World Commerce & Travel*	PhotoDisc
Figures C-1 and C2	Russell McDougal	
Figures C-3, C-5, C-13, and C-14	Denise McClelland	
Figures C-8 and C-10	Denise McClelland	
Figure C-16	*V. 5, World Commerce & Travel*	PhotoDisc
Figure C-17, top	Dan Norris, *Sampler One*	Color Bytes
Figure C-17, bottom	Bob Barber, *Sampler Two*	Color Bytes
Figure C-18	*William Morris — Selected Works*	Planet Art
Figure C-20, upper left	Jon Eisberq	FPG International
Figure C-20, upper right	Michael Ian Shopenn	AllStock
Figure C-20, lower left	Phil Borges	Tony Stone Worldwide
Figure C-20, lower right	Gerald Zanetti	The Stock Market
Figure C-21, left	Blake Sell	Reuter
Figure C-21, right	Phelan Ebenhack	Reuter

(continued)

Images	Photographer/Product	Company
Figure C-22, left		The Bettmann Archive
Figure C-22, right		Bettmann-UPI
Figure C-23, top	Mike Powell	AllSport
Figure C-23, bottom	David Cannon	AllSport
Figure C-24, left	Eric Feferberg	Agence France-Presse
Figure C-24, right	Pierre Guillaud	Agence France-Presse
Figures 2-2, 2-4, 2-5, and 2-9 through 2-11	*V. 1, Business & Industry*	PhotoDisc
Figures 3-1 and 3-20	*Photo CD Snapshots*	Eastman Kodak
Figure 3-9	*V. 11, Retro Americana*	PhotoDisc
Figures 3-22, 3-23, 3-25, and 3-26	Denise McClelland	
Color Plate 3-1	*V. 9, Holidays & Celebrations*	PhotoDisc
Figure 4-7	*V. 5, World Commerce & Travel*	PhotoDisc
Figures 4-10, and 4-12 through 4-14	Denise McClelland	
Color Plate 4-2	*V. 5, World Commerce & Travel*	PhotoDisc
Figures 5-2 through 5-4 and 5-7	Carlye Calvin, *Sampler One*	Color Bytes
Colors Plates 5-1 and 5-2	Carlye Calvin, *Sampler One*	Color Bytes
Figure 6-5	*V. 11, Retro Americana*	PhotoDisc
Figure 6-6	Denise McClelland	
Figure 6-15	Mark Collen	
Color Plate 6-1	Mark Collen	
Figures 7-6 through 7-8, 7-29, and 7-30	Russell McDougal	
Figures 7-13 and 7-14	*V. 5, World Commerce & Travel*	PhotoDisc
Figure 7-15	*V. 12, Food & Dining*	PhotoDisc
Color Plate 7-1	*V. 12, Food & Dining*	PhotoDisc
Color Plates 7-4 and 7-5	*V. 5, World Commerce & Travel*	PhotoDisc
Figures 8-4, 8-15, 8-17 through 8-20, 8-24, 8-25, 8-28 through 8-30, 8-36, and 8-37	*V. 4, Technology & Medicine*	PhotoDisc

Images	Photographer/Product	Company
Figures 8-6 through 8-8	Russell McDougal	
Figures 8-9 and 8-32 through 8-34	V. 4, Technology & Medicine	PhotoDisc
Figures 8-10 through 8-14	V. 4, Technology & Medicine	PhotoDisc
Figure 8-18 (face)	V. 5, World Commerce & Travel	PhotoDisc
Figures 8-21 and 8-22	Russell McDougal	
Figure 8-27 (background)	V. 4, Technology & Medicine	PhotoDisc
Figures 9-1, 9-2, 9-13, and 9-19 through 9-23	V. 11, Retro Americana	PhotoDisc
Figures 9-3 through 9-10	V. 4, Technology & Medicine	PhotoDisc
Figures 9-15 and 9-18		The Bettmann Archive
Color Plate 9-1	V. 11, Retro Americana	PhotoDisc
Color Plate 9-2		The Bettmann Archive
Figures 10-2, 10-30, 10-32, and 10-36 through 10-38	Russell McDougal	
Figures 10-5, 10-6, 10-39, and 10-40	V. 11, Retro Americana	PhotoDisc
Figures 10-7 and 10-9 through 10-12	V. 6, Nature & the Environment	PhotoDisc
Figures 10-27 and 10-29	V. 5, World Commerce & Travel	PhotoDisc
Color Plates 10-1 and 10-2	V. 6, Nature & the Environment	PhotoDisc
Figures 11-2 through 11-5, 11-12, and 11-23	Denise McClelland	
Figures 11-6 and 11-7	Russell McDougal	
Figures 11-8 through 11-11 and 11-18 through 11-21	Michael Probst	Reuter
Figure 10-17, top	Wraptures	Form and Function
Figure 10-17, bottom	Folio 1	D'pix
Figures 12-2, 12-11 through 12-16, and 12-20 through 12-22	Carlye Calvin, Sampler One	Color Bytes
Figures 12-23 through 12-25	V. 11, Retro Americana	PhotoDisc

(continued)

Images	Photographer/Product	Company
Figures 13-1, 13-2, 13-4, 13-5, 13-8 through 13-15, 13-18 through 13-21, 13-25 through 13-28, 13-30, 13-31, 13-41, 13-43, 13-44, and 13-46 through 13-48	V. 5, World Commerce & Travel	PhotoDisc
Figure 13-3	V. 5, World Commerce & Travel	PhotoDisc
Figures 13-6, 13-7, 13-22, 13-24, and 13-40	V. 11, Retro Americana	PhotoDisc
Figures 13-16, 13-17, 13-32 through 13-38, and 13-45	V. 5, World Commerce & Travel	PhotoDisc
Color Plates 13-1 and 13-2	V. 5, World Commerce & Travel	PhotoDisc
Color Plates 13-3 through 13-5 and 13-8	V. 9, Holidays & Celebrations	PhotoDisc
Color Plate 13-6	V. 5, World Commerce & Travel	PhotoDisc
Color Plate 13-7	V. 5, World Commerce & Travel	PhotoDisc
Figures 14-1 through 14-4, 14-6 through 14-8, 14-11, 14-13, 14-14, 14-20, 14-21, and 14-36	V. 5, World Commerce & Travel	PhotoDisc
Figures 14-5, 14-9, 14-10, and 14-27	V. 11, Retro Americana	PhotoDisc
Figure 14-12	Mark Collen	
Color Plates 14-1 through 14-3, 14-8, and 14-9	V. 9, Holidays & Celebrations	PhotoDisc
Color Plates 14-4 through 14-6	V. 7, Business & Occupations	PhotoDisc
Color Plate 14-7	Mark Collen	
Figures 15-1, 15-42, 15-43, and 15-45	V. 9, Holidays & Celebrations	PhotoDisc
Figures 15-3 through 15-31 and 15-33 through 15-41	V. 5, World Commerce & Travel	PhotoDisc
Color Plates 15-1 and 15-2	V. 5, World Commerce & Travel	PhotoDisc
Color Plates 15-3 and 15-4	V. 9, Holidays & Celebrations	PhotoDisc

Images	Photographer/Product	Company
Figures 16-1, 16-2, 16-4 through 16-6, 16-12, 16-14, 16-15, 16-17, and 16-21 through 16-25	*V. 5, World Commerce & Travel*	PhotoDisc
Figure 16-10	*V. 9, Holidays & Celebrations*	PhotoDisc
Colors Plates 16-1 through 16-3 and 16-6 through 16-8	*V. 5, World Commerce & Travel*	PhotoDisc
Color Plates 16-4, 16-5, 16-9, and 16-10	*V. 9, Holidays & Celebrations*	PhotoDisc
Color Plate 16-11	*French Posters*	Planet Art
Figures 17-3 through 17-10, 17-12, 17-13, 17-15, and 17-16	Russell McDougal	
Figures 17-18 through 17-21	Carlye Calvin, *Sampler One*	Color Bytes
Figure 17-23	*V. 11, Retro Americana*	PhotoDisc
Color Plates 17-1 and 17-2	Russell McDougal	
Color Plates 17-3 through 17-5	Carlye Calvin, *Sampler One*	Color Bytes
Figures 18-1, 18-2, 18-4, and 18-6	Russell McDougal	
Figures 18-7 and 18-8	Carlye Calvin, *Sampler One*	Color Bytes
Color Plates 18-1 and 18-3	Russell McDougal	
Color Plates 18-4 and 18-5	Carlye Calvin, *Sampler One*	Color Bytes

Products and Vendors

The following is a list of all the products mentioned in this book, along with vendors, prices, and phone numbers. This list is in no way intended to serve as a recommendation for any of these products; it's provided merely a reference so that you can find out more information on your own.

I've also taken the liberty of including a few products that I did not mention in the book. Some arrived on my desk after the book was finished, others didn't strike me as important enough to mention on their own. Nonetheless, these products relate directly to Photoshop or to some peripheral Photoshop concern, such as Photo CD, scanning, or printing.

Product	Vendor	List price	Phone
Alias Sketch	Alias Research	$695	416/362-9181
The Allsport Library	Allsport USA	NA	310/395-2955
Animation System	Electric Image	$7,495	818/577-1627
Arcus II flatbed scanner	Agfa	$3,495	508/658-5600
ArtPad drawing tablet	Wacom	$199	201/265-4226
ArtZ drawing tablet	Wacom	$449	201/265-4226
ATM	Adobe Systems	$60	415/961-4400
The Black Box	Alien Skin	$89	919/832-4124
Cachet	Electronics for Imaging	$595	415/286-8600
Canvas	Deneba	$399	305/596-5644
CD Stock (all four-disks)	3M	$650	612/628-6295
CD Stock (individual disks)	AllStock	$195	206/622-6262
	FPG International	$195	212/777-4210
	The Stock Market	$195	212/684-7878
	Tony Stone Worldwide	$195	312/787-7880
CD-ROM Toolkit	FWB	$79	415/474-8055
ClarisDraw	Claris	$399	408/987-7000

(continued)

Product	Vendor	List price	Phone
Collage	Specular International	$399	413/253-3100
Colorfinder	Trumatch	$85	212/351-2360
Color It	MicroFrontier	$150	708/559-1300
ColorMatch	DayStar Digital	$239	404/967-2077
ColorSync (part of QuickDraw GX)	Apple	$150	408/996-1010
ComputerEyes/Pro	Digital Vision	$400	617/329-5400
DeBabelizer	Equilibrium	$299	415/332/4343
Dimensions	Adobe Systems	$199	415/961-4400
DrawingPad drawing tablet	CalComp	$395	714/821-2000
EfiColor for Photoshop	Electronics for Imaging	$199	415/286-8600
EfiColor Works	Electronics for Imaging	$399	415/286-8600
Folio 1 Media Kit	D'pix	$300	415/664-4010
Folio 1 Print Pro CD	D'pix	$500	614/299-7192
FreeHand	Aldus	$595	206/628-2320
Gallery Effects: Classic Art 1	Aldus	$199	206/628-2320
Gallery Effects: Classic Art 2	Aldus	$99	206/628-2320
Gallery Effects: Classic Art 3	Aldus	$199	206/628-2320
Illustrator	Adobe Systems	$595	415/961-4400
ImageEditor	PictureWorks	$249	510/735-2018
Infini-D	Specular International	$695	413/253-3100
Kai's Power Tools	HSC Software	$199	310/392-8441
LapisColor 24	Focus Enhancements	$399	617/938-8088
LeMansGT	Radius	$2,499	408/434-1010
Lumina digital camera	Leaf Systems	$6,900	508/460-8300
MacRenderMan	Pixar	$695	510/236-4000
MacroMind Director	Macromedia	$1,195	415/252-2000
MacVision Color Digitizer	Koala Acquisitions	$799	408/776-8181
MultiSpin 74 CD-ROM drive	NEC Technologies	$615	708/860-9500
NuVista+	TrueVision	$3,595	317/841-0332
Ofoto	Light Source	$395	415/461-8000

Product	Vendor	List price	Phone
PageMaker	Aldus	$895	206/628-2320
Paint Alchemy	Xaos Tools	$99	415/558-9831
Painter	Fractal Design	$499	408/688-8800
Persuasion	Aldus	$495	206/628-2320
Photo CD Access	Eastman Kodak	$40	716/724-4000
PhotoDisc, Vol.'s 1-2, 4-13	PhotoDisc	$395 each	206/441-9355
PhotoDisc, Volume 3	PhotoDisc	$295	206/441-9355
PhotoEdge	Eastman Kodak	$139	716/724-4000
PhotoMatic	DayStar Digital	$279	404/967-2077
Photoshop	Adobe Systems	$895	415/961-4400
PhotoSpot	Second Glance	$199	714/855-2331
PhotoStyler	Aldus	$795	206/628-2320
PixelPaint Professional	Pixel Resources	$379	404/449-4947
Planet Art Image Collection	Planet Art	$90 each	213/651-3405
PlateMaker	IN Software	$295	619/743-7502
Pocket Tint Chart	NAA	$175	703/648-1000
PowerLook 30-bit scanner	Umax Technologies	$3,495	510/651-8883
PowerPoint	Microsoft	$495	206/882-8080
Premier	Adobe Systems	$495	415/961-4400
PressLink media service	PressLink	NA	305/376-3818
PressView 21 Display System	SuperMac Technology	$3,999	408/541-6100
Process Color Imaging Guide	Pantone	$75	201/935-5500
Process Color System Guide	Pantone	$75	201/935-5500
Pro Imager 8000	PixelCraft	$12,995	510/562-2480
Professional DCS 420	Eastman Kodak	$10,995	716/724-4000
QuarkXPress	Quark	$895	303/894-8888
QuickTake digital camera	Apple	$749	408/996-1010
RAM Doubler	Connectix	$99	415/571-5100
Ray Dream Designer	Ray Dream	$349	415/960-0768
Remedy font	Emigre	$95	916/451-4344
Renaissance	Eastman Kodak	$695	716/724-4000

(continued)

Product	Vendor	List price	Phone
Samplers One and Two	ColorBytes	$399	303/989-9205
ScanMaker III 36-bit scanner	Microtek	$3,499	408/297-5000
ScanPrepPro	ImageXPress	$295	404/564-9924
SD-510 drawing tablet	Wacom	$695	201/265-4226
Shoebox	Eastman Kodak	$395	716/724-4000
ShowPlace	Pixar	$695	510/236-4000
Sketcher	Fractal Design	$149	408/688-8800
StrataVision 3d	Strata	$695	801/628-5218
StudioPro	Strata	$1,495	801/628-5218
SummaSketch drawing tablet	SummaGraphics	$649	203/881-5400
SwatchPrinter Software	Trumatch	$48	212/351-2360
Terrazzo	Xaos Tools	$149	415/558-9831
TextureScape	Specular International	$195	413/253-3100
Thunder II•GX 1360	SuperMac Technology	$3,299	408/541-6100
Thunder II•GX 1600	SuperMac Technology	$3,999	408/541-6100
Typestry	Pixar	$299	510/236-4000
VideoSpigot	SuperMac Technology	$449	408/773-4498
Wraptures One and Two	Form and Function	$95 each	415/664-4010

Index

• M •

For the perfect image <u>on-line,</u> just say the word.

Now, instant access to thousands of premium images from nearly 30 of the world's preeminent professional stock agencies is right at your fingertips. Seymour™ utilizes cutting-edge technology to bring you an unequaled, on-line creative tool for research, visual brainstorming, comps, layouts and publishing.

Simply type in a single word or an entire phrase that describes the image you're looking for, and, in seconds, Seymour will display thumbnail-sized pictures from the PNI Image Library for your review.

Unlike other on-line services, Seymour understands everyday conversational English and can recognize modified phrases. There's no need to learn a new software language or create Boolean searches.

Best of all, if you want to order an image you've found, Seymour lets you price and license right from your desktop, so you don't have to deal separately with each photo agency. Pick your delivery format — PNI's exclusive on-line delivery system, CD-ROM, SyQuest™ cartridge or original film — and your search is complete. Call, write, or fax PNI and put Seymour to work for you today.

Just say the word... it's that easy.

Picture Network International
2000 15th Street North
Arlington, VA 22201
Tel (703) 312-6210
    (800) PNI-PICS
Fax (703) 522-1236

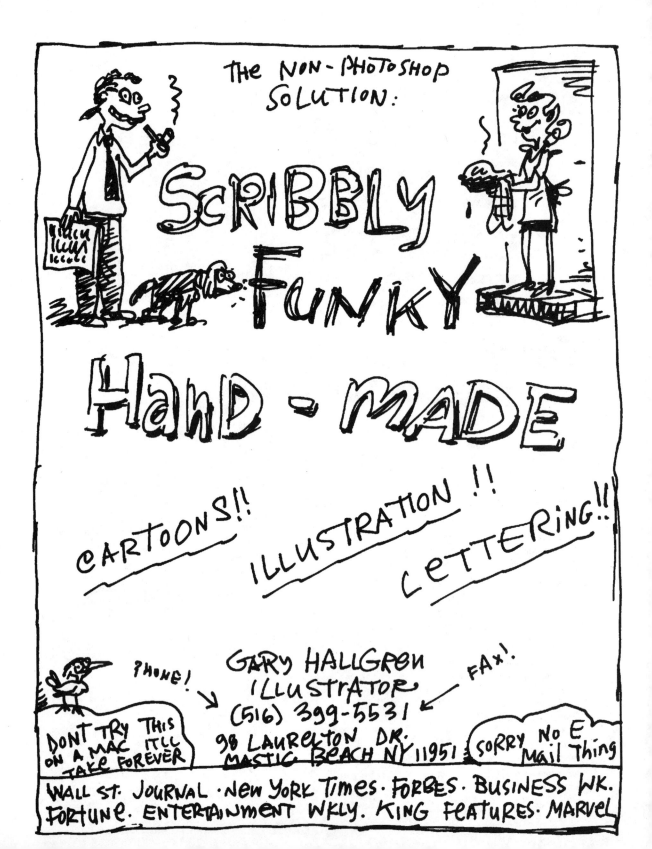

Upgrade to the Latest Version of the Incredible KAI'S POWER Tools™!

You're entitled to fantastic savings on an even more powerful version of HSC Software's Kai's Power Tools for Macintosh and Windows — the award-winning set of extensions and filters for killer digital imaging. Order direct from HSC and save $100!

More Extensions! Amazing effects from the Fractal and Texture Explorers are built on the presets from the Gradient Designer.

More One-Step Filters! Over a dozen, including the Seamless Welder and Vortex Tiling.

More Power! Real Time Previews, Apply Modes & Enhanced Speed.

More Creative Options! Yours when you upgrade.

Call 1.800.472.9025 to Order!
Mention this code: PSB99

Or Fax to 805.566.3885

Or Mail to
HSC Software Corp.
6303 Carpinteria Ave.
Carpinteria, CA 93013

Yes! Please send me the **Kai's Power Tools** upgrade at the special price of just $99.95, $100 off the suggested retail price of $199.

■ Kai's Power Tools 2.1 for Macintosh/Power Macintosh
■ Kai's Power Tools 2.0 for Windows

When ordering, ask for your special pricing on KPT Bryce™ for Macintosh, the amazing 3-D landscape terrain generator!

Price	$ 99.95
Sales Tax[1]	$ _____
Shipping & Handling[2]	$10.00
Total	$ _____

1. California residents add 8.25% state sales tax. Offer subject to change without notice. Please allow three to four weeks for delivery.
2. For international orders outside the U.S. and Canada, please call 805.566.6699 for shipping and handling prices.

Customer Information (please print clearly)

Name_____ Company_____

Address_____

City_____ State/Province_____ Zip/Postal Code_____

Phone (_____) _____ Fax (_____) _____

Payment Information

■ Check enclosed *(payable to HSC Software Corp.)*

■ Bill my credit card.   ■ Visa ■ Mastercard

Card number | | | | | | | | | | | | | | | | | | Expiration date_____

Cardholder name_____ Signature _____

HSC is a registered trademark and Kai's Power Tools and KPT Bryce are trademarks of HSC Software Corp. All other product names are trademarks of their respective owners.

PSB 9/94

*"I love it! This product is in the must-have category
if you use Adobe Photoshop!"
- Flash Magazine, May/June 1994*

The Black Box is a set of six Photoshop-compatible filters that will save you hours of tweaking with channel operations. Why waste precious time trying to duplicate a channel recipe when you can get better looking special effects by simply clicking the OK button? These filters condense chapters of Photoshop tips into simple tools that take care of the details for you.

As a special offer you can get The Black Box for $20 off the retail price!
Just mention special offer PSB23A to get this price.
To order the Mac/PowerPC or Windows version of The Black Box for $69 (regularly $89),
call (919) 832-4124, fax (919) 832-4065,
or send a check including $5 for shipping to:
Alien Skin Software, Raleigh, NC 27607.

Only one copy per customer.

Twelve Free Photo CD Scans...

Quality, excellent service and support... just a few of the reasons Photoshop users, designers, photographers and publishers from around the country choose PALMERS for their Photo CD scanning. Your image is taken seriously regardless of whether you need one scan or thousands.

Introduce yourself to the difference. Give us a try. Twelve scans from your 35mm film at no charge. A disc and shipping charge of only $10 dollars.

Send twelve slides or selected frames from your 35mm film - black & white or color with a check or money order for $10.00 (California residents add your sales tax). That's it! No risk for a try from America's Premier Photo CD service.

For More Information
800 735 1950

2313 C Street
Sacramento
CA 95816
916 441 3305

P A L M E R S

Yes!
Send Me The Stuff!

Name	Title
Company	Telephone
Address	Fax
City	Business Type
State/Zip	Scans per Month

This offer is good for 35mm film and one use only, although please pass it along to your friends.

A new breed of textures & backgrounds

On Photo CD

Enhance your desktop creation with uncommonly elegant lighting, color and style. "Art Textures & Backgrounds"– Volume One by FotoSets.™ Transcend the look of common stock photos or computer effects. The FotoSets volume, created with intricate lighting and unique materials, cannot be duplicated on the computer or found in stock libraries.

The disc contains 100 distinctly styled color photos of artistic surfaces, 3D sets and objects. They are ideal design elements in desktop publishing, multimedia and illustration. Create dramatic effects for fonts, fills, text, collage and more. For samples of similar images, see FotoSets on the companion CD ROM.

Specifications

Photo CD format. Each of the 100 images has five resolutions ranging from display quality up to magazine quality at 18 MB (3072 X 2048 pixels). The disc works with any Photo CD enabled XA drive, graphics program, PC, MAC or UNIX (check with your manufacturer). You'll need a minimum of 4.5 MB RAM. More RAM is required for loading and manipulating larger files.

ORDERING COUPON

With this coupon receive FotoSets "Art Textures & Backgrounds"–Volume One for $249 ($100 off regular $349 price). While supplies last.

Send me: ☐ "Art Textures & Backgrounds"–Volume One $ 249.00
Sales tax (California only) $ 21.17
Standard shipping $ 13.50
Total $

☐ Free brochure. For overview and royalty free license information.

Ship to:

NAME _____

STREET _____
Cannot deliver to P.O. Box

CITY _____ STATE _____ ZIP _____

PHONE _____ COUNTRY _____

METHOD OF PAYMENT: ☐ CHECK ☐ MC ☐ VISA

CARD NUMBER _____ EXP. DATE _____

NAME ON CARD _____

CARD HOLDER'S BILLING ADDRESS _____

CITY _____ STATE _____ ZIP _____

**ORDER BY FAX 1-415-621-2917
OR PHONE 1-800-577-1215 · 1-415-621-2061**

FotoSets · 4104 Twenty-fourth Street · San Francisco, CA 94114 · Facsimile 415-621-2917 · Telephone 415-621-2061

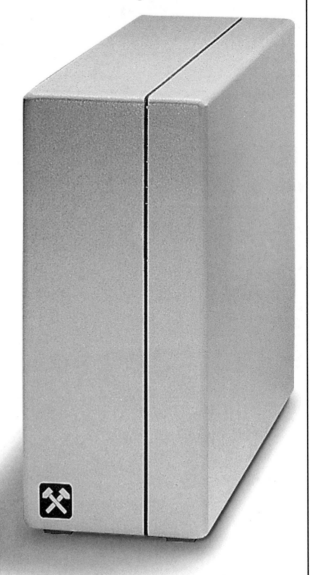

See the movie, try the magic, get the power.

Your copy of the *Tempo Photoshop 3.0 Magic Macros* is right in the CD-ROM at the back of this book. Try out the simplicity, the ease—not to mention the *fun*—of macros that make your life easier. Then come back to this coupon. Go ahead, we'll wait.

Well, how'd you like it? The Photoshop Magic macros are downright *inspiring!* And now for the cool part... as a Tempo/RT Demo user, the full power, speed and convenience of TempoEZ or Tempo II Plus are yours for a fraction of list price! So you can save time, save effort and save money too!

Your one command can apply filters to hundreds of Photoshop files. Tempo can even run the *right* macro

on each file, based on the file's name or some characteristic of the file. Tempo can create new files automatically, naming each in sequence.

The only limit to the power of Tempo macros—in *any* program—is the extent of your needs. And Tempo's ability to share information with AppleScripts makes it the ideal complement for linking scriptable and non-scriptable programs as well.

Watch it happen, then make it happen

Run the "Macro Treatments" movie included in the Tempo Photoshop Magic 3.0 folder to see some of the possibilities of Tempo working with Photoshop. Then write, call, E-Mail or fax your order now to put the power of Tempo II Plus to work for you!

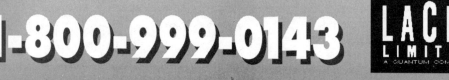

Manage and edit your images!

New software for Macintosh and Windows applications.

The demo version of PictureWorks IMAGE*editor* XTension for QuarkXPress included in this Photoshop 3.0 Bible CD-ROM is only the beginning of what you can do with your images using PictureWorks software products.

The Image Editing XTension for QuarkXPress®

- Rectangle Selection
- Lasso Selection
- Paintbrush
- Smudge Brush
- Pencil
- Eyedropper
- Elliptical Selection
- Magic Wand Selection
- Brush Size/Shape Options
- Eraser
- Crop images
- Supports RGB, CMYK, Grayscale, Black/White Modes
- Sophisticated Paste Controls
- Access QuarkXPress's Color Palette to load and save custom colors

The Color Balance XTension for QuarkXPress®

- Color Balance
  - Cyan/Red slider controls
  - Magenta/Green slider controls
  - Yellow/Blue slider controls
- Color Adjust
  - Hue • Brightness • Color • Contrast
- Tone Adjust
  - Highlight • Histogram• Input/Output
  - Auto Controls
- Individual Color Adjustments

The Image Effects XTension for QuarkXPress.

- Smooth
- Emboss
- Quake
- Outline
- Custom
- Histogram
- Sharpen
- Mosaic
- ZigZag
- Lighten
- Hue/Saturation
- Threshold
- Antique
- Noise
- Cartoon
- Darken
- Remap Controls
  - Negate, Solarize, Posterize
  - Freehand, Control
  - Brightness, Contrast
- Access your favorite Photoshop™ plug-ins

PhotoNow!

The TWAIN Module for the Apple™ QuickTake Camera

- View and open pictures from QuickTake camera
- View and open QuickTake pictures on directories or disk
- Open pictures in native QuickTake format
- Take pictures from your applications
- Rotate pictures
- Delete pictures from camera
- Set the flash
- Set the self-timer
- View the camera battery level
- Choose high/low resolution

For more information about how the PictureWorks family of image editing products can improve your performance, please fill out the form below and mail or fax to:

Picture WORKS

PictureWorks Technology, Inc.
125 Town and Country Drive
Danville, CA 94526
fax: 510-835-2019

Call for special offers and promotions! 800-326-5700

Name_____ Title_____

Company_____

Address_____

City_____ State____ Zip_____

Phone _____ Fax _____

Please send more information on:

☐ IMAGE XTensions for QuarkXPress
☐ Apple QuickTake photo editing products:

_____

Please indicate for Macintosh or Windows

PHOTODISC™

Telephone:
800.528.3472 / 206.441.9355
Fax:
206.441.9379

Call for current
special discounts and
free
thumbnail catalogs.

Save **$20**
on the PhotoDisc Starter Kit

This coupon is worth $20 towards the purchase of a
PhotoDisc Starter Kit. Your price: $29 (save 40%).
Over 4,000 low-res images, browsing software & 109-page
color catalog. Perfect for browsing & comping.

Call to order 1-800-528-3472. Free information kit available. Good only on orders made
directly through PhotoDisc. One per customer. Not redeemable for cash. Expires 12/31/96.
Offer Code #AP30.

Save **$25**
on any PhotoDisc Volume

This coupon is worth $25 towards the purchase of one
PhotoDisc Volume. Your price: $274 (regularly $299).
336 high-resolution images, royalty-free and ready to use.
Color corrected for outstanding 5"x7" or 8"x10" output.

Call to order 1-800-528-3472. Free information kit available. Good only on orders made
directly through PhotoDisc. One per customer. Not redeemable for cash. Expires 12/31/96.
Offer Code #AP30.

The **Best Photographs** Are Also

the Easiest to Find

with FPG's CD Selects Vol. 1

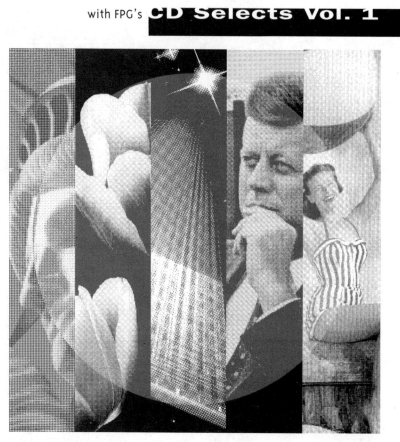

You get 5,700 of FPG International's top selling photographs, right on your desktop for immediate use in your comps. CD Selects Vol. 1 is easy to use and contains great photos from FPG's 5 divisions:

CHROMES - subject coverage in contemporary color.
GALLERY - selections in artistic contemporary black-and-white.
F/X - state-of-the-art special effects, composites and computer graphics.
ARCHIVE - historical black-and-white from the 1850s through the 1950s.
RETRO - nostalgic color from the 1950s, 60s and 70s.

This vast and varied collection of images is at your fingertips - for inspiration, research, or use in comps. CD Selects Vol. 1 is compatible with both Macintosh and PC systems.

Call FPG today for more information on pricing and ordering CD Selects Vol. 1. at :

FPG

212 **777 4210**
fax 212 995 9652

FPG International   **32 Union Square East**   **New York, NY**   **10003-3295**

About PressLink®

PressLink is the premier online service for the publishing professional. All of your editorial needs -- news, photos, graphics,
research libraries and electronic mail -- are available in the PressLink Media Mall™.
Nearly 200,000 photo and graphic files reside in the digital archives managed by
PressLink's information providers: the largest single collection of digitally copyrighted
material available to the professional publishing community.

To activate the PressLink communications software on the CD-ROM that accompa-
nied this edition of the Macworld Photoshop Bible, complete this form and fax to PressLink.

Special PressLink Offer -- Expires March 31, 1995

Return this order form to PressLink to activate your software. We'll send you a startup kit complete
with manuals and a quick-start guide to get you online quickly. As a bonus, we'll include at no additional cost our new image-viewing software — PressLink Explorer™. Explorer allows you to view
images in a contact-sheet environment and will help you manage your digital collection.

U.S. subscribers will be billed $49.95 for the PressLink Startup Kit. Canadian and International rates
available upon request.

Name: _____

Company: _____

Address: _____

City: _____ State: ____ Zip: _____

Your phone: _____ Your fax: _____

Charge to: MasterCard ____   Visa ____

Account number: _____

Expires: _____

Signature: _____

Complete and mail or fax to:

Macworld/Photoshop Bible Offer
PressLink, Inc.
11800 Sunrise Valley Drive
Suite 1130
Reston, VA 22091-5302

Fax: 703-758-8368
Voice: 703-758-1740

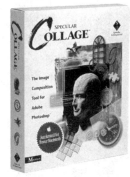
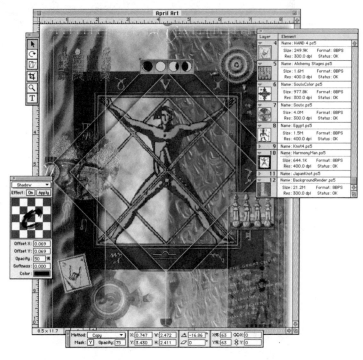

Notes

Notes

Notes

Notes

Title	Author	ISBN	Price
			12/20/94
INTERNET / COMMUNICATIONS / NETWORKING			
CompuServe For Dummies™	by Wallace Wang	1-56884-181-7	$19.95 USA/$26.95 Canada
Modems For Dummies™, 2nd Edition	by Tina Rathbone	1-56884-223-6	$19.99 USA/$26.99 Canada
Modems For Dummies™	by Tina Rathbone	1-56884-001-2	$19.95 USA/$26.95 Canada
MORE Internet For Dummies™	by John R. Levine & Margaret Levine Young	1-56884-164-7	$19.95 USA/$26.95 Canada
NetWare For Dummies™	by Ed Tittel & Deni Connor	1-56884-003-9	$19.95 USA/$26.95 Canada
Networking For Dummies™	by Doug Lowe	1-56884-079-9	$19.95 USA/$26.95 Canada
ProComm Plus 2 For Windows For Dummies™	by Wallace Wang	1-56884-219-8	$19.99 USA/$26.99 Canada
The Internet For Dummies™, 2nd Edition	by John R. Levine & Carol Baroudi	1-56884-222-8	$19.99 USA/$26.99 Canada
The Internet For Macs For Dummies™	by Charles Seiter	1-56884-184-1	$19.95 USA/$26.95 Canada
MACINTOSH			
Macs For Dummies®	by David Pogue	1-56884-173-6	$19.95 USA/$26.95 Canada
Macintosh System 7.5 For Dummies™	by Bob LeVitus	1-56884-197-3	$19.95 USA/$26.95 Canada
MORE Macs For Dummies™	by David Pogue	1-56884-087-X	$19.95 USA/$26.95 Canada
PageMaker 5 For Macs For Dummies™	by Galen Gruman	1-56884-178-7	$19.95 USA/$26.95 Canada
QuarkXPress 3.3 For Dummies™	by Galen Gruman & Barbara Assadi	1-56884-217-1	$19.99 USA/$26.99 Canada
Upgrading and Fixing Macs For Dummies™	by Kearney Rietmann & Frank Higgins	1-56884-189-2	$19.95 USA/$26.95 Canada
MULTIMEDIA			
Multimedia & CD-ROMs For Dummies™, Interactive Multimedia Value Pack	by Andy Rathbone	1-56884-225-2	$29.95 USA/$39.95 Canada
Multimedia & CD-ROMs For Dummies™	by Andy Rathbone	1-56884-089-6	$19.95 USA/$26.95 Canada
OPERATING SYSTEMS / DOS			
MORE DOS For Dummies™	by Dan Gookin	1-56884-046-2	$19.95 USA/$26.95 Canada
S.O.S. For DOS™	by Katherine Murray	1-56884-043-8	$12.95 USA/$16.95 Canada
OS/2 For Dummies™	by Andy Rathbone	1-878058-76-2	$19.95 USA/$26.95 Canada
UNIX			
UNIX For Dummies™	by John R. Levine & Margaret Levine Young	1-878058-58-4	$19.95 USA/$26.95 Canada
WINDOWS			
S.O.S. For Windows™	by Katherine Murray	1-56884-045-4	$12.95 USA/$16.95 Canada
MORE Windows 3.1 For Dummies™, 3rd Edition	by Andy Rathbone	1-56884-240-6	$19.99 USA/$26.99 Canada
PCs / HARDWARE			
Illustrated Computer Dictionary For Dummies™	by Dan Gookin, Wally Wang, & Chris Van Buren	1-56884-004-7	$12.95 USA/$16.95 Canada
Upgrading and Fixing PCs For Dummies™	by Andy Rathbone	1-56884-002-0	$19.95 USA/$26.95 Canada
PRESENTATION / AUTOCAD			
AutoCAD For Dummies™	by Bud Smith	1-56884-191-4	$19.95 USA/$26.95 Canada
PowerPoint 4 For Windows For Dummies™	by Doug Lowe	1-56884-161-2	$16.95 USA/$22.95 Canada
PROGRAMMING			
Borland C++ For Dummies™	by Michael Hyman	1-56884-162-0	$19.95 USA/$26.95 Canada
"Borland's New Language Product" For Dummies™	by Neil Rubenking	1-56884-200-7	$19.95 USA/$26.95 Canada
C For Dummies™	by Dan Gookin	1-878058-78-9	$19.95 USA/$26.95 Canada
C++ For Dummies™	by Stephen R. Davis	1-56884-163-9	$19.95 USA/$26.95 Canada
Mac Programming For Dummies™	by Dan Parks Sydow	1-56884-173-6	$19.95 USA/$26.95 Canada
QBasic Programming For Dummies™	by Douglas Hergert	1-56884-093-4	$19.95 USA/$26.95 Canada
Visual Basic "X" For Dummies™, 2nd Edition	by Wallace Wang	1-56884-230-9	$19.99 USA/$26.99 Canada
Visual Basic 3 For Dummies™	by Wallace Wang	1-56884-076-4	$19.95 USA/$26.95 Canada
SPREADSHEET			
1-2-3 For Dummies™	by Greg Harvey	1-878058-60-6	$16.95 USA/$21.95 Canada
1-2-3 For Windows 5 For Dummies™, 2nd Edition	by John Walkenbach	1-56884-216-3	$16.95 USA/$21.95 Canada
1-2-3 For Windows For Dummies™	by John Walkenbach	1-56884-052-5	$16.95 USA/$21.95 Canada
Excel 5 For Macs For Dummies™	by Greg Harvey	1-56884-186-8	$19.95 USA/$26.95 Canada
Excel For Dummies™, 2nd Edition	by Greg Harvey	1-56884-050-0	$16.95 USA/$21.95 Canada
MORE Excel 5 For Windows For Dummies™	by Greg Harvey	1-56884-207-4	$19.95 USA/$26.95 Canada
Quattro Pro 6 For Windows For Dummies™	by John Walkenbach	1-56884-174-4	$19.95 USA/$26.95 Canada
Quattro Pro For DOS For Dummies™	by John Walkenbach	1-56884-023-3	$16.95 USA/$21.95 Canada
UTILITIES / VCRs & CAMCORDERS			
Norton Utilities 8 For Dummies™	by Beth Slick	1-56884-166-3	$19.95 USA/$26.95 Canada
VCRs & Camcorders For Dummies™	by Andy Rathbone & Gordon McComb	1-56884-229-5	$14.99 USA/$20.99 Canada
WORD PROCESSING			
Ami Pro For Dummies™	by Jim Meade	1-56884-049-7	$19.95 USA/$26.95 Canada
MORE Word For Windows 6 For Dummies™	by Doug Lowe	1-56884-165-5	$19.95 USA/$26.95 Canada
MORE WordPerfect 6 For Windows For Dummies™	by Margaret Levine Young & David C. Kay	1-56884-206-6	$19.95 USA/$26.95 Canada
MORE WordPerfect 6 For DOS For Dummies™	by Wallace Wang, edited by Dan Gookin	1-56884-047-0	$19.95 USA/$26.95 Canada
S.O.S. For WordPerfect™	by Katherine Murray	1-56884-053-5	$12.95 USA/$16.95 Canada
Word 6 For Macs For Dummies™	by Dan Gookin	1-56884-190-6	$19.95 USA/$26.95 Canada
Word For Windows 6 For Dummies™	by Dan Gookin	1-56884-075-6	$16.95 USA/$21.95 Canada
Word For Windows For Dummies™	by Dan Gookin	1-878058-86-X	$16.95 USA/$21.95 Canada
WordPerfect 6 For Dummies™	by Dan Gookin	1-878058-77-0	$16.95 USA/$21.95 Canada
WordPerfect For Dummies™	by Dan Gookin	1-878058-52-5	$16.95 USA/$21.95 Canada
WordPerfect For Windows For Dummies™	by Margaret Levine Young & David C. Kay	1-56884-032-2	$16.95 USA/$21.95 Canada

Fun, Fast, & Cheap!

CorelDRAW! 5 For Dummies™ Quick Reference
by Raymond E. Werner

ISBN: 1-56884-952-4
$9.99 USA/$12.99 Canada

Windows "X" For Dummies™ Quick Reference, 3rd Edition
by Greg Harvey

ISBN: 1-56884-964-8
$9.99 USA/$12.99 Canada

Word For Windows 6 For Dummies™ Quick Reference
by George Lynch

ISBN: 1-56884-095-0
$8.95 USA/$12.95 Canada

WordPerfect For DOS For Dummies™ Quick Reference
by Greg Harvey

ISBN: 1-56884-009-8
$8.95 USA/$11.95 Canada

Title	Author	ISBN	Price
DATABASE			
Access 2 For Dummies™ Quick Reference	by Stuart A. Stuple	1-56884-167-1	$8.95 USA/$11.95 Canada
dBASE 5 For DOS For Dummies™ Quick Reference	by Barry Sosinsky	1-56884-954-0	$9.99 USA/$12.99 Canada
dBASE 5 For Windows For Dummies™ Quick Reference	by Stuart J. Stuple	1-56884-953-2	$9.99 USA/$12.99 Canada
Paradox 5 For Windows For Dummies™ Quick Reference	by Scott Palmer	1-56884-960-5	$9.99 USA/$12.99 Canada
DESKTOP PUBLISHING / ILLUSTRATION/GRAPHICS			
Harvard Graphics 3 For Windows For Dummies™ Quick Reference	by Raymond E. Werner	1-56884-962-1	$9.99 USA/$12.99 Canada
FINANCE / PERSONAL FINANCE			
Quicken 4 For Windows For Dummies™ Quick Reference	by Stephen L. Nelson	1-56884-950-8	$9.95 USA/$12.95 Canada
GROUPWARE / INTEGRATED			
Microsoft Office 4 For Windows For Dummies™ Quick Reference	by Doug Lowe	1-56884-958-3	$9.99 USA/$12.99 Canada
Microsoft Works For Windows 3 For Dummies™ Quick Reference	by Michael Partington	1-56884-959-1	$9.99 USA/$12.99 Canada
INTERNET / COMMUNICATIONS / NETWORKING			
The Internet For Dummies™ Quick Reference	by John R. Levine	1-56884-168-X	$8.95 USA/$11.95 Canada
MACINTOSH			
Macintosh System 7.5 For Dummies™ Quick Reference	by Stuart J. Stuple	1-56884-956-7	$9.99 USA/$12.99 Canada
OPERATING SYSTEMS / DOS			
DOS For Dummies® Quick Reference	by Greg Harvey	1-56884-007-1	$8.95 USA/$11.95 Canada
UNIX			
UNIX For Dummies™ Quick Reference	by Margaret Levine Young & John R. Levine	1-56884-094-2	$8.95 USA/$11.95 Canada
WINDOWS			
Windows 3.1 For Dummies™ Quick Reference, 2nd Edition	by Greg Harvey	1-56884-951-6	$8.95 USA/$11.95 Canada
PRESENTATION / AUTOCAD			
AutoCAD For Dummies™ Quick Reference	by Bud Smith	1-56884-198-1	$9.95 USA/$12.95 Canada
SPREADSHEET			
1-2-3 For Dummies™ Quick Reference	by John Walkenbach	1-56884-027-6	$8.95 USA/$11.95 Canada
1-2-3 For Windows 5 For Dummies™ Quick Reference	by John Walkenbach	1-56884-957-5	$9.95 USA/$12.95 Canada
Excel For Windows For Dummies™ Quick Reference, 2nd Edition	by John Walkenbach	1-56884-096-9	$8.95 USA/$11.95 Canada
Quattro Pro 6 For Windows For Dummies™ Quick Reference	by Stuart A. Stuple	1-56884-172-8	$9.95 USA/$12.95 Canada
WORD PROCESSING			
Word For Windows 6 For Dummies™ Quick Reference	by George Lynch	1-56884-095-0	$8.95 USA/$11.95 Canada
WordPerfect For Windows For Dummies™ Quick Reference	by Greg Harvey	1-56884-039-X	$8.95 USA/$11.95 Canada

FOR MORE INFORMATION OR TO ORDER, PLEASE CALL ▶ 800 762 2974

For volume discounts & special orders please call
Tony Real, Special Sales, at 415. 655. 3048

"*Macworld Complete Mac Handbook Plus CD* covered everything I could think of and more!"

Peter Tsakiris, New York, NY

"Thanks for the best computer book I've ever read — *Photoshop 2.5 Bible*. Best $30 I ever spent. I *love* the detailed index...Yours blows them all out of the water. This is a great book. We must enlighten the masses!"

Kevin Lisankie, Chicago, Illinois

"*Macworld Guide to ClarisWorks 2* is the easiest computer book to read that I have ever found!"

Steven Hanson, Lutz, FL

Macworld QuarkXPress 3.2/3.3 Bible

by Barbara Assadi & Galen Gruman

ISBN: 1-878058-85-1
$39.95 USA/$52.95 Canada

Includes disk with QuarkXPress XTensions and scripts.

Macworld PageMaker 5 Bible

by Craig Danuloff

ISBN: 1-878058-84-3
$39.95 USA/$52.95 Canada

Includes 2 disks with Pagemaker utilities, clip art, and more.

Macworld FileMaker Pro 2.0/2.1 Bible

by Steven A. Schwartz

ISBN: 1-56884-201-5
$34.95 USA/$46.95 Canada

Includes disk with ready-to-run databases.

Macworld Word 6 Companion, 2nd Edition

by Jim Heid

ISBN: 1-56884-082-9
$24.95 USA/$34.95 Canada

Macworld Guide To Microsoft Word 5/5.1

by Jim Heid

ISBN: 1-878058-39-8
$22.95 USA/$29.95 Canada

Macworld ClarisWorks 2.0/2.1 Companion, 2nd Edition

by Steven A. Schwartz

ISBN: 1-56884-180-9
$24.95 USA/$34.95 Canada

Macworld Guide To Microsoft Works 3

by Barrie Sosinsky

ISBN: 1-878058-42-8
$22.95 USA/$29.95 Canada

Macworld Excel 5 Companion, 2nd Edition

by Chris Van Buren & David Maguiness

ISBN: 1-56884-081-0
$24.95 USA/$34.95 Canada

Macworld Guide To Microsoft Excel 4

by David Maguiness

ISBN: 1-878058-40-1
$22.95 USA/$29.95 Canada

FOR MORE INFORMATION OR TO ORDER, PLEASE CALL ▶ **800. 762. 2974**

For volume discounts & special orders please call Tony Real, Special Sales, at 415. 655. 3048

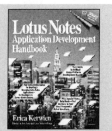

12/20/94

Order Center: **(800) 762-2974** *(8 a.m.–6 p.m., EST, weekdays)*

Quantity	ISBN	Title	Price	Total

Shipping & Handling Charges

	Description	First book	Each additional book	Total
Domestic	Normal	$4.50	$1.50	$
	Two Day Air	$8.50	$2.50	$
	Overnight	$18.00	$3.00	$
International	Surface	$8.00	$8.00	$
	Airmail	$16.00	$16.00	$
	DHL Air	$17.00	$17.00	$

*For large quantities call for shipping & handling charges.
**Prices are subject to change without notice.

Ship to:

Name _____

Company _____

Address _____

City/State/Zip _____

Daytime Phone _____

Payment: ☐ Check to IDG Books (US Funds Only)

☐ VISA   ☐ MasterCard   ☐ American Express

Card # _____ Expires _____

Signature _____

Subtotal _____

CA residents add
applicable sales tax _____

IN, MA, and MD
residents add
5% sales tax _____

IL residents add
6.25% sales tax _____

RI residents add
7% sales tax _____

TX residents add
8.25% sales tax _____

Shipping _____

Total _____

Please send this order form to:
IDG Books Worldwide
7260 Shadeland Station, Suite 100
Indianapolis, IN 46256

Allow up to 3 weeks for delivery.
Thank you!

IDG BOOKS WORLDWIDE REGISTRATION CARD

RETURN THIS REGISTRATION CARD FOR FREE CATALOG

Title of this book: Macworld Photoshop 3 Bible, 2nd Ed.

My overall rating of this book: ❑ Very good [1] ❑ Good [2] ❑ Satisfactory [3] ❑ Fair [4] ❑ Poor [5]

How I first heard about this book:

❑ Found in bookstore; name: [6] _____

❑ Book review: [7]

❑ Advertisement: [8]

❑ Catalog: [9]

❑ Word of mouth; heard about book from friend, co-worker, etc.: [10]

❑ Other: [11]

What I liked most about this book:

_____

_____

_____

What I would change, add, delete, etc., in future editions of this book:

_____

_____

_____

Other comments:

_____

Number of computer books I purchase in a year: ❑ 1 [12] ❑ 2-5 [13] ❑ 6-10 [14] ❑ More than 10 [15]

I would characterize my computer skills as: ❑ Beginner [16] ❑ Intermediate [17] ❑ Advanced [18] ❑ Professional [19]

I use ❑ DOS [20] ❑ Windows [21] ❑ OS/2 [22] ❑ Unix [23] ❑ Macintosh [24] ❑ Other: [25]_____
(please specify)

I would be interested in new books on the following subjects:
(please check all that apply, and use the spaces provided to identify specific software)

❑ Word processing: [26] _____

❑ Spreadsheets: [27] _____

❑ Data bases: [28] _____

❑ Desktop publishing: [29] _____

❑ File Utilities: [30] _____

❑ Money management: [31] _____

❑ Networking: [32] _____

❑ Programming languages: [33] _____

❑ Other: [34] _____

I use a PC at (please check all that apply): ❑ home [35] ❑ work [36] ❑ school [37] ❑ other: [38] _____

The disks I prefer to use are ❑ 5.25 [39] ❑ 3.5 [40] ❑ other: [41]_____

I have a CD ROM: ❑ yes [42] ❑ no [43]

I plan to buy or upgrade computer hardware this year: ❑ yes [44] ❑ no [45]

I plan to buy or upgrade computer software this year: ❑ yes [46] ❑ no [47]

Name: _____ Business title: [48] _____ Type of Business: [49] _____

Address (❑ home [50] ❑ work [51]/Company name: _____)

Street/Suite# _____

City [52]/State [53]/Zipcode [54]: _____ Country [55] _____

❑ **I liked this book!** You may quote me by name in future IDG Books Worldwide promotional materials.

My daytime phone number is _____

IDG BOOKS

THE WORLD OF COMPUTER KNOWLEDGE

❏ YES!

Please keep me informed about IDG's World of Computer Knowledge.
Send me the latest IDG Books catalog.